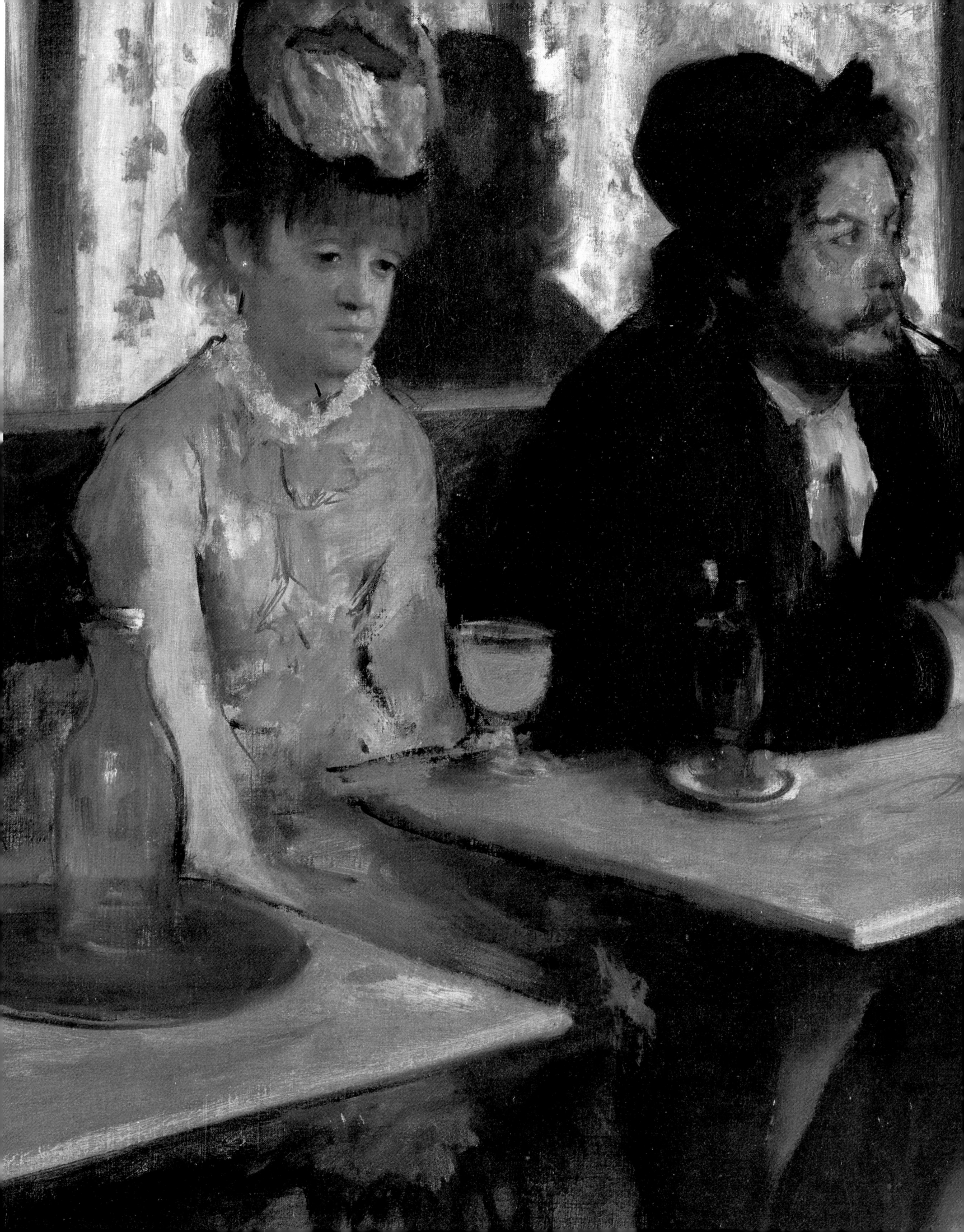

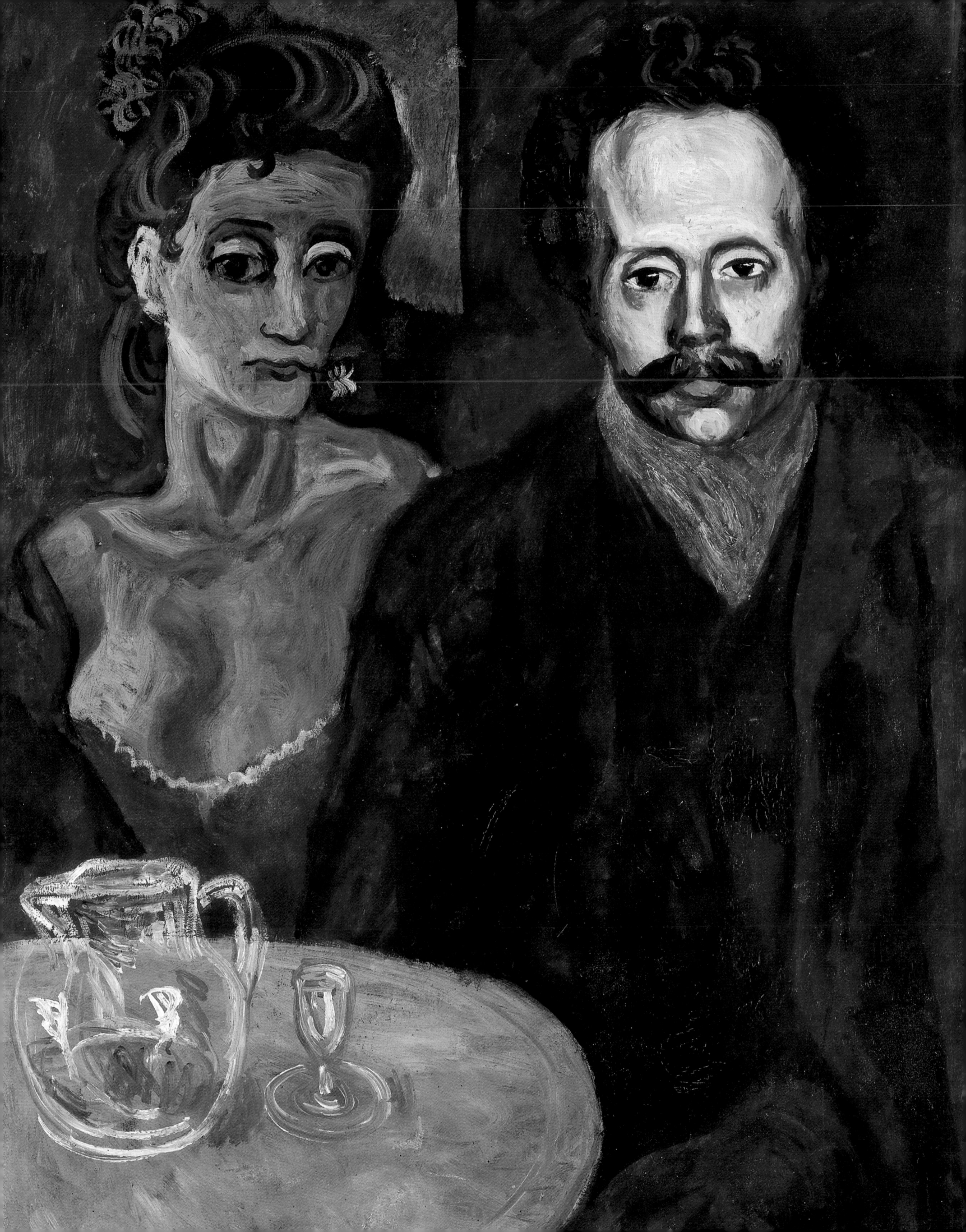

PICASSO LOOKS AT DEGAS

ELIZABETH COWLING AND RICHARD KENDALL

WITH ADDITIONAL CONTRIBUTIONS BY **CÉCILE GODEFROY, SARAH LEES, AND MONTSE TORRAS**

STERLING AND FRANCINE CLARK ART INSTITUTE | WILLIAMSTOWN, MASSACHUSETTS

MUSEU PICASSO | BARCELONA

DISTRIBUTED BY YALE UNIVERSITY PRESS | NEW HAVEN AND LONDON

This book is published on the occasion of the exhibition *Picasso Looks at Degas*

Sterling and Francine Clark Art Institute
Williamstown, Massachusetts
13 June–12 September 2010

Museu Picasso, Barcelona
14 October 2010–16 January 2011

Picasso Looks at Degas was organized by the Sterling and Francine Clark Art Institute and the Museu Picasso, Barcelona. It is supported in part by a grant 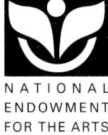 from the National Endowment for the Arts, an indemnity from the Federal Council on the Arts and the Humanities, and with the special cooperation of Fundación Almine y Bernard Ruiz-Picasso para el Arte.

NATIONAL ENDOWMENT FOR THE ARTS
A great nation deserves great art.

Produced by the Sterling and Francine Clark Art Institute in association with the Museu Picasso, Barcelona, under the direction of Curtis R. Scott

Coordinated by Katherine Pasco Frisina
with Teresa E. O'Toole
Spanish and Catalan editions coordinated
by Marta Jové

Research assistance by Elizabeth O'Grady
and Sharon Brower
Translations by C'est-à-dire, Inc., and Lucie Maguire
Copyedited by Sharon Herson (USA)
and líniazero edicions (Spain)
Index by Kathleen M. Friello

Designed by Susan Marsh
Composed in Gotham by Matt Mayerchak
Map adapted by Mary Reilly
Production by The Production Department,
Whately, Massachusetts
Printed on 135 gsm Fedrigoni Tatami
Color separations and printing by Trifolio, Verona

Cover illustrations:
Front, (top) Detail of Pablo Picasso, *Woman Plaiting Her Hair* (fig. 206); (bottom) Detail of Edgar Degas, *Combing the Hair (La Coiffure)* (fig. 227)
Back, (left) Pablo Picasso in Montmartre, c. 1904 (fig. 64); (right) Edgar Degas in Paris, 1889, by Giuseppe Primoli, courtesy Fondazione Primoli, Rome

Details:
Page i: Edgar Degas, *In a Café (L'Absinthe)* (fig. 104);
Page ii: Pablo Picasso, *Portrait of Sebastià Junyer i Vidal* (fig. 105); Page vi: Pablo Picasso, *The Dwarf* (fig. 120); Page viii: Edgar Degas, *Two Dancers in the Wings* (fig. 154)

Library of Congress Cataloging-in-Publication Data

Cowling, Elizabeth.
  Picasso looks at Degas / Elizabeth Cowling and Richard Kendall ; with additional contributions by Cécile Godefroy, Sarah Lees, and Montse Torras.
      p. cm.
  "This book is published on the occasion of the exhibition Picasso Looks at Degas, Sterling and Francine Clark Art Institute, Williamstown, Massachusetts, 13 June–12 September 2010, Museu Picasso, Barcelona, 14 October 2010–16 January 2011."
  Includes bibliographical references and index.
  ISBN 978-0-931102-85-1 (clark (cloth) : alk. paper)
— ISBN 978-0-931102-86-8 (clark (pbk.) : alk. paper)
— ISBN 978-0-300-13412-4 (yale : alk. paper)
1. Picasso, Pablo, 1881–1973—Exhibitions. 2. Degas, Edgar, 1834–1917—Influence—Exhibitions. 3. Degas, Edgar, 1834–1917—Exhibitions. I. Kendall, Richard. II. Sterling and Francine Clark Art Institute. III. Museo Picasso. IV. Title.
  N6853.P5A4 2010
  709.2–dc22

                                    2010006046

Printed and bound in Italy

10 9 8 7 6 5 4 3 2 1

Distributed by Yale University Press
New Haven and London
www.yalebooks.com

CONTENTS

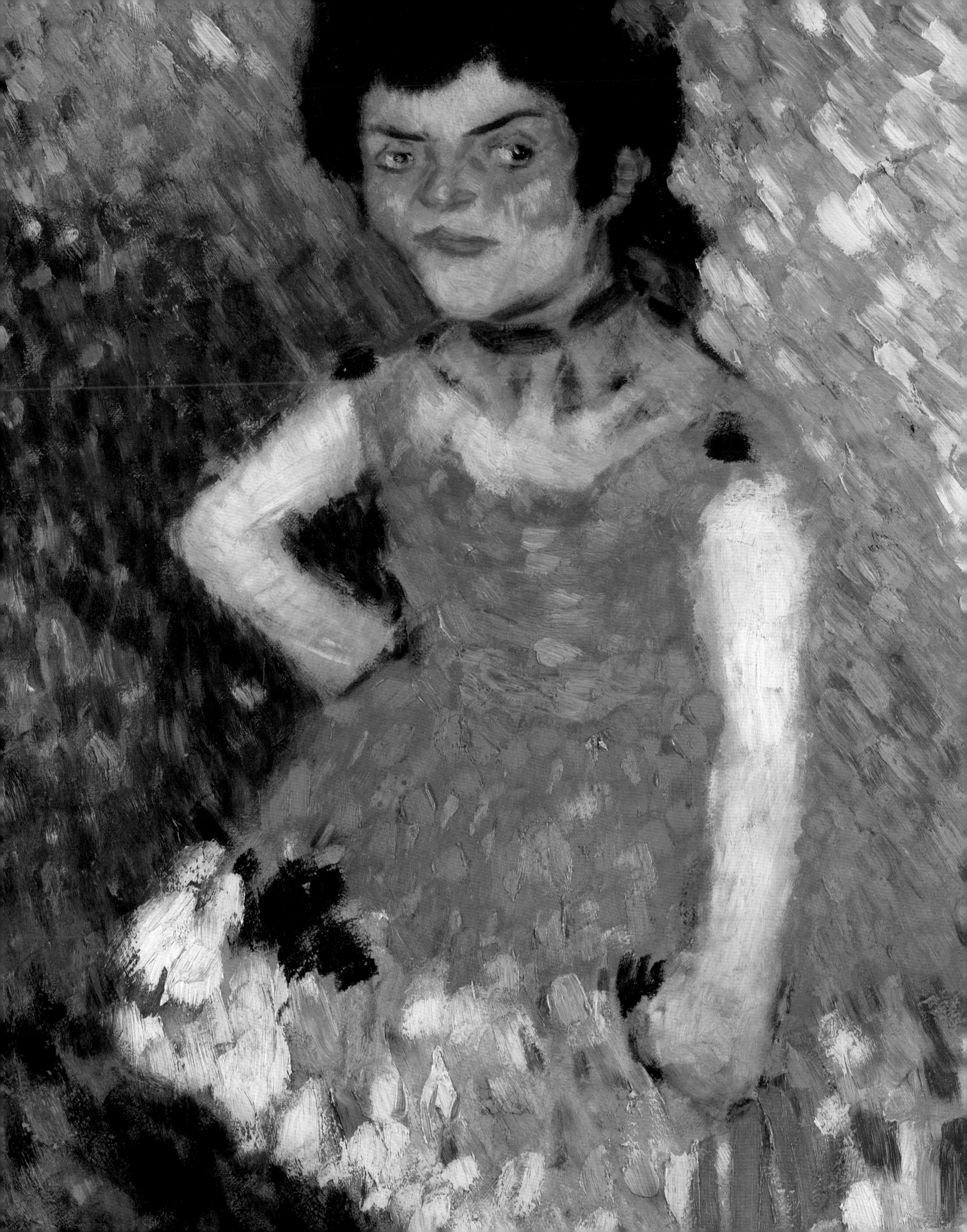

DIRECTORS' FOREWORD

Pablo Picasso was an artist who observed and absorbed the work of other artists throughout his long life. Of all the masters he admired, Edgar Degas played an unexpectedly important role during much of the younger artist's career. Although the two were neighbors in Montmartre for several years before Degas's death in 1917, there is no evidence that they ever met. Yet the café habitués, stage performers, bathers, and ballerinas that Degas typically depicted also appear repeatedly in Picasso's images, and Degas the man appears in person in a substantial series of etchings Picasso made in 1971, just two years before his death.

This fascinating aspect of Picasso's artistic personality has been a longstanding focus of study for curators Elizabeth Cowling and Richard Kendall. Both bring extensive expertise on Picasso and Degas, respectively, to the exploration of ways in which Picasso found inspiration not just in the work but in the personality of his predecessor. Together, they have produced an insightful and provocative exhibition and catalogue that will shed considerable new light on both masters.

The exhibition has benefited immeasurably from the support of many individuals and organizations. Foremost among these is the Fundación Almine y Bernard Ruiz-Picasso para el Arte, which has offered its special coopera-

tion to the initiative. We are also deeply grateful to Claude Picasso and the Picasso Administration for their support of the project. It is only with the generous participation of numerous institutions and private collectors who agreed to lend some of their most important works that *Picasso Looks at Degas* could be realized, and we offer them all our warmest thanks. The exhibition has also been supported by an indemnity from the Federal Council on the Arts and Humanities, and, at the Clark, by a grant from the National Endowment for the Arts.

Picasso Looks at Degas presents the first full-scale examination of the Spanish artist's work to audiences at the Clark and offers a comparably in-depth view of the French artist's work in Barcelona for the first time. Our collaboration on this project has thereby broken new ground for both institutions, and it is our hope that the exhibition will provide new insights into the multifaceted creativity of these two great artists.

Michael Conforti
Director
Sterling and Francine Clark Art Institute

Pepe Serra
Director
Museu Picasso

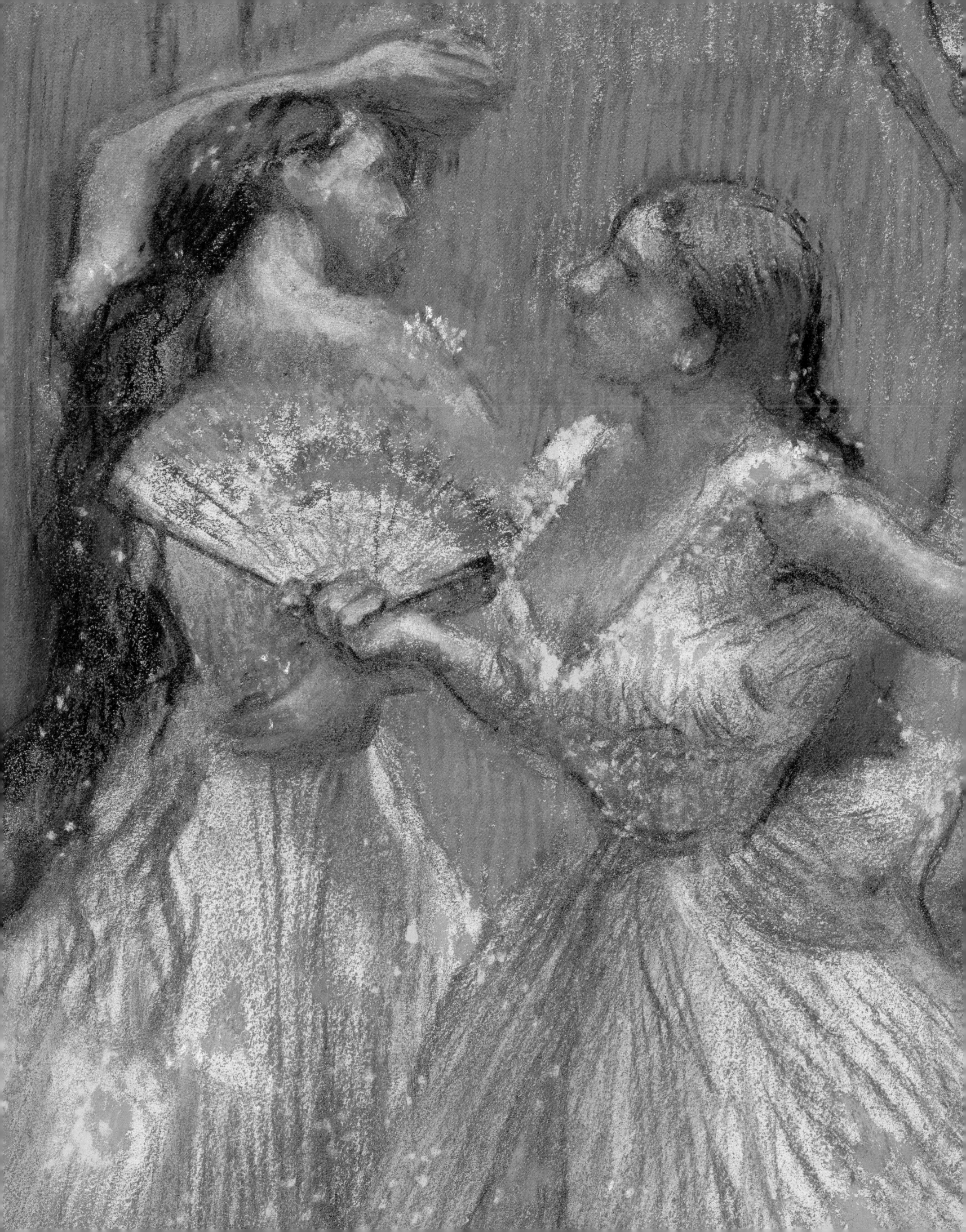

LENDERS TO THE EXHIBITION

Albertina, Vienna

Allen Memorial Art Museum, Oberlin College, Ohio

The Art Institute of Chicago

The Baltimore Museum of Art

Gretchen and John Berggruen

Bibliothèque de l'Institut national d'histoire de l'art, Paris

Birmingham Museums and Art Gallery, England

The British Museum, London

Brooklyn Museum, New York

Dumbarton Oaks House Collection, Washington, D.C.

El Conventet Collection

Fundación Almine y Bernard Ruiz-Picasso para el Arte

Hamburger Kunsthalle

Hirshhorn Museum and Sculpture Garden, Smithsonian Institution, Washington, D.C.

The Kreeger Museum, Washington, D.C.

Kunsthalle Bremen

Kunstmuseum Basel

Los Angeles County Museum of Art

The Metropolitan Museum of Art, New York

Musée d'Orsay, Paris

Musée national Picasso, Paris

Museo del Novecento, Milan

Museu de Montserrat

Museu Picasso, Barcelona

Museum Boijmans Van Beuningen, Rotterdam

Museum Ludwig, Cologne

Museum of Fine Arts, Boston

The Museum of Modern Art, New York

The National Gallery, London

National Gallery of Art, Washington, D.C.

National Gallery of Canada, Ottawa

National Gallery of Ireland, Dublin

The National Gallery of Scotland, Edinburgh

The National Museum, Belgrade

The Phillips Collection, Washington, D.C.

Marina Picasso

Sainsbury Centre, Norwich, England

Solomon R. Guggenheim Museum, New York

Sterling and Francine Clark Art Institute, Williamstown, Massachusetts

Nicholas Stogdon

Tate, London

Vanech Family

Private collections

Special thanks to the following galleries and dealers for their assistance with loans from private collections: Acquavella Gallery, New York; Galerie Jan Krugier & Cie., Geneva; Guggenheim Asher Associates, Los Angeles; Halcyon Gallery, London; Sotheby's, New York

ACKNOWLEDGMENTS

The exhibition *Picasso Looks at Degas* and its accompanying catalogue have emerged from discussions between the curators that began more than a decade ago. In recent years, both projects have been energetically supported and informed by our friends and colleagues in numerous institutions in the United States and Europe. Crucial to this endeavor has been the encouragement of the director of the Sterling and Francine Clark Art Institute, Michael Conforti, and the senior curator, Richard Rand, while Kathleen Morris skillfully oversaw our efforts and coordinated them with her counterparts in Spain. Without the exceptional enthusiasm and understanding of the director of the Museu Picasso in Barcelona, Pepe Serra, and his predecessor Maria Teresa Ocaña, this ambitious enterprise would not have been possible. In lending works by Picasso from their own museum with such generosity and offering assistance with research and the negotiation of loans from public and private collections, they have helped to make *Picasso Looks at Degas* into a truly international event.

On hearing of our project, Bernard Ruiz-Picasso immediately expressed his desire to collaborate by lending, in addition to works of art, precious unpublished documents from the archive of his grandmother, the Russian ballerina and Picasso's first wife, Olga Khokhlova. His researcher Cécile Godefroy has contributed a groundbreaking essay to the catalogue on Olga's career as a dancer and explored new evidence for her influence on Picasso's imagery. The participation of the Fundación Almine y Bernard Ruiz-Picasso para el Arte has greatly enhanced the exhibition. We are likewise delighted to acknowledge the staunch support of Claude Picasso and the Picasso Administration, and the generosity of Marina Picasso. Diana Widmaier-Picasso has kindly shared her expert knowledge of her grandfather's work throughout.

At the Clark, we have benefited from the assiduous curatorial skills of Sarah Lees, who has patiently coordinated our efforts and contributed to our discussions on every aspect of the exhibition, and written a thoughtful catalogue essay on the two artists' forays into photography. As the exhibition came together, we have also depended on the expertise of Jay A. Clarke, Manton Curator of Prints, Drawings, and Photographs, and the professionalism and experience of Mattie Kelley and Monique LeBlanc for the intricate orchestration of loans from many countries. Production of the catalogue was overseen by Curtis Scott and supervised with infinite good humor, patience, and precision by Katie Frisina, assisted by Teresa E. O'Toole and Elizabeth O'Grady. For their work on many aspects of this catalogue, we also wish to thank Michael Agee, Sophie Brisebois, Sharon Brower, June Cuffner, Kathleen M. Friello, Marta Jové, Susan Marsh, Matt Mayerchak, Susan Medlicott, Rosa Mercader, Mary Reilly, Nerissa Dominguez Vales, and Paul White.

Many other members of the Clark staff have contributed their expertise and hard work to the realization of the exhibition and catalogue. We wish to recognize Karen Bucky, Michael Cary, Michael Cassin, Julie Chase, Paul Dion, Jay Dubé, David Edge, Maria Gamari, Diane Gottardi, Frank Gregory, Sarah Hammond, Monica Henry, Sarah Hoffmann, Tim Johnson, Becca Johnston, David Keiser-Clark, Tony King, John Ladd, Helen Ledbury, Mary Leitch, Tom Loughman, Sally Morse Majewski, Tom Merrill, Jim Moran, Leslie Paisley, Bill Powers, Susan Roeper, Patrick Rhine, Vicki Saltzman, John Skavlem, Janet Thompson, Ronna Tulgan-Ostheimer, Elizabeth Tunick, and Sandra L. Webber.

At the Museu Picasso, Barcelona, the project was skillfully and tirelessly coordinated by Montse Torras, who has also contributed valuably to the catalogue. The hard work of many other staff members was also indispensable to the realization of the exhibition, among them Manel Baena, Lluís Bagunyà, Anna Bru de Sala, Anna Fàbregas, Reyes Jiménez, and Anna Vélez. We are also grateful to Clara Grífol for her assistance with the exhibition.

As our research progressed, we learned much from exchanges with fellow curators and authorities on the art of Edgar Degas and Pablo Picasso. We are especially grateful to: Simon André-Deconchat, Olivier Berggruen, Yve-Alain Bois, Sylvie Brame, Neil Cox, Marie-Noëlle Delorme, Jill DeVonyar, Ann Dumas, Dominique Dupuis-Labbé, John Elderfield, Michael FitzGerald, Susan Grace Galassi, John Golding, Christopher Green, Hélène Klein, Bernardo Laniado-Romero, Brigitte Léal, Laurence Madeline, Marilyn McCully, Cristina Mendoza, Peter Read, Theodore Reff, John Richardson, Edouard Sebline, and Richard Thomson.

An exhibition of this kind depends on the generosity and patience of many institutions and their staffs, and of private collectors in several countries, some of whom have preferred to remain anonymous. We extend our thanks to: Ignazio Amuro, Richard Armstrong, Arxiu Historic de la Ciutat, Anne Baldassari, Mandy Bartram, Gabriella Belli, Daniella Berman, Biblioteca de Catalunya, Antje Birthälmer, Doreen Bolger, Marie Bourke, Eva Buch, Gudrun Buehl, Rupert Burgess, Bernhard Mendes Bürgi, Connie Butler, Isabelle Cahn, Lisa Cain, Thomas P. Campbell, Jacquie Cartwright, Elisenda Casanova, Michael Clarke, Catherine Clement, Judy Cline, Guy Cogeval, Evelyne Cohen, Caroline Collier, Stephane Cosman Connery, Alexander Corcoran, Fionnuala Croke, James Cuno, Kathy Curry, Tatjana Cvjeticanin, Susan Dackerman, Ivan Delgado, Isabelle Dervaux, Charles Desmarais, Sofía Díez, Judith Dolkart, Mercè Doñate, James David Draper, Douglas Druick, Sonja Eiböck, Carol Eliel, Patrick Elliott, Sjarel Ex, Evelyne Ferlay, Michael Findlay, Jay M. Fisher, Valerie Fletcher, Eliza Flynn, Emily Foss, Joanna Foyster, Sylvie Fresnault, Barbara Freund, Julia Friedrich, Olivier Gabet, Isabelle Gaëtan, Matthew Gale, Galerie Schmidt,

Hubertus Gaßner, Carmen Giménez, Lukas Gloor, Carmen Godia, Michael Govan, Darrell Green, Judy A. Greenberg, Antony Griffiths, Gloria Groom, Stéphane Guégan, Marta-Volga Guezala, Florence Half-Wrobel, Claire Hallinan, Margarete Heck, Katharina Hein, Miri Hirschfeld, Anne Hoenigswald, Joe Holbach, David Jaffé, Nichola Johnson, Kimberly Jones, Raymond Keaveney, Erich Keel, Kasper König, Richard Koshalek, Dorothy Kosinki, Diana Kunkel, Ulf Küster, Josep de C. Laplana, Arnold L. Lehman, John Leighton, Margareta Leuthardt, Dominique Lobstein, Glenn Lowry, Rachel Lucera-Fein, Neil MacGregor, Maria Isabel Marín, Caroline Mathieu, Lucia Matino, Ceridwen Maycock, Nesta Mayo, James Mayor, Suzanne Folds McCullagh, Rita McLean, Henriette Mentha, Michael Merisi, Odile Michel, Lourdes Moreno, Christian Müller, Nathalie Muller, Jodi Myers, David C. Norman, Didier Ottinger, Kim Pashko, Varshali Patel, Nicholas Penny, Therese Marie Peskowits, Christine Pinault, Martine Poulain, Earl A. Powell III, Marina Pugliese, Jutta Putschew, Michael Raeburn, Sonìa Villegas Ramos, Eliza Rathbone, Janice Reading, Christopher Riopelle, Malcolm Rogers, Cora Rosevear, Katy Rothkopf, Marylou Rybicki, Robert Salmon, Claudio Salsi, Dieter Scholz, Veronica Sekules, Carel van Tuyll van Serooskerken, George Shackelford, Karen Shahadi, Nicole Simões da Silva, Jodi Simpson, Janice Slater, Kim Smit, Whitney Snyder, Nancy Spector, Gregory Spurgeon, Lucille Stiger, Denny Stone, Andrew Straus, Jeanne Sudour, Anna Swinbourne, Emily Talbot, Pierre Théberge, Alicia B. Thomas, Nancy Thomas, Gary Tinterow, Keri Towler, Lluís Utrilla, Caroline Villiers-Stuart, Margreet Wafelbakker, Meike Wenck, Alice Whelihan, Stephanie Wiles, Amy Wright, Jan Ziolkowski, Marta Zlotnick.

In addition, the curators wish to thank those friends and relatives who have sustained them during their labors: Michael Bury, Peter Bury, Jill DeVonyar, Ruth Rattenbury, Gabrielle Turner, Jessie Turner.

NOTE TO THE READER

All works by Edgar Degas and Pablo Picasso include reference numbers for the standard catalogues on these artists. References are listed in the exhibition checklist and/or index at the back of this volume (see pp. 337–53).

Abbreviations for Degas sources are as follows:

B. R. Philippe Brame and Theodore Reff, *Degas et son oeuvre: A Supplement* (New York: Garland Publishers, 1984)

D. Malcolm Daniel, *Edgar Degas, Photographer* (New York: Metropolitan Museum of Art, 1998)

J. Eugenia Parry Janis, *Degas Monotypes: Essay, Catalogue and Checklist* (Cambridge, Mass.: Fogg Art Museum, 1968)

L. Paul André Lemoisne, *Degas et son oeuvre*, 4 vols. (Paris: P. Brame et C. M. de Hauke, aux Arts et métiers graphiques, 1946–49)

R. John Rewald, *Degas, Works in Sculpture: A Complete Catalogue* (New York: Pantheon Books, 1944)

R. S. Sue Welsh Reed and Barbara Stern Shapiro, *Edgar Degas: The Painter as Printmaker* (Boston: Museum of Fine Arts, 1984)

Vente I *Catalogue des tableaux, pastels et dessins par Edgar Degas. . . .* (Paris: Galeries Georges Petit, 6–8 May 1918)

Vente II *Catalogue des tableaux, pastels et dessins par Edgar Degas. . . .* (Paris: Galeries Georges Petit, 11–13 December 1918)

Vente III *Catalogue des tableaux, pastels et dessins par Edgar Degas. . . .* (Paris: Galeries Georges Petit, 7–9 April 1919)

Vente IV *Catalogue des tableaux, pastels et dessins par Edgar Degas. . . .* (Paris: Galeries Georges Petit, 2–4 July 1919)

Vente Estampes *Catalogue des eaux-fortes, vernis-mous, aquatintes, lithographies et monotypes par Edgar Degas, et provenant de son atelier.* (Paris: Galerie Manzi-Joyant, 22–23 November 1918)

Abbreviations for Picasso sources are as follows:

B. Anne Baldassari, *Picasso photographe, 1901–1916* (Paris: Réunion des musées nationaux, 1994)

Baer Brigitte Baer and Bernhard Geiser, *Picasso: Peintre-Graveur*, 7 vols. (Bern: Kornfeld, 1986–96)

PF1. Josep Palau i Fabre, *Picasso. Life and Work of the Early Years, 1881–1907*, trans. Kenneth Lyons (London: Phaidon, 1981)

PF3. Josep Palau i Fabre, *Picasso: des ballets au drame (1917–1926)*, trans. Robert Marrast (Cologne: Könemann, 1999)

S. Werner Spies, *Picasso: The Sculptures* (Ostfildern/Stuttgart: Hatje Cantz, 2000)

Z. Christian Zervos, *Pablo Picasso*, 33 vols. (Paris: Cahiers d'art, 1932–72)

Picasso Looks at Degas uses Catalan spellings of names for most painters, sitters, and all other people from Catalonia. Translations from original or secondary sources in French, Spanish, and Catalan are by the authors unless otherwise indicated. Cécile Godefroy's text was translated from the French by C'est-à-dire, Inc. Montse Torras's text was translated from the Catalan by Lucie Maguire.

Dimensions provided for prints correspond to image size, not sheet size. Dates and dimensions for Degas's monotypes correspond to those in Jean Sutherland Boggs et al., *Degas*, exh. cat. (New York: Metropolitan Museum of Art, 1988). All other dates and dimensions were provided by the owners of the works.

PICASSO LOOKS AT DEGAS

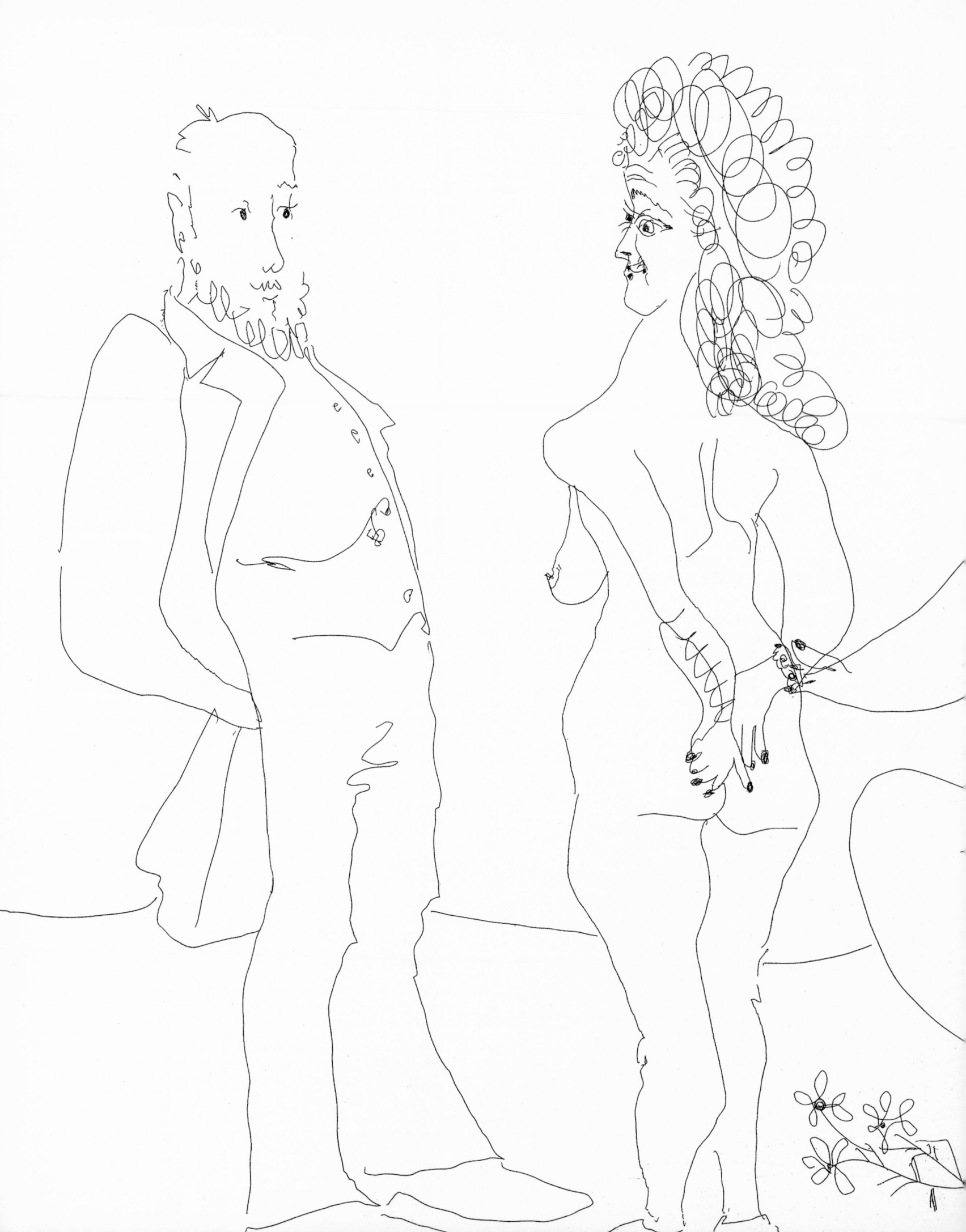

INTRODUCTION

ELIZABETH COWLING AND RICHARD KENDALL

In summer 1901, Picasso exhibited a group of his paintings in Paris for the first time. Though still only nineteen years old and virtually unknown in the city, Picasso's remarkable, multifaceted talent was soon noticed: "[Picasso] has emerged as a brilliant artist. He paints — and beautifully," wrote the respected critic Félicien Fagus. "Like all pure painters he loves color for itself." Listing some of the varied subjects in Picasso's display — flowers, racecourses, bullfighting rings, female nudes, dancers — Fagus added that "it is easy to detect numerous likely influences: Delacroix, Manet, . . . Monet, Van Gogh, Pissarro, Toulouse-Lautrec, Degas."[1]

More than a century after the 1901 exhibition, Picasso's voracious appreciation for the art of his predecessors — not just in his youth, but throughout his unusually long career — has become a central feature of his legend. Articles, books, and catalogues have been devoted to Picasso's fascination with the work of such individuals as Ingres, Delacroix, Manet, Van Gogh, Rodin, and Cézanne, while large-scale exhibitions have recently surveyed his relationship with the Old Masters, reaching back to the Renaissance. Strangely, this wide-ranging investigation has omitted several of the artists who were proposed as "influences" in 1901, among them the three representatives of the Impressionist movement: Monet, Pissarro, and Degas. Any doubts about the critic's meaning were removed the following year, when Picasso again showed some pictures in Paris. Noting the dis-

tinctive "temperament, race, and individuality" of the new wave of Spanish artists in Paris, Fagus insisted that Picasso and his colleagues had been "stimulated by Manet, Monet, Degas, Carrière, our Impressionists."[2]

In 2010, it is startling to find that these claims have yet to be examined. There have been no studies of Picasso's early engagement with Impressionism and no focused examinations of his debt to Monet, Pissarro, and Degas. The case of Degas is especially surprising. Following Fagus, biographers and scholars have recorded a number of precise moments of contact between Picasso's paintings, drawings, and prints and certain works by Degas, as well as broader parallels in their identities as artists. Most spectacularly, Picasso himself acknowledged this relationship in 1958 when he became the proud owner of a group of Degas's monotypes depicting brothels. In 1971, Picasso went a step further, beginning a series of drawings and prints in which he created variations on Degas's caustic imagery, introducing — sometimes playfully, sometimes cruelly, sometimes sympathetically — the figure of Degas himself into dozens of these new compositions. The last of them were made only months before Picasso's death in April 1973, bringing full circle the curiosity about Degas and his art that Fagus had identified seven decades earlier.

In *Picasso Looks at Degas*, the broad arc of Picasso's career provides the structure for a detailed, episodic study of this intricate story.

Detail of Pablo Picasso,
Degas among Prostitutes.
First Appearance of Degas
(270)

3

Beginning with his childhood and teenage years in Spain, the catalogue and the exhibition it accompanies trace his earliest contacts with Degas's art. Picasso initially encountered works by Degas and his peers in black-and-white illustrations, and only began to see their original pastels and paintings when he visited Paris several times from 1900 onward. Dating from this moment are his first tentative gestures toward some of Degas's signature themes: the cabaret singer, the prostitute, and, as Fagus indicated, racecourses, female nudes, and dancers. After settling in Montmartre in 1904, Picasso became acquainted with several people who knew Degas, including the dealer Ambroise Vollard, who briefly represented both artists, and Benedetta Canals, who modeled for them both. Although the two men seem never to have met, Picasso was well aware that Degas lived and worked very close to the Bateau Lavoir, the squalid artists' colony where he painted some of his most important early pictures. Here the young Spaniard brazenly confronted Degas in his art, portraying laundresses, bohemians in cafés, entertainers in mid-performance, and naked women bathing and combing their hair — all subjects that were very publicly associated with Degas. Here, too, Picasso experimented with sculpture and prints, sometimes with explicit references to works by his French predecessor, activities he would return to over the decades as his fame increased and his wealth enabled him to move to more salubrious premises. Celebrated for his audacious multiplicity of styles, from the near-abstraction of Cubism to surrealistic experiments with color and line by way of a seemingly limitless range of naturalist modes, the mature Picasso continued to revisit Degas's work in his imagination. Whether represented in delicate drawings that recalled Picasso's youth or in dramatic canvases and sculptures that seemed to push these media to their limits, bathers and ballet dancers in particular emerged from his studio to pay subtle,

sporadic homage to his Impressionist forebear.

In *Picasso Looks at Degas*, works by Picasso are often juxtaposed with works by Degas that he saw or could have seen. Never straightforwardly imitative, Picasso's response to Degas was mercurial and competitive, always involving an element of willful transformation and sometimes bordering on parody or pastiche. A parallel narrative in the exhibition concerns the gradually revealed affinity between these two artists as professionals and as human beings, an affinity that Picasso was surely aware of. In their youth, for example, both had experienced a traditional training dominated by the practice of drawing from the human figure and by reverence for great works of art from the past. Not coincidentally, Degas and Picasso subsequently emerged as the finest draftsmen of their respective generations — some would say of all time — who continued to place drawing at the center of their creative endeavors throughout their long careers. The female body, too, remained a persistent and often obsessive concern for both men, ruling over their oeuvres in all media. For the reputedly celibate Degas, this fascination was most famously expressed in his scenes of ballet dancers in their classrooms and in pictures and sculptures of intimate bathing, while for the notoriously lustful Picasso, it took on the myriad shapes of life in the studio or the home, private fantasy, and antique reverie.

The careers of Degas and Picasso were not only long and extremely productive but also heterogeneous. *Picasso Looks at Degas* is inevitably selective, highlighting a series of moments when Picasso manifestly turned to the art of his predecessor and engaged with a specific motif, technique, or group of works that caught his attention. Owing to the inaccessibility or fragility of key works, not every aspect of this engagement proved susceptible to reconstruction. Thus, the shared theme of the horse and rider called out for exploration but regretfully had to be abandoned. Conversely, concentration on our overarching theme necessitated a sharply focused approach to each artist's career. Many important features of their achievement are simply omitted, and other preoccupations of Picasso — thematic, stylistic, and technical — are bypassed. Also marginal to our project are Picasso's many other intense dialogues with the art of the past and of his near-contemporaries, even when they overlap with or echo his interest in Degas. As Picasso discovered when the contents of Degas's studio were auctioned after his death in 1917, canvases by El Greco, Delacroix, and Ingres, among works by numerous other artists in Degas's personal collection, signaled crucial shared allegiances, while his unashamed reworking of compositions by Titian, Rembrandt, and Ingres — to name but a few — anticipated Picasso's own absorptive approach. Indeed, beneath the surface the two artists shared a common attitude to the relationship between "influence" — or more accurately "appropriation" — and personal expression; a statement on this subject made by Picasso might almost have come from Degas: "What does it mean . . . for a painter to paint in the manner of So-and-So or to actually imitate someone else? What's wrong with that? On the contrary, it's a good idea. You should constantly try to paint like someone else. But the thing is, you can't! . . . You try. But it turns out to be a botch. . . . And it's at the very moment you make a botch of it that you're yourself."[3]

Picasso's restless, inventive relationship with the art of the past, which can still surprise those more attuned to his modernity, opens a window onto the creative processes that sustained his career. The masterly achievements of Poussin and Delacroix, Velázquez and Goya challenged him not only to make grand statements for the twentieth century but also to find ways of confronting the new sensibility that his artist-heroes could never have imagined. In this endeavor Degas became an ally, a direct precursor who had pioneered new forms as a painter of the modern city and a near-contemporary in the age of anxiety. Before Picasso was born, Degas had developed a compulsive relationship with his subject matter that was to become a defining studio strategy, producing subtle and intricate series of drawings, sequences of prints, and reiterations of his favorite images and compositions. Fifty years later, this way of working in improvised cycles became habitual for Picasso, sometimes resulting in more than a hundred variants of his initial motif. Both artists reached for what they sought, not through a cerebral process, but through intuition, constant experimentation, and nuanced repetition, and both were suspicious of theories and critical rhetoric.

Sharing the older artist's absorption in the dynamism of the creative process, Picasso was just as averse as Degas to the notion of perfection or completeness. In this respect, both knowingly transgressed against their academic training. Inevitably Picasso preferred his predecessor's most spontaneously executed or "unfinished" works — large-scale paintings or charcoal and pastel drawings that blatantly reveal signs of revision or were left unresolved, and the tiny monotypes executed at speed with fingers and rags that capture fleeting movements and sensations.

Like Degas before him, Picasso also became the great untaught sculptor of his age, glorying in the freedom to improvise that his amateurism sanctioned. Typically visualized at the outset in paintings and drawings, the resulting sculptures might then feed back into both artists' two-dimensional works, generating further innovations in style, technique, and imagery. Sympathizing warmly with his creative restlessness, Picasso liked to quote approvingly Degas's wry observation to Vollard that, far from wanting to find his "true style," he would have been "bored to death" if he had ever done so. "That," Picasso would remark, "is the fundamental difference between an idiot and a true painter."[4]

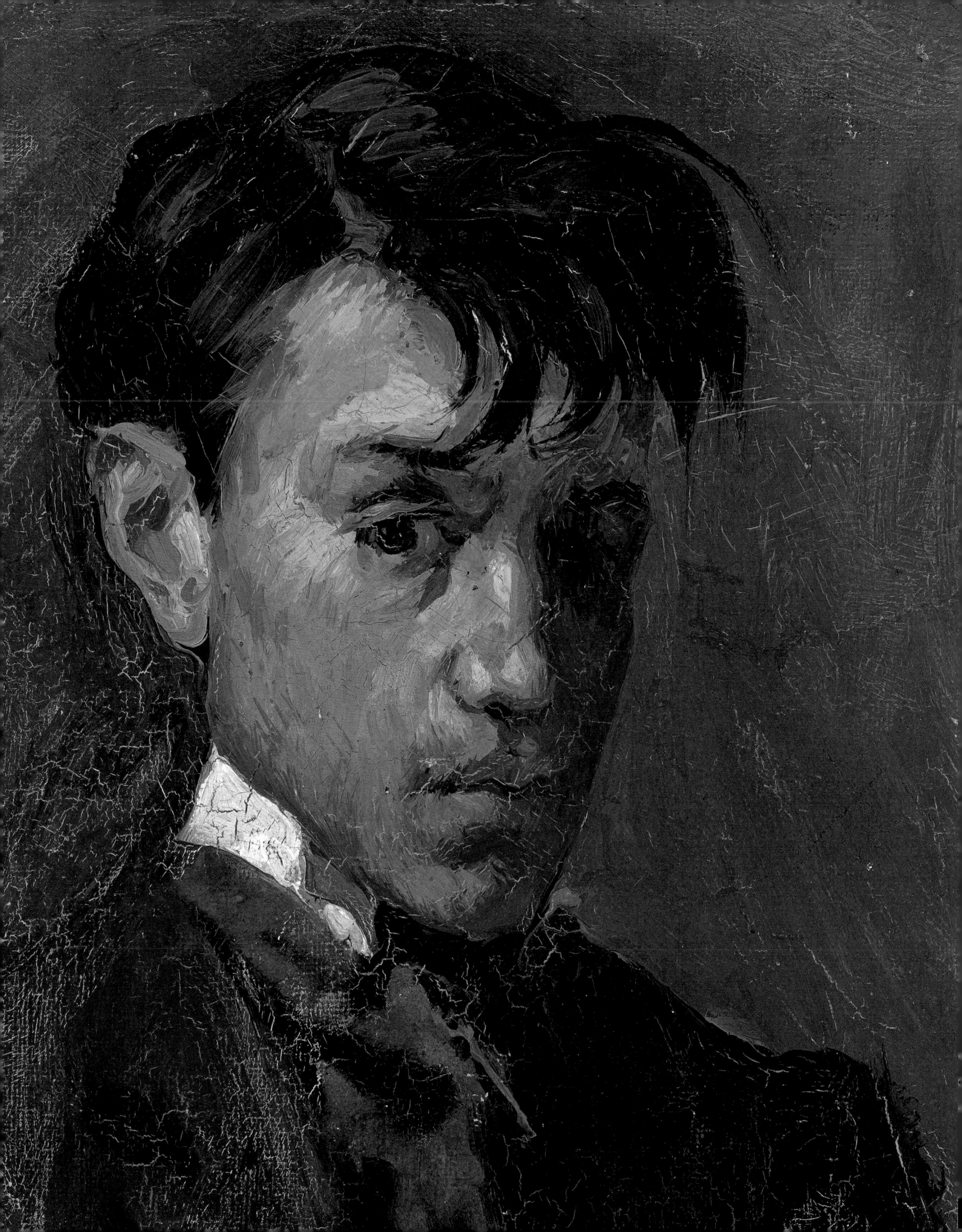

CHAPTER 1

ACADEMIES AND "MAD REVOLUTIONARIES"

RICHARD KENDALL

A vivid paradox that linked the careers of Degas and Picasso at the deepest level was their traditionalism. While both artists would later be counted among the most conceptually original and technically anarchic figures of their generations, Degas and Picasso began their training in a conventional manner. Like most of their peers in the nineteenth century, their early art education was based on copying: week after week, they were required to make drawings from historic works of art, accurately transcribing the objects and images placed in front of them. As students made progress they were permitted to work from live models, who might also be posed to reflect some notable sculpture or painting from the past. Rigorous and demanding, these rituals contributed fundamentally to the artistic formation of Degas and Picasso in ways that persisted in their maturity. Even in old age, they both retained a fascination with scrutinizing and drawing the human figure, along with a compulsion to reinterpret great works from previous centuries in two and three dimensions.

Such parallels invite a closer examination of the early years of these two artists, separated as they were by almost a half century. Initially, both young men came to terms with the academic tradition that dominated their training, emerging as outstanding draftsmen who were vividly conscious of their skills. For Degas, who was born in Paris in 1834, his progression from this traditional vocabulary to the stark realism of the 1860s — which formed the basis of Impression-

ism in the following decade — was protracted and personally challenging. In the final decade of the century, the teenage Picasso took a comparable step in a matter of months and with few regrets. Like Degas, he effectively became a "Painter of Modern Life," in Charles Baudelaire's celebrated phrase, relishing the urban landscape of Barcelona as Degas had once flourished in the boulevard cafés and theaters of Paris.[1] The extent to which the adolescent Picasso — who was born in 1881 — knew about the work of his French predecessor during these years has never been studied, though his subsequent fascination with certain aspects of Degas's art has long been acknowledged. This chapter follows the earliest phases of Picasso's drawing and painting, and their echoes of the work and youthful experience of Degas, beginning with their common educational grounding. It also attempts a broad summary of knowledge about modern French painting in Spain during these years and of the awareness of Impressionism in the circles around Picasso. Such an inquiry suggests, contrary to received wisdom, that Picasso and his friends were significantly informed about these topics in the 1890s, and specifically conscious of Degas's reputation and the character of his art before 1900.

Malaga and Corunna: Studying the Past

Picasso's earliest surviving exercises in conventional draftsmanship preceded his formal art education. Around 1890, at the age of nine,

Detail of Pablo Picasso,
Self-Portrait
(25)

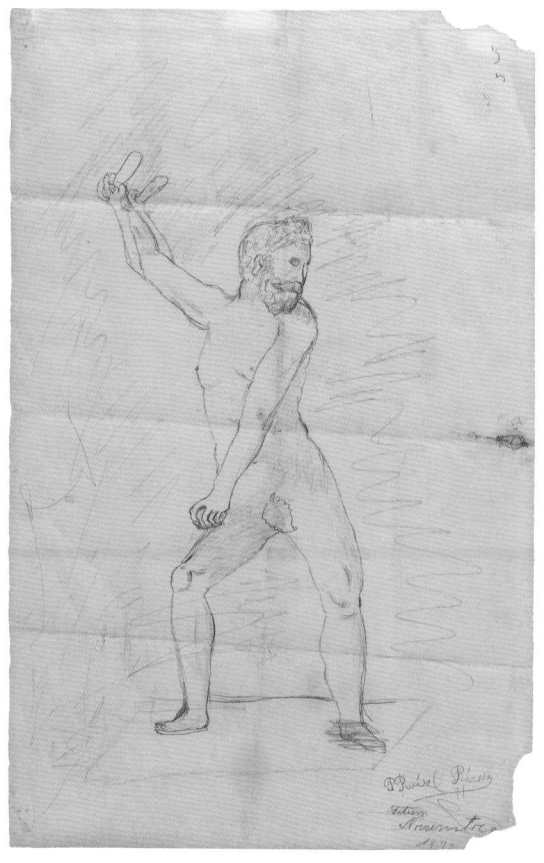

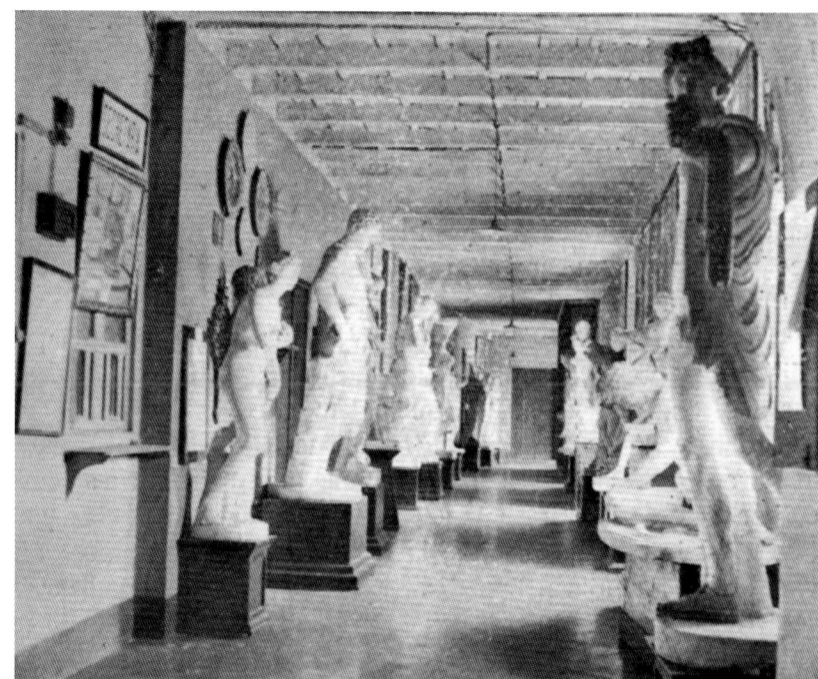

he is said to have made a drawing of Hercules (**1**) from a statue in the family home, perhaps inspired by his father, José Ruiz Blasco, who was an art teacher in the town of Malaga in southern Spain.[2] Don José had a modest local reputation as a painter and useful contacts elsewhere, but earned his living teaching traditional skills. Copies from plaster casts of Classical sculpture, and from prints and reproductions of other notable works, dominated the curriculum at the academy in Malaga (**2**) — where don José taught — and at the École des Beaux-Arts in Paris, which Degas had attended in the 1850s. At this date, the practice of drawing from live models was generally reserved for advanced classes, but even here the use of impersonal lines and shading was insisted upon, and attempts at individual expression were firmly discouraged. Today such discipline seems unimaginably oppressive, yet in their different

ways Degas and Picasso appear to have relished its challenges in their youth, as they pitted themselves against their peers and their illustrious forebears alike. When they first emerged as young independent artists, the human body — often naked — also persisted as a fundamental theme in their own paintings and sculpture. Inextricable from this practice was a dedication to draftsmanship that would only increase with age. As Paul Valéry said of the elderly Degas, in words that apply equally at times to Picasso: "The sheer labor of Drawing had become a passion and a discipline to him, the object of a *mystique* and an ethic all sufficient in themselves, a supreme preoccupation which abolished all other matters."[3]

A curiously echoing pair of drawings allows us to compare these two young artists directly. Degas made *Study after a Rider from the Parthenon Frieze* (**3**) in 1855, the year

1

Pablo Picasso

Hercules, 1890. Pencil on paper, 49.6 x 32 cm. Museu Picasso, Barcelona (MPB 110.842)

2

Plaster casts of classical sculpture at the Escuela de Bellas Artes (San Telmo) in Malaga

3

Edgar Degas

Study after a Rider from the Parthenon Frieze, c. 1855. Pencil on gray paper, 23 x 30.2 cm. Kunsthalle Bremen, Kupferstichkabinett, Der Kunstverein (1956/536)

4

Pablo Picasso

Academic Study: Greek Horseman (Copy of a Plaster Cast; Parthenon, West Frieze [VI], Figure 11), 1895. Pencil and Conté crayon on paper, 28.3 x 29.9 cm. Museu Picasso, Barcelona. (MPB 110.694V)

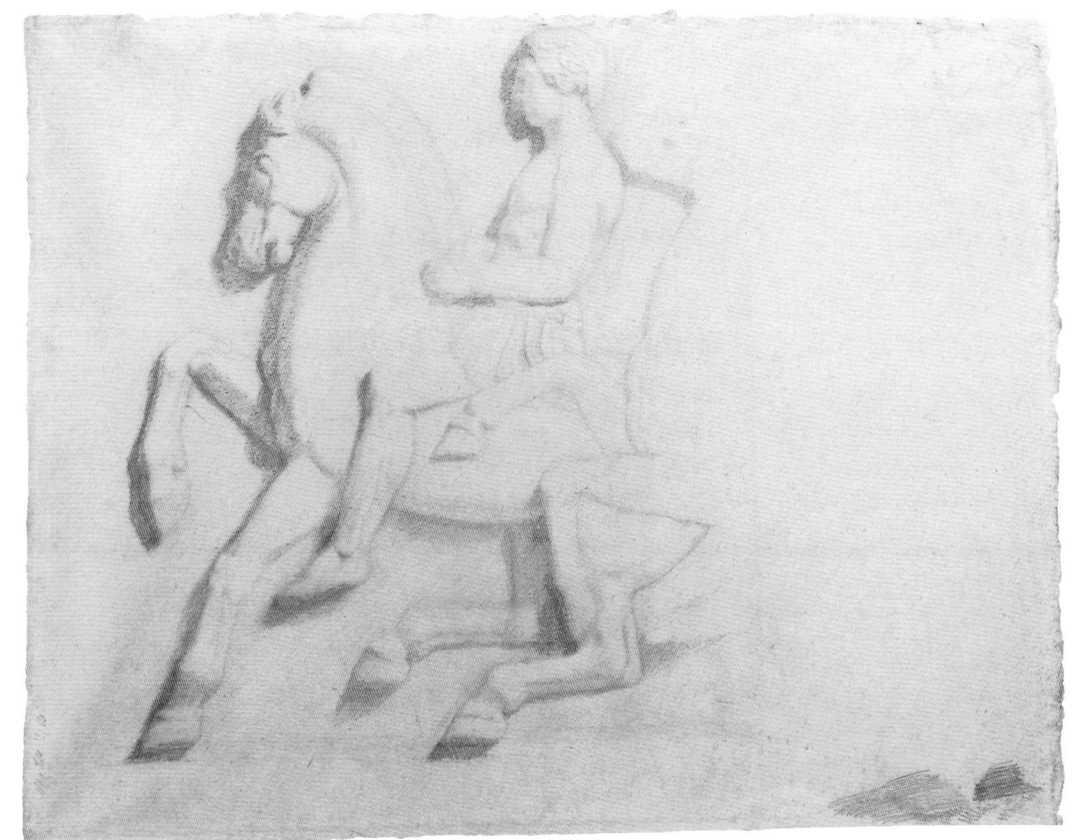

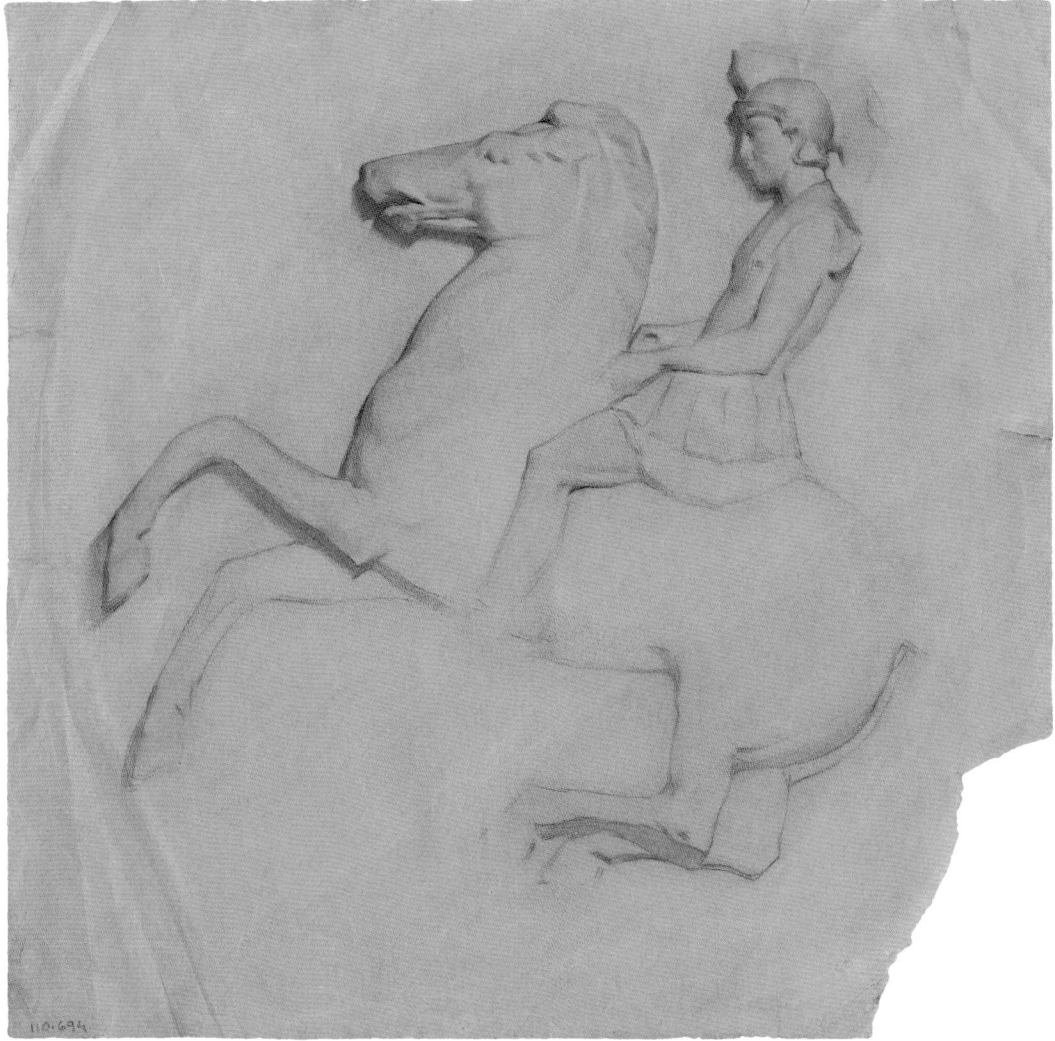

of his twenty-first birthday.[4] In contrast to the
extensively documented early life of Picasso,
no childhood sketches from Degas's hand are
known. The first traces of his artistic activity
are small, informal pencil copies of paintings in
the Louvre and elsewhere that were accumulated a year or two before the Parthenon study.[5]
His high school records indicate that Degas
showed ability if not brilliance in art classes,
yet by 1855 he had clearly made considerable
advances in both skill and application.[6] These
drawings by Degas and Picasso were based
on casts from marble reliefs that once graced
the Parthenon in Athens, among the most copied creations of antiquity at this date. Degas's
pencil study combines precisely articulated
form within the horse's head and finely hatched
modeling throughout, effectively rendering the
three-dimensional character of the panel and
its partly eroded surface. As current teaching
recommended, he also labored to capture the
broader masses and rhythms within the carved
block, qualities that were frequently admired
in the original work. Almost half a century later
Picasso was presented with much the same
challenge, when he began the drawing known
as *Academic Study: Greek Horseman (Copy of a
Plaster Cast; Parthenon, West Frieze [VI], Figure
11)* (**4**). Around fourteen at this time, Picasso
created a variant that is more intensely detailed
than Degas's and more confident despite his
tender years.[7] This superb sheet was just one of
a number of bravura performances by the child-
artist that announced his exceptional technical
command, his powers of observation and visual
judgment, and his uncanny ability to assimilate
the styles of others. While the mature Degas
would later be called "the most intelligent, the
most reflective, the most demanding, the most
merciless draftsman in the world," Picasso was
already outperforming his peers and would
soon set the pace for followers old and young.[8]

These two copies introduce us to several
defining elements in Picasso's early relationship

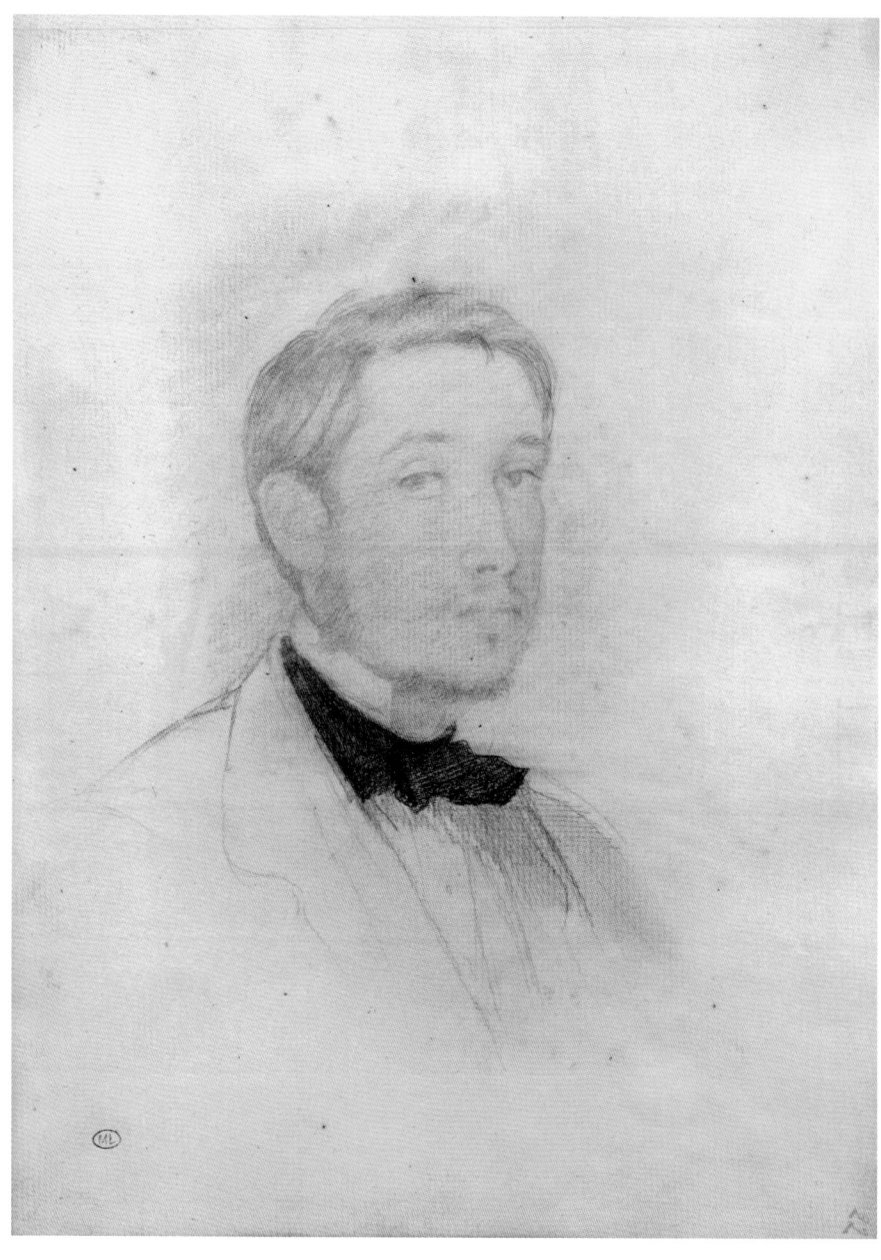

5

Edgar Degas

Self-Portrait, 1856.
Pencil and ink on paper,
17.8 x 25.3 cm. Musée
d'Orsay, Paris, housed in
the Department of
Graphic Arts, Musée
du Louvre (RF 5634 34)

6

Edgar Degas

*Studies of the Borghese
Gladiator*, c. 1856–57. Red
and black chalk on beige
laid paper, 31 x 24.1 cm.
Sterling and Francine
Clark Art Institute,
Williamstown,
Massachusetts
(1971.41)

with the art of Degas. As he grew up in provincial Spain — in Malaga and later in Corunna — Picasso had no direct contact with major centers of European culture or with the progressive tendencies that were then transforming painting and sculpture. The controversial rise of Realism in mid-nineteenth-century France was certainly echoed in Spanish art, though detailed and substantial information about the emergence of Impressionism in the 1870s, for example, probably failed to reach don José and his son until their move to Barcelona in 1895. It is highly unlikely, therefore, that when Picasso made his Parthenon study he was aware of Degas's mature achievement, and it was literally impossible for him to have known about his predecessor's early drawings, which had never been

exhibited.[9] Nevertheless, this phase in Picasso's career helps to articulate a specific connection between the emerging art of the two men. Evident in their drawings from the Parthenon frieze and in slightly later studies from the nude model (see 48, 49) was their mastery of line and form as applied to the human — and animal — body. That both artists persisted in this discipline even when their art education was left behind underscores its significance for Degas and Picasso and separates them from many of their contemporaries. In Degas's case, for example, we find that the majority of his Impressionist colleagues — including Renoir, Monet, and Sisley — had missed out on, or chosen to avoid, this traditional education entirely. Others — notably Pissarro — experienced only briefly the academic approach to drawing from the figure. By the time Picasso and his peers were undergoing instruction, a gradual decline in the dominance of life drawing was already evident; many of his Barcelona friends spent less time in the life class than he did, and certain individuals, such as Carles Casagemas and Ricard Opisso, appear to have bypassed it altogether. No doubt combined with a number of other factors, this early division of ways seems to have left its mark on the careers of Degas and Picasso. As artists in their own right, both continued to place drawing at the center of their studio practice, and both remained committed to the human figure as their prime preoccupation. Whether depicting dancers or harlequins, ladies of fashion or women at their *toilette*, it was Degas and Picasso who could claim to be the preeminent draftsmen and figurative painters of their respective generations.

If some aspects of academic routine engaged Degas and Picasso in their youth, others clearly provoked them. Little in Degas's background marked him out as a radical (**5**), yet within a few months of registering at the École des Beaux-Arts, he chose to abandon its formal courses in favor of self-imposed discipline. With

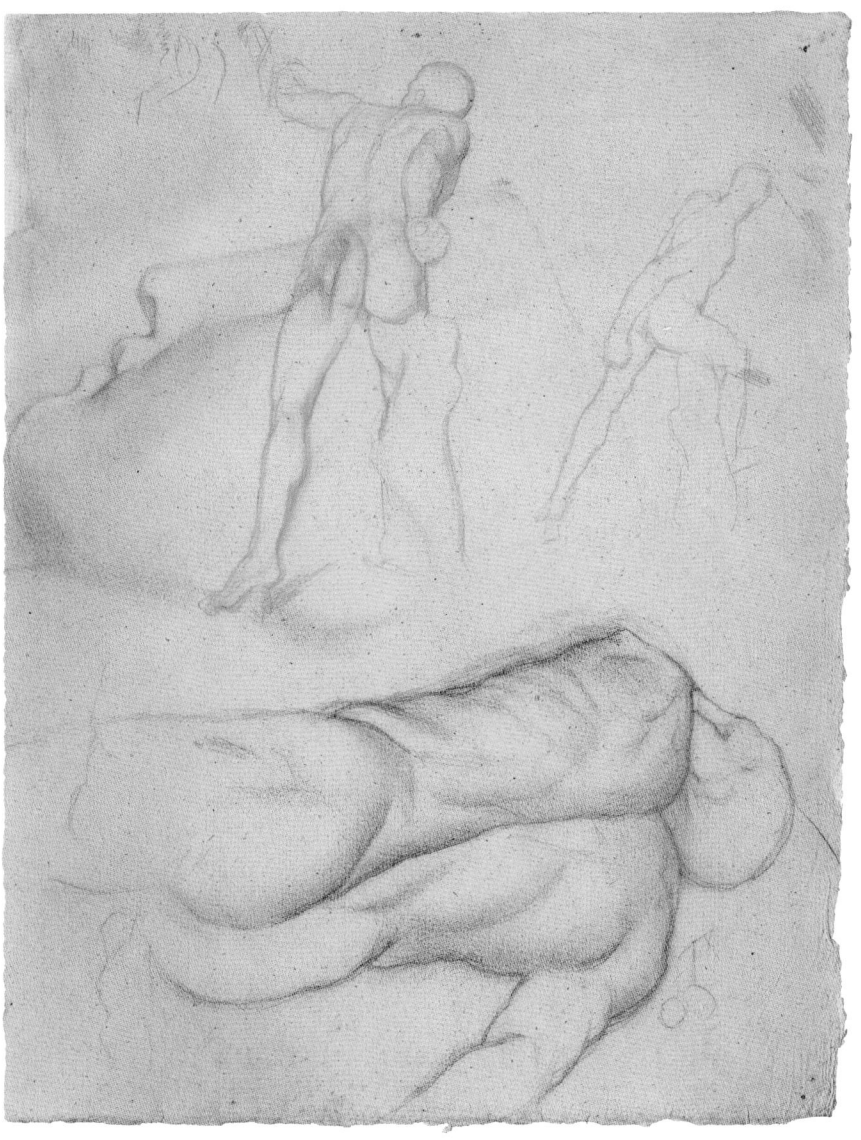

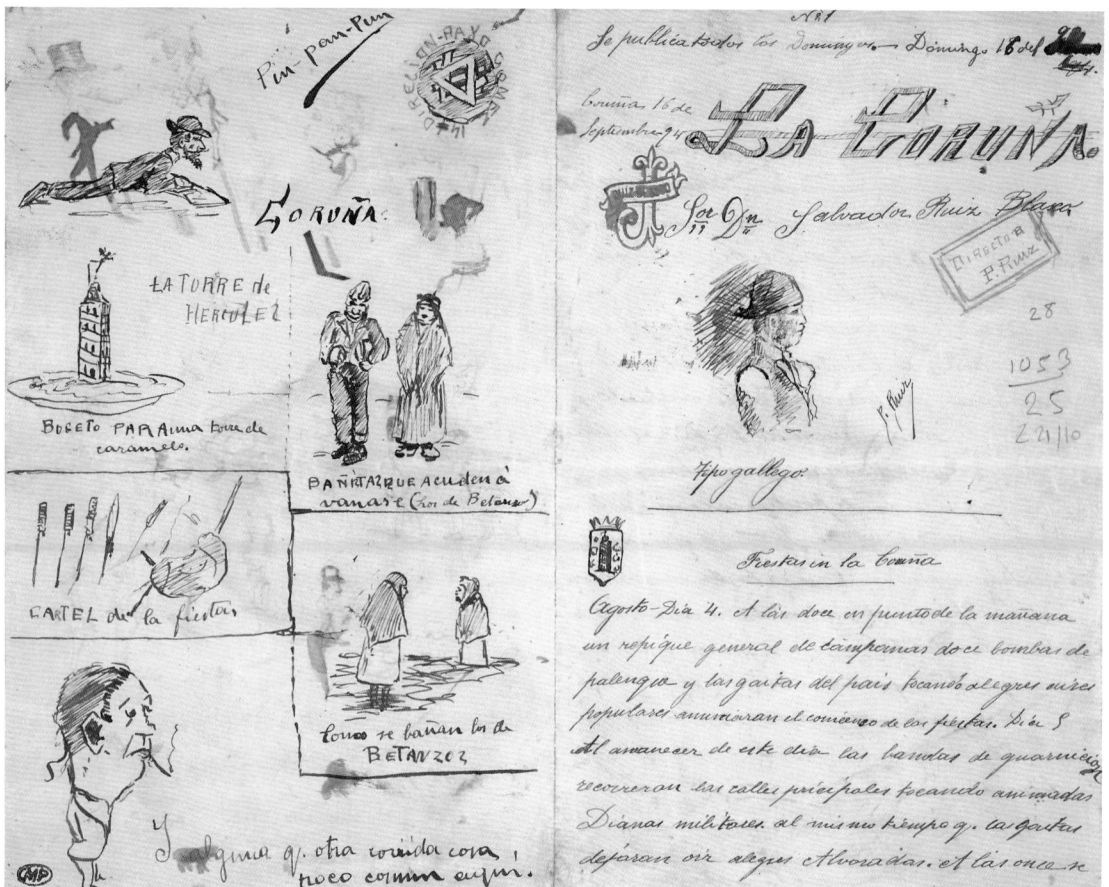

7

Pablo Picasso

"La Coruña"
(manuscript newspaper),
16 September 1894.
Pen, brown ink, and pencil
on paper, 21 x 26 cm.
Musée national Picasso,
Paris (MP 402r)

the moral and financial support of his art-loving father, Degas contrived his own intensive program of study in a traditional vein, first in France and then during three years in Italy, where he could experience Classical and Renaissance art in situ. As he traveled, Degas made many hundreds of drawings and paintings that included a high proportion of self-directed copies, ranging from quick sketches in notebooks to meticulous, detailed compositions on canvas. Among them were studies from such canonical works as the *Roman Borghese Gladiator* (**6**), frescoes by Giotto and Raphael, oil paintings by Bellini and Leonardo, and sculptures by della Robbia and Donatello, as well as less predictable items such as a Mughal miniature and Egyptian wall-paintings.[10] These same crowded notebooks also reveal the first stirrings of Degas's response

as a draftsman to the modern world. Alternating with his copies and at times sharing the same page, we find quick sketches of faces and figures he encountered, attempts at local hillscapes and sunsets, and scenes of dancing and horse racing that presaged his mature oeuvre.[11]

Forty years later Picasso, too, found himself leading a double life as a maker of drawings, the prodigy of the Academy by day but a fantasist and chronicler of his banal surroundings when class was over. After his improvisations in Malaga, he turned even more energetically at Corunna — where the family moved in 1891 — to transcribing houses, animals, matadors in the bullring, and picturesque themes from his imagination. The family's coastal surroundings were tackled in studies of boats and in little paintings of rocks and sea, while local inhabi-

8

Pablo Picasso

Going to School: Lola,
Sister of the Artist, 1895.
Pen and black ink on
paper, 22.9 x 15.1 cm.
Musée national Picasso,
Paris (MP 406)

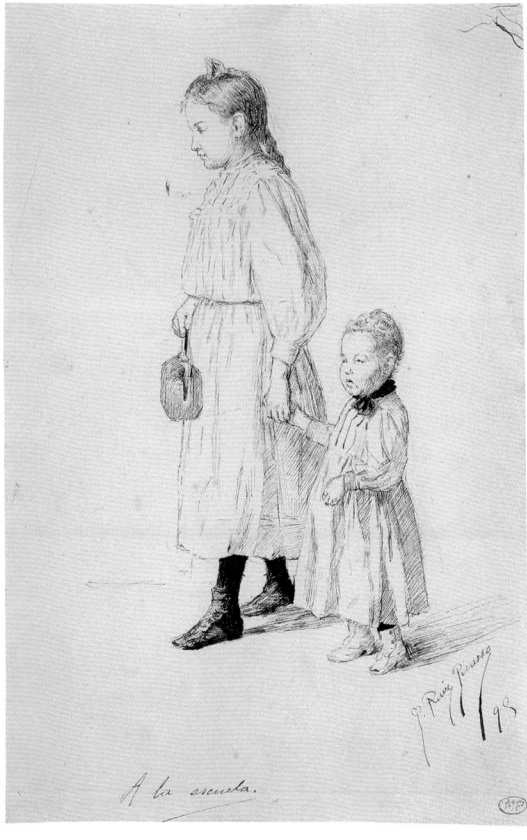

tants featured in rustic narratives made for his own amusement.[12] A cartoon-like manner also appeared in the pages of two mock "newspapers" that Picasso devised, one entitled *La Coruña* (**7**), revealing a taste for the graphic arts that would bear rich fruit in his late adolescence.[13] Again, he could not have known that he was following a path that Degas had pioneered in the 1870s, when the Impressionist brazenly adopted several new media to extend the reach of his art. Using lithography, gillotage, and the multiple print, Degas projected his draftsmanship into the broader marketplace and collaborated with ephemeral publications as he engaged with the wider world.[14]

Picasso's *Greek Horseman* was probably completed in the year that his household made a second, definitive move, leaving for Barcelona after four years in Corunna. They had been lured to Corunna at the northwest extremity of Spain

by improved job prospects for don José, who became teacher of figure and ornamental drawing at the Instituto da Guarda, effectively a high school.[15] The Corunna sojourn coincided with Picasso's emergence as an occasionally wild teenager, but also as a strong-minded, exceptionally versatile young artist. Attempts to submit him to orthodox schooling had little success but were counterbalanced by a strong loyalty to his father — himself a minor painter — and a respectful fascination with the tools of his profession.[16] Now studying under his father's guidance, Picasso continued to copy the prints and plaster casts that surrounded students at this date, as he followed a syllabus that dated back to the Renaissance.[17] In vivid contrast, he also advanced rapidly in the visual mastery of the people and commonplace sights he saw around him. Like countless talented youngsters — including Degas — Picasso found willing models at home, repeatedly drawing his parents and his sister Lola, who posed patiently over the years. His delicate composition *Going to School: Lola, Sister of the Artist* (**8**) introduces us to a less-familiar process — pen-and-ink — and a note of tenderness in Picasso's emotional range. Similar qualities of directness and intimacy are evident in drawings that Degas had made of his siblings and other relatives in the late 1850s. In his vigorous *Giulia Bellelli, Study for "The Bellelli Family"* (**9**), Degas represented a cousin he had visited on his Italian tour, her forceful character drafted in dark, brushed lines in oil on paper with added color. Though a light pencil drawing is visible beneath the brushwork, this is less an exercise in academic technique and more a spirited attempt to pin down a vibrant personality. Around this date Degas's father wrote to his son to encourage his efforts in portraiture, predicting that it would one day be "the most beautiful jewel in your crown," and implicitly urging him toward a remunerative career.[18] Perhaps mindful of this advice, Degas was already planning a huge, innovative group portrait in a domestic

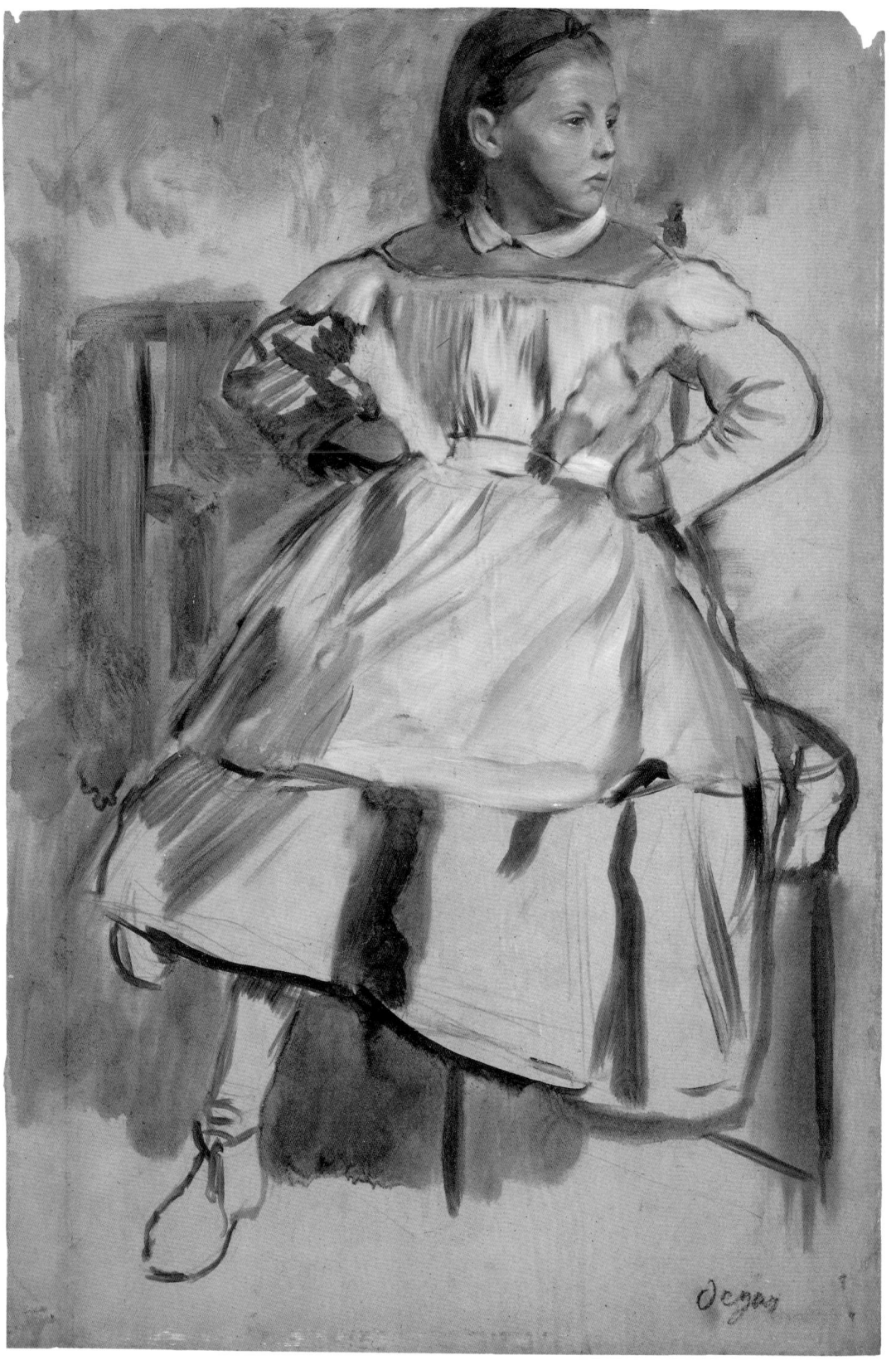

9
Edgar Degas
Giulia Bellelli, Study for
"The Bellelli Family,"
c. 1858–59. Essence and
pencil on buff wove
paper, 36.2 x 24.8 cm.
Dumbarton Oaks House
Collection, Washington,
D.C. (HC.P.1937.12.[E])

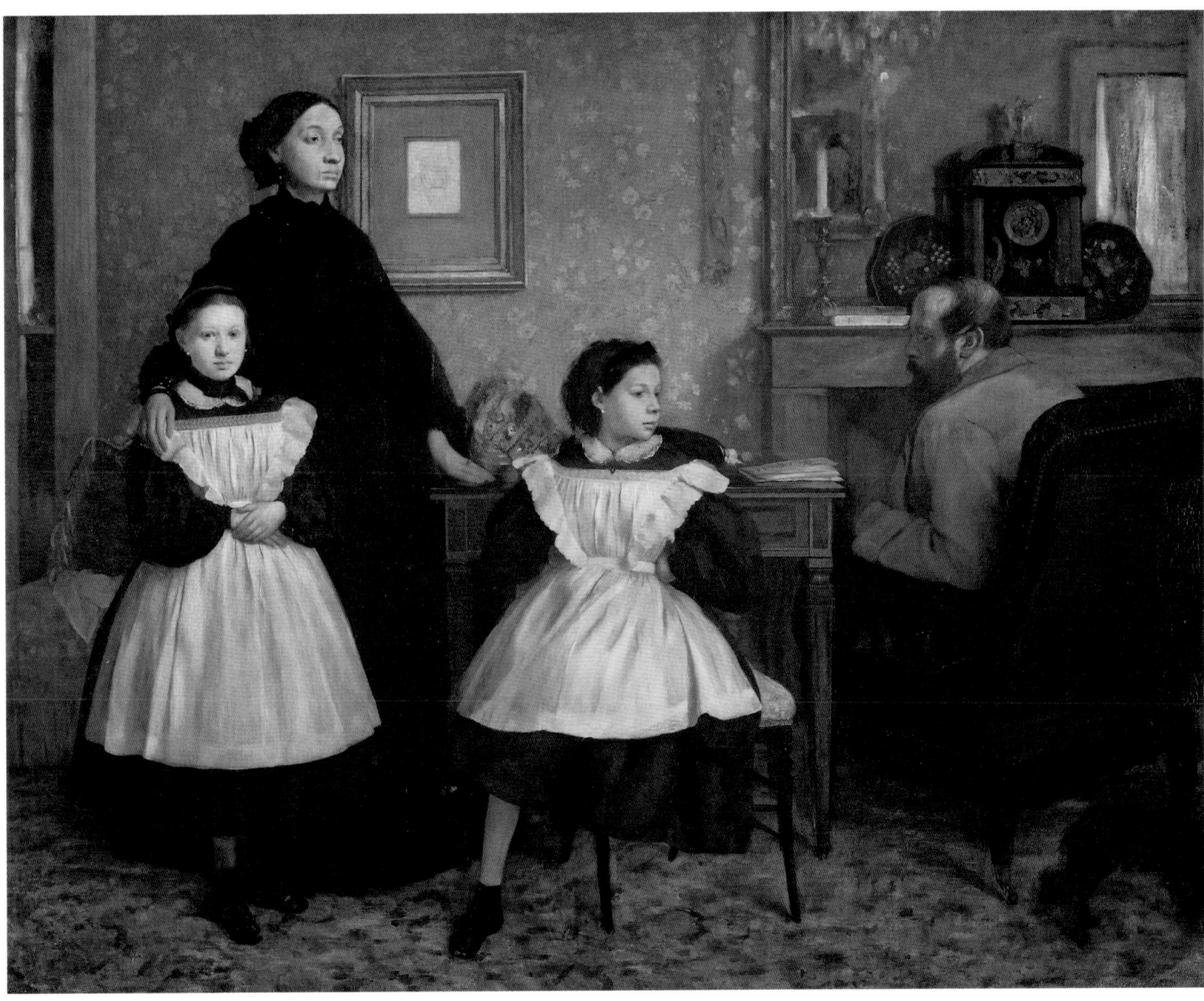

10

Edgar Degas

The Bellelli Family,
1858-67. Oil on canvas,
200 x 250 cm.
Musée d'Orsay, Paris
(RF 2210)

interior, which would include the figure of his cousin Giulia. The finished canvas, now known as *The Bellelli Family* (**10**), was eventually accepted for exhibition at the Paris Salon of 1867, an important step in Degas's advancement in the French capital.[19]

The early careers of Degas and Picasso were both informed and overshadowed to varying degrees by their fathers. By the mid-1890s, don José had a similar future in mind for his gifted son, who was now being actively coached for worldly success. Portraiture was

traditionally seen as a reliable means of ensuring an income for a painter — and perhaps for his larger family — that lay beyond the vagaries of artistic fashion. It also had a proud tradition in Spain, the country that had produced Diego Velázquez and Francisco de Goya, and welcomed El Greco and Peter Paul Rubens to its shores. Encouraging Pablo to draw and paint from a range of characters in Corunna, don José introduced the young prodigy to this possibility and simultaneously promoted his talents in the town.[20] Picasso once more rose to the challenge, creating some of his first works of art that stand on their own merits, irrespective of his age. The impact of *Girl with Bare Feet* of 1895 (**11**) depends on an impressive mastery of proportion and foreshortening, natural daylight and down-to-earth color, and a sensitivity to his model that hints at some identification between the fourteen-year-old painter and his sitter. John Richardson has stressed that such achievements did not come as easily to Picasso as legend tells us, and there are many traces of hard labor and unresolved effort in similar projects from this period.[21]

Also indicative of don José's plan is a cluster of much smaller paintings and drawings made by Picasso during these same months. Consisting of roughly drafted compositions of figures in interiors and in rural settings, these were the kinds of studies that artists conventionally made when conceiving a grander work of art. Some are awkward and most are unfinished, but one vivid example in oil on board captures the drama surrounding an elderly bedridden woman and the two individuals who appear to await her death (**12**). Variants of this theme would be revisited by Picasso more than once in subsequent years, most successfully in the large, ambitious painting *Science and Charity* (**13**), which he completed in Barcelona in 1897.[22] By a strange coincidence, this picture was executed on a canvas with nearly the same dimensions — two meters by two and a half — as Degas's *The Bellelli Family*. Like the latter, no doubt, its scale was intended to catch the eye in a major public forum and draw attention to a new talent. *Science and Charity* also echoed Degas's achievement by winning prizes in Madrid and Malaga, though its ponderous subject appears to have similarly discouraged purchasers.[23]

Advised by perceptive but cautious fathers, the young Degas and the teenage Picasso each found themselves advancing along official channels toward a career as a figure painter-portraitist.[24] Degas's emergence as an artist

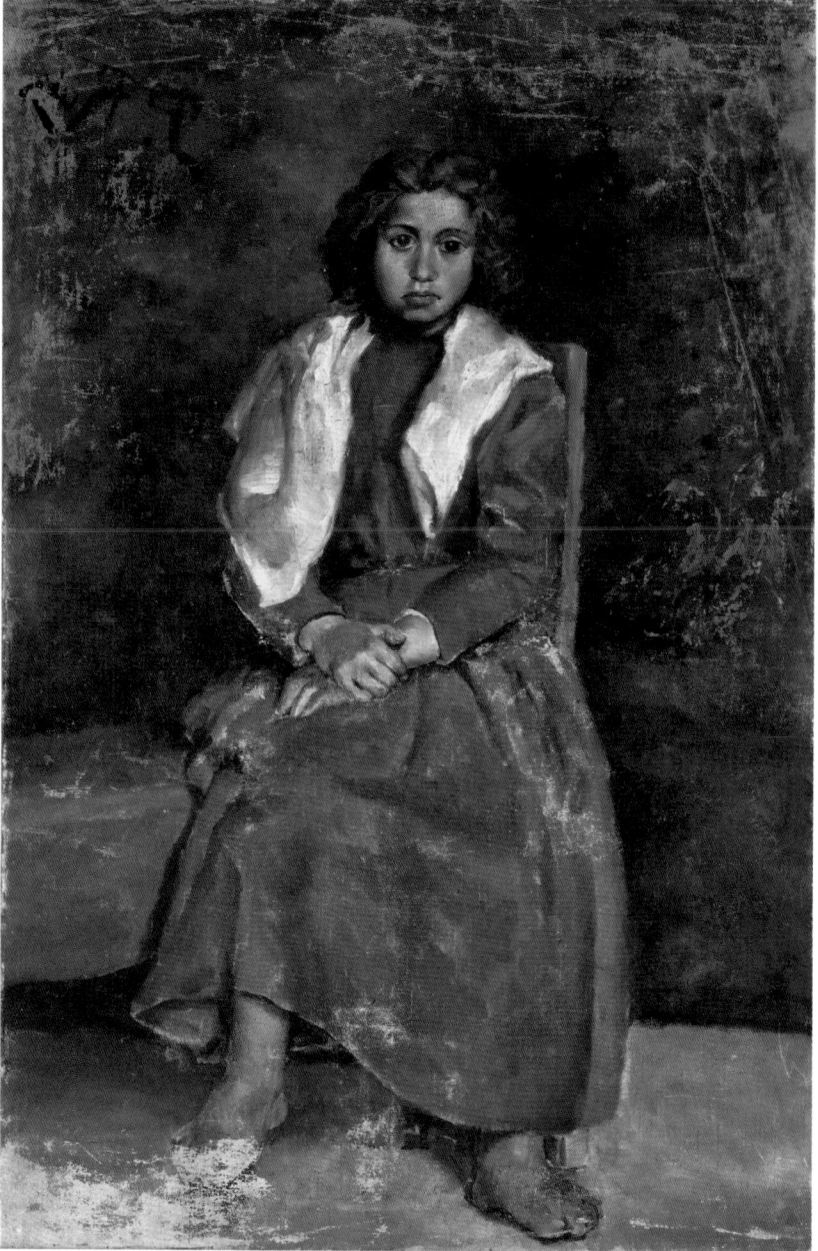

after he returned from Italy had been dominated by his experience of Renaissance art, which he gradually absorbed into a new and audacious role as a painter of modern Paris. Now mixing with such rising stars as Édouard Manet, James Tissot, and James McNeill Whistler, Degas stood aloof from most of the controversies they provoked. Tellingly, he also continued to make drawings in the galleries of

11

Pablo Picasso

Girl with Bare Feet, 1895.
Oil on canvas, 75 x 50 cm.
Musée national Picasso,
Paris (MP 2)

12

Pablo Picasso

The Sick Woman, 1894.
Oil on wood, 14 x 21.5 cm.
Private collection

13

Pablo Picasso

Science and Charity,
1897. Oil on canvas,
197 x 249.5 cm. Museu
Picasso, Barcelona
(MPB 110.046)

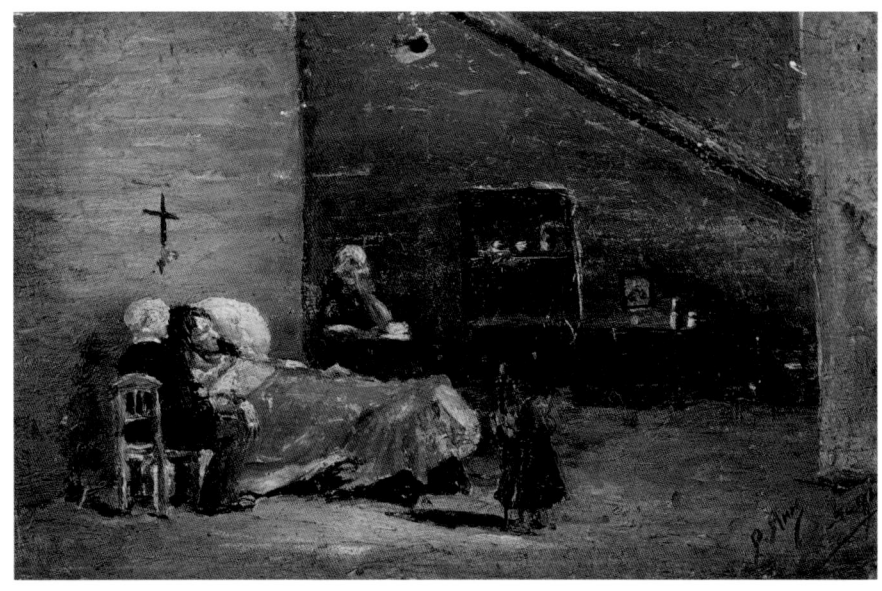

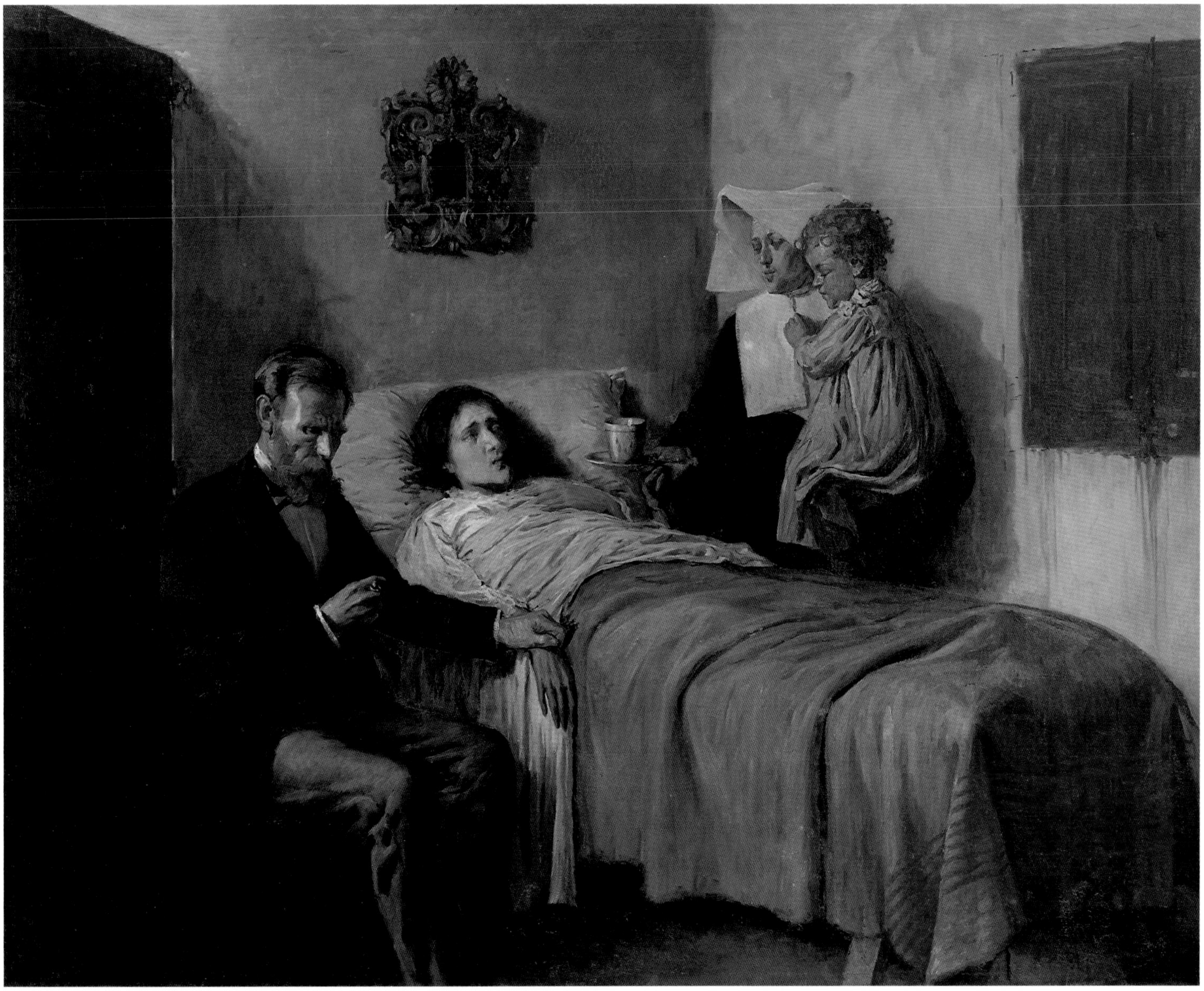

the Louvre until the mid-1860s, sustaining the dialogue with Luca Signorelli, Sebastiano del Piombo, and their Renaissance peers that had begun more than a decade earlier.[25] Expressive of these activities was a sequence of canvases on contemporary themes that echoed the historic works he had encountered, such as portraits of friends that recalled pictures by Titian and Raphael, and Parisian racecourse scenes that ingeniously reworked frescoes by Benozzo Gozzoli.[26] Though Degas brought his distinctive intelligence and wit to these works, his tactics were hardly unusual for a young French artist at this moment. Brought up on the vast holdings of the Louvre and encouraged to study other collections elsewhere, most graduates of the École des Beaux-Arts prided themselves on their continuity with the past. For them and for thousands of equivalent figures throughout Europe, the great tradition resided in the arts of Greece and Rome, where "the cult of beauty" — as it was defined by the authoritative theorist Charles Blanc — still offered guidance in modern times.[27] Even those who espoused the cause of radicalism during these years, from the urbane Manet to the proudly provincial Paul Cézanne, often chose to cite the hermetic language of tradition in the very works that brought them notoriety.

This precedent throws into relief a distinctive aspect of Picasso's formation, which here contrasts starkly with that of Degas. A child of the Spanish provinces in the 1880s and early 1890s, Picasso had been denied the firsthand exposure to great Classical art that Degas enjoyed in Paris and during his Italian tour, and Picasso had seen few Old Master paintings of consequence.[28] Nor was he able to study or copy in large public collections in the manner of his contemporaries in many of Europe's great capitals. Perhaps too young to take on the sustained program of copying that was expected of Degas's generation, Picasso does not seem to have attempted any such tasks even on a

modest scale. In Malaga and Corunna, his only comparable encounters had been with Spanish paintings from previous centuries that could be found in local museums and churches, and with whatever reproductions of famous works he happened to come across. Classrooms and teaching studios at this period often featured monochrome engravings of Spanish works from the Prado and instructive prints of other kinds, but again there is little evidence of protracted engagement with such imagery in Picasso's early drawings and paintings.[29] His father and his other teachers presumably extolled the galleries they had visited elsewhere and the masterpieces they had encountered, but this was a poor substitute for the prodigy under their guidance. As a consequence, Picasso's youthful oeuvre lacks the extensive drawn and painted copies from past art that had distinguished Degas's beginnings and provided the historical grounding for many of his early pictures. So marked was this discrepancy that Picasso's work in his early maturity shows few traces of a response to the art of the Renaissance, much of which he later dismissed as "pathetic."[30]

Encounters with the Modern

A readily accessible and less forbidding source of imagery at this time was the illustrated publication, a factor that has been underexplored in Picasso's early self-education. Spain already had a well-established modern printing industry, which used the latest engraving and photomechanical techniques to produce a wide variety of journals with an emphatically visual character. Mainly published in Madrid and Barcelona, many could be obtained by subscription or bought elsewhere and were augmented in municipal libraries by similar magazines from abroad.[31] Picasso's delight in illustrated satirical journals had been expressed in his witty pastiches of 1893 and 1894, such as *La Coruña*, and persisted throughout adolescence. As a rising young painter at a distance from Spain's

14

Historia y Arte, December
1895, p. 196. Courtesy
Biblioteca Virtual de
Prensa Histórica, Madrid

15

Front cover of *La
Ilustración Artística* 658,
(6 August 1894). Courtesy
Arxiu Històric de la Ciutat,
Barcelona

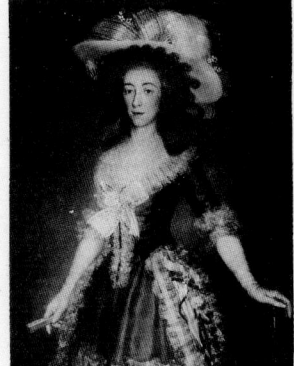

NUEVOS DATOS SOBRE GOYA Y SUS OBRAS

GOYA.—LA CONDESA DE BENAVENTE

196

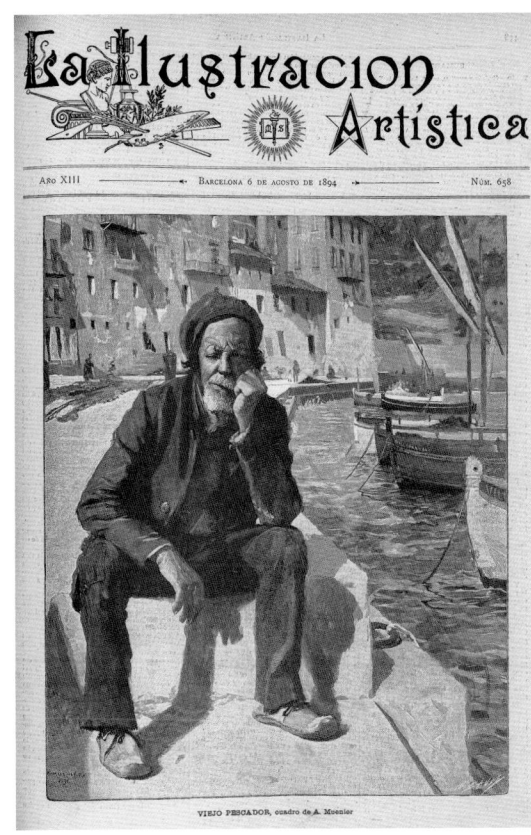

VIEJO PESCADOR, cuadro de A. Mesaler

art centers, he surely went further, to take in the general interest periodicals and perhaps the specialist art titles that had become increasingly available. An example of the latter was the short-lived monthly *Historia y Arte*, which combined poetry, features on ancient objects, occasional articles on painting and sculpture, and some illustrations of historic works of art. In 1895, for example, Picasso's last year in Corunna, *Historia y Arte* included images of Antonio Canova's *Mars and Venus*; several pictures by Francisco de Goya (**14**); and a Hieronymus Bosch-like scene by Jeronimo van Alken, as well as paintings by several modern Spaniards, among them Joaquin Sorolla y Bastida.[32]

Much more widely read was the weekly *La Ilustración Artística* (**15**), whose sixteen pages were divided between sentimental stories, articles on varied cultural matters, and a profusion of photographs and high-quality engravings.

For today's historians, *La Ilustración Artística* offers a broad but vivid conspectus of the years in which Picasso grew up, as recorded in the popular press and its unpretentious visual material. Produced in Barcelona over several decades, it was directed at a middle-class readership and openly celebrated the nation's modern history and current achievements.[33] Every issue contained reproductions of Spanish paintings, principally from the nineteenth century, while the country's religious life was reflected in scenes of piety and ceremonial, and in extensive sacred imagery. Illustrations of older art appeared from time to time; during 1894, for example, *La Ilustración Artística* printed a full-page image of Bartolomé Esteban Murillo's *Saint John the Baptist* and *Virgin in Prayer* by Sassoferrato, as well as a range of secular portraits by Raphael, Franz Hals, Hans Holbein, and others.[34] At a time when art books were still rare and costly, such pictures would have had considerable significance for painters living outside the major cities of Spain, where *La Ilustración Artística* was certainly read. Records at the Biblioteca de Circulo de Artesanos — a public library in Corunna — show that this magazine was available in the town throughout the sojourn of Picasso and his family.[35] A less predictable side of the same publication was its wide coverage of contemporary art, both from Spain and beyond the nation's borders. A single issue might embrace reproductions of paintings and sculptures by a half dozen living Spanish artists, in a spectrum of styles from historical pastiche to near-photographic realism. Their subjects were equally diverse: a modern rendering of the Madonna and Child might be followed by a contemporary street scene, often with captions showing that they were fresh from the easel or from that year's Exposición des Bellas Artes in Barcelona. Also represented were young artists from elsewhere in Europe, notably England and Germany, some of whom sent their canvases to the annual Barcelona show. Even at a distance from major centers, it seems, readers of *La Ilustración Artística* could follow the fluctuations of metropolitan taste and see the pictures that were being bought and collected at that moment.

Where Degas's family had encouraged him toward the Italian masters, don José appears to have chosen Spanish art — occasionally from earlier eras, but mainly from this modern context — as the model for his multitalented son. The historic painting of Spain had long been a source of national pride and was still interminably recommended to students for their emulation; Picasso himself complained of the monotonous references to Diego Velázquez during his studies in Madrid in 1898.[36] In the course of the nineteenth century, the Spanish school enjoyed a surge of popularity throughout Europe, where thinly veiled references to paintings by Velázquez as well as Goya, Murillo,

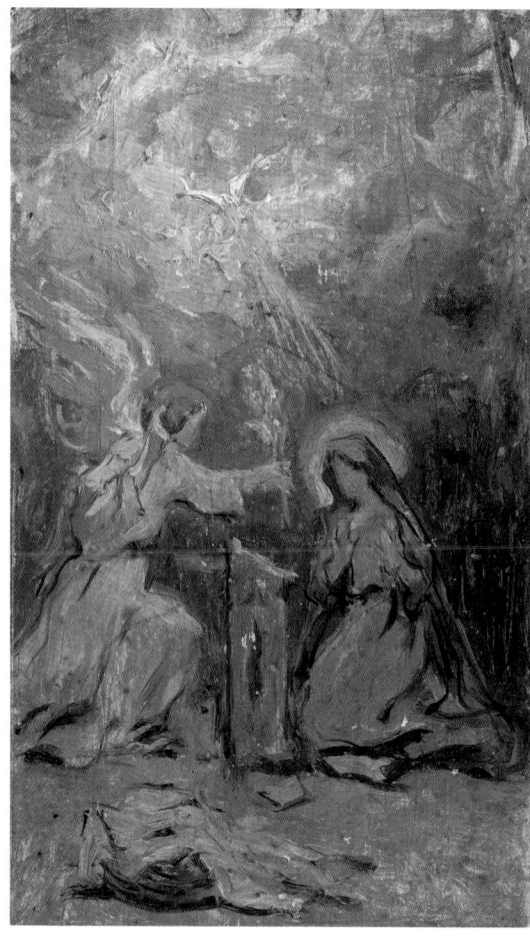

and Francisco de Zurbarán became commonplace and a Spanish "style" was adopted by novices and contemporary masters alike. A curious feature of Picasso's adult interest in the art of Degas was the fact that many French painters in the wider Impressionist circle, among them Manet, Whistler, Degas, and Mary Cassatt, had fallen under a similar influence at various points in their careers.[37] For Picasso's generation, paradoxically, this circumstance was almost reversed, as they turned away from their national forebears toward other European models of the day, such as those of France, England, and Germany. Relatively few scenes that may have been prompted by traditional Spanish prototypes can be identified among the young Picasso's informal sketches on paper and canvas from the Corunna years. These include small-

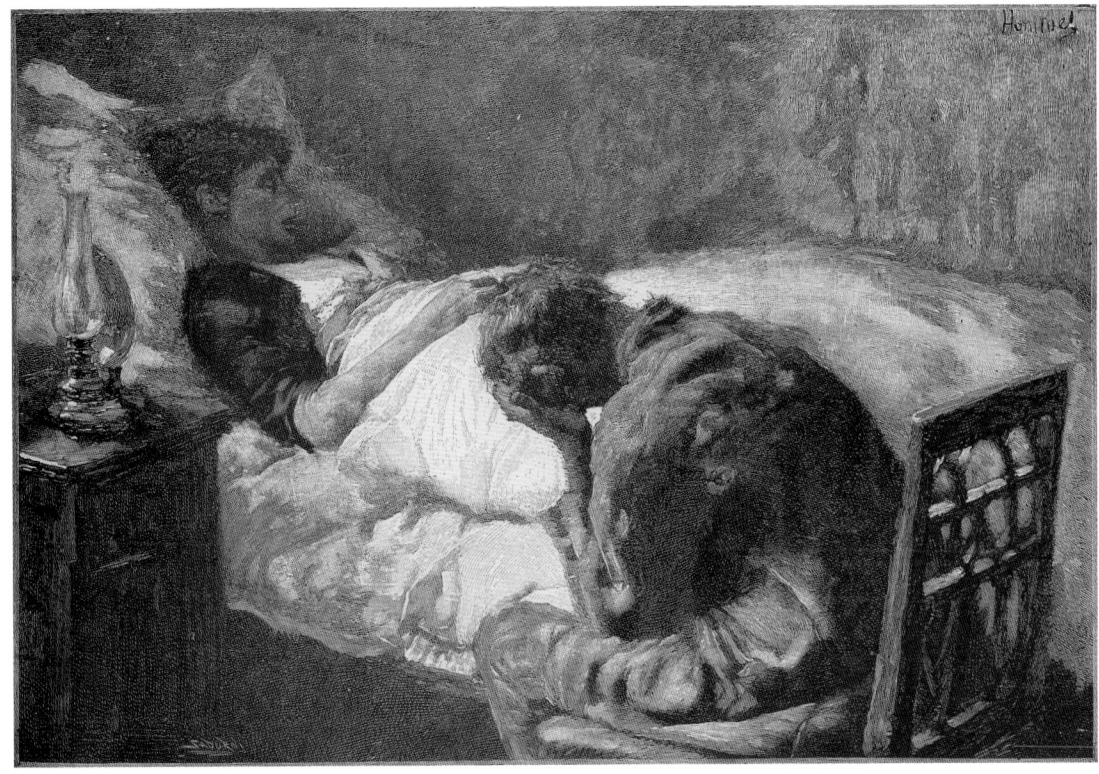

17

Theodor Hummel

(German, 1864–1939)

United at the Mother's Deathbed. Reproduced in *La Ilustración Artística* 658 (6 August 1894), p. 499. Courtesy Arxiu Històric de la Ciutat, Barcelona

scale compositions of battles and knights in armor — some linked with Don Quixote — and of seventeenth-century swordsmen, episodes from the life of Columbus, and drawings of stylized saints and martyrs.[38] Also suggestive of a nationalistic taste is the scattering of religious motifs that Picasso experimented with: a *Nativity* in a broad-brushed, "Old Master" manner; oil studies of a priest and an ornate altar; and the painting *Annunciation* (**16**).[39] Picasso's father and his family — if not the young artist — are said to have been conventionally religious, and it seems likely that these traditionally inclined pictures were undertaken to please those around him and extend his marketable repertoire.[40] Yet this pattern was remarkably limited within Picasso's overall production; few if any of his Corunna sketches of historical or ecclesiastical themes were developed as substantial canvases, and it was essentially to other genres and current modes that father and son chose to turn.

Several key compositions begun by Picasso

in 1894 and 1895 show him rejecting history in favor of modernity. Concerned as ever for his son's advancement, don José appears to have directed him toward styles then fashionable in Barcelona, of the type that appeared regularly in the pages of *La Ilustración Artística* and other widely read magazines. Picasso's little sketch of *The Sick Woman* (see 12), for example, painted in Corunna but ultimately developed and expanded into *Science and Charity* (see 13), brought together popular sentiment, theatricality, and an element of contemporary religion in a broadly realistic context, ingredients almost guaranteed to find favor in the current Spanish art market. The roots of this image are not in the Old Masters but in works such as Theodor Hummel's recent *United at the Mother's Deathbed*, which was shown in Barcelona in 1894 and reproduced in *La Ilustración Artística* on 6 August (**17**). More sophisticated in every way than Picasso's first attempt at a similar theme, Hummel's emphasis on the tragic end of a relationship between a young woman and her child anticipates many features of the completed *Science and Charity*. The same magazine offers other parallels with early figure scenes by Picasso, showing a marked taste for pictures of poor but endearing Spanish children, such as the model in Picasso's *Girl with Bare Feet* (see 15). In a comparable way, the frequent appearance of engravings and photographs of elderly workers and weatherworn mariners — one of whom is portrayed on the cover of the same issue of *La Ilustración Artística* with the title *The Poor Fisherman* (see 15) — may have played some role in the emergence of Picasso's painting with a similar title (see 19).

A pervasive quality of the European art world in the 1890s that proved to have even greater repercussions for Picasso's future had almost certainly entered his consciousness by this date. This was the dominance of Paris, not just as a lure for young painters but as a center of vital, sometimes disruptive creativity in the arts as a whole. One of the few teachers of whom Picasso spoke well in later years, Isidoro Brocos, had studied in Paris as a young man in the mid-1870s and may have been Picasso's first personal contact with that city. While Picasso was still in Corunna, two young painters whose circle he was soon to join — Santiago Rusiñol and Ramon Casas — had already followed in Brocos's footsteps and would have been even better informed about current Parisian matters. The topicality of French culture during this decade is markedly evident at many levels, not just in the experimental journals that are so characteristic of the period but also in mainstream Spanish publications. Once again, *La Ilustración Artística* is symptomatic of the phenomenon, offering articles, features, and images that dealt with subjects as disparate as the street life of Paris, Sarah Bernhardt's glamorous apartment in the city, and the work of living French painters. In 1894, no fewer than three covers for *La Ilustración Artística* were devoted

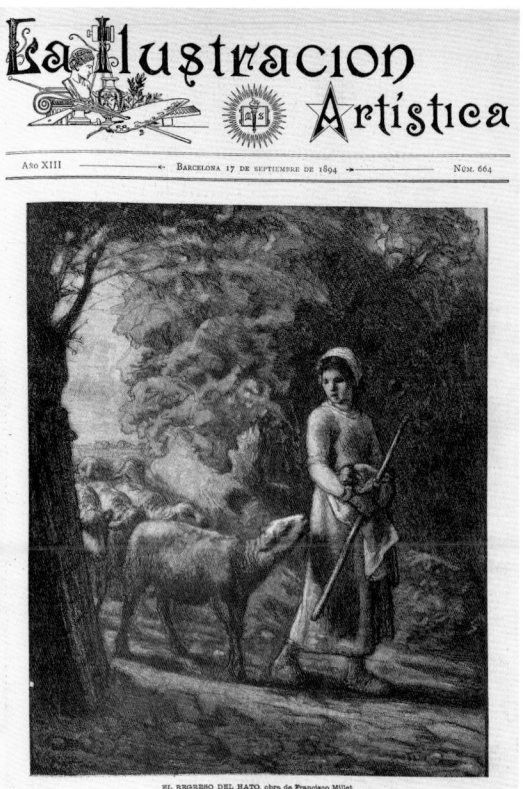

18

Front cover of *La Ilustración Artística* 664 (17 September 1894), p. 499. Courtesy Arxiu Històric de la Ciutat, Barcelona

to engravings of pictures by Benjamin Constant, a former student at the École des Beaux-Arts in the generation that followed Degas's.[41] Constant had traveled in Spain as a young man but later found favor in France as a portraitist and designer of murals for public buildings. Less predictable in this magazine were works by Jean-François Millet (**18**) and Camille Corot, chosen as cover designs in 1894 and 1895, given that both men had been seen as radicals in their time and were represented here by somber, black-and-white drawings.[42]

More directly instructive for modern Picasso scholars was an article that appeared in July 1894, dedicated to the art of Pierre Puvis de Chavannes.[43] Illustrated with six of his paintings and murals, this substantial tribute reflected the qualities of gravity and compositional inventiveness in Puvis's work that would be seized upon by Picasso and his peers at the turn of the century. Three months earlier, *La Ilustración Artística* had published an essay that is even closer to the present inquiry, with the title *La pintura impressionista francesca*.[44] Written by the leading Spanish intellectual and educational theorist Francisco Giner de los Ríos, this text had been prompted by a gallery of French paintings at the current Fine Arts Exhibition in Madrid. Giner acknowledged that the works on view did not "convey the fullest sense of the blossoming of that art which now enjoys such a magisterial influence throughout the world," even though his essay suggests a generous — even bewildering — breadth in the Madrid installation.[45] In short, the author's notion of "Impressionist Painting" seemed to encompass almost every current tendency in French art except for the most profoundly conservative. Within a single paragraph we find the names of such painters as Léon Bonnat, William Bouguereau, and Édouard Detaille, despite the known opposition of such individuals to Impressionism, as well as "landscapists and seascapists like Pissarro, Monet, Sisley."[46] After attempting an outline history of the new movement, Giner defined the Impressionist school as a descendant of Realism but again struggled to include Millet, Puvis de Chavannes, and Albert Besnard ("perhaps the most extreme Impressionist") within his idea of the new mode. On other issues he was more accurately informed, citing the role of "plein-air" — or outdoor painting — and Chevreul's optics in the innovative approaches of the Frenchmen and accepting that Monet should be regarded as "one of the foremost Impressionists."[47] Far from hostile to Impressionism, such texts nevertheless reveal the limited information available to the Spanish public at this date about works by "Pissarro, Monet, Sisley" and their colleagues. Absent from Giner's account of this largely landscape-based group of individuals were many of Impressionism's leading participants, notably those associated with Degas and with the depiction of the human figure. As we shall see, this distinction between the "pleinairistes"

and the painters of the modern city life — while never exclusive or clear-cut — played an important role in the reception of Impressionist art generally, and also in its impact on modern developments in Spain.

It was not until Picasso finally left Corunna in summer 1895 that he experienced the great European masters firsthand. His family was now following don José to a better teaching post in Barcelona, where he would eventually end his career. Required to change trains in Madrid, father and son rushed to look at the spectacular rooms of paintings at the Prado, dominated then as now by works from the Spanish and Italian schools. There are no firsthand accounts of what took place, but two small drawings of minor figures in pictures by Velázquez seem to have been made by Picasso on this visit.[48] Instead of proceeding directly to Barcelona, the family had decided to return to Malaga for a long vacation in the company of their relatives and acquaintances. Perhaps inspired by what he saw in Madrid and certainly better informed about his ancient craft, it was at Malaga that Picasso painted one of the masterpieces of his early years: *The Old Fisherman* (**19**). Several elements of his prior exposure to the arts came together in this arresting canvas, which is precocious by any standards. True to his academic training, Picasso had first made a sequence of drawings of the partly unclothed figure (**20**), a destitute named Salmerón who was known to local friends. From these poses Picasso chose one that stressed the old man's craggy features and angular, undernourished frame, perhaps recalling the fisherman by Mueller on the cover of *La Ilustración Artística* (see 15). As he tackled the canvas itself Picasso became more Old Masterly, invoking traditional *chiaroscuro* in the bright light falling from above on the deeply shadowed room and dramatizing the figure in rich flourishes of white, gray, and bronze oil paint. Some hesitation is indicated in changes made to the position of the arm at right, yet the young artist's bold use of pictorial

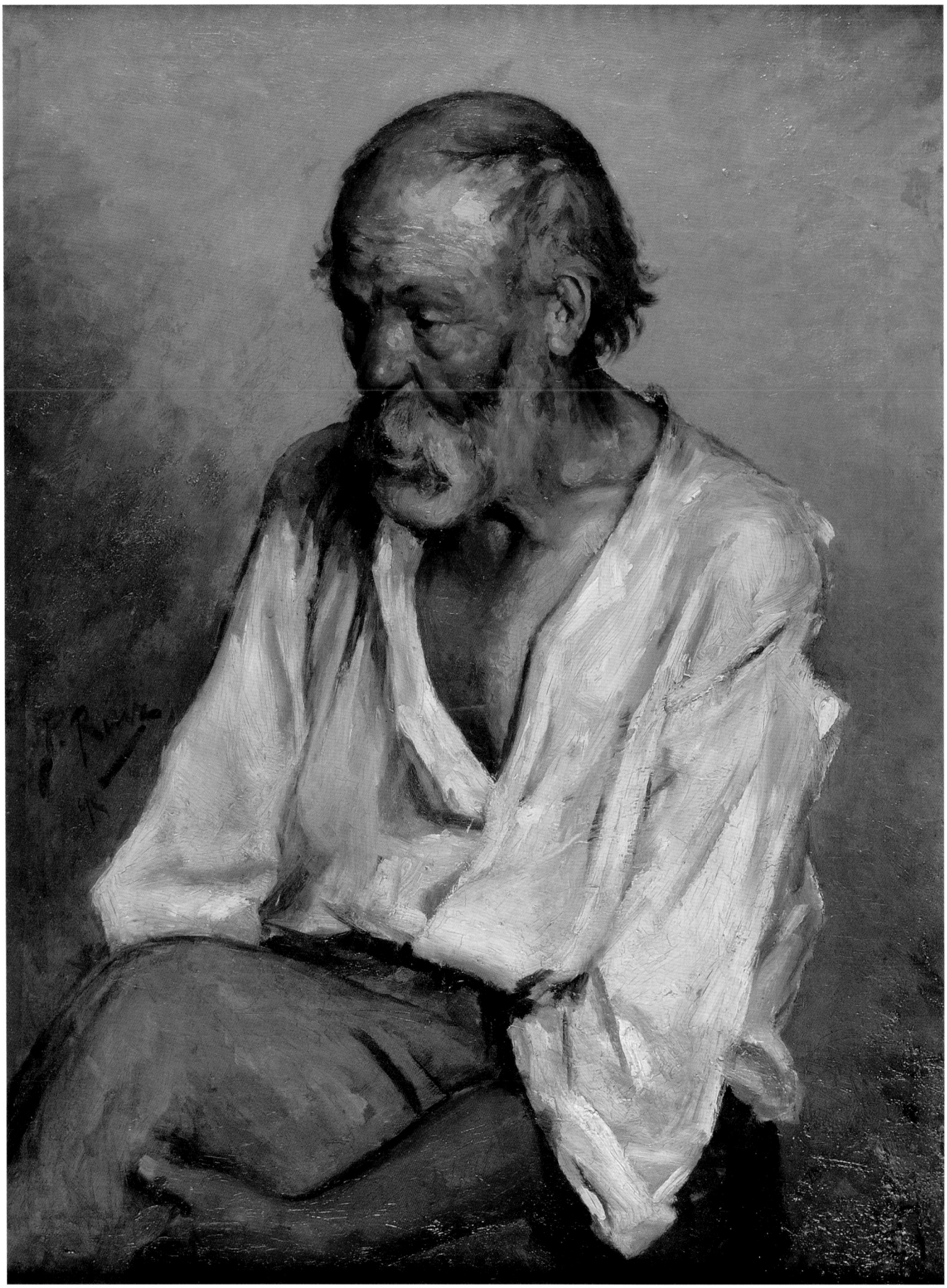

19

Pablo Picasso

The Old Fisherman, 1895.
Oil on canvas,
83 x 62.5 cm. Museu
de Montserrat.
Gift of X. Busquets
(N.R. 200.502)

20

Pablo Picasso

Old Fisherman, Seated,
14 August 1895. Pencil
on paper, 12 x 8 cm.
Museu Picasso, Barcelona
(MPB 111.167)

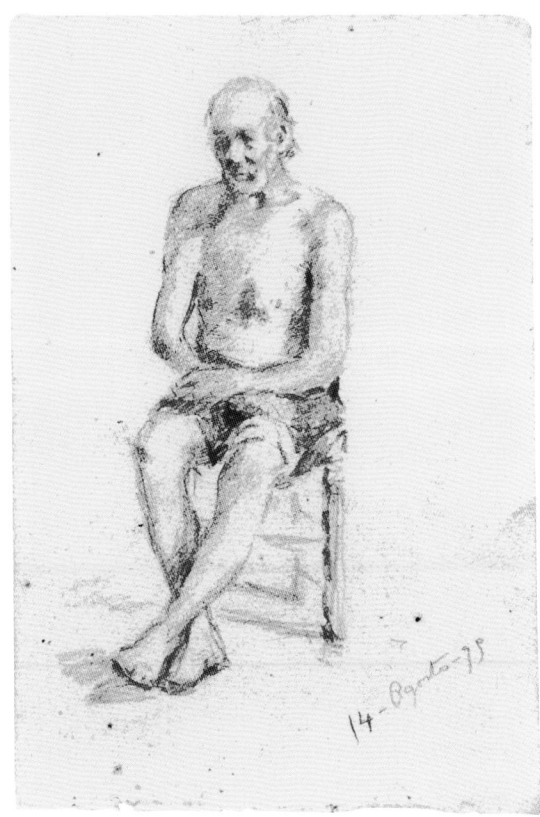

devices associated with his predecessors seems to exude confidence. Echoes of well-known depictions of hermits, peasants, and Christian martyrs seen in the Prado have been noted in this work, which nevertheless remains grittily contemporary.[49]

Studies based on picturesque human types often played an important role in the artist's education in mid-nineteenth-century Europe, when they were seen as useful additions to the pictorial repertoire and challenges to individual skill. During his Grand Tour of Italy in the 1850s, Degas had engaged with this genre when he joined a group of talented young contemporaries at the French Academy in Rome and shared some of their classes. In several watercolors and two substantial oil paintings he made detailed studies of gypsies and other characters in local costume, dating his pictures and proudly adding "Rome" to the inscriptions.[50] His

Roman Beggar Woman (**21**), completed in 1857, is considerably more painstaking than Picasso's *The Old Fisherman*, while similarly evoking the grimness of vagrant life through its shadowy voids and subdued earth tones. Given the very limited education in the practice of painting that Degas had experienced, his picture is also a remarkably accomplished work and one that — like Picasso's — largely avoids the sentimental clichés associated with such subjects. Despite his model's squalid setting, Degas — again foreshadowing Picasso — was able to suggest some dignity in the elderly model's demeanor and to implicitly link the figure with grander historical precedents. There is no record of Degas exhibiting this highly finished and subtly detailed canvas, which joined a large number of works from his early years that followed him from studio to studio as his career advanced. It would thus have been seen only by individuals who knew him personally or managed to penetrate his seclusion in later life. Like *The Bellelli Family* and other pictures of this kind, *The Roman Beggar Woman* represents a generic precedent for Picasso's early attempts at historically informed painting, but not a specific prototype known to the young Spaniard.

As aspiring but still unknown young artists, Degas and Picasso each strove to widen their artistic repertoires within the conventions of the day. Much of the government-sponsored imagery in France and Spain, which often took the form of state commissions for murals and other monumental canvases, was still concerned with dramatic episodes from ancient and modern history. Around 1860, when Degas began his large oil painting *Semiramis Building Babylon* (**22**), he may have had such a project in mind for one of the existing or still unbuilt civic structures in Paris.[51] In the approved manner, he made scores of exquisite drawings for the composition and its participants, including the exotic retinue of Queen Semiramis, the warlike Babylonian ruler.[52] One of Degas's studies, *Two*

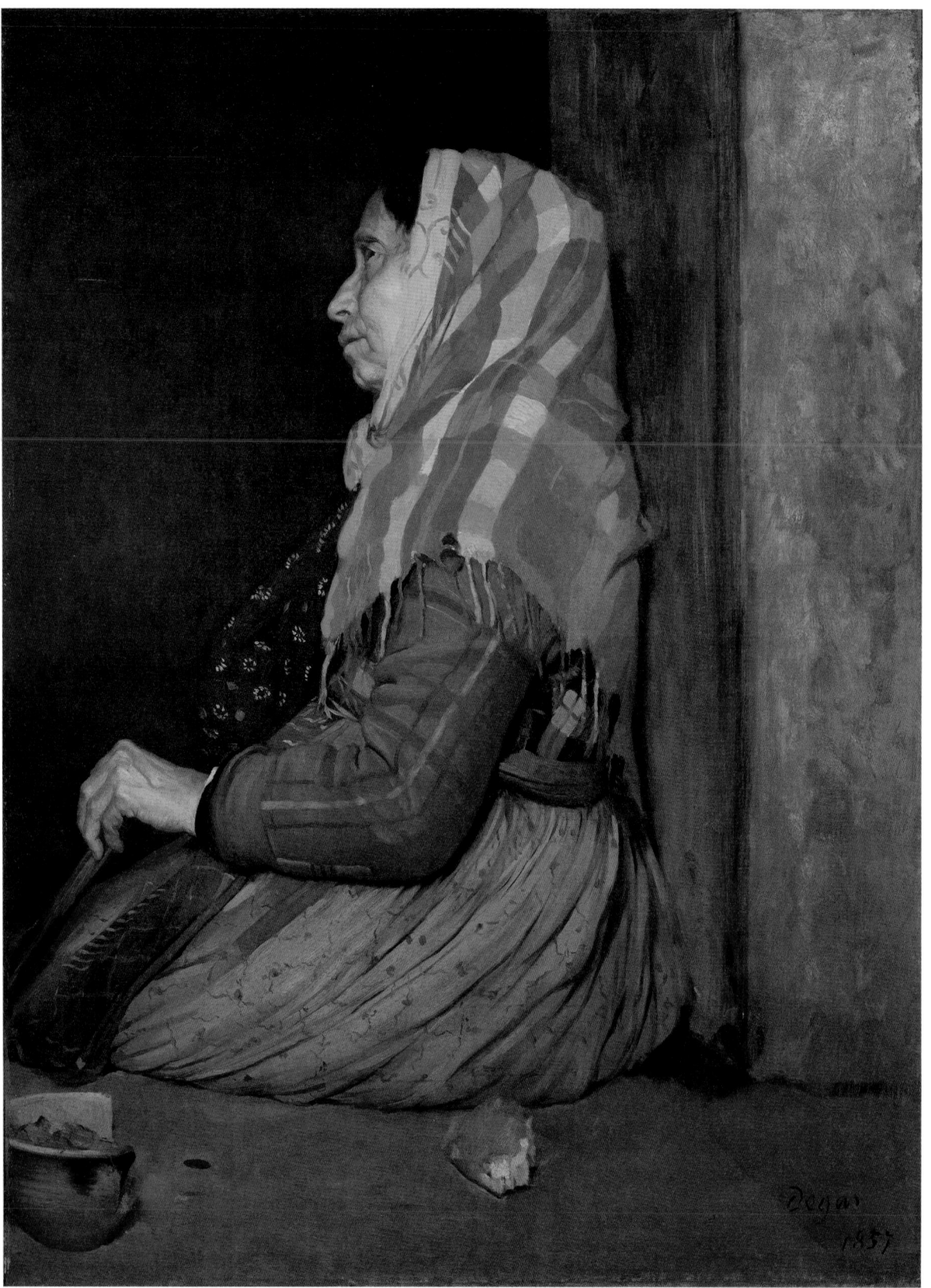

21

Edgar Degas

Roman Beggar Woman,
1857. Oil on canvas,
100.3 x 75.2 cm.
Birmingham Museums
and Art Gallery, England
(1960P44)

22

Edgar Degas

*Semiramis Building
Babylon*, 1861. Oil on
canvas, 151 x 258 cm.
Musée d'Orsay, Paris
(RF 2207)

23

Edgar Degas

*Two Women Restraining
Horses*, c. 1860–62.
Pencil on tracing paper,
30.6 x 31 cm. Musée
d'Orsay, Paris, housed
in the Department of
Graphic Arts, Musée du
Louvre (RF 15 528)

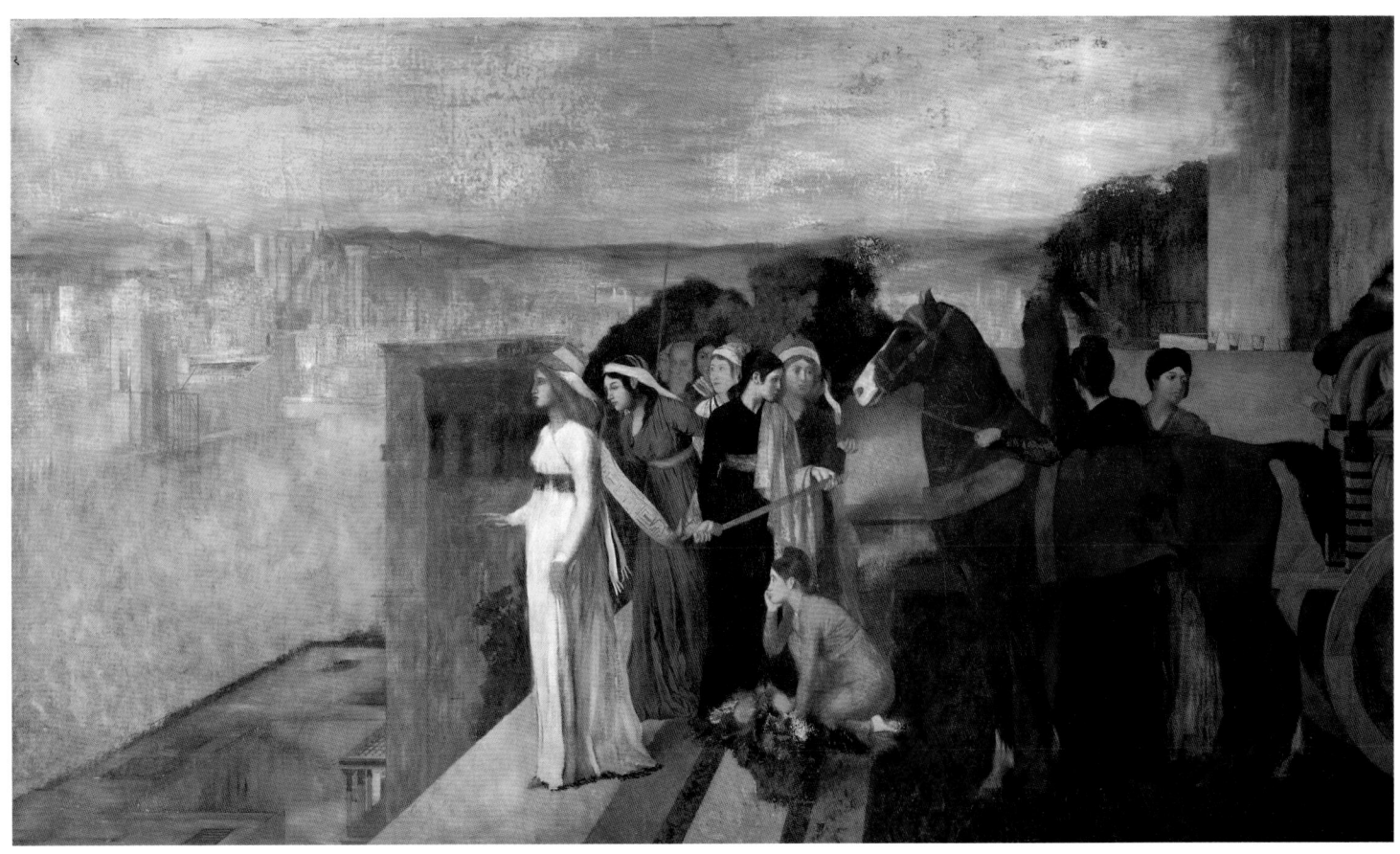

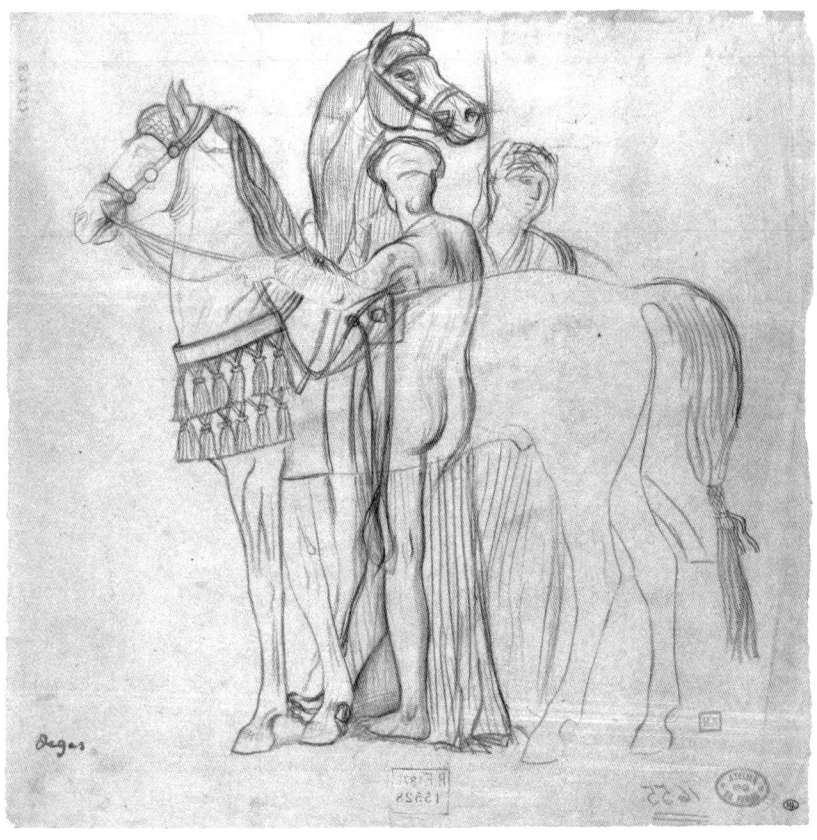

Women Restraining Horses (**23**), is clearly part of a work in progress in which some areas are elaborately developed and others left incomplete, even incoherent. At the center of the sheet, for example, Degas acknowledged his schooling by initially depicting one woman naked, though he subsequently equivocated and retained elements of her nude body and pleated costume on both sides of the drawn horse. Even more unpolished as a drawing is Picasso's *Battle of Covadonga* (**24**), which also seems to have been a rough draft for a historical scene. Using pen and ink with considerable freedom, Picasso revealed a young artist's high spirits and taste for adventure in a vivid melée of soldiers and horses that nevertheless shows skill in foreshortening and expressive anatomy. As with Degas's theme, the subject of Picasso's

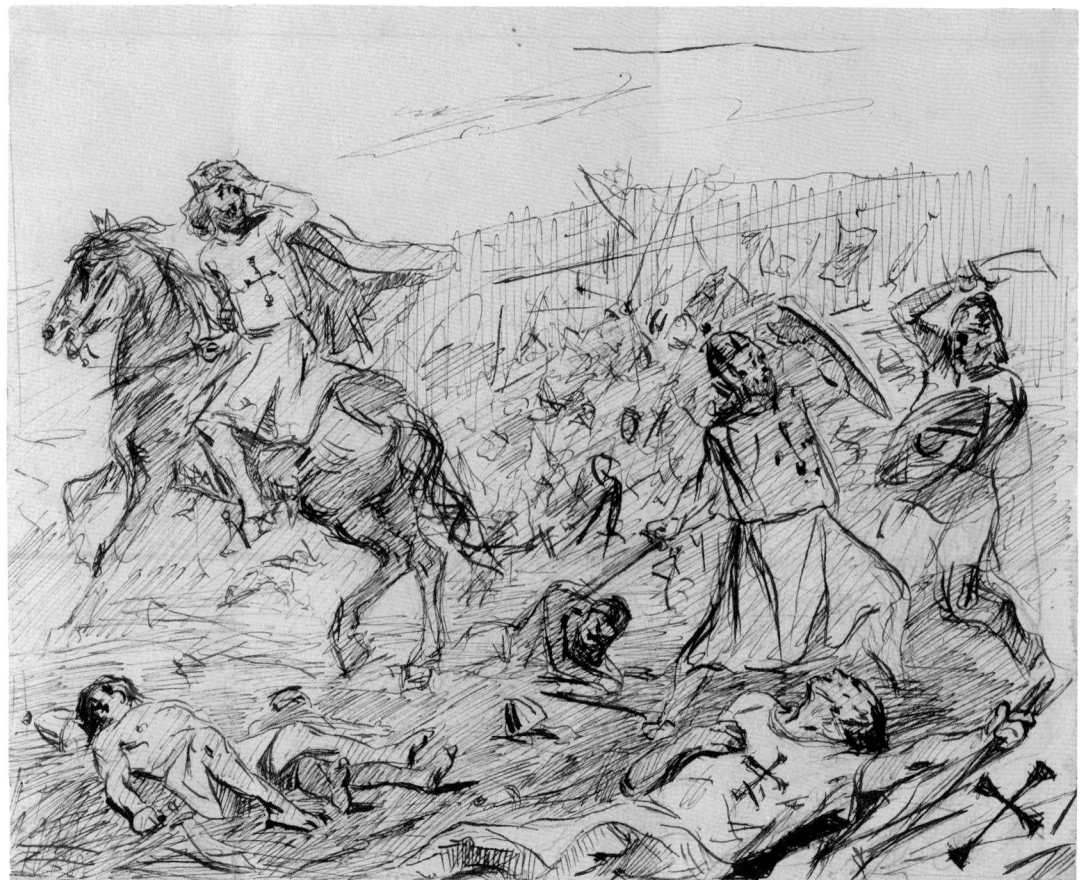

24

Pablo Picasso

Battle of Covadonga,
1895–96. Pen and
sepia ink on paper,
17.9 x 22.4 cm. Museu
Picasso, Barcelona
(MPB 110.639)

sketch was a combination of fact and myth, though here with a specific resonance in the story of the ancient foundation of Spain.[53] Picasso had been fascinated by battle scenes since childhood, sharing a widespread interest in depictions of war and military skirmishes that was reflected in both Spanish art and the popular media. Unlike Degas, however, no large-scale expressions of this grandiose theme survive from Picasso's hand, though one such canvas is said to have been destroyed.[54]

Barcelona: 1895–1900

The pivotal event in Picasso's early career was undoubtedly the move to Barcelona, where he arrived with his family in September 1895. Not yet fourteen, before the turn of the century his personal life and future prospects would undergo a series of radical shifts as he tired of

the academic system and rejected the conventional art market, and began to identify with the city's avant-garde. His father had chosen to settle in Barcelona when its cultural and commercial fortunes were booming, providing the ideal context for the advancement of his gifted son. The newcomers from Corunna witnessed the dramatic reconstruction of parts of the Catalan capital, where older areas were being demolished to open up modern squares and boulevards that echoed the redesigned center of Paris. In 1888, Barcelona had staged its own Universal Exhibition, which "reflected a growing confidence among Catalans that they had finally arrived as a European power," in the words of a recent writer.[55] The progressive journal *L'Avenç* extended this buoyant spirit to the entire region, announcing "the growth in our homeland of a certain literature, a certain science and a certain art," all of which were described as "essentially modernist."[56] An ill-defined "Modernisme" became the rallying cry of the moment, echoed in a wave of identification with progressive developments in Europe's other great cities. This was also a period of severe political turbulence at home and abroad, when Spain lost its major overseas territories and anarchism threatened its domestic security. Picasso clearly flourished in these turbulent surroundings, engaging briefly with radical politics and relishing the often extreme visual and literary license that Barcelona now offered. Already known for Antoni Gaudí's fantastical, unfinished cathedral, the *Sagrada Familia*, the city now witnessed the latest Symbolist poetry and theater, outlandish innovations in design and fashion, and spectacular advertising, color printing, and illustration imported from France and beyond. At a more banal level, another symbol of Barcelona's internationalism was the opening of the first direct rail link with Paris, the route Picasso would take in 1900 when he first crossed the Spanish border.

Though he initially lived in the shadow of his parents, Picasso's growing confidence is suggested in the compelling *Self-Portrait* (**25**) painted in the months that followed their move. Fusing the awkwardness of youth with a burgeoning self-knowledge, this picture might almost be a warning to those around him of things to come. Contrary to most artists' self-portraits, the depiction of his eyes suggests that Picasso is almost avoiding his own glance and looking slightly downward and sideways, as if uncomfortable with his precocity. Though the canvas is smaller and darker overall, its palette of colors is much the same as that in *The Old Fisherman* and similarly recalls the mannered studio lighting of tradition. Elizabeth Cowling has noted that Picasso would have seen self-portraits with similar qualities during his summer visit to the Prado.[57] Arguably as forceful in this work is the sense that it belongs to the

age of photography, when freshly scrubbed and smartly dressed adolescents were thrust in front of studio cameras. Caught between similar extremes is Degas's *Self-Portrait* of about 1857 in the Sterling and Francine Clark Art Institute (**26**), which was executed when Degas was almost a decade older than Picasso at the time of the Barcelona canvas. Already the veteran of at least a dozen self-portraits, Degas gazes calmly into a mirror, yet even he opted for a coy, partial concealment within the shadow cast by his hat. Degas had been accustomed since birth to the great metropolis of Paris, perhaps the most photograph-obsessed city in Europe at this date, and was already functioning in a self-conscious world of multiple visual languages that embraced the ancient and the newly minted. A black-and-white etching made around the same time as the painting (**27**) was part of this wider exploration, varying the scale and pose of *Self-Portrait* while bringing it even closer to a daguerreotype. Apparent in both these and Picasso's pictures is an unmistakable touch of stage management, in which costume, posture, and expression have been rehearsed for their encounters with the modern world.

Picasso was now enrolled at the Escola Provincial de Belles Arts in Barcelona, housed in an older part of the city and known as La Llotja, where his father taught figure drawing. The boy's exceptional gifts and previous training resulted in his immediate promotion to the senior class. Here he returned to the process of copying plaster casts — his *Greek Horseman* (see 4) was probably made at this moment — and increasingly focused on drawing the male body.[58] Female models were not permitted at La Llotja and remained absent from Picasso's art until he moved to Madrid two years later. The newcomer rose to his task with barely a false move, displaying a casual mastery of what many considered to be the definitive challenge of the nineteenth-century artist. Several exceptionally refined figure drawings survive from

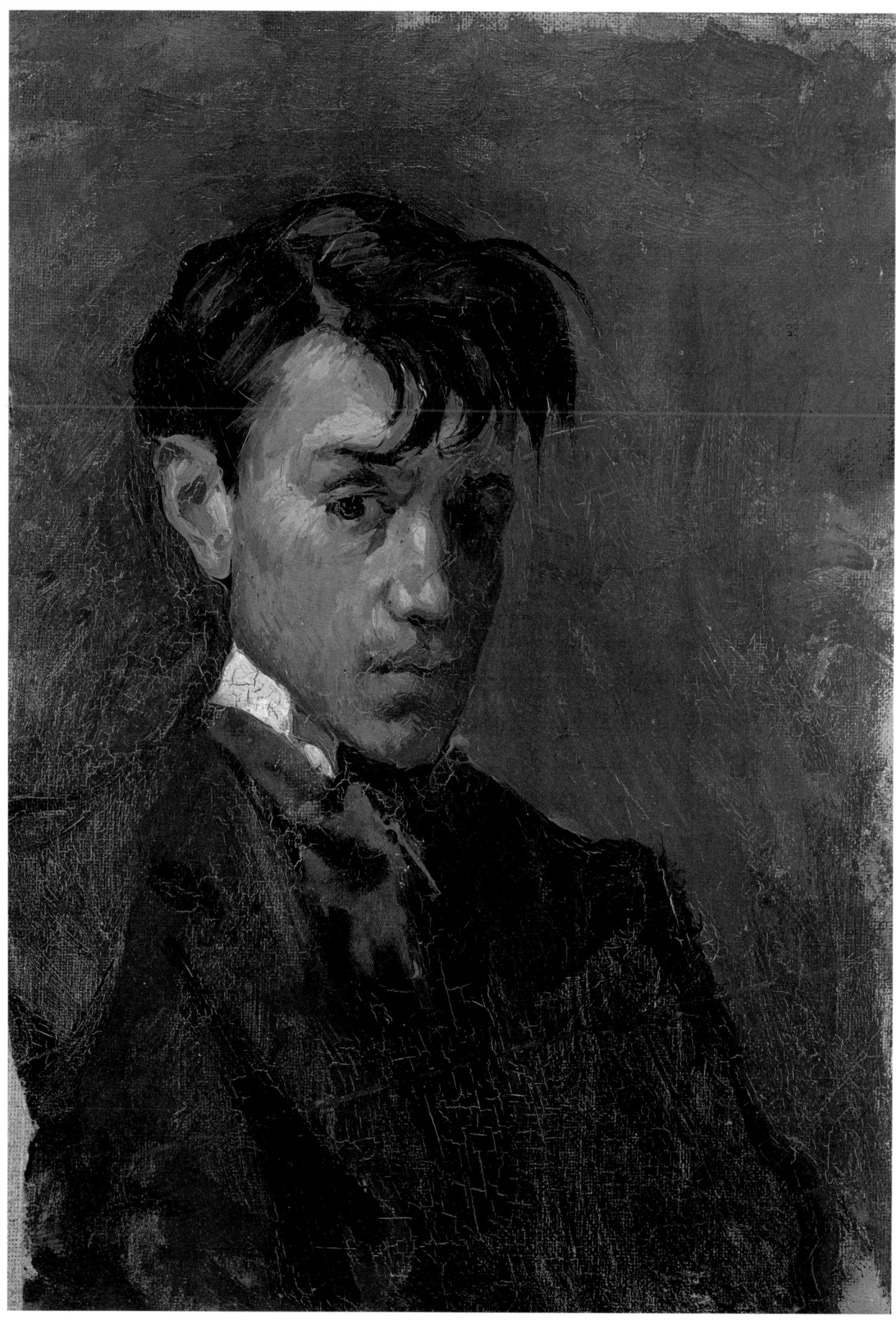

25

Pablo Picasso

Self-Portrait, 1896. Oil on
canvas, 32.9 x 24 cm.
Museu Picasso, Barcelona
(MPB 110.076)

26

Edgar Degas

Self-Portrait, c. 1857–58.
Oil on paper, mounted
on canvas, 26 x 19 cm.
Sterling and Francine
Clark Art Institute,
Williamstown,
Massachusetts
(1955.544)

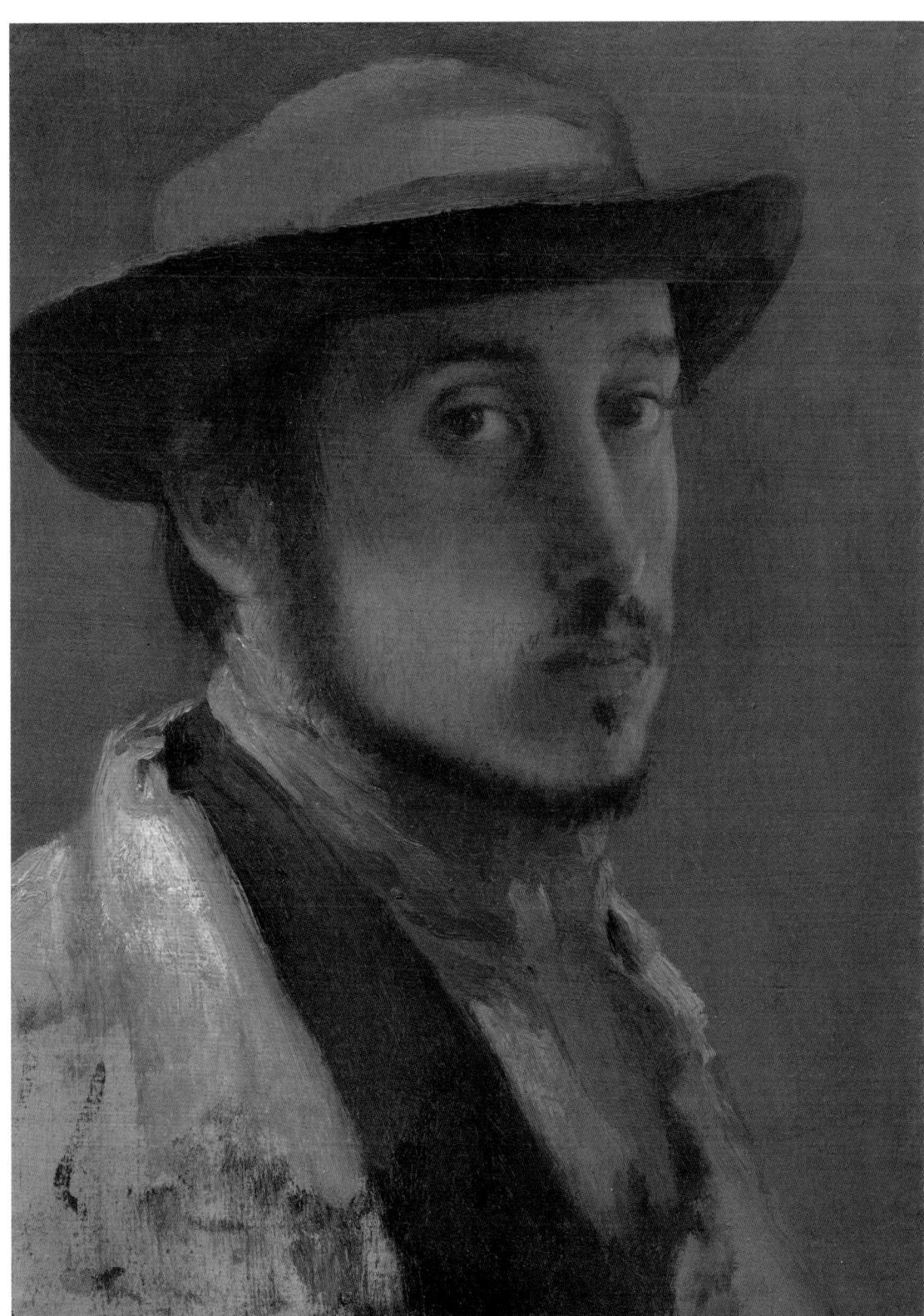

this phase, including a pair in which Picasso showed the same individual from two different angles.[59] One of these, *Academic Study from Life* (**28**), is a classic of the genre, emblematic of those made at art academies throughout the Western world across the centuries. Here Picasso used a crisp, finely inflected contour to define the man's body, while subtle passages of internal modeling indicate his musculature and hint at arrested movement. Also recalling time-honored practice, the model at La Llotja was posed in a heroic stance that was suitable for incorporation into a large-scale narrative composition. Other studies by Picasso follow the next steps in this process, when the studio model was rendered in oil paint on canvas.[60] Forty years earlier in Rome, Degas had followed an almost identical sequence of operations as he worked on a group of early historical scenes in the privacy of his studio. *Study for "Dante and Virgil"* (**29**) was among several preparatory drafts in which he explored poses, gestures, and elements of costume for an ambitious painting that represented the Italian poet Dante Alighieri led through the underworld by his great Roman predecessor.[61] Degas, like Picasso, worked from a model positioned in an active stance, here tentatively advancing and reaching toward the left. All these features then became absorbed into more complete studies in oil on card and ultimately on canvas, resulting in one of Degas's first independent creations. The completed picture was sent to his father in Paris, presumably to demonstrate Degas's progress and justify the allowance he was still receiving.[62]

At La Llotja and while under his father's supervision, the human form remained at the center of Picasso's curriculum. Following the pattern established at Corunna, however, don José did little to encourage his son to work in the manner of the Old Masters and still directed him toward the fashionable realism of the day. Their goal was to see Pablo's paintings exhibited in Barcelona, where they might attract the

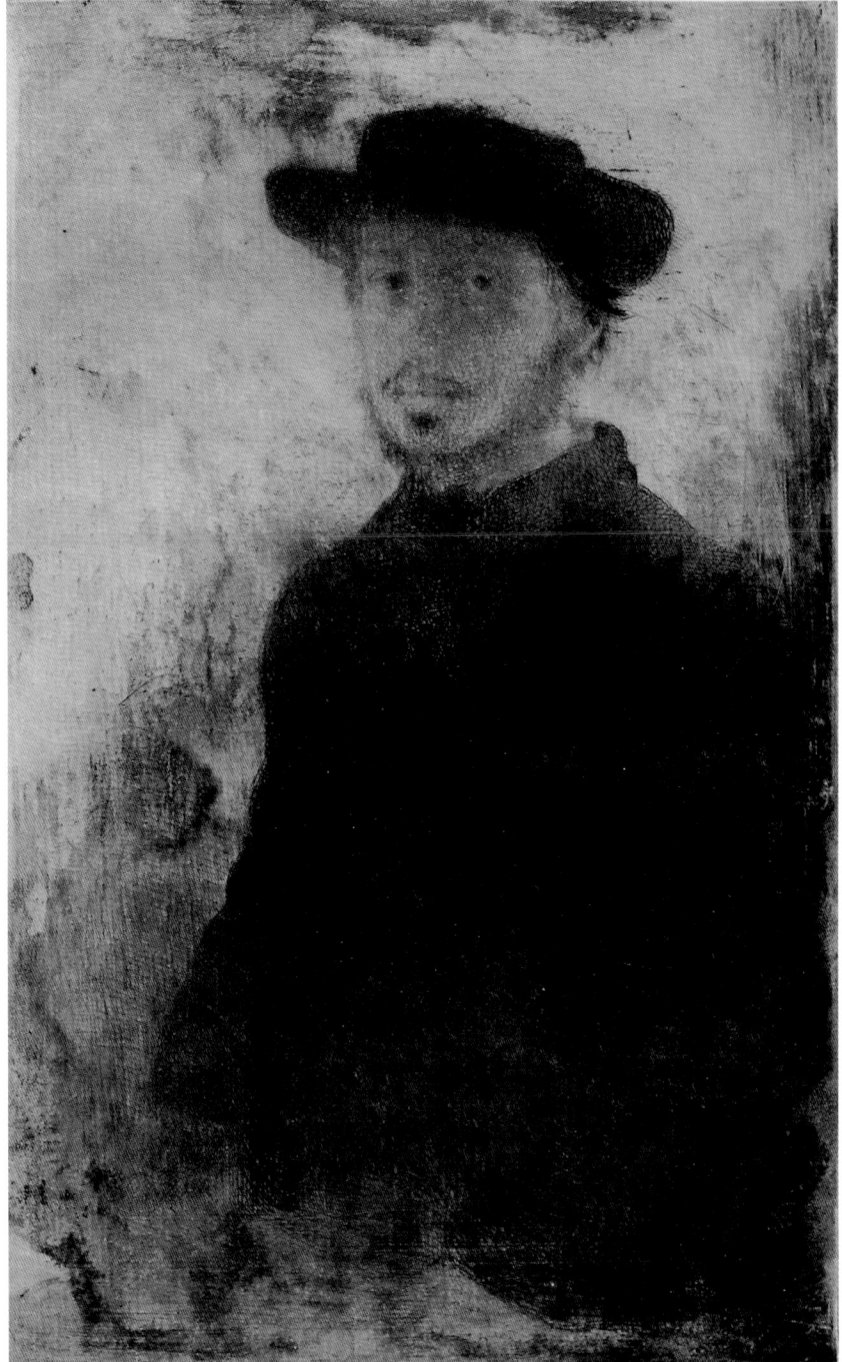

27

Edgar Degas

Self-Portrait, c. 1857.
Etching and drypoint,
23 x 14.4 cm. Sterling and
Francine Clark Art
Institute, Williamstown,
Massachusetts
(1955.1402)

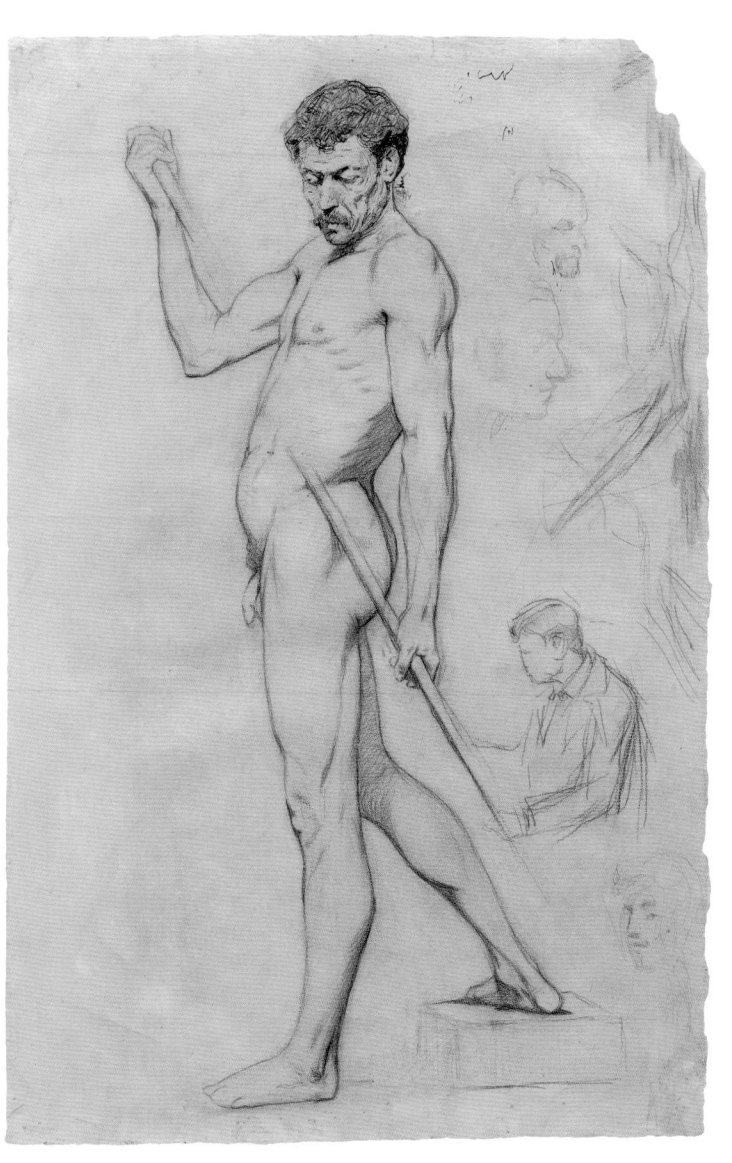

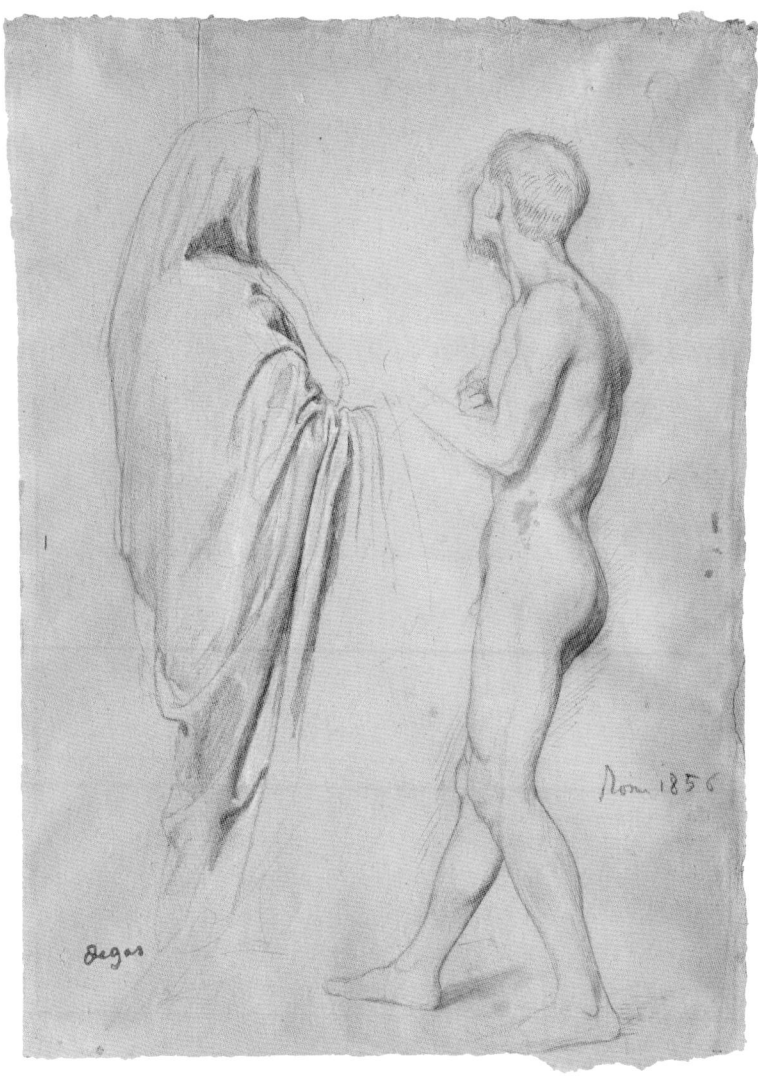

28

Pablo Picasso

Academic Study from Life: Male Nude, from the Side, with a Pole; Sketch of Head and Bust of Male Figures, 1895–97. Pencil, Conté crayon, and ink on paper, 48.3 x 31.5 cm. Museu Picasso, Barcelona (MPB 110.849)

29

Edgar Degas

Study for "Dante and Virgil," 1856–57. Pencil and chalk on paper, 30.8 x 22.5 cm. Sterling and Francine Clark Art Institute, Williamstown, Massachusetts (1955.1403)

approval of the art establishment and eventually sell to collectors and institutions. Portraiture clearly remained among the more sympathetic modes for the boy himself. Several fine pictures of his mother and sister illustrate his advancing subtlety and technical range, while a succession of animated watercolors show his father as an anxious, prematurely aging head of the household (see 246). Don José had now set aside his own ambitions as a painter and staked the family fortunes on the versatility of his only son. Pablo continued to dazzle those around him, executing small paintings of historic buildings, still-life objects, and figures on the theater stage, as well as occasional religious motifs both ancient and modern.[63] Small studies for a *Crucifixion*, an *Exodus*, and a *Martyrdom of Saint Sebastian* may have helped to secure a commission to copy works by Murillo, but they were also accompanied by scenes of piety set in the contemporary world.[64] The latter reached their climax in the almost six-foot-high *The First Communion* of 1896 (**30**), a work whose polished details suggest that don José — who posed for one of the figures — may have contributed to its final state. Grandly conceived but based on an incident in a child's life that most Spaniards could relate to, this milestone in Picasso's youthful career was executed in a blandly realistic, almost illustrational technique. Submitted to the 1896 Exposición des Bellas Artes in Barcelona, *The First Communion* was accepted and offered for sale at the considerable price of 1500 pesetas; the efforts of don José and his son to achieve public recognition had been vindicated.[65]

First Contacts with Impressionsism

In these same months, there were already signs of tension in Picasso's fledgling career. Some of the private experiments he now undertook turned away from the human body and even the act of drawing to explore the colors and textures of the landscape. Earlier attempts of this kind had revealed Picasso's unexpected

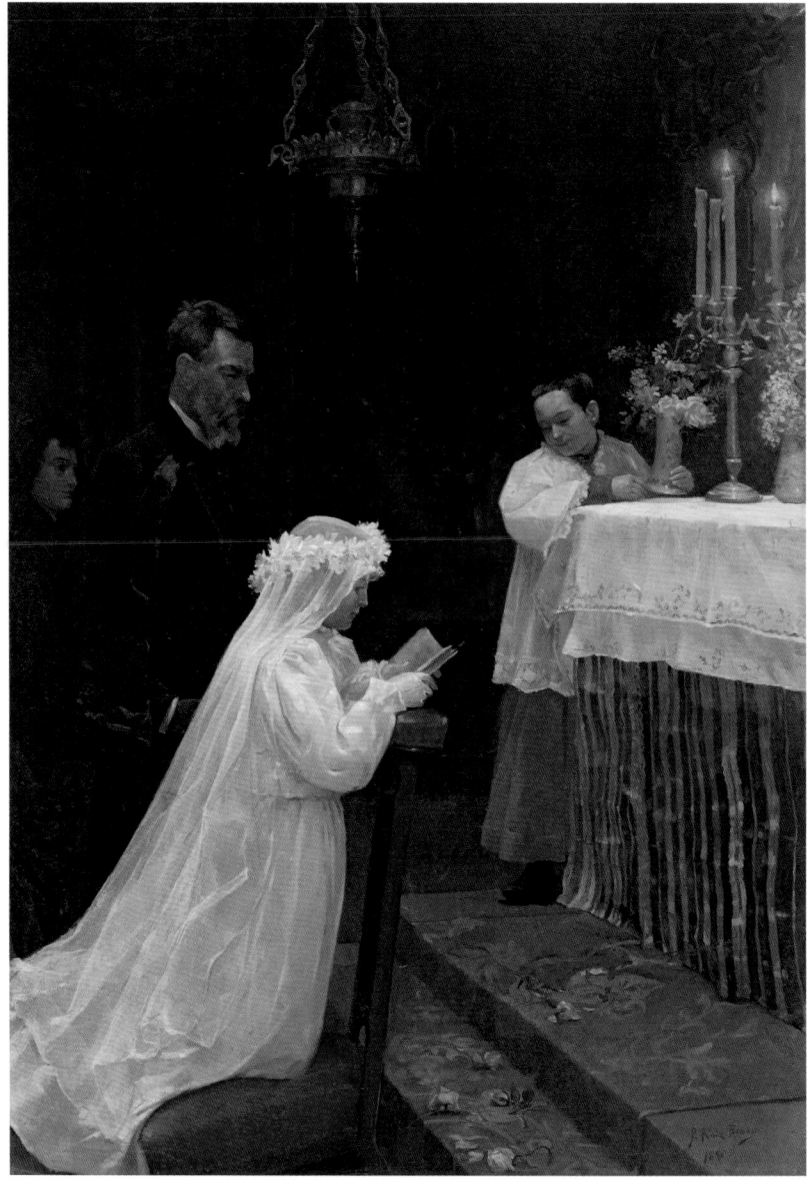

sensitivity when painting open-air scenes, a practice that was not taught in most academic courses at this time.[66] The confidence he showed and the freshness of his handling indicate that the teenager was already familiar with the plein-air tradition, one that had influenced many landscape artists in Europe — including Spain — since at least the eighteenth century.[67] Typically used as an informal or preparatory activity, plein-air painting relied on a direct response to natural form and an

30

Pablo Picasso

The First Communion, 1896. Oil on canvas, 166 x 118 cm. Museu Picasso, Barcelona (MPB 110.001)

emphasis on shifting light and weather, often captured at speed with deft brush marks. In a small canvas entitled *Garden* and dated "April 1896" (**31**), however, Picasso went beyond this technique and took a much bolder step toward some of the novel notions of modern painting that he must already have encountered. This little-discussed work depicts a sunlit area that is not only free of figures but of most of the narrative devices in the pictorial repertoire.[68] The antithesis of his *First Communion*, yet apparently painted alongside it, *Garden* also represented its opposite in terms of execution. Now the picture was built up from broad strokes and dabs of color, dominated by touches of green and gold but with added flurries of blue and scarlet. This procedure had no counterpart in Picasso's previous oeuvre and raises the possibility that he was emulating the techniques of certain French Impressionists. As Giner had indicated two years earlier, the landscapists within the movement tended to use the "tache" (dab) or "pointille" (dot), strokes that facilitated "the breaking down of a tone into its elemental colors and their juxtaposition so that from a distance they merge and reform."[69] More accessible accounts of these same processes were no doubt available to Picasso, such as brief references in *La Ilustración Artística* during 1895 to "Impressionist" art in Paris.[70] These remarks explained that this method of outdoor painting relied on a new kind of "touch" with the brush and a different approach to color, along with the "violent contrasts" produced by attention to "natural daylight."[71]

Garden would be less significant if it stood alone, but in the course of 1896 Picasso produced approximately a dozen such scenes that exploited variations on the same loose, fragmentary application of paint. Some were executed during the summer of that year, when the artist and his family again paid a nostalgic visit to Malaga. Freed from the constraints of La Llotja and prompted by the glaring sunlight

and reddish-brown rocky terrain, the teenager applied color in hatchings and flicks of the brush that summarized not only the landscape but also its vibrancy. While most of these pictures were small, an ambitious canvas entitled *Mountain Landscape* (**32**) is almost the same size as his celebrated *The Old Fisherman*, painted the previous year.[72] Scholars have connected this unexpected cluster of landscapes with the "Saffron" group, a loose confederation of Barcelona-based artists who first came together in 1893. At the 1896 Exposición des Bellas Artes in the city, Joaquim Mir — the leader of this tendency — drew attention to their aims when he showed his intensely hued painting *The Rector's Orchard*.[73] Picasso could have seen Mir's composition — which was shown before he left for Malaga — and perhaps similar works by his associates, such as Isidre Nonell's *Morning Sun*, a variant on the distinctive Impressionist subject of haystacks in a field.[74] Contacts of this kind may well have emboldened Picasso in his own experiments and urged him toward a more audacious palette and bold facture. Yet most of the "Saffron" pictures by Mir, Nonell, and others lack the dab-like brushstrokes of Picasso's *Garden*, which appears to depend on knowledge of Impressionist canvases. This may have resulted from contact with French works shown in Spain — such as those discussed by Giner in 1894 — or conceivably from an attempt by Picasso to reconstruct this technique from firsthand descriptions of Impressionist paintings. Whatever their precise origins, paintings such as *Garden* surely represent one of the first plausible signs of Picasso's response to the art of his older contemporaries in Paris.

Perhaps the most notable aspect of this sequence of events was the fact that, in the early 1890s, French Impressionism was already two decades old. The first exhibition by the artists who acquired the name "Impressionists" had taken place in Paris in the spring of 1874, to

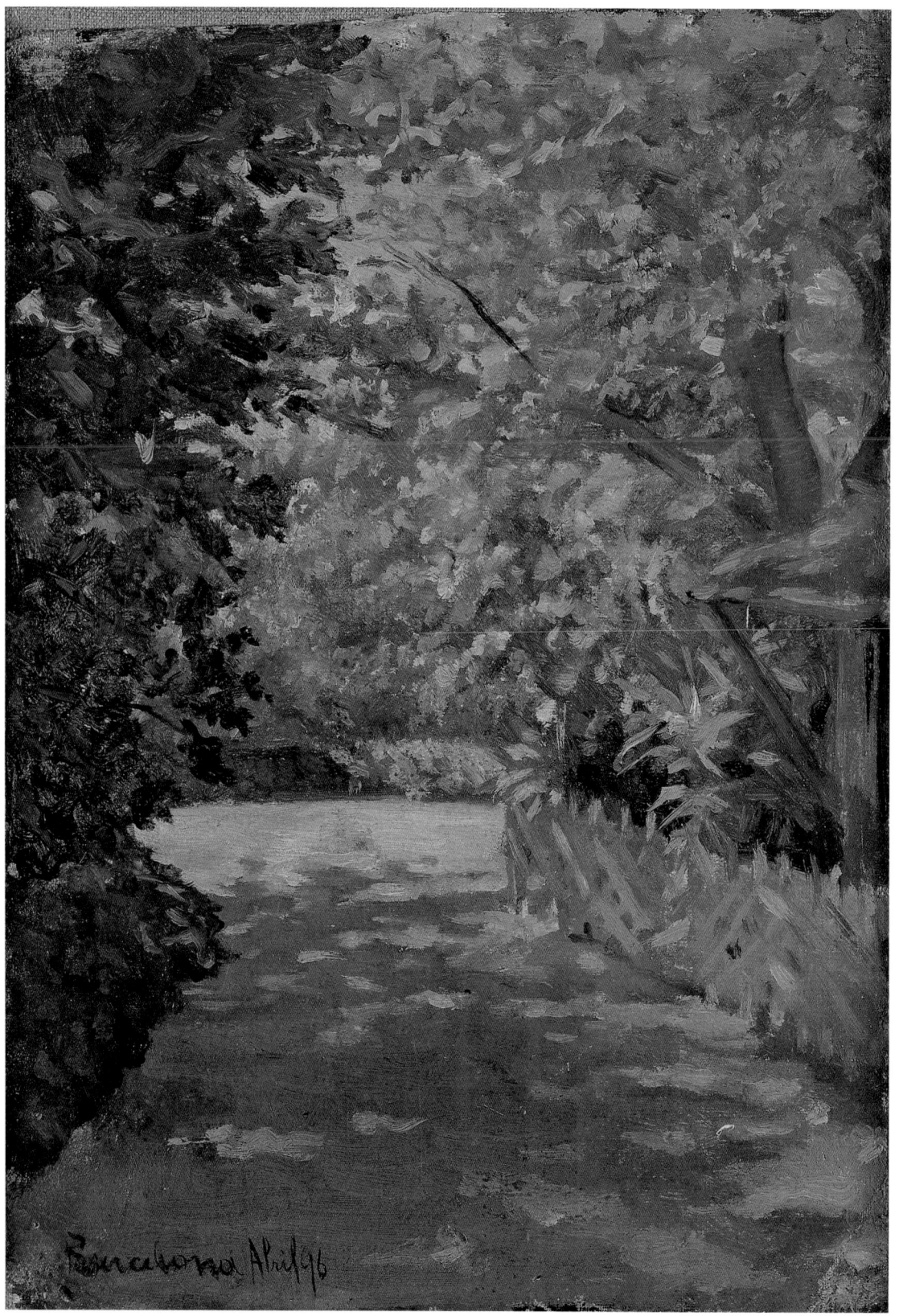

31

Pablo Picasso

Garden, April 1896. Oil on canvas, 38.5 x 27.4 cm. Museu Picasso, Barcelona (MPB 110.070)

32

Pablo Picasso

Mountain Landscape, June–July 1896. Oil on canvas, 60.5 x 82 cm. Museu Picasso, Barcelona (MPB 110.008)

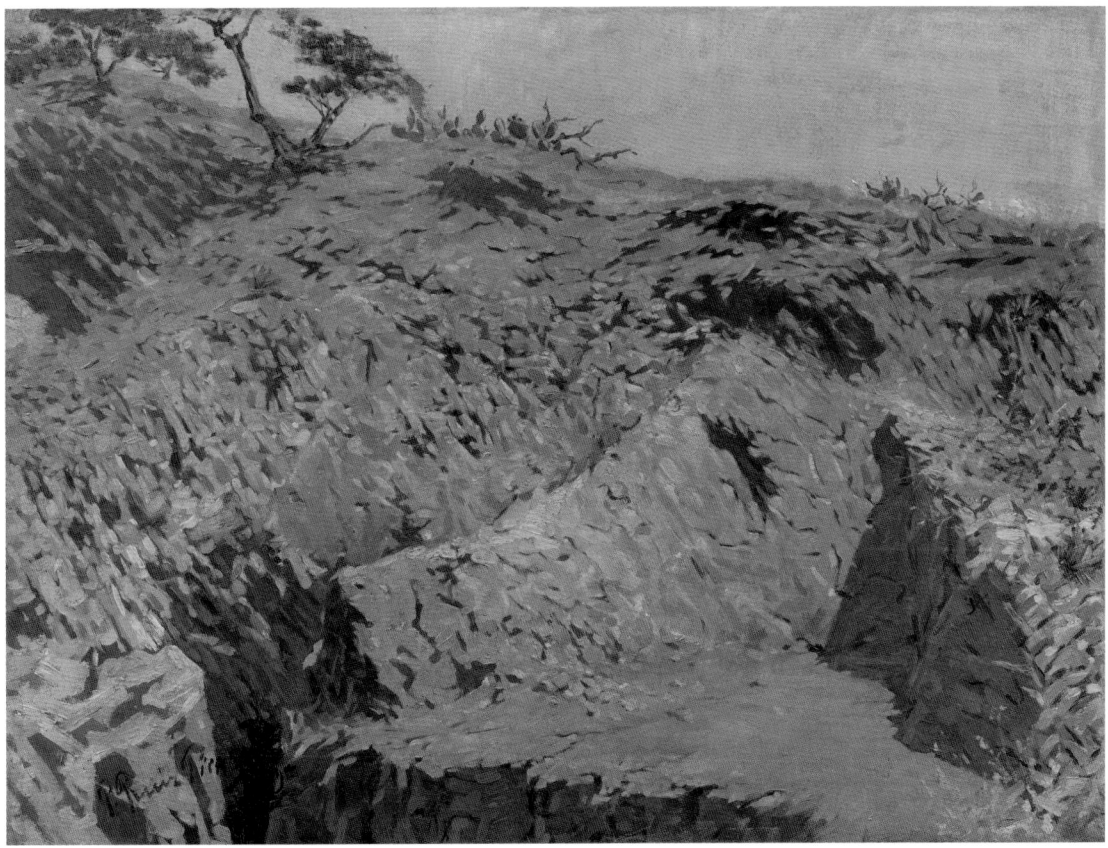

be followed by seven further collective displays at irregular intervals, the last in 1886.[75] Participation had varied and key figures dropped out, reappeared, and were joined by new and usually younger colleagues, while the character of their artistic enterprise changed in a number of ways. By the time Giner wrote his article, several of the leading painters had acquired substantial reputations in their native country and discussions of their work could be found in respected newspapers and journals, in a few cases with monochrome illustrations. Visitors to France — Walter Sickert from England, Max Liebermann from Germany, Giovanni Boldini from Italy — sometimes sought out individual Impressionists and took home accounts of the new school, along with idiosyncratic variants of their themes and methods. While Spanish artists certainly went to France during this period — among them Isidoro Brocos, Picasso's teacher in

Corunna — there was a crucial exodus in the 1880s and 1890s of aspiring young painters from Barcelona, many of whom later became known personally to Picasso. Among the most prominent was Ramon Casas, who first traveled to Paris in 1881, the year that the sixth Impressionist exhibition took place.[76] Born into a wealthy Catalan family, Casas studied there at leisure and by 1883 had shown his first pictures in the French capital. Three years later his close friend, Santiago Rusiñol, followed, and in 1890 the two lived in Montmartre with a third Spanish artist, Miquel Utrillo. Never intimately involved with the senior Impressionists, this trio nevertheless met prominent individuals in the group and their acolytes, frequented the same neighborhoods, galleries, and exhibitions, and visited collectors who owned Impressionist works. Studying with mainstream teachers who favored a polished, even slick brand of realism,

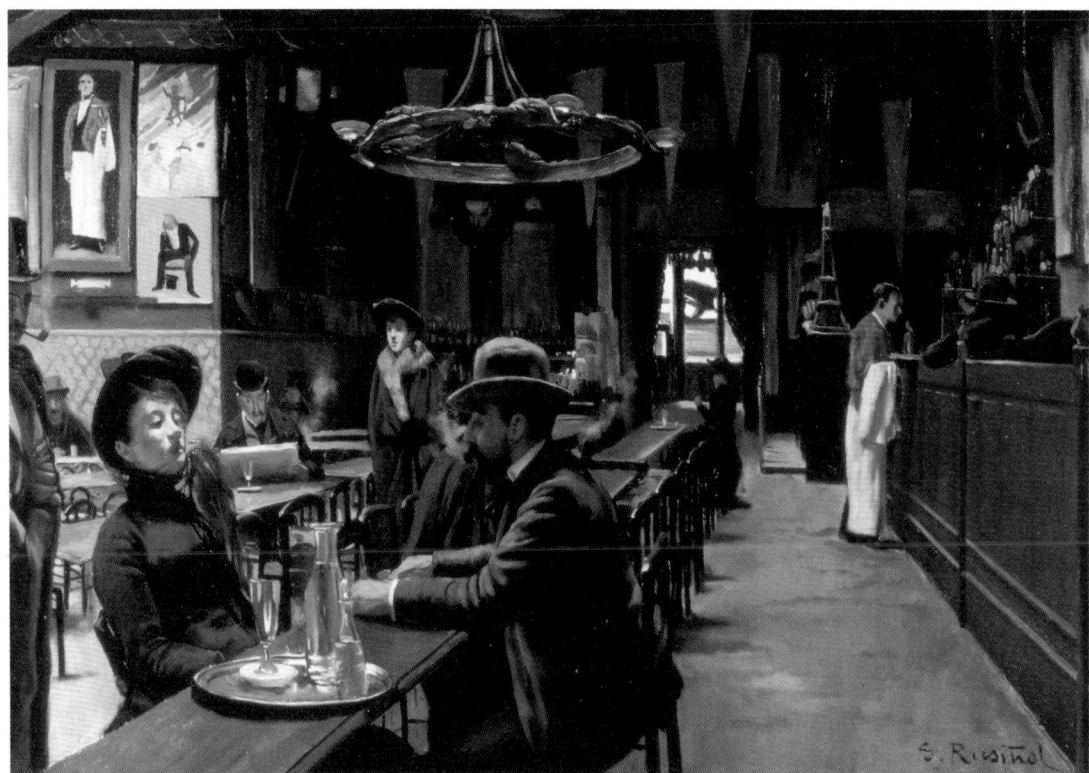

33

Santiago Rusiñol

(Spanish, 1861–1931)

Café de Montmartre,

1890. Oil on canvas,

80 x 116 cm. Museu

de Montserrat. Gift of

Joseph Maria Sala i Ardiz

(N.R. 200.532)

34

S. Azpaizu

*Concert at the Café

des Ambassadeurs*.

Reproduced in

La Ilustración Artística 701

(3 June 1895), p. 390.

Courtesy Arxiu Històric de

la Ciutat, Barcelona

they each painted a number of resonant landscapes and cityscapes based on Paris itself.
More significantly, much of their output emphasized urban narratives, evoking the often bleak
atmosphere of Parisian bars and drinking halls,
and recording the dissolute men and women,
performers on stage, and backstreet loiterers
they found there (**33**).[77]

For the generation that followed Casas and
Rusiñol, information about the pleasures and
pitfalls of Paris was readily available in Barcelona, even in a family journal such as *La Ilustración Artística*. During 1895, the year Picasso
arrived in the Catalan city, several long articles
about Paris had appeared under the title
Cronica Parisienne, apparently aimed at readers
and their families who were planning vacations.
These texts dealt mainly with such bracing
activities as walking on the famous boulevards,
visiting parks, and making trips to the surrounding countryside, with canoeing and other sports
recommended for all. Attention to the city's

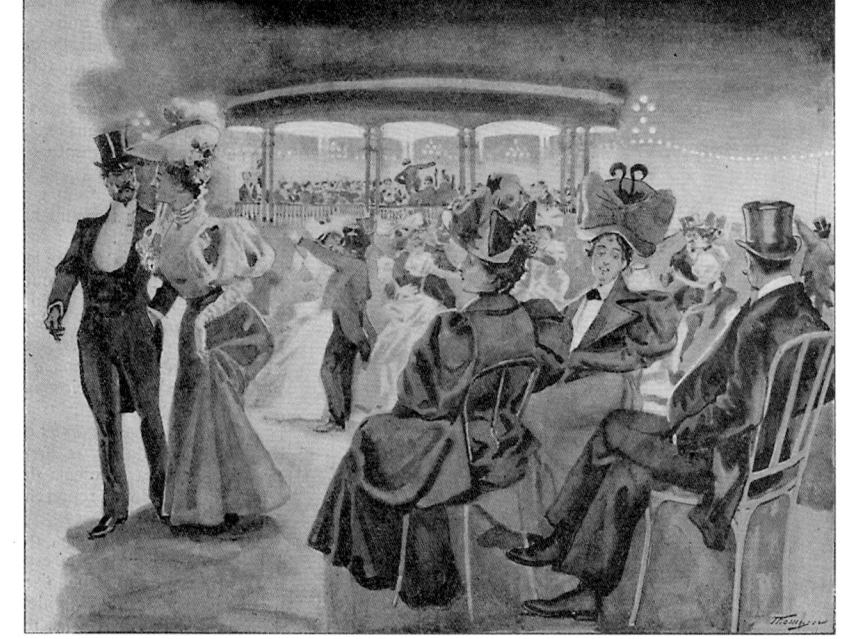

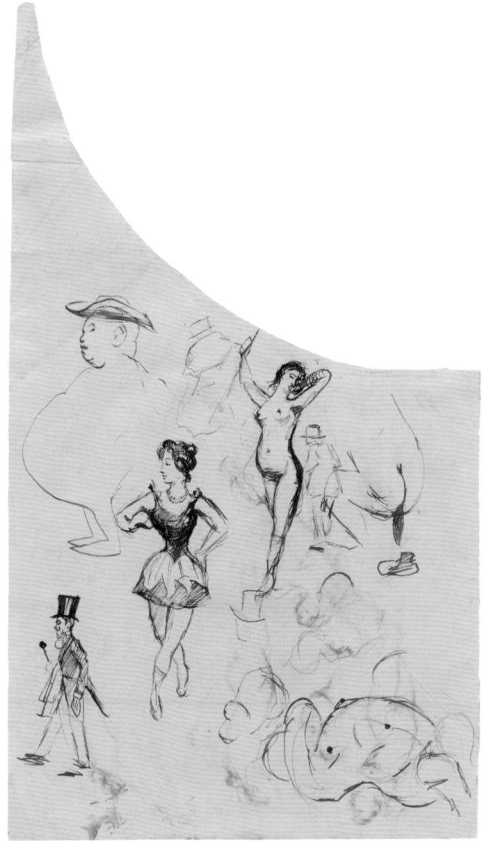

35

Pablo Picasso

Dancer, Nude Woman, and Other Studies, 1895–96. Pen and ink on paper, 37.8 x 22 cm. Museu Picasso, Barcelona (MPB 110.379)

36

Pablo Picasso

Café-Concert, 1896–97. Oil on wood, 10.1 x 15.5 cm. Museu Picasso, Barcelona (MPB 110.137)

great monuments was advised and a description of a "vernissage" or exhibition opening at the annual Salon acknowledged the nation's artistic life. Altogether less expected in these conventional pages were evocations of adult attractions, principally the more salubrious cafés, theaters, and nightclubs for which Paris was famous throughout Europe. Illustrations that were remarkably bold by the standards of the day showed singers and dancers on the stage at various cabarets, including the Ambassadeurs, the site of many of Degas's cabarets scenes and etchings (**34**).[78] Accompanying texts also mentioned the off-beat Chat Noir on the rue Victor Massé, where Miquel Utrillo pioneered his shadow dramas; the Moulin Rouge, associated with Toulouse-Lautrec and with Rusiñol and Casas; as well as the Folies-Bergère, the Eldorado, and the Alcazar. For assiduous readers of *La Ilustración Artística,* other features revealed a lively sense of the wider cultural landscape in Paris, from references to French

writers and composers to news about current exhibitions. Long lists of contributors to these events included several artists known to the Impressionist generation — Alfred Roll, Eugène Carrière, Albert Besnard — and others who were specifically close to Degas, such as Georges Jeanniot, Albert Bartholomé, and Jean-Louis Forain.[79]

Before he met members of the circle around Casas and Rusiñol, Picasso had the opportunity to see examples of their painting at various exhibitions that took place in Barcelona after 1895.[80] An awareness of their Paris-inflected art was thus added to a heterogeneous range of factors that contributed to his own changing vocabulary as the adolescent artist began to make drawings and small pictures in response to the city. Landscape had quickly faded from his concerns, to be replaced by a fascination with café interiors and scenes of cheap popular entertainment. In one of Picasso's early attempts of this kind, a dancer gyrates in some kind of stage show and other women display themselves naked (**35**), and in a tiny but evocative oil painting on panel Picasso captured a café-concert singer in mid-action, viewed over the heads of her audience (**36**).[81] Lacking inscriptions and dates, these works are distinct in style from both his earlier manner and his more confident approach of the later 1890s, when such motifs would play a dominant role in Picasso's art. No doubt partly informed by imagery from France and elsewhere, these novel sketches clearly reflected the teenager's familiarity with Barcelona's street life, as his own later reminiscences and those of his former companions confirmed. One such friend, Jaume Sabartés, recalled that Picasso was seen "making notes at a café concert," and others confirmed his fondness for the Eden Concert, a well-documented cabaret that was perhaps the subject of his small painting.[82] It is also said that a fellow-student at La Llotja, Manuel Pallarès, soon introduced him to the bars and brothels of the notoriously squalid area of old Barcelona known as the Bario Xino. Ever precocious, Picasso apparently acquired his own mistress by the time he reached the age of fifteen.[83]

If Picasso's furtive sketches of this metropolitan underworld from 1896 and 1897 are slight in scale and few in number, their implications are far-reaching. Earlier drawings made in Corunna had already spelled out the boy's delight in urban types and scurrilous caricature, as well as a surprising interest in backstage theater imagery.[84] The Barcelona studies take these tastes to a more challenging and topical level, adding an Art Nouveau line to his striptease artists and hazy, atmospheric colors and textures to his cabaret interior. The most likely source for these devices was modern French art, transmitted through such intermediate forms as the paintings of expatriate Spaniards, etchings and lithographs of various kinds from Paris and elsewhere, and the posters and illustrated French magazines that were now popular throughout Europe. The latter were well known in Barcelona and appealed to several audiences. Titles such as *La Caricature*, *Le Mirliton*, and *Gil Blas Illustré* offered bold design — sometimes enhanced by bright color — and salacious texts, gossip from the streets, and reports on prominent personalities and the arts of the day. The vividly pictorial *Gil Blas Illustré* (**37**, **38**) had been launched in 1891 and soon published stories by the controversial novelists Émile Zola and Guy de Maupassant, and the art writer and occasional pornographer Félix Champsaur. Its graphic star was Théophile Alexandre Steinlen, some of whose powerful, fluent illustrations were devoted to the harsh lives of the Parisian poor and their cheap entertainments. Steinlen was a disciple of the great lithographer Honoré Daumier and shamelessly echoed his scenes of city life, from the grim to the lighthearted. Though they were never personally close, Steinlen also knew and made reference to the art of Degas and his entourage to a significant extent. Certain images that had originated with Daumier — such as the laundress carrying her bundle — were given new life by Degas and subsequently popularized in the illustrations of Steinlen, who made no attempt to hide his sources. Another case was Degas's *In a Café (L'Absinthe)* (see 104), intended for the 1876 Impressionist exhibition and later cited blatantly in Steinlen's own scenes of cafés and their forlorn customers, which were widely circulated in print form (**39**). The familiarity of the Picasso household with *Gil Blas Illustré* and Steinlen's work is put beyond dispute by a drawing of 1899, where his father is shown with a copy of the magazine in his coat pocket (**40**).

The Influence of Degas

Where *Garden* takes us back to the Impressionist landscape painters, so Picasso's first sketches of lowlife in Barcelona have their roots in an alternative aesthetic, one that was represented on the printed page by Zola, Maupassant, and

37

Front cover of *Gil Blas Illustré* 9, no. 15 (14 April 1899). Courtesy The New York Public Library. General Research Division, Astor, Lenox, and Tilden Foundations

38

Front cover of *Gil Blas Illustré* 9, no. 22 (2 June 1899). Courtesy The New York Public Library. General Research Division, Astor, Lenox, and Tilden Foundations

39

Théophile Alexandre Steinlen

(Swiss, 1859–1923)

L'Assommoir, 1900. Lithograph, 196 x 137 cm. Petit Palais, Geneva (inv. 12636)

40

Pablo Picasso

The Artist's Father, with a Copy of the Magazine "Gil Blas" in His Pocket, 1899. Conté crayon on paper, 30.5 x 24.7 cm. Museu Picasso, Barcelona (MPB 110.032)

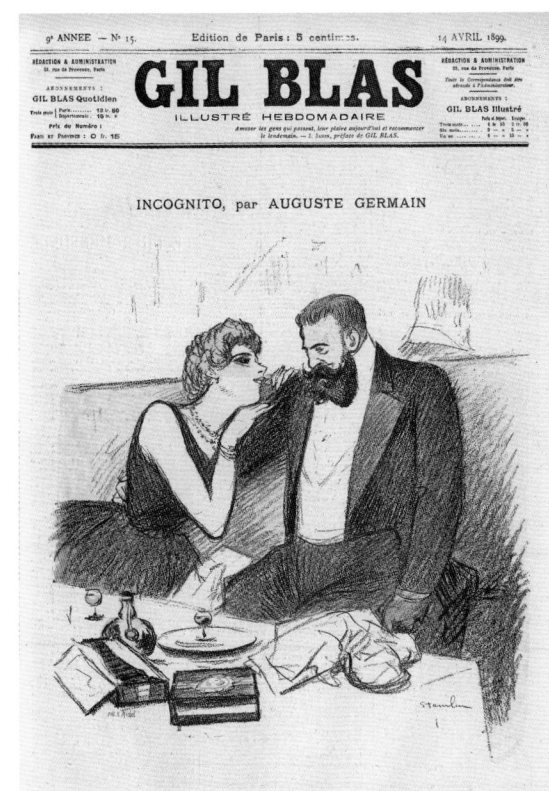

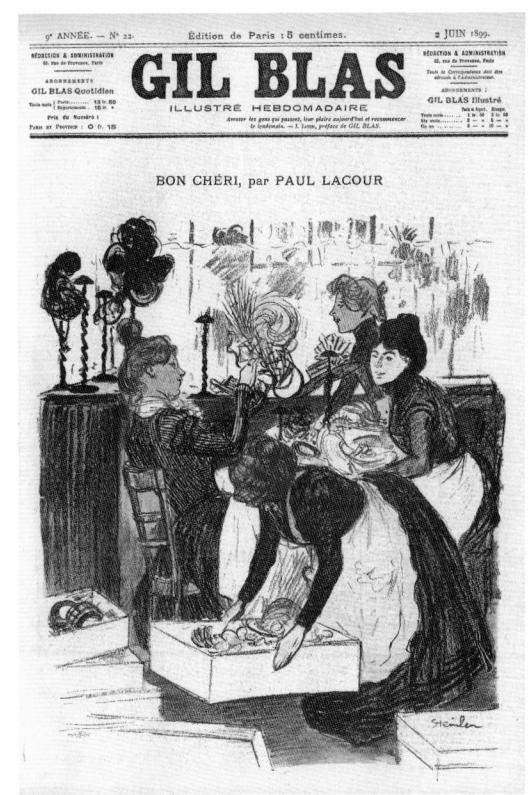

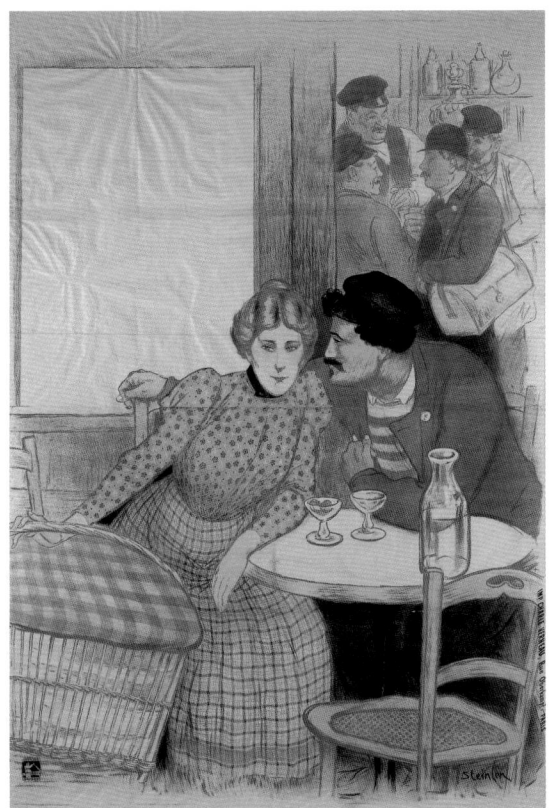

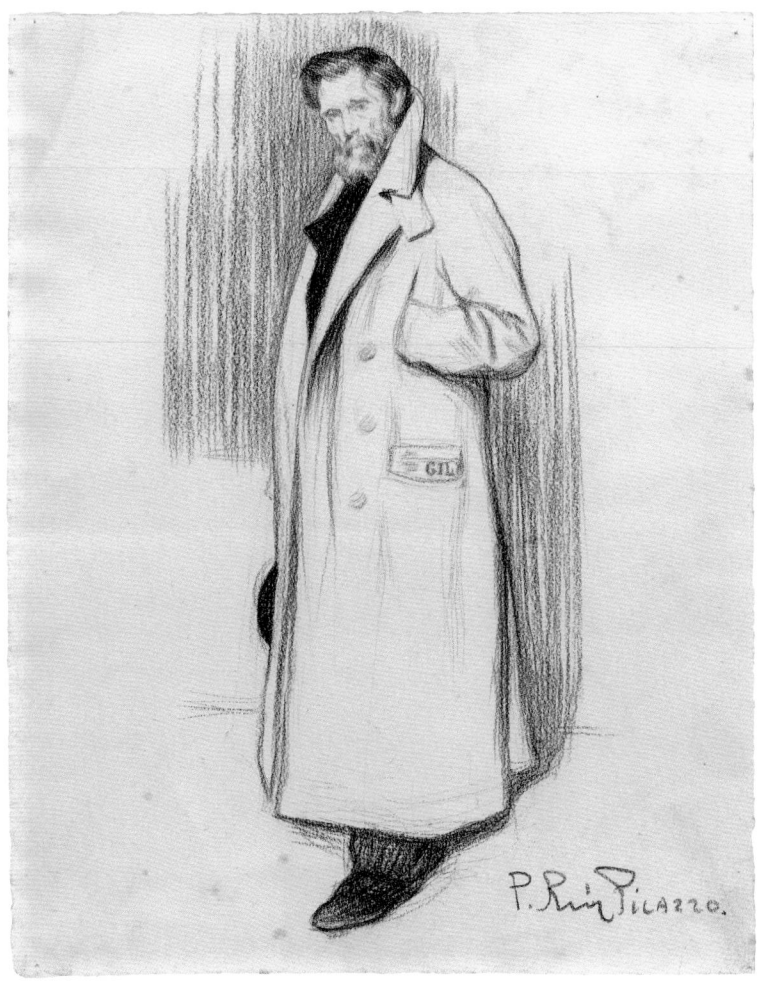

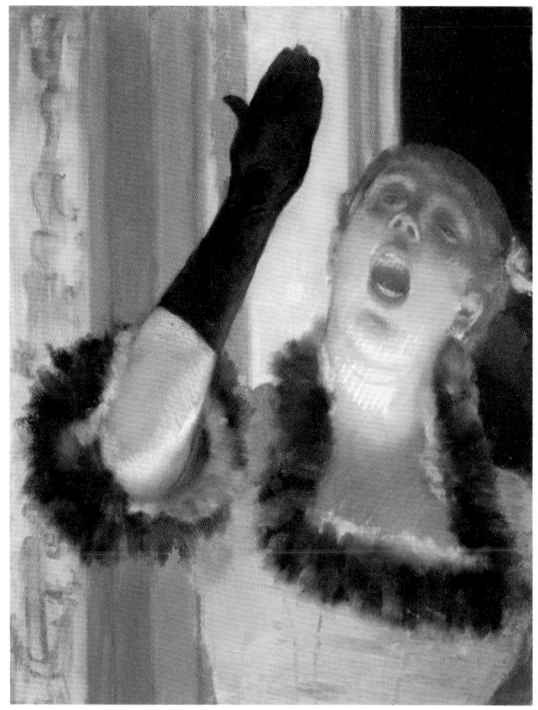

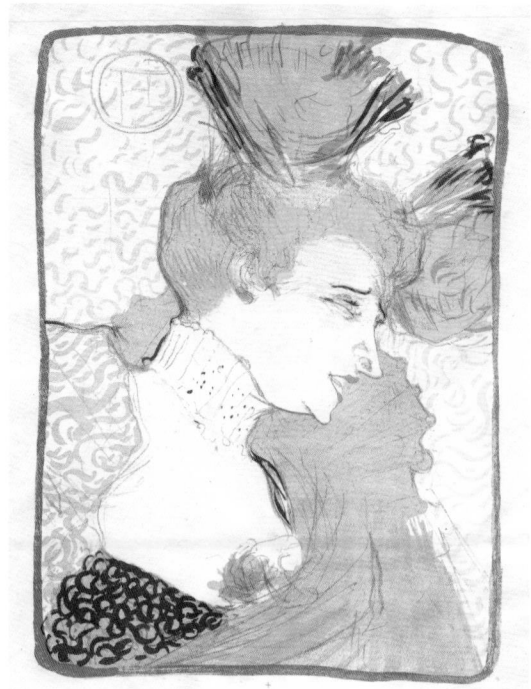

Steinlen. All three of these individuals were identified in some way with Impressionism, typically with its urban, narrative aspect rather than the rural vocabulary that had already defined the movement for many of its admirers. As Giner's text made clear, this broad division of emphasis within the Impressionist camp could sometimes have the effect of excluding Degas and his followers altogether, even though many were founding members and major exhibitors who had contributed to the movement in definitive ways. While Monet was typically hailed in France as the leader of the landscape faction, Degas and his allies were characterized as artists engaged with the human dramas of Paris, or "the reality of the streets," in the words of one of their sympathetic critics, Edmond Duranty.[85] At the pioneering Impressionist exhibitions in the 1870s, it was Degas's pictures that marked out this territory in visually radical compositions and startling new combinations of media. Between 1874 and 1879, he showed scenes of office workers and crowds at the racetrack, cabaret singers (**41**) and prostitutes, drinkers and laundresses, morally dubious nude women in their tubs and tired dancers backstage, subjects that often had notorious counterparts in the literature of the day. Degas's perceived skills and his preoccupation with urban themes also tended to link him with draftsmanship, to strongly drawn paintings and emphatic pastels, prints, and monotypes. Younger artists with similar talents and aspirations were soon attracted to Degas's side and often shared his taste for these media. Jean-Louis Forain, Marcellin Desboutin, and Jean-François Raphaëlli all took up the challenge of printmaking and illustration in these years, while Degas's self-proclaimed disciple, Henri de Toulouse-Lautrec — though never an exhibitor with the Impressionist group — later achieved international fame through his lithographs and posters of dancers, courtesans, and nightclub performers (**42**).

Despite the often harsh critical reception of Impressionism in its early days and the occa-

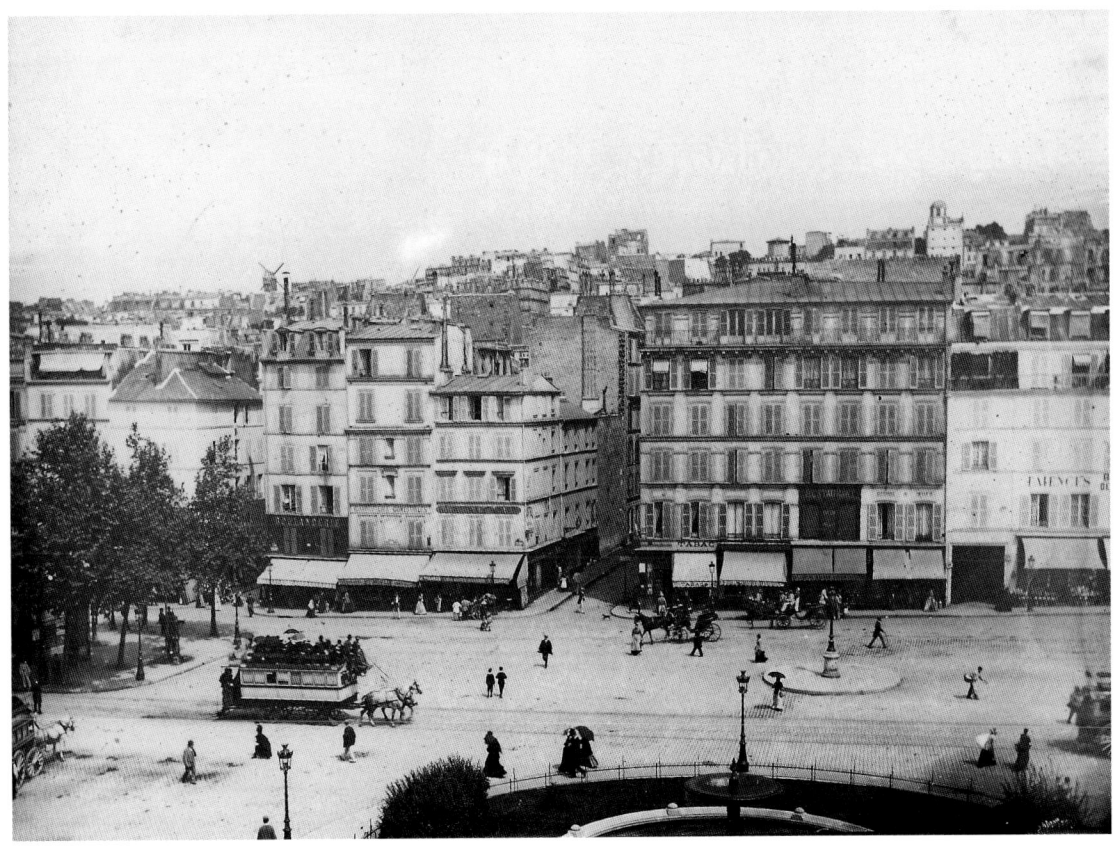

sional absence of Degas's name from less well-informed accounts of the movement, such as Giner's, there is persistent and widespread evidence of the visibility of works by Degas and his followers from the 1870s onward. Degas's pictures were displayed prominently in seven of the eight Impressionist exhibitions and were among the most widely admired by contemporary critics. "What precision there is to his drawings!" one leading writer exclaimed in 1874, while in 1876 another approved of Degas's "intimate acquaintance with modern life," and a third announced in 1877 that he was "definitely the most original" of the artists in the group.[86] The controversy that surrounded certain of Degas's notorious themes, notably the ballet, the nude, and the *chanteuse*, added to his renown and his scandalous reputation, without discouraging more courageous collectors. Substantial numbers of his paintings, pastels, and

other works on paper were sold throughout this period and attracted the support of the leading Impressionist dealer, Paul Durand-Ruel, and several other Parisian entrepreneurs. Though Degas could be famously acerbic with his opponents, he was often sympathetic to younger painters and enjoyed the loyalty of many admirers and a number of imitators. A very visible presence in Paris, Degas lived near Place Pigalle at the heart of Montmartre, the celebrated artists' quarter that remained his home throughout a long professional career (**43**). After moving from studio to studio, he had settled on the rue Victor Massé, a street celebrated for such nightclubs and cabarets as the Bal Tabarin and the Chat Noir.[87]

Some of the distinctive qualities of Degas's art would certainly have been known to the painters from Catalonia who worked in Paris from the 1880s onward. Though he had long refused to participate in the annual Salons

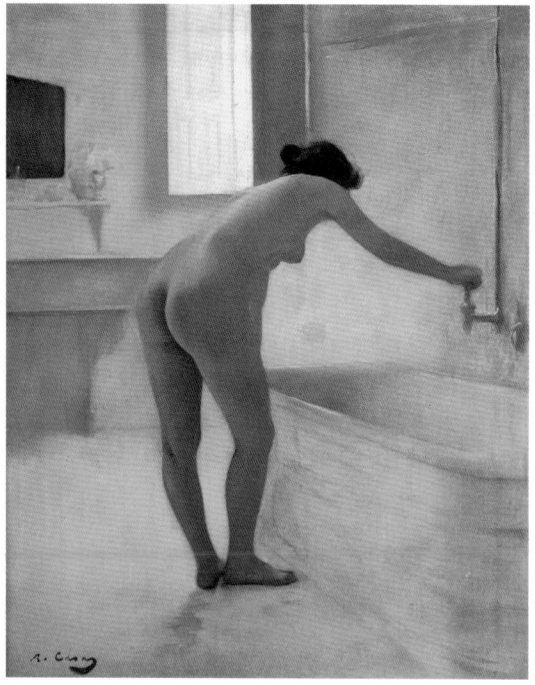

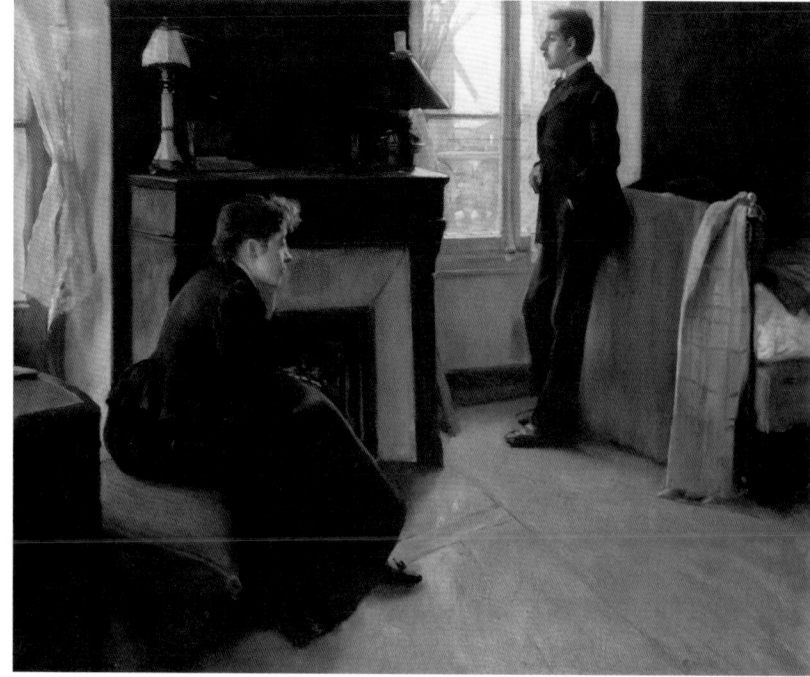

endorsed by the state, Degas contributed substantially to the Impressionist exhibitions of 1880, 1881, and 1886, and showed significant groups of new and older pictures in dealers' galleries until the mid-1890s.[88] After this period he exhibited less, while remaining a familiar figure on the city's streets and accessible to old acquaintances and young admirers until his death in 1917. Among traces of Degas's influence on his followers, a number of documents and specific pictures show that he excited the sustained interest of Casas, Rusiñol, and Utrillo. By 1882, for example, Casas had painted two remarkable café interiors that point to an awareness of Degas's *In a Café (L'Absinthe)* (see 104) and he later created a series of strongly drawn, Degas-like bather and *toilette* scenes (**44**), one of which was shown in Barcelona in 1894.[89] Rusiñol's familiarity with Degas's world is the most fully recorded. From 1889, Rusiñol studied with Henri Gervex, a close friend of Degas at this moment, and executed a sequence of painstakingly realistic canvases that were indebted to both men.[90] Several of Rusiñol's accomplished

views of Montmartre and its pleasure-seekers indicate a knowledge of Degas's innovatory approach to space and tonality, and his signature use of asymmetry and cropped forms. Again, some of these were sent for exhibition to Barcelona.[91] In one bleak picture of 1891, *Summer Cloud* (**45**), Rusiñol represented an alienated bourgeois couple in a darkened room, in what has been seen as a direct homage to Degas's now notorious *Interior (The Rape)*, a work known exclusively in Degas's lifetime to those with access to his studio.[92] The second period spent by Rusiñol in Paris, from 1893 onward, resulted in less confrontational pictures but increasing contact with Degas's social and professional circle. Rusiñol's correspondence is littered with references to painters, sculptors, and graphic artists who knew and admired Degas, among them Forain, Steinlen, Toulouse-Lautrec, Whistler, Carrière, and Puvis de Chavannes, the latter a favorite of Rusiñol's and a colleague and near neighbor of Degas.[93] An even more intimate connection that brought together some of these figures was Suzanne Valadon, a Parisian model and

44

Ramon Casas

(Spanish, 1866–1932)

The Bath, c. 1895. Oil on canvas, 95.5 x 75.5 cm. Private collection

45

Santiago Rusiñol

Summer Cloud, 1891. Oil on canvas, 66.5 x 71.5 cm. Private collection

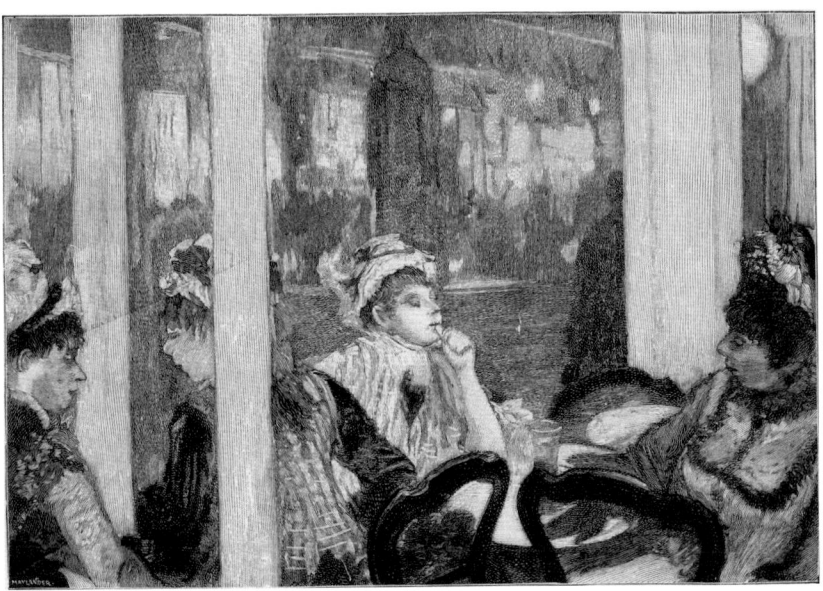

46

Edgar Degas

*Women on the Terrace
of a Café in the Evening.*
Reproduced in Roger
Marx, "Cartons d'Artistes
Degas," in *L'Image* 11
(October 1897), p. 323.
Courtesy Sterling and
Francine Clark Art
Institute, Williamstown,
Massachusetts

struggling artist who had a child by Utrillo and posed for several of Rusiñol's major paintings.[94] She also sat for Degas in this same decade and earned his affection and respect; in a letter of 1895, Degas complimented her highly when he admired the "bold and supple lines" of Valadon's drawings (see 130).[95]

A further factor in the spread of information about Degas's work among Spanish painters was the international art press, which had already recognized his achievement in substantial articles, some accompanied by illustrations. Several texts offered considered accounts of Degas's career written by individuals who knew him well, extending his reputation at home and abroad. The majority of early essays appeared in French journals, but significant exceptions to this rule occurred before the turn of the century. Barcelona and its institutions prided themselves on their wide European reach, which was reflected in the availability of periodicals of many kinds in their libraries. At the Ateneo, for example, a prominent literary and artistic club of the kind that Picasso's father may have frequented, members could read a range of titles from the popular *Gil Blas* to the scholarly *Gazette des Beaux-Arts*, from the English *Art*

Journal to the ultra-modern *L'Image*, a magazine published in Paris in 1897.[96] In the *Art Journal* of 1894 they would have found an essay by the respected French critic Théodore Duret, offering a judicious summary of Degas's art and accompanied by six black-and-white engravings. These embraced several of Degas's most characteristic themes: ballet dancers, racecourses, a laundress, and the drinkers in his lowlife scene, *In a Café*.[97] In October 1897, Roger Marx took a similar approach in the magazine he edited, *L'Image*, adding to this repertoire of reproductions a scene of intimate bathing and a depiction of Parisian prostitutes (**46**). This was based on the pastel over monotype *Women on the Terrace of a Café in the Evening* (see 74) that had recently been placed on public display at the Musée du Luxembourg in Paris.[98]

The internationalism of this period was embodied in the figure of the widely traveled and multitalented Rusiñol, who was also active in publication from an early date. Writing essays for a number of periodicals, Rusiñol sometimes dispatched two or three articles a month from Paris to the Barcelona newspaper *La Vanguardia*. Further contributing to the circulation of news about French culture, Rusiñol's journalistic activities added to his status as a tastemaker and cultural entrepreneur when he returned to live in Spain in 1894.[99] A significant presence in the Barcelona art world, Rusiñol also established a center for innovative cultural activities of many kinds at the nearby coastal town of Sitges. In June 1897, he joined Casas, Utrillo, and Pere Romeu as founders of Els Quatre Gats café and beer hall in Barcelona, which frankly imitated the Chat Noir on the rue Victor Massé in Paris, near Degas's studio.[100] In addition to its function as a gathering place, Els Quatre Gats presented mildly anarchistic performances, occasional art displays, and back-lit silhouette and puppet shows. It may have been on these premises that Picasso first encountered Rusiñol, during one of the young artist's reported visits to the café in

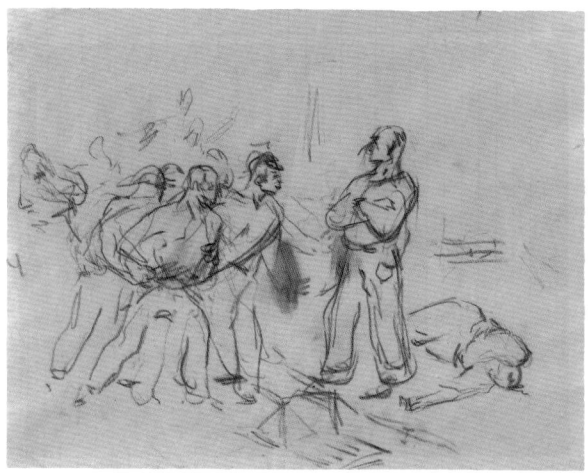

47

Pablo Picasso

The Brawl, 1897.

Conté crayon on paper,

20.1 x 26.2 cm. Museu

Picasso, Barcelona

(MPB 110.335)

its opening year, but it would be many months before their friendship blossomed.[101]

Several definitive shifts in Picasso's identity as a young artist can be located in 1897. Now with a modest studio space in Barcelona, he spent the beginning of the year completing the last "set piece" he was to make under his father's direct supervision, *Science and Charity* (see 13), which received an honorable mention when it was exhibited in June. Opening in this same month, Els Quatre Gats offered a profoundly contrasted prospect as a focus for the city's literary and visual avant-garde. In yet another paradoxical twist at this moment, Picasso was persuaded by don José to take one more step toward official acclaim by leaving Barcelona to study at the Real Academia de Bellas Artes de San Fernando in Madrid. Conceding reluctantly and now away from the critical eye of his father for the first time, Picasso soon rebelled against the Academy's antiquated procedures and arbitrary exercises. A rare surviving letter to a friend reveals Picasso's low esteem for his teachers: "They have no common sense . . . it's always the same: painting, Velázquez; sculpture, Michelangelo."[102] Perversely, he skipped classes but spent time looking and drawing in the Prado, compensating for gaps in his education by tackling the Spanish and European masters on his own terms. But his

drawings from Goya are untidy and fragmented, and several other studies were left unfinished.[103] Much of Picasso's attention was now given to the city and its populace, in a group of mainly small, fluent oil paintings of Madrid's gardens and parks that took him briefly back to landscape and color, and to brushwork that recalls Rusiñol.[104] In yet another mode, rough sketches show Picasso brazenly experimenting with the style and subject matter of Steinlen, dashing off scenes of brawling workers that directly cite one of Steinlen's signature motifs (**47**).[105] Within a few months it was clear that he had finally lost patience with the academic process. After falling seriously ill, he left Madrid and spent the rest of 1898 recuperating with his friend Pallarès in the countryside. Just as he was poised to relaunch himself in Barcelona, Picasso was taken out of circulation for almost a year.

Early Independence

The analogy between Picasso's rejection of the Madrid academy in 1898 and Degas's abandonment of the École des Beaux-Arts in 1855 is not close in terms of their relative ages or personal circumstances. Yet both artists, after submitting to a traditional education in their student years, had chosen not only to step outside this system but to challenge many of the principles on which it was founded. Now armed with a sophisticated mastery of drawing and the intricacies of the human body, Degas and Picasso were more than able to compete with their peers. Despite these advantages, their attempts to establish themselves and redefine their careers in distinctive terms took some time. With the arguable exception of certain portraits, Degas was almost thirty before he painted his first substantial modern pictures, while the prodigious Picasso was around a dozen years younger when he attained the same goal. Uniting them was an ambition to make paintings and drawings that were distinct from most of their previous efforts, now addressing the world that surrounded them in forms that were appropriate to their times. Both finally turned away from subject matter that was sanctioned by the past, from rhetoric and bland sentimentality, and even from the facile realism that the art market continued to favor. When Degas stopped work on his unresolved *Semiramis Building Babylon* (see 22) and several comparable canvases, some of his paintings had already begun to confront the local racetracks he visited with friends and views of his fellow artists in their Paris studios. In the mid-1860s, he turned to his first pictures of ballerinas on the stage and in their dressing rooms. Intriguingly, Picasso would deal with several of these same themes as he gradually defined his own cast of topical characters around the turn of the century. Newly prominent with both artists was an element of autobiography; no longer drawing and painting past events, they made pictures about the people around them, the urban locations they knew well, and the everyday dramas of the cities — Paris and Barcelona — where they lived.

Traces of this new independence can be found in drawings made by Degas and Picasso as they embarked on their solitary careers. In the early 1860s, Degas chose to hire his own model and draw her in his Montmartre studio, effectively refashioning academic practice for his own ends. *Standing Nude* (**48**) shows the young woman in a relaxed, almost domestic mode, as if she were lost in thought or about to bathe or dress herself. Degas's fastidious, densely shaded account of her body recalls the rich tonality of his slightly earlier *Self-Portrait* (see 26), while its assertively monochromatic character is even more suggestive of a photograph. His plans for this impressive sheet are unknown: it would be some years before such figures appeared in Degas's pastels of Parisian bedrooms and paintings of bathing parties beside the ocean. Picasso's *Female Nude* (**49**) is more straightforwardly quotidian, the roughly drafted chair locating the scene in an anonymous modern room. Dating from 1898 or 1899

in Madrid or Barcelona, it was probably made at an independent art class where Picasso could work cheaply and informally from a model.[106] Now beyond the reach of the Academy, he defied its edicts by superimposing on the woman's physique the fashionably stylized outlines of Art Nouveau or Jugendstil. Picasso's figure is thus poised between a living individual and a modish cipher, a hybrid image that lent itself to the book and poster designs that he and his friends had begun to imitate.

Now commanding many and varied pictorial styles, Picasso could still charm those around him. The suave lines and classical economy of the 1899 portrait of the artist's father (see 40) were an acknowledgment of the son's long training, here used to flatter the professor from La Llotja as a dignified citizen. A touch of irreverence, however, proved irresistible: the copy of *Gil Blas Illustré* in don José's pocket stood for everything the former student had been taught to despise. In the late 1890s, each weekly issue of this magazine had a brash cover design by Steinlen at his most facetious, followed by short stories and decorative or amusing illustrations that were sometimes frankly erotic.[107] Typical of the gaudily designed pages of many such publications were their echoes of styles and imagery from recent French art. During 1899, don José and his son would have found in *Gil Blas Illustré* a number of Degas-like genre scenes, including views of assignations (see 37) and hat shops (see 38), that ultimately derived from Degas's pictures of the previous two decades. Though seemingly trivial, *Gil Blas Illustré* and similar titles were among the secondary modes that disseminated the radical language of Impressionism at this period. As we have seen, Picasso had been notably open to sources of this kind from an early age, exhibiting a catholicity of taste that expanded to a remarkable degree in Barcelona. Illustration and commercial advertising had become major vehicles for graphic experimentation, soon providing yet another

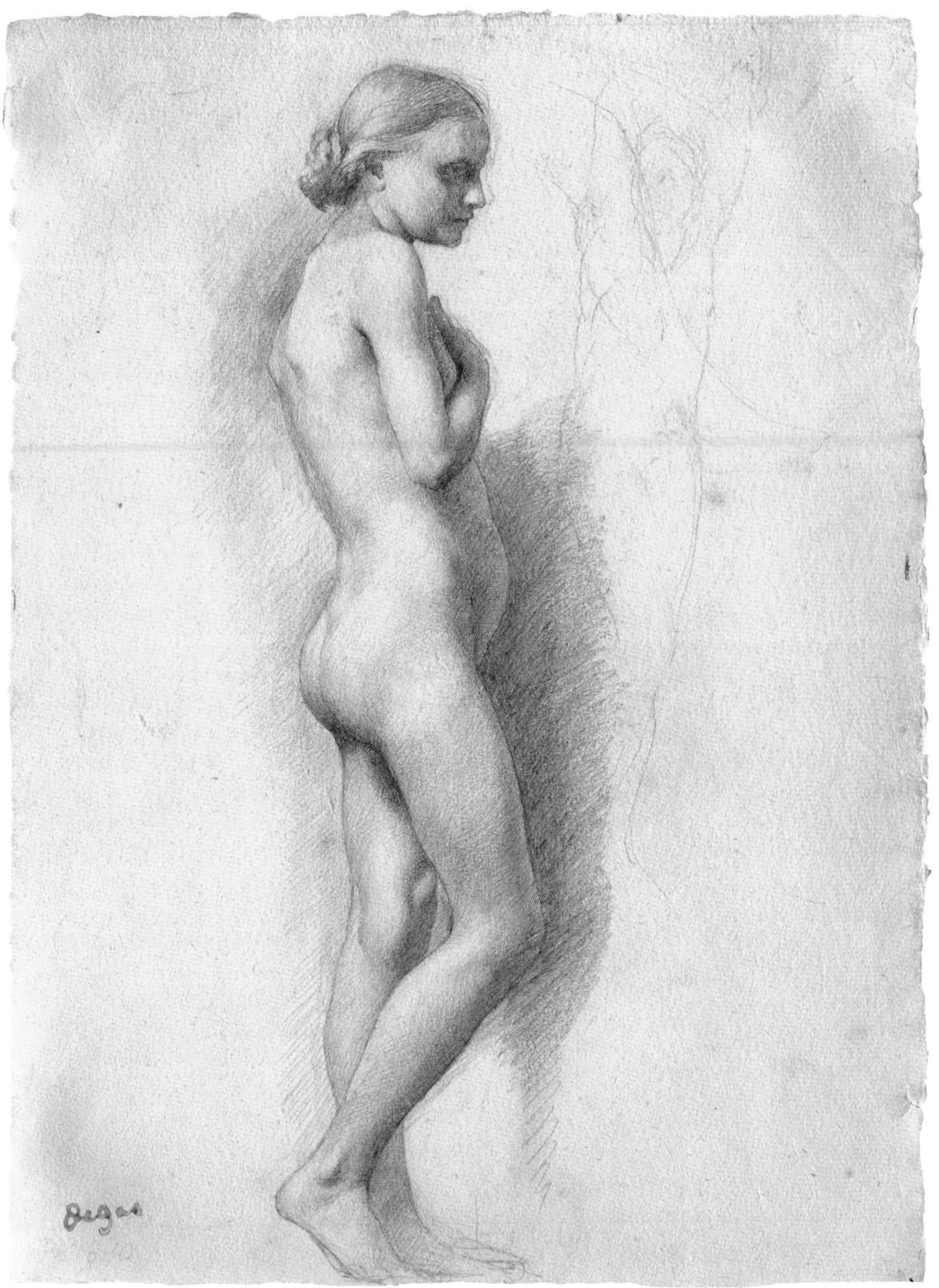

48

Edgar Degas

Standing Nude, c. 1860–65.
Pencil on paper,
29 x 21.7 cm. Sterling
and Francine Clark Art
Institute, Williamstown,
Massachusetts
(1955.1847)

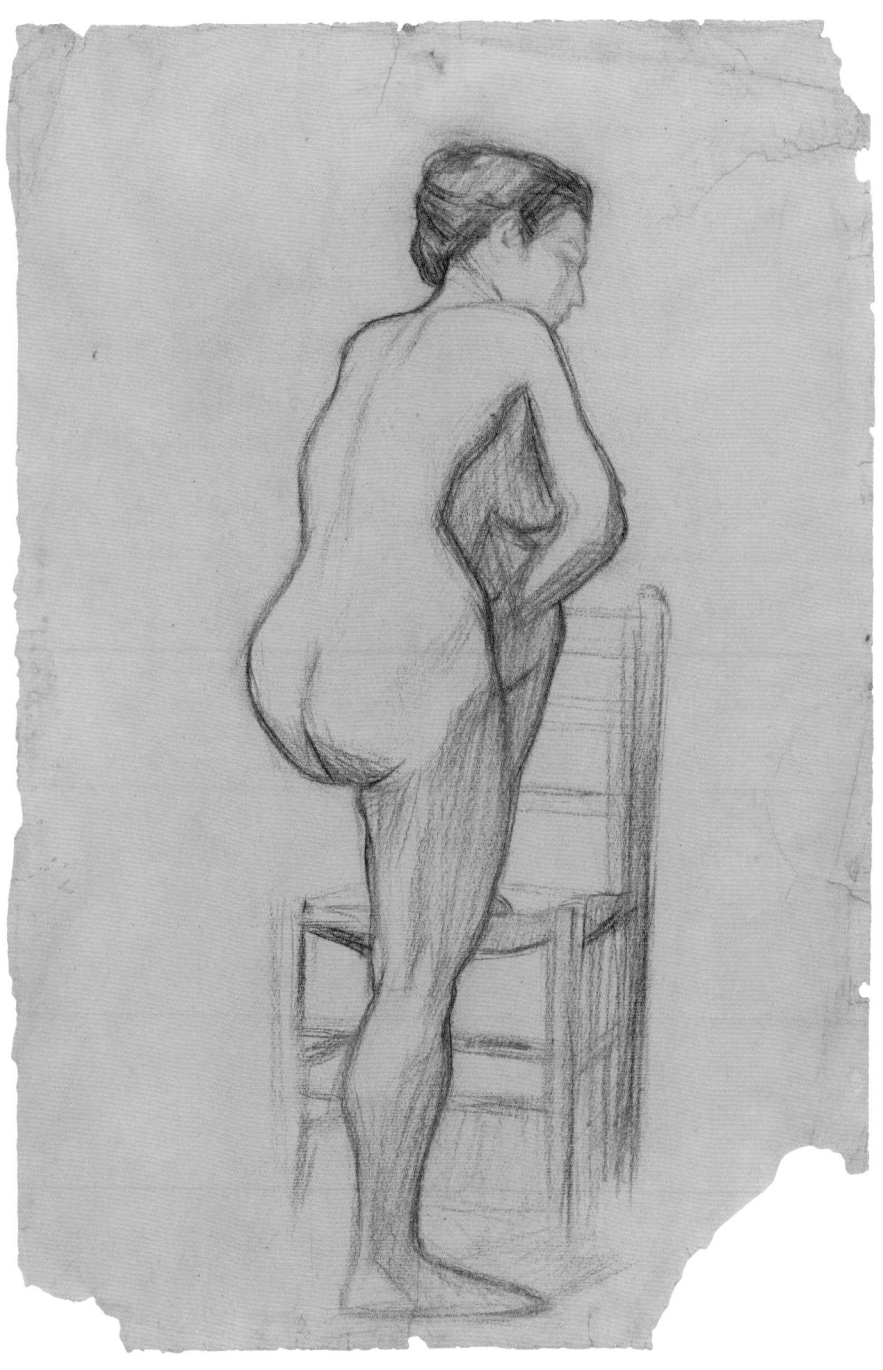

49

Pablo Picasso

Female Nude, c. 1899.
Charcoal on paper,
48.5 x 33 cm. Museu
Picasso, Barcelona
(MPB 110.595)

outlet for his prodigious skills. In 1898, Picasso's first drawing to be reproduced appeared in a local magazine, followed by his attempts at poster designs and contributions to other vanguard journals at the turn of the century.[108] Consciously or otherwise, he was following the example of many of the Impressionist artists who welcomed the publicity offered through timely illustrations made by their own hands. In this context, Degas stood out as a model for his relentless advocacy of the graphic arts, making drawings for several periodicals, planning a number of illustrative projects, and dabbling in photomechanical reproduction.[109]

The new generation of periodicals that appeared in Barcelona in these years not only allowed Picasso and his companions to show their talents but also to identify with a wider Catalan and European modernism. The largely literary *Luz*, for example, founded in November 1897, carried articles by Rusiñol, stories by the Belgian Symbolist Émile Verhaeren, and observations on such contemporary French writers as Émile Zola, Alphonse Daudet, and Paul Verlaine. The dominant graphic style was a somewhat insipid Art Nouveau, exemplified in the illustrations of Eugène Grasset, while drawings by those closer to Picasso — Utrillo, Canals, Opisso, Nonell, and Ramon Pichot — pointed to bolder developments ahead. A parallel theme in *Luz* was the visual art of France, represented in the work of such figures as Steinlen, Forain, and Jules Chéret, in an issue devoted entirely to the recently deceased Puvis de Chavannes, and in knowing references to such prominent writers on Impressionism as François Thiébault-Sisson, Gustave Geffroy, and Arsène Alexandre. Soon after its demise in late 1898, *Luz* was followed by the more rudimentary *Quatre Gats*, a bimonthly publication edited by Romeu that reflected the interests of his café's artistic clientele. Each issue consisted of a single sheet folded into four pages, with color added occasionally to invigorate illustrations by Mir, Nonell,

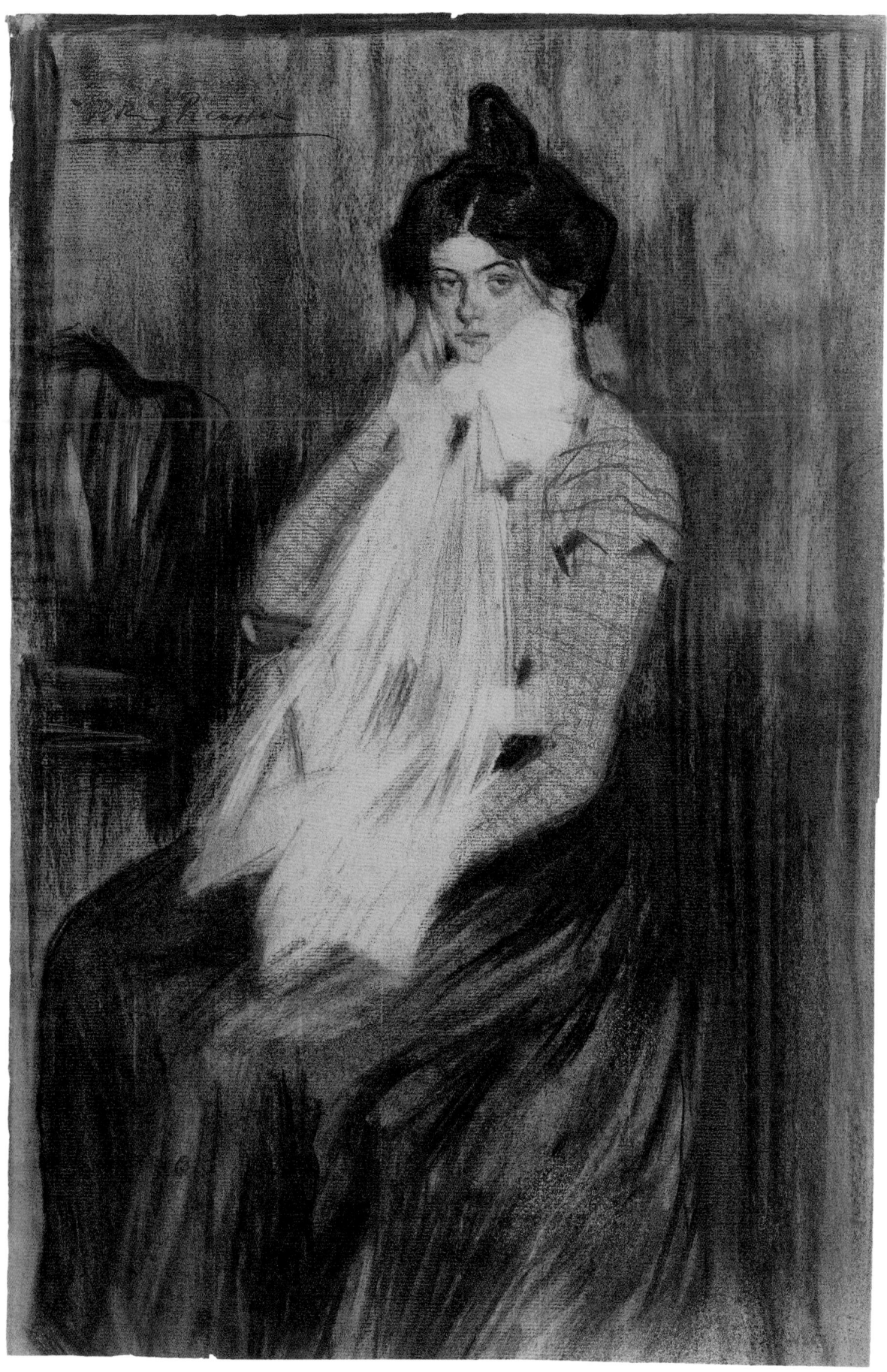

50

Pablo Picasso

Lola, the Artist's Sister,
1899. Charcoal and
colored pencil on paper,
45 x 29.5 cm. Museu
Picasso, Barcelona
(MPB 4.265)

51

Edgar Degas

*Portrait of Thérese
Degas-Morbilli (Study for
"Portrait of M and Mme
Morbilli")*, c. 1865. Pencil
and charcoal on paper,
35.2 x 23.3 cm. Musée
d'Orsay, Paris, housed in
the Department of
Graphic Arts, Musée du
Louvre. Gift of Mme
Arlette Devade, née
Nepveu-Degas, 1990
(RF 42 663)

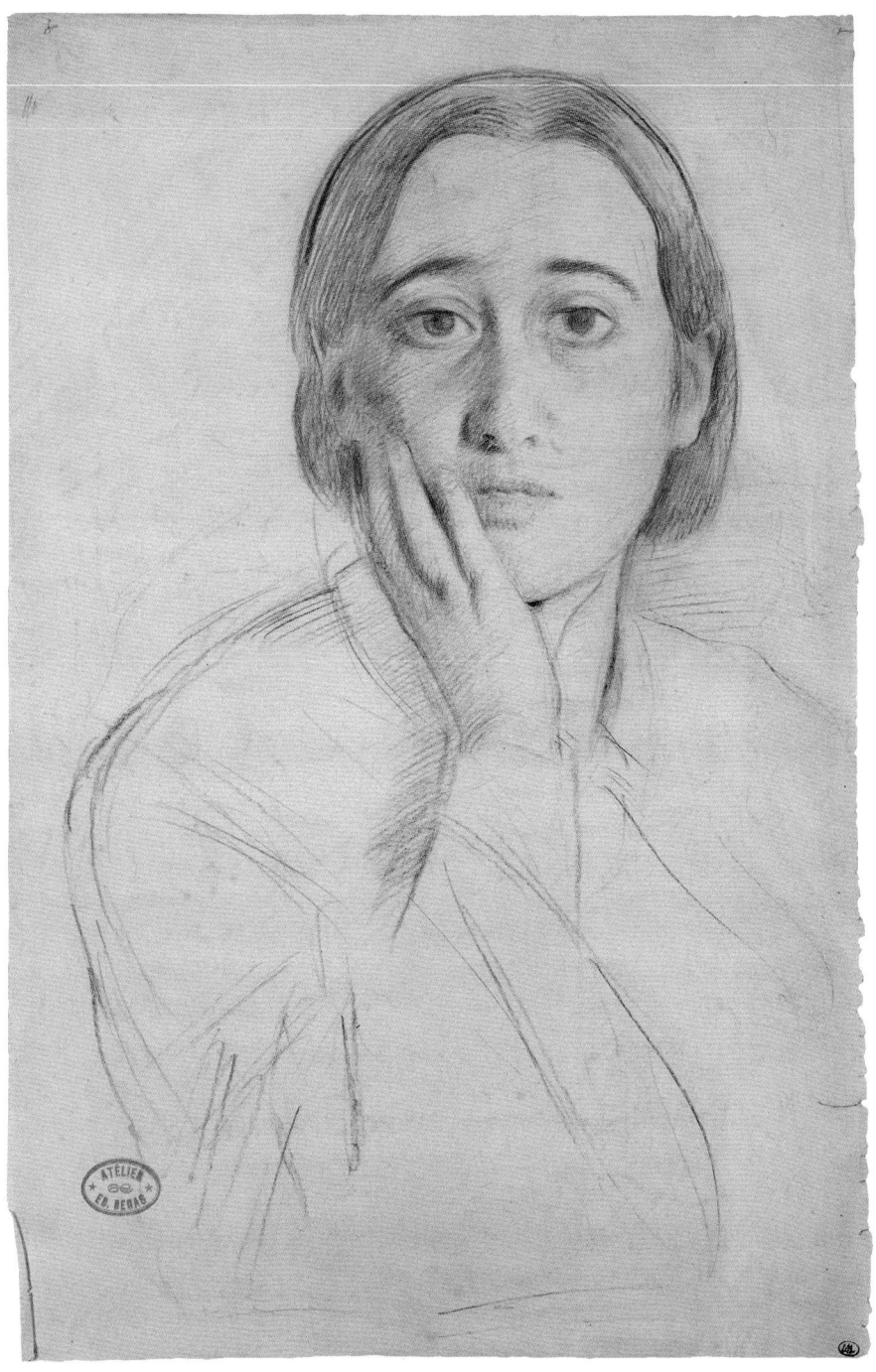

encouraging Rodin to form a new group which will include Degas, Monet and other great artists who are not known to the public."[110]

While the more anemic aspects of Art Nouveau played an occasional role in the work of the *Quatre Gats* artists, the style was more evident in Picasso's paintings and drawings in heavy, sinuous contours that contained and energized some of his drawn figures. The superb charcoal and colored pencil portrait *Lola, the Artist's Sister* (**50**) is a sophisticated case in point.[111] Here the child from Corunna has become a remote *femme fatale*, her body subsumed in an upward, wave-like rhythm that embraces her shadowy setting, voluminous gray skirt, and cascading white scarf. This Lola is a creature of her times, a reflective, morose being, rather than a mere socialite who glowers at her brother as she returns his gaze. Modish accessories such as the background chair and even Lola's exotic hairstyle — which might almost be a sculpture by Émile Gallé — remind us forcefully of Barcelona's fashionable status at this moment. The leap back to Paris in the 1860s, when Degas drew his own sister, Thérèse, in an uncannily similar pose (**51**) seems to take us to a remote age. In the refined, understated drawing belonging to the Louvre, Thérèse appears overwhelmed by reticence and propriety. Made around 1865 in preparation for a large double portrait on canvas, this project was part of Degas's determined effort to launch himself as a contemporary, even stylish, portraitist in the terms of his own day.[112] Bold in its psychological directness, the painting explored Thérèse's evident anxiety even as it included the dominant figure of her husband and recorded their recent marriage. The fine nuances and light touch of his drawing are powerful reminders of Degas's long apprenticeship as a draftsman and of his father's vision of portraiture as "the jewel" among his son's potential achievements. Yet in contrast to Picasso's study, the delicacy of Degas's sheet is almost overwhelmed in his finished picture,

Casas, or Rusiñol. Less emphatically international than *Luz*, *Quatre Gats* nevertheless printed a short statement in March 1899, under the heading "Paris Salons," that claimed to report a rebellion of young painters: "These young people together with other slightly older artists are

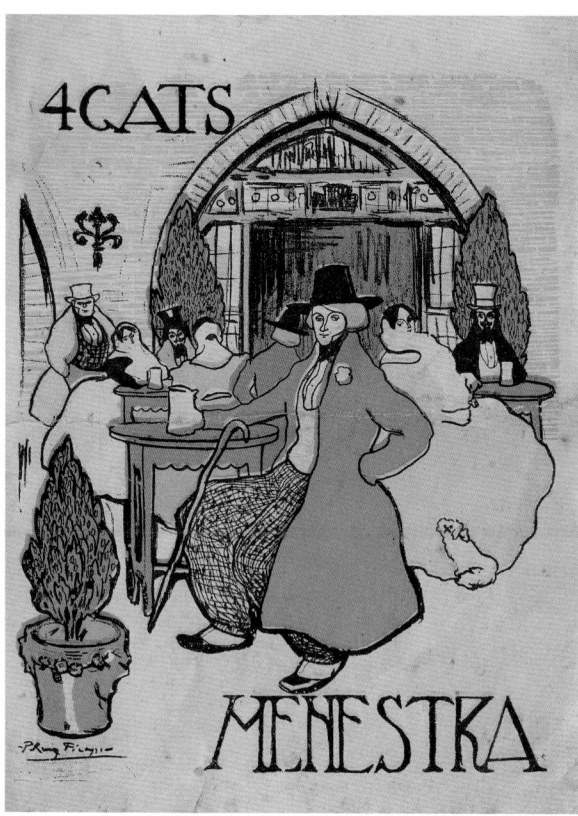

where his relatives appear as solemn, formally dressed individuals in a gloomy bourgeois salon.

Els Quatre Gats

Picasso was now part of the crowd that included Casas, Rusiñol, and Utrillo, and many other established and aspiring Catalan artists who gathered at Els Quatre Gats. Still only seventeen, he was regularly exposed to their skeptical and adventurous attitudes, their evident public achievements, and their considerable awareness of art beyond the Spanish border. In return, their respect for Picasso's draftsmanship was signaled in a commission to design the café's menu card, on which the figure of an outrageously overdressed dandy at the center of this composition could conceivably be understood as an expression of Picasso's own burgeoning self-esteem (**52**). Among the transformative effects of Els Quatre Gats was Picasso's enthusiasm for the work of painters whom he had only

recently discovered. This extended from the seventeenth-century portraits and religious scenes of El Greco to the decorative patterning of Aubrey Beardsley, and from the austere murals of Puvis de Chavannes to the melancholy paintings and prints of the Norwegian artist Edvard Munch. True to form, Picasso absorbed what he heard and cannibalized what he saw, making saintly looking portraits of friends, scenes of languishing adolescents, and a number of haunted likenesses of himself. Distinctive in Picasso's approach to his predecessors and senior contemporaries was a free and inventive — rather than merely slavish — response to their work. Within months, for example, Picasso's specifically El Greco-like mannerisms were abandoned, but the deeper lessons of his use of pictorial space and depiction of ecstatic feeling lingered for decades. Even the influence of Munch, which surfaced in several guises, soon became absorbed into Picasso's growing battery of styles, infusing his remarkable *Self-Portrait* in charcoal and crayon (**53**) with northern European intensity, yet blending uneasily with the image of the artist as a young Spanish roué.

The company at Els Quatre Gats was also a vital source of information about current French art and artists. Rusiñol's generation, with their firsthand knowledge of Impressionist Paris, was now augmented by younger painters with more recent experience of the city, some of many months' duration. A case recorded in some detail is that of Nonell, whom Picasso got to know in the intervals between the older man's several visits to France. Nonell and Picasso were to develop "a warm admiration for each other and each other's work" at this time, despite Nonell's greater age and restless travels.[113] In rarely cited letters written from Paris to the Barcelona art critic Raimon Casellas, Nonell used plain but vivid language that probably reflected the tone of many such communications from their itinerant friends. After his first visit to the Louvre, in March 1897, Nonell remarked that

52

Pablo Picasso

Menu for Els Quatre Gats, 1899–1900. Chromolithograph, 32.8 x 21.8 cm. Museu Picasso, Barcelona (MPB 110.995)

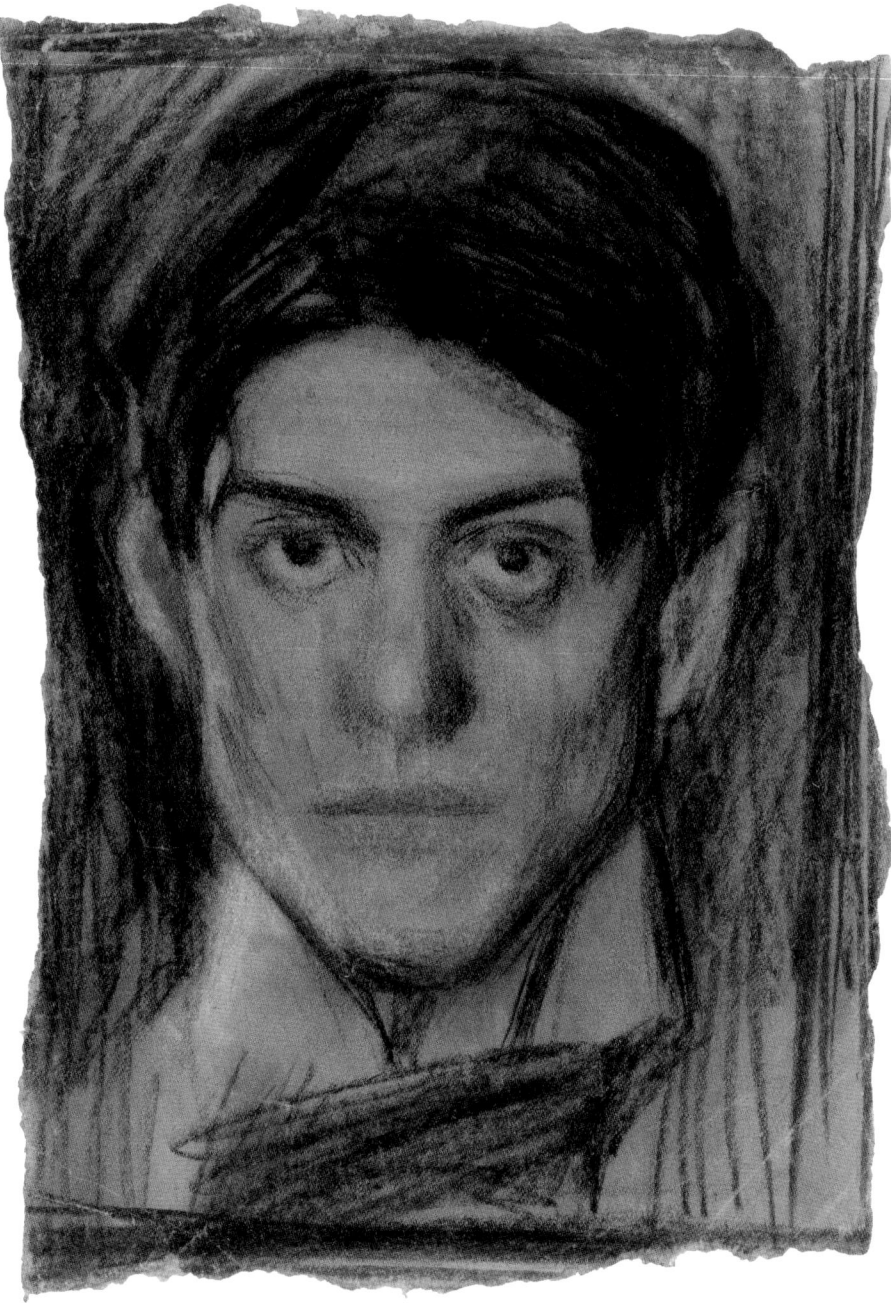

53

Pablo Picasso

Self-Portrait, 1899–1900.
Charcoal and crayon on
paper, 22.5 x 16.2 cm.
Museu Picasso, Barcelona
(MPB 110.632)

many pictures had left him "completely cold"; "Millet and Corot's work almost made me shrug my shoulders in resignation," he confessed.[114] "Puvis de Chavannes, Whistler, Sargent and Carrière," however, pleased him considerably, among whom Puvis was identified as "the greatest of the painters I have seen." Before his first trip to France, Nonell's own art had emerged from its "Saffron" phase toward a harsh, almost maladroit social realism. By late 1897, his colleagues were told that he was about to show some of these recent pictures in the exhibition of "Impressionist and Symbolist" works at the gallery of Le Barc de Bouteville.[115] Nonell's first contacts with Impressionism had been disconcerting. In 1897, he told his Barcelona correspondent: "Initially I found the [works of] C. Monet, Degas, Pissarro, Manet, Renoir etc quite weak," but less than a month later he announced, "Lately I find I'm really keen on Monet and Degas too."[116] The following year, Nonell explained his earlier coolness: "[A]ccustomed as I am to seeing the gentle art produced by every single one of the Barcelona painters . . . Degas, Monet, Pissarro and Manet seemed to my eyes to be mad revolutionaries."117 "Apart from the Degas pictures which are frequently at the Durand-Ruel gallery, I have seen those in the Count Camondo collection. Most of them are impressive studies of dancers (as you well know)."[118] As part of his extensive collecting activities, Isaac de Camondo had brought together an extraordinary group of Impressionist works that included almost twenty major pictures by Degas, among them a remarkable *Laundress* and his celebrated *In a Café* (see 104).[119]

Reverberations from encounters with the art of Degas and his admirers are clearly apparent in the output of Nonell and those around him. Nonell admitted that he found lesser figures such as Forain, Steinlen, and Henri-Gabriel Ibels "tiresome" or "uneven," and acknowledged that the draftsman in this circle who "interested me

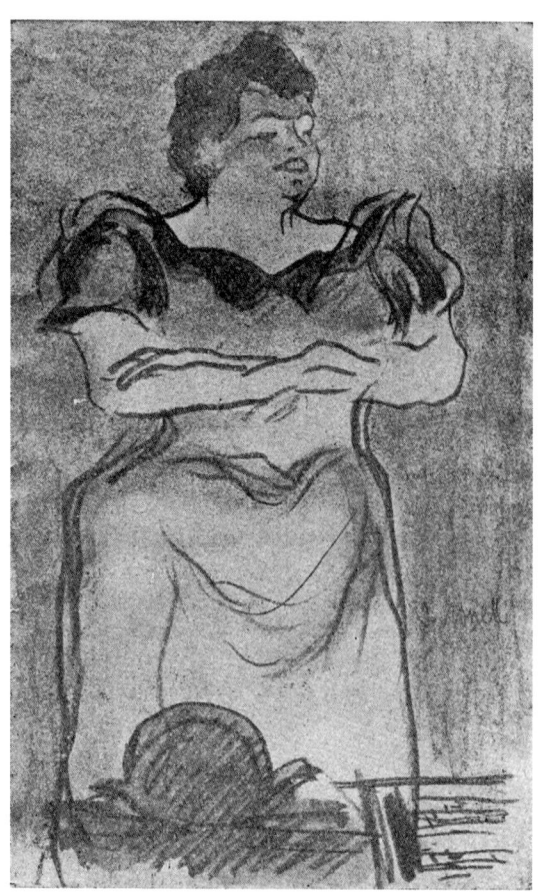

most" was Lautrec.[120] Nonell's overtly Francophile drawing, *Cabaret Singer* (**54**), dating from 1897 or 1898, includes some graphic flourishes in the manner of Lautrec but manifestly has its roots in the café-concert imagery of Degas.[121] Picasso was typically alert to all these sources, whether first- or secondhand, and his debt to a range of French painters and printmakers was evident in much of his graphic work at the end of the century. References to Steinlen, who was the conduit for a number of Degas's motifs, are almost uncomfortably apparent in a group of Picasso's heavily stylized drawings of women on the street and men with horses, presented in formats that recall the covers of *Gil Blas Illustré*.[122] Lautrec, Forain, and Degas himself seem to have provided the inspiration for several variants on the crowded café and the insalubrious bar, some featuring — for the first time in Picas-

so's oeuvre — characters who were unquestionably prostitutes (**55**).[123] Picasso's mastery of line was put to many new uses in works of this type, prominently in the coarse, expressive drawings of half-naked whores in shadowy rooms that have few equivalents outside Degas's monotype repertoire. More squalid than anything by Lautrec, Picasso's experiments culminated in such compositions as the stark, unforgiving *The Divan* (**56**) of about 1899, which seems to announce his arrival as an artist of urban vice. This is an astonishingly confident performance for a teenager, strongly — almost brutally — drawn with a powerful sense of the collision between two individuals in an act of lust. Clashing colors add further to its energy, underscored by near-violent strokes of charcoal that deny everything he had learned at La Llotja.

Even before the new century dawned, the gifted child-artist from Malaga had transformed himself beyond recognition. Once committed to drawing and painting within the polite modes of the day, he now reveled in a kind of international eclecticism that was yet to declare itself in substantial canvases or in a definitive style. Among his countless artist-heroes was the group around Edgar Degas, who had chosen to focus their graphic skills on what Degas once called "the human animal."[124] Increasingly well informed about this circle, Picasso may also have responded to specific works by Degas

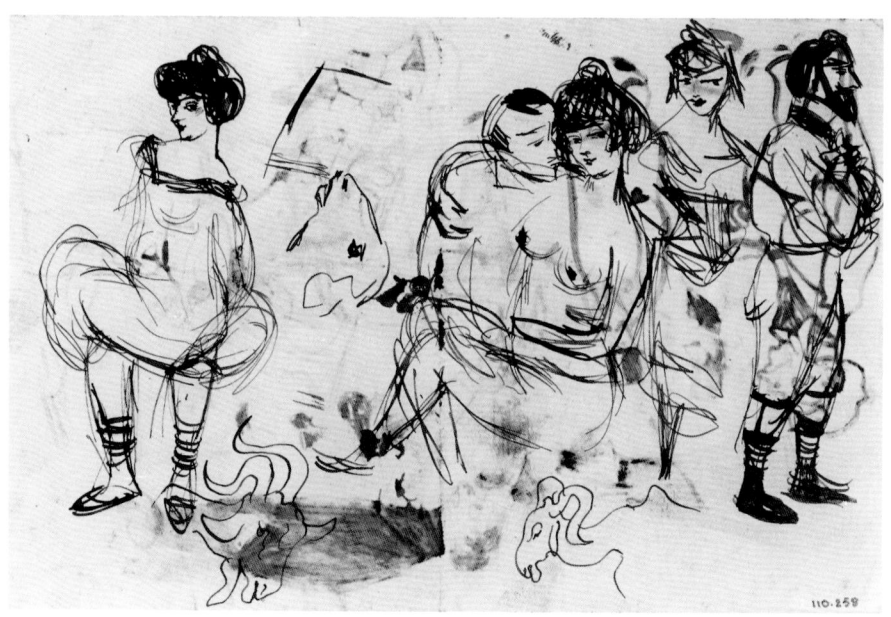

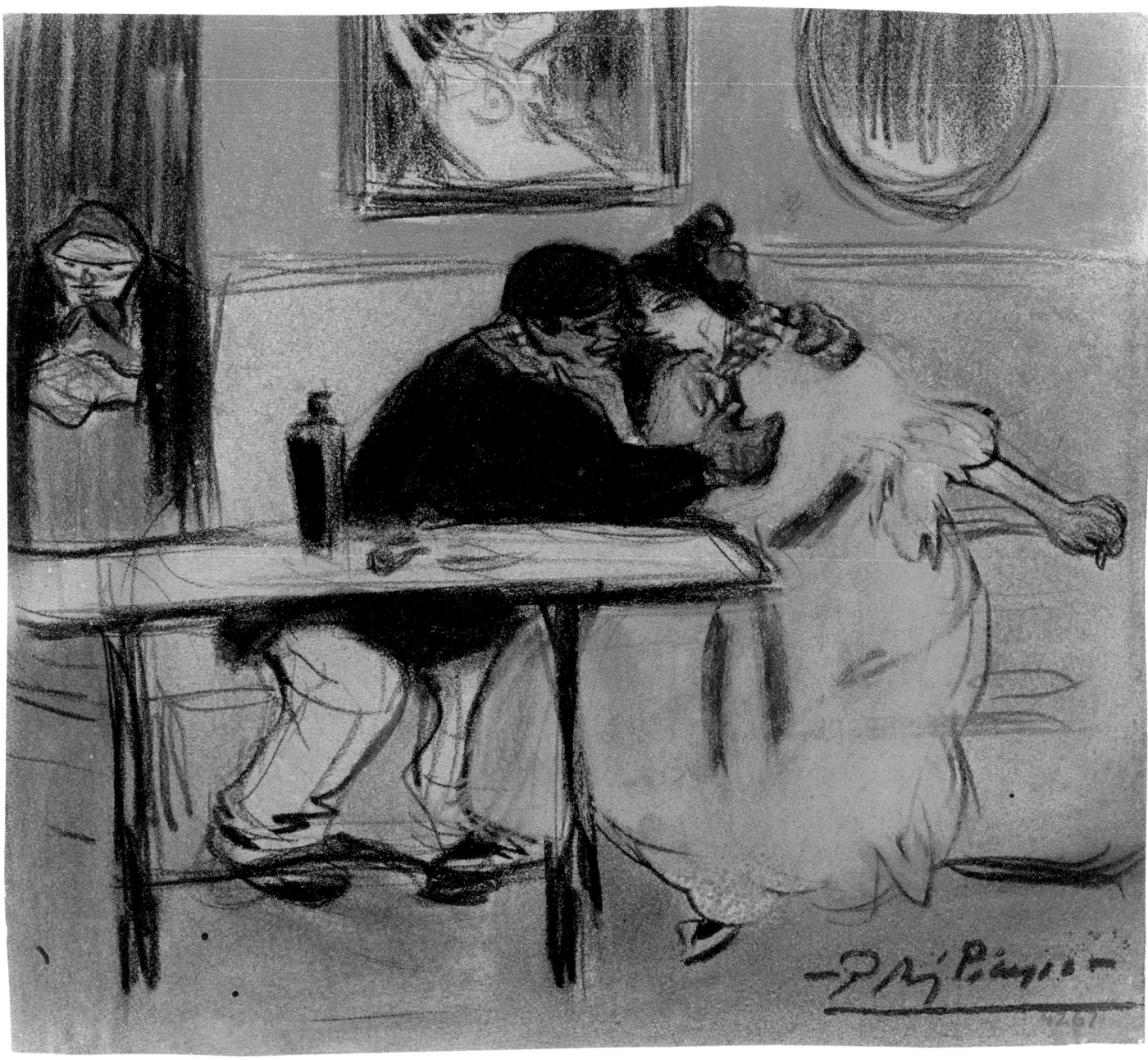

56

Pablo Picasso

The Divan, c. 1899.
Charcoal, pastel, and
colored pencil on
varnished paper,
26.2 x 29.7 cm. Museu
Picasso, Barcelona
(MPB 4.267)

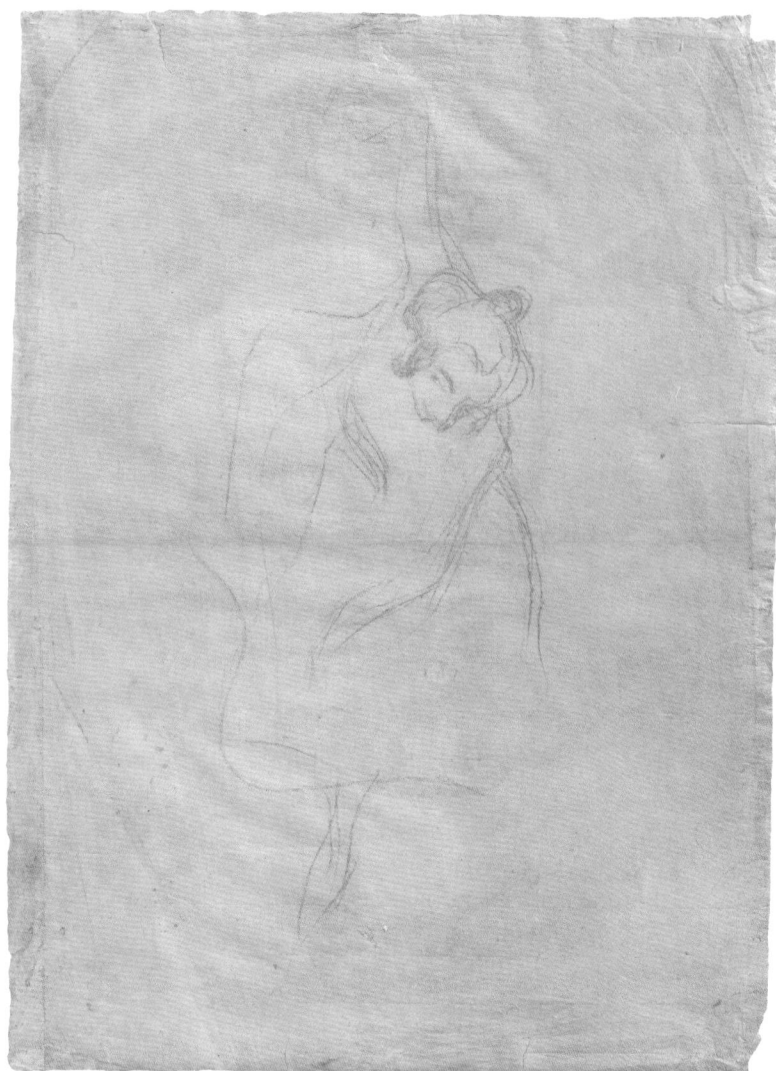

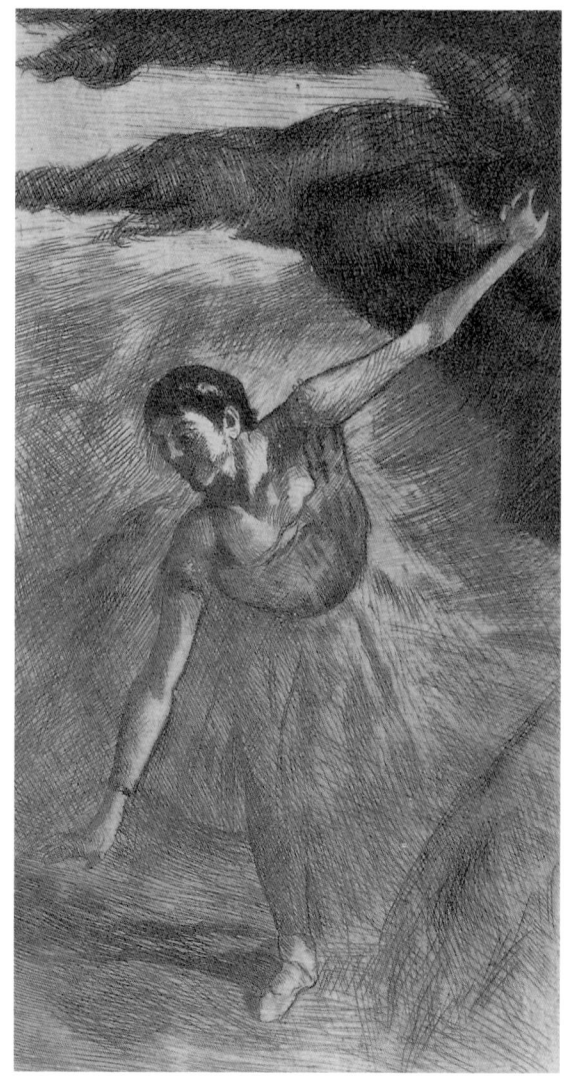

known through prints and reproductions, as he had responded to pictures by Beardsley and Toulouse-Lautrec, Munch and Steinlen. A little-noticed drawing of a ballerina from the fin-de-siècle (**57**), for example, is striking in itself but becomes more so when understood as a view from high above the stage. Degas had long been celebrated for his introduction of precisely this device, which appeared several times in illustrations that were currently in circulation, in such publications as Georges Lecomte's 1892 book *L'Art Impressioniste* (**58**) and Roger Marx's 1897 *L'Image* article (see 97).[125] Picasso's fluent drawings of cabaret singers have a similar reso-nance, though they are perhaps indebted to intermediary images by Ibels or Lautrec as much as to works by Degas himself.[126] More deeply suggestive are three or four café scenes, from small sketches to a large painting on canvas, where somber figures huddle around tables and stare back at the viewer in ways reminiscent of Degas's *In a Café*. Seen firsthand by Nonell in the Camondo collection and known in reproduction by readers of contemporary periodicals, this iconic work soon became central to Picasso's competitive thinking.

Picasso was finally celebrated in one of the new breed of Barcelona publications in January

57

Pablo Picasso

Dancer, 1899–1900.
Conté crayon on paper,
62.2 x 47.5 cm. Museu
Picasso, Barcelona
(MPB 110.877R)

58

Edgar Degas

Dancer. Reproduced in
Georges Lecomte, *L'Art
impressionniste* (Paris:
Typographie Chamerot et
Renouard, 1892), p. 153.
Courtesy Sterling and
Francine Clark Art
Institute, Williamstown,
Massachusetts

59

Ramon Casas

Front cover of *Pèl &
Ploma* 15 (9 September
1899). Courtesy Getty
Research Institute,
Los Angeles

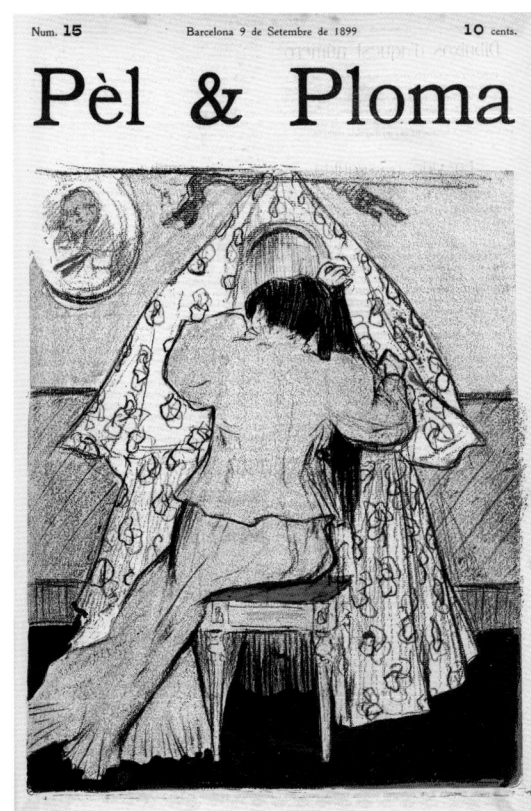

1900, when his design for a poster to mark the new century was mentioned in *Pèl & Ploma*.[127] This magazine had recently taken the place of *Quatre Gats* and was altogether more sophisticated in appearance and content. Loosely based on the Parisian journal *La Plume*, it contained articles and commentary by Utrillo and suave illustrations by Casas, with occasional contributions from others. Overtly Francophile and increasingly wide-ranging as the months passed, *Pèl & Ploma* initially carried several features on the 1900 Universal Exhibition — the event that first lured Picasso to France — and on the Salons, as well as reports on notable sales and collections of pictures in Paris. Frequent references to senior or mid-career Parisian painters — Whistler, Carrière, Besnard, and Jacques-Émile Blanche — assumed a familiarity with their work among Catalan readers, while the established status of other key figures was taken for granted. In June 1899, an article con-

trasted the modest experiences of ordinary Parisians with the imaginative creations of "a Zola or a Degas or a Mirbeau" and in May 1900 a discussion of the Exposition pointed out that the achievements of "artists like Rodin, Claude Monet, Degas, Renoir, Besnard, Dalou, Sisley" did not ensure a line of greatness in French art.[128] The influence of some of these figures was graphically evident in *Pèl & Ploma* itself; the cover of the issue of 9 September 1899, for example, consisted of a *toilette* composition by Casas that seems like an over-upholstered hair-combing scene by Degas (**59**). Picasso first contributed to these pages after returning from his trip to Paris in late 1900, when he was represented by a small caricatural drawing of Rusiñol.[129] In May 1901, he was rewarded with a short article about his own pictures written by Utrillo, in which Picasso was included among "the up-and-coming talents" in Barcelona. Utrillo noted that Picasso had acquired the nickname "Little Goya" in Paris, where he could also be seen wearing "ultra-Impressionist ties."[130]

In February 1900, a month after the launch of *Pèl & Ploma*, the first significant exhibition of Picasso's work opened at Els Quatre Gats when he was still eighteen years of age. It was dominated by more than a hundred drawings and probably included *Portrait of Joan Vidal i Ventosa* (**60**) and the portrait *Santiago Rusiñol* (**61**), both depicting the artist's local friends.[131] Apart from the novelty of the event and the youth of the artist, two other features of this show were exceptional. Almost all of the drawings were portraits of Picasso's male acquaintances in the same three-quarter-length format; and the entire installation was an informal replica of a show held just four months earlier by Ramon Casas, by now a senior figure in Barcelona's artistic life. Casas, too, had presented an extensive series of charcoal drawings, showing them at the Sala Parés, the city's principal art gallery. Confident and stylish, Casas's portraits appear to have provoked Picasso into a public response

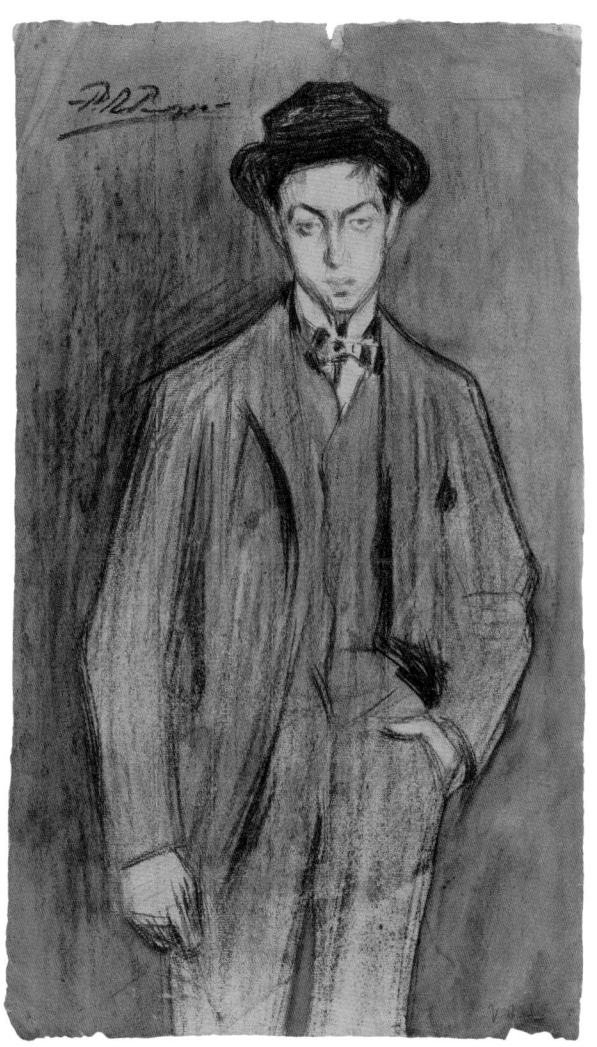 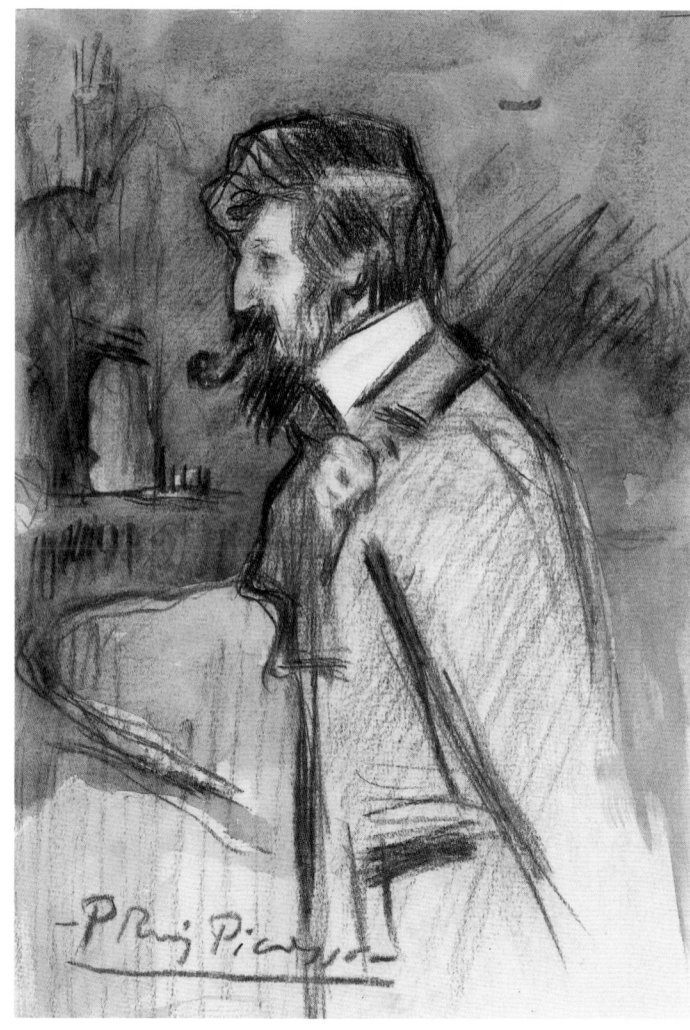

that could be seen as respectful but also bra-zen. His *Portrait of Joan Vidal i Ventosa*, for example, was more confrontational than any-thing by Casas and suggested awkwardness rather than urbanity. Likewise, *Portrait of Santiago Rusiñol* seems oblique, almost casual, and entirely lacking in reverence for his occasional mentor. Both artists had chosen to play with a virtual cliché of the period, represented in an earlier generation by the caricatural portraits of national figures made for magazines by Carlo Pellegrini and other illustrators (**62**). Probably unknown to Casas and Picasso was the fact that Degas had trodden the same ground before them. His witty *Carlo Pellegrini*, painted on

paper in the late 1870s (**63**), is assumed to have been given by Degas to the caricaturist himself in an exchange of works and remained Degas's only exercise in this mode.[132] More imaginatively than either of his Spanish successors, Degas loomed over his subject and almost turned him away from the viewer, leaving gesture and cos-tume to convey much of his personality. Where Casas and even Picasso were content to offer variations on an existing form, two decades earlier Degas had chosen to challenge the convention itself.

This limited event in Barcelona tells us much about the young artist who would soon tackle Paris and some of its competing personalities,

60

Pablo Picasso

Joan Vidal i Ventosa,
1899–1900. Charcoal,
black pencil, and wash
on paper, 47.5 × 28 cm.
Museu Picasso, Barcelona
(MPB 70.802)

61

Pablo Picasso

*Portrait of Santiago
Rusiñol*, c. 1900. Charcoal
and watercolor on paper,
33 × 23 cm. El Conventet
Collection

62

Carlo Pellegrini

(Italian, 1839–1889)
*Portrait of Lord
Wharncliffe*, 1875.
Watercolor on paper,
30.5 × 17.8 cm. National
Portrait Gallery, London
(NPG 4699)

63

Edgar Degas

Carlo Pellegrini,
c. 1876–77. Oil on paper
mounted on board,
63.2 × 34 cm. Tate,
London. Presented by the
Art Fund, 1916 (N03157)

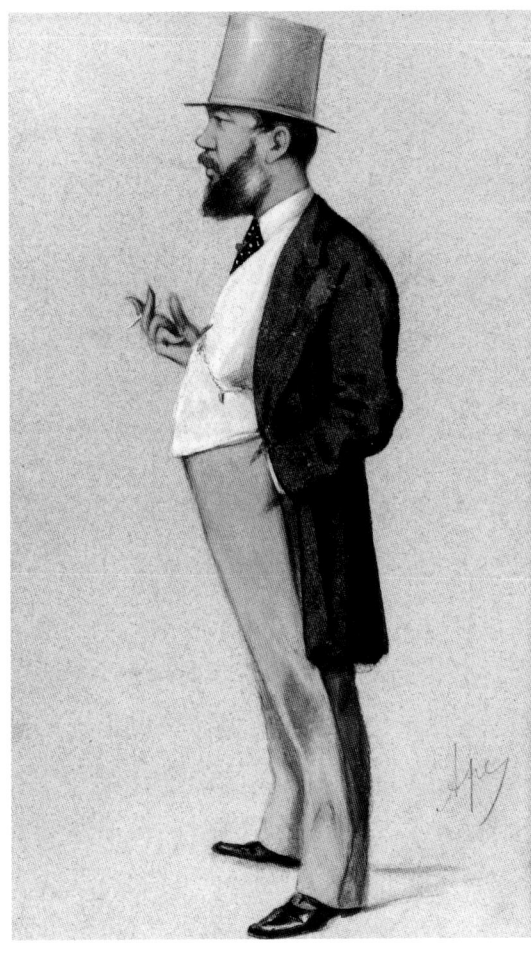

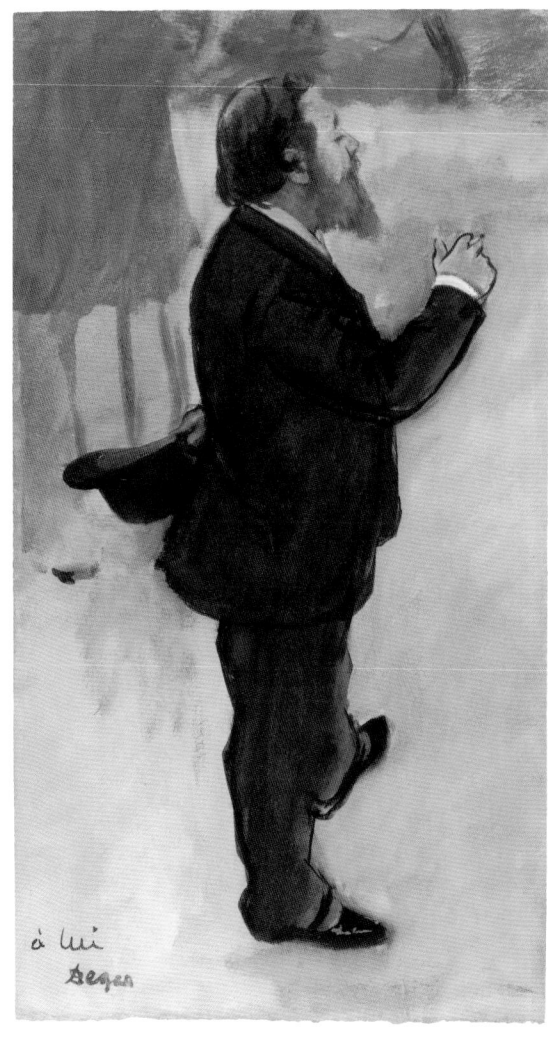

disparate styles, and clashing pictorial modes.
As in his gallery of Catalan portraits, Picasso
surrounded himself over the next two or three
years with the Parisian equivalents of the young
writer Ventosa and the mature painter Rusiñol
— the subjects of two of his recent drawings
— and continued to delight in similar games of
imitation and mockery. Less conspicuous was a
small show at Els Quatre Gats of Picasso's pastels of Hispanic country subjects and brightly
colored *corrida* scenes, some of which would
reappear in his early Paris exhibitions.[133] Very
soon he would turn his back on such material
to focus on the new metropolitan motifs he
encountered and the new visual models he con-

fronted. Already well aware of the reputations
of "Monet, Degas, Renoir," within a year Picasso
would be making pictures that frankly challenged their supremacy. As with Casas, he
chose to approach their work directly and fight
them on their own ground, measuring himself
against their most conspicuous achievements.
A token of his determination was the roughly
contemporary *The Divan* (see 56), a work
entirely alien to the Casas-like portraits and
already engaged with some of the toughest
art emerging from Paris. Setting out with this
exceptional armory, Picasso was now ready to
take on the "mad revolutionaries" who had so
shocked his friend Nonell.

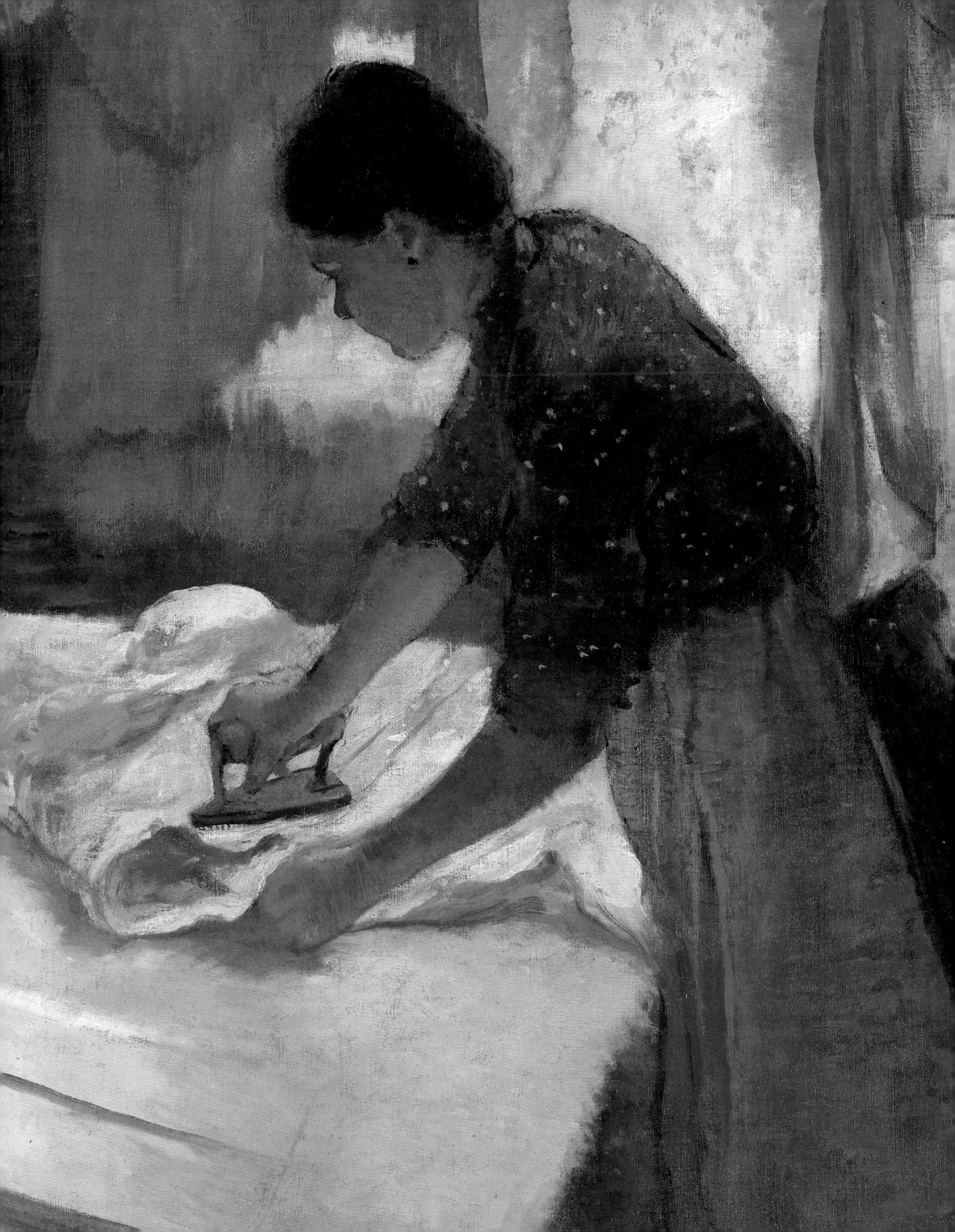

CHAPTER 2

NEIGHBORS IN MONTMARTRE

RICHARD KENDALL

One of Picasso's young companions at Els Quatre Gats café in Barcelona before the turn of the century, Jaume Sabartés, remembered that "Paris had fascinated us and filled us with feverish curiosity and an anxious longing."[1] In October 1900, Picasso traveled to Paris for the first time, transforming his relationship with modern French art and redirecting the course of his career. Clearly determined to satisfy his "feverish curiosity," he plunged into the city's network of museums and public exhibitions, commercial galleries and dealers, and the scattered artists' studios of Montmartre and elsewhere (**64**). An early outing was made to the vast Exposition Universelle in central Paris that marked the centennial year, where extensive displays of painting and sculpture from France and other countries included his own now-lost canvas *Last Moments*.[2] In a satirical drawing made afterward, Picasso showed himself with other painters and their girlfriends as they left this event and suggested the boisterousness of such excursions, which nevertheless coexisted with a deep seriousness of purpose on Picasso's part.[3] Before returning to Spain in late December, he had "spent a great deal of time" at the Louvre and at the Musée du Luxembourg, where Gustave Caillebotte's bequest of forty major Impressionist pictures was on view.[4] Astonishingly, this energetic young stranger had also sold some paintings to a minor art dealer in the city, Berthe Weill, and contracted to provide three works each month to Pere Mañach, a

Spanish entrepreneur who would soon arrange Picasso's inaugural exhibition in the city. Living mainly among the Catalan expatriate community, Picasso joined their sorties to the cafés, bars, cabarets, and vaudeville theaters for which Paris was famed. Known to him previously through travelers' tales and the magazine illustrations and reproduced pictures he had seen in Barcelona, these subjects clearly filled his imagination and invaded his own art.

It was now Picasso's turn to recount his adventures to those at home. In a mainly facetious letter signed jointly with Carles Casagemas, the young artist who had accompanied him to Paris, the two teenagers boasted soon after their arrival that "we have already started work and have a model. . . . So long as there is daylight . . . we stay in the studio painting and drawing."[5] The studio in question was situated on the rue Gabrielle on the heights of Montmartre and had been formerly occupied by Nonell, who is described in their letter as "a very congenial guy." Casagemas and Picasso also listed the notorious places of entertainment they had seen or visited: the Moulin Rouge, the Cabaret des Arts, Le Néant, and several other bars and dance halls, which these penniless foreigners considered expensive. Unlike Nonell's correspondence of 1897 and 1898, however, their letter revealed nothing about the works of art they had encountered or dramatic shifts in their taste in these first few days. Picasso's improvised drawings on these pages indicate that

Detail of Edgar Degas,
Woman Ironing
(110)

many of his earlier enthusiasms persisted. A shadowy café scene made with colored pencils is a direct extension of his Barcelona repertoire, as is the figure of a flamboyantly dressed cabaret singer that owed much to his idea of both Degas and Lautrec (**66**).[6] According to Sabartés, one of Picasso's ambitions in Paris was "to fill his eyes with the spectacle of the street," a project already evident in a tiny sketchbook used during these weeks and in other studies that punctuated the letter (**65**).[7] Noting what he saw with a sharp eye and a brilliant economy of touch, Picasso asserted himself as a Baudelairean observer of city life in ways that recalled the Degas of three decades earlier. Though fashions had clearly changed, Degas's *Young Woman in Street Costume* was the direct antecedent of Picasso's sketch. It was also one of several sheets of this kind in private hands in Paris that Picasso and his colleagues might have known. Acquired at an unknown date by the art dealer Paul Durand-Ruel, it may have been visible when his collection was opened to visitors on Tuesdays each week or when it appeared in his gallery; the work was also included in the album of color reproductions of Degas's drawings edited by Michel Manzi in 1898 (**67**).[8]

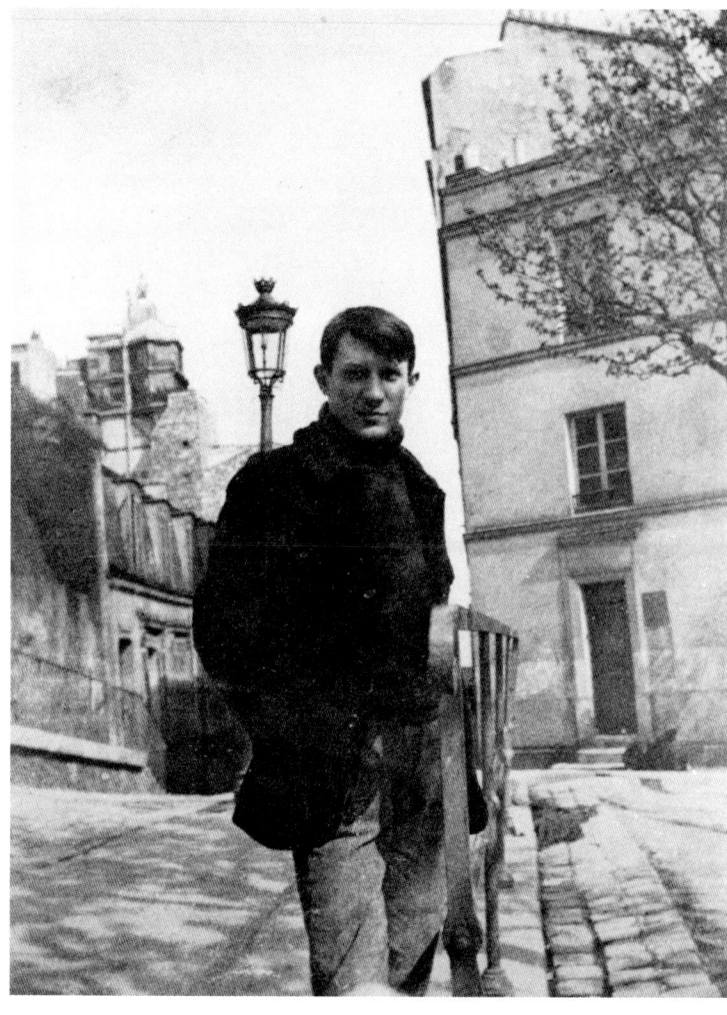

Picasso Discovers Degas

The story of Picasso's contact with the art of Degas during his early Paris visits is intricate and challenging, but ultimately productive. Neither in these months nor at any time in his youth did Picasso comment directly on his interest in Degas, any more than he held forth on his passion for Cézanne, Manet, or El Greco. Yet Parisian critics identified Degas as one of the principal contemporary models behind the pictures that Picasso was now making, a view that was repeatedly endorsed by other witnesses. Subject matter was a major indication: "the spectacle of the street" extended to the city's night life and to depictions of local characters, whether shown in parks or restaurants, or in the artist's own studio. Degas's career during the Impressionist years had largely been built on this controversial material, leaving a rich, if circuitous, trail of drawings, prints, pastels, and oil paintings that was still visible in Paris in the early twentieth century. Always a prolific artist, Degas had exhibited his work frequently between the 1870s and 1890s, placing pictures in leading collections and selling major and minor works through dealers to private individuals. The challenge for a young artist after 1900 was to make contact with Degas's art in a world when the first books and substantial articles were only just beginning to appear. This chapter follows the parallel narratives of Picasso's development and his documented or

65

Pablo Picasso

Letter from Casagemas and Picasso to Ramon Reventós [Woman with a Dog], 1901. Charcoal and colored pencil on paper, 21 x 13 cm. Collection of Dr. Jacint Reventós, Barcelona

66

Pablo Picasso

Letter from Casagemas and Picasso to Ramon Reventós [Singer], 1901. Charcoal and colored pencil on paper, 21 x 13 cm. Collection of Dr. Jacint Reventós, Barcelona

67

Edgar Degas

Young Woman in Street Costume, c. 1879. Reproduced in *Degas: Vingt Dessins, 1861–1896* (Paris, New York: Goupil et Cie, 1897), pl. 11. Courtesy Sterling and Francine Clark Art Institute, Williamstown, Massachusetts

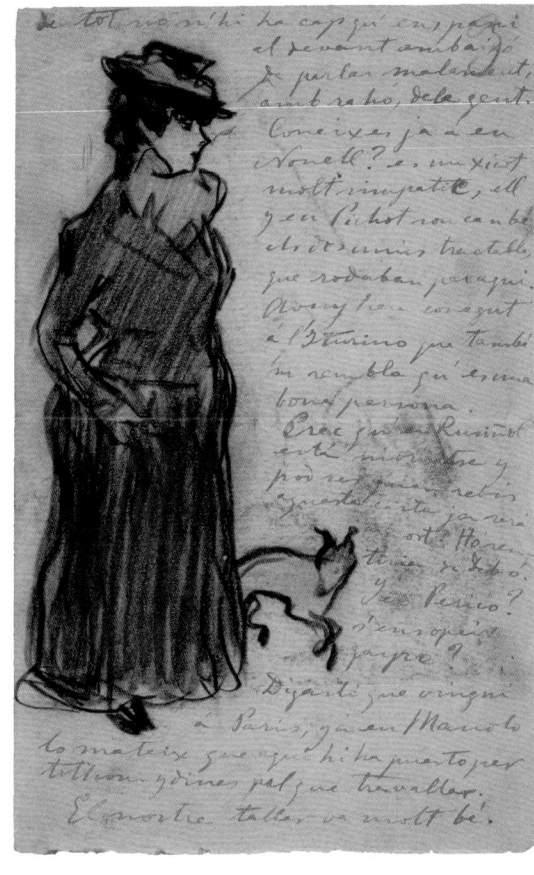

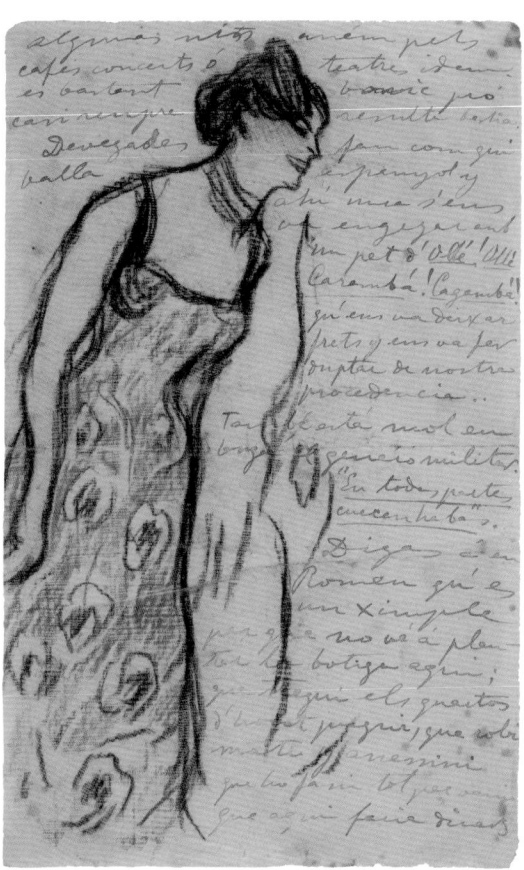

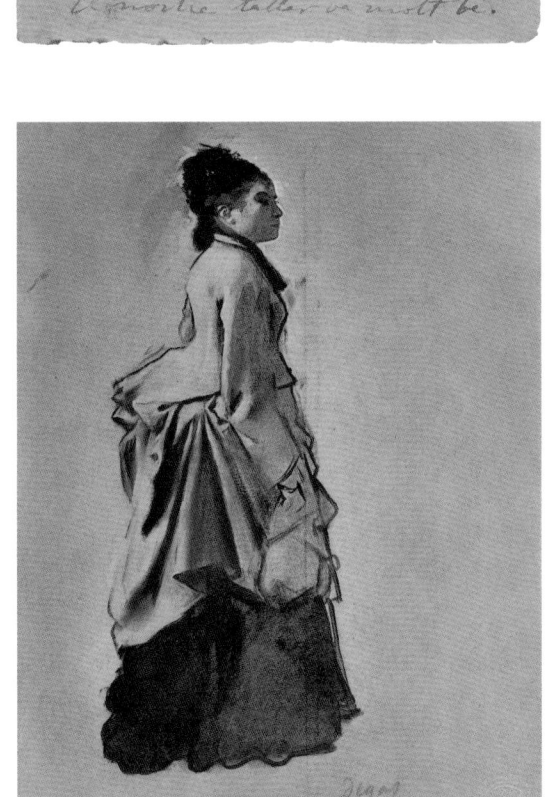

conjectural engagement with the imagery of his Impressionist predecessor. Those cases that are demonstrable require the patient reconstruction of events and encounters, the consideration of accessibility, and the tracking down of specific objects through archives and other records, even the study of his studio methods and preferred materials.

A telling novelty in Picasso's technique in 1900 was the appearance of pastel, a medium that had flared briefly in some *corrida* pictures before he left Barcelona but was otherwise little used in the Els Quatre Gats milieu.[9] Applied freely to pencil drawings in his small Paris sketchbook, pastel allowed Picasso to bring animation and particularity to the briefest study of his fellow pedestrians.[10] On a more ambitious scale, pastel also brought its fragile glamour to a group of cabaret pictures dominated by *The*

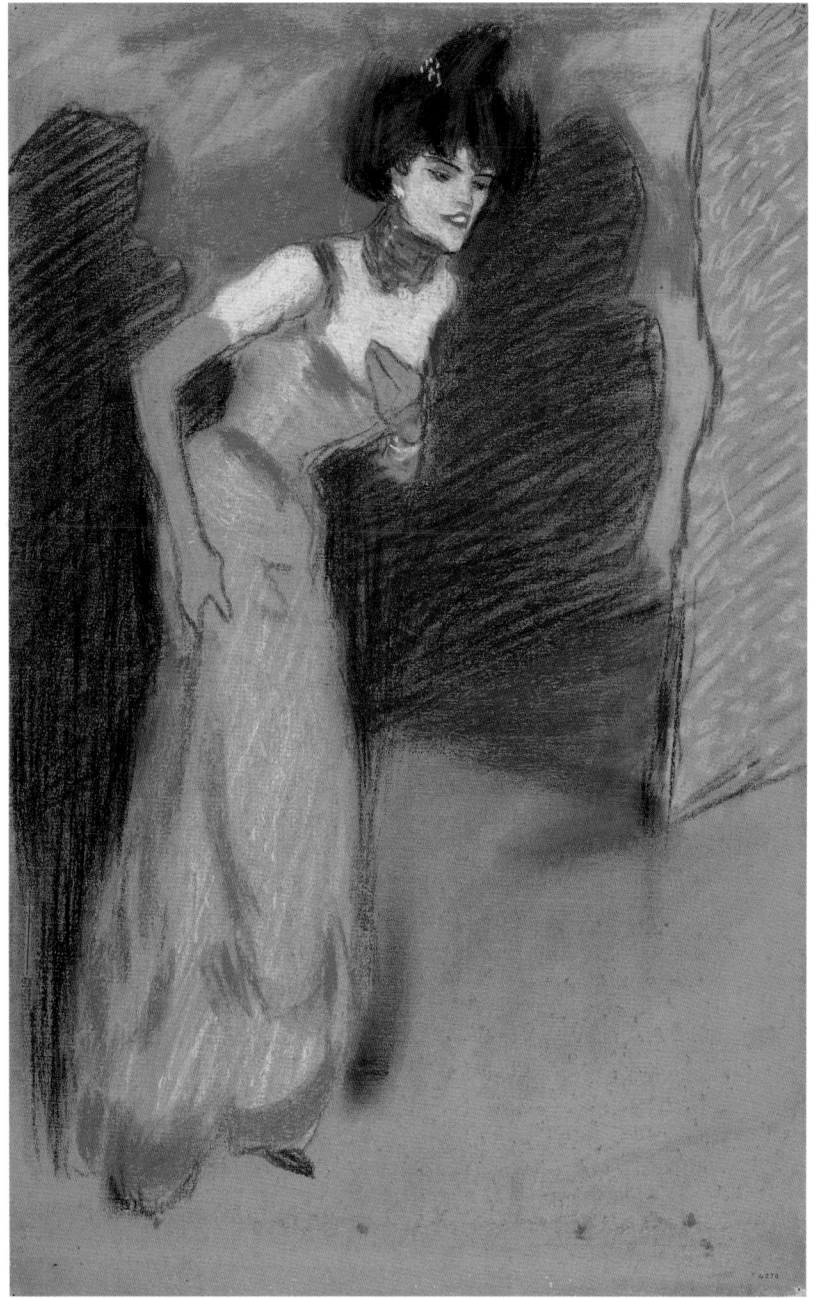

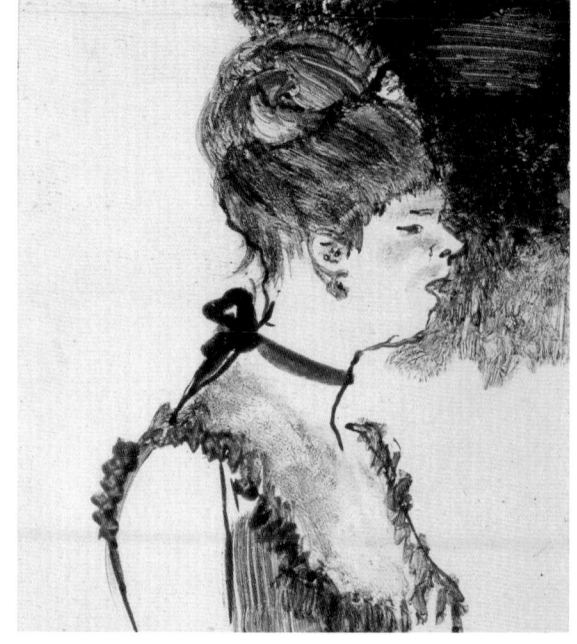

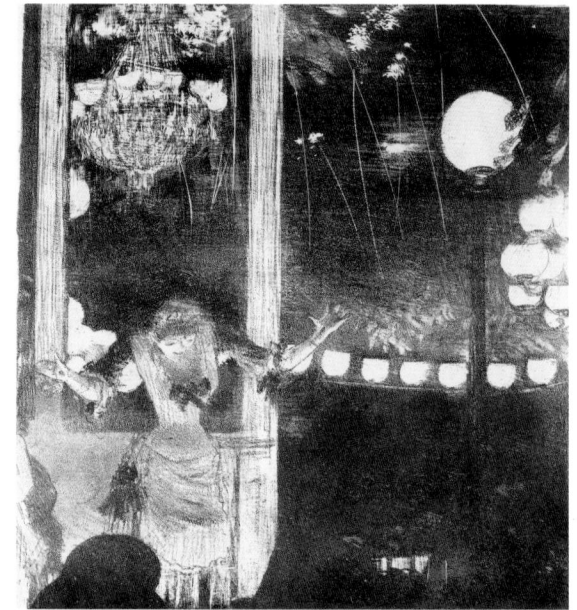

68

Pablo Picasso

The End of the Performance, 1901. Pastel on canvas, 73 x 47 cm. Museu Picasso, Barcelona. (MPB 4.270)

69

Edgar Degas

Café-Concert Singer, c. 1878–80. Monotype in black on cream laid paper, 8 x 7.2 cm. The Art Institute of Chicago. Potter Palmer Collection Fund (1963.822)

70

Edgar Degas

Mlle Bécat at the Café des Ambassadeurs, c. 1877–78. Lithograph in black on grayish white wove paper, 20.5 x 19.3 cm. The Art Institute of Chicago. William McCallin McKee Memorial Collection (1932.1296)

71

Edgar Degas

Song of the Dog, c. 1876–77. Crayon lithograph, 37 x 26.6 cm. Lent by Nicholas Stogdon

72

Edgar Degas

At the Café des Ambassadeurs, 1885. Pastel over etching, 26.5 x 29.5 cm. Musée d'Orsay, Paris (RF 4041R)

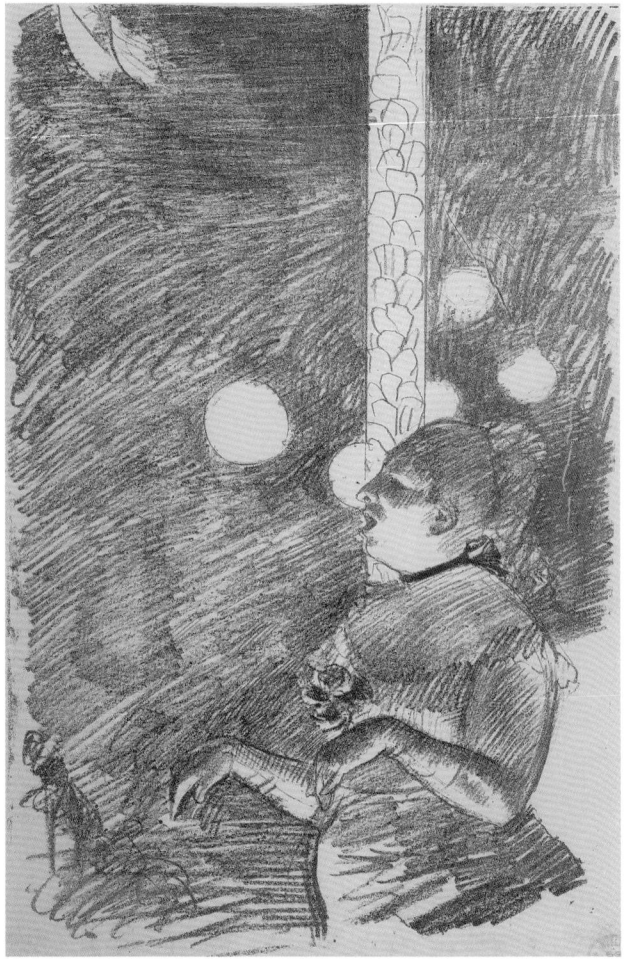

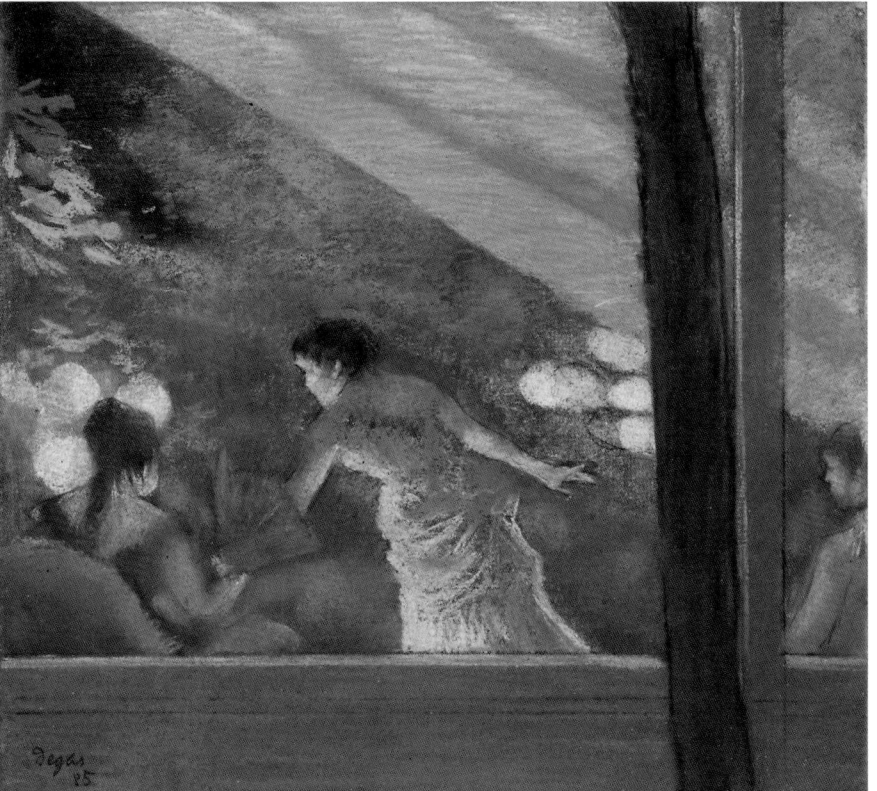

End of the Performance (**68**), a bold composition executed on canvas in 1901.[11] Again fusing motifs from Degas, Lautrec, and their many imitators, this arresting work had its deepest roots in a suite of prints made by Degas in the 1870s, such as *Café-Concert Singer* (**69**), *Mlle Bécat at the Café des Ambassadeurs* (**70**), and *Song of the Dog* (**71**). Black-and-white prints of this kind — such as monotypes, lithographs, and etchings — allowed the artist to exploit his powers of draftsmanship and simultaneously explore vivid effects of light and shadow. After printing them on paper, Degas often departed from conventional practice by developing such images with pastel, from light veils of color to dense encrustations that virtually covered the monochrome base. Clearly proud of his innovative pictures, Degas showed several pastelized prints in the series of Impressionist exhibitions, where some were bought immediately.[12] As Nonell would have observed when he saw Isaac de Camondo's pictures in 1898, the collector had a marked taste for Degas's enhanced prints that was revealed in no less than nine major examples, principally divided between bathing nudes and ballet scenes. Around the turn of the century, Camondo had also acquired one of the most spectacular of the pastelized prints of a cabaret scene, *At the Café des Ambassadeurs* (**72**), which is remarkable both for its subtly variegated hues and for the audacious viewpoint adopted by the artist.[13] Here the singer leans away from us, the mirror image of Picasso's comparable figure in *The End of the Performance* but similarly surrounded by a blaze of color.

Now living in the city where Degas had worked and exhibited for four decades, and where he still resided in his Montmartre apartment, Picasso finally began to see a haphazard selection of his pictures firsthand. The two works by Degas that appeared among the French contributions to the Exposition Universelle, one of them his startling diagonal composition in pastel *Dancer in Green*, may have been noted by Picasso when he visited this display soon after arriving in Paris.[14] If he followed in Nonell's footsteps, Picasso would also have come face-to-face with Degas's monotypes in the Camondo collection, as well as a stunning array of dance pictures and the now renowned oil painting *In a Café (L'Absinthe)* (see 104). As we would expect on a first Paris visit, Picasso is said to have done "the rounds of the commercial galleries, above all the more progressive ones on the rue Laffitte," which included the premises of Durand-Ruel and Vollard, where other works by Degas could occasionally be seen.[15] Degas's own correspondence from this same period shows that a considerable number of his drawings, pastels, and oil paintings were currently passing through the hands of Durand-Ruel, who exhibited, sold, or stored them in his gallery.[16] Acting as Degas's principal representative for much of his career, Durand-Ruel had shown his extraordinary pastel landscapes in 1892 and four years later a more comprehensive survey of works that included a "new series of nudes."[17] In 1898, he also staged a major show of Impressionist art that embraced Degas's "racetrack scenes, landscapes, dancers," while continuing to present "one-man" exhibitions by Pissarro, Monet, and Renoir.[18] Durand-Ruel's premises — referred to by the English artist John Rothenstein as "a kind of second Louvre" — were just a few blocks south of Montmartre on the rue Laffitte, the street of galleries known to other young artists at this time as "a pilgrim's resort."[19] Visitors of many kinds came to inspect whatever was on view there, even to examine works kept behind the scenes in these galleries. Degas himself (**73**) haunted the rue Laffitte and, as Ambroise Vollard recalled, "liked going there when he had finished work for the day," walking down the steep hill from his Montmartre studio to inspect the latest offerings and occasionally buying a picture for his own expanding collection.[20]

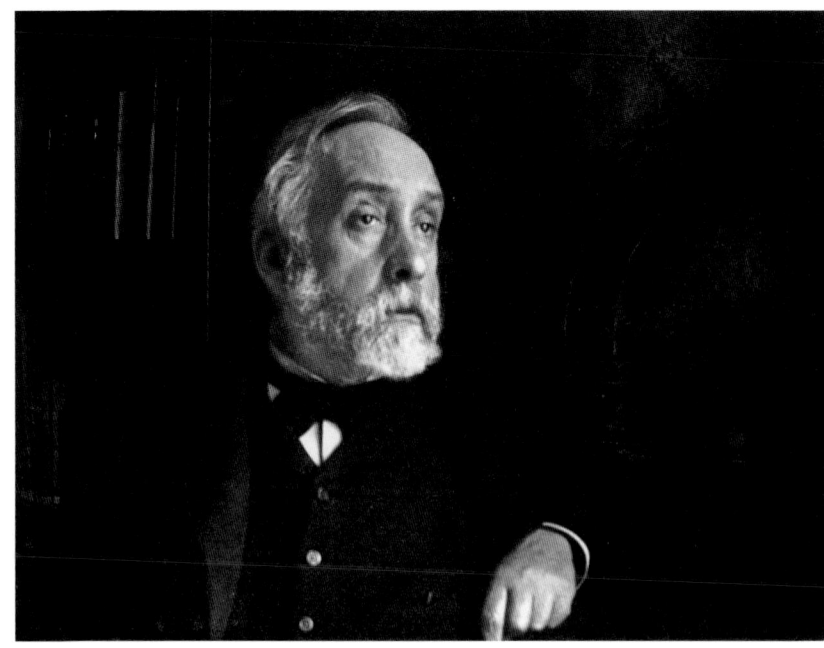

Significant to Picasso in a broader sense was the Musée du Luxembourg, where the Caillebotte bequest offered a virtual conspectus of Impressionist art from the 1870s and 1880s. Here Picasso could finally confront Monet's canvases of Argenteuil and Pissarro's of Pontoise, Renoir's *Moulin de la Galette* and Cézanne's *L'Estaque*, as well as works by Manet and Sisley. Degas was represented at the Luxembourg by seven major pictures that emphasized his bather and theater compositions, one of which was the now iconic *The Star*.[21] All seven were pastels and all but two had been made over monotypes, including the exceptionally large *Women on the Terrace of a Café in the Evening* (**74**). There is no doubt that Picasso saw these works and had the opportunity to scrutinize their dense, intricate surfaces, which reveal much about the often unorthodox interplay of line and color in Degas's mature craft. It is against such a background that *The End of the Performance* and similar creations are best understood, as explorations of contemporary iconography and innovative studio practice. Compared to the finest pastels by Degas that he now saw, Picasso's first attempts in the medium

73

Edgar Degas

Self-Portrait in Library, 1895. Photograph, 18.3 x 24.3 cm. Musée d'Orsay, Paris (RF Pho 1994-44)

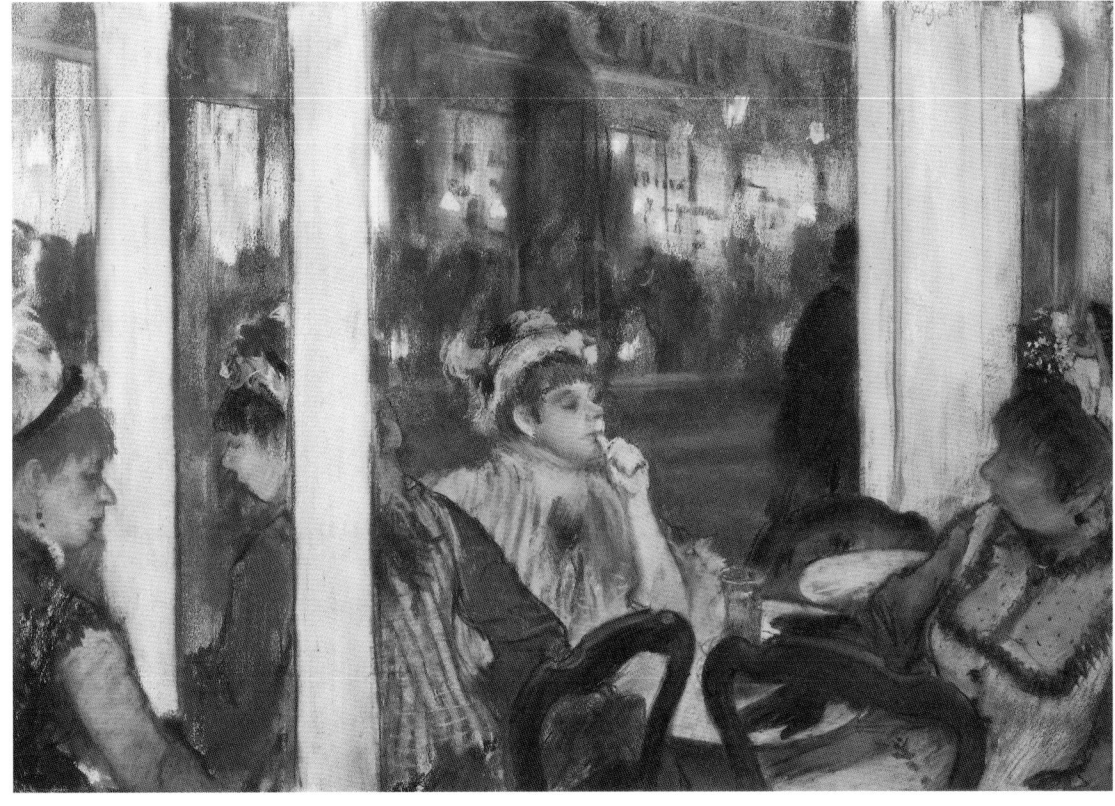

were rudimentary but also expressive of his own approach to picture-making. Both artists were masters of line, instinctively recording their observations and developing their ideas in the language of draftsmanship, a practice that had been nourished by their academic education.[22] Color, while sometimes overwhelmingly evident in the mature pictures of Degas and Picasso, was characteristically "imposed" on this linear and tonal substructure during most phases of their careers. Even as a young man, Picasso may have sensed a kinship with Degas as he encountered these qualities in his art, not least in the pastel-enhanced monotypes. In these highly distinctive works, Degas declared himself as a draftsman first and foremost, who has skillfully integrated color into a sequence of compositions whose black-and-white foundation had already been resolved. The same principle can also be observed in some of Degas's later oil paintings, such as *Combing the Hair* (see 227), where les-

sons learned from the pastelized monotypes often paid spectacular dividends.[23]

An illuminating example of such technical cross-fertilization in the work of Picasso is *Stuffed Shirts* (**75**), a dazzling miniature frieze in oil on wooden panel that has been variously ascribed to his 1900 and 1901 Paris sojourns. By contrast with certain of the lugubrious canvases he had labored over in Barcelona, such as *Last Moments*, this small painting belonged both literally and figuratively to a new era. Yet almost every element in *Stuffed Shirts*, from the charismatic singer and her faceless male audience to the lateral view of the stage and the darkened wings at left, can be found in works by Degas and his followers. What gives them new life in Picasso's painting is his vivacious handling, especially the flickering, impulsive touches of the brush that are concentrated in areas such as the woman's dress. Even in these painterly passages, however, we are reminded of strokes of

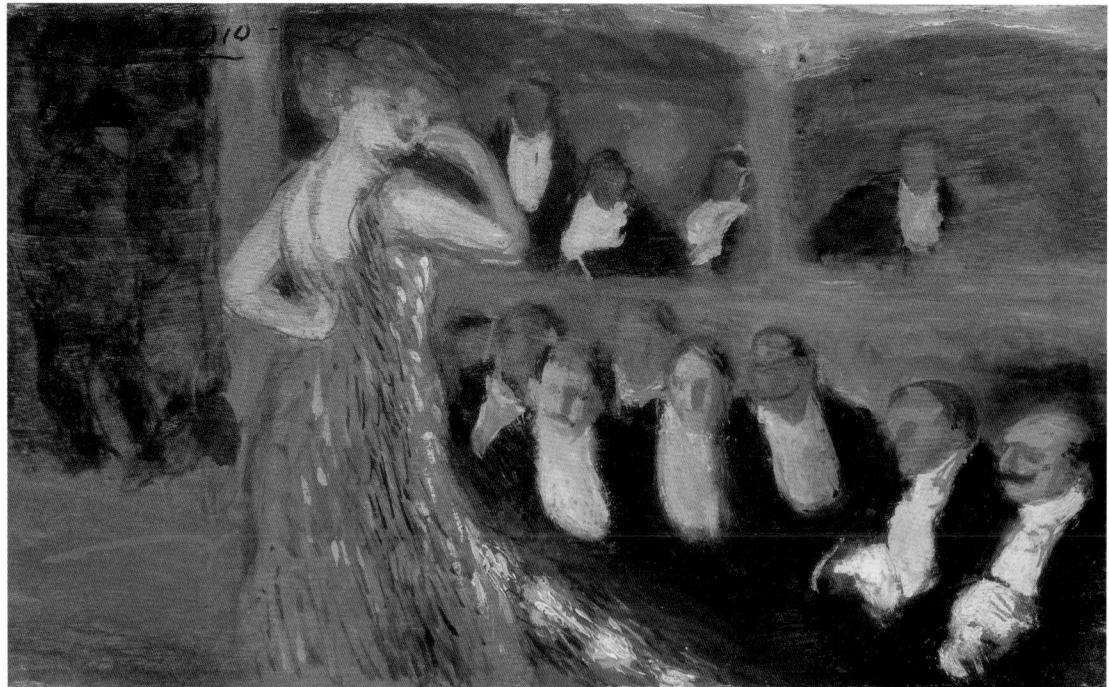

75

Pablo Picasso

Stuffed Shirts, 1900
or 1901. Oil on panel,
13.6 x 22.5 cm. Museum of
Fine Arts, Boston. Gift of
Mrs. Charles Sumner Bird
(Julia Appleton Bird)
(1970.475)

pastel that have been applied to tinted paper or to the surface of monotypes. Degas's *Singers on the Stage* (**76**), for example, seems to anticipate not only Picasso's design and his dominant range of orange-golds and whites, but even the last-minute flourishes of blue and bright red in the little Boston picture. This case is among those where a family resemblance between works by the two artists becomes exceptionally tantalizing, here made more so by a trail of connections that could conceivably have linked them. At this date, *Singers on the Stage* was in a notably informal Paris collection, that of the energetic dentist-collector Georges Viau, who hung some of his pictures in his office and had many friends in the contemporary art world. Viau welcomed artists to his several residences and bought from both the Impressionist generation and younger figures, such as Lautrec and Steinlen. More specifically, works by Joachim Sunyer — a painter and illustrator who knew Steinlen and had been part of the Catalan community in Paris for some years — were included in Viau's collection. Sunyer soon became promi-

nent in Picasso's circle and partly preceded him as a painter of modern life and as a follower of Degas.[24] Familiar with the city and the language, he would also have been able to make the introduction to the hospitable Viau.[25]

Before traveling back to Spain in late December, the prodigiously energetic Picasso completed a number of larger compositions in oil paint on canvas and pastel on card. Stimulated by what he had seen and already focused on the next steps in his career, he clearly wished to tackle the older generation on a large scale and make works that would impress dealers and prospective buyers. While some of the resulting pictures grew out of the process of drawing, others were notable for their sheer painterliness and seem to have been improvised on whatever support came to hand, even over earlier pictures. Stylistic consistency troubled Picasso even less. In shameless variants of scenes of impoverished lovers by Steinlen, daytime pleasure-seekers by Renoir, and the decadent night-owls of Munch, he wrestled with his heroes on their own territory. Many such ele-

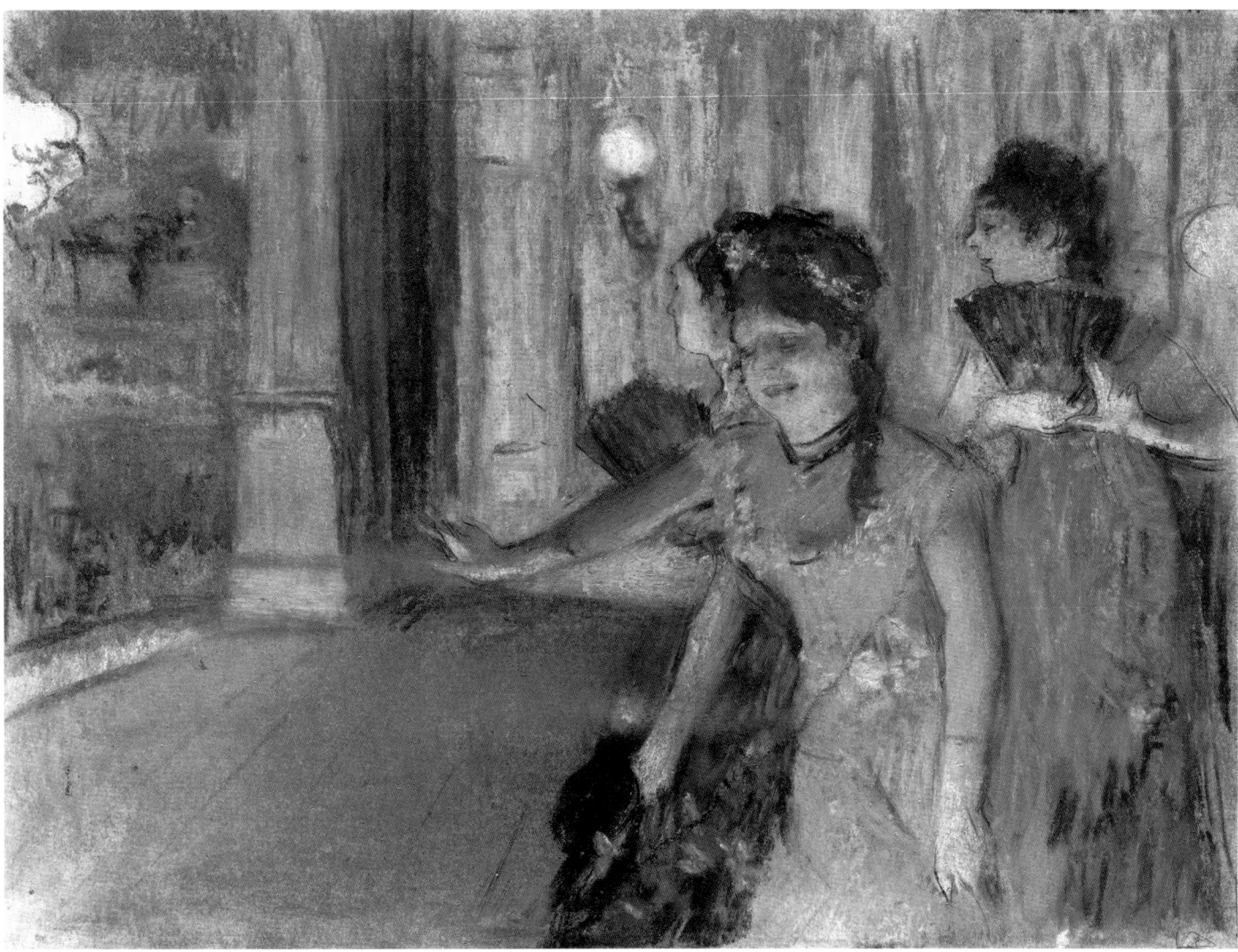

76

Edgar Degas

Singers on the Stage,
c. 1877. Pastel over
monotype on ivory
wove paper, laid down
on board, 16 x 21 cm.
The Art Institute of
Chicago. Bequest of
Mrs. Clive Runnells
(1977.773)

ments were fused in the grandest composition made during his stay, *Le Moulin de la Galette* (**77**), now in the Guggenheim Museum in New York. With a title stolen from Renoir's painting at the Musée du Luxembourg, a cast of fashionable characters that owed something to both Manet and Lautrec, and a nocturnal setting reminiscent of Degas's café-concert prints (see 70, 71), this four-foot-wide self-advertisement was quickly sold by Berthe Weill.[26] Less apparent to French eyes would have been the significance of *Le Moulin de la Galette* in the contemporary Spanish context. A decade earlier, Rusiñol, Casas, and Utrillo had lived in the

old Montmartre mill that gave this attraction its name, yet their realistic pictures of its interior now seemed dull against the glamorous decadence that fascinated their young successor.

It was in this same flurry of painting that Picasso grappled for the first time with the theme of brightly colored dancers on a Paris stage. Popular entertainers rather than ballerinas, some are shown reenacting the time-worn drama of Harlequin and Columbine while others almost disappear in waves of garish yellows and greens, swamped by their voluminous skirts.[27] If Picasso had Degas in mind at all, it was perhaps to distance himself from the pictures of classical

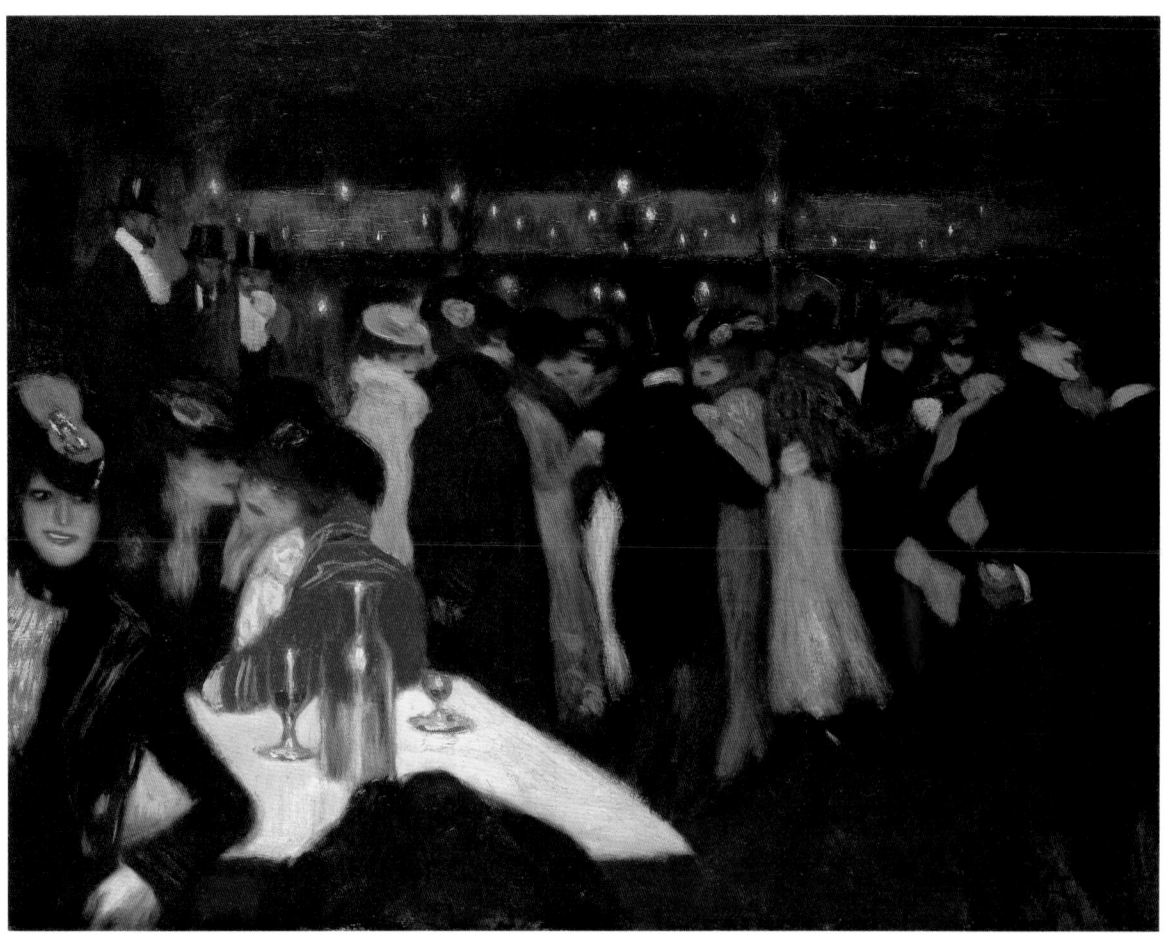

77

Pablo Picasso

Le Moulin de la Galette,
1900. Oil on canvas,
88.7 x 115.5 cm. Solomon
R. Guggenheim Museum,
New York. Thannhauser
Collection, Gift, Justin K.
Thannhauser, 1978
(78.2514.34)

78

Pablo Picasso

The Dressing Room, 1900.
Pastel, 47.5 x 52.5 cm. Museu
Picasso, Barcelona (4.275)

79

Pablo Picasso

In the Café, 1900. Oil on
canvas, 25.5 x 37.7 cm.
Yale Collection of American
Literature, Beinecke Rare
Book and Manuscript Library,
New Haven

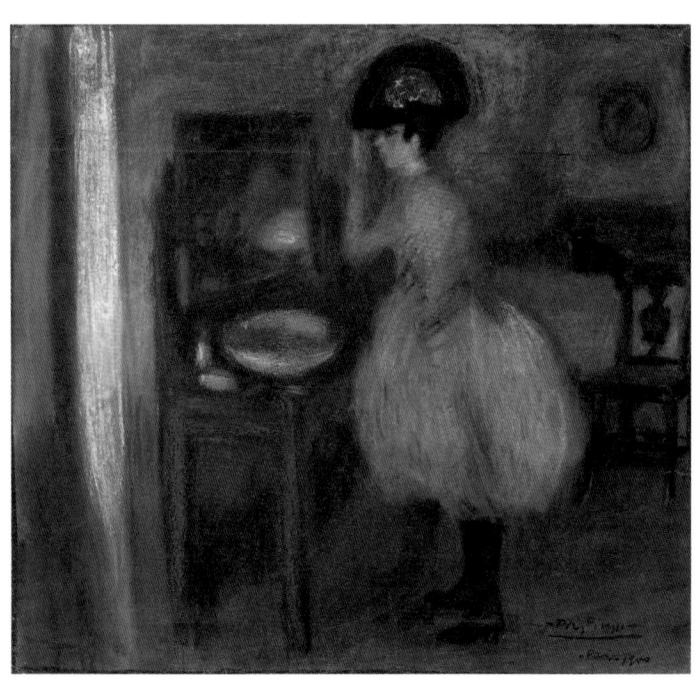

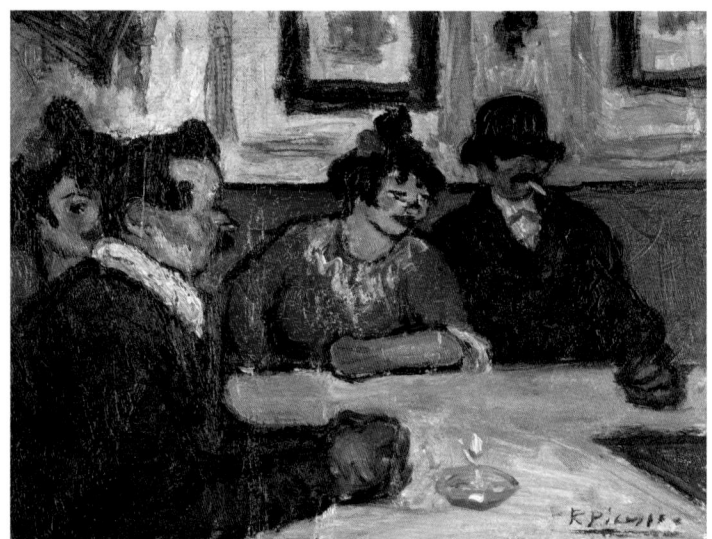

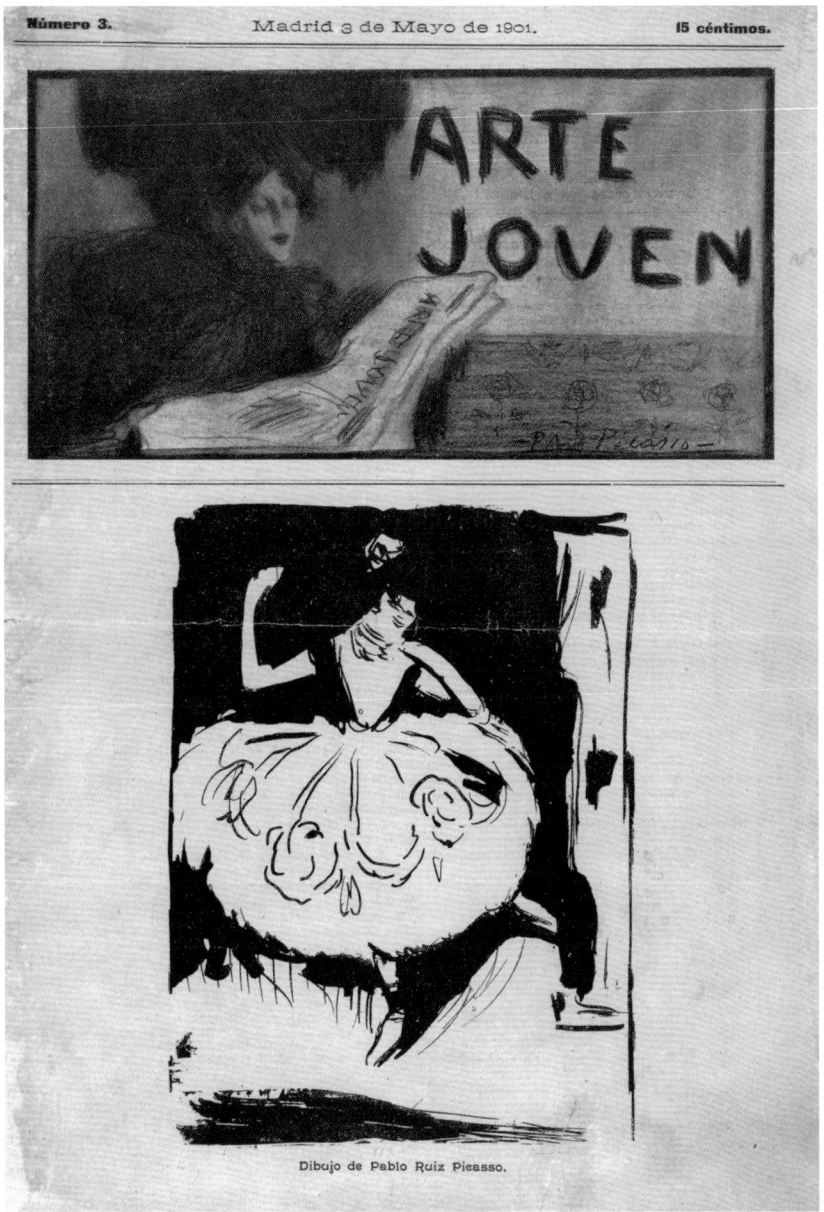

ARTE JOVEN

Dibujo de Pablo Ruiz Picasso.

80

Pablo Picasso

Front cover of *Arte Joven*
3 (3 May 1901). Courtesy
Dartmouth College
Library, Hanover,
New Hampshire

ballet that had become his predecessor's exclusive preserve. When the occasional ballerina appeared in Picasso's new work, their theatrical settings tended to be spartan and the young ladies themselves were brazen rather than demure.[28] It would be more than a decade before he found the confidence to tackle ballet directly, spurred on by his marriage to the young star of the Ballets Russes, Olga Khokhlova. In 1900, other subjects associated

with Degas seem to have been less daunting, especially those explored previously in Barcelona. A shadowy boudoir or backstage scene in pastel (**78**) is too awkward to be an act of homage but may represent a not entirely successful attempt at layered colors on a dark base in the manner of Degas. Such somber works could also have been part of what Josep Palau i Fabre called Picasso's "black period," which is sporadically evident in these months.[29] In this bleaker mode, Picasso painted a group of dusky street vistas in Montmartre and drab bar interiors, the latter typified by a small canvas known as *In the Café* (**79**). This willfully awkward composition shares its grid-like design with Degas's pastel at the Luxembourg, *Women on the Terrace of a Café in the Evening* (see 74), a deeply influential work that exemplified the more desperate side of Parisian pleasure-seeking.

Far from returning in triumph to his colleagues in Barcelona, Picasso left Paris in late December 1900 and went immediately to Malaga, then spent five months in Madrid. During this unexpected exile he made paintings and pastels to fulfill his agreement with Mañach and helped to launch the short-lived journal *Arte Joven* in the Spanish capital. Notionally the journal's artistic director, Picasso made contributions consisting mainly of drawings in a variety of styles and techniques that appeared on its eight cheaply printed pages. When it was launched, *Arte Joven* announced a policy of "forever fleeing the ordinary, the vulgar" and mocked the view that Spanish art had suffered from "this ragbag of impressionists" who "adulterated" native talent.[30] Caught up in a moment of radicalism, Picasso chose to reproduce some of the coarsest illustrations he had made to date, all of which were published in black and white. Using rough lines in charcoal, crayon, or pen-and-ink for his original drawings, he quickly sketched groups of bearded, ill-dressed figures on street corners and vulgar diners at the table. There

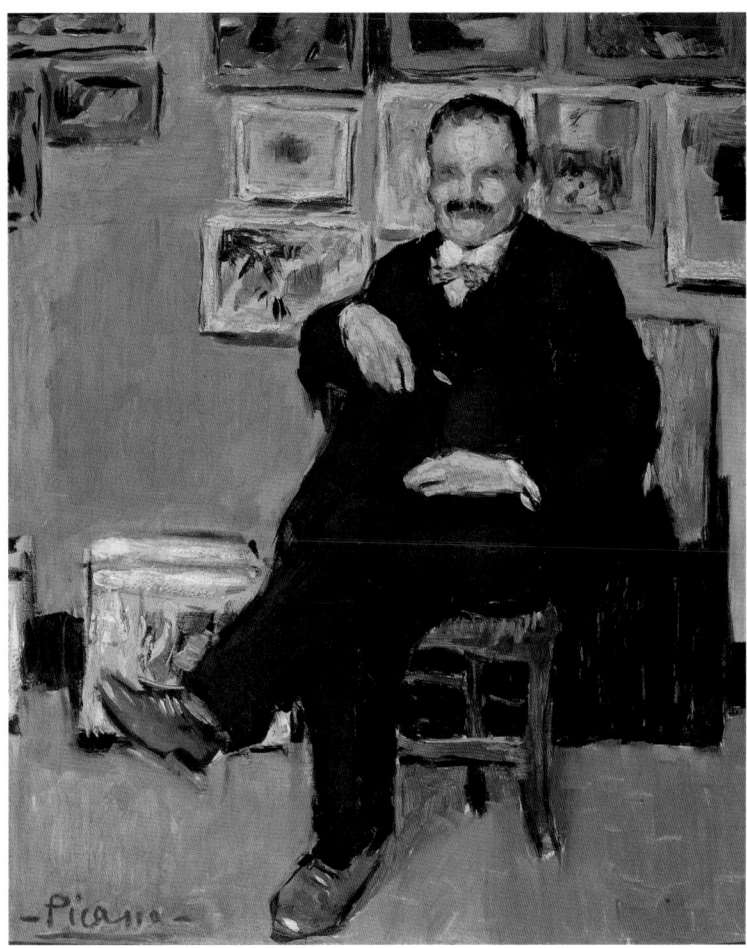

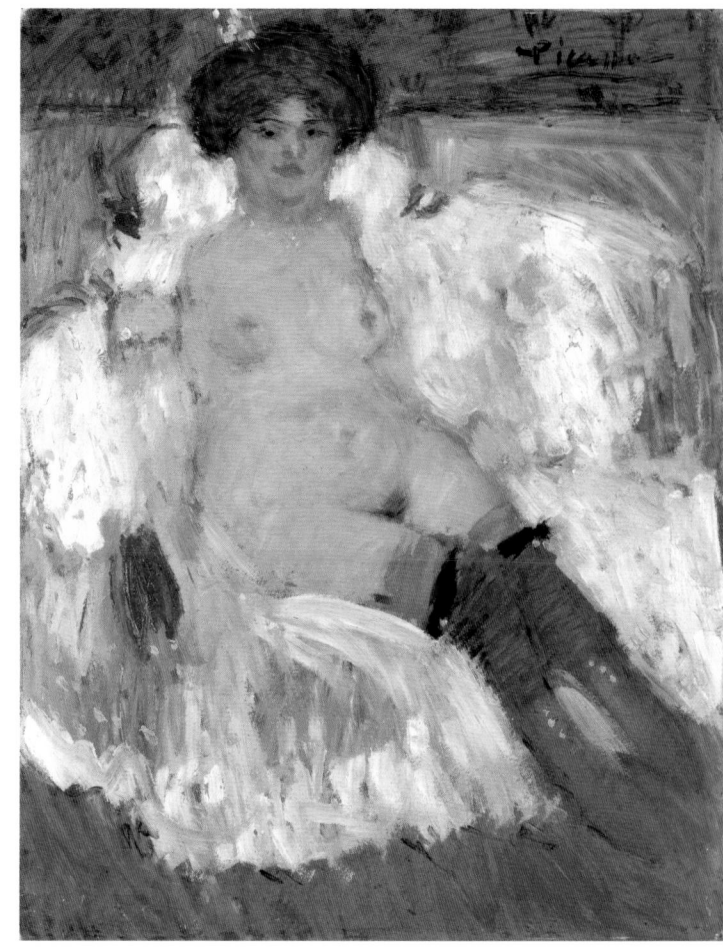

is something frankly defiant about a brash bar interior that echoes the little *In the Café* painted in Paris but also a glimpse of stylish minimalism from heady days in Montmartre in the vivacious ballerina on the cover of the third issue (**80**).[31] For all its amateurism, *Arte Joven* allowed Picasso to explore the obstreperous side of his draftsmanship and enjoy a brief spell of minor prominence as a graphic prodigy in Madrid.

The Vollard Exhibition: 1901

Many of the paintings that Picasso executed while working on *Arte Joven*, and during a brief spell in Barcelona before traveling back to Paris, would appear in the first substantial exhibition of his work outside Spain. This took place at

Ambroise Vollard's gallery on the rue Laffitte, where it opened in June 1901.[32] When he arrived in Paris a month earlier, Picasso is said to have painted up to three additional canvases a day to fill the gallery walls, a possibility endorsed by other sources. In *Recollections of a Picture Dealer*, Vollard (**81**) recalled his first meeting with "the young Spaniard, dressed with the most studied elegance," who had already "finished about a hundred paintings" for the occasion.[33] By today's standards, the exhibition was haphazard and crowded, and Vollard himself considered that it "was not a success." A minimal catalogue listed the titles of works on display, many of which have been identified from references in the press and through assiduous subsequent research.[34] Following the pattern

81

Pablo Picasso

Portrait of a Man (Ambroise Vollard?), 1901. Oil on cardboard, 46 x 37 cm. E. G. Bührle Collection, Zurich

82

Pablo Picasso

Nude with Red Stockings, 1901. Oil on cardboard on wood, 67 x 51.5 cm. Musée des Beaux Arts de Lyon (1997-44)

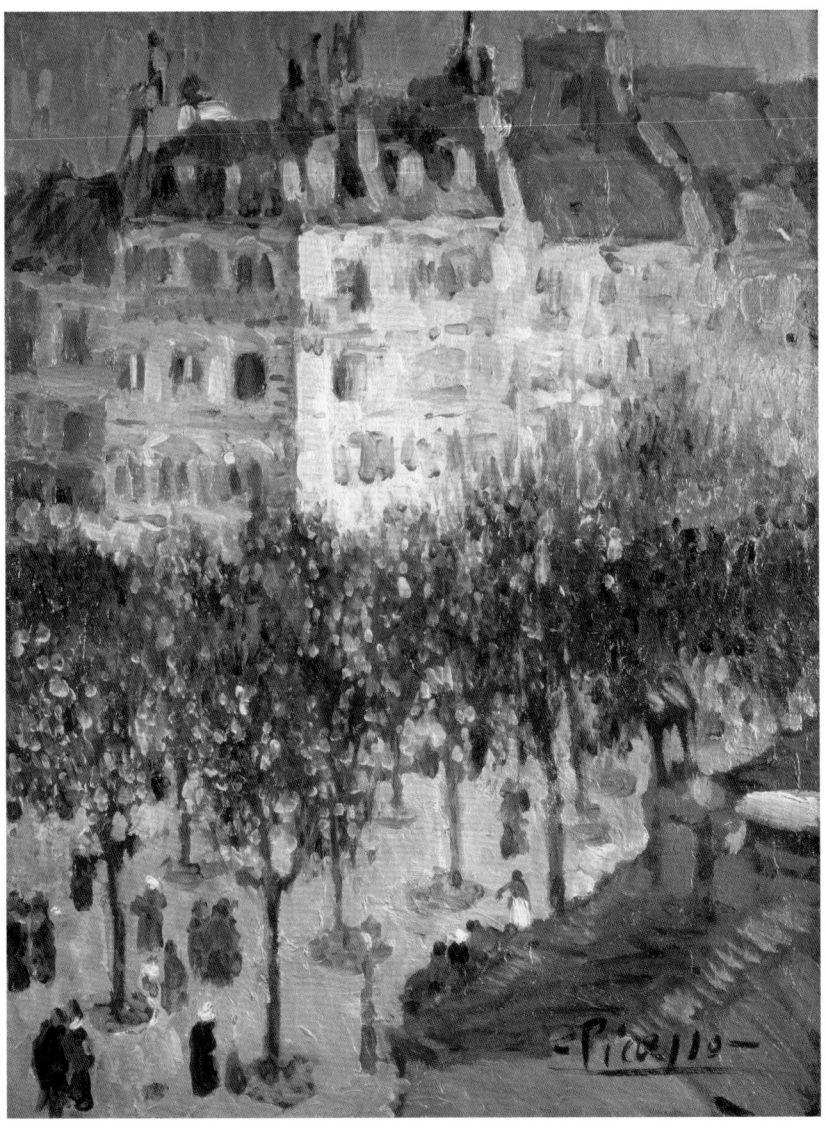

83

Pablo Picasso

Boulevard de Clichy, 1901.
Oil on canvas,
61.5 x 46.5 cm.
Location unknown

of Picasso's early years, the overwhelming majority of paintings represented the human figure, here shown old and young, clothed and unclothed, in a dazzling variety of social, domestic, and professional circumstances. Again in keeping with his recent practice, most of the models were women, though a scattering of men and a few children, even babes in arms, ensured that both sexes and every generation were represented. In devising his own *Human Comedy* or panorama of modern life, Picasso depicted subjects of all classes as they strolled in streets and parks, lingered elegantly at the

racetrack and danced in nightclubs, or retreated to assignations in restaurants and bars. Some of them had clearly posed for their portraits in anonymous rooms, returning Picasso's gaze while they drank, smoked, or exulted in their finery. Self-consciousness was a persistent issue, as if many of these individuals were complicit in the audacious project the young artist had set himself. Picasso's rapport was at its most complex in several pictures of nudes, most of whom acknowledged his presence and offered themselves frankly for inspection (**82**). The main exceptions to this broad pattern were a group of city and rural views, including some from Spain, and several multihued paintings of flowers.

Just as profligate in the Vollard installation was Picasso's display of painting styles, all but a few deriving from avant-garde French art of the previous three decades. The earlier years of Impressionism, for example, were reflected in atmospheric city views and freely executed landscapes, while some pictures of rocks and sea broadly resembled those of Monet in the 1880s. Here, as elsewhere in the exhibition, Picasso often used exaggeratedly bold brushwork and dense paint, perhaps to caricature the manner of his predecessors or attempt to beat them at their own game. Genuine respect for Pissarro seems to be implicit in the young artist's *Boulevard de Clichy* (**83**), a view of a bustling Paris street seen from the building in Montmartre that Picasso now inhabited. The fact that Pissarro's recent pictures of similar subjects had been shown at Durand-Ruel's gallery on the rue Laffitte is intriguing testimony to his admirer's alertness and to his precocious familiarity with "the second Louvre."[35] Awareness of the Nabi painters — principally Pierre Bonnard, Édouard Vuillard, and Maurice Denis — can also be found in Picasso's more domestic motifs in the Vollard show, such as infants playing outdoors and mothers relaxing in well-furnished rooms. Steinlen and Lautrec

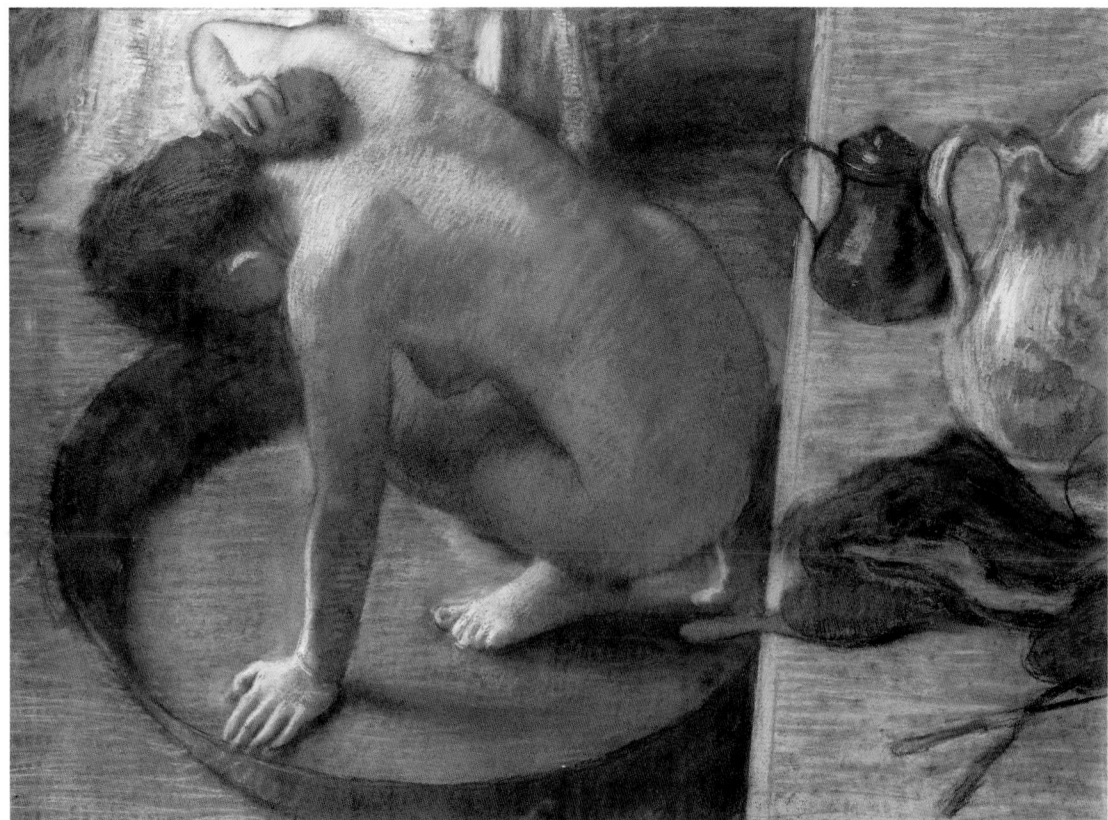

84

Edgar Degas

The Tub, 1886.

Pastel, 60 x 83 cm.

Musée d'Orsay, Paris

(RF 4046)

were inevitably invoked in pictures with a more linear emphasis, the latter prompting experiments with planes of thinly washed color, such as those in *Stuffed Shirts* (which may have appeared under the title *La Chanteuse*).[36] In yet another mode, Picasso built up several vivacious images from broad slab-like strokes of yellow, green, scarlet, and white, as in his arresting picture of a dancer, *The Dwarf* (see 120). Perhaps attempting to digest the pointillism of Seurat along with the expressive handling of Van Gogh, he also hinted at other influences in his frequent use of oil on card — chosen for reasons of economy — that resulted in dry surfaces reminiscent of works in pastel.

Critical response to Picasso's 1901 exhibition was meager, dominated by a short article written by Félicien Fagus for *La Revue Blanche*. Fagus, a pseudonym of the author Georges Faillet, was quick to spot the painterly talents of this "brilliant and impetuous" novice and admire the dazzling effects of his pictures, "the multicolored specks of a crowd," "the yellow and white of a woman's hat," "the naked bodies of women."[37] He also proposed some of his modern sources, among them "Monet . . . Van Gogh, Pissarro, Toulouse-Lautrec, Degas, Forain, and Rops perhaps," before warning Picasso of the dangers of "facile virtuosity." Fagus's decision to include Degas in this list, which is initially surprising, demands careful examination. Picasso's racecourse pictures, for example, have often been associated with Degas but were dominated by fashionable crowds rather than horses and have little in common with Degas's many works on this theme. Several paintings described as "Drinkers" and one entitled *L'Absinthe* appear to have been much closer to Degas's known territory and can be understood as gestures toward his celebrated canvas

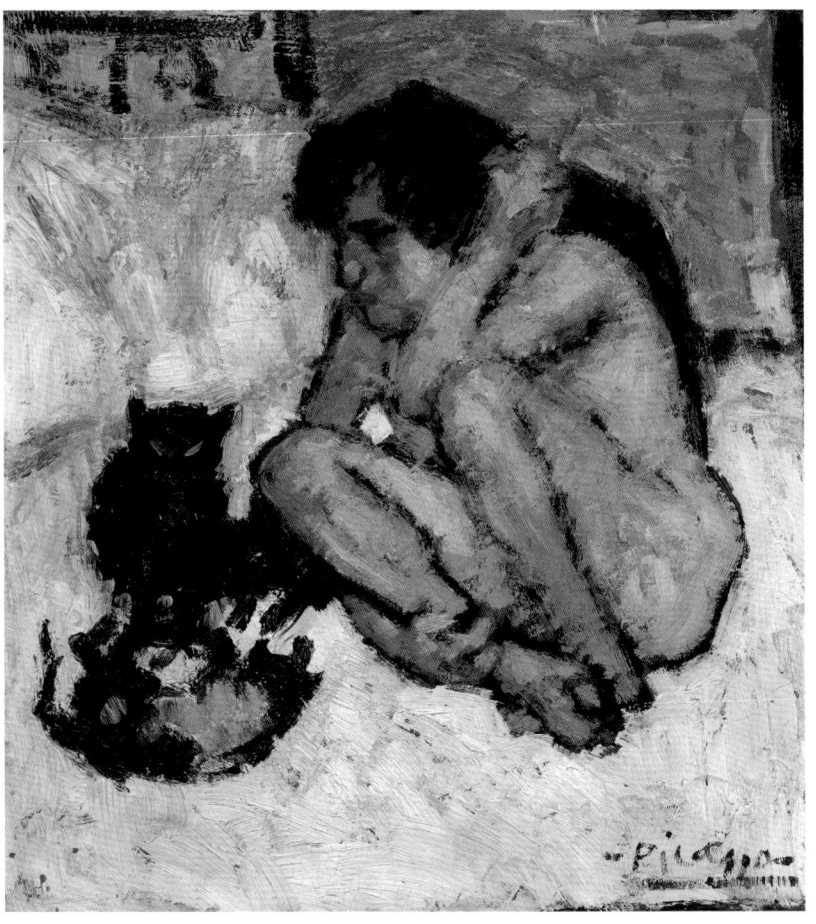

85

Pablo Picasso

Crazy Woman with Cats, 1901. Oil on pulp board, 45.1 x 40.8 cm. The Art Institute of Chicago. Amy McCormick Memorial Collection (1942.464)

themselves, brush their hair or have it brushed."[39] Attracting wide and sometimes vitriolic attention in the press, this near-obsessive series of pictures confirmed Degas's status as a leading artist of the nude in modern, urban surroundings. This reputation was further enhanced in shows that took place over subsequent years, including two in galleries on the rue Laffitte, in 1888 and 1896, respectively.[40] Controversial though they were, several of the large pastels of nudes that Degas made in the 1880s were bought by private individuals, such as Henri Lerolle and Émile Boussod. The picture owned by Boussod, *The Tub* (**84**), was later sold to the tirelessly acquisitive Camondo, in whose collection it hung at the turn of the century.[41] Against this background, those in Paris who knew Camondo's pictures or similar works by Degas in private hands may reasonably have sensed that paintings by Picasso in the Vollard show, such as *Crazy Woman with Cats* (**85**) and *Nude with Red Stockings* (see 82), indicated he was following in Degas's footsteps.

Another little-discussed aspect of Picasso's show at Vollard's was a selection of drawings that were probably displayed — in the manner of the day — unframed and in a portfolio. The critic Gustave Coquiot, who produced a prefatory article about the exhibition and also claimed to have organized it, concluded his text with a short paragraph about these "delicious" studies on paper; noting that some showed "once again the young flesh of little prostitutes," Coquiot implied that this subject had already been broached in other works on the gallery walls.[42] For certain exhibition visitors, such an association may again have suggested links with Degas's art. When his "suite of nudes" was shown in 1886, "the dubious boudoirs of registered houses" and women described as "sluts" had similarly been invoked in the contemporary press, though this assumption was not universally shared.[43] Beyond dispute, however, is that some pictures by Degas, including pastels that

in the Camondo collection. Unlikely though it appears at first glance, Picasso's *The Dwarf* was also among the possible links with Degas, as we shall later discover. In a more oblique sense, pictures with titles such as *Femme nue* and *Femme de nuit* may have indicated to Fagus an awareness of a quite different aspect of Degas's career. For at least two decades, Degas had enjoyed a reputation as an artist preoccupied with the female form. In six of the seven Impressionist exhibitions to which he contributed, Degas showed compositions based on naked women, typically in bedroom or bathroom contexts.[38] At the final group exhibition of 1886, his submissions were dominated by an extensive "suite of nudes" in pastel, described by the artist in the accompanying catalogue as "women who bathe themselves, dry themselves, wipe

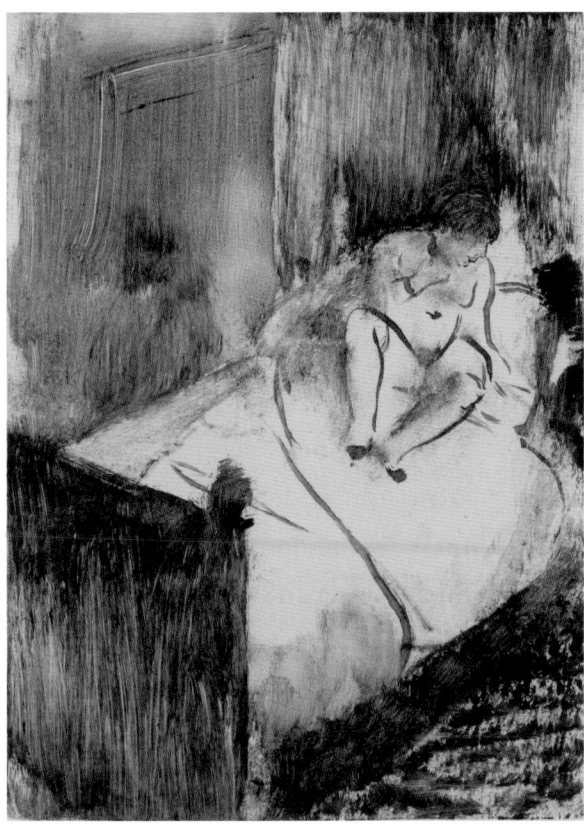

Picasso had seen in the Caillebotte bequest, represented naked women who were implicitly under voyeuristic observation, presumably in brothels.[44] Even more literal in this respect was an earlier sequence of works by Degas that was little known to the public at large, in which he had tackled the subject of prostitution very frankly. Around 1876 Degas had made more than one hundred black-and-white monotypes that showed prostitutes with or without their clients, such as *Rest on the Bed* (**86**) and *Conversation* (see 275), and groups of "filles" — as they were known — passing the time together in various states of undress (see 250, 272). The purpose of his project is unclear, though Degas may have exhibited a few of these brothel prints at the 1877 Impressionist exhibition and certainly gave a number to his friends.[45] Over the years, two monotypes linked with the theme were bought by Camondo and others were acquired by dealers, among them younger or less estab-

lished figures who were willing to take "minor" works by the master toward the end of the century. It is thus distinctly possible that Picasso — who had shown a lively interest in the prostitutes of Barcelona and drawn them on several recent occasions — learned about Degas's monotypes on his early visits to Paris.

One of the young dealers in question was Vollard, a relative newcomer to the business who opened his gallery on the rue Laffitte in 1893. Among his early customers was Degas himself, who in October 1894 began to acquire items from Vollard for his private collection in exchange for works of his own, a practice he continued for many years.[46] As a result, Vollard, too, found himself in possession of several pictures by Degas and in time became a modest dealer in his art, as well as a longstanding personal acquaintance of the aging painter; they are recorded dining together as late as 1912.[47] Degas sometimes attended the informal dinners held in the basement of Vollard's gallery and inevitably kept an eye on the exhibitions that appeared on his walls. At first, Vollard presented exhibitions of artists who were still young or little known at the time, such as Van Gogh, Gauguin, and the Nabis, and in 1899 showed a group of drawings by Nonell.[48] Though he never became Degas's exclusive dealer, Vollard clearly earned his trust. The two collaborated around 1914 on a catalogue of almost one hundred of Degas's drawings, prints, and paintings that Vollard had accumulated, which became the largest illustrated volume of the artist's oeuvre available at that date.[49] After Degas's death, Vollard also wrote a book filled with colorful recollections about their dealings and mentioned him freely in his memoirs, where fragments of information fill out our knowledge of Degas's life and work. Vollard remembered, for example, that Degas executed his monotypes of brothel scenes "after dinner," using "printer's ink on a copper plate" and "sometimes touched them up with pastel."[50] "These little master-

86

Edgar Degas

Rest on the Bed,

c. 1876–77. Monotype,

16.2 x 12.1 cm. Städelsches

Kunstinstitut und

Städtische Galerie,

Frankfurt

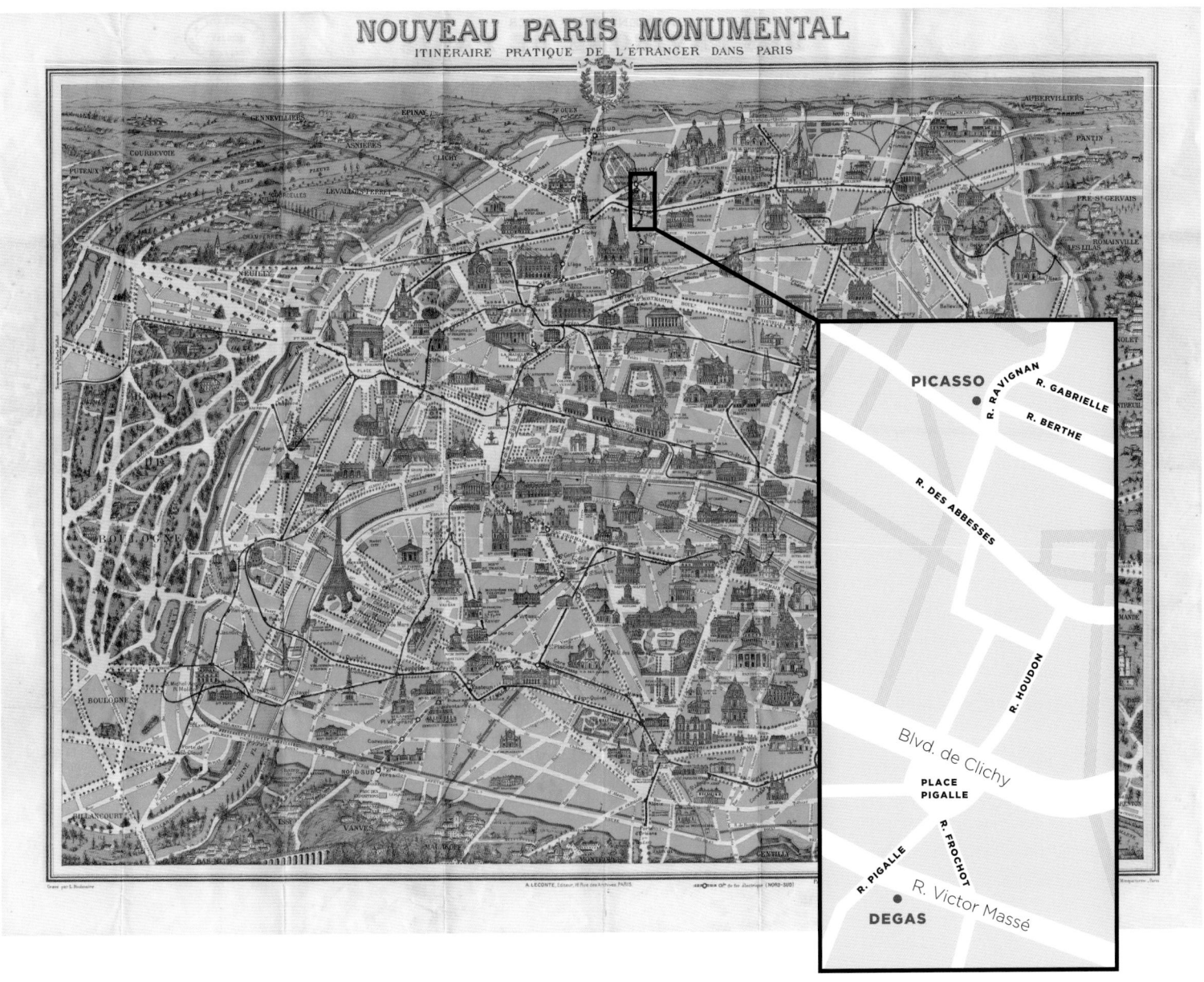

NOUVEAU PARIS MONUMENTAL
ITINÉRAIRE PRATIQUE DE L'ÉTRANGER DANS PARIS

87

Map of Paris, c. 1900,
with locations of Picasso's
and Degas's studios

pieces" continued to fascinate Vollard in later life, when he reproduced a substantial number in luxurious books that spread the artist's and the monotypes' fame.[51]

For a few brief weeks in 1901, therefore, when Vollard helped to launch Picasso's career in Paris, he effectively became an informal representative for both the elderly Degas and the youthful Spaniard. Given his long-established habit and his familiarity with the dealer, it is almost certain that Degas saw Picasso's exhibition in the rue Laffitte gallery, though nothing is known of his response; some years later, when Degas examined a show of Cubist pictures, he is said to have announced that it looked "harder to do than painting."[52] The Vollard exhibition was nevertheless a significant — even historic — moment, when a representative of late Impressionism encountered the beginnings of an entirely new art. Yet there is no firm evidence that the three men met together at this or any other time. For several years, Picasso remained hampered by his lack of French and was still capable of youthful shyness: he apparently hid in his bed when Berthe Weill first called.[53] For Picasso and his young entourage, however, it is clear that the visibility of Degas's art and person had a considerable resonance. Degas's reputation as a radical figure of his day was already formidable, in ways that increasingly added to his stature among the young. In his seminal article about Degas published in 1894 in the *Art Journal*, Théodore Duret defined Degas as "one of those artists who live in the closest contact with contemporary life, penetrating to the very heart of their own time[s]."[54] Such terms surely appealed to Picasso, as would Duret's stress on Degas's achievements as a draftsman, whose "love and knowledge of drawing" identified him with the tradition of Poussin and Ingres, and their "common tendency to lead everything up to drawing."[55]

Picasso and his Catalan friends currently occupied cheap lodgings in Montmartre, a few minutes away from the Place Pigalle. They would soon have learned that Degas lived nearby, on the rue Victor Massé where his studio had been for a decade (**87**), a street that was also the site of the renowned Chat Noir cabaret, the model for Els Quatre Gats.[56] While Degas had once been famous for his pastels and prints of such establishments, his art had now entered a distinctive late phase in which topical scenes had been largely replaced by two dominant motifs: the bathing nude and the dancer in the wings. In declining health and suffering from limited eyesight, he also chose to exhibit less and became known as a difficult, work-obsessed recluse. Still important to Degas's routines was walking, which made him a familiar figure on the Place Pigalle and adjoining streets. This was an area long associated with artists and performers of every kind, from musicians and dancers to sculptors, printmak-

ers, and painters, the latter provided for by several legendary suppliers of artist's materials. It was also known for its rudimentary bars and restaurants, and its accommodations that ranged from the modest to the squalid. Picasso found a sparse room here during his 1901 visit to Paris, on a thoroughfare that ran through this neighborhood, the Boulevard de Clichy, and it was from a high window in the building he occupied that he painted his Pissarro-like *Boulevard de Clichy* (see 83).[57] Here also Picasso arranged his crude furniture and belongings as the setting for a small but critical canvas painted in these months, *The Blue Room (The Tub)* (**88**).

Not for the first time, Picasso brought together in *The Blue Room* a number of elements that recalled the recent past as he strove toward a new painterly synthesis. His intensely evocative picture shows one of his Monet-like landscapes and Lautrec's *May Milton* poster hung on the wall, marking some of his former enthusiasms, while the colorful bunch of flowers at right recalls several works exhibited at Vollard's. The room itself is dominated by cool tones, though a richly hued carpet and bright sunshine entering at left hint at comfort and optimism, even domestic bliss. Picasso's current mood was probably dependent on the model for the standing figure, believed to be Blanche, the latest in a succession of his companions.[58] Unlike the nudes he had exhibited a few months earlier, this figure does not crouch in shame or mindlessly display her attributes, but calmly washes in the silver-yellow light. To those contemporaries who knew Degas's art well, her pose may have looked distinctly familiar. Blanche leans forward with one shoulder dropped and her head slightly lowered, subtly arching her back as she concentrates on her toilette. Variants of this position had appeared in many of Degas's works of art from the 1890s, including a series of six variously developed and modified lithographs, among them the superb,

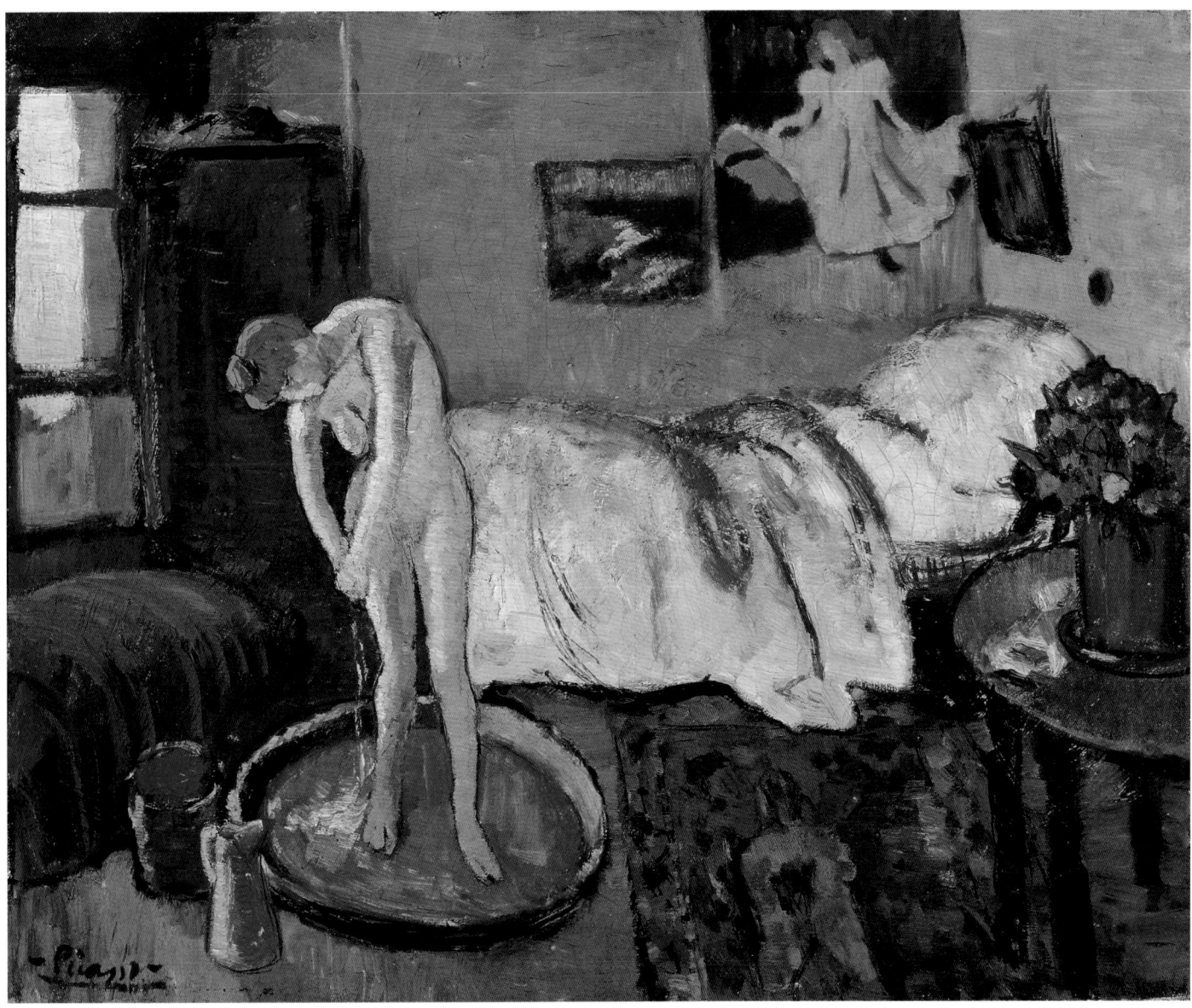

88

Pablo Picasso

The Blue Room (The Tub),

1901. Oil on canvas,

50.5 x 61.6 cm.

The Phillips Collection,

Washington, D.C.

Acquired 1927 (1554)

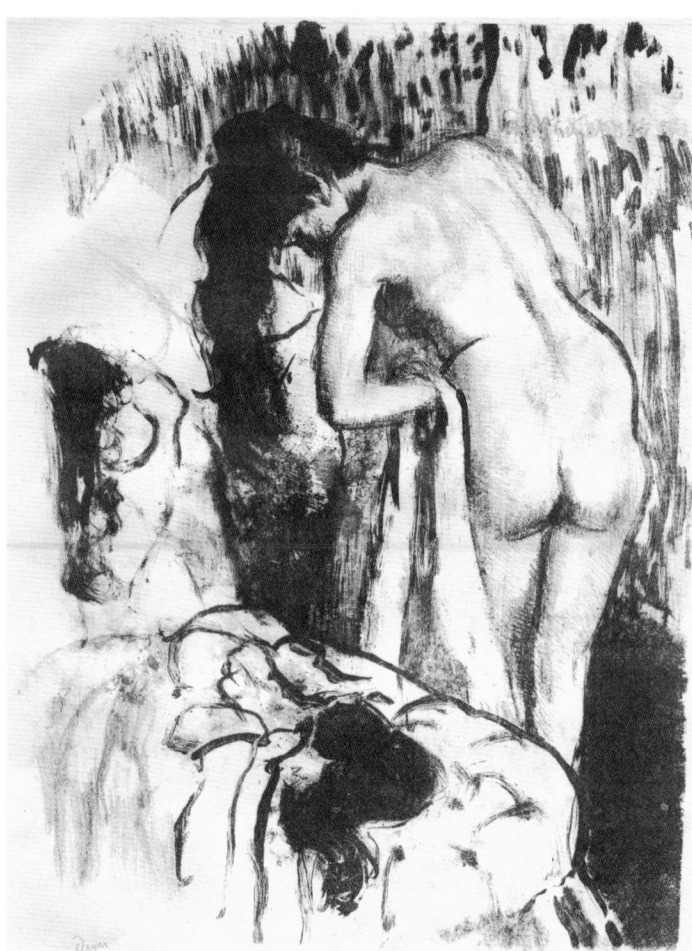

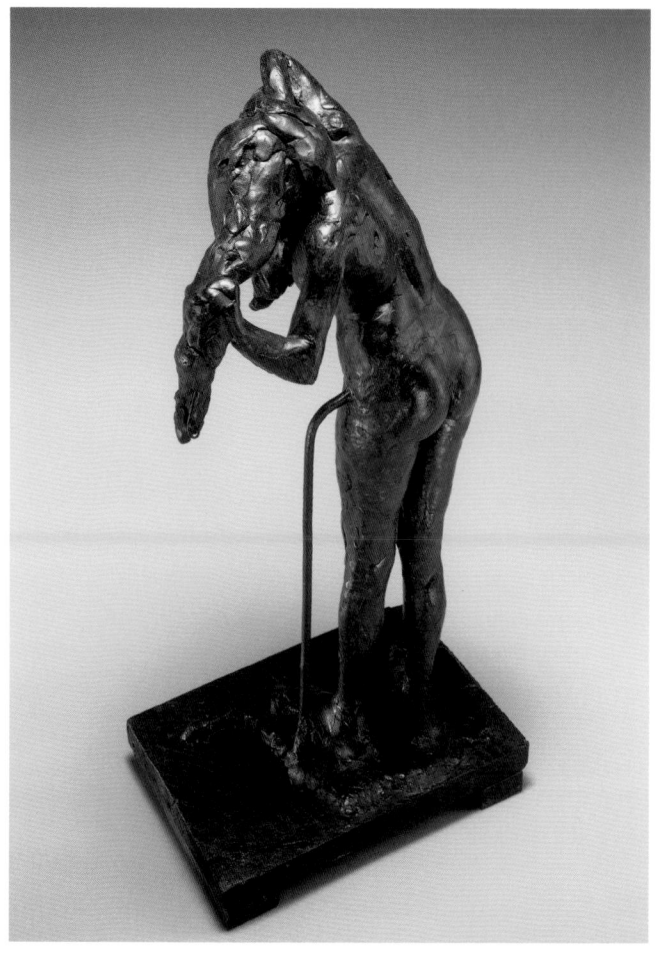

almost minimal *Woman Drying Herself* (**89**). Comparable figures could also be found among Degas's wax sculptures from this same period, in which naked women are shown reaching down to attend to their bodies or upward to adjust their hair.[59] An example is *Woman Arranging Her Hair* (**90**), an original wax from Degas's studio that was cast in bronze after the artist's death (see 205). As so often in his oeuvre, both the lithographs and the waxes were also surrounded by preparatory drawings of similar motifs and by pastels that reiterated the same subjects in bright color. Like the female figures in his 1886 "suite of nudes," the finely inflected poses of these standing women had taken on an obsessive significance in Degas's later creative process.

The resemblance between a subject, a composition, and even an individual pose in a picture by Picasso and their equivalent in works by Degas offers a number of historical and interpretive challenges. With the single exception of the *Little Dancer Aged Fourteen* (see 141), which was shown at the 1881 Impressionist exhibition, none of Degas's wax sculptures had been seen in public at this date and not a single example had been cast in bronze. They were thus literally unknown to the wider world, even to most of those who admired the artist and had followed his career for decades. Yet it is clear that a restricted number of individuals saw these waxes firsthand in Degas's rue Victor Massé studio and were aware of their role in the artist's mature oeuvre.[60] Over the years Degas had

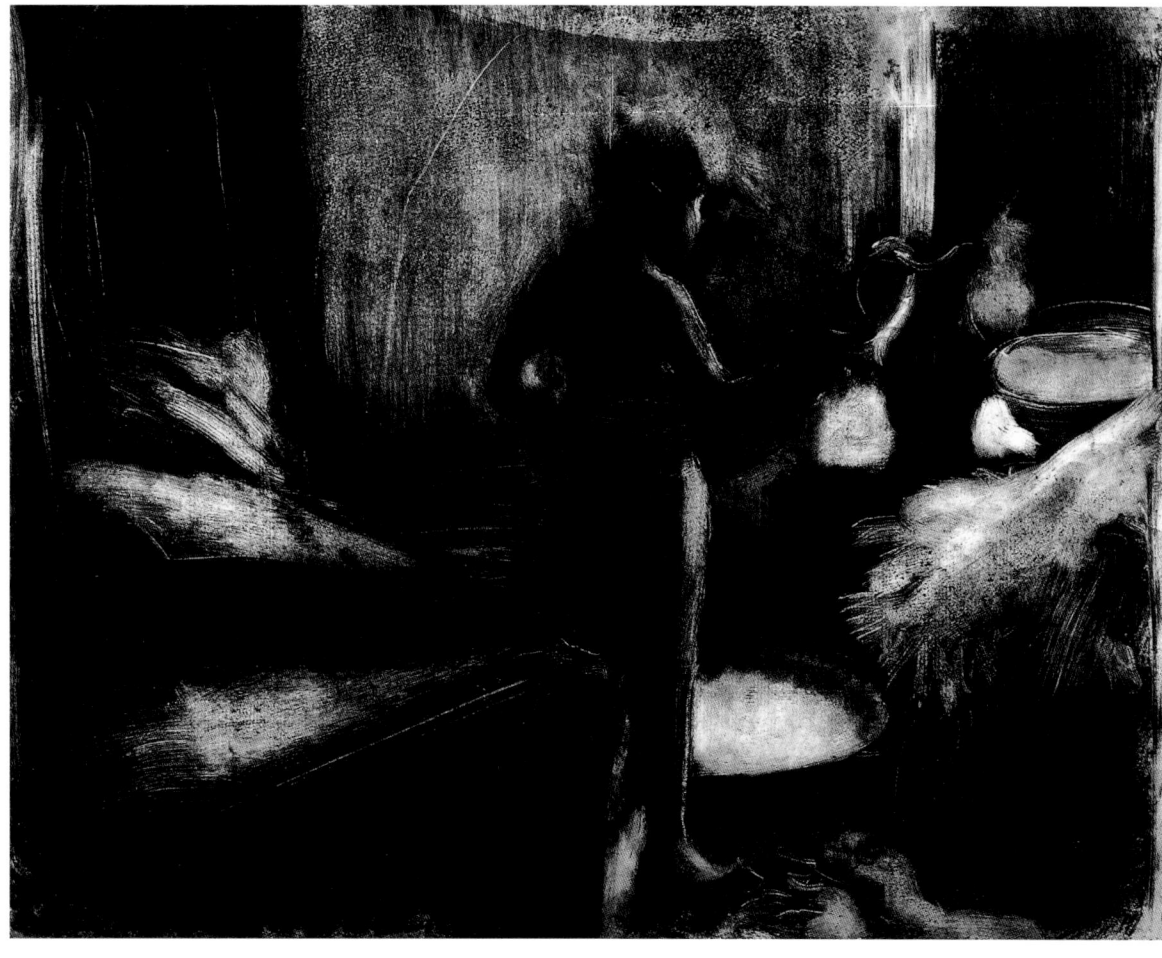

made more than seventy sculptures that ranged in scale from handheld objects to heavy, bulky depictions of women drying themselves and thus constituted a body of work that could hardly be concealed from his visitors.[61] Contemporary reports of many kinds reveal that — despite his partially self-generated reputation for reclusiveness — Degas welcomed certain people to his apartment and allowed some of them into his studio, which occupied the upper floor in the same building.[62] Among these individuals were family and close friends, artists and protégés, a few privileged dealers and their representatives, models with their acquaintances — in 1904, Benedetta Canals and Fernande Olivier found Degas at work there — and a number of acute observers who wrote down their

memories, such as Paul Lafond and Paul Valéry.[63] Just as important in the years around 1900 were documented visits by several younger artists, for whom Degas retained a pronounced fondness until his final years. In addition to the old guard of local painters and sculptors — such as Forain, Bartholomé, and Pierre-Alexandre Jeanniot — there were now others: Maurice Denis, Suzanne Valadon, and Georges Rouault, and amateurs such as Julie Manet and Jeanne Baudot. From further afield came the Britons John Rothenstein and Walter Sickert, and the expatriate Alphonse Legros, all anxious to see the aging master in the "indescribable disorder" of his working spaces, and sometimes recording their impressions.[64]

In time, certain of these accounts found

their way into the artistic community and joined the received wisdom of the age. Some of them were specific about the nature of Degas's unexhibited works: Fernande Olivier reported that Degas was "making small statuettes" and noted that Suzanne Valadon was currently his model, while Vollard later remembered that the artist used a "wooden horse" as he worked on his equestrian sculptures.[65] Others mentioned the easels "loaded with charcoal sketches" and the late pastels of dancers, "in one version the petticoats . . . yellow, in another purple."[66] The "lithographic and etching presses" observed by Lafond must have been visible to all who entered the rue Victor Massé studio, along with accompanying evidence of Degas's recent excursions into printmaking.[67] *Woman Drying Herself* and its other lithographic variants were manifestly made in such circumstances but again were not widely known in the artist's lifetime. There are many documented instances, however, when Degas gave proofs of his prints to colleagues, thus allowing these works a limited circulation outside the studio.[68] From the number of etchings, lithographs, and even monotypes that reached the art market, it is also clear that Degas collaborated with dealers and perhaps individual collectors in this respect.[69] It is thus historically plausible that the echo of Degas's standing bathers in *The Blue Room* was communicated through prints of this kind, perhaps encountered by Picasso in private hands or in the "second Louvre." An additional and unusually challenging source is suggested by a Degas monotype with a similar title to Picasso's painting (**91**). Made around 1876, this horizontal composition also shows a standing nude, a shallow basin, and an unmade bed in a spacious though cluttered room. This monotype was among Degas's largest experiments in the medium and is surprisingly close in scale to Picasso's canvas. When seen side by side with the image of the light-filled room on the Boulevard de Clichy, Degas's print resembles

a penumbrous draft for the painting or even a photographic negative of Picasso's picture. Supporting the link between these curiously twinned works are indications that Degas's print *The Tub* was in circulation during his lifetime, finding its way into the collection of Jacques Doucet, the eventual owner of Picasso's *Les Demoiselles d'Avignon*.[70] It was also known indirectly in a colored lithograph, one of the suite of reproductive prints made after Degas's pictures by William Thornley in 1888.[71]

Still underestimated at this period is the role of high-quality reproductions of artists' work in the dissemination of their imagery. In the last decades of the nineteenth century, several of the Impressionists had collaborated with specialists in lithography and photomechanical techniques to produce half-tone or full-color illustrations for journals and periodicals. Monet, Pissarro, and Degas were all in the vanguard of such experimentation, which helped to spread the fame of their art and attract buyers for individual paintings.[72] Two projects exemplify Degas's involvement in this process and his success in reaching new audiences. In 1888, Degas worked closely with the artist and printmaker William Thornley as the latter patiently created a set of lithographs based on freehand, linear translations of fifteen of Degas's paintings and pastels.[73] Printed in one and sometimes two colors, some sets of Thornley's prints included Degas's signature and implicitly carried the artist's authorization. Almost a decade later, Degas was again personally involved with a second collection of high-quality prints of his own work, this time focused exclusively on drawings and pastels. Entitled *Degas: Vingt Dessins, 1861–1896,* this publication used the latest technology for color reproduction and was overseen by Michel Manzi, an artist and illustrator known personally to Degas.[74] Manzi's remarkable sequence of facsimiles were sold in a specially designed portfolio and brought many examples of Degas's draftsmanship to public notice for

92

Edgar Degas

Laundress. Reproduced in *Degas: Vingt Dessins, 1861–1896* (Paris, New York: Goupil et Cie, 1897), pl. 8. Courtesy Sterling and Francine Clark Art Institute, Williamstown, Massachusetts

93

Edgar Degas

Woman Drying Her Back with a Towel. Reproduced in *Degas: Vingt Dessins, 1861–1896* (Paris, New York: Goupil et Cie, 1897), pl. 18. Courtesy Sterling and Francine Clark Art Institute, Williamstown, Massachusetts

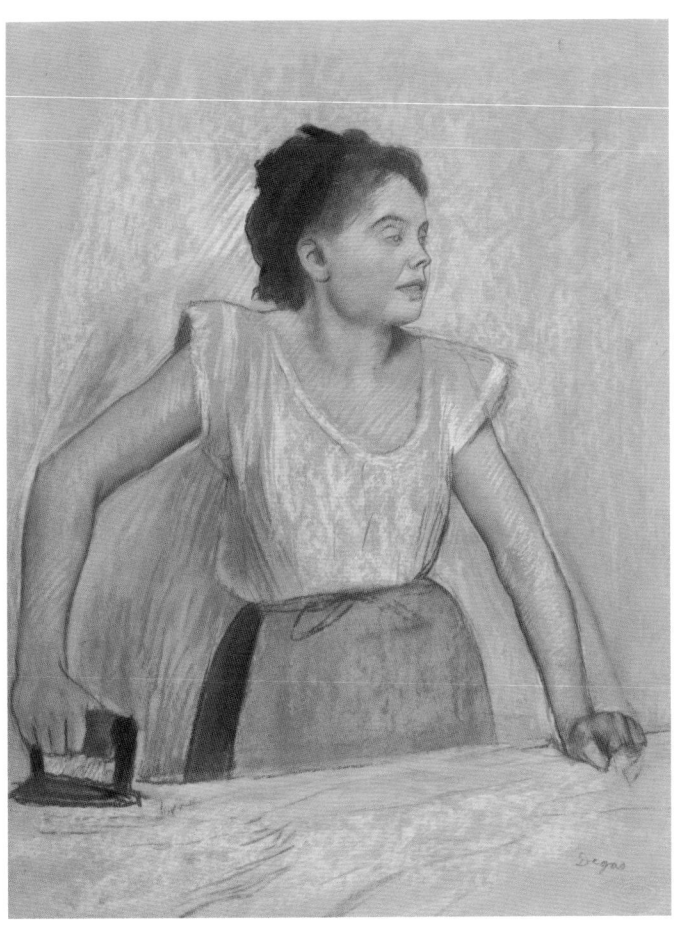

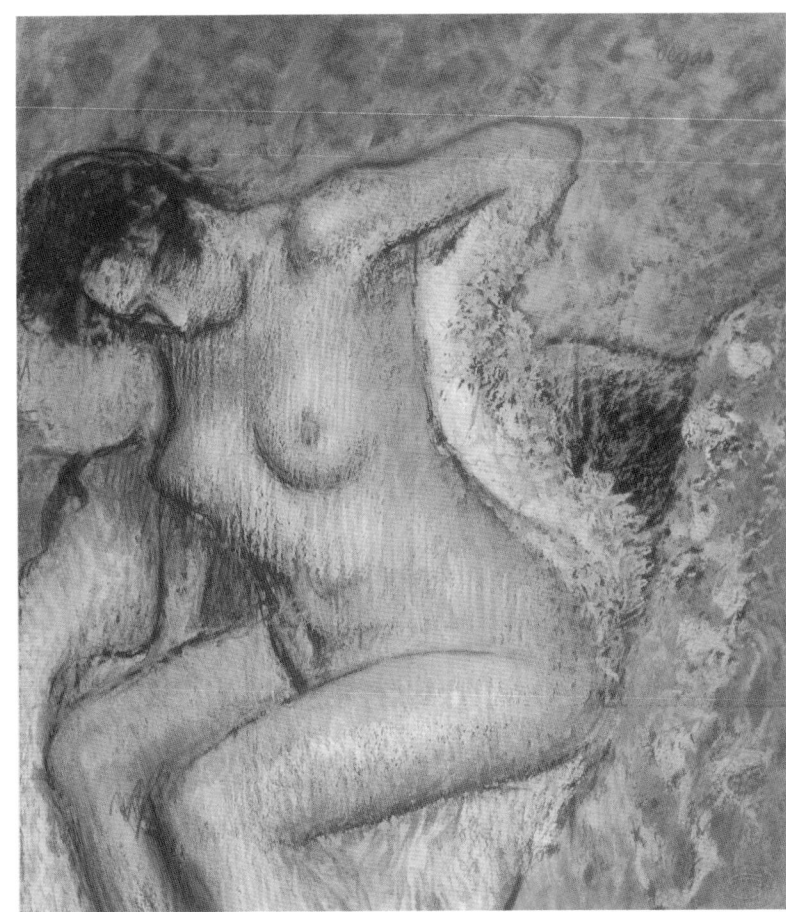

the first time. In addition to exquisite studies from his youth, it also included more recent pastels, among them a resonant *Laundress* (**92**) and a richly developed *Woman Drying Her Back with a Towel* (**93**). As we shall discover, the importance of this publication for Picasso is not hypothetical: a copy was owned and proudly shown to visitors in the early twentieth century by his friend Leo Stein, Gertrude's brother.

The cool hues of Picasso's *The Blue Room*, which was probably painted in the fall of 1901, were among early signs of a shift in his palette and ultimately of a new approach to painting. The "Blue Period" was marked not just by new chromatic emphases but by a shift away from Parisian portraits and cityscapes, or what Sabartés had called "the spectacle of the street." A pervasive factor was Picasso's reengagement

with the work of El Greco, who had been "rediscovered" toward the end of the nineteenth century as a major figure in the history of Spanish art. An active pioneer in this process was Rusiñol, who bought two El Grecos in Paris in 1894 and had them carried through the streets of Sitges at that year's "Modernist Festival."[75] His enthusiasm was clearly infectious and showed in Picasso's work during his period as a student in Madrid in 1897, when he even signed one of his own drawings "I am El Greco."[76] Now searching for an idiom of his own in Paris, Picasso was newly attracted to El Greco's acid colors, attenuated forms, and mysterious narratives, resulting in pictures that were "bleak in mood, focusing on the misery of the human lot rather than the frenetic round of social pleasure."[77] In France, the uncanonical qualities of El Greco had also been quietly celebrated for some time, inspiring scholars, collectors, and dealers to seek out his pictures. Somewhat paradoxically, one of these enthusiasts was the lifelong advocate for the art of Renaissance Italy, Edgar Degas. In 1894, Degas had also acquired an El Greco, the large oil painting entitled *Saint Ildefonso*, which he bought from Durand-Ruel for the sum of two thousand francs, followed by a second magnificent canvas purchased from an artist colleague in 1896.[78] A passionate collector who would eventually own hundreds of drawings and paintings by his artist-heroes, principally Delacroix and Ingres, Degas nevertheless accumulated such works in private and showed them mainly to close friends. If Picasso was aware of their shared taste for El Greco, or of the presence of these two canvases at the heart of Montmartre while he was living there, it must again have been through the network of models, dealers, and collectors who spanned their worlds. The coincidence can nevertheless be added to a list of overlapping passions for past art that Degas and Picasso would share, which included several names that were far from predictable at this date.

Portraiture and Decadence

Early in 1902, Picasso returned to Barcelona, continuing a pattern of temporary residence in the two capitals that was repeated several times before he settled in Paris in 1904. Blues and grays were now dominant in his paintings but gradually accommodated warmer tones in works that could be wistful as well as overtly tragic. A common thread throughout these years was the human face and body as expressive entities, when a particularized figure such as that of Blanche in *The Blue Room* could be enlarged and transposed into a more timeless scene, as in that of the young group in Picasso's monumental 1903 painting, *La Vie*. In his early twenties, Picasso was the age that Degas had been when he studied briefly at the École des

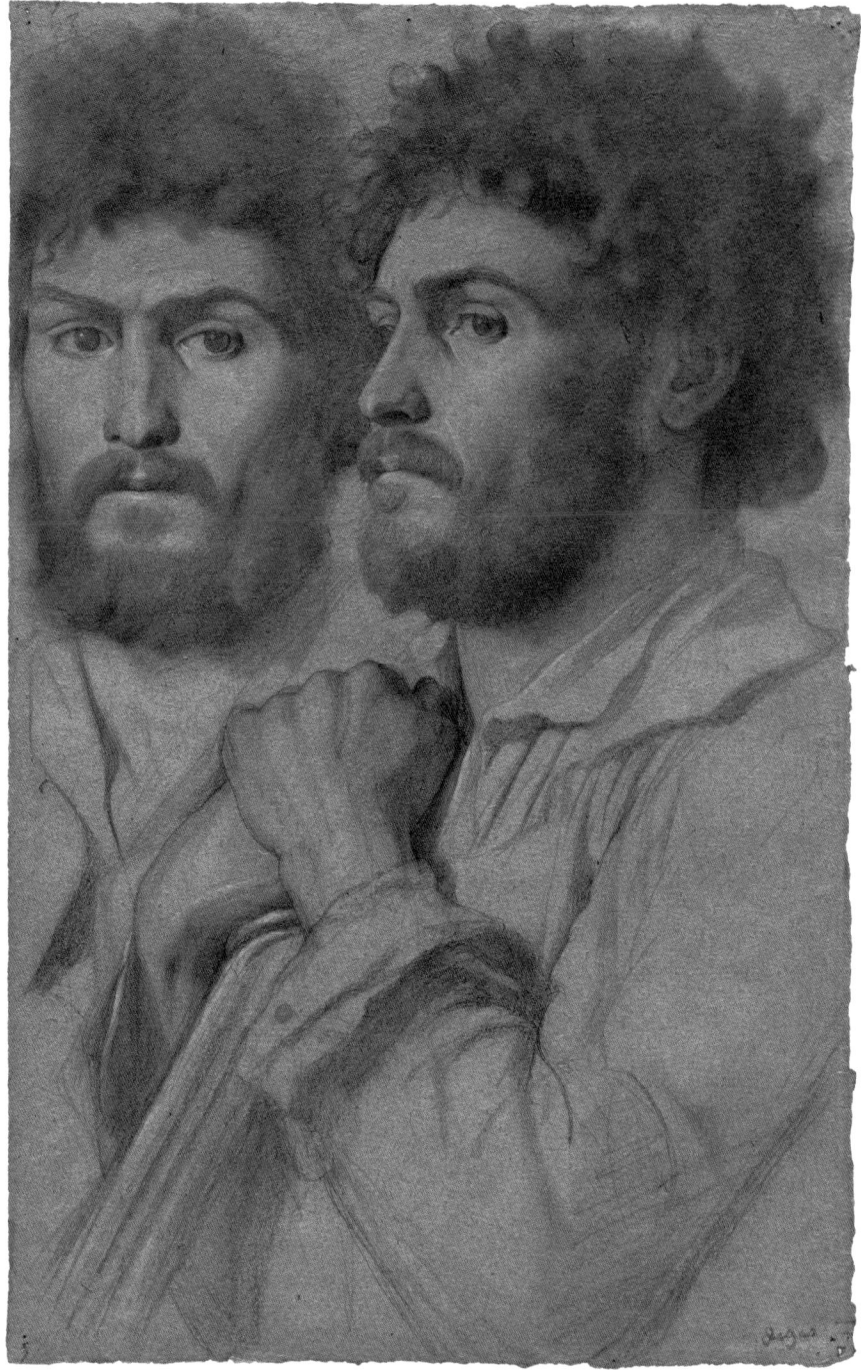

94

Edgar Degas

Two Portrait Studies of a Man, c. 1856–57. Pencil and stumping with slight touches of white heightening on burnt-rose paper. 44.8 x 22.6 cm. Sterling and Francine Clark Art Institute, Williamstown, Massachusetts (1955.1393)

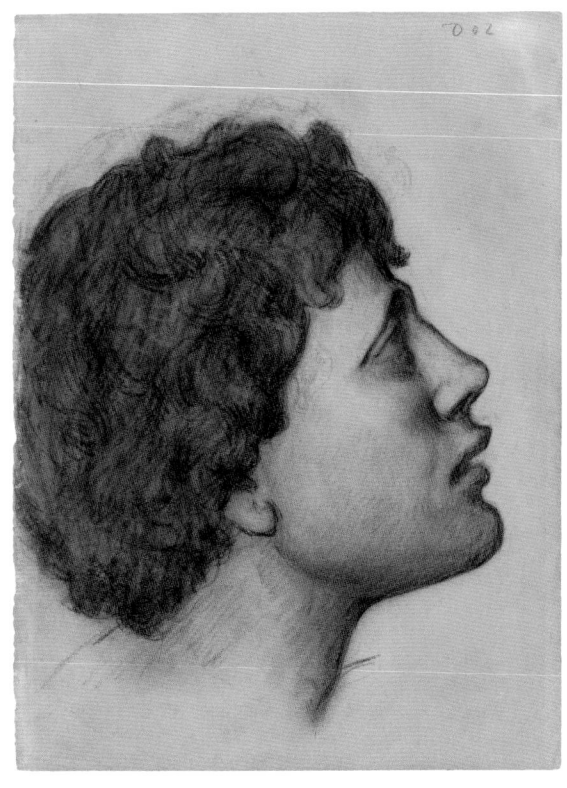
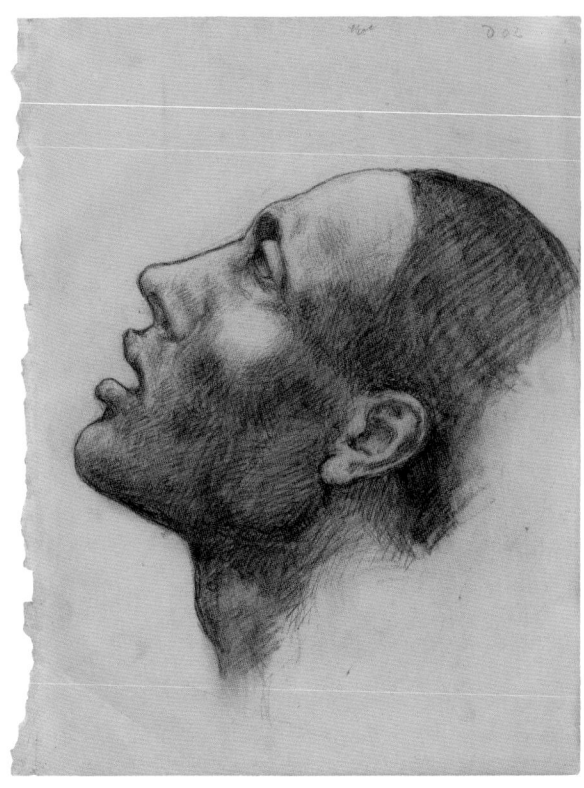

Beaux-Arts in Paris, working from Classical sculpture and attempting his first self-portraits. At some fundamental level, Picasso again found himself reaching back to his instruction at the hands of his father as he made his own power-fully articulated drawings — from models or from memory — to underpin these newly ambi-tious narratives. In this phase Picasso would have immediately grasped the point of a draw-ing such as Degas's *Two Portrait Studies of a Man* (**94**), the kind that academic artists had once made as they learned to master human expression. This superbly confident and minutely detailed sheet combines frontal and oblique views of the same individual, a testa-ment to his application and his technical com-mand. Yet Degas seems to have used neither face in a finished painting, keeping the drawing in his studio into old age with hundreds of other examples of his youthful draftsmanship.[79] Half a century later, Picasso conducted a similar exer-cise on two separate sheets of paper, in *Boy's*

Head (**95**) and *Study of a Head Gazing Upward* (**96**). Taking his idea a stage further than Degas had done, he integrated similar heads into sev-eral designs for a multifigure composition, *Scene of Despair*, though this plan, too, remained among many that were left unresolved.[80] Char-acteristically, line was still being used by Picasso to explore and define the subject for a painting, with color added to certain drafts or integrated into the scene as it advanced.

While Picasso was still in Barcelona, a sec-ond exhibition of his work was arranged by Mañach in April 1902, at the modest little Paris gallery recently opened by Berthe Weill. Evi-dently a believer in Picasso and his country-men, Weill admired the drawings of Nonell and Sunyer, and bravely staged a second show of Picasso's paintings in 1904.[81] Located at 25, rue Victor Massé, her gallery was just a few doors away from Degas's apartment and studio at number 37 on the same street. As historical coincidences go, this might have been among the most illuminating and productive, but events were to prove otherwise. Though inevitably aware of the exhibition, Degas may not have seen the works on show, many of them left over from Vollard's exhibition. "Whenever he passed my shop (he was my neighbor) and saw me on the threshold," Weill wrote in her memoirs, "his looks became furious, he visibly turned his head, salivating with contempt."[82] The cause of these outbursts was not the nature of Weill's exhibitions or her personality but Degas's anti-Semitism, which had been tragically exacerbated in the previous decade by the Dreyfus affair. Regardless of Degas's attitude, the display of Picasso's work — now graced by *The Blue Room* — attracted significant interest in the city. One critic noted that "amateurs" (collectors) were already "making the pilgrimage" to the rue Victor Massé, and Fagus again insisted in print that Picasso and his fellow Spaniards had been "stimulated by Manet, Monet, Degas, Carrière, our Impressionists."[83]

Fagus's twice-repeated implication that Picasso had a kinship with modern French art — "our Impressionists" — may have encouraged Parisians to pay attention to his work. Several early patrons and supporters of Picasso already owned Impressionist pictures, and a fascinating subgroup turn out to be established collectors or advocates of Degas. A striking example was Olivier Sainsère, a senior government official who owned four substantial ballet pastels by Degas but was also "one of his first buyers" when Picasso began to show his work in Paris, according to Weill.[84] Even before Vollard's 1900 show had opened, Sainsère snapped up Picasso's painting entitled *Danseuses*, perhaps intrigued by the prospect of owning dance images by artists from successive generations.[85] Sainsère continued to buy from Picasso in his Bateau-Lavoir days, and Weill recalled a later attempt to get Sainsère to purchase another Degas pastel for five hundred francs.[86] Other figures involved with Weill and with the careers

and work of Degas and Picasso were Viau, Manzi, Frank Burty de Haviland, Daniel Halévy, Paul Valéry, and Eugène Rouart, the latter a son of Degas's closest friend, Henri Rouart.[87] Also significant in this circle was the art writer and administrator Roger Marx, the author of the most informed and thoughtful article on Degas to have appeared in print. This was published in the innovative periodical *L'Image* in 1897 and was accompanied by seven superb wood

L'Image. Octobre 1897.

CARTONS D'ARTISTES

Degas

PAR ROGER MARX.

Quand un peintre a renouvelé l'inspiration, l'optique et les procédés de son art, quand il s'est révélé le vrai maître du Moderne, on ne saurait céder à son désir hautain de silence et d'oubli, sous peine de rompre le lien historique et de rendre inintelligible le développement de l'école française; y souscrire serait encore abdiquer toute liberté et toute justice au profit de l'étranger qui, affranchi du secret, acclame hautement en Degas un « réformateur » et « l'égal des plus grands peintres de tous les temps, dans leurs chefs-d'œuvre ».

La haute portée de ses initiatives vient de ce qu'elles émanent d'un artiste *complet*, exceptionnellement savant, curieux et lucide. Il y eut révolution à la fois dans l'ordre intellectuel et technique, et l'époque où elle se produisit ne saurait indifférer. Degas naît un peu après Manet, en 1834; sa jeunesse, qui assiste aux dernières luttes entre les romantiques et les classiques, voit d'autre part s'épanouir librement le génie de Daumier et de Corot; elle tient en défiance l'exclusivisme des systèmes; elle se forme et s'informe de tous côtés, à l'école des beaux-arts, par les voyages, dans la fréquentation des maîtres. La tradition de M. Ingres arrive à Degas, plus ou moins adultérée, à travers l'enseignement de M. Lamothe; en Italie, où il séjourne en 1857, il tient commerce avec les primitifs et les Florentins; si on le surprend à peindre *Sémiramis construisant les murs de Babylone*, les *Jeunes filles spartiates s'exerçant à la lutte*, simultanément presque, il interprète Lawrence, il donne une copie chaleureuse de l'*Enlèvement des Sabines*, tant il est exact que Poussin est l'ancêtre et le guide avec lequel renoue tout régénérateur de vraie lignée française. L'éducation se poursuit, sévèrement menée par un artiste qui se soumet à la rude discipline d'une étude

Onzième Numéro.

41

97

Opening page of Roger Marx, "Cartons d'Artistes Degas," in *L'Image* 11 (October 1897), p. 321. Courtesy Sterling and Francine Clark Art Institute, Williamstown, Massachusetts

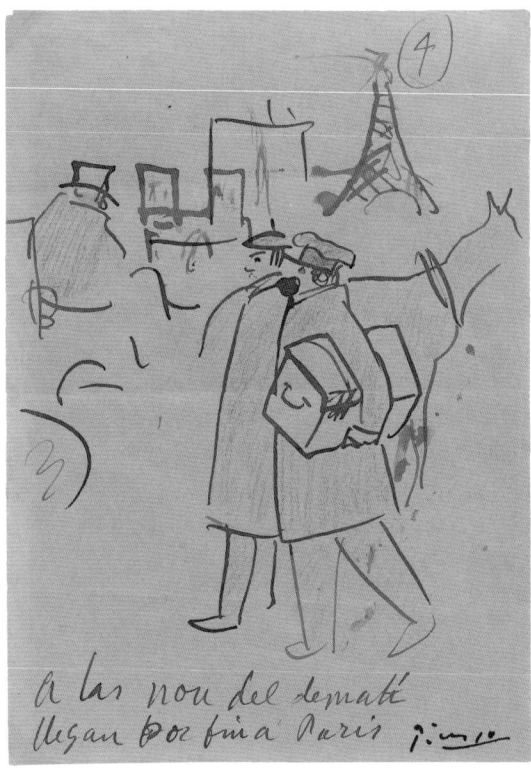

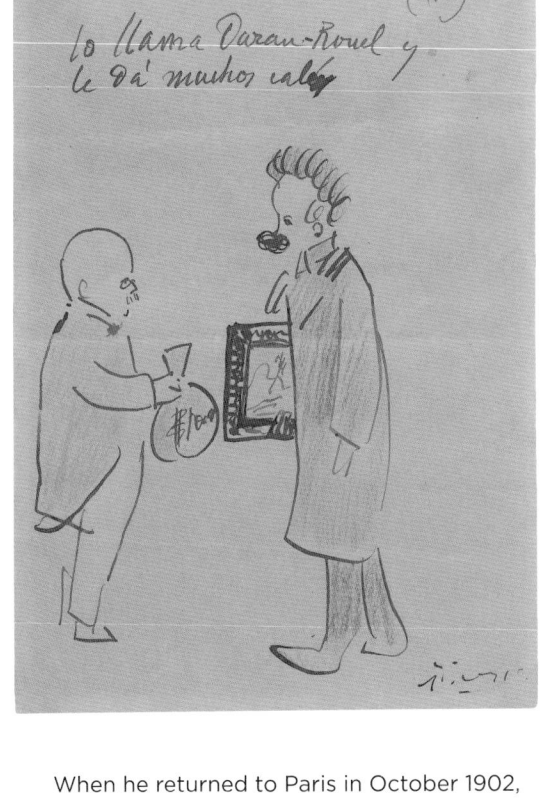

engravings of Degas's pictures, most of them from Camondo's holdings.[88] In his text, Roger Marx showed a level of knowledge that suggests he had visited the painter's studio, not least in his awareness of the never-exhibited *Semiramis Building Babylon* (see 22). More important for younger readers was the author's insistence on Degas's status as "the true master of the Modern," who had simultaneously created a revolution in "the intellectual and technical order."[89] Roger Marx himself owned the superb drawing *Three Studies of a Dancer in Fourth Position* (see 129), which he reproduced in two parts in *L'Image* (**97**); it was conceivably a gift from the artist to mark his important article. He was also an obsessive collector of prints who acquired a substantial group of Degas's etchings and lithographs during these years. Berthe Weill tells us that Roger Marx closely followed her gallery activities and also wrote a preface for a Matisse exhibition that she presented in 1904.[90]

When he returned to Paris in October 1902, Picasso went "the very first day, to show his work to the impresario of Impressionism, Durand-Ruel, though evidently without success: there are no traces of the dealer buying or displaying his pictures."[91] Though Picasso never felt comfortable with the "bourgeois" Durand-Ruel, he undoubtedly kept abreast of his stock and in 1904 again took his new work to show the dealer in the hope of making money, an event anticipated in a series of caricatures made for his friends (**98, 99**).[92] Now taking the initiative in advancing his own career, Picasso was increasingly ambitious in the scale of certain of the projects he engaged with, including several based on key works by Degas. An image that had already begun to haunt an entire sequence of pictures was that of the drinker, seated in solitude or with a companion of the opposite sex. Though never much attracted to alcohol, Picasso spent a great deal of time in cafés and bars, meeting with friends and —

according to Weill — often drawing in such places during the evenings.[93] Between 1900 and 1903, he chose to devote more than a dozen major canvases to this subject, from the Casas-like *Interior of the Quatre Gats* to a group of visually radical and sometimes technically coarse portraits in the Blue Period manner.[94] The subject of these pictures is not the act of drinking, which is never described, but almost invariably Picasso's sense of his models' private isolation, even when they are in company. The critic Charles Maurice identified this quality as a "negative sense of life" when he reviewed the second exhibition of Picasso's work at Weill's gallery in late 1902. Referring to the pastel *Couple at a Music Hall* (**100**), Maurice found it "as disturbing and provocative" as Baudelaire's *Fleurs du mal*, despite the presence in the back-ground of a dancer "who performs, far off, in bright light."[95] With the exception of this refer-ence to the Degas- or Lautrec-like dancing figure, Picasso focused most of this series of pictures on sedentary individuals in almost bare surroundings, where they stare blankly into space or back at the viewer. The largest of this group may also have been the last to be painted. Completed in Barcelona in 1903, *Portrait of Sebastià Junyer i Vidal* (see 105) is a shadowy but imposing portrait of one of his local acquaintances, accompanied by "a scrawny prostitute with a telltale red flower in her hair."[96] In front of them is a marble-topped table, a jug, and a small glass, but almost nothing in the composition directs us to a personal or contex-tual narrative. Yet Picasso's peers would have had no doubt that this picture and others in the sequence were intended to invoke a major historical precedent.

More than three decades earlier, the subject of isolated figures of various kinds lingering over their drinks had attracted attention in the art of Manet, Degas, and their acolytes. Some of these compositions were austere, while others were seen to be endearing: Manet's painting of

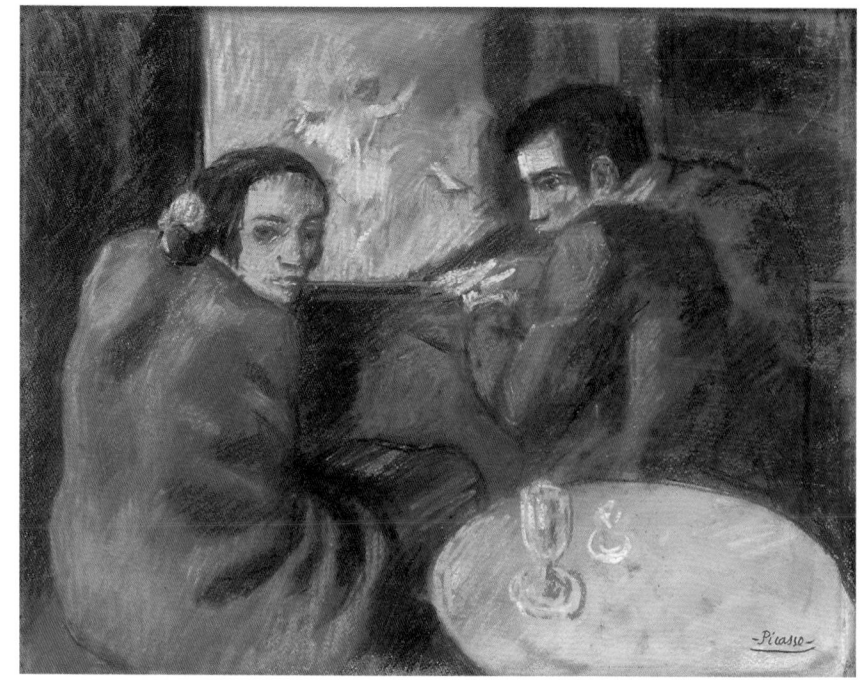

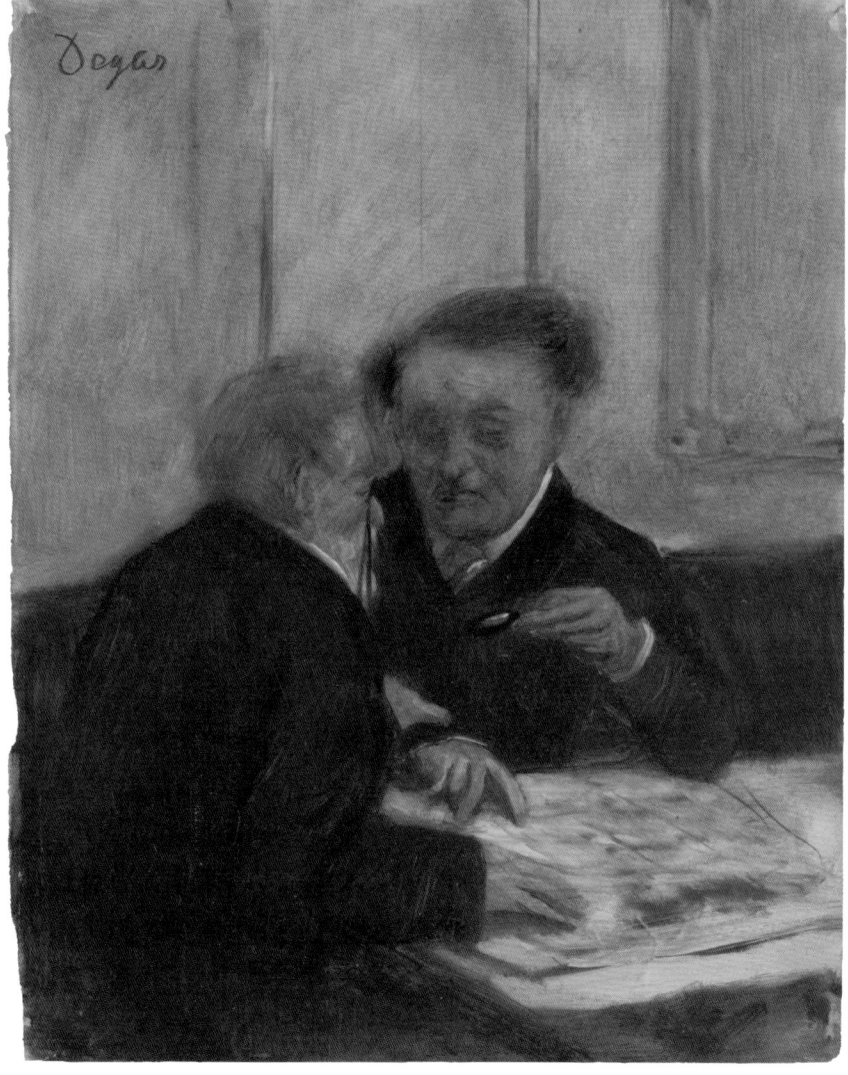

100

Pablo Picasso

Couple at a Music Hall, 1902. Pastel on cardboard, 31 x 40 cm. Nationalgalerie, Museum Berggruen, Staatliche Museen zu Berlin

101

Edgar Degas

At the Café Châteaudun, c. 1869–71. Pencil and oil (essence) on paper, mounted on canvas, 23.7 x 19 cm. The National Gallery, London. Presented by Mr. and Mrs. Charles Wilmers, 1991 (NGL 6536)

102

Edgar Degas

In a Café. Reproduced in Théodore Duret, "Degas," in *The Art Journal*, 1894, p. 206. Courtesy Sterling and Francine Clark Art Institute, Williamstown, Massachusetts

103

Pablo Picasso

Study for "Couple in a Café" and Other Studies, 1903. Pen and sepia ink on paper, 13.5 x 9 cm. Museu Picasso, Barcelona (MPB 110.482)

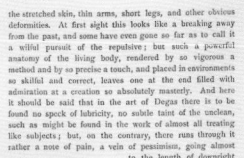

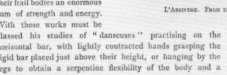

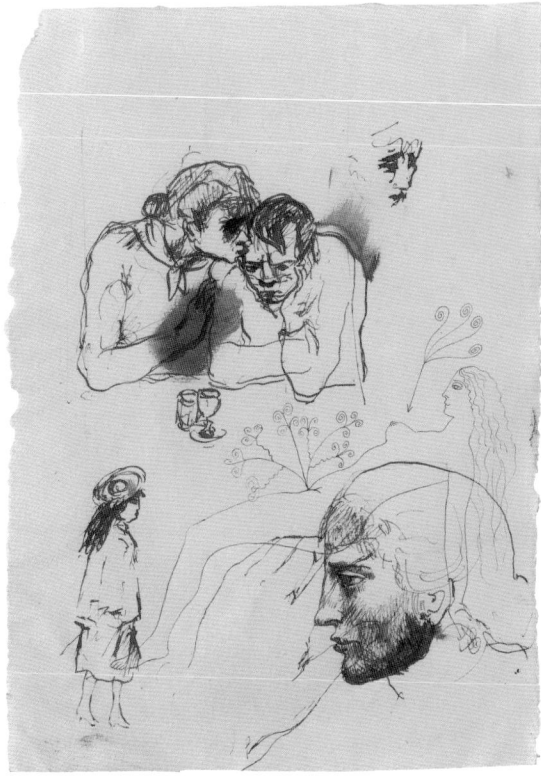

a lone beer drinker, *Le Bon Bock*, was even called "charming" by a reviewer in 1873.[97] Around 1870, Degas had used some sketchbook drawings made in a Paris café as the basis for his intriguing but somewhat uncharacteristic little painting on paper *At the Café Châteaudun* (**101**).[98] Here the scene is mundane and exclusively masculine, as two gentlemen fussily consult a newspaper in a brightly lit room and disregard the protocol of ordering refreshments. Within three years, however, Degas passed beyond the anecdotal quality of this picture in a much larger work that would become the classic statement of a newly defined genre. Initially entitled *Dans un Café* but now also known as *L'Absinthe* (see 104), it was completed in the spring of 1876 and added to his list of potential submissions for the second Impressionist exhibition.[99] The subsequent history of *In a Café* was complicated by the almost two decades the painting spent in British private collections, when it created a

scandal and shocked one critic with "the disgusting novelty of its subject."[100] In 1893, the canvas was bought by Isaac de Camondo and displayed in his Paris home, to be bequeathed to the Louvre in 1908. For Picasso's generation, the accessibility of *L'Absinthe* in Paris at the turn of the century was crucial. Not only was it seen by visitors to Camondo's collection, but this increasingly notorious work was described as "a masterpiece" by Théodore Duret and subsequently cited as "one of the most well-known works of Degas."[101] In his important article of 1894, in which *In a Café* was reproduced in black and white (**102**), Duret was frank about the questionable nature of Degas's composition, "a study of . . . two people from a class of shady individuals who spend their lives in the cafés of Paris, trifling away their days."[102]

When Picasso took on the challenge of *In a Café* in the early twentieth century, he chose to raise his private, often small-scale engagement with Degas to a public contest of the most

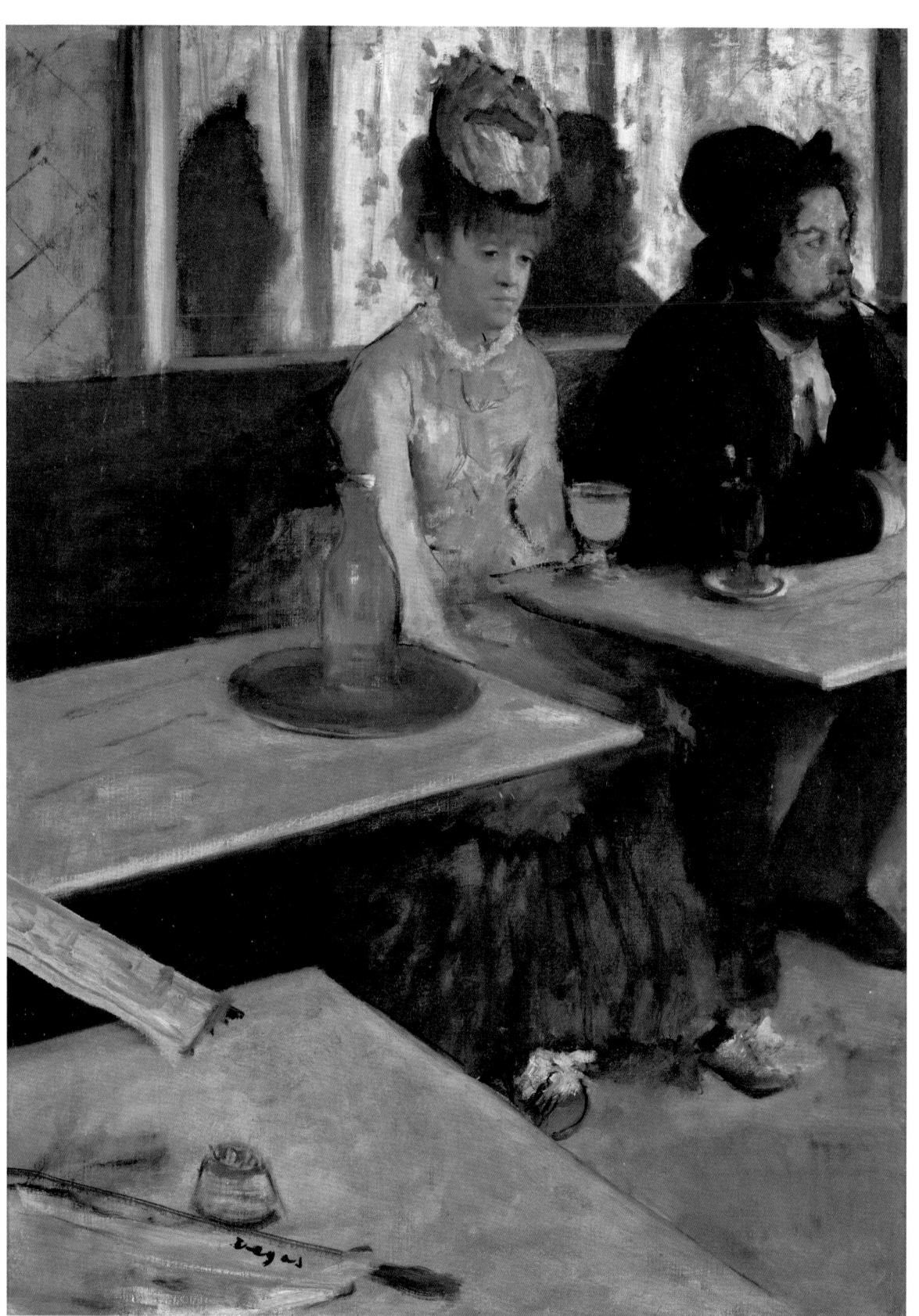

104

Edgar Degas

In a Café (L'Absinthe),
1875–76. Oil on canvas,
92 x 68.5 cm. Musée
d'Orsay, Paris. Bequest of
Count Isaac de Camondo,
1911 (RF 1984)

105

Pablo Picasso

*Portrait of Sebastià
Junyer i Vidal*, 1903.
Oil on canvas,
126.4 x 94 cm.
Los Angeles County
Museum of Art.
David E. Bright Bequest
(M.67.25.18)

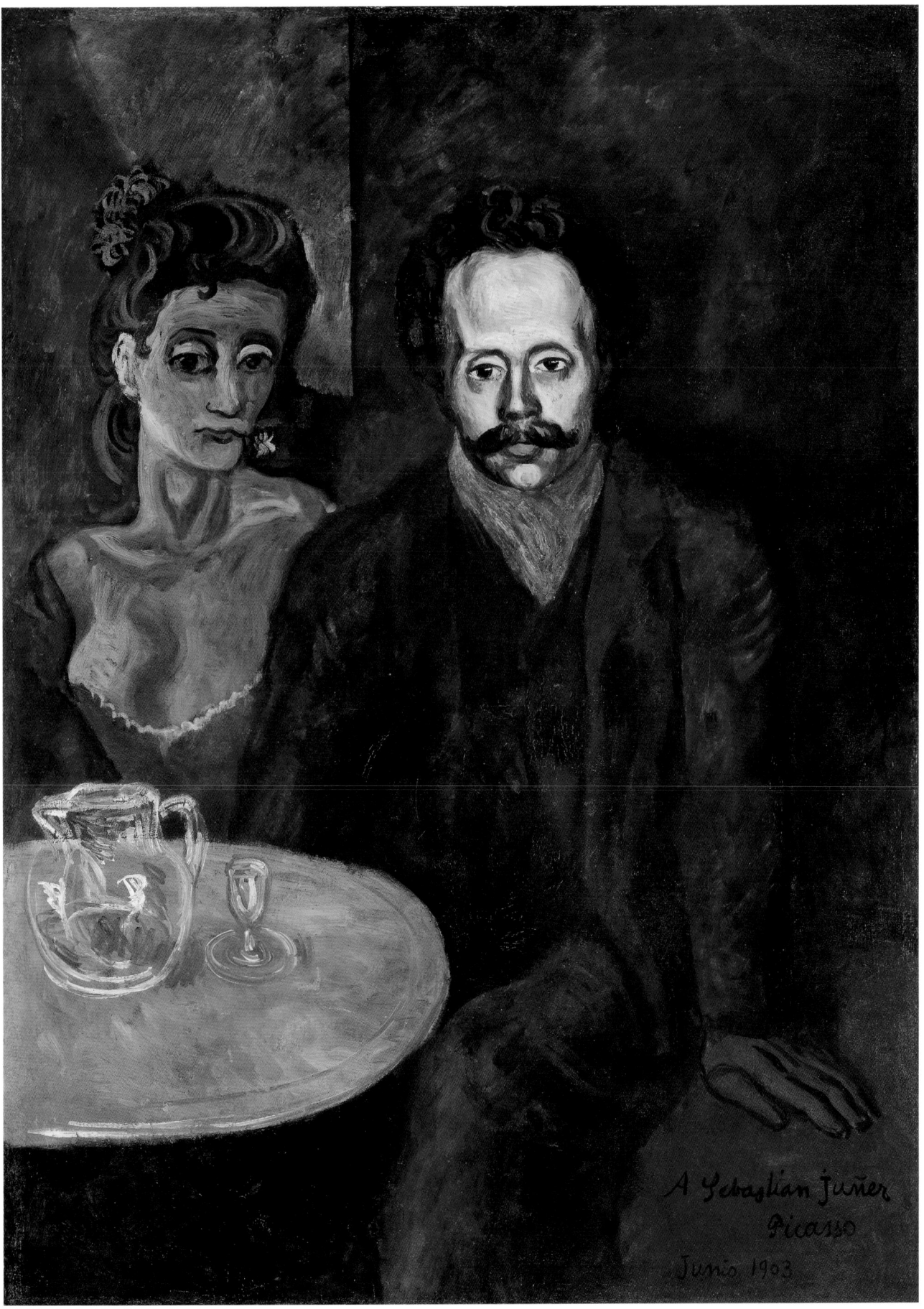

specific kind. In a sequence of variants he tackled the human drama, the pictorial dynamic, and the distinctive setting of Degas's painting with great deliberation, but — just as importantly — confronted its status as one of Degas's acknowledged masterworks. Sabartés remembered how Picasso would become obsessed by another artist's picture: "He would analyze it minutely, penetrate to its heart and tear it out, the better to understand its beat."[103] A few small sketches on paper (103) show Picasso's determined approach to one variant of this motif and reveal his analytical, competitive mind in action. In the much larger *Portrait of Sebastià Junyer i Vidal*, he opted for a broad restatement of Degas's *In a Café* with its dark-clad male figure at right and a paler image of his female companion at left (104). Responding to the latter, a "shady individual" who would probably have been seen as sexually available in the Paris of 1876, Picasso chose to be explicit, introducing the "scrawny prostitute" whose identity is unknown (105). His presentation of the heavily mustachioed man beside her may have been more calculated: Degas's own model was the printmaker and occasional writer Marcellin Desboutin, for whom Picasso substituted a close equivalent from his own circle, a minor artist turned journalist. Though Picasso spelled out these similarities very frankly, Sabartés was surely right in insisting that he "would never copy anybody."[104] Unlike Degas's indolent daytime drinkers, the two characters in Barcelona are surrounded by impenetrable darkness, from which they peer steadily and almost disconcertingly back at the viewer. Where Desboutin and his consort — her "dull eyes in vacant thought," in Duret's phrase[105] — seem bored or distracted, Picasso's models are direct, even confrontational. In almost every sense, this is a more unequivocal and aggressive painting than Degas's, though not necessarily the knock-out blow that Picasso had planned. Technical examination has revealed many compositional

changes during the painting of this canvas and the likelihood that the prostitute was added at the last minute, though the artist signed and dated the work with a flourish at lower right.[106]

In a comparably ambitious project undertaken during these same years, Picasso adopted the theme of the laundress and began "analyzing it minutely" as he again prepared to compete with his predecessor on a large scale. The laundress had become even more well known as Degas's territory, from its first appearance around 1869 to his repeated revisitations of the subject over the following decades, the last in the mid-1890s. In this sporadic series Degas created at least a dozen substantial variants in oil and pastel, each exploring single or paired women laboring at their ironing tables and slaking their thirst from large bottles.[107] Some of these pictures attracted comment at the Impressionist shows of the 1870s and quickly found buyers, among them several works that remained in Paris private collections at the end of the century. A prominent figure in this process was Paul Durand-Ruel, who handled no less than four laundress paintings across the years and still owned three when Picasso came to the city.[108] Camondo acquired just one (106), a study in oil paint on unprimed canvas that is now famous for its tactile surface and for the grittiness of the scene it represents, with one woman slumped over her iron and another leaning back in exhaustion. Adding to the visibility of these pictures was the representation in printed form of three variants of Degas's laundress compositions before 1900: the first in Duret's 1894 article, the second chosen by Degas himself for the 1898 Manzi portfolio (see 92), and a third printed in Max Liebermann's book on the artist that was published in 1899 (107).[109] In principle, Picasso and his friends had access to all three of these images, as well as the four canvases belonging to Camondo and Durand-Ruel, and perhaps others passing through galleries and sale rooms.

106

Edgar Degas

Women Ironing, 1884–86. Oil on canvas, 76 x 81 cm. Musée d'Orsay, Paris (RF 1985)

107

Edgar Degas

Women Ironing. Reproduced in Max Liebermann, *Degas* (Berlin: Bruno and Paul Cassirer, 1899), p. 24. Courtesy Sterling and Francine Clark Art Institute, Williamstown, Massachusetts

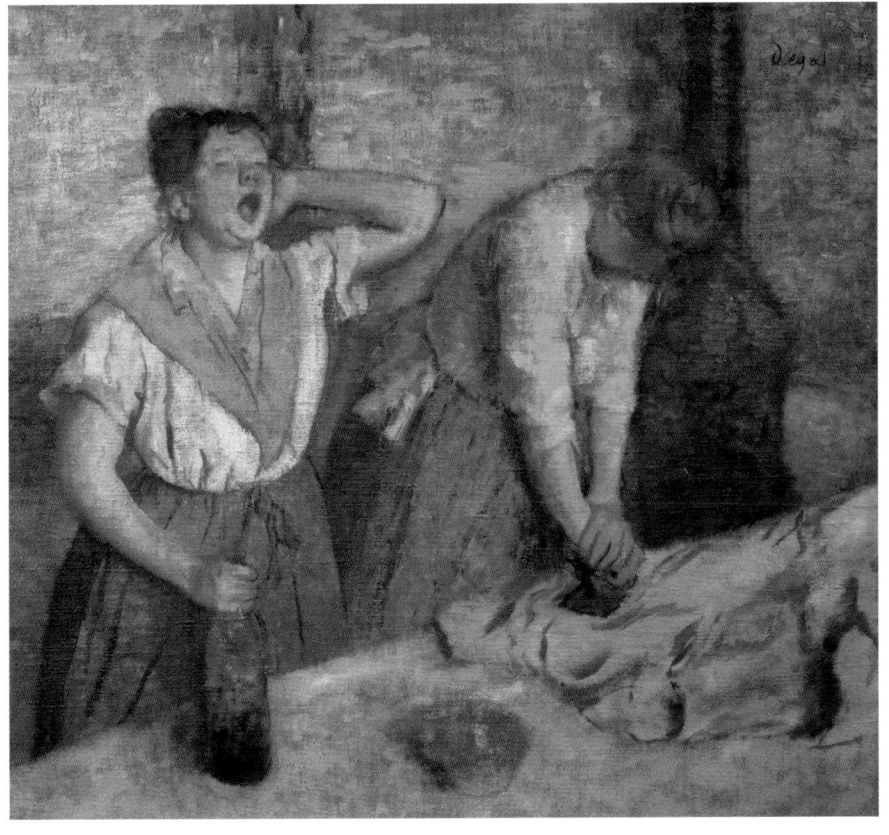

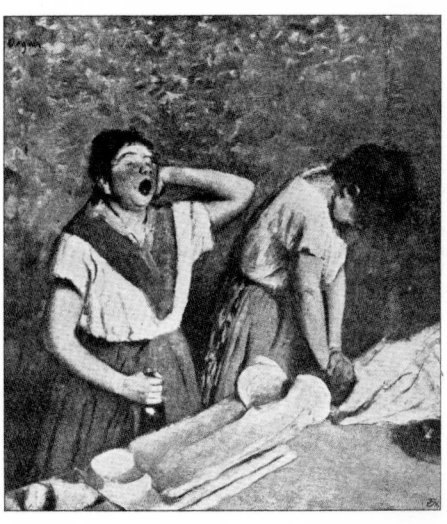

108

Pablo Picasso

Study for "Woman Ironing," 1904.

Pen and ink on paper,

37 x 26.9 cm.

Musée national Picasso,

Paris (MP 480)

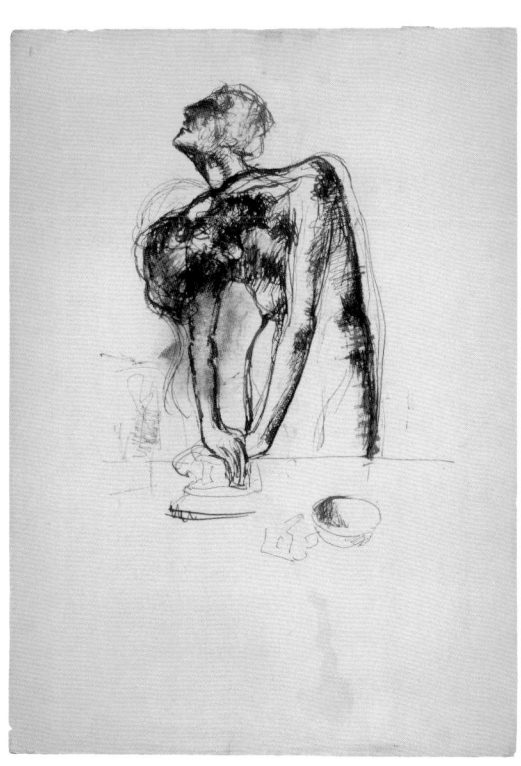

Picasso's first response to this formidable precedent was a small, dark painting of a woman ironing that he completed in 1901 and dedicated to Sabartés.[110] Here the model is shown hunched forward like Blanche in *The Blue Room* but now struggling in a cramped, dismal room. Three years later, Picasso opted to carry the challenge to a much higher level as he prepared for another epic struggle with Degas, selecting a canvas that was almost as large as that used for *Portrait of Sebastià Junyer i Vidal*. This time we know that the painting was rehearsed on paper, in a pen-and-ink study that shows two figures who have become curiously merged (**108**). The woman who strains her head upward as if in exhaustion or despair was defined first, then partly concealed by the second character who almost slumps over her iron.[111] Both of the poses that these women adopt are exaggerated variants of laundress

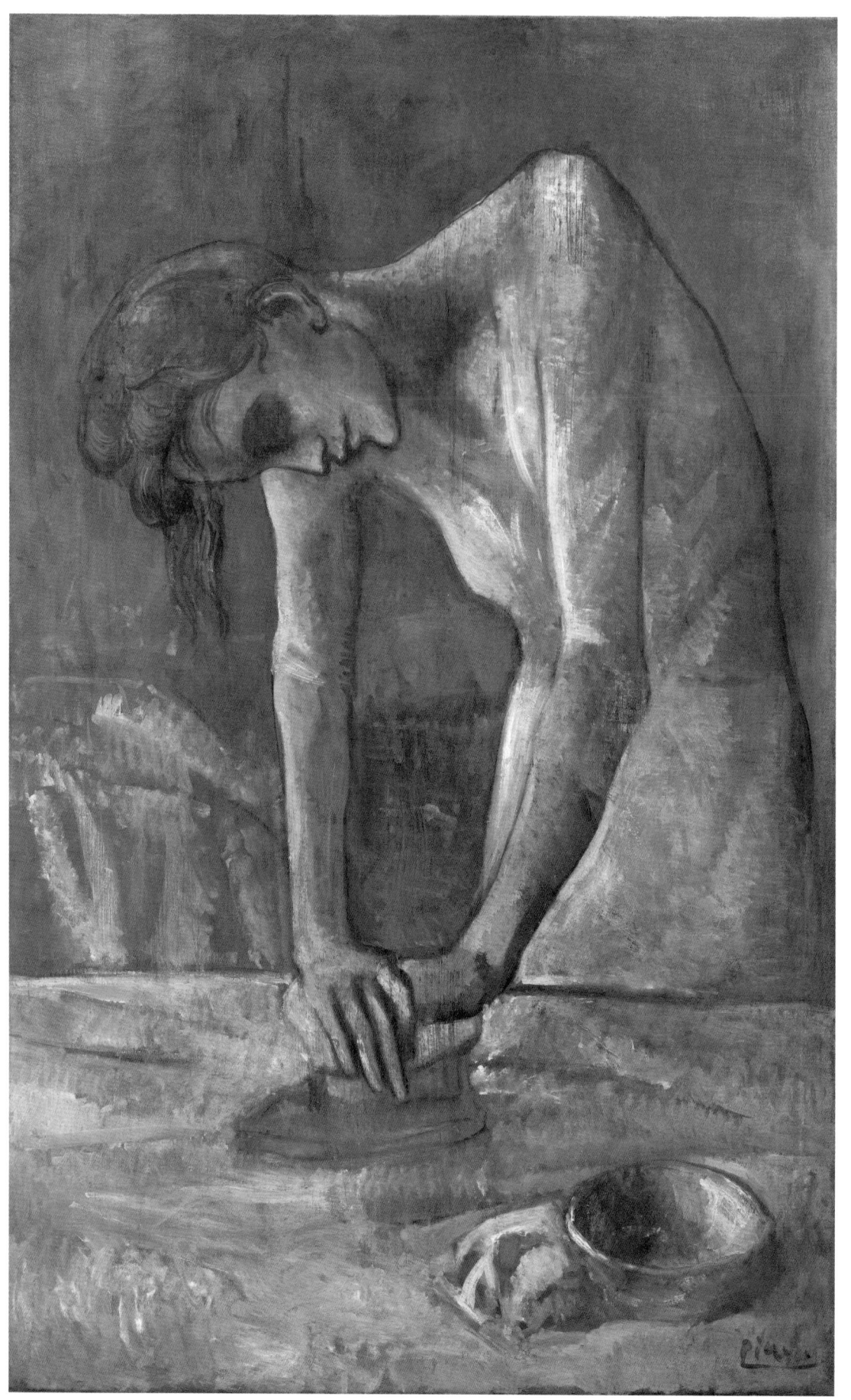

109

Pablo Picasso

Woman Ironing, 1904. Oil on canvas, 116.2 x 73 cm. Solomon R. Guggenheim Museum, New York. Thannhauser Collection, Gift, Justin K. Thannhauser, 1978 (78.2514.41)

110

Edgar Degas

Woman Ironing, 1876–87. Oil on canvas, 81.3 x 66 cm. National Gallery of Art, Washington, D.C. Collection of Mr. and Mrs. Paul Mellon (1972.74.1)

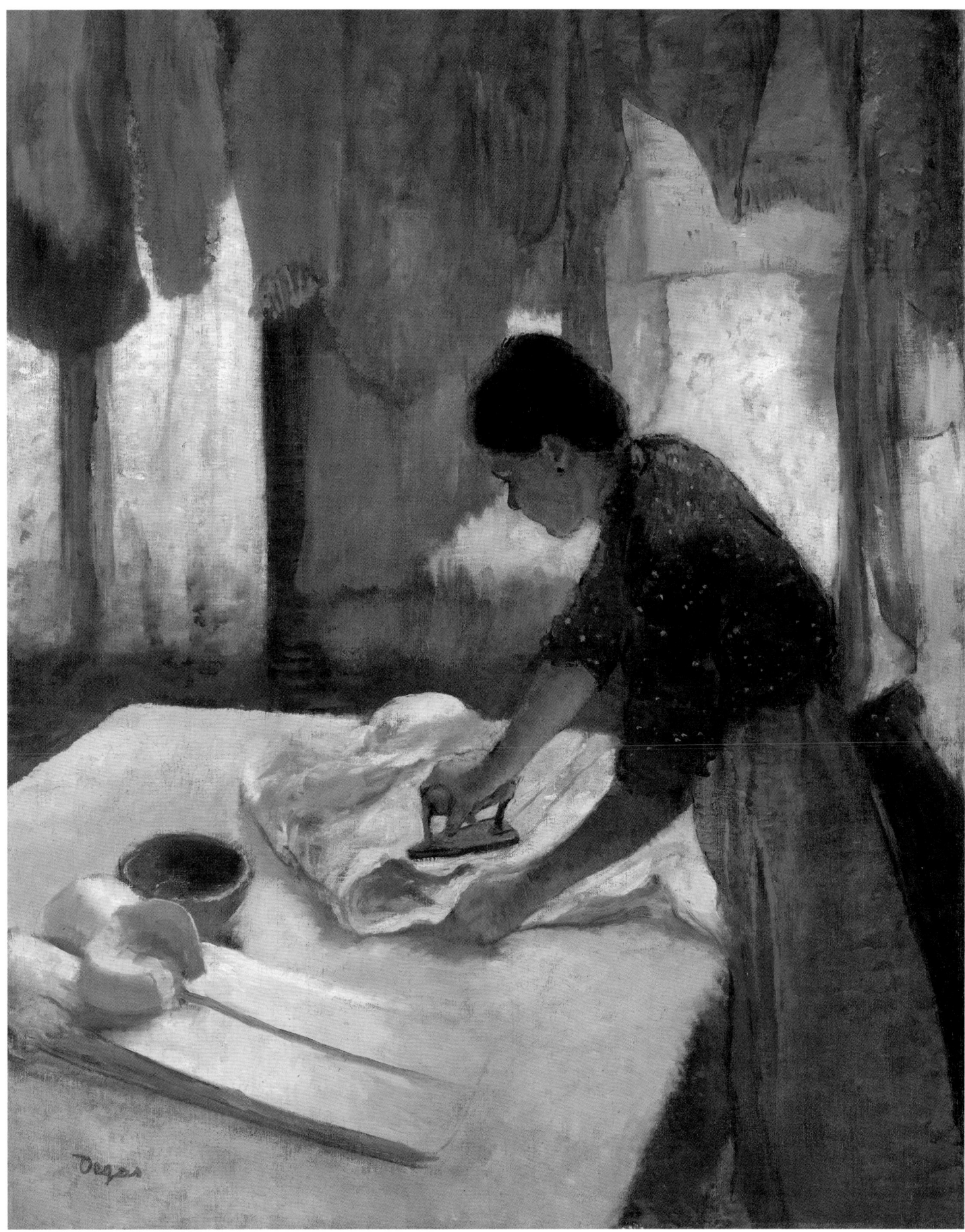

figures in pictures by Degas, in each case accessible to Picasso at this date. Citing the position used by Degas in several of his laundry scenes, in which a woman yawns and rests from her work, Picasso tipped the head of the background figure further and elongated her neck. In a similar way, his foreground laundress drops her head even lower than the equivalent individuals leaning over their ironing in Degas's pictures, emphasizing the emaciation of her body.

As he turned to his canvas, Picasso chose to concentrate on the most prominent of the two women in the drawing and further accentuate the physical labor demanded of her profession (**109**). This figure now tilts forward like many of Degas's laundresses and her hands grip the iron in a remarkably similar way, yet her gaunt appearance contrasts sharply with that of her predecessors. Seen beside Degas's variously muscular or amply fed individuals, Picasso's model appears frankly undernourished and perhaps consumptive. In this and many other features of his picture, Picasso demonstrated that he had not only grasped Degas's visual and thematic vocabulary but moved beyond it, making *Woman Ironing* into his own distinct creation and using it as a vehicle for his own current concerns. The work by Degas that it most resembles illustrates this polarity, sharing several aspects of the design and physical character of Picasso's *Woman Ironing*, while representing its virtual opposite as a finished statement. This painting, now in the National Gallery of Art in Washington, D.C. (**110**), belongs to a minority of Degas's laundress compositions as a representation of a single figure. As in Picasso's *Woman Ironing*, a solitary, blue-and-white-clad laundress works alone at a broad expanse of table, her figure dominating the pictorial rectangle and drawing our attention to the powerful action of her hands on the iron. Less apparent in reproduction are the physical similarities between these two canvases: an irregular reddish-brown

underlayer in the Washington picture was probably the result of reworking by Degas over several years, yet a comparable tinted substratum can also be detected in the Picasso and accounts for the hint of warmth within its steely grays. Elizabeth Cowling has also pointed out that the "chalky texture" of Picasso's *Woman Ironing* makes it look "as if it might have been executed in charcoal and pastel," further extending its resemblance to Degas's images of this motif on paper.[112] Beyond these common features, however, Degas's composition retains its identity as a scene of Parisian street life, while his follower's variant aspires to and arguably achieves a greater universality. The possibility that Picasso's image was an oblique act of homage to the Washington work by Degas nevertheless remains. The latter picture passed through several hands in the later nineteenth century but was in Durand-Ruel's possession by 1898 and stayed in his family for several decades.[113] Picasso's familiarity with this picture is thus historically plausible as well as visually suggestive: even his somewhat unexpected decision to include a well-defined water bowl at lower right in *Woman Ironing* points to the same conclusion. Though such bowls appear in several other Degas versions of this theme, they are notably less articulated or less prominent than that in the National Gallery painting.

Manifestly a response to Degas, *Woman Ironing* — like so many of Picasso's pictures at this period — was also a testimony to other figures in his established and rapidly growing pantheon. The attenuated features of his model have been linked with El Greco's saints, but the chalky palette of the picture might equally derive from a Puvis de Chavannes mural, such as those that Picasso had admired from afar in Barcelona and could now see firsthand in Paris. More challenging in this respect is the steeply angled ironing table, which seems to push against the body of the laundress and almost flatten her against the background wall. Defying the perspective traditions of several centuries of European art, this device is especially jarring beside the spatial orderliness of Degas's ironing scenes, as exemplified in the Washington canvas. Such extreme departures in these years remind us of Picasso's simultaneous interest in artists as different as Gauguin and Cézanne, both of them the focus of growing cults in Paris and both of profound importance to Picasso's unfolding career. He was also capable of startling regression, as in a 1904 pastel known as *The Ironer's Room*, where an almost illustrational manner describes furniture and domestic accessories in banal detail.[114] Such an output could baffle his past supporters but exhilarate the most intrepid of Picasso's new admirers. Among these was the Stein family, led by the writer Gertrude Stein and her brother Leo, who is said to have made his mark as a fearless collector by buying Picasso's work at Berthe Weill's gallery.[115] While the story of their early support for his Blue Period works has often been told, the parallel role of Leo Stein as a proponent of Degas is largely unknown. Leo had formerly studied art in Paris and at that time bought Manzi's portfolio *Degas: Vingt Dessins, 1861–1896*, which he eagerly showed to those around him.[116] Leo and Gertude also added to their collection an unidentified Degas entitled *After the Bath* as Leo tirelessly promoted the Impressionist's importance as a modern artist.[117] Asserting that "the big four are Manet, Renoir, Degas and Cézanne," he claimed Degas as "incomparably the greatest master of composition of our times," as well as an exemplar "of movement of line, with a colossal feeling for form and superb color."[118] As Degas has so often been marginalized in accounts of this period, it is at least refreshing to find his work discussed in this new, proto-formalist language at the heart of the Parisian avant-garde. Perhaps because of the artist's anti-Semitism, however, the Steins gradually stepped back from such fierce advocacy of

his work while their friends, the Cone sisters of Baltimore, continued to include Degas amongst their collection of Picassos and Matisses.[119]

Fernande and Benedetta

Early in the Steins' friendship with Picasso, he brought his new and rather nervous lover, Fernande Olivier, to meet them at their Paris home and marvel at their picture-filled walls; as well as works by Cézanne and Picasso, "an El Greco; some Renoirs . . . two fine Matisses, one Vallotton" were noted by Fernande.[120] In time, Fernande felt at ease with the Steins, attaching her greetings to Picasso's letters to his new patrons and apologizing for his "more or less fantastical French."[121] During the tempestuous decline of her relationship with Picasso, she confided in Gertrude and asked for help in raising money by giving French lessons.[122] Fernande had begun her life in the city as a young model, working for artists both famous and obscure who included several from Degas's generation, among them Alfred Cormon, Charles Carolus-Duran, Jean-Jacques Henner, and Alfred Roll. Now she was posing for Picasso and becoming a popular presence in the casual world of the Bateau Lavoir, a ramshackle cluster of studios in Montmartre with a shifting population of French and Spanish men and women, artists, writers and — according to Fernande — laundresses.[123] Situated within a five-minute walk of Degas's apartment, Picasso and his friends would occasionally encounter the older generation on their doorstep. According to Maurice Raynal, who was then an aspiring artist, "Though sometimes from the windows of the studios in the Bateau Lavoir we watched Degas or Renoir coming up or going down the steps that led to it, the idea of getting to know them personally never crossed our minds."[124] Instead, they sometimes indulged in vulgar games, "doing Degas" by imitating the old gentleman's dignified manner while "he" delivered a stream of obscenities aimed at their own pictures; according to his

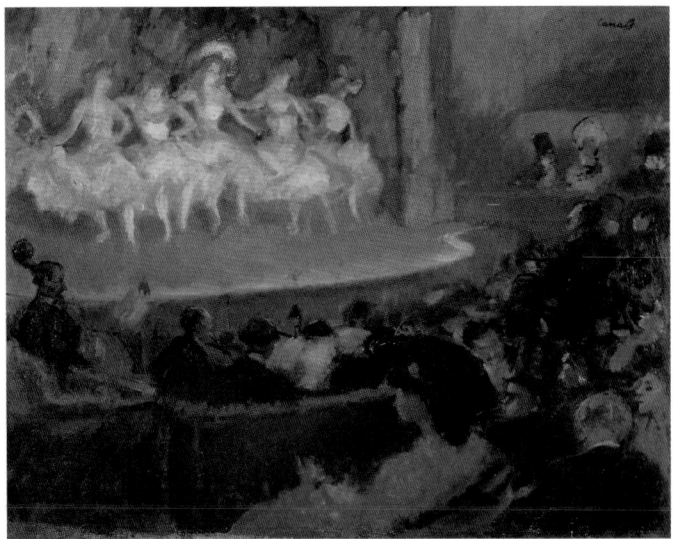

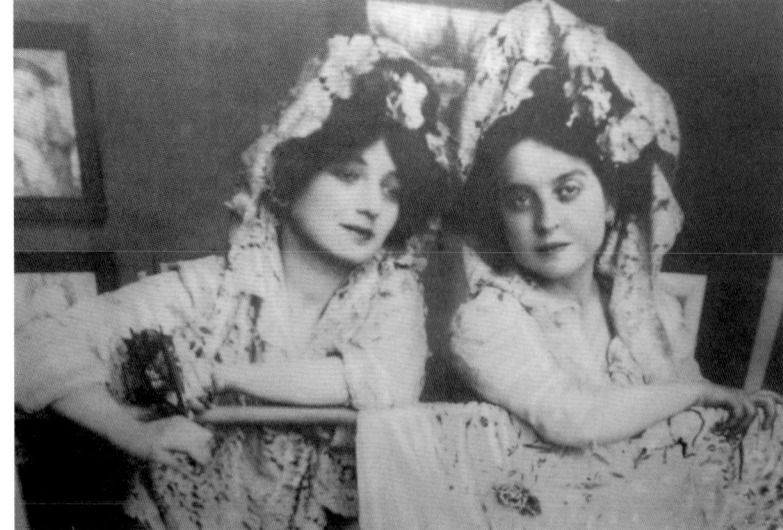

close friend André Salmon, Picasso was "enchanted" by this farce.[125]

Fernande soon moved in with Picasso and met his anarchic circle, joining him at the dinners in Vollard's basement where Degas had once sat, his place now taken by Redon, Matisse, and their peers.[126] Attached to the group around Picasso was now another colleague from Barcelona days, the painter Ricard Canals. Canals had accompanied Nonell to Paris in 1897 and rapidly fallen under the influence of Degas's toilette and bather scenes, attracting the support of Durand-Ruel, who showed his work in New York in 1902.[127] He was currently painting cabarets and music-halls (111), and sometimes his strikingly good-looking Italian wife, formerly Benedetta Coletti. "Life at the Canals is delightful," Fernande wrote in her *Souvenirs intimes*, recalling her first welcome from the "beautiful, redhead[ed]" Benedetta.[128] Soon close friends, the two women shared a history of professional modeling, which included posing for Degas and his sculptor friend, Bartholomé. Unlike some other models and those familiar with Degas's studio, Benedetta left behind no recollections of these experiences, of the years when she posed, or the works for which she had modeled. But it was presumably in this capacity

that she and Fernande made a memorable expedition: "I visited Degas's studio with Benedetta Canals, who used to model for him," Fernande noted in 1904, "he's not painting at the moment but is working on small statuettes from his model S. V. [Suzanne Valadon]. . . . He's a strange old man, with a tough, sarcastic quality that comes from his strength, and a kindness that comes from his humility."[129]

Nothing more was recorded about their interview with Degas, though we might assume that observations of this kind made at 37, rue Victor Massé were of some interest to Canals, Picasso, and the company at the Bateau Lavoir. Neither does Picasso seem to have attempted a similar visit, just as he kept his distance from Cézanne, Pissarro, and Monet in their final years, though he later tried to see Bonnard.[130] Benedetta's history with the "strange old man" living nearby, however, does seem to have stimulated Picasso's sense of rivalry. As Pierre Daix has suggested, Picasso may have deliberately planned a picture of his friend's wife "that would eclipse all those for which she had posed," presumably including the unidentified works by Degas.[131] One of these previous efforts was that painted by Canals himself, showing Benedetta with Fernande in Spanish mantillas at a *corrida*, a

111
Ricard Canals
(Spanish, 1876–1931)
Café-Concert, 1903. Oil on canvas, 50 x 65.8 cm. Museu Nacional d'Art de Catalunya, Barcelona (MAM 65624)

112
Benedetta Canals and Fernande Olivier in Spanish costume. Collection of Gilbert Krill

113
Pablo Picasso
Portrait of Benedetta Canals, 1905. Oil and charcoal on canvas, 90 x 69.5 cm. Museu Picasso, Barcelona (MPB 4.266)

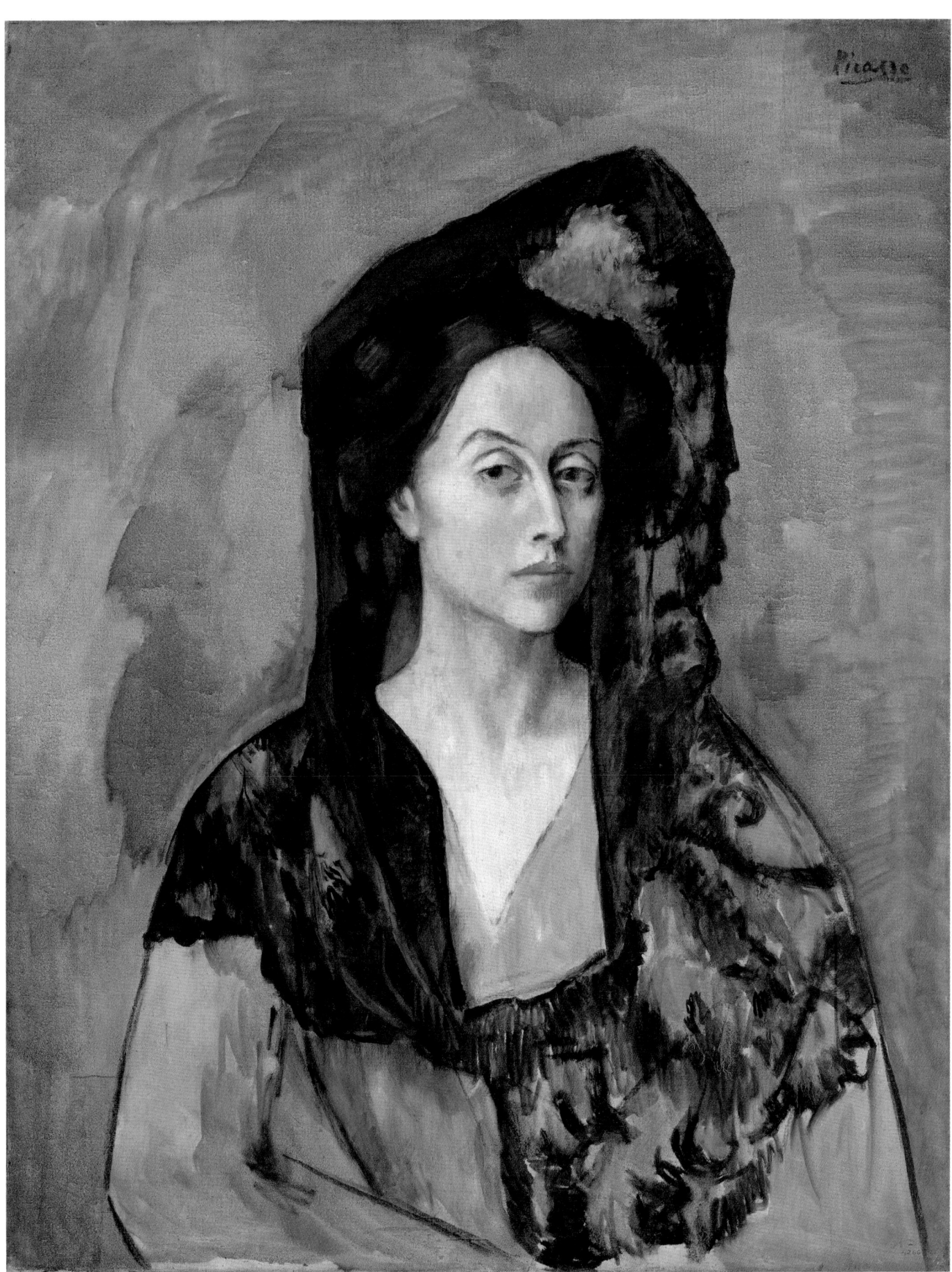

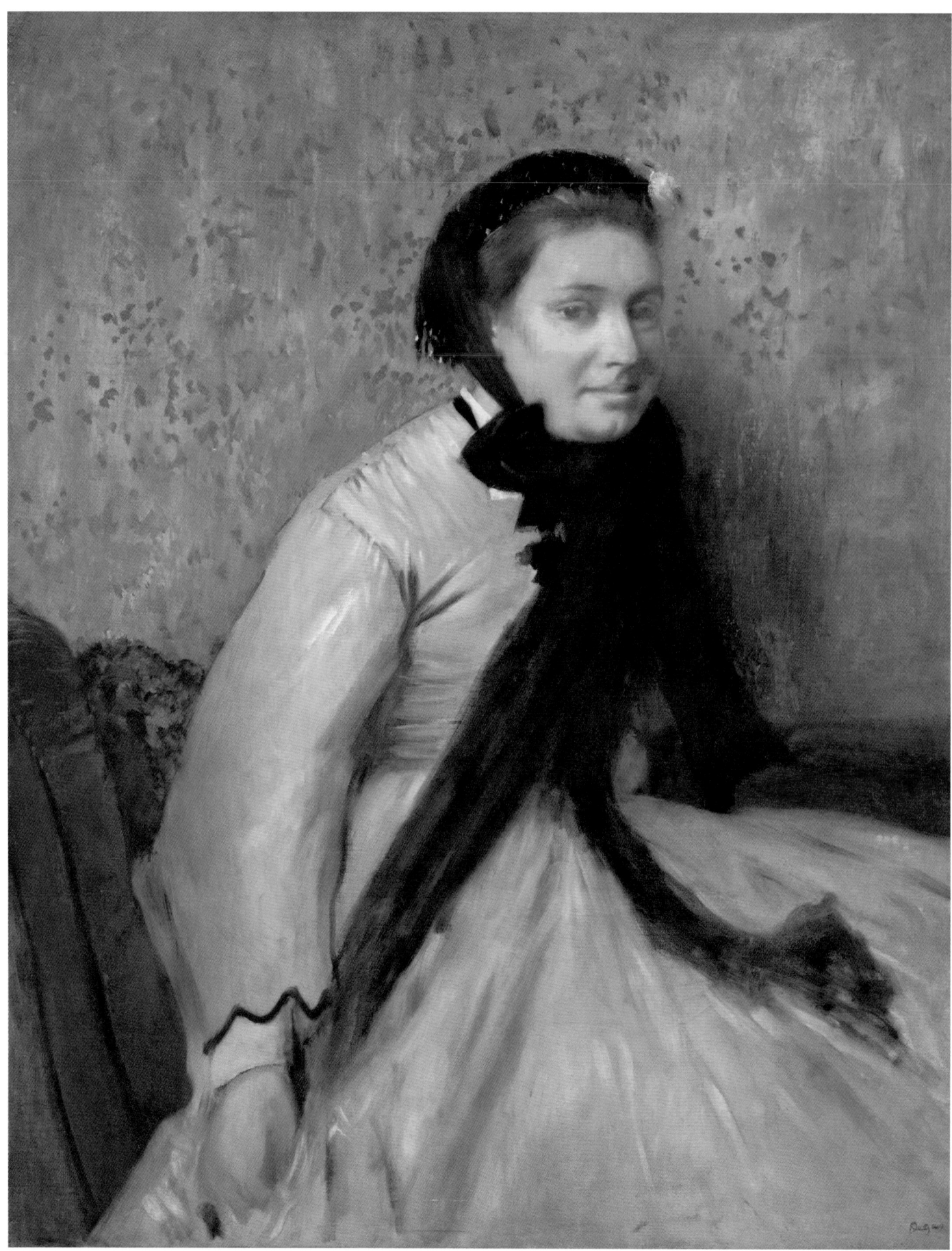

114

Edgar Degas

Portrait of a Woman in Gray, c. 1865. Oil on canvas, 91.4 x 72.4 cm. The Metropolitan Museum of Art, New York. Gift of Mr. and Mrs. Edwin C. Vogel, 1957 (57.171)

115

Edgar Degas

Woman with an Umbrella (Berthe Jeantaud), c. 1876. Oil on canvas, 61 x 50.2 cm. National Gallery of Canada, Ottawa. Purchased 1969 (inv. no. 15838)

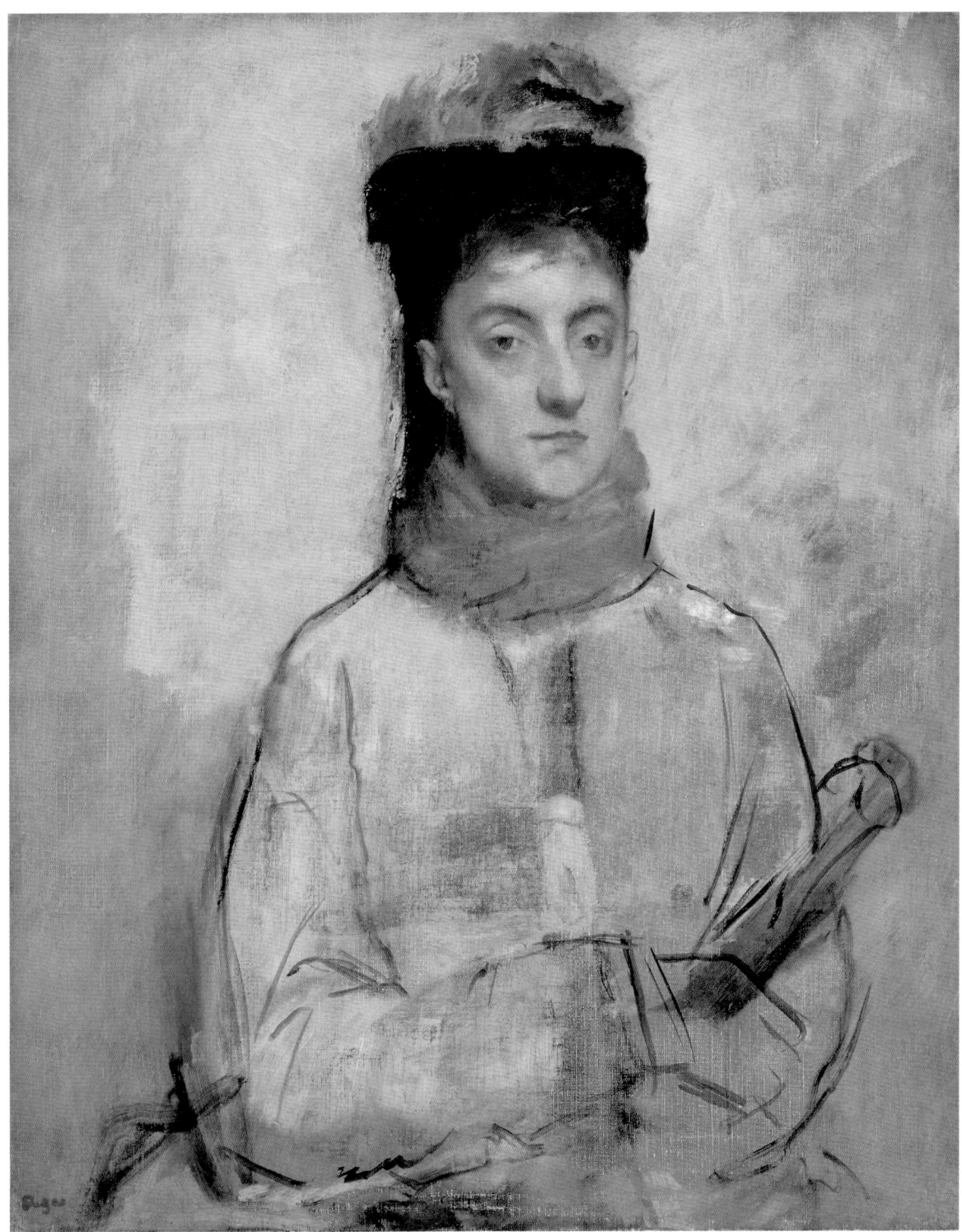

moderately distinguished work that was partly derived from a photograph (112). Unlike his previous assaults on *L'Absinthe* and *Woman Ironing*, Picasso's justly celebrated *Portrait of Benedetta Canals* (113) — which pointedly shows her in a mantilla — is unashamedly fresh and sensuous, a tribute to his subject's elegance and her gracious disposition. Carried out in fine veils of naturalistic color and delicate passages of texture, this work also parts company with the physical character of his earlier ripostes to Degas. Almost the same width as *Woman Ironing* but not as tall, the airy canvas of 1905 seems spacious where the preceding work is claustrophobic, rhythmic where the Guggenheim picture is angular. Again Picasso proved to be a man of the moment, favoring the pinkish palette that he used throughout much of this year but minimizing the moodiness of his harlequins and the exaggeratedly slender limbs of his circus performers. Yet the spirit of El Greco still hovers a little over Benedetta, in the slim, tapering features that contrast markedly with her appearance in the Canals photograph. On this occasion, Picasso embraced a relatively straightforward realism, perhaps anxious to measure up to Degas's portraits of his own acquaintances.

Attempts to identify Benedetta among the many hundreds of Degas's figure studies from the turn of the century have proved fruitless, since most of the dancers and bathers who dominated his art during this period are essentially anonymous. What remains, however, is her role among those with access to Degas's premises and specifically as a conduit between Degas and the "Bande à Picasso." As we know from photographs and verbal accounts, a notable aspect of Degas's apartment and studio was the presence of many works of portraiture, with pictures of his own hanging beside examples by his peers and illustrious forebears.[132] Still a relatively unsung facet of his achievement at this date, portraiture had featured

prominently in Degas's early years and appeared in most of his public exhibitions, but had yet to be appropriately represented in major collections. Among the several hundreds of canvases stored beneath his roof were many that embodied his successes in the genre, as well as those marking his frustrations. *Portrait of a Woman in Gray* (114), for example, is a vivid demonstration of Degas's achievement in the mid-1860s, a sympathetic attempt to capture the soft, mobile features of an anonymous sitter as she poses in her stylish outfit. Almost the same size as *Portrait of Benedetta Canals*, Degas's painting has a richer surface but makes a similar play with the woman's black, gauzy scarf as a foil to her pale dress, hinting at the vogue for Spanish costume in these years. The modernity of this image is unmistakable, in its broad informality and the way in which the woman appears to have settled fleetingly on a couch before rushing back to the streets of Paris. The smaller but no less compelling *Woman with an Umbrella (Berthe Jeantaud)* (115) is clearly less finished and also remained with the artist until his death. Like Picasso's picture of Benedetta, Degas chose to depict this subject frontally and almost symmetrically, suggesting an encounter with a strong personality and perhaps some kind of unstated challenge. Nothing is known of the circumstances in which the painting — which is believed to represent the wife of one of Degas's friends — was left incomplete, except that the canvas had already been used to sketch out an earlier and quite different likeness.[133] For those visitors to Degas's apartment who may have seen it around 1900, the strong modeling of the face, the crisp, vibrant brushwork, and contrasting passages of detail and imprecision may have seemed more appropriate to their own times than to the mid-1870s, when it is thought to have been painted. Degas has sacrificed everything, it seems, to the imperative need to pin down this rather severe personality. As hap-

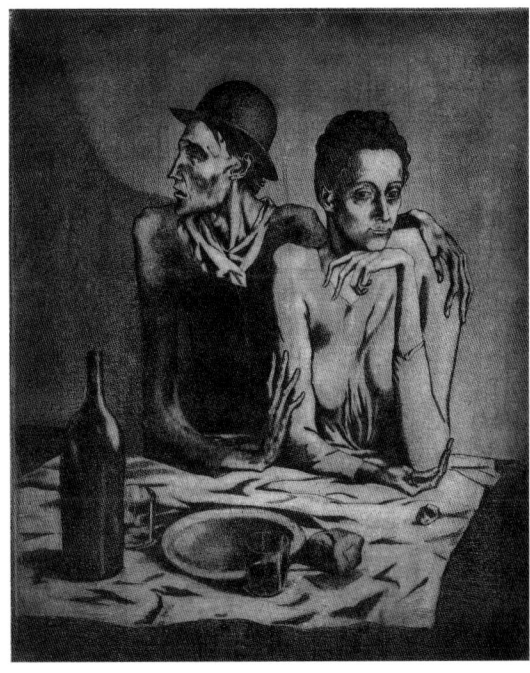

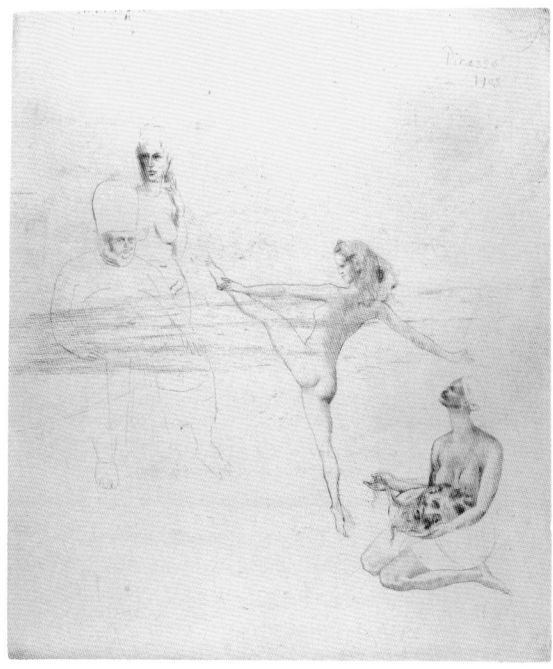

pened before and would occur again, either the artist's own dissatisfaction with his picture or a dispute with the lady in question had probably brought the process to an end.

After painting *Woman Ironing* and *Portrait of Benedetta Canals*, Picasso continued his dialogue with Degas's art more obliquely and often on a smaller scale. In the summer of 1904, he had returned briefly to both Degas's *In a Café* and *Woman Ironing* in a single image, that of his first etching, *The Frugal Repast* (**116**). Now Degas's "shady characters" in a Parisian café have become long-fingered destitutes seated at a deep table with the ironers' signature wine bottle and water bowl in front of them. Ricard Canals helped Picasso with the unfamiliar technique, and Fernande remembered that it was followed by another print, "a drypoint, Salomé dancing before Herod," in which a naked, muscular Salomé performs a frankly indecent *battement* in front of the diminutive ruler (**117**).[134] This whimsical choice of subject is perhaps best understood in the context of Picasso's current passion for the circus, expressed among other ways in rapid drawings of bareback riders and

trapeze artists who can seem indistinguishable from ballet dancers.[135] As Picasso must have known, Degas's later dance pictures and lithographs were typically begun from nude models in his studio, a situation recycled here by Picasso as a titillating display. The acrobat-dancers that intrigued Picasso may well have been studied at the Cirque Medrano, once known as the Cirque Fernando, a permanent place of entertainment in Montmartre that had briefly attracted Degas more than two decades earlier. In his spectacular 1879 oil painting *Miss La La at the Cirque Fernando*, Degas showed the performer suspended by her teeth high above the audience, a challenge to the artist's skills that might have tested even Picasso.[136] Degas's canvas was briefly in Durand-Ruel's hands in 1904, potentially adding to the hundreds of works by the older master that Picasso had now become acquainted with.[137] By this date, it is clear that Degas's imagery was an established and familiar part of his thinking, though some subjects — the bather, the woman at her toilette, and the dancer — would still return to haunt him over the decades.

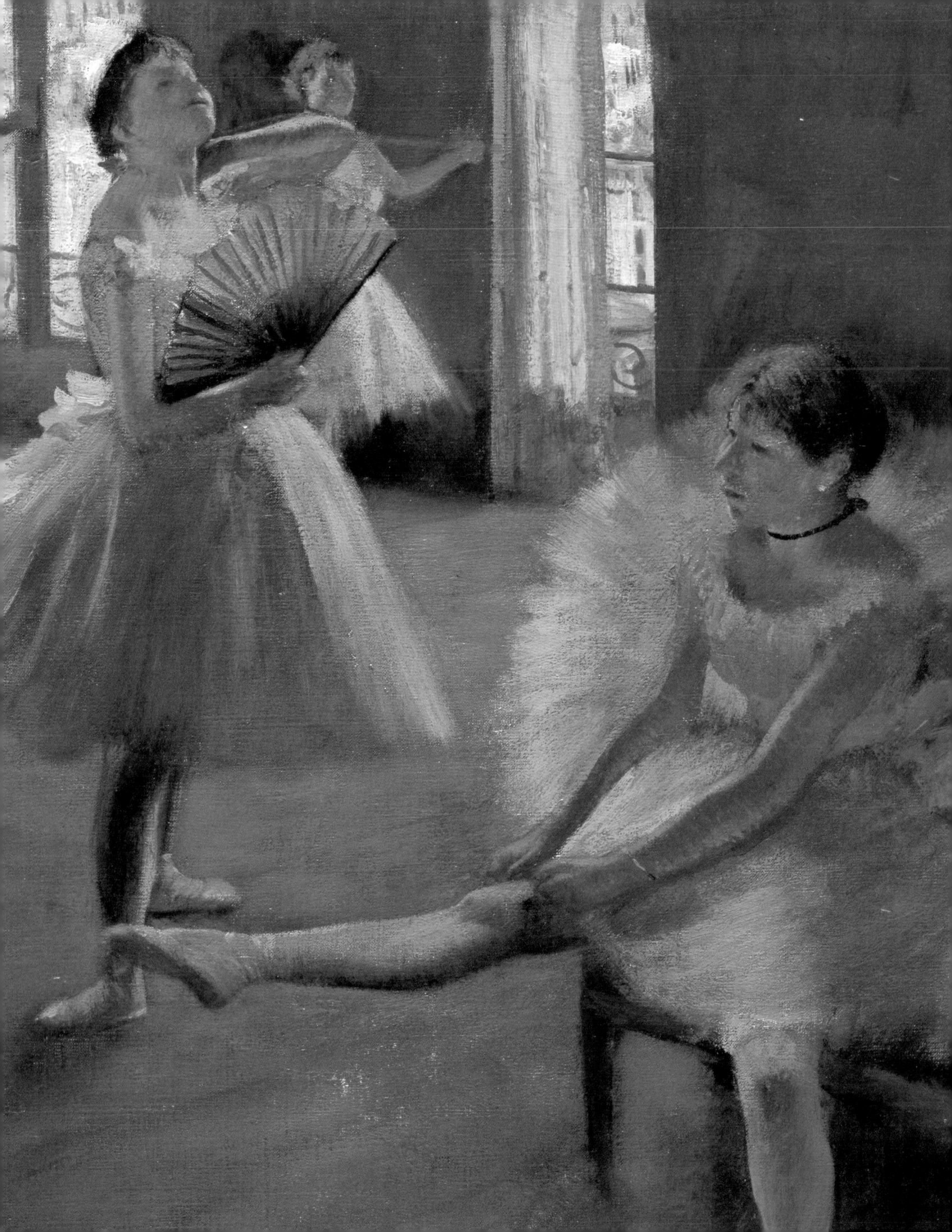

CHAPTER 3

THE BALLET: "WORK, PLEASURE AND VICE"

RICHARD KENDALL

In 1917, two entirely separate events took place that would open a new chapter in Picasso's relationship with Degas's art. Temporarily resident in Rome as he worked on Serge Diaghilev's theatrical extravaganza *Parade*, Picasso fell in love with Olga Khokhlova (**118**), an accomplished young ballerina who had been trained in Saint Petersburg.[1] Though they were not married until the following year, Olga soon became a conspicuous presence in Picasso's life and gradually appeared in his drawings and paintings (see 144, 149, 161, 300). Probably unknown to both of them, during these same months the health of the eighty-two-year-old Degas — often called "The Painter of Dancers" — was in serious decline in Paris: "He does not go out. He dreams, he eats, he sleeps," wrote one of his visitors.[2] On 28 September 1917, Degas died in his apartment on the Boulevard de Clichy in Montmartre, where he had lived since moving from the rue Victor Massé in 1912. Among the mourners at his funeral were aging colleagues from the Impressionist years, including Claude Monet and Mary Cassatt, and representatives of the two dealers who had consistently promoted his career, Joseph and Georges Durand-Ruel, and Ambroise Vollard. Within days of this gathering, preparations were underway for a series of enormous sales at which the accumulated work of Degas's career would be dispersed. Beginning in May 1918 and occurring sporadically until June 1919, some two thousand of the paintings and works on paper by Degas that

had been stored in his studio were shown in temporary displays in Paris and then sold. Suddenly much of his life's achievement was briefly accessible to the public, who turned out to see these unfamiliar pictures despite the grim continuation of the First World War. By this date, Picasso and Olga were also among the residents of the city: they were married in Paris on 12 July 1918, between the first and second auctions of Degas's estate.

One of the principal surprises of the Degas sales was the sheer quantity of his works devoted to the ballet, which accounted for more than a third of the total number of lots. This exceptional oeuvre embraced canvases from the large to the minute, drawings of dancers that dated from the beginning of his professional career and from his last active months, the pastels for which Degas was renowned, and many prints and monotypes of dance motifs that had remained largely unknown. Scattered through this abundance were a few of the earliest ballet pictures that had established his reputation as a dance artist, a process that almost coincided with the launch of Impressionism itself. At the first exhibition of the Impressionist collective in 1874, Degas had asserted his taste for this novel subject in scenes of a ballet classroom, a rehearsal on stage, and a view in the wings.[3] Over subsequent Impressionist shows he expanded this repertoire and developed its potential for visual innovation and topical commentary, with critics admiring the "absolute

Detail of Edgar Degas,
Dancers in the Classroom
(158)

reality" of his vision or scorning his "scattered and disorderly" compositions.[4] Exhibiting his drawings alongside other works, Degas also presented the individual dancers who posed in his studio, while in numerous pastels and occasional prints he explored their professional and private lives.

As the first artist in history to specialize in the ballet, Degas had knowingly engaged with an activity that was seen by many of his contemporaries to challenge the bounds of decency.[5] Dancers at the Paris Opéra — the prestigious theater in central Paris where Degas watched the ballet and sometimes went backstage — were rigorously taught and many achieved the highest technical standards. Some were also reputed to have "the lightest of morals" and exploited their glamorous profession to attract wealthy lovers.[6] By the 1880s, Degas had tackled this and almost every other aspect of the dance world, in brilliantly colored compositions of the great *étoiles* of the day in their moments of glory and tiny black-and-white monotypes that spelled out the flirtations of their colleagues. In a way that is hard to grasp after more than a century, he also managed to show the dancer as both a vulnerable individual and an emblematic figure of her times, created by a vast entertainment industry and alternately adored and vilified by her public. In later years, Degas's interests shifted from the spectacle itself toward small groups of anonymous dancers who typically rested or waited in the wings. Growing old with the artist, these figures had heavier limbs and indulged in fewer acrobatics, and were now represented in tremulous charcoal drawings that showed the dancers as primal, decontextualized beings. Complaining to Vollard around the turn of the century about the clichés that threatened to dominate his achievement, Degas insisted that one of his main interests had always been in "rendering movement."[7]

Prior to his meeting Olga in 1917, there is almost no evidence of Picasso having an inter-

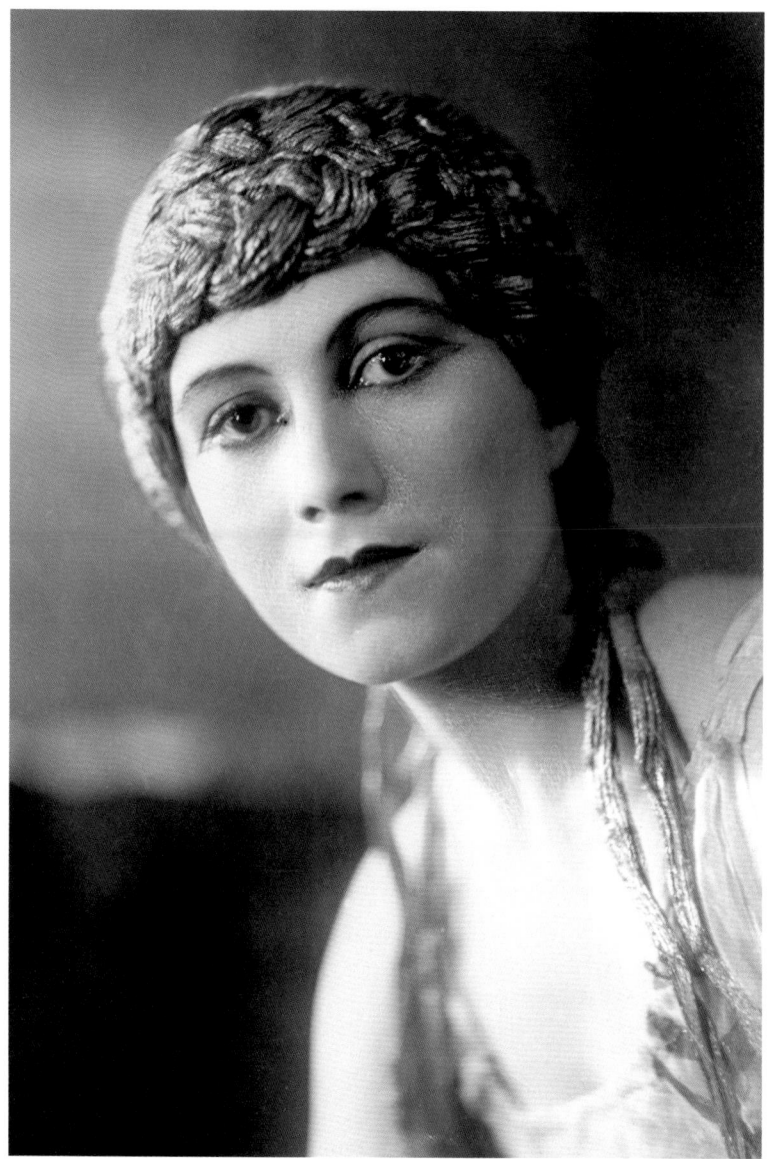

est in classical ballet. On the rare occasions that a young woman in a tutu features in his early work, she is almost invariably performing in a vaudeville or cabaret — as in the pastel of 1901 *Dancer* (**119**) — or is accompanied by acrobats in an outdoor display. The individuals who appear in these pictures had probably received little or no traditional ballet training and were not expected to execute flawless *arabesques* or *battements*. In the handful of such images that Picasso made in Barcelona, his models seem to

118

Olga Khokhlova as a nymph in *L'Après-midi d'un faune (The Afternoon of a Faun)*, c. 1916. Reproduction from a glass negative, 11.9 x 7.4 cm. Archives Olga Ruiz-Picasso, Courtesy Fundación Almine y Bernard Ruiz-Picasso para el Arte

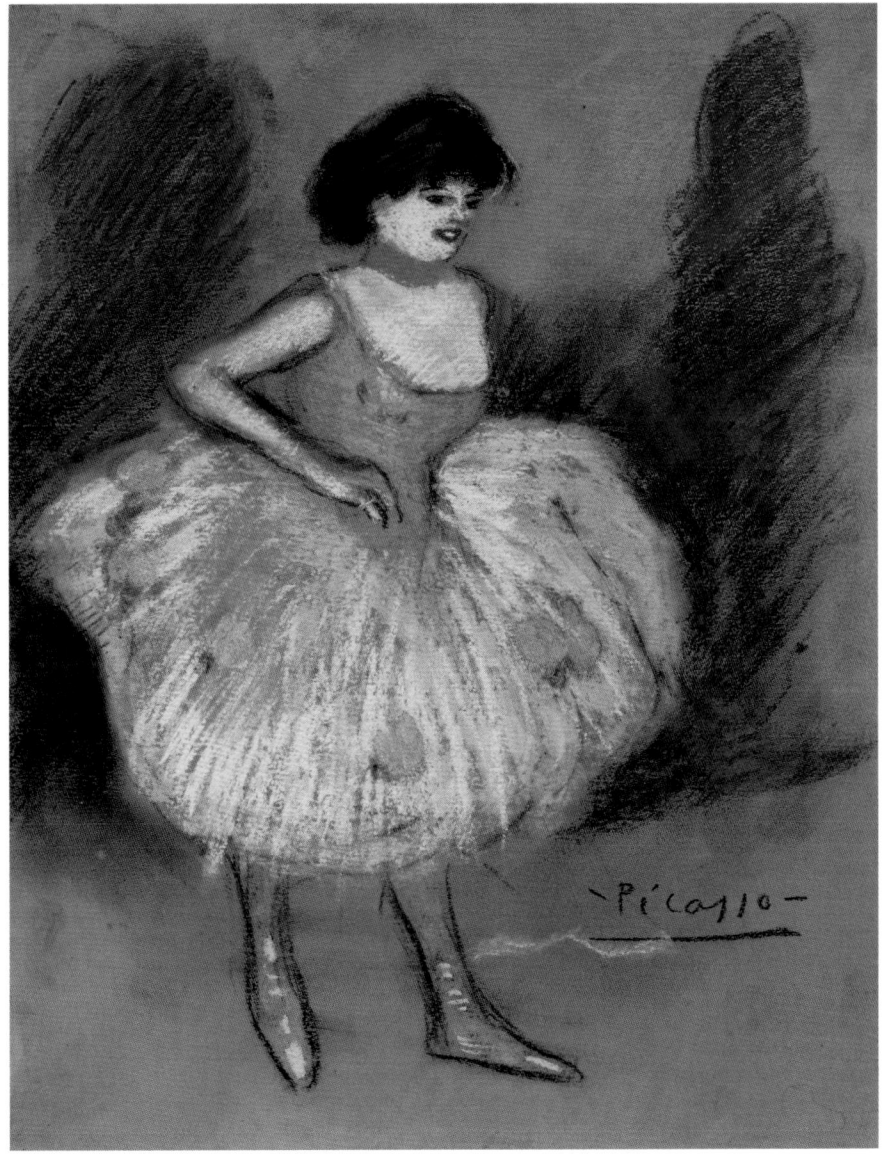

119

Pablo Picasso

Dancer, 1901. Pastel,
45.1 x 32.3 cm.
Location unknown

of conventional ballet or from a determination to distance himself from Degas's signature theme is not clear, though subsequent events suggest a mixture of both motives. The most challenging picture in this context is unquestionably *The Dwarf* (**120**), formerly known as *The Dwarf Dancer*, which has been seen as a response to painters as varied as Velázquez and Goya, Van Gogh and Signac.[9] Less commented upon is the diminutive performer's identity, as expressed in her remarkable posture and costume, and especially her multicolored dress. Though far from orthodox in its glaring hues and brash ornamentation, this outfit has the short, conical shape of a traditional tutu rather than the voluminous folds of a cancan skirt. Both shape and decoration are vividly paraphrased in Degas's *Dancer Leaving Her Dressing Room* (**121**), a richly developed pastel that belonged to Degas's friend Henri Rouart and was known to many of his contemporaries through a Thornley lithograph. Consistent with this association with the ballet are the "turned-out" feet and pale slippers with silky ribbons in *The Dwarf*, the model's amateurish or relaxed "second position," and the resulting poise that sustains her in a meteor shower of color. While this confident girl in her hybrid costume can be seen as a distant relative of the classical dancer, she is clearly worlds away from the ballerinas of the Paris Opéra.

During Picasso's early visits to Paris in 1900 and 1901, the range of compositions by Degas that were now accessible to him included a substantial number of his predecessor's ballet pictures. Both the Caillebotte and Camondo collections were rich in dance pastels, while Camondo owned four of the finest of Degas's ballet canvases then in private hands.[10] On a more modest scale, the scintillating little study *The Dance Class* (**122**) could be found hanging on the walls of one of Degas's less-celebrated admirers, in this case a certain Adolphe Tavernier. In addition to other works held by collectors or those occasionally visible in "the second

belong with the other urban entertainers who feature in his drawings and colored sketches of the period, though a study such as *Dancer* (see **57**) suggests that he may occasionally have encountered a more sophisticated ballet vocabulary.[8] As he looked around him in Paris, Picasso seized joyfully on the cancan and exploited a range of Lautrec-like mannerisms in his ink drawings and freely brushed paintings of stage spectacles, while continuing to avoid the ballet itself. Whether this resulted from a dislike

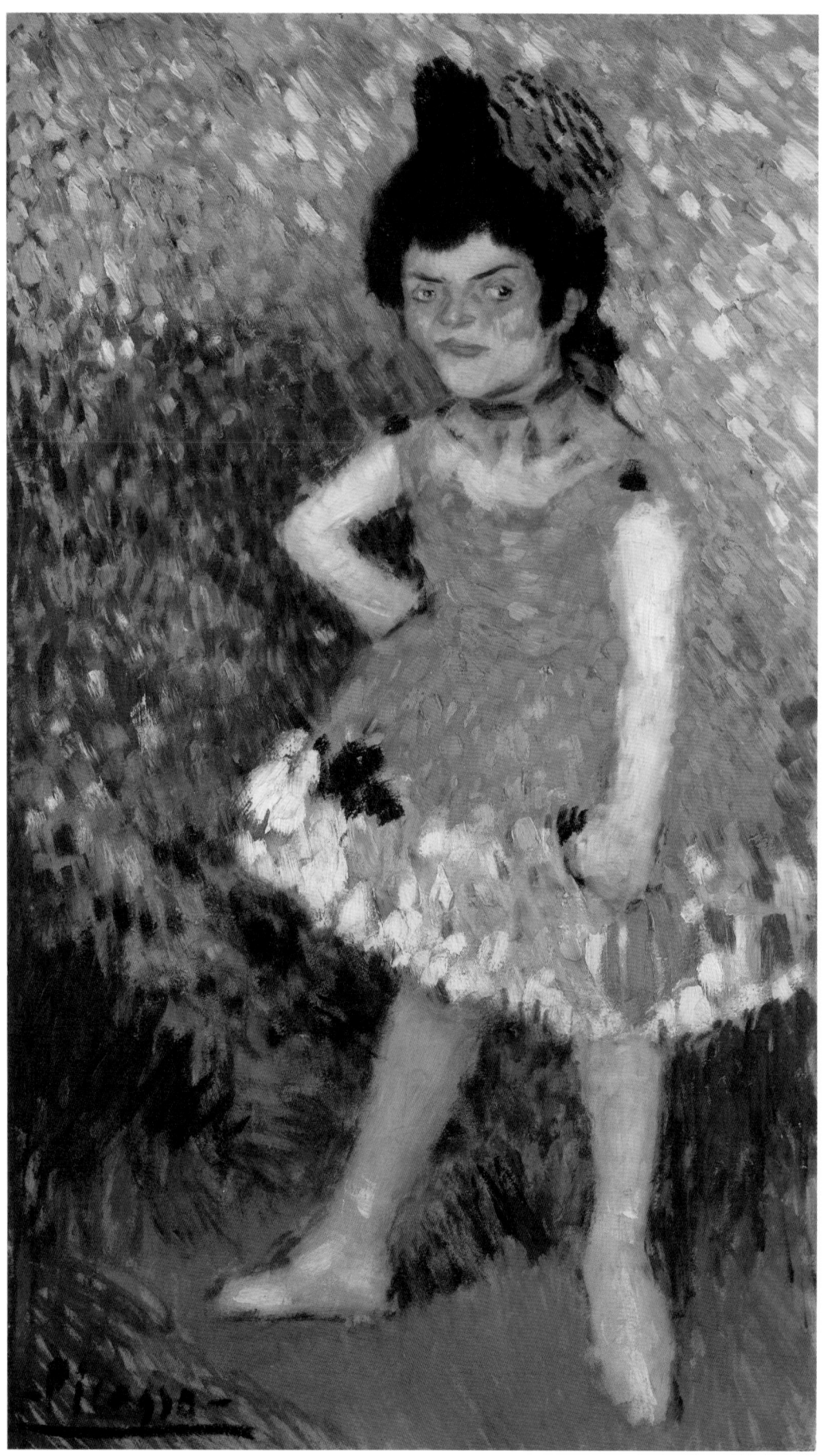

120

Pablo Picasso

The Dwarf, 1901. Oil on
cardboard, 105 x 60 cm.
Museu Picasso, Barcelona
(MPB 4.274)

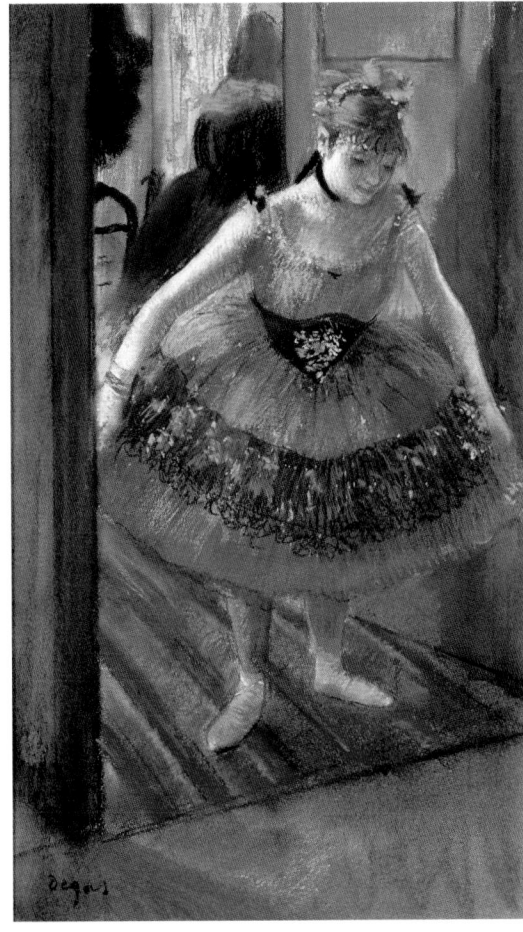

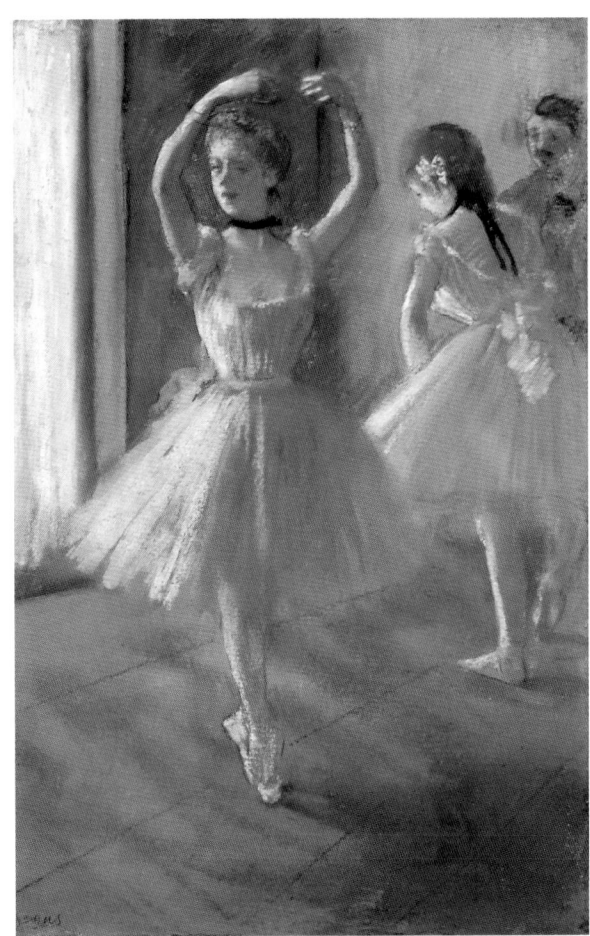

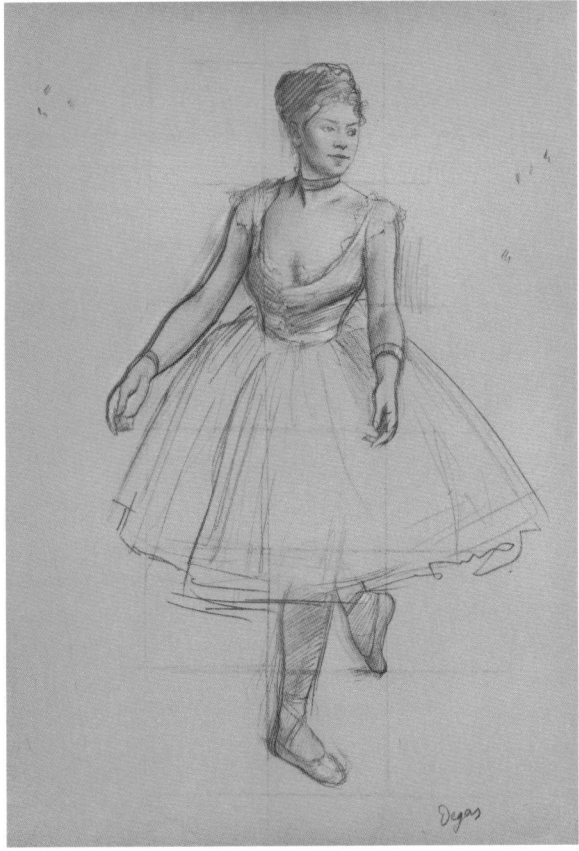

Louvre" on the rue Laffitte, this repertoire was extended by a growing number of reproductions in books and magazines, and the high-quality Thornley and Manzi portfolios. The twenty works printed in color in the latter, for example, included seven pictures of ballerinas, such as *Dancer in Position, Three-Quarter View* (**123**) and *Study of Leg and Arm Movements for a Dancer with a Tambourine*.[11] As he encountered these works of art or their facsimiles, Picasso could expand on what little he had learned in Barcelona about "The Painter of Dancers" and ponder the significance of the older man's idiosyncratic career. Degas's leading proponents had recently stressed the importance of dance imagery to his achievement and begun to articulate it in increasingly modern terms. Duret wrote of Degas that by "studying more and

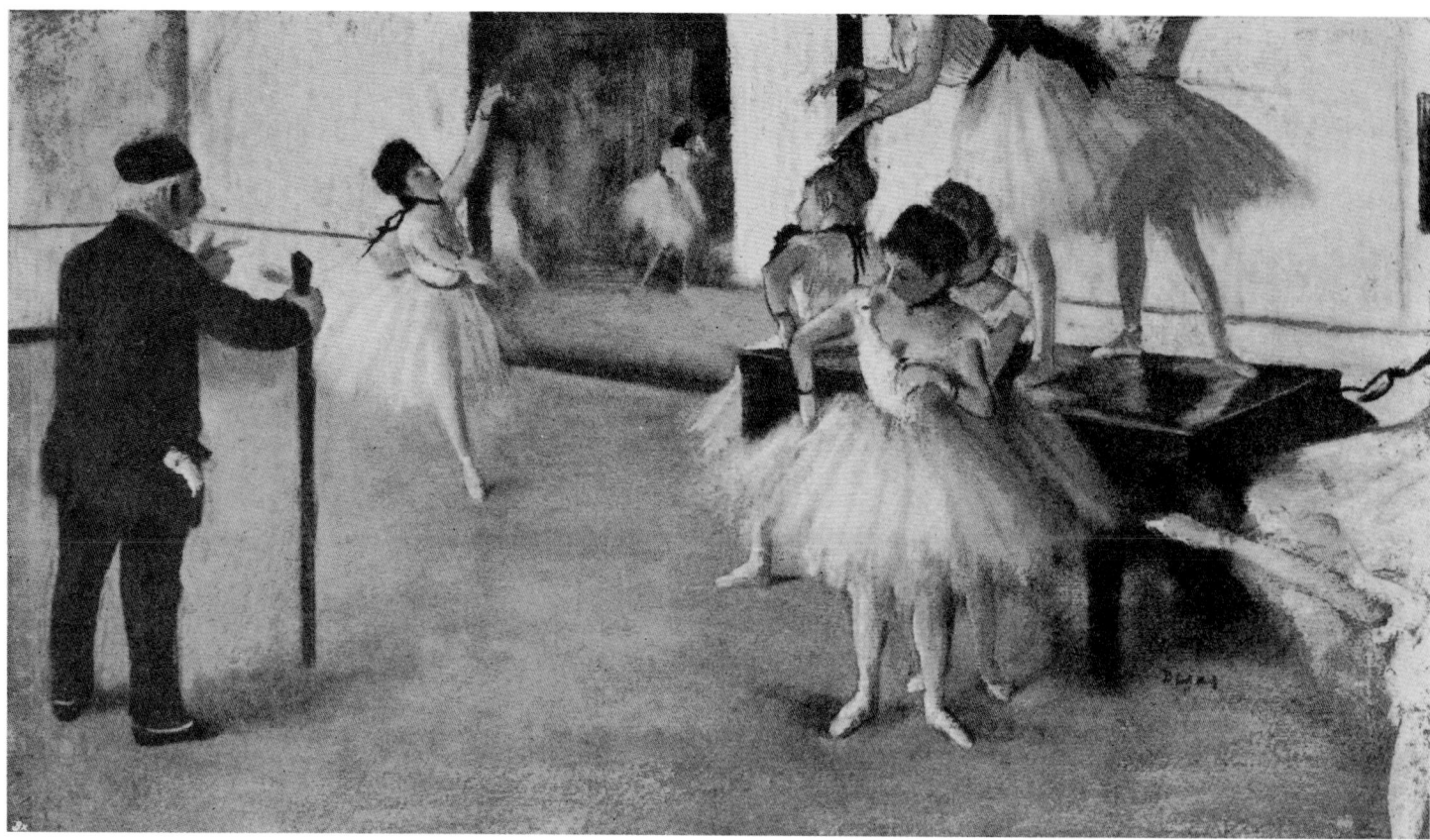

more closely the *being* apart from the dancer, he has ended by making his studies of 'danseuses' convey a world of meaning to which at first they were strangers."[12] Using phrases that could equally apply to Degas's laundress pictures, Duret argued that the artist showed his ballet subjects "as creatures agonized by their work . . . which has drawn from their bodies an enormous sum of strength and energy." Revealingly, of the six illustrations in Duret's article, half were dance works, while a full three-quarters of the pictures reproduced by Roger Marx in 1897 were devoted to this theme. Roger Marx's text echoed many of Duret's sentiments, arguing that — as a ballet artist — Degas was "an ironist" even as he was "an aesthete," involved in painting pictures "of work, pleasure and vice."[13]

Degas's ability to combine the off-duty awkwardness of the ballerina with her public grace was encapsulated in a pastel known as *The*

Dance Lesson, a work that was illustrated in Max Liebermann's 1899 book (**124**).[14] In this unusually anecdotal picture the leaping figure at left is performing for her instructor as if in front of an audience, while the anarchic cluster of girls at right await their turn. The most prominent dancer in this latter group appears to adjust her skirt while standing squarely on the floor, absorbed by the practical realities of her situation and offering a contrast to her airborne colleague. Such down-to-earth dancers seem to have been more to Picasso's taste and may well have contributed to his first large-scale venture into this territory. Though *The Dwarf* is implicitly on stage and distinctly more brazen than Degas's model at right in *The Dance Lesson*, her frontal position, crooked right arm, and ungainly stance have much in common with this figure in *The Dance Lesson*. Picasso's dancer is certainly no weightless sylph but might plausi-

124

Edgar Degas

The Dance Lesson. Reproduced in Max Liebermann, *Degas* (Berlin: Bruno and Paul Cassirer, 1899), p. 13. Courtesy Sterling and Francine Clark Art Institute, Williamstown, Massachusetts

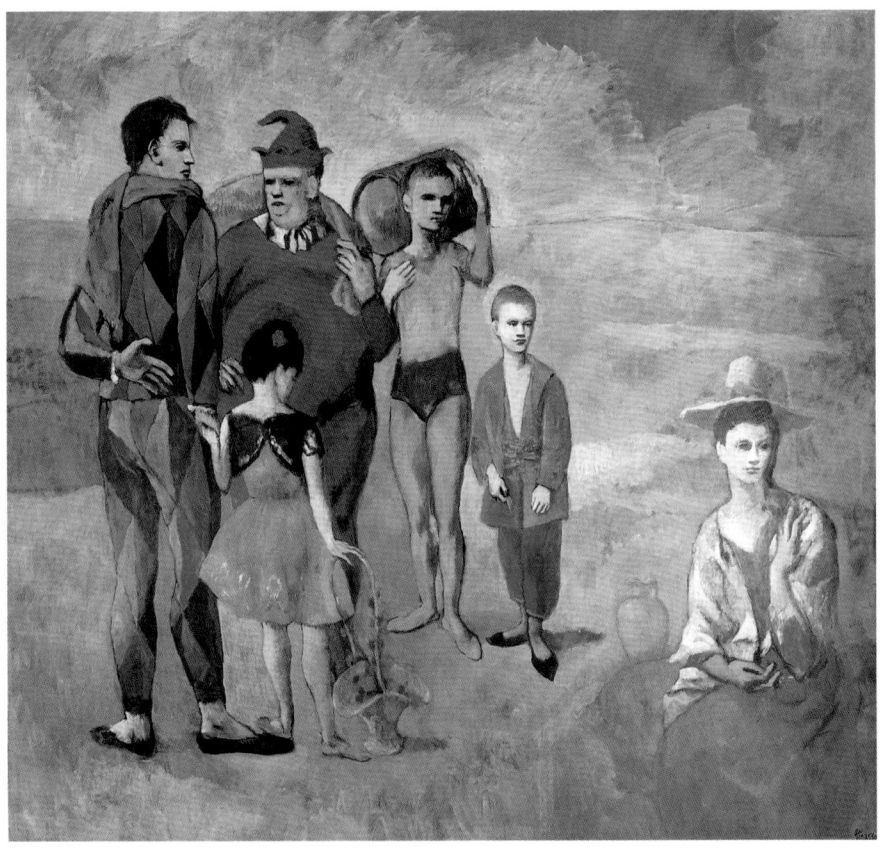

125

Pablo Picasso

Family of Saltimbanques,
1905. Oil on canvas,
212.8 x 229.6 cm.
National Gallery of Art,
Washington, D.C.
Chester Dale Collection
(1963.10.190)

café-concerts or the theater," adding that "yesterday we saw a horror show at the Théâtre Montmartre."[15] Soon Picasso got to know several leading actors in Paris but claimed to find French classical drama "boring"; it is said that one of his close companions in these years, the poet Max Jacob, occasionally "dragged him" against his will to the opera.[16] Many opera performances at this period still included traditional ballets, and it was perhaps in such a setting that Picasso was first introduced to their fairy-like executants and fantastical decor. Yet it would be more than a decade before a few glimpses of such productions appeared in Picasso's own works, which occasionally starred his future wife. In his pre-Olga years Picasso continued to step around the ballet, perhaps from a continued aversion to the genre but conceivably to avoid another direct confrontation with Degas on his own territory. When there were exceptions to this rule, his references to Degas were typically muted or oblique. The pale young dancer in Picasso's magnificent 1905 *Family of Saltimbanques* (**125**), for example, is surely a subdued gesture toward his elderly near-neighbor in Montmartre, a link made more explicit in an earlier state of this canvas when racehorses appeared in the background.[17] Other variants of the composition insist on the fragility of this miniature ballerina, who comes from the opposite end of the spectrum to that occupied by *The Dwarf*. Yet unmistakable in the solemn frieze of *Family of Saltimbanques* is Picasso's interest — already rehearsed in *The Dwarf* — in ballet dancers who were children or adolescents, and thus distinct from the predominantly adult stars at the Paris Opéra.[18]

bly be seen as an alternative embodiment of the "work, pleasure and vice" identified in Degas's art by Roger Marx, with an enigmatic expression and exaggerated stance that "convey a world of meaning." In this challenging sense, *The Dwarf* both identifies with Degas and mocks him, transposing the subtle paradoxes of the Paris Opéra to the farcical stage of a cabaret and spelling out the sexuality that is merely implicit in most of Degas's ballet scenes.

With a face from a Lautrec painting, a proto-Fauvist background, and a Degas-like pose, *The Dwarf* remained a solitary experiment in Picasso's early Parisian oeuvre. An enthusiast for public spectacles of many kinds, Picasso continued to favor the popular entertainments that he had already enjoyed and portrayed in Barcelona. In October 1900, the letter that he and Casagemas wrote to their friends announced, "Some nights we go to

The Little Dancer Aged Fourteen

Degas's single most famous ballet work, made at the height of his public career, was a depiction of a young teenager. This was the sculpture known as the *Little Dancer Aged Fourteen* (**126**), standing more than three feet high and mod-

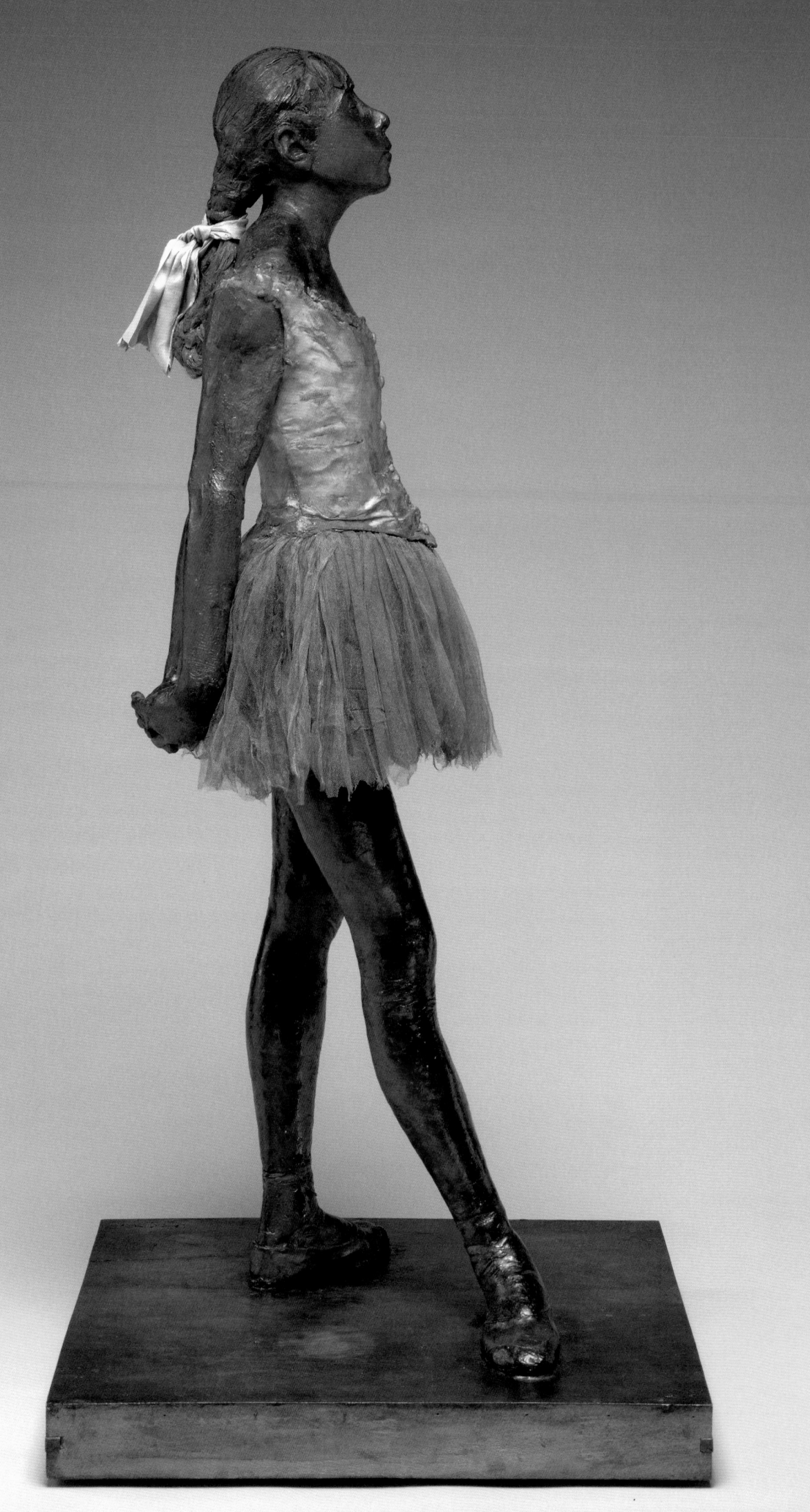

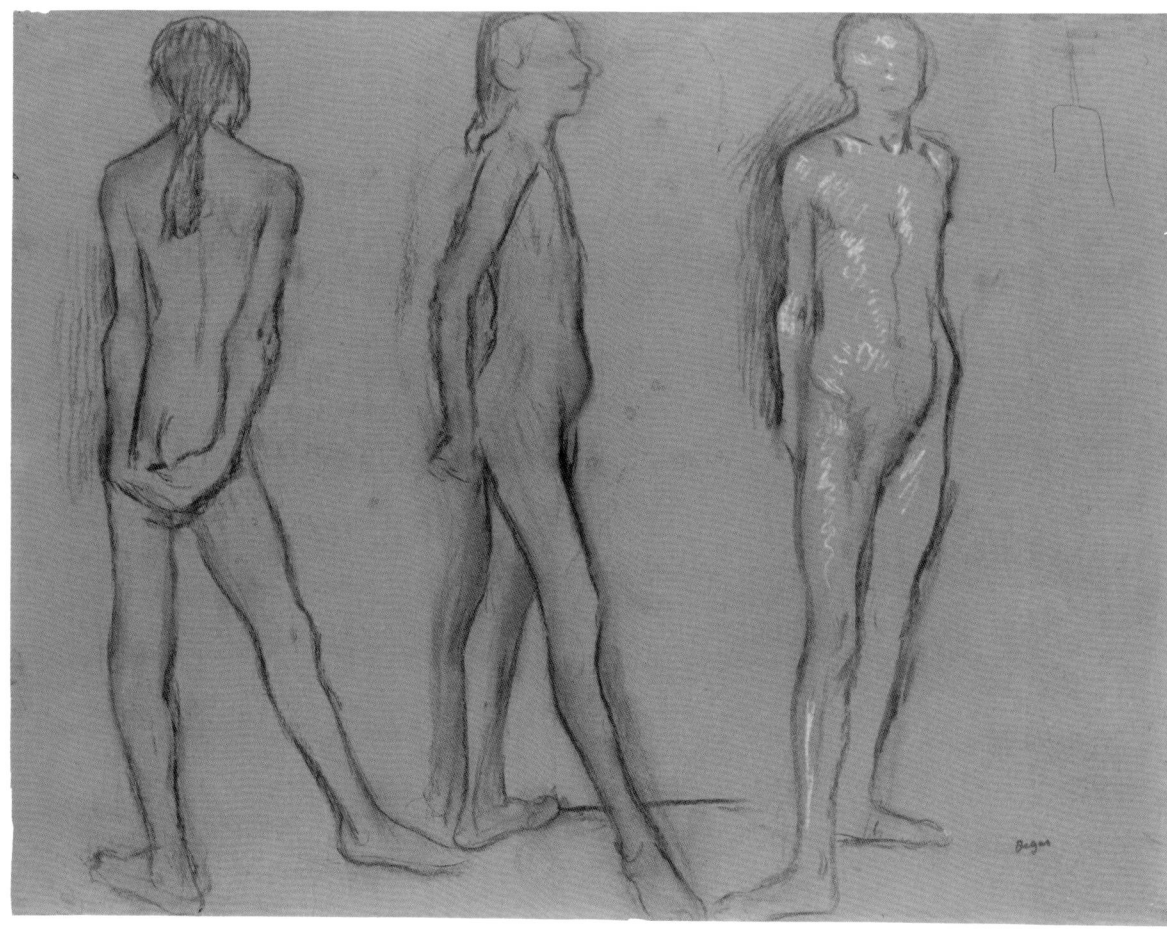

eled in wax, with a fabric tutu, miniature slippers, and a hair wig tied with a silk ribbon. Many
of these features were discussed — and have
continued to be analyzed and evaluated — by
critics and commentators who have associated
Degas's figure with funeral effigies and medical models, Egyptian statues and ethnographic
specimens, and with divergent attitudes to adolescent sexuality in nineteenth-century France.[19]
On a purely practical level, it was also remarkable as Degas's first major exercise in a medium
in which he was entirely untaught. The sculpture
was planned in several drawings that showed
Degas's subject, Marie van Goethem, a trainee
from the Paris Opéra, posing both in the nude
and in her standard practice tutu.[20] One early
draft of this kind, *Studies for the "Little Dancer*

Aged Fourteen" (Nude) (**127**), emphasizes the
slenderness of the girl's body and limbs, and her
lack of physical development at this stage in her
youth. Several erased and redrawn lines in the
drawing reveal changes made by the artist as he
accustomed himself to her unfamiliar physique,
studied in views from the back, front, and side.
Degas was clearly anticipating the step toward
sculpture and — as an amateur — beginning to
grasp the dancer's form in the round. As he prepared for the final work, he made a wax version
of this naked figure on a smaller scale than the
Little Dancer Aged Fourteen, a study that was
never exhibited but later cast in bronze after
his death. In the spare, elegant forms of this
*Nude Study for the "Little Dancer Aged Four-
teen"* (**128**), Degas again insisted on his model's

113

attenuated, childlike body, notable in the thin arms that extend behind her back and join in her clasped hands.

A similar procedure was followed in the creation of the larger, dressed sculpture of the *Little Dancer Aged Fourteen*. Almost a dozen sheets of drawings have been linked with this and the unclothed figure, representing intermediary steps in the process of defining the girl's body from a succession of viewpoints. *Three Studies of a Dancer in Fourth Position* (**129**) is characteristic of the group, combining a near-scientific precision with a lively and informed understanding of the model's identity as an aspiring ballerina. When the wax body was completed and all its accessories integrated or added, the *Little Dancer Aged Fourteen* was placed in a glass case and displayed at the 1881 Impressionist exhibition. Degas's bold, unsentimental approach to his subject and its remarkable naturalism immediately provoked a wide range of specialist and vernacular responses. Discussed in at least twenty contemporary newspapers and magazines, the figure became the focus of extreme vilification and of equally extravagant praise, creating a sensation that would reverberate down the years. Enthusiasts were thrilled by "its singular truthfulness" and "extreme realism," and the prominent novelist and critic Joris-Karl Huysmans claimed that it was "the first truly modern attempt at sculpture."[21] The opposition was even more vehement, describing the model portrayed by Degas as "frightful" and "ugly," even "depraved . . . a flower of the gutter"; "Can art descend any lower?" a commentator exclaimed in the English press.[22] When the exhibition closed, the contentious *Little Dancer Aged Fourteen* had failed to attract a buyer and was returned to Degas, who in later life transported it with his other effects as he moved from studio to studio. There it was observed by a succession of the artist's visitors, among whom were the writers George Moore and Paul Valéry, and painters Walter Sickert and

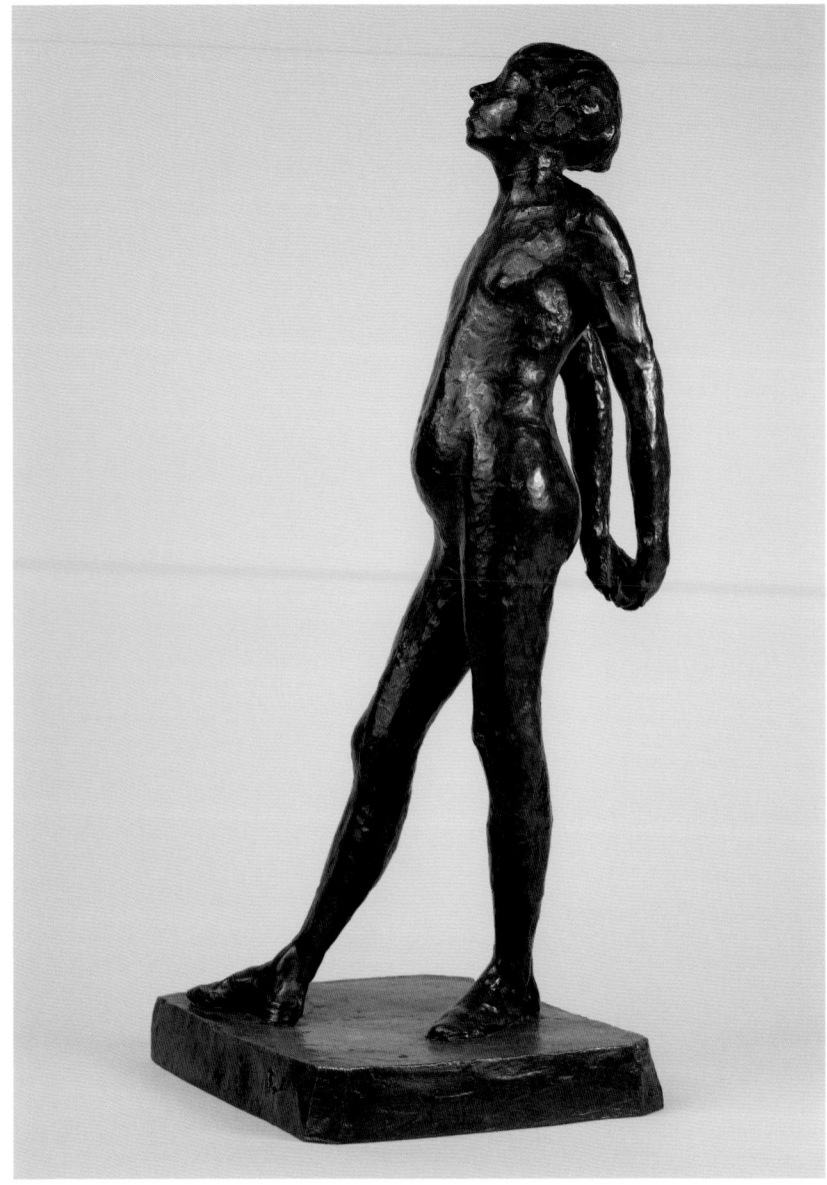

Pierre-Auguste Renoir, who recalled in later years "the ballet dancer in wax."[23] As the most celebrated work in three dimensions to emerge from the Impressionist circle, it soon became something of a legend. The prominent American admirer of Degas's art, Louisine Havemeyer, saw the sculpture at the turn of the century in Degas's rue Victor Massé studio and tried unsuccessfully to buy it, noting sadly "how faded the gauze was and how wooly the dark hair appeared."[24]

128

Edgar Degas

Nude Study for the "Little Dancer Aged Fourteen," c. 1878. Bronze, height: 72.4 cm. The National Gallery of Scotland, Edinburgh (NG1624)

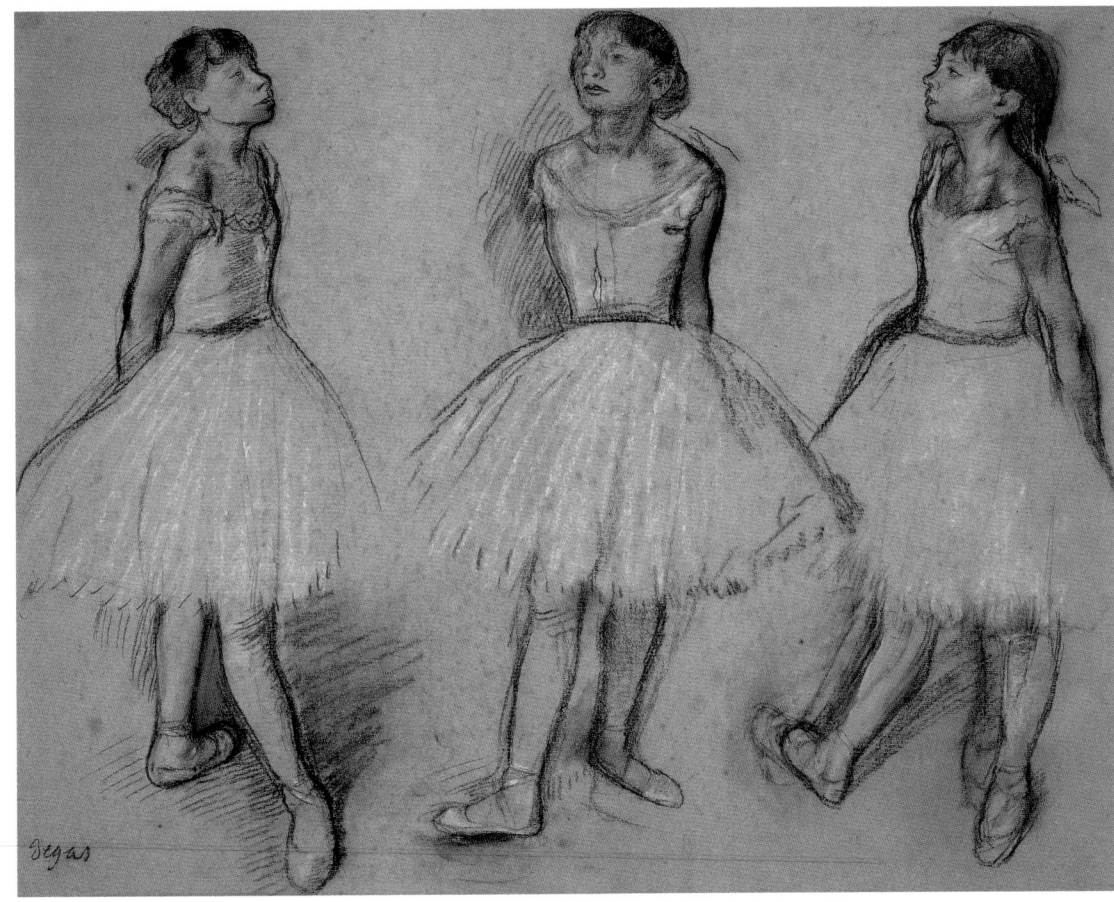

129

Edgar Degas

Three Studies of a Dancer in Fourth Position, c. 1879–80. Charcoal and pastel with stumping, and brush and black wash, on grayish-tan laid paper with blue fibers, laid down on gray wove paper, 48 x 61.6 cm. The Art Institute of Chicago. Bequest of Adele R. Levy (1962.703)

Such stories inevitably joined the art-world gossip of Montmartre and still lingered when Picasso and his comrades settled a few streets away. Picasso may also have received more detailed accounts of the pictures and sculptures in Degas's studio from those who went there in person, such as Ambroise Vollard, Benedetta Canals, and Fernande Olivier. Another witness known to him was Suzanne Valadon, whose life became interwoven over the years with both Degas and the circles around Picasso. Valadon had been the lover of Miquel Utrillo, the Catalan artist who was a stalwart of Els Quatre Gats after contributing to shows at the Chat Noir on the rue Victor Massé in the 1890s. In this decade Valadon went frequently to Degas's studio on the same street, where he encouraged her attempts to achieve recognition as a maker of

drawings, prints, and paintings. A familiar figure in Montmartre for many years, Valadon displayed her drawings at the bohemian bar known as the Lapin Agile, a favorite haunt of the Picasso crowd between 1904 and 1905.[25] Even more pertinent in the present context is the recently published indication that Valadon was posing for Degas's wax figures when Fernande Olivier and her friend visited him in 1904.[26] In 1908, Valadon herself recalled the *Little Dancer Aged Fourteen* in a drawing appropriately entitled *Puberty* (**130**), in which she seems to pay homage to the pose of the nude study as well as the larger dressed figure, both familiar to her from visits to Degas's premises. Along with these firsthand accounts and visual responses, Degas's sculpture also achieved currency through the preparatory drawings that he had made for the work. By the turn of the century, several of these sheets had already been sold or given away by the artist, one finding its way into the collection of Jacques Doucet, the first owner of *Les Demoiselles d'Avignon*, and another, *Three Studies of a Dancer in Fourth Position* (see 129), was acquired by Roger Marx.[27] It was Roger Marx who broadcast Degas's sculpture to a wide audience for the first time, when he reproduced this superb drawing in the journal *L'Image* in 1897 (see 97).

Unmistakable in all the drawings for the *Little Dancer Aged Fourteen* — and in the wax itself — is the pronounced anatomical and spatial character of Degas's posed model. The upper part of the girl's body is almost entirely symmetrical, from her firmly held shoulders and forward-facing head to the echoing forms of the arms, both of which fall downward and backward in a near-straight line, with hands clasped behind her back. Below the waist, by contrast, the figure is distinctively asymmetrical, with the right leg projected forward and to the side, and the left leg held close to vertical and carrying most of the body weight. Precisely replicated in the wax sculpture, this configuration follows a standard posture known to all ballet students as a casual "fourth position," which in visual terms fuses balance and formality with the dynamism implied in the advancing leg. It is difficult to exaggerate the distinctiveness of this form, which is almost entirely unknown in the world of sculpture in previous centuries.[28]

The presence of many of these characteristics in Picasso's *The Dwarf* — a painting that is almost exactly the same height as Degas's wax figure — seems to suggest that Picasso knew the *Little Dancer Aged Fourteen* in one of its incarnations as early as 1901. In Picasso's picture, the tutu and lower limbs follow those of Degas's figure extremely closely, their forms perhaps communicated through Roger Marx's drawing where the lower part of the right-hand figure is strikingly similar to *The Dwarf*. The

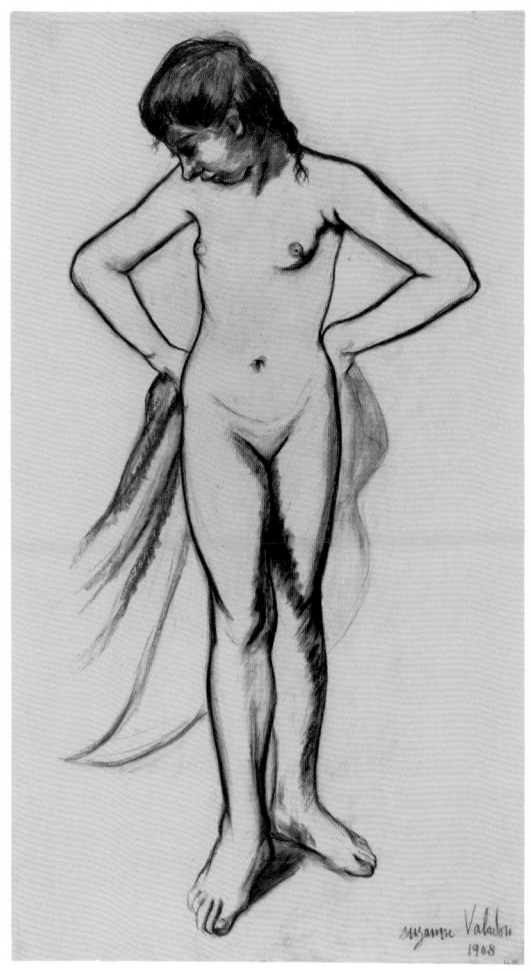

torso in Picasso's picture similarly follows the published drawing, though the left arm has been pulled forward and a sharp bend introduced into the right arm. Once these similarities and variations have been noted, the sense that *The Dwarf* is some kind of descendant of Degas's notorious sculpture — or of the drawings that were in circulation at this date — is difficult to set aside. Though it is probable that Picasso had not seen the *Little Dancer Aged Fourteen* firsthand, it may well have been described to this highly competitive young artist by his acquaintances and mentors, or otherwise encountered in Degas's preparatory sheets. As with his slightly later responses to the artist's iconic *In a Café* (see 104) and *Women Ironing* (see 106), Picasso appears to have taken on the

Pablo Picasso

Three Studies of a Nude Woman, c. 1903. Pen and ink on paper, 17.9 x 23 cm. Museu Picasso, Barcelona (MPB 110.496)

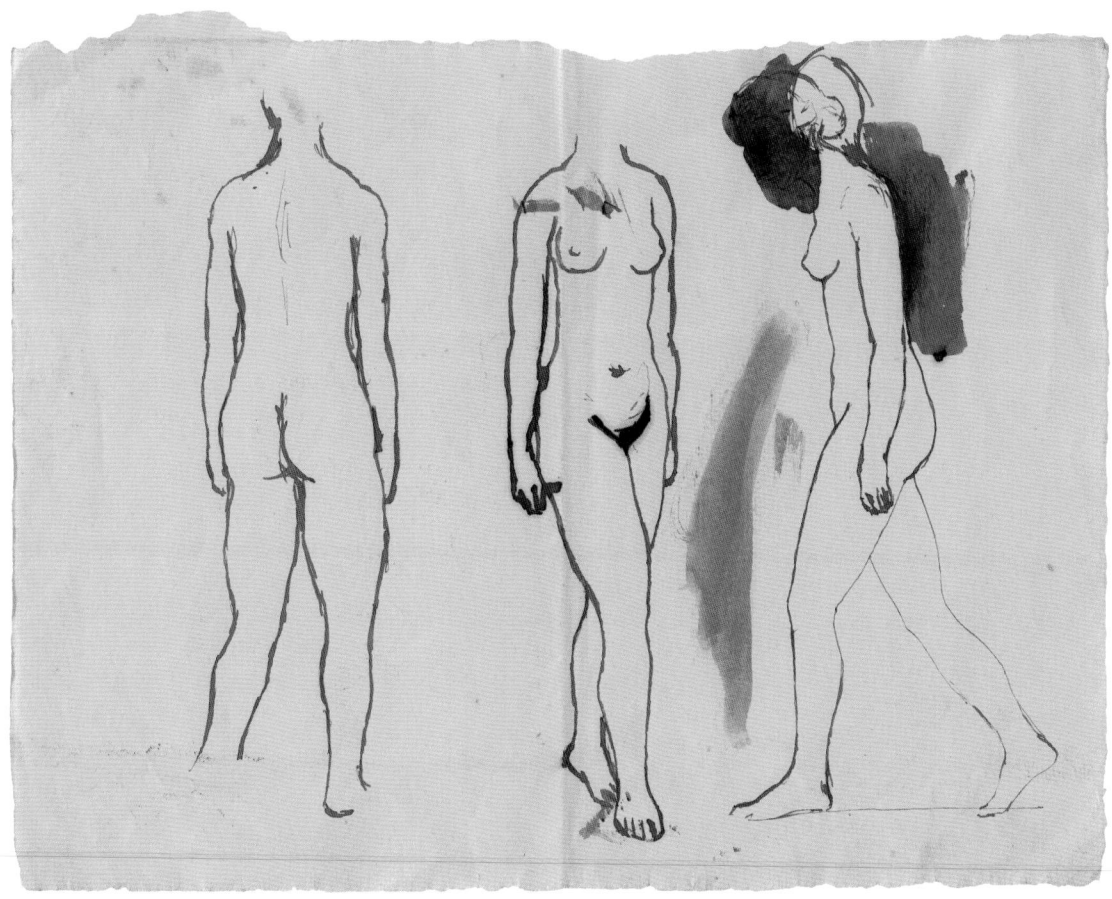

challenge of Degas's sculptural masterpiece at this moment, choosing to confront it in the medium in which he felt most at home: oil paint. In *The Dwarf*, Picasso's oblique restatement of the wax figure can be seen as witty or impertinent, perversely flattering or frankly combative. It would be four or five years before he returned to the fray, when the *Little Dancer Aged Fourteen* provoked a series of profoundly different images in an even more ambitious context.

By 1902, if not before, Picasso had become fascinated by the idea of making his own sculpture in response to some of his new experiences. Inspired by seeing the work of Auguste Rodin and perhaps by a meeting with Aristide Maillol, he was advised by Catalan sculptor-friends as he learned the basic skills and experimented with a range of materials.[29] Picasso began on a small scale, modeling a clay figure

of a seated woman and making some wood carvings, but by 1906 he had advanced considerably in his ambitious *Head of a Woman (Fernande Olivier)* (see 188) and *Woman Plaiting Her Hair* (see 201). In that year "sculpture was very much on his mind," in Elizabeth's Cowling's words, as shown in sheet after sheet of powerfully articulated drawings, many of which included multiple viewpoints of a single model.[30] An earlier attempt of this kind, *Three Studies of a Nude Woman* (**131**), was never achieved in the round but is self-evidently a beginner's attempt to comprehend the human form in a series of linked images.[31] Just as Degas had done three decades earlier in his *Studies for the "Little Dancer Aged Fourteen" (Nude)* (see 127), Picasso now recorded his naked model in back, front, and profile views, here choosing a striding figure with her arms by

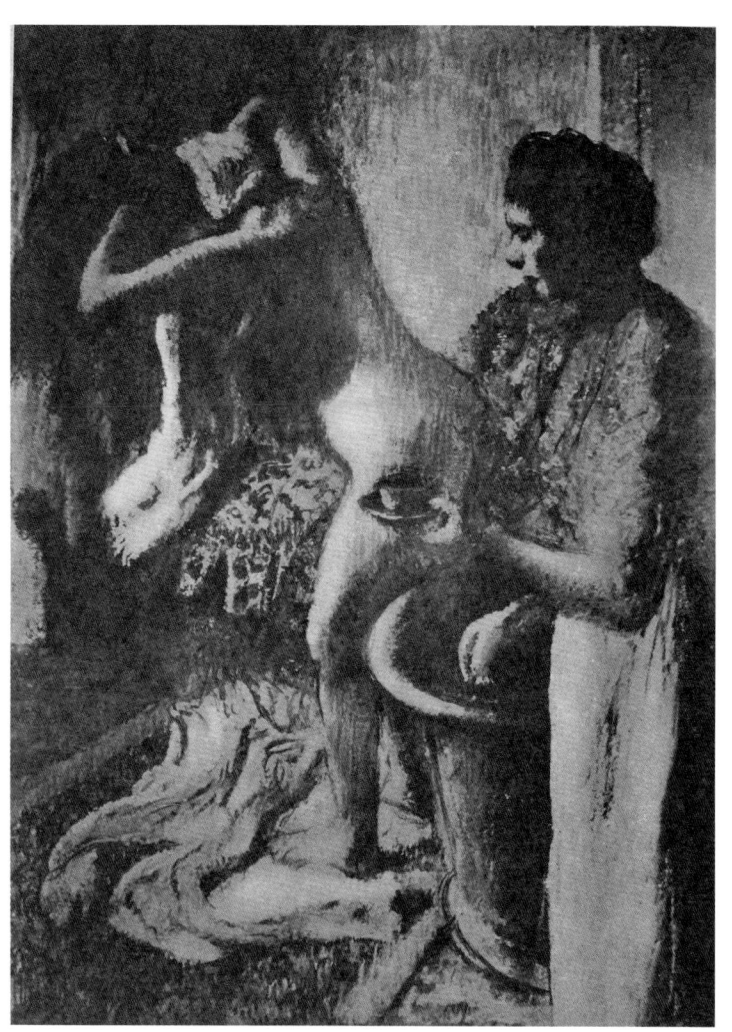

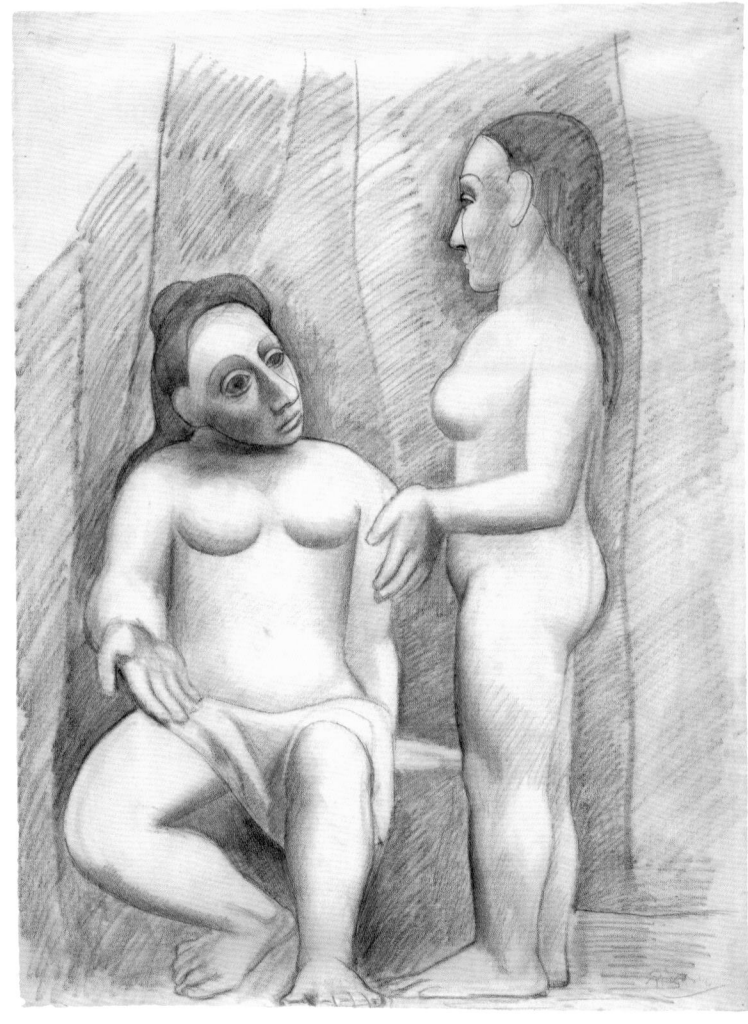

132

Edgar Degas

The Breakfast after the Bath, c. 1895. Pastel, 121 x 92 cm. Reproduced in Ambroise Vollard, *Degas* (Paris: Galerie A. Vollard, 1914), pl. 7. Courtesy Sterling and Francine Clark Art Institute, Williamstown, Massachusetts

133

Pablo Picasso

Seated Nude and Standing Nude, 1906. Charcoal on paper, 63.6 x 47.6 cm. Philadelphia Museum of Art. The Louise and Walter Arensberg Collection, 1950 (1950-134-162)

134

Edgar Degas

The Green Skirt, c. 1895. Pastel and charcoal on paper, 45 x 37 cm. Burrell Collection, Glasgow. Culture and Sport Glasgow (Museums) (35.242)

135

Pablo Picasso

Seated Nude (Study for "Les Demoiselles d'Avignon"), 1907. Oil on canvas, 121 x 93.5 cm. Musée national Picasso, Paris (MP 10)

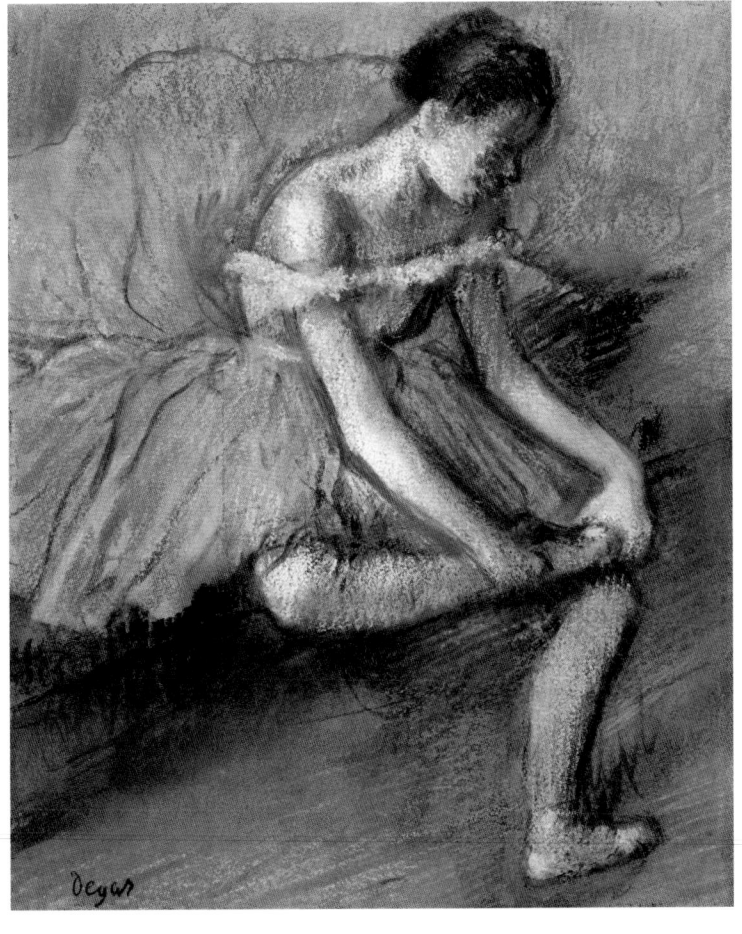

her sides. Such drawings are by no means common, and Picasso's choice of this format increases the probability that he had seen or become aware of Degas's sheets. From 1906 onward, other works on paper and related paintings showed his progress in the new discipline, as he engaged confidently with female and occasionally male figures in emphatically sculptural terms. Few of these projects were realized as physical objects, but Picasso's numerous drawings allow us to follow his thinking and to identify some of his historical sources. An almost repetitive sequence of paired standing women, for example, offers variations on the idea of multiple viewpoints and was clearly indebted to Egyptian, and perhaps African and Gothic, forms, though rendered in a radically volumetric manner that was entirely Picasso's own.[32] Among more contemporary influences were passing references to Degas, the leading painter-sculptor of the older generation who was also self-taught, whose drawings and pastels lay behind a Picasso seated figure with a standing "maid" (**132, 133**) and an androgynous individual who sits cross-legged, like dozens of Degas's ballet dancers (**134, 135**).[33]

Les Demoiselles d'Avignon

The most intriguing character of this kind to emerge from Picasso's sketchbooks and portfolios at this period was one that is much more familiar today, Degas's *Little Dancer Aged Fourteen*. As Picasso labored tenaciously through hundreds of drawings toward the elaborate brothel composition that became *Les Demoiselles d'Avignon* (**136**), devouring the work of Cézanne, Gauguin, and El Greco, Egyptian figurines and tribal masks on the way, he became fixated at a relatively early stage on the figure of a naked, stylized young woman who steps forward into the composition. Precise dating is especially hazardous in this context, but varied pictorial statements of this individual are

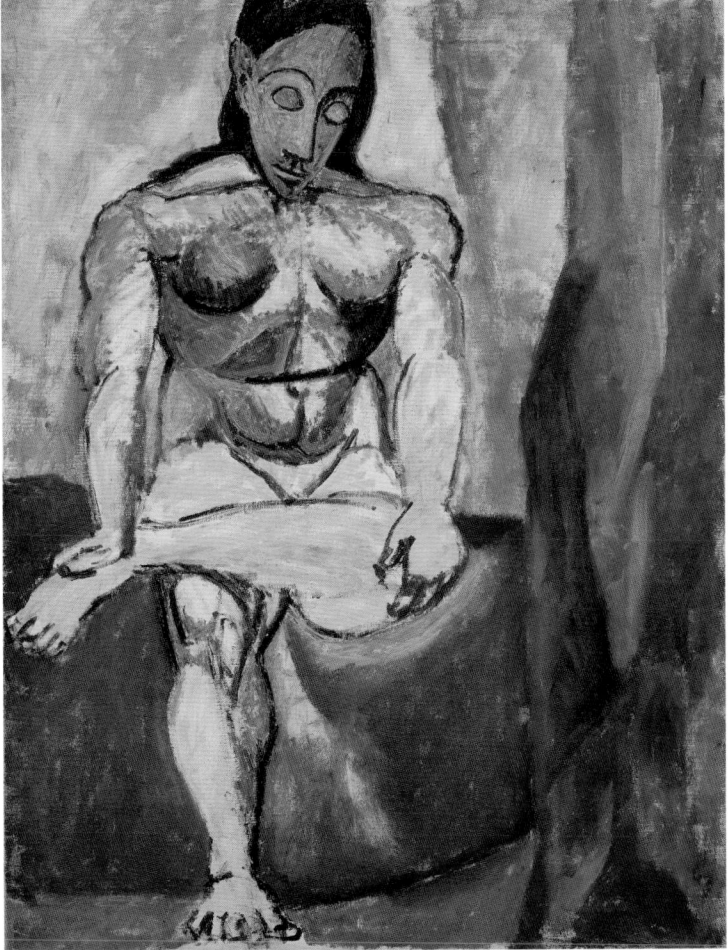

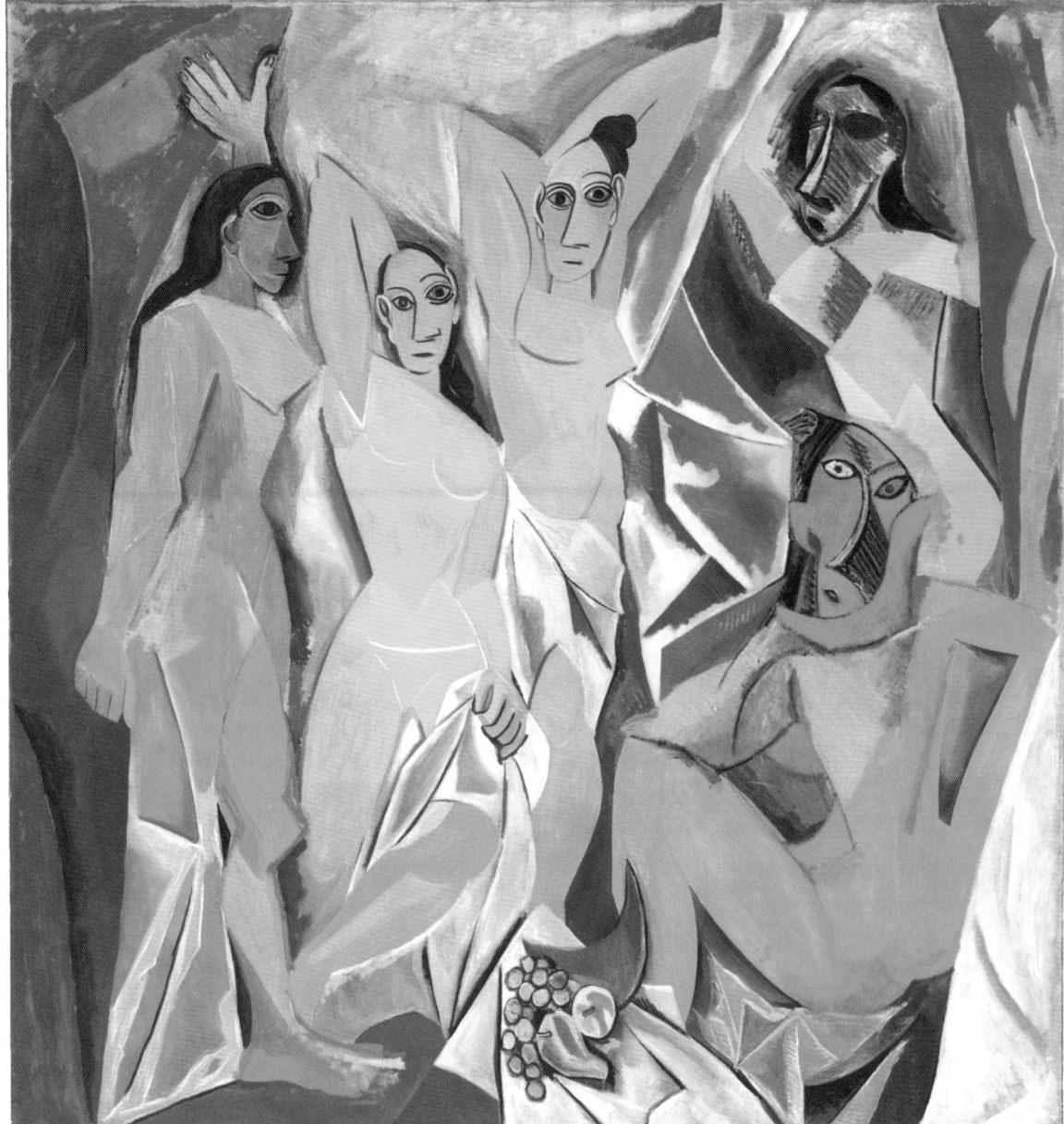

136

Pablo Picasso

Les Demoiselles d'Avignon,
1907. Oil on canvas,
243.84 x 233.68 cm.
The Museum of Modern
Art, New York. Acquired
through the Lille P. Bliss
Bequest

generally located in late 1906 or the early
months of 1907. In each case, the figures in question advance on a single leg and in at least two
examples the woman steps forward with arms
behind her back and right leg extended.[34]
Though partly covered by drapery, the body
of the woman in *Study for "Les Demoiselles
d'Avignon": Nude Woman Parting a Curtain* (**137**),
for example, is essentially arranged in the pose

of Degas's *Little Dancer Aged Fourteen*. Simultaneously or perhaps a little later, this stepping
character became the male "student" who is
famously present in the charcoal and pastel
Study for "Les Demoiselles d'Avignon" belonging to the Kunstmuseum Basel (see 242). A
suite of drawings apparently made in the spring
of 1907 includes both variants in schematic
designs for the entire picture,[35] while another

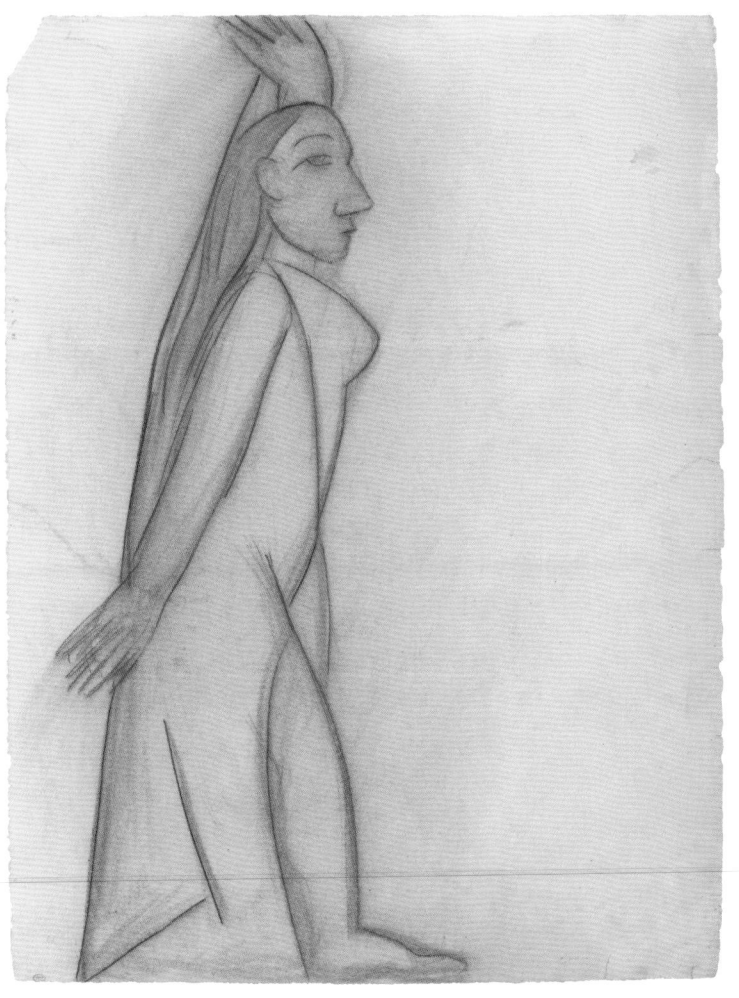

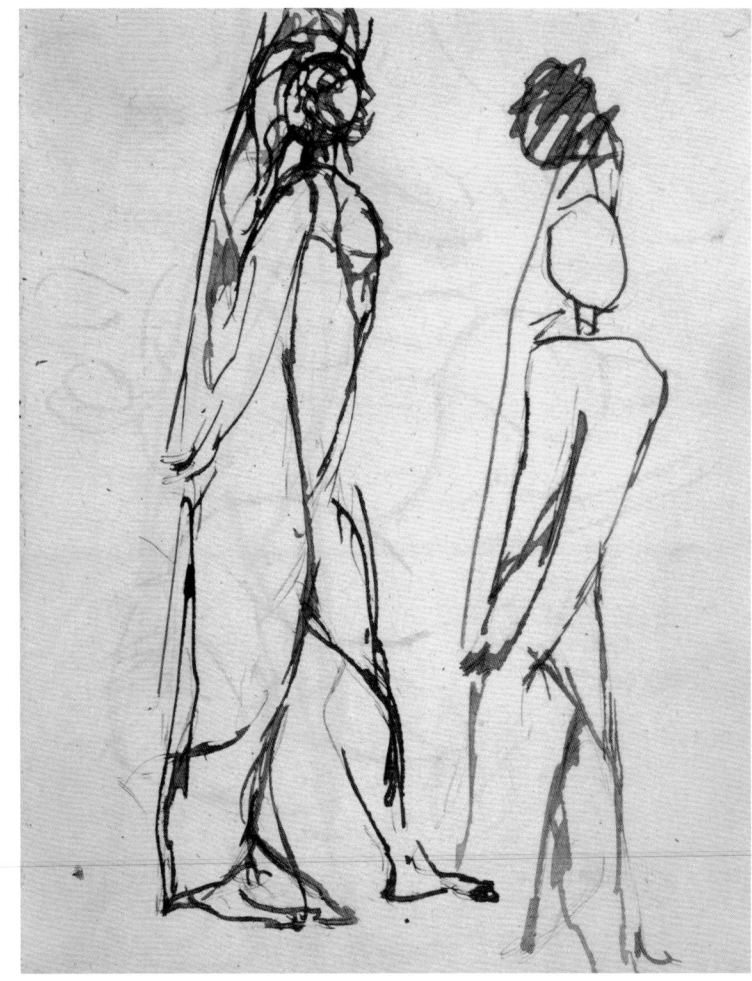

137

Pablo Picasso

Study for "Les Demoiselles d'Avignon": Nude Woman Parting a Curtain, 1907. Charcoal on paper, 63.4 x 48 cm. Musée national Picasso, Paris (MP 541)

138

Pablo Picasso

Two Standing Nudes in Profile, 1907. Ink on paper, 14 x 10 cm. Musée national Picasso, Paris (MP 1862)

related sketch depicts the "stepper" from behind, her arms held low and hands clasped, exactly as in Degas's wax figure (**138**). By June 1907, Picasso had settled on a female cast throughout the canvas and an entirely new player had appeared. In *Yellow Nude* (**139**), the heavy limbs of Picasso's previous sheets have been replaced by tapering legs and short arms, all belonging to a model in a lithe, open posture. This small-breasted, awkward individual stands typically with her right leg forward and both arms behind her back, in the definitive manner of the *Little Dancer Aged Fourteen*. More than twenty drawings and other works on paper from this period explore versions of this same pose, as the model temporarily raises one

arm above the head or retracts her right leg but is essentially recognizable as the prepubescent figure with a slightly awkward stance.[36] Apparently suffering from chronic equivocation, as elsewhere in this much pondered and reworked creation, Picasso may have considered these alternative sketches for development in separate paintings. The scale and emphatic color of *Yellow Nude*, for example, certainly appear to point in this direction, but it would be another iteration of this figure that finally achieved an independent status.

Picasso's experimentation with both a naked and clothed variant of the *Little Dancer Aged Fourteen* in the context of *Les Demoiselles d'Avignon* invites analysis. In conventional terms

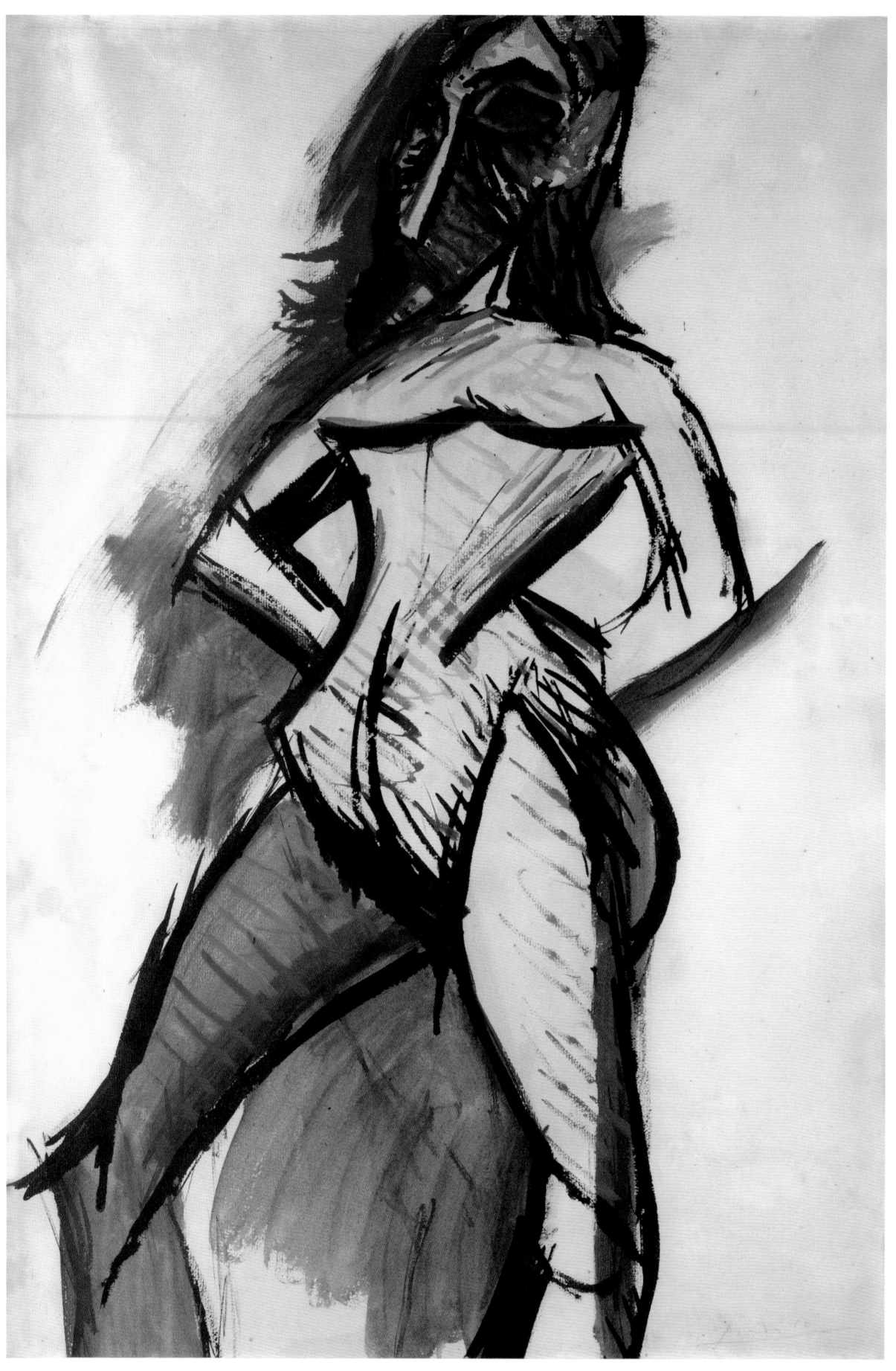

it might be argued that he was still following his art-school training by developing a composition from drawings of nude models, who were then "clothed" as the work was completed. Degas himself had observed this protocol in his plans for the *Little Dancer Aged Fourteen*, producing *Studies for the "Little Dancer Aged Fourteen" (Nude)* (see 127) and at least one other sheet that defined the position of the girl's naked body.[37] The possibility that Picasso was aware of such earlier works on paper — and even the wax original of the sculpture that resulted — might shed light on his proposal to add a naked variant of Degas's figure to his monumental canvas. Tantalizing though it is, this scenario remains historically problematic. The two known drawings of Marie van Goethem in the nude remained with Degas until his death and were never reproduced or exhibited; it is also beyond doubt that the wax *Nude Study for the "Little Dancer Aged Fourteen"* stayed in his studio, seen only by his visitors and introduced to the public for the first time when the bronze casts of Degas's sculptures were displayed in 1921.[38]

A more persuasive explanation for Picasso's choice of a nude dancer figure in *Les Demoiselles d'Avignon* is that of sexual fantasy. This is consistent with his documented interest in adolescent girls and his portrayals from Barcelona onward of real or imaginary intimacy with very young women.[39] The reputed availability of low-ranking dancers as lovers, legendary in Degas's time and still persistent in the early twentieth century, no doubt fueled this preoccupation. It may also have encouraged Picasso's perception — shared with some of the 1881 critics — that the model for the *Little Dancer Aged Fourteen* was implicitly "depraved." Though he could not have known it, the van Goethem family turns out to have been living on the extreme margins of respectability, with Marie and her dancer-sister appearing less frequently at the Opéra and soon resorting to prostitution in the taverns of Montmartre.[40] Similar cases no doubt came

to Picasso's ears in Paris and may already have coalesced in his mind with Degas's history as a maker of brothel monotypes.[41] Given his obsessive fascination with such matters, did Picasso — a known habitué of brothels — contemplate a child-prostitute in his "imaginary bordello" as he wrestled over his large canvas during 1907?[42] William Rubin has pointed out that this was a phase of considerable private anxiety for the artist, during which his intimate relationship with Fernande was undergoing the crisis that led to their separation: "I'm devastated," she wrote to Gertrude Stein in August.[43] This quarrel, Rubin argues, may also have been exacerbated by the presence in their lives of a young girl that Fernande and Picasso had adopted, who was beginning to attract the artist's prurient attention.[44]

Some light is shed on the role these issues played in both the artist's imagination and the development of *Les Demoiselles d'Avignon* by an often overlooked painting made at this time. *Standing Nude* (**140**) is arguably Picasso's most direct homage to Degas's the *Little Dancer Aged Fourteen* (**141**). Like the earlier *The Dwarf*, this vertical canvas differs in height from the wax figure by just a couple of inches. Even more than in the 1901 work, Picasso's model is now positioned in the unmistakable stance defined by Marie van Goethem in the late 1870s, when she stood with shoulders level and balanced, and with both arms reaching down and behind her back. Below the waist, the left leg of the model in *Standing Nude* is close to perpendicular, while the right reaches out and away from the body. Given the rarity of this configuration in the sculptural canon, we must surely consider it as a private reference by Picasso to the celebrated sculpture of his predecessor, who was still living close to the Bateau Lavoir at this moment. Similarly telling was Picasso's emphasis on the relative youth of the figure in *Standing Nude*; unlike the voluptuous, Amazon-like creatures who populate many of his early sketches for *Les Demoiselles d'Avignon* and still partly dominate the finished composition, this individual is small-breasted and timid in her demeanor.

Yet *Standing Nude* was executed in the harsh, faceted manner used in the final stage of the large painting, leaving much of the body articulated with "gouged" marks, as if cut into wood. This quality immediately relates *Standing Nude* to the figure at upper right in *Les Demoiselles d'Avignon* (see 136), who shares the same facial features — especially the long nose and pointed chin — and their "chiseled" treatment. Most of the other forms in *Standing Nude*, however, either did not survive Picasso's repeated transformations or were never introduced into this section of the canvas, leaving us to speculate about his motivations for painting the smaller work. It appears from drawings and various hybrid figures related to this less-familiar composition that Picasso briefly contemplated its wholesale inclusion in "his strange picture," as Gertrude Stein called it.[45] Having tried to accommodate a variant of the *Little Dancer Aged Fourteen* at the left-hand margin, he clearly experimented with the idea of using it again — seen from the opposite angle — as Rubin's "curtain-turner" figure at upper right.[46] There is now a serious case for seeing *Standing Nude* not only as part of the larger story of *Les Demoiselles d'Avignon* but as evidence that Picasso returned for a final bout with Degas and his *Little Dancer Aged Fourteen* in 1907, and pondered its inclusion — not once, but perhaps twice — in his "imaginary bordello."

An unexpected coda to this complex narrative emerges from one of the sketchbooks used by Picasso as he painted *Les Demoiselles d'Avignon*, which includes the name and address of Eugène Rouart.[47] This was the second son of Henri Rouart, one of Degas's closest friends through much of his life and the subject of two of his most touching, intimate portraits.[48] Degas also made pastels and paintings of Rouart's wife and several of his children, who in turn built

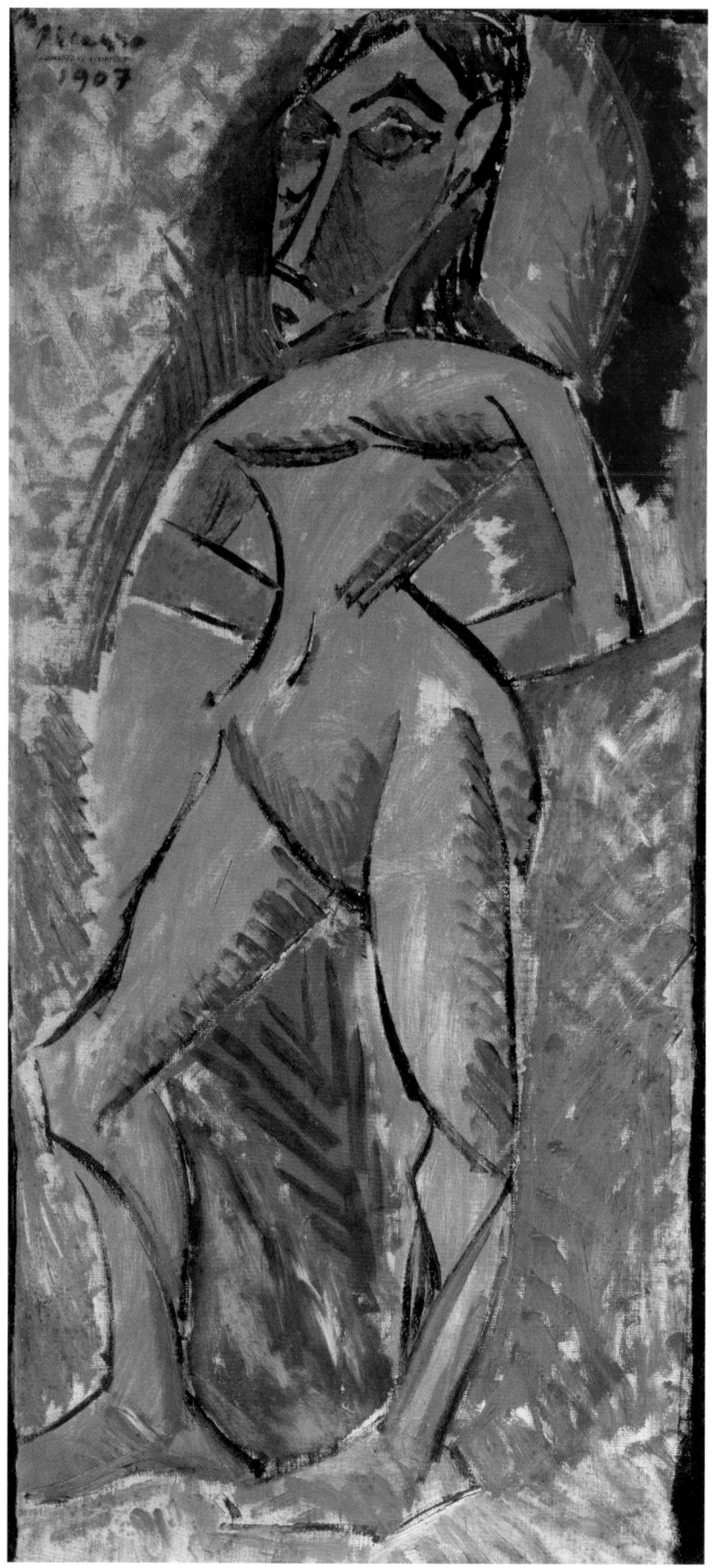

140

Pablo Picasso

Standing Nude, 1907.
Oil on canvas, 93 x 43 cm.
Museo del Novecento,
Milan (8750)

141

Edgar Degas

*Little Dancer Aged
Fourteen*, 1879–81. Bronze,
with gauze tutu and silk
ribbon, on wooden base,
height: 99 cm. Sterling
and Francine Clark Art
Institute, Williamstown,
Massachusetts
(1955.45)

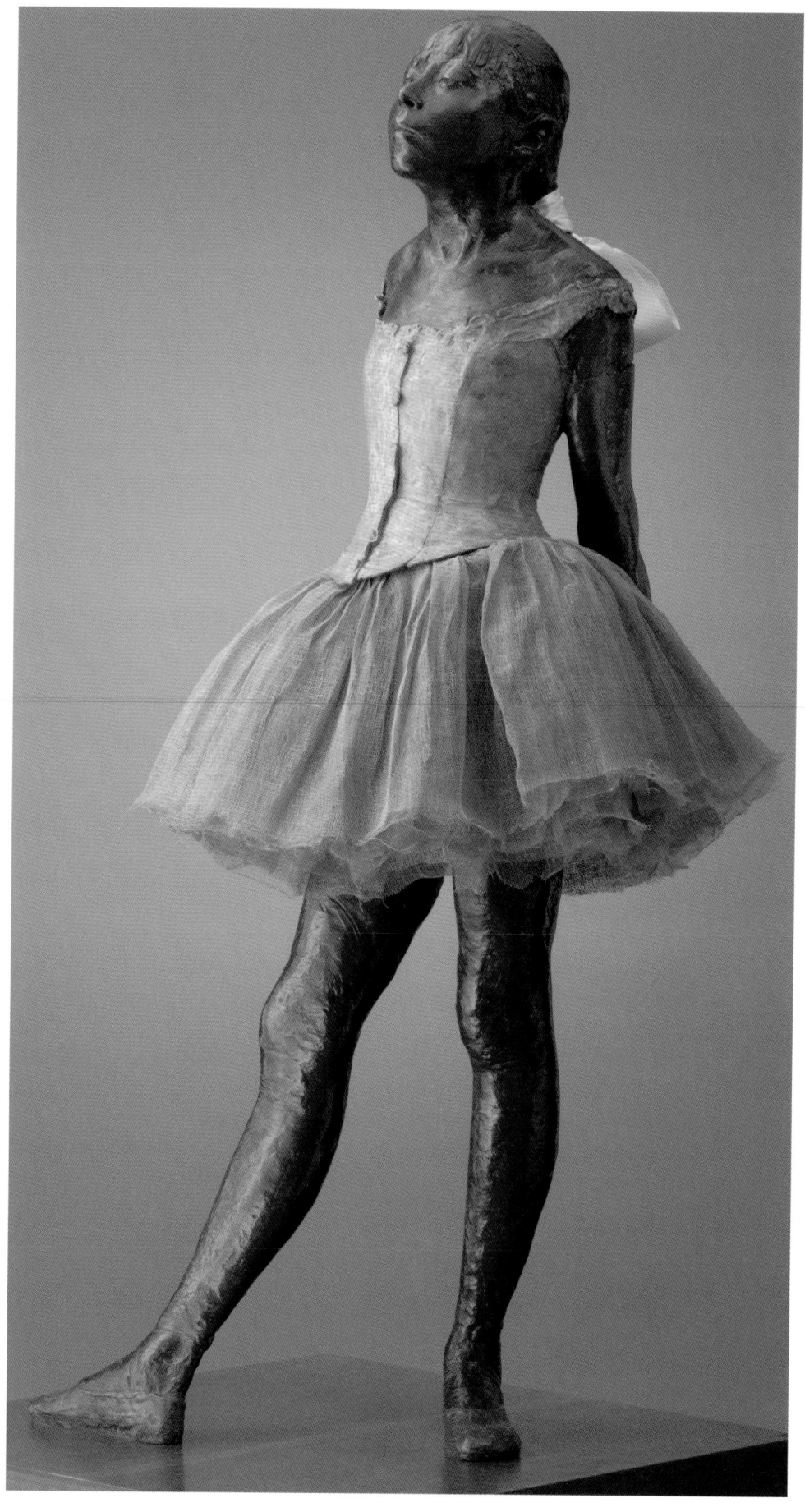

up collections of the artist's work.[49] Henri was a successful industrial engineer and an amateur painter who showed his landscapes alongside Degas at seven of the eight Impressionist exhibitions.[50] As his business thrived, Rouart filled his house with pictures by nineteenth-century artists and with many choice works on canvas and paper by Degas.[51] His son Eugène, a writer and friend of André Gide in his youth, later became "an audacious entrepreneur" who introduced modern agricultural methods into his large country property.[52] As a collector, he appears to have neglected the family's taste for Degas and set out to support contemporary art. In the spring of 1907, Eugène visited Picasso at the Bateau Lavoir and soon after wrote to ask him, "Would you be willing to part with your canvas representing the large red clown and the little harlequin?" referring to a work that is now in the Barnes Foundation.[53] This initiative was successful, and it appears from his correspondence that Eugène also saw *Les Demoiselles d'Avignon* as it was evolving in Picasso's studio and may even have contemplated buying it.[54] The bizarre coincidence of a figure so close to Degas possessing Picasso's most radical painting to date was not to transpire: Eugène's interest gradually shifted elsewhere and the monumental canvas remained with the artist until its acquisition by Jacques Doucet in 1924.

Olga and the Ballet Russes

Like so many of his encounters with the dance, Picasso's return to ballet imagery in 1917 was largely inadvertent. He had been invited by Serge Diaghilev to join a star-studded team of young talents who were collaborating on *Parade*, "the first incursion of truly radical modernism into the ballet."[55] With music by Erik Satie, book by Jean Cocteau, and choreography by Léonide Massine, *Parade* was soon launched in Paris under the flag of multidisciplinary artistic innovation. By this date Picasso had been hailed internationally as the inventor of Cubism,

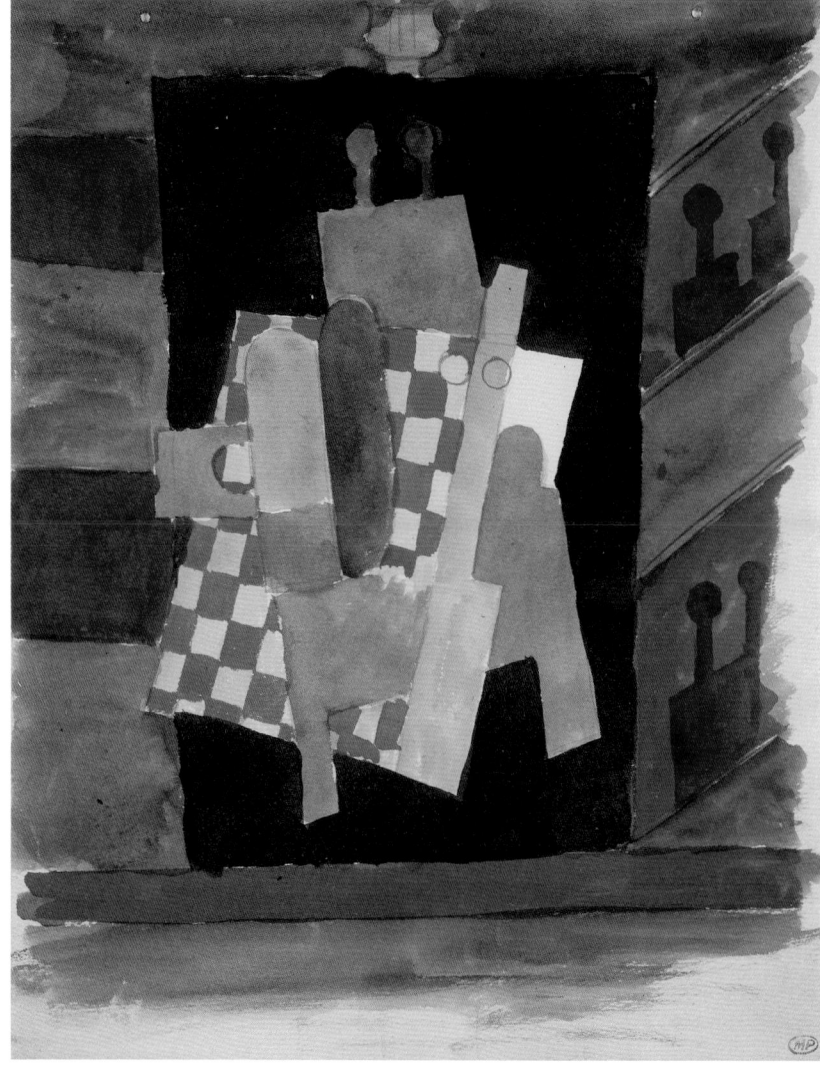

a visual revolution in which — to quote Roland Penrose — "Every aspect of painting had undergone an inquisitorial revision. Form, color, light, space, surface textures, signs, symbols and the meaning of reality had all been stripped of their former conventions and reinstated and developed with fresh significance."[56] Buoyed by his status as the Cubist pioneer but already concerned by the narrowness of some its interpreters, Picasso toyed with such whimsical hybrids as the semi-abstracted *Ballet and Spectators* of 1916 (**142**). His serious admirers were initially shocked, however, by the decision to join

142

Pablo Picasso

Ballet and Spectators, 1916. Gouache and pencil on paper, 29 x 22.5 cm. Musée national Picasso, Paris (MP 1546)

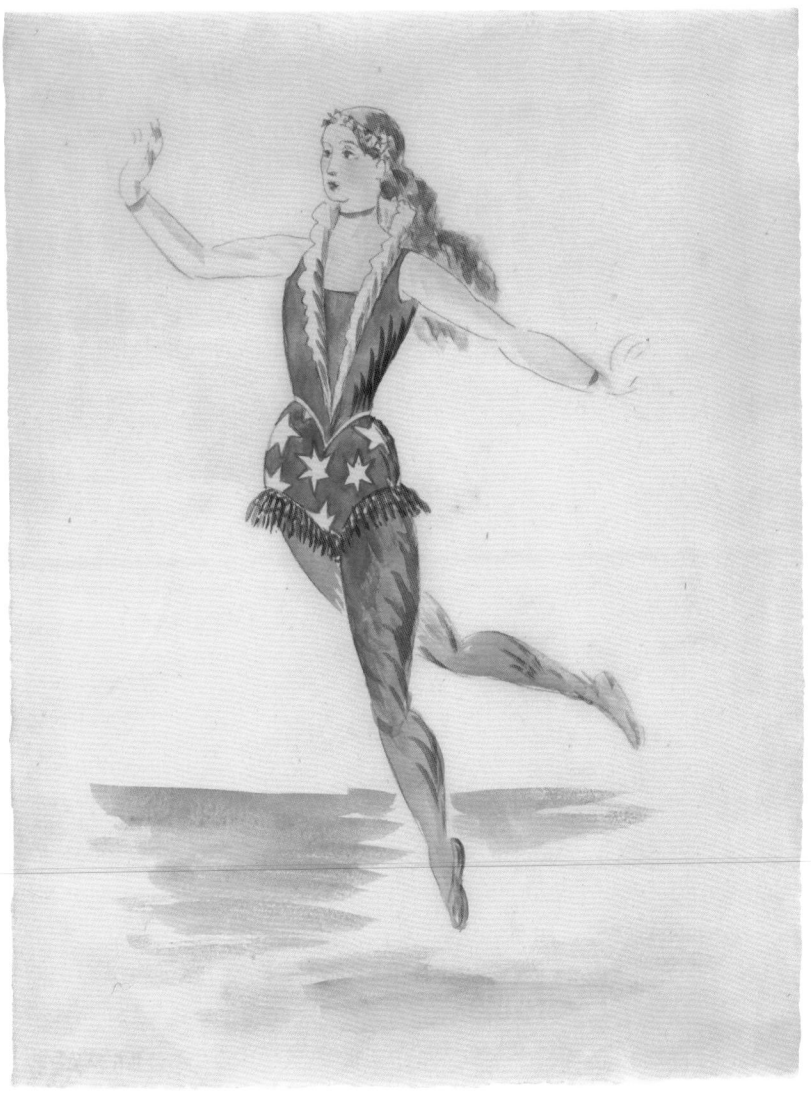

figure echoed in the production itself by a scantily clad female acrobat (**143**) and a character called "The Little American Girl." Though little or no conventional ballet featured in *Parade*, the airborne, innocent figure on the white horse had brought the subject back into Picasso's vocabulary after a decade's absence.

When Picasso first met Olga Khokhlova in Rome in 1917, she was rehearsing not an avant-garde production but Michel Fokine's *Les Sylphides*.[58] This was a modern tribute to the Romantic ballet of the 1830s, when the epoch-defining and similarly named *La Sylphide* had launched its own "revolution in the art of dancing" and established the legendary Marie Taglioni as a star.[59] Picasso's sighting of Olga in *Les Sylphides* thus took place in a quasi-traditional setting, danced to the music of Chopin and presented in the time-honored style of the "ballet blanc." The all-white costumes and ethereal qualities of the Diaghilev production are vividly conveyed in the publicity photograph for the Ballets Russes, where Olga is reclining in the foreground (see 304). Almost dissolved against their bleached surroundings, the dancers in their full-length tutus evoke the perfections of a past era. Clearly captivated, Picasso also learned that the chaste character of the ballerinas' stage roles could persist in daily life: Olga is said to have been one of the few targets of his passion who resisted the artist's advances.[60] But this introduction to Olga seems to have had a larger significance, defining her image for Picasso as he began to make her the subject of drawings and paintings. Olga's pale, elegant yet severe presence is now well known from a succession of pictures made in their early married life, such as the superb *Seated Woman (Olga Picasso)* (**144**). Initially drawn in firm charcoal lines, this study of his wife in a strikingly Degas-like position was subsequently and uncharacteristically developed in Conté crayon and gouache, perhaps recalling the use of pastel or from a desire to soften and animate

143

Pablo Picasso

Study for the Female Acrobat's Costume, 1916–17. Watercolor and pencil on paper, 27.5 x 20.7 cm. Musée national Picasso, Paris (MP 1571)

Diaghilev's frivolous-seeming enterprise, which soon sent Picasso back to his old passion for popular theater. As he began work in Rome on the stage sets and costume designs for *Parade*, Picasso went to "a tiny, dirty little-known theater music-hall" that thrilled both him and Cocteau.[57] A mixture of such commonplace associations, mass-media clichés, and vanguard devices permeated Picasso's resulting designs, which were at their least provocative in the vast drop-curtain that he created for *Parade*. Dominating this composition at left was a white horse surmounted by a white-clad ballerina, a

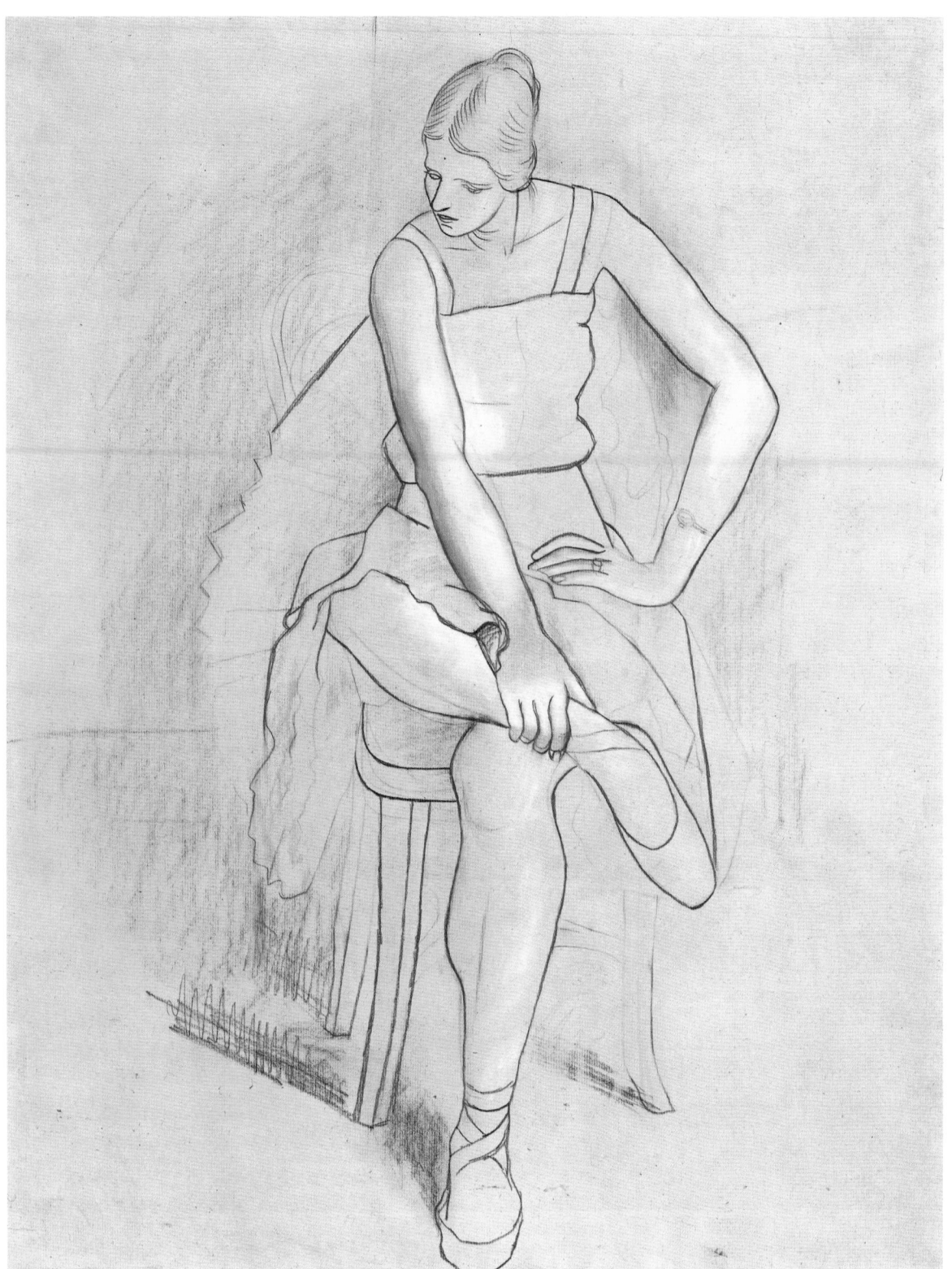

144

Pablo Picasso

Seated Woman (Olga Picasso), 1920. Conté crayon and gouache on paper, 63 x 48 cm. Collection of Marina Picasso

145

Pablo Picasso

Dancers, 1917? Watercolor on paper, 26.5 x 19.7 cm. Musée national Picasso, Paris (MP 845r)

146

Pablo Picasso

Two Dancers, 1919. Pencil on paper, 26.5 x 39.2 cm. Musée national Picasso, Paris (MP 852)

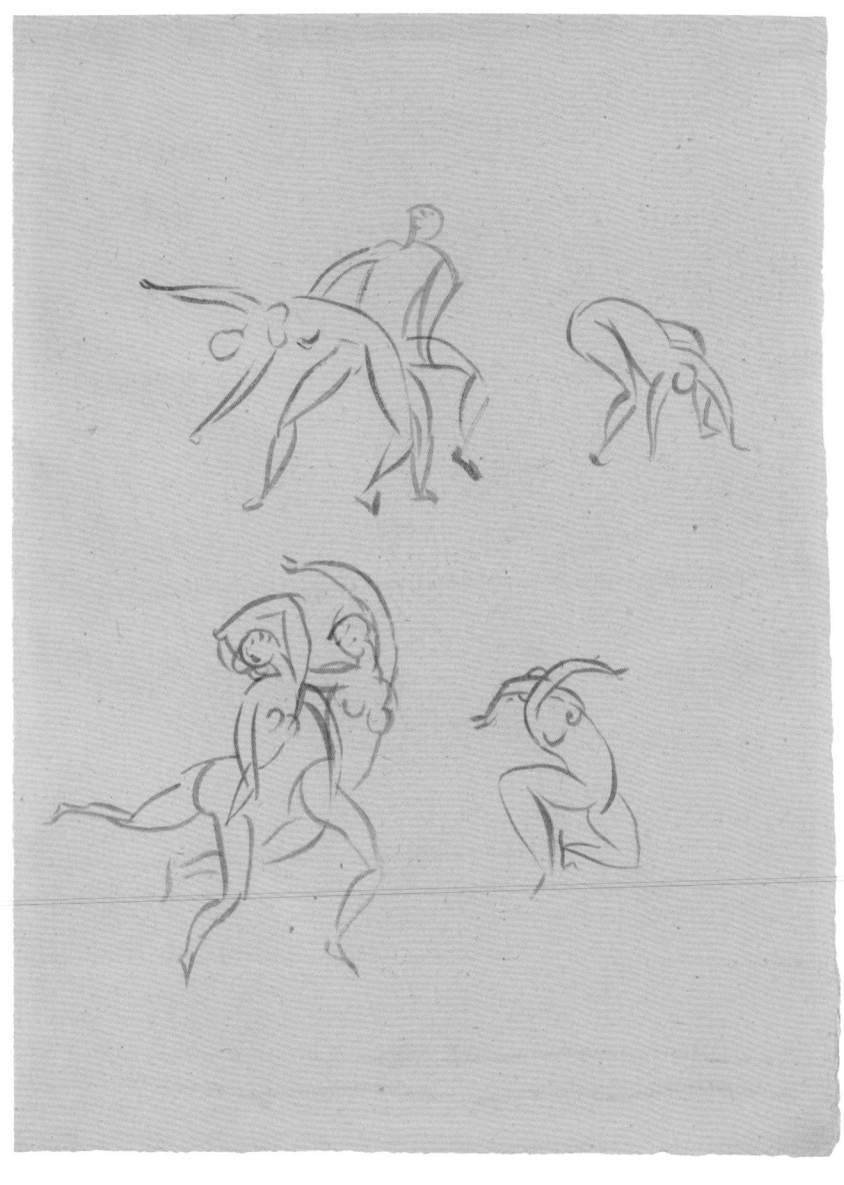

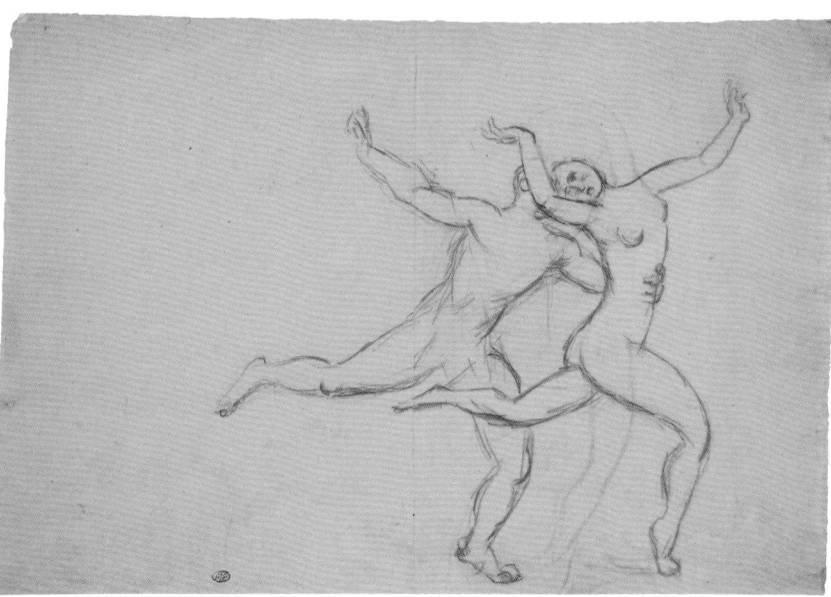

the image. Other pictures can tell a different story: casual photographs from their sojourn in Rome reveal Olga smiling broadly offstage, while another shows her blithely rehearsing for Stravinsky's radical *Firebird* with her hair loose and wearing a shapeless shift.[61]

Before leaving Rome, Picasso painted the large canvas *Harlequin and Woman with a Necklace* in which both figures are involved in stylized, geometric dancing. The scale of this picture alone suggested that the theme was perhaps returning to his art at a serious level: "Dance had evidently seeped into Picasso's vision" once again, as Richardson observes.[62] In his new, semi-public life, however, the artist found himself pulled in many directions and challenged both personally and artistically. The task of balancing his role as one of Diaghilev's designers with the high demands of Cubism would engage and entertain Picasso for several years, during which ballet appeared only sporadically in his pictures. *Parade* had opened in Paris on 18 May 1917, when its conjunction of new musical, choreographic, and visual modes prompted reactions from the ecstatic to the enraged. But Picasso's appetite for further theatrical productions was to prove almost insatiable; in succeeding years he designed costumes, scenery, and even publicity materials for Diaghilev and Massine's *The Three-Cornered Hat* in 1919; *Pulcinella*, with music by Stravinsky in 1920; and the Massine-Satie *Mercure* in 1924. Soon Picasso's décor threatened to attract as much acclaim as the music and dance at such events, while further projects beckoned. Throughout this period, the extent to which Picasso — an artist dedicated above all to the human figure — concentrated on the geometric or otherwise fanciful trappings of these theatrical spectacles at the expense of their performers can approach the perverse. Some quick sketches of naked dancers (**145**) may be part-observed, part-imaginary, while a more studied drawing that is clearly related to the 1919

129

La Boutique Fantastique (**146**), designed by André Derain, falls back on an undemanding classicism. During this period, Douglas Cooper asserts, Picasso was "constantly in the theater watching performances or in the practice studios watching the dancers exercise. He was never without a sketchbook in his hand."[63] Some of the drawings were used to illustrate Ballets Russes programs, but these small works were almost his only attempts to deal directly with the challenge of representing the ballet.

Like his predecessors in this field, Picasso had come up against one of the defining paradoxes of the dance. However mesmerizing firsthand, ballet is defined by an almost continuous pattern of movement that taxes all but the most acute observers and deft draftsmen. Faced with such a challenge, Picasso may well have recalled the sensation caused in 1910 by Matisse's *Dance*, his friend and rival's mural-sized painting that was inspired by a group of dancing Catalan fishermen, rather than ballerinas, but regarded by many as a triumphant breakthrough for the artist.[64] Picasso himself was now ideally placed to respond, fully at home in the theaters of Europe — thanks to Diaghilev and company — and able to see dancers of every kind and portray them as he wished. None of his major pictures, however, had confronted the ballet in performance, and he had certainly produced no works with the visceral power of *Dance*. As the partly abstracted *Harlequin and Woman with a Necklace* indicates, Picasso could tackle dancers in the stylized idioms of later Cubism while remaining uncertain in his depiction of events on the stage, such as the occasions when he saw Olga and her colleagues in more traditional roles. It is hardly a coincidence that all his depictions of Olga, before she decided to retire from dancing at the time of their marriage, show her at rest or holding a pose for effect.

A characteristic strategy of Picasso's that he used in more than one situation of this kind was to fall back on humor. In *Two Dancers* (**147**),

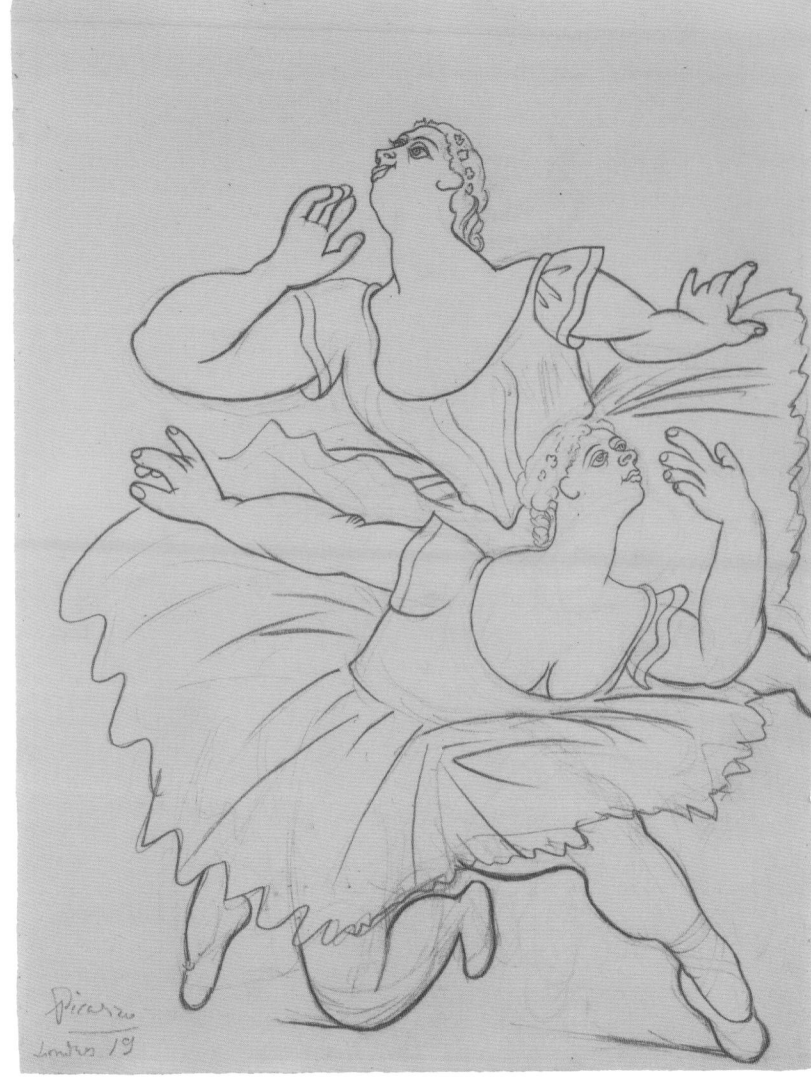

made in London in 1919, the artist celebrated his exuberant models in their capacity as popular entertainers, reveling in their extravagance as much as their traditional skills. The Diaghilev company was in London for a season, presenting *The Three-Cornered Hat* and *La Boutique Fantastique*, and briefly reviving the enthusiasm of Picasso who "appeared on opening night with paint and brushes to add his latest ideas to the costumes of the dancers."[65] During this period Picasso is said to have "filled several albums with drawings of groups of dancers performing, at rest, or in classical poses," some of

147

Pablo Picasso

Two Dancers, 1919 (Summer). Pencil on paper, 31 x 23.9 cm. The Museum of Modern Art, New York. The John S. Newberry Collection, 1963 (178.1963)

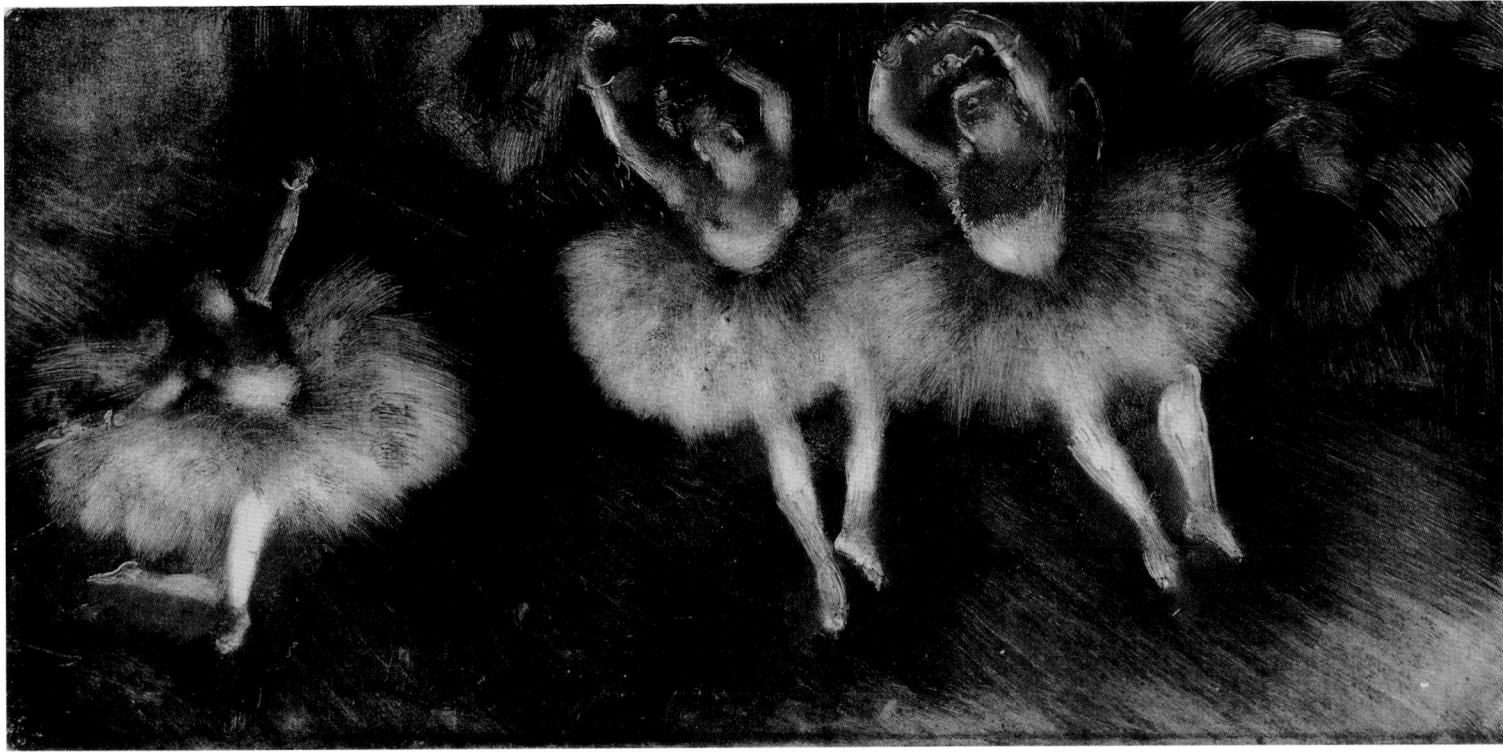

148

Edgar Degas

Three Ballet Dancers,
c. 1876–77. Monotype,
20 x 41.7. Sterling and
Francine Clark Art
Institute, Williamstown,
Massachusetts
(1955.1386)

them apparently providing the stimulus for *Two Dancers*.[66] This drawing is a picture of ebullience, where the women are unquestionably performing on stage, their energy expressed in billowing curves and counter-curves, overlapping volumes and echoing spaces. Though apparently frivolous, *Two Dancers* is a serious drawing that Picasso first drafted in lighter lines and subsequently refined, then proudly signed and dated. By this time, he must have been conscious that his most famous precursor in the field, Edgar Degas, had also explored the less solemn aspects of the ballet on occasion. In the monotype *Three Ballet Dancers* (**148**), Degas took a similar delight in his acrobatic trio who jump and gesticulate on the Paris Opéra stage and exude an irresistible joie-de-vivre. After more than a decade's experience of drawing and painting dancers at close quarters, Degas was sufficiently well informed to improvise this scene directly into the ink spread on a monotype plate. It is even possible that Picasso had

seen this particular work, in the original or in reproduction. The signed monotype was given by Degas to his friend Alphonse Cherfils and subsequently acquired by Durand-Ruel, then illustrated in 1919 — the year of Picasso's *Two Dancers* — in Paul Lafond's pioneering biography of Degas.[67]

Several drawings in a broadly comparable style from this same year show members of Diaghilev's company in their dancing attire. In the justly celebrated *Three Ballet Dancers: Olga Khokhlova, Lydia Lopokova, and Lubov Tchernicheva* (**149**), Picasso was less lighthearted than in *Two Dancers* and even more disciplined in his draftsmanship. A shadowy network of sketched and partly erased lines shows the evolution of this tightly structured group who are again presented in the outfits of the "ballet blanc," complete with miniature wings and wreaths of tiny flowers in their hair. Further refined by Picasso's stylized handling, this self-conscious cluster of dancers emphasizes the

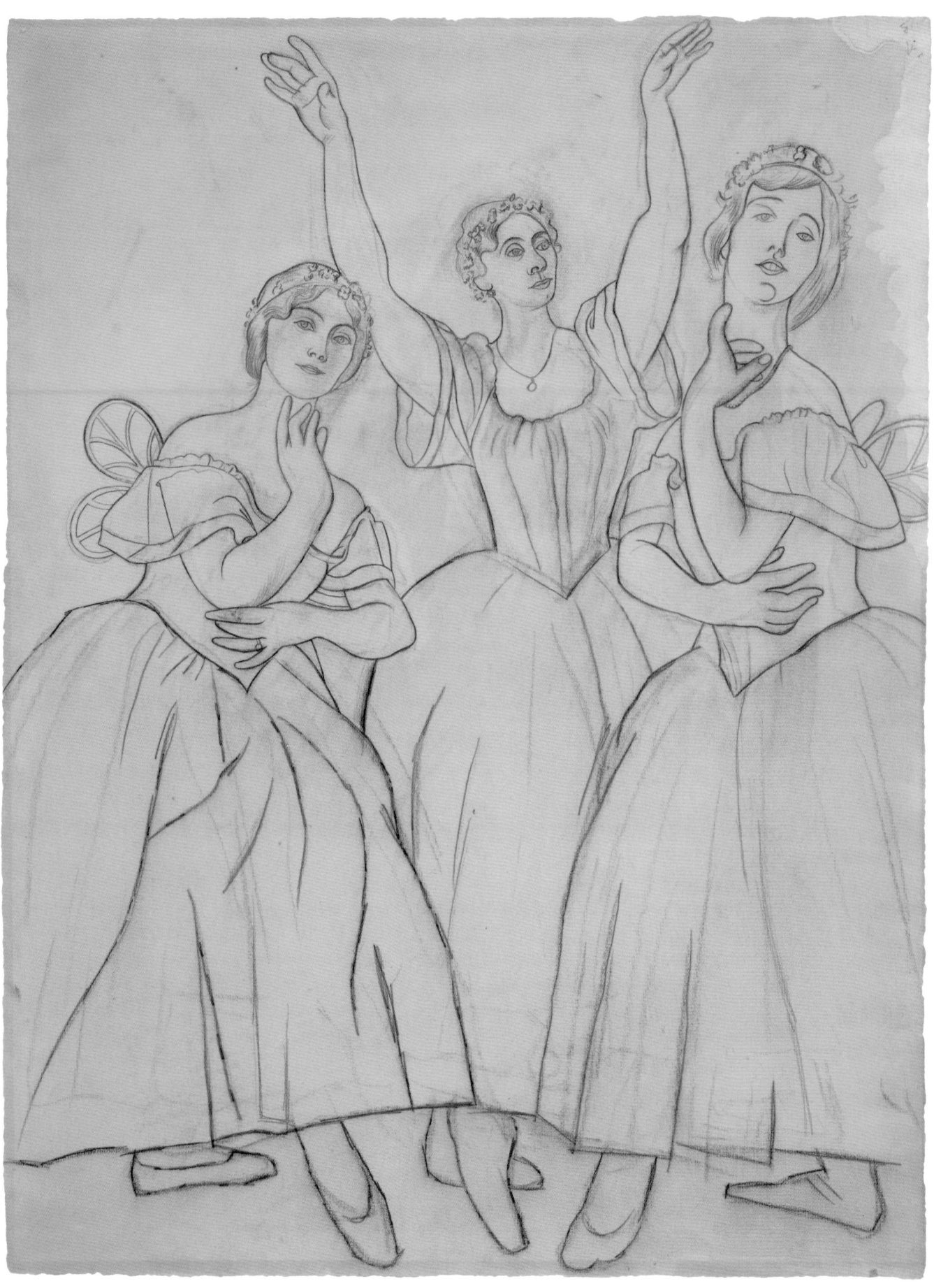

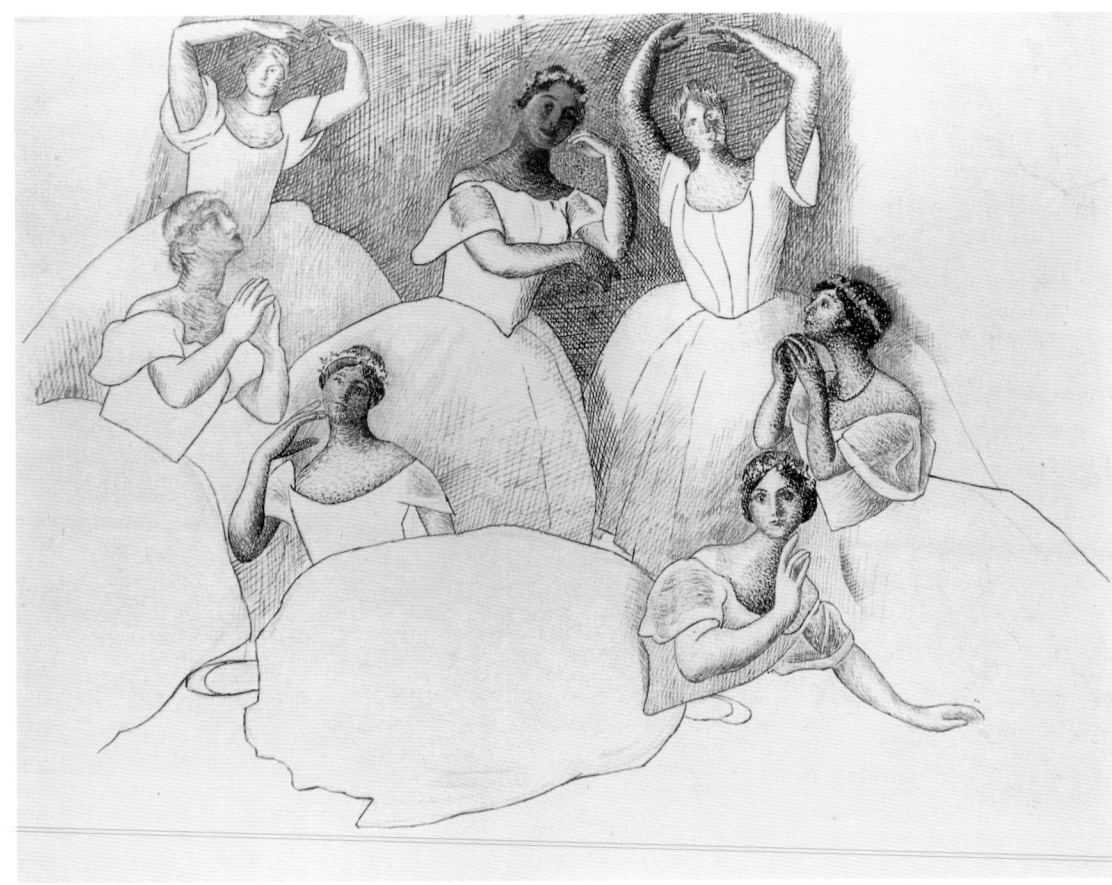

ethereal qualities of the ballet rather than the boisterousness of *Two Dancers*. In reality, the three graceful figures were posed for the camera rather than for roles on stage. At this date Picasso used photographs as his starting point for several drawings of this type, one of them exploiting the print that showed Olga reclining in the foreground with the cast of *Les Sylphides* (**150**; see also 304, 305).[68] As many artists had already discovered, photography had the potential to solve some of their problems, though here — almost perversely — Picasso was exploiting the medium to study a stationary subject. A similar graphic manner was chosen for a group of portraits of his theatrical collaborators, including Satie, Cocteau, Massine, and Diaghilev himself, that allowed Picasso to be both solemn and a little ironic. It has often been noted that this style relates to Picasso's

current passion for the art of Jean-Dominique Ingres, the great nineteenth-century classicist whose work had enjoyed a major revival after an ambitious retrospective in Paris in 1905.[69] Predominantly known for his formal portraits and paintings of exotic or classicized nudes, Ingres was now openly discussed in terms of his erotic fascination with the female body. Central to Ingres's artistic persona was a dedication to drawing, an aspect of his achievement that had deeply influenced Degas from youth onward, after he met the aging artist and was memorably advised by him to "always make lines, many lines."[70]

The major shift in Picasso's strategy as a ballet artist in the postwar years was undoubtedly his decision to revisit the work of Degas. Now enjoying the bourgeois comforts of life in Paris with Olga, Picasso was among those who first benefited from the new awareness of Degas's art that followed his death in September 1917. One response to this event was a series of new publications on the Impressionist painter, which transformed the trickle of books and articles in the early years of the century into a steady stream. The first biography of Degas appeared in two volumes in 1918 and 1919, and substantial surveys of his work came out in French, German, and English, typically containing a selection of monochrome illustrations.[71] Books devoted to Degas's prints and his achievement as a draftsman soon followed and were among many studies that now exploited the evidence of the posthumous studio sales, which began in spring 1918. With the single limitation of color, which was still beyond all but the most lavish publications, examples of work by Degas from most periods of his career could now be perused on the printed page.

Confronting the Degas Legacy

The sales of Degas's art were complex and protracted, but received a great deal of attention in war-threatened Paris and even outside the country. Among the visitors to the displays that preceded each auction was probably Picasso himself: a comparison of the dates of these sales with the artist's known movements at this period shows that he was in Paris for the first three auctions.[72] Each of the principal studio sales included some three or four hundred pictures, the equivalent of four massive retrospectives taking place in a little over a year. The items in each sale were arranged by the organizers so that a selection of paintings, pastels, and drawings appeared on each occasion, though the sheer quantity of the latter meant that large numbers of works on paper were concentrated in the final auctions.[73] Similarly spread across the months was the output of every phase in Degas's life, from his art-school days and Italian tour of the 1850s to the public spectacle of Impressionism, then into his slow

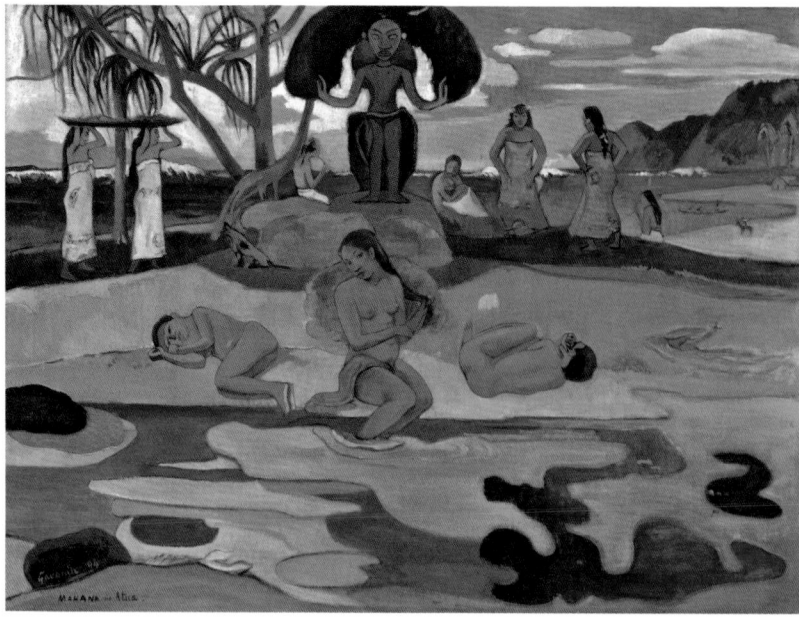

retreat from the art world and even his own studio in the new century. The only aspects of his marathon production left unrepresented were the artist's sketchbooks and his considerable body of sculpture, the latter unveiled several years later when the fragile waxes were cast in bronze. There were also separate sales of prints and Degas's holdings of works by other artists, a collection of more than a thousand works that astonished all but a few who had been intimate with Degas's home in the rue Victor Massé. Major canvases by El Greco, Ingres (**152**), and Delacroix were now sold side by side with pictures by his contemporaries — Manet, Pissarro, Cassatt, Cézanne, Morisot, Gauguin (**151**), and others — many of which now hang in the world's great museums. Along with this evidence of his own taste, those who wished to engage firsthand with Degas's principal obsessions as an artist — the nude, the ballerina, the racehorse, the portraits of contemporaries and scenes of Parisian life, even the little-known landscapes — could linger at their leisure in the rooms full of pictures assembled for each sale.

A distant sense of these developments and of their importance in the French art world can

151

Paul Gauguin

(French, 1848–1903)

Day of the God (Mahana no Atua), 1894. Oil on canvas, 68.3 x 91.5 cm. The Art Institute of Chicago. Helen Birch Bartlett Memorial Collection (1926.198)

be gleaned from the illustrated catalogues that accompanied each of the four principal sales of Degas's own work.[74] All the lots appeared in black-and-white photographs that ranged from the crisp and legible to the shadowy (**153**), beginning with his more important pictures and culminating in page after page of drawings. These pictures were displayed and sold in the galleries of Georges Petit, one of a trio of dealers handling the project that included the Durand-Ruels and Ambroise Vollard. If Picasso was almost certainly aware of these events, he characteristically failed to mention them to his biographers, yet vivid traces of their currency survive in his intimate circle. The first sale, for example, is colorfully recorded in the writings of perhaps Picasso's closest friend at this time, "the only human being in whom he had complete faith," the poet Guillaume Apollinaire.[75] As an occasional critic, Apollinaire had been casually tracking Degas's fortunes for some

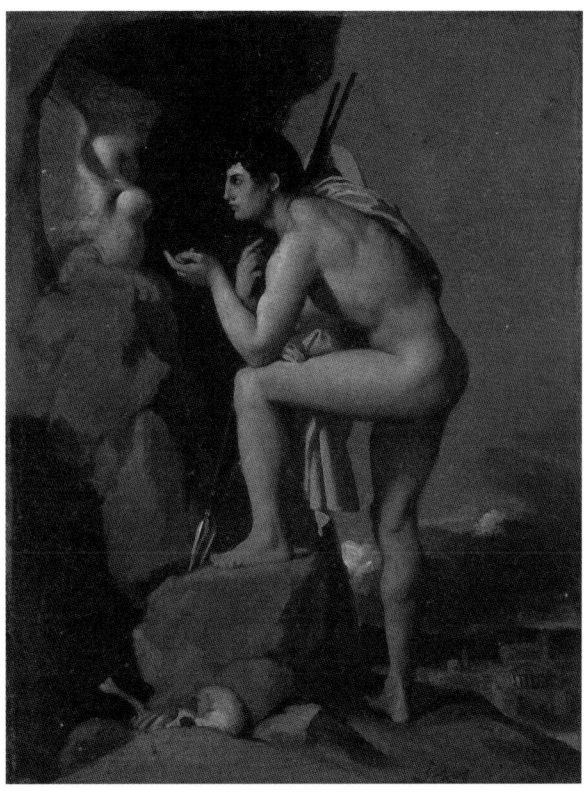

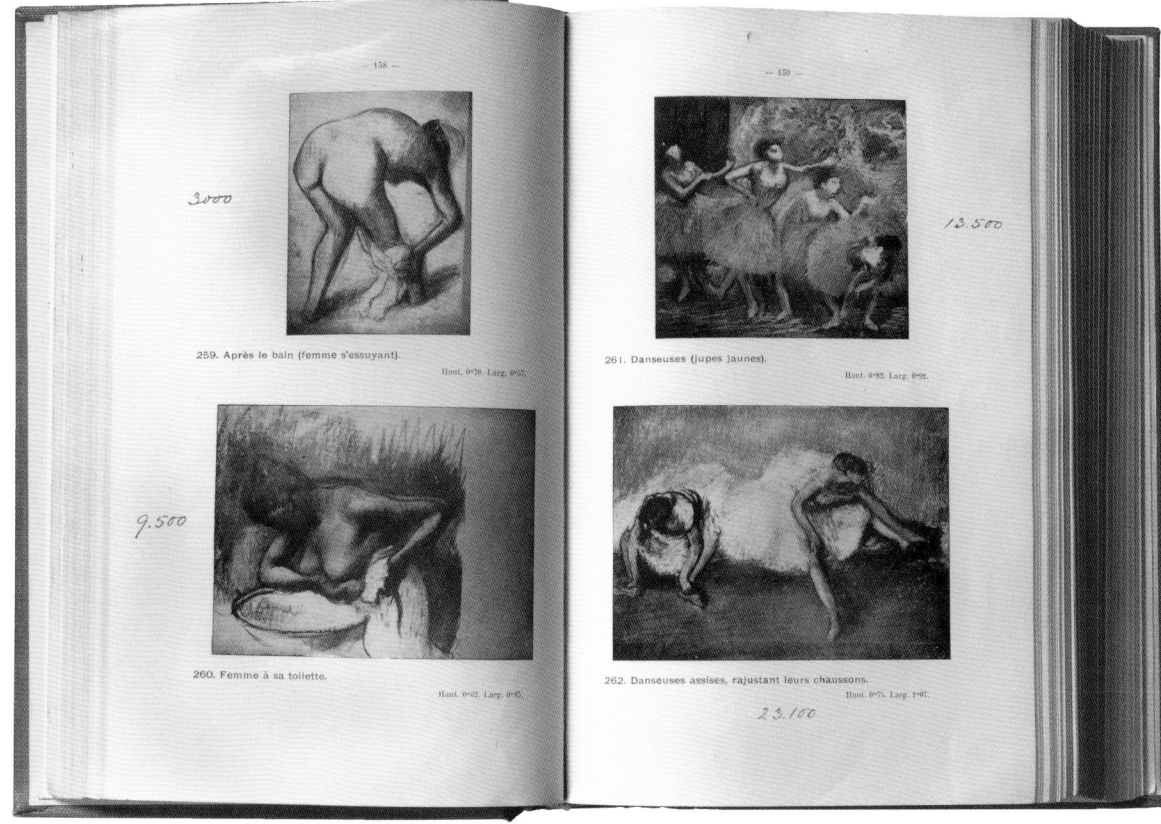

259. Après le bain (femme s'essuyant).

260. Femme à sa toilette.

261. Danseuses (jupes jaunes).

262. Danseuses assises, rajustant leurs chaussons.

time, noting the appearance of individual works in earlier exhibitions and auctions, and views about his art among the younger generation. On 11 May 1918, a few days after the first sale of Degas's own pictures, Apollinaire wrote some gossipy paragraphs that began: "Opinions flew thick and fast among the crowd attending the Degas exhibition at the Georges Petit Gallery."[76] Reporting on a supposedly overheard conversation about the recent auction of the artist's old and modern masters, he continued: "'Did you notice,' said a painter to his poet friend, 'that in Degas's collection, which was sold recently, there were works by practically everyone — Gauguin, Cézanne, Jeanniot — but *there was not a single Toulouse-Lautrec*? Today I finally understand why.'" It is of course very tempting to see "the poet" as Apollinaire and "the painter" as Picasso himself, but no further clues were forthcoming. Instead, we are left to imagine Picasso's fascinated encounter with Degas's two El Grecos, his portraits and drawings by Ingres, and his less expected taste for newer art, "works by practically everyone."

Responding to the first auction of Degas's own paintings, pastels, and drawings, Apollinaire noted the "curious and unfavorable opinions expressed by one part of the crowd," adding that "Degas remained controversial even after his death."[77] But he also reported the thrilled surprise of others around him when the same pictures were shown prior to the sales: "Would you believe it!" the critic Clément-Janin is heard to exclaim, "These wonders have been hidden from us all this time!"[78] In his article entitled "The Degas Sale," Apollinaire aspired to a more balanced view of the artist's lifetime accomplishment as represented in the May auction.[79] Degas's works "varied greatly in technique and inspiration," he explained, yet "all of them confirmed the prodigious mastery that made the master of ballerinas a unique artist, a cruel but subtle observer who was able to express, without banality, the dazzling, elusive essence of

gracefulness." Apollinaire went on to argue that it was "regrettable that the state did not make a bid for more of these infinitely precious works," before remarking on Degas's skill as a pastelist. In conclusion, he added that future audiences would "look at *The Dancers at the Bar*, *The Green Chartreuse*, or *Two Women Ironing* to try and imagine all the bitterness and all the exquisite charm of the nineteenth century." Even allowing for Apollinaire's use of one or two clichés that had been in circulation for some time, this was a powerful endorsement of Degas from a commentator at the heart of the Parisian avant-garde.

As Apollinaire's texts so vividly suggest, the first Degas sale brought Picasso and his peers face-to-face with "the master of ballerinas." More than a third of the items listed and illustrated in the May 1918 catalogue are based on the ballet, apparently arranged at random by the organizers but representing most of the significant subjects of Degas's dance art. A few works in the sale were probably known to Picasso from other contexts, such as *The Dance Lesson* (see 124) and the pastel that Manzi had titled *Study of Leg and Arm Movements for a Dancer with a Tambourine*.[80] Most of the ballet pictures, however, had never been seen outside Degas's studio and illuminated aspects of his career that were less familiar to — or in some cases, entirely unsuspected by — the Parisian audience. Especially noteworthy was the fact that a high proportion of these works came from the last two decades of Degas's active life, the 1890s and 1900s, when he exhibited less and less frequently and finally withdrew from the public arena. Surrounded — then as now — by misinformation about the artist's health, eyesight, and sociability, these decades were in fact enormously productive and arguably among his most creative.[81] They were also replete with contradiction, not least Degas's gradual retreat from the Paris Opéra and its ballerinas in the very years when the theme of the dance took hold of his art as never before. Several accounts tell us that female models — such as Benedetta Canals and Suzanne Valadon — still came to his studio to pose, while witnesses described the tutus, silk slippers, and other accessories that Degas continued to arrange in some of his late compositions.[82] Other visitors recalled easels loaded with pastels of dancers and the decaying waxes that occupied him well into the twentieth century: in 1910, he wrote to a friend, "I do not finish with my damned sculpture."[83]

Though essentially a continuation of Degas's earlier practice, the dance works of his last years represent a departure that was both unexpected and curiously poignant. Toward the end of the century, it was the dancers backstage who effectively supplanted almost all his other obsessions, to the point where few new pictures of ballet performances were now undertaken. The dancers of these late years typically stand by a scenery flat or sit on a low bench, sometimes with one or two companions but often alone. At a time when the artist himself had slowed down physically, his dancer-models rest their aching bodies and massage their limbs as they recover from working in the classroom or performing on stage. A superb example of the genre that was probably made around 1895 is *Two Dancers in the Wings* (**154**), a drawing that Degas greatly enriched with pastel and sold during his lifetime.[84] At left is part of the scenery that we glimpse from the back while in the distance at right is the stage itself, which is empty as far as the wings at the opposite side. Probably representing an interval during a performance when the company awaits the raising of the curtain, Degas used this composition to reflect on the inertia and weariness of the foreground dancers. One figure stands patiently at center while the other leans almost desperately against the set and gathers her strength for the next act, their isolation from the rest of the company adding to the atmosphere of stoicism. Even more extreme is *Group*

of Dancers (**155**), a work executed around 1900 and sold in the first studio sale. Here Degas's fascination with the rhythms of the ballerinas was so intense that their clothes were added almost as an afterthought, in a powerful statement about human vitality itself. Strongly articulated as figures but remote from the life of the stage, they bring to mind an enigmatic remark of the poet Stéphane Mallarmé, a friend of Degas's at this period: "A danseuse is not a woman dancing, because she is not a woman and she does not dance."[85]

A particular focus of Picasso's interest at the first posthumous sale would surely have been Degas's drawings. As Picasso was already aware, even a pastel as rich in color as *Two Dancers in the Wings* had been created on a foundation of line, in this case a characteristic study in charcoal that established the positions of the figures and defined their relationships to each other and to their surroundings. A powerful example of a drawing for another ballet motif that appeared in the first sale in May 1918 was *Three Nude Dancers* (**156**), a work representing a favorite theme from Degas's late years: the seated dancer.[86] *Three Nude Dancers* follows his almost invariable practice of this period, when the artist drew each of his figures naked before adding costumes, ballet slippers, and other accessories. A distant echo of his months at the École des Beaux-Arts in 1855, this ritual had faded significantly in the Impressionist years but took on a revitalized role in Degas's later art. In *Three Nude Dancers*, sensuous charcoal marks and flourishes explored his models' naked bodies, fixing their contours and progressively articulating the spaces around and between them. Such works often provided the starting point for a progression from drawing to pastel, when Degas used tracing paper to make two or more variants of a charcoal composition that could then be developed in startlingly different combinations of color. Following *Three Nude Dancers*, for example, he created one

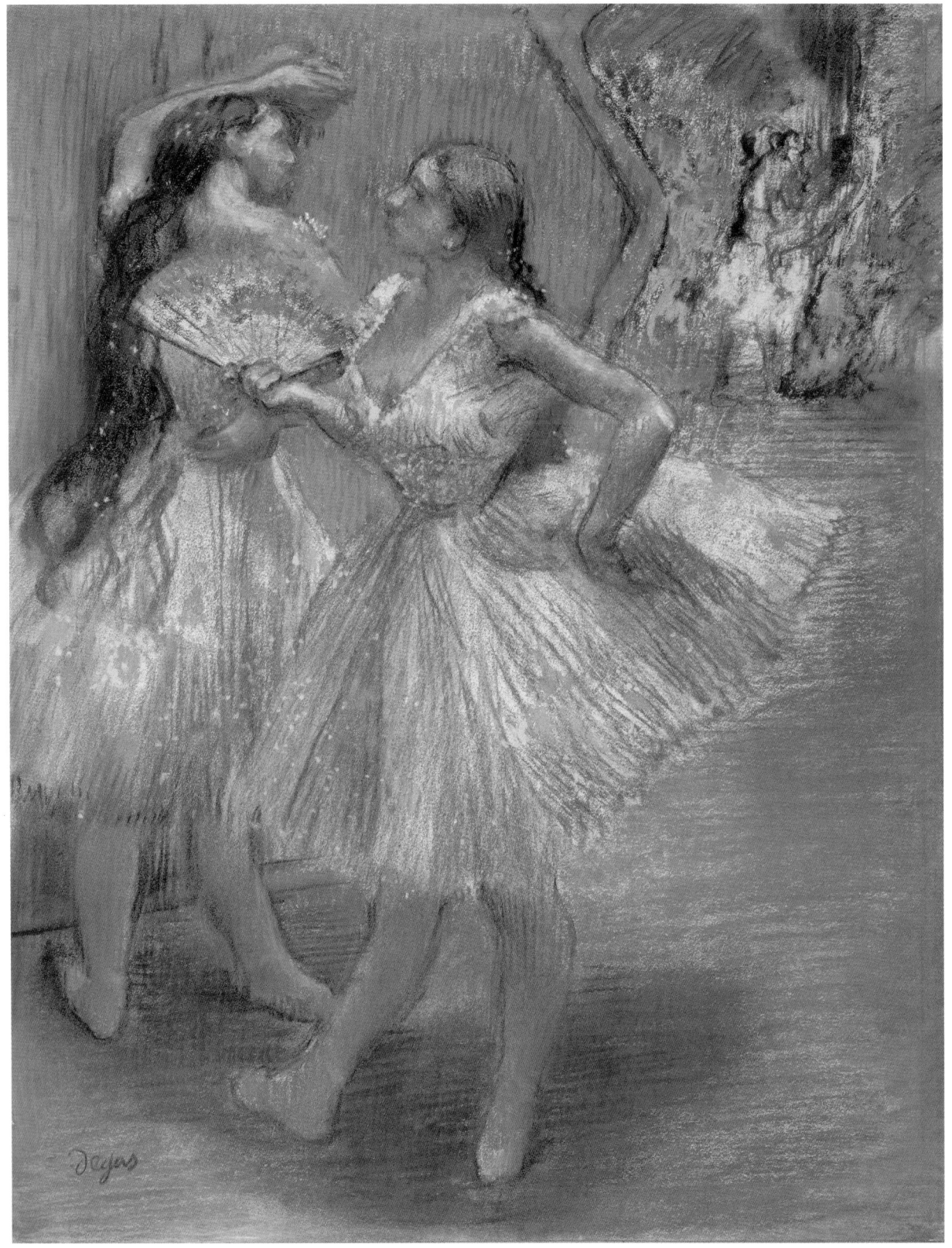

154

Edgar Degas

Two Dancers in the Wings,
c. 1888. Pastel on paper
mounted on cardboard on
a wooden stretcher,
59 x 46.4 cm.
Private collection

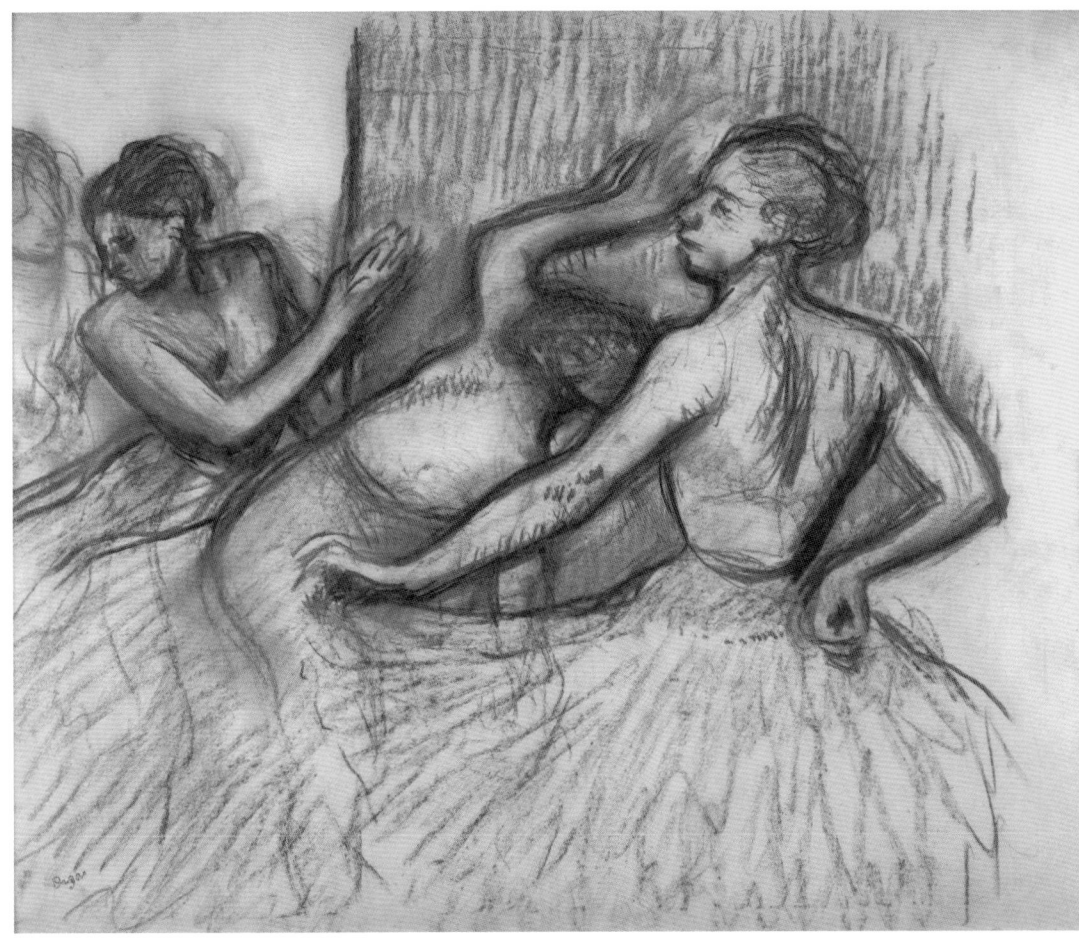

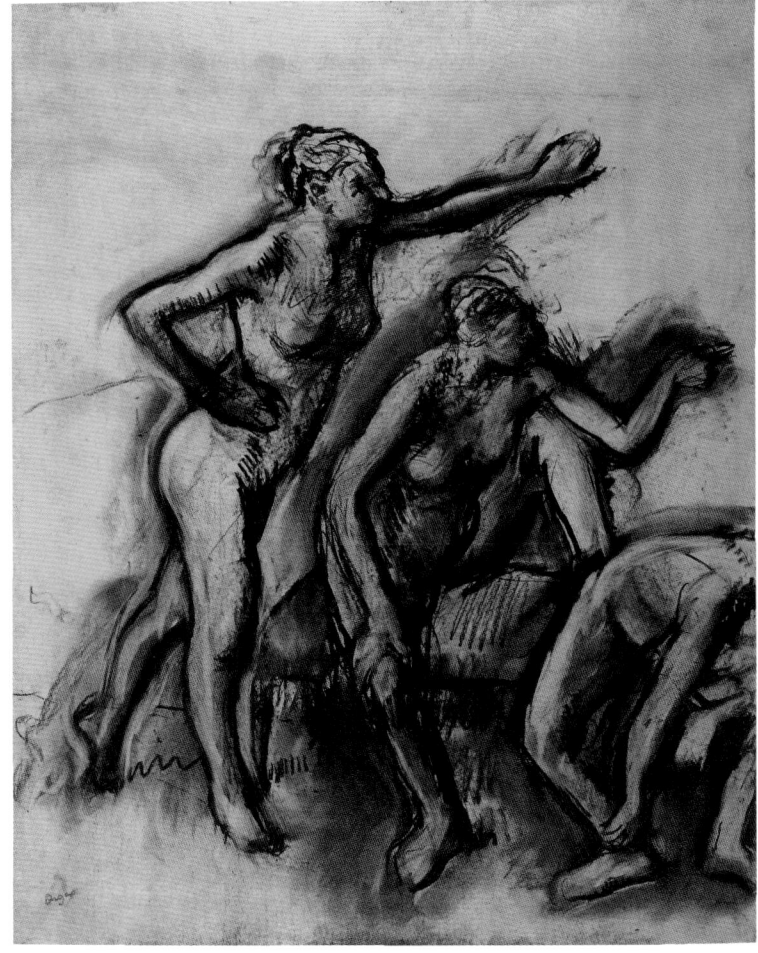

version of this scene in bright mineral green and another in brilliant pinks and golds, keeping both in his studio among the works that later appeared at the 1918–19 sales.[87] For Picasso and his colleagues, such sheets would have been among the first examples of Degas's late drafts-manship — and of his eccentric approach to pastel-making — that they had seen. In later life Degas released relatively few new pictures onto the art market, keeping them for the endless process of revision that filled his days or as ref-erence points for future works. As Apollinaire's article indicated, the unfamiliar manner of draw-ings such as *Three Nude Dancers* disconcerted conservative visitors to the Degas studio sales, while attracting younger Parisians who were attuned to their significance. Remote from the acute realism of the ballet classroom pictures

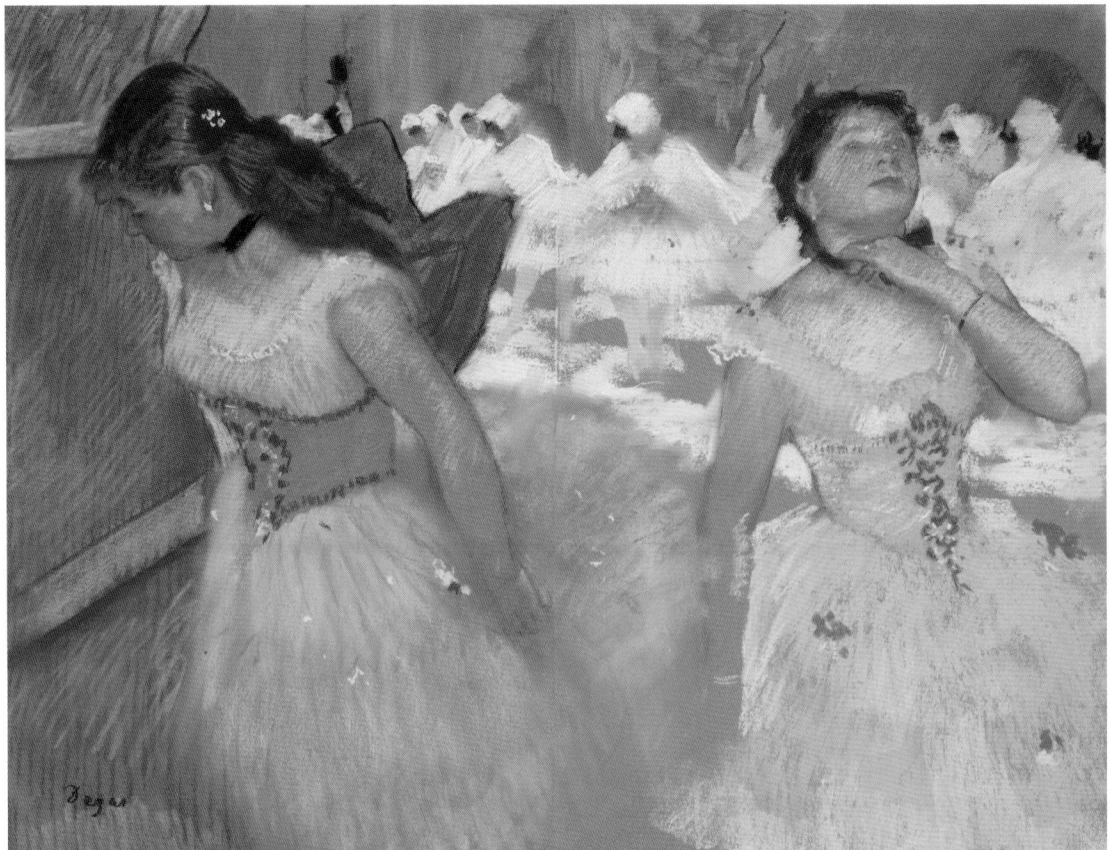

157

Edgar Degas

Entrance of the Masked Dancers, c. 1884. Pastel on gray-brown paper, 49 x 64.7 cm. Sterling and Francine Clark Art Institute, Williamstown, Massachusetts (1955.559)

of the 1870s, such drawings seemed to aspire toward a more timeless depiction of the human figure, in which Degas used nothing but the simple expedient of ". . . lines, many lines," in Ingres's formulation. Notionally a cluster of ballerinas in the wings, Degas's *Three Nude Dancers* presents the human body devoid of temporal trappings, as it might have appeared in a carved Classical relief or equally in a candid photograph from the early twentieth century.

In a way that Picasso would have grasped instinctively at this moment, Degas had come to understand that attempts to capture the dancer in flight or even in graceful arabesque were at best paradoxical, at worst frankly contrived. Developments in nineteenth-century photography, which Degas had followed from an early age and explored firsthand around 1896, may have played a part in this thinking. Conversant

with the experiments of Étienne-Jules Marey and Eadweard Muybridge, Degas and his contemporaries acknowledged that their rivals' new techniques far exceeded the draftsman's own capacity to "freeze" the human figure in motion. Artists could now choose to exploit the evidence of high-speed photographs or rethink their craft by acknowledging the role of personal perception and experience in their creative endeavors. A vivacious pastel from Degas's middle years, the *Entrance of the Masked Dancers* (**157**), is a brilliant assertion of the dynamic spirit of the ballet within these limitations. While the smaller figures in the distance execute modest dance steps, the principal dancers in the foreground surge toward us as they leave the stage in a blaze of color. Spectacular in summarizing the energy of an Opéra production, this pastel is nevertheless one of

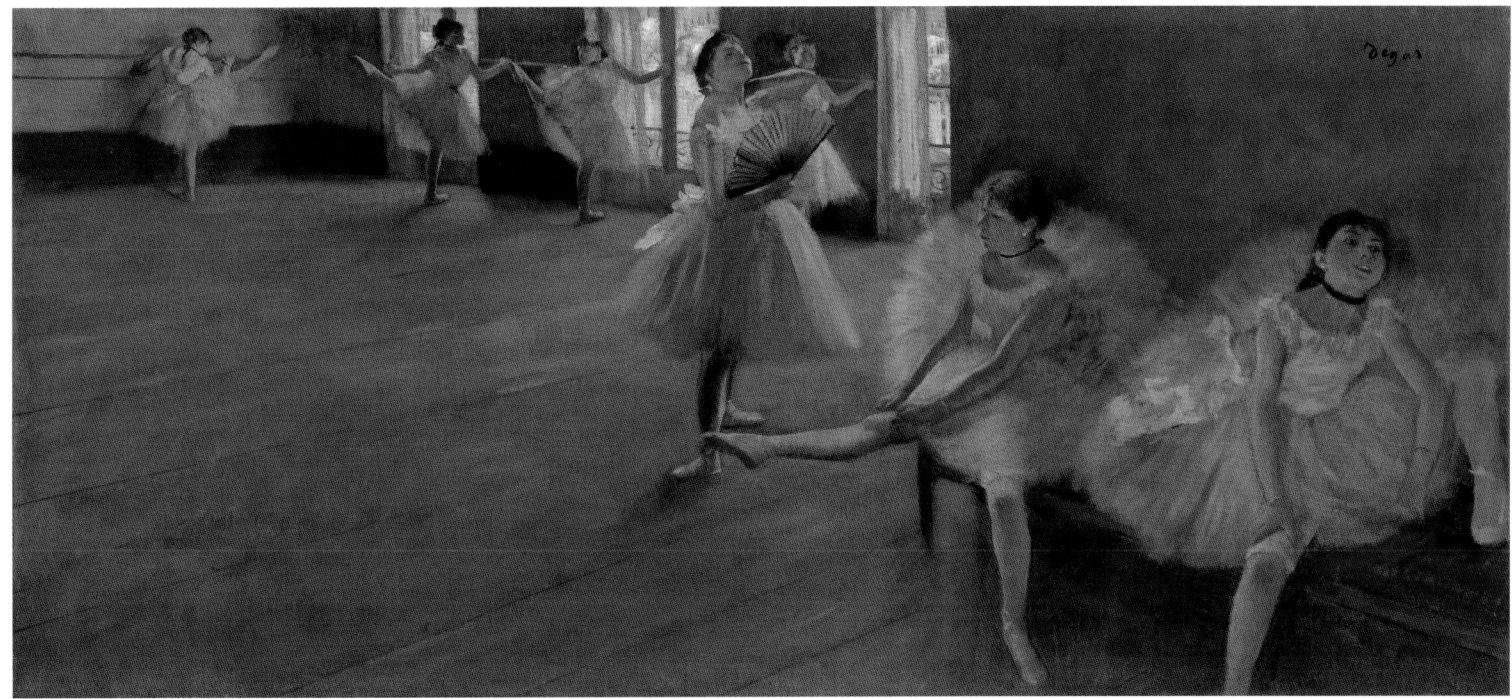

158

Edgar Degas

Dancers in the Classroom, c. 1880. Oil on canvas, 39.4 x 88.4 cm. Sterling and Francine Clark Art Institute, Williamstown, Massachusetts (1955.562)

159

Edgar Degas

A Coryphée Resting, c. 1880. Pastel, 46.4 x 61.3 cm. John G. Johnson Collection, Philadelphia Museum of Art (J#970)

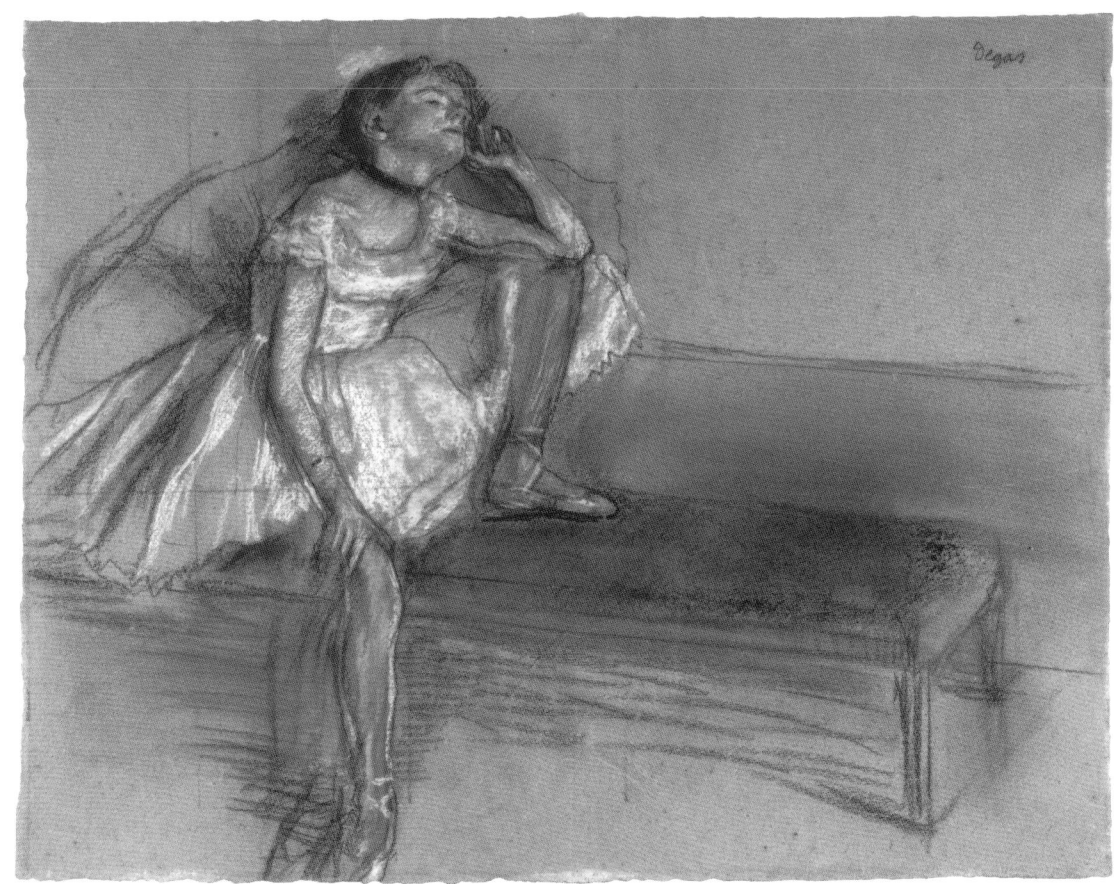

hundreds that show such a scene before or after the main dance events have taken place, or — literally or metaphorically — at an oblique angle to the ballet itself. Alongside such works, Degas developed other kinds of compositions that allowed him to address the ballerina's earthbound activities to the virtual exclusion of her acrobatics. *Dancers in the Classroom* (**158**) was one of an irregular series of frieze-like paintings and pastels that dwelled on the daily tedium experienced by the corps-de-ballet. A subtly atmospheric and understated picture, this work was apparently snapped up by an avid collector soon after it was painted around 1880, but its subject would be refined and reformulated by Degas in several other versions of the motif that continued into the twentieth century. These included works in oil paint on canvas and pastel on paper, many left unfinished at the artist's death and appearing at the first studio sale in 1918, where Apollinaire and his peers would have seen them.[88]

In *Dancers in the Classroom*, Degas brought together several of his characteristic devices for defining the young ballerinas of his day: the central figure preening self-consciously, those in the distance stretching at the barre or following their daily exercises, and the girls at right either waiting or resting their weary bodies. None of these figures is dancing and all could be studied by the artist from stationary, posed models, as he had done when drawing Marie van Goethem.[89] This was an aspect of the ballet that could be controlled, allowing Degas to move his dancer-models around like the proverbial chess pieces on a board and manipulate their positions to suit his pictorial needs. One such individual clearly required his attention: in *A Coryphée Resting* (**159**), the multiple lines around the girl's arms and legs record Degas's struggles as he endeavored to fix her in a suitable pose for *Dancers in the Classroom*. Technical examination of the canvas has revealed that this position was among several used by the artist for

the individual at extreme right, whose configuration changed repeatedly as the painting advanced. Other related canvases show similar rooms and reintroduce some of the characters from *Dancers in the Classroom*, or present new permutations of ballet students and assorted musical instruments. Common to them all is a sense of lassitude; these rooms are places where time passes slowly and weariness sets in, where companions gather to stand around in groups or slump together on benches as the hard work proceeds. For Picasso several decades later, they also offered a way out of his dancing dilemma.

Picasso Returns to the Ballet

The spectacle of the Degas sales must have been sobering for Picasso and his generation. Here was a great modern artist whose achievements had been founded on discipline and a mastery of line that linked him directly to the Italian Renaissance. Far from constricting his

160

Pablo Picasso

Three Dancers, 1919–20. Pencil on paper, 39.5 x 26.3 cm. Private collection. Courtesy Fundación Almine y Bernard Ruiz-Picasso para el Arte (2304)

161

Pablo Picasso

The Three Dancers, 1925. Oil on canvas, 215.3 x 142.2 cm. Tate Britain, London. Purchased with a special Grant-in-Aid and the Florence Fox Bequest with assistance from the Friends of the Tate Gallery and the Contemporary Art Society, 1965 (T.729)

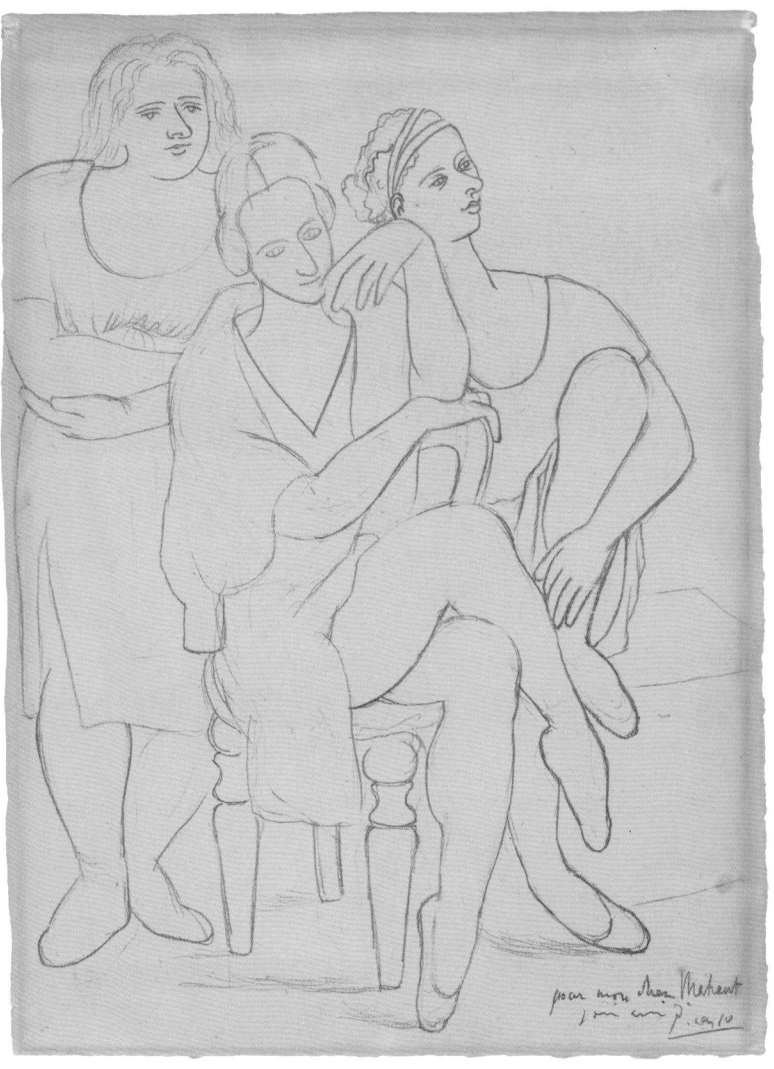

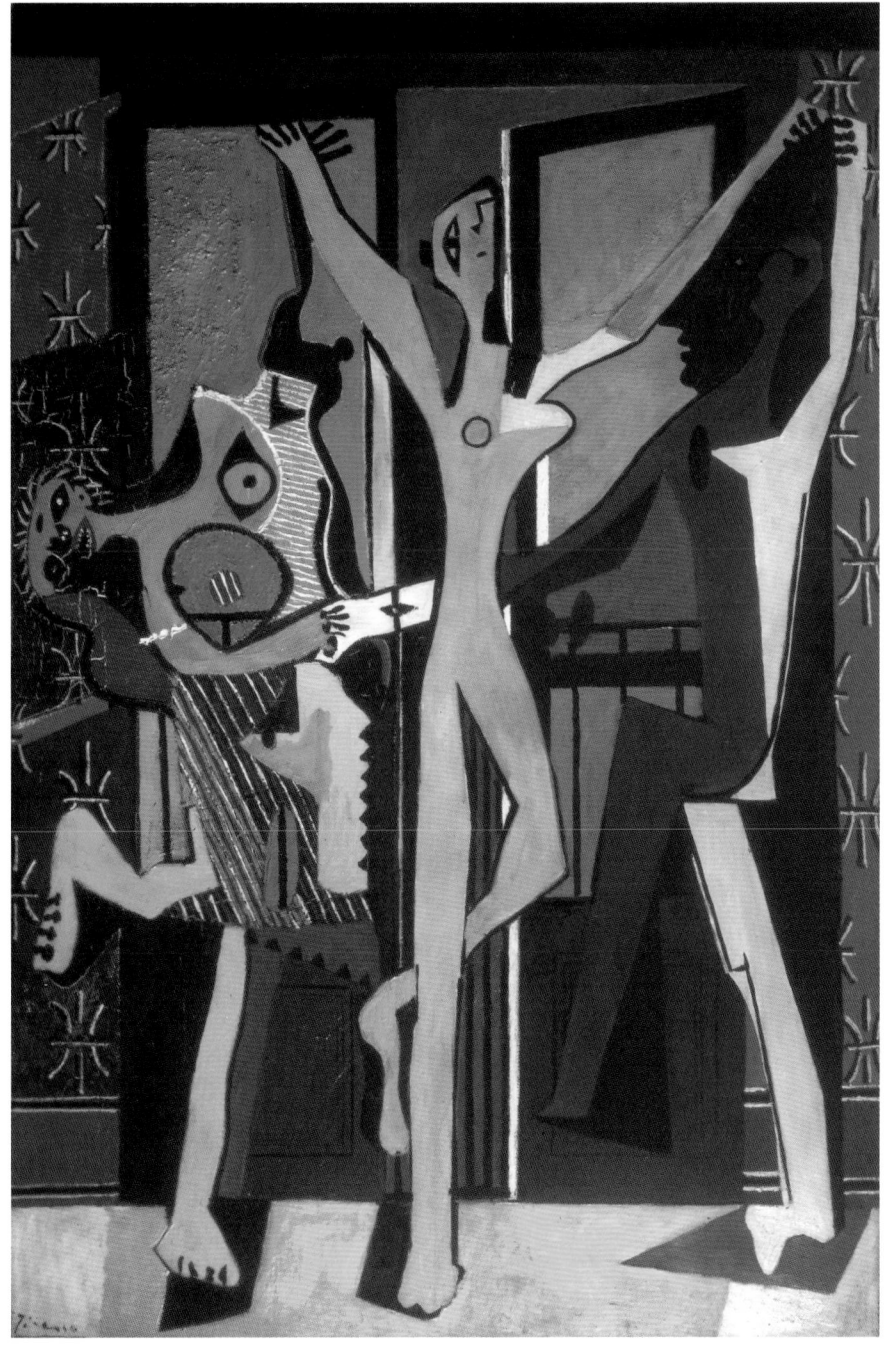

no hurry to respond to the Degas revealed at the 1918–19 auctions. His ballet drawings of 1919, such as *Two Dancers* (see 147) and *Three Ballet Dancers: Olga Khokhlova, Lydia Lopokova, and Lubov Tchernicheva* (see 149) — made before the cycle of sales was complete — owed more to Ingres than to Degas and may even have represented an initial move to resist Degas, "the Painter of Dancers." In a different sense, *Three Dancers* (**160**) seemed to play with such studies of tired ballerinas as *Coryphée Resting*, again incorporating believable individuals he surely knew. More than half a decade passed before the first clear signs of an engagement with the new Degas appeared, characteristically transformed by Picasso's ingenious, convoluted mind. In 1925, two utterly contrasting initiatives brought the dance back into his art, one focused on a single, large-scale oil painting, the other spelled out in a sequence of small, easily overlooked drawings.

Late in 1924, Picasso heard that his close friend from Barcelona days, Ramon Pichot, was seriously ill. Still strongly attached to his Catalan circle, Picasso visited Pichot in Paris and was greatly moved when he died in March 1925. Associating his old colleague with an earlier, unresolved project to paint a mural-like picture of the *Three Graces*, Picasso now took up this idea again and transformed it intermittently but fiercely as the months passed.[90] Among other memories of Pichot was an occasion when "he danced a wonderful religious Spanish dance ending in making himself a crucified Christ upon the floor."[91] The result was *The Three Dancers* (**161**), Picasso's "most impassioned and disturbing statement of the Dionysiac motif of wild dancing to date," which has also been traced back to a group of relatively serene studies from 1923 — one linked by Elizabeth Cowling to a sketch of Lupokova performing on stage.[92] *The Three Dancers* was modified and transformed repeatedly as it progressed, leaving a partly encrusted surface that amplifies the

development, this long apprenticeship had prepared Degas for the rigorous studio practice that marked him out from his contemporaries and informed some of the most profound innovations of his late career. In a manner that was distinctive of his mature years, Picasso was in

tormented character of this canvas and invokes its painful evolution. The haunting image that Picasso signed has no pretension to clarity, least of all as a statement about dance. Incorporating elements of primitive ritual and orgiastic revels, jazz and ballet, the setting is incongruously domestic with patterned walls that belong to none of them. Picasso insisted that it be called *The Death of Pichot* and explained that the shadowy form at right represented his friend, while the figure at left has often been identified as that of his ballerina-wife, Olga Khokhlova.[93]

Widely seen as a turning point in his career, one that "had nothing in common with the snobbism of Russian Ballet," this forceful seven-foot-high painting may also have allowed Picasso to get even with Matisse and his *Dance*, and perhaps to reflect again on Degas.[94] Few of Degas's late canvases were large, but certain works that appeared in the 1918–19 sales had been often repainted in a similar way and had both a substantial scale and an imposing presence. One of these, *Dancers at the Barre* (**162**), was executed around 1900 or even later and shows Degas striving toward a near-minimal statement of a theme that he had pursued for decades. In effect, his subject was plucked from the background of works made twenty years earlier, such as *Dancers in the Classroom* (see 158), where timeless figures stretched their legs and arms, and expressed their exhaustion after the rigors of their training. In *Dancers at the Barre* these individuals became the sole focus of Degas's energies in a painting that has been visibly drawn and redrawn, brushed and repeatedly rebrushed with color. The two ballerinas from the turn of the century are also sparer and tenser than the dainty girls in *Dancers in the Classroom*, suggesting muscular adults who have served out their time but still work their bodies at the barre. This is ballet as endurance and self-mortification, associated with pain as much as the giving of pleasure. Grimly sympa-

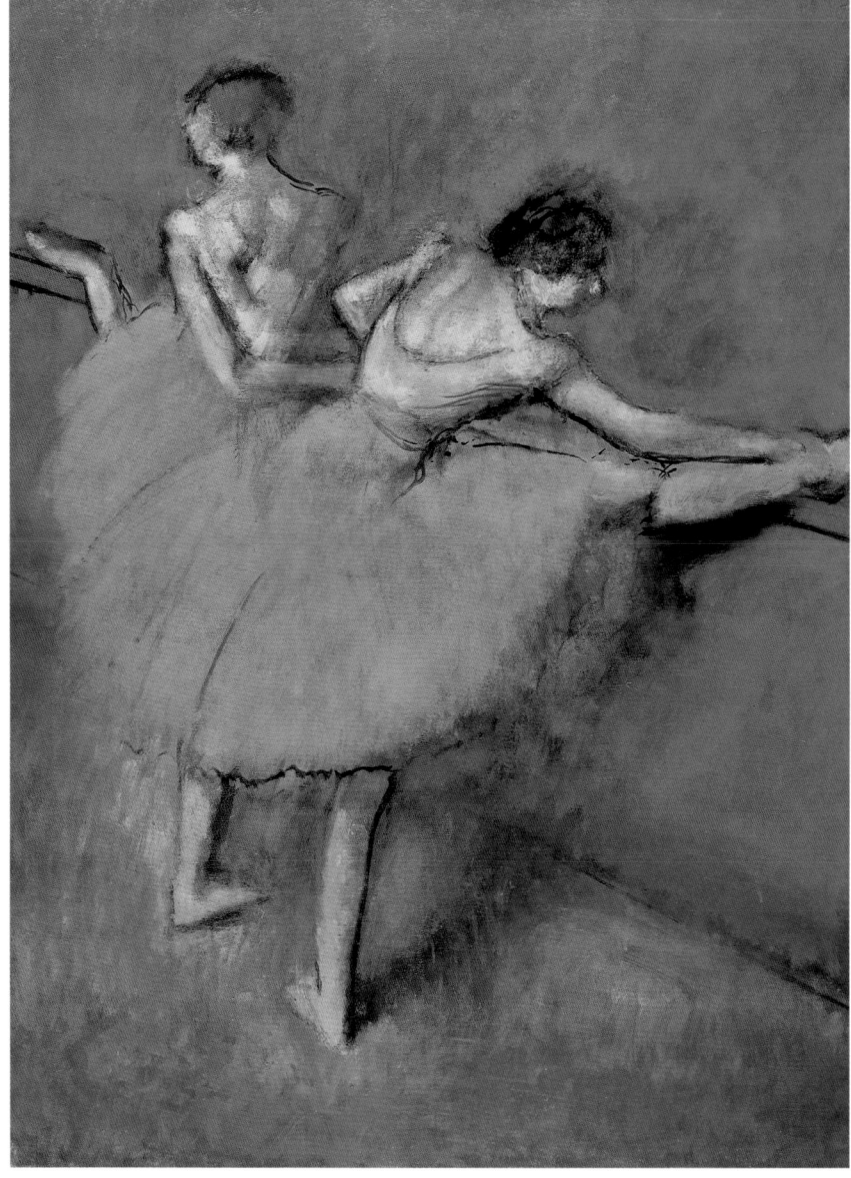

thetic with this mood is the bare wall and featureless floor tilted roughly toward the viewer, as well as the stark diagonal that runs across the picture and results in a cruciform composition. When it was seen by countless Parisians at the first 1918 sale, *Dancers at the Barre* no doubt disconcerted many of them. It may have lingered, too, in Picasso's mind and resurfaced as he struggled with the similarly proportioned and structured *The Three Dancers*. Both works seem to defy the association of their subjects

162

Edgar Degas

Dancers at the Barre,
c. 1900. Oil on canvas,
130.2 x 97.8 cm.
The Phillips Collection,
Washington, D.C.
Acquired 1944
(no. 0479)

with mere stage entertainment and reach toward an altogether tougher, more universal statement.

Picasso Draws the Ballet Classroom

With the resolution of *The Three Dancers* still underway, Picasso's labyrinthine creative processes also allowed him to embark on other works whose scale, subject, and handling might almost be from another artist's hand. The year 1925 was one of several in this decade when he holidayed on the fashionable Mediterranean coast, now accepting Diaghilev's invitation to join his company and entourage at Monte Carlo. Arriving with Olga and their son Paulo, Picasso opted not to become involved with theater or

163

Pablo Picasso

Three Dancers Resting, 1925. Pen and ink on paper, 35 x 25 cm. Private collection

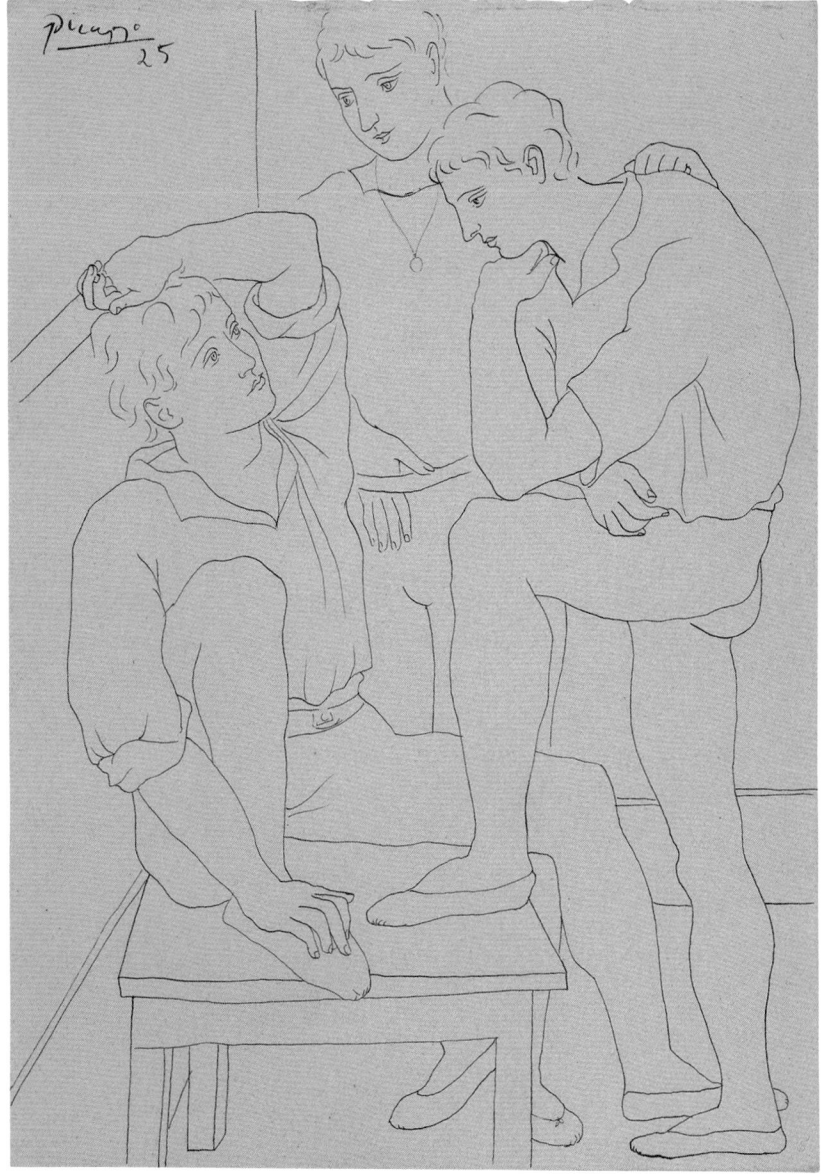

costume design but agreed to make drawings for a program: he had now "turned against the ballet; it was too distracting and time-wasting," Richardson tells us.[95] Weary also of the interminable socializing, Picasso chose to pass some of his days with the dancers and quietly investigate an as-yet unexplored aspect of Degas's draftsmanship. In works such as the pen-and-ink *Three Dancers Resting* (**163**) Picasso sprang two new surprises: for the first time in his career, he concentrated on the quintessential Degas theme of the classroom, while simultaneously distancing himself from Degas by concentrating on young men rather than girls or women. Continuing his earlier practice of watching the corps-de-ballet in private, he now made dozens of sheets that — in Douglas Cooper's view — challenged his predecessor: "Not even Degas . . . studied and noted dancers' movements with quite the same degree of intensity," he claimed in 1968.[96] In the restrained, exquisitely controlled *Three Dancers*, Picasso showed his male subjects far from the stage, relaxing and waiting as a class or rehearsal progresses. Here the position of the left-hand figure with his legs spread and arms akimbo might be a deliberate homage to the central ballerina in Degas's more gestural *Three Nude Dancers* (see 156), the drawing that had featured among those in the May 1918 sale. The standing figure at right is less immediately Degas-like but remarkably reminiscent of a work by his hero Ingres, whose celebrated painting of *Oedipus and the Sphinx* (see 152) shows Oedipus in precisely this pose. In 1918, Picasso could have seen that Degas himself owned a small version of this picture, and it may have amused Ingres's younger admirer to fuse these two references into a single private joke.[97] As so often, part of his subtlety is found in technique, here based on a fine needle-like line that reaches back beyond Ingres to the classical tradition that all three of these artists revered, with other resonances in Degas's early draftsmanship and Ingres's pencil portraits, yet distinct from both.

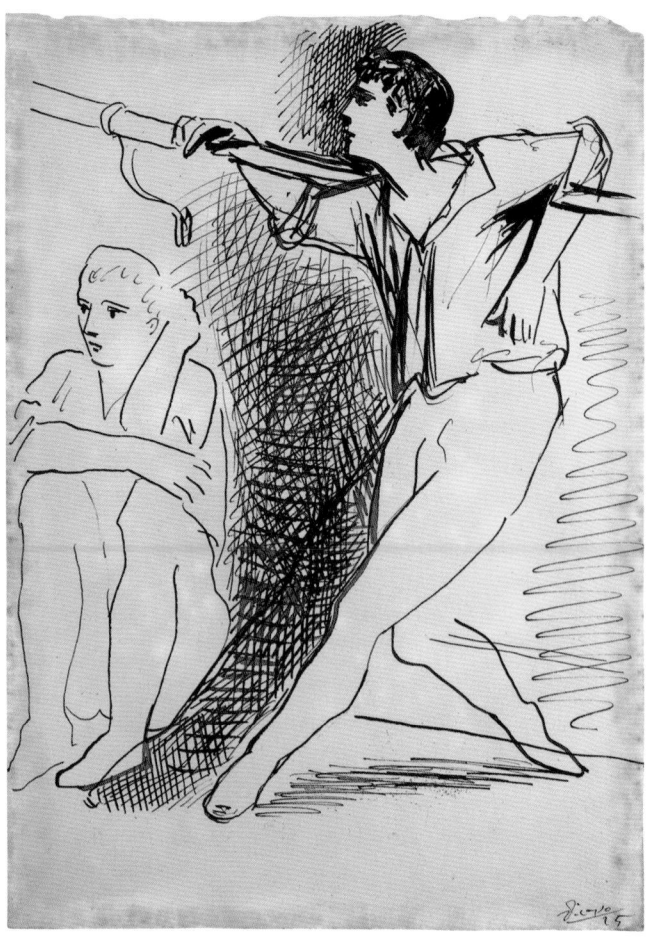

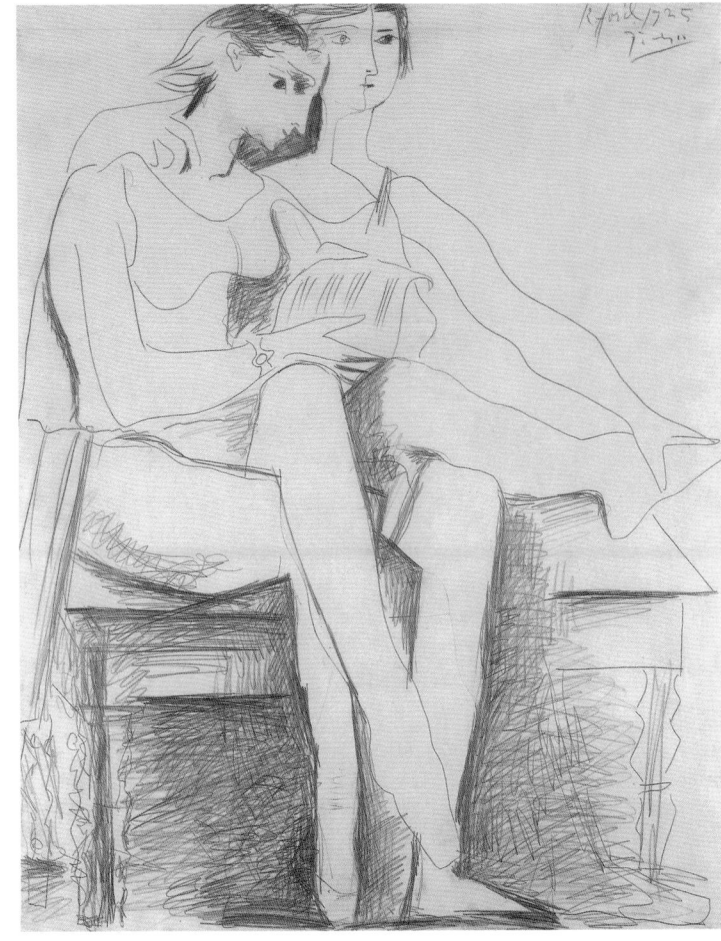

There were other variations on this same teasing game with Picasso's predecessors in the summer of 1925. Drawings of young men at the barre (**164**) are explicitly based on the signature motif that inspired both Degas's *Dancers in the Classroom* and his *Dancers at the Barre*. In several studies of young women from the Diaghilev troupe, Picasso also seemed to challenge Degas more directly. For *Two Seated Dancers* (**165**), he chose the relative softness of pencil to evoke a sympathetic human moment in the classroom, where a pair of young female ballerinas embrace gently as one rubs her tired foot. Strongly reminiscent of such working drawings as Degas's *A Coryphée Resting* (see 159), this composition now left Ingres far behind and allowed the overlapping planes of Cubism

to assert themselves. Close scrutiny of *Two Seated Dancers* shows that it was begun in a purely linear mode, then developed with pencil hatchings and strengthened contours into a complex design that is easily imagined as a sculptural relief. Clearly intrigued by its possibilities, Picasso returned to this same group in a half dozen linked but graphically contrasted studies that ranged from the calmly linear to the nervously sculptural.[98] In *Two Dancers* (**166**), bolder strokes and passages of shadow create a dramatic, even agitated atmosphere that distantly echoes his seminal painting *The Three Dancers*. Equally captivating in this work are the crossed and interlocking legs, masterfully drawn and here suggesting the play of forms in space as much as patterns on paper. Picasso's tour of

164

Pablo Picasso

Two Dancers Resting, 1925. Pen and ink on paper, 34.9 x 24.9 cm. Collection of Richard and Mary L. Gray / Courtesy the Gray Collection Trust (590034)

165

Pablo Picasso

Two Seated Dancers, 1925. Pencil on paper, 50 x 40 cm. Private collection

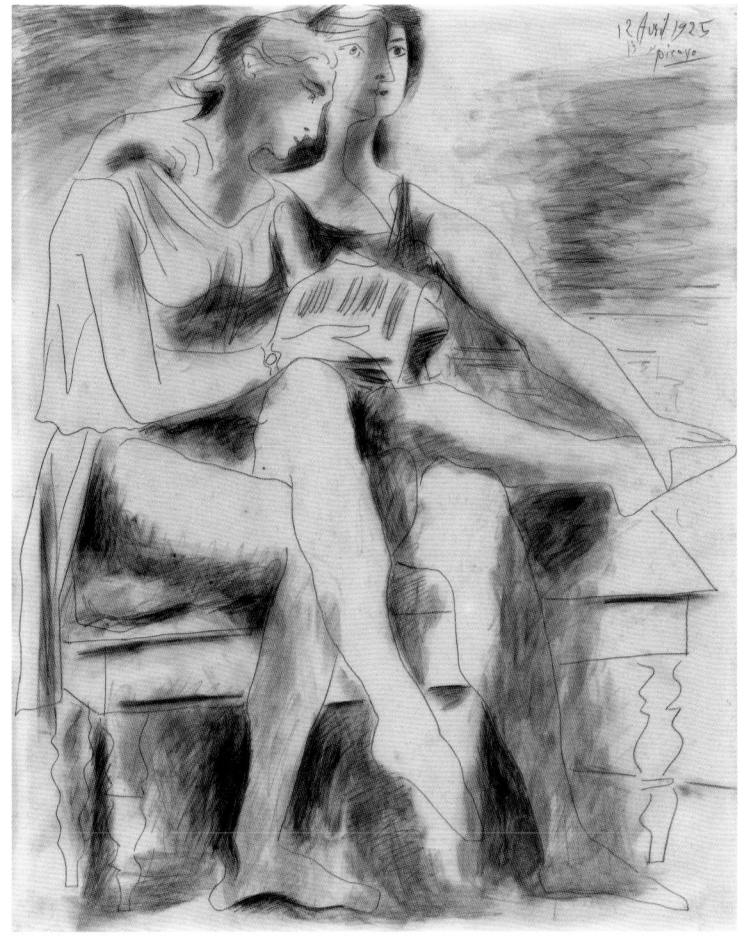

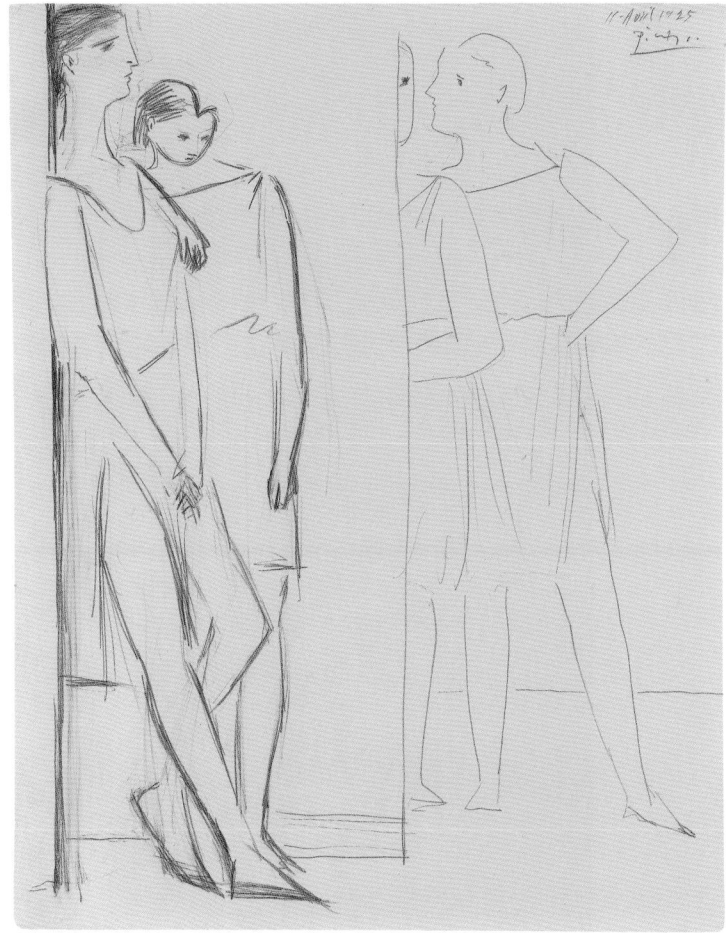

166

Pablo Picasso

Two Dancers, 12–13 April 1925. Pencil on paper, 51 x 41 cm. National Gallery of Ireland, Dublin (NGI.3271)

167

Pablo Picasso

In the Wings, 1925. Pencil on paper, 50.9 x 40.5 cm. Collection of the Vanech Family

the backstage world was given a further twist when he offered yet another nod toward "the Painter of Dancers," now in a calmer mode. *In the Wings* (**167**) approaches Degas on his most specific territory, known to all those who were familiar with his art and epitomized in pastels such as *Two Dancers in the Wings* (see 154). Picasso's elegant drawing includes a figure at right who stands calmly waiting for her next entrance on the stage, even crooking her right arm like the dancer in Degas's richly colored pastel. At left in the Picasso, two economically stated young women echo the tiredness of the other figure in Degas's pastel, leaning on the scenery and allowing it to support their weight. The costumes of all three are not tutus but dresses in the neo-Greek mode that was much

in vogue at this time, yet their identity as descendants of Degas and his coryphées is surely beyond doubt.

During the 1920s Picasso emerged as the outstanding figure in postwar European art, whose dazzling but unpredictable work created endless controversy as he moved from style to style, theme to theme, and medium to medium. In a 1923 interview given to the New York magazine *The Arts*, he famously challenged the idea of cultural progress, insisting that "the several manners I have used in my art must not be considered as evolution, or as steps toward an unknown ideal of painting."[99] Two years later, this coexistence of styles was perfectly summarized in the large, violent canvas of *The Three Dancers*, on one hand, and the

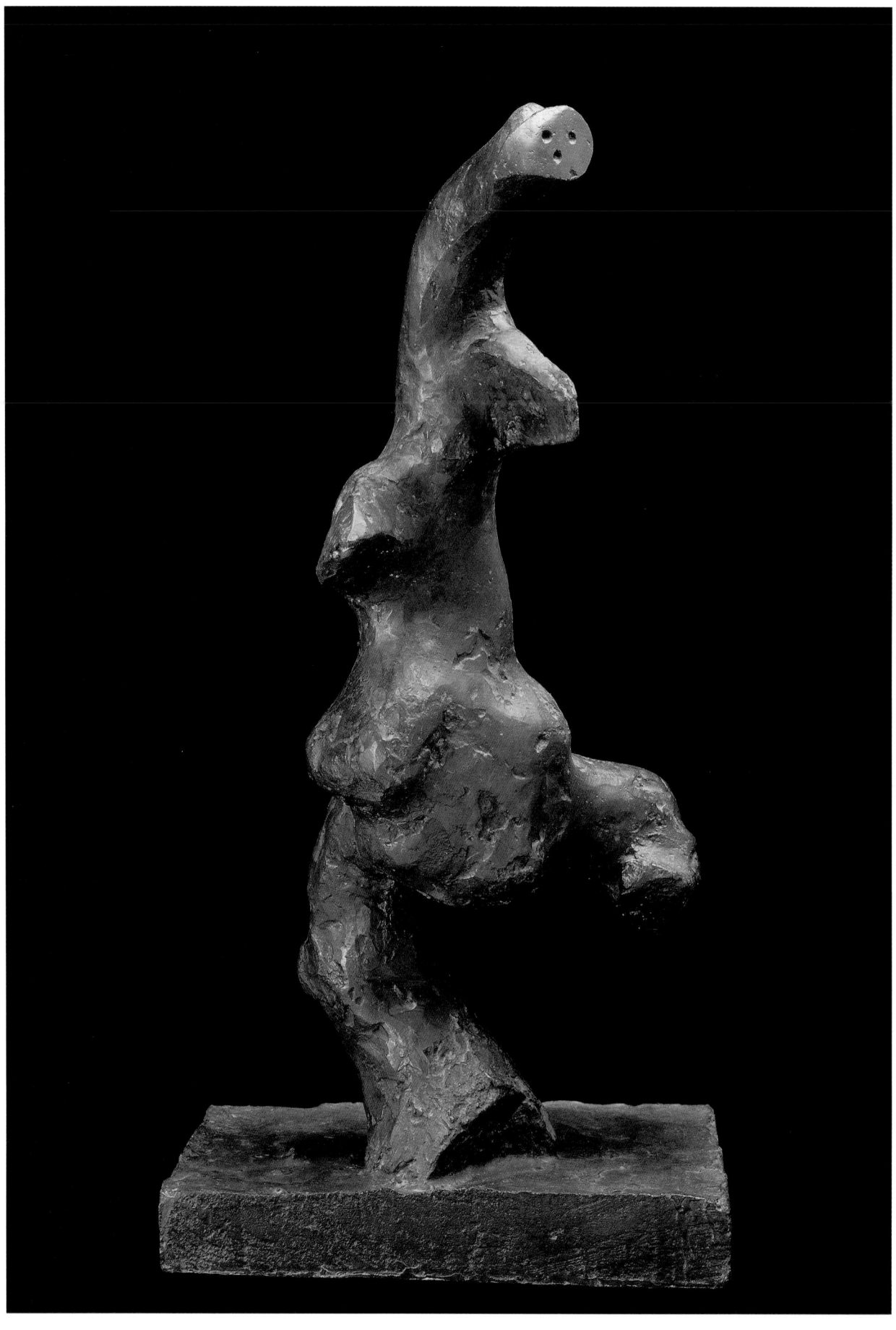

sketchbook-size drawings of Diaghilev's calmly resting troupe, on the other. A timely exhibition of almost sixty paintings held in 1926 at the Rosenberg gallery in Paris showed examples of Picasso's work from a twenty-year period and allowed him to glory in the diversity that angered his critics. His personal life seems to have been equally multifarious. Some of the delightful amateur photographs that were taken of Olga in 1925 show her posing in a tutu and smiling in the Mediterranean sunshine (see 309), yet the painted image of her at left in *The Three Dancers* is grotesque and terrifying. Olga's varying fortunes were reflected in countless pictures during these years, from chaste portraits in the manner of Ingres to the large, collage-like Cubist canvas entitled *Still Life (Easel and Dancer's Tights)* of 1926.[100] In the late 1920s, the mood of these works became angrier as the relationship between Picasso and Olga declined; some drab collages included scraps of faded tulle — the material used in tutus — amongst crude stitching and harsh abstract forms, while the oil painting *Large Nude in a Red Armchair (Olga)* of 1929 shows a hysterical, amoeba-like female nude spread-eagled against a bourgeois interior.[101]

A Dialogue in Sculpture

One symptom of their estrangement was Picasso's purchase of a house of some antiquity at Boisgeloup between Paris and the Normandy coast, where he began making large heads and figures in plaster. Sculpture had remained a persistent if occasional interest since the Bateau-Lavoir days, manifesting itself in radical Cubist assemblages and more recently in welded constructions that sometimes incorporated found objects. Still unconcerned by his amateur status Picasso had turned to several sculptor friends to help him, currently his fellow Spaniard, Julio González, who carried out the welding in Paris and facilitated other anarchic inventions. Where Picasso's recent three-

dimensional work had often been spacious and witty, many of the forms that now dominated his Boisgeloup studios were massive and solid-looking: oversize heads with bulbous features, anthropomorphic shapes, and reliefs and busts representing a handsome young woman. This was Marie-Thérèse Walter, the latest object of Picasso's passion, who had already appeared in drawings and pictures of variously erotic beach scenes that began in 1927. Alongside the bigger sculptures, Picasso had also modeled several figures on an almost miniature scale by his current standards, from a mere eight inches in height to just over two feet, initially made in plaster but subsequently cast in bronze. One of the largest, known simply as *Bather* (**168**), is equipped with rudimentary legs, arms, and a face, while the smallest is a sculpture that defies anatomical convention, entitled *Metamorphosis I* (**169**). A clue to the origins of this work is again the connection with bathing and the beach, and thus with Marie-Thérèse and their clandestine sexual encounters beside the sea. In 1927, these were still imaginary, but in 1928 Picasso installed her at Dinard on the Brittany coast, the same town where he, Olga, and Paulo were spending their summer. Following the habit of these years, the artist transmuted some of his bizarre experiences into tense drawings and occasionally euphoric paintings, and into the agonized forms of *Metamorphosis I*.

A drawing of 1927 for the solid, earth-hugging mass of this sculpture shows a relatively light, surrealistic figure — who consists mainly of limbs — running or jumping on a beach.[102] Picasso's association of beach vacations with sex reached back to his childhood, but it was paralleled by a more ambiguous sense of the seashore as a place of free, unhampered physical behavior of many kinds. His celebrated small painting *Bathers*, made in Biarritz in 1918, had already brought together three women who sit in their swimming suits, display themselves languorously, or fuse an eccentric

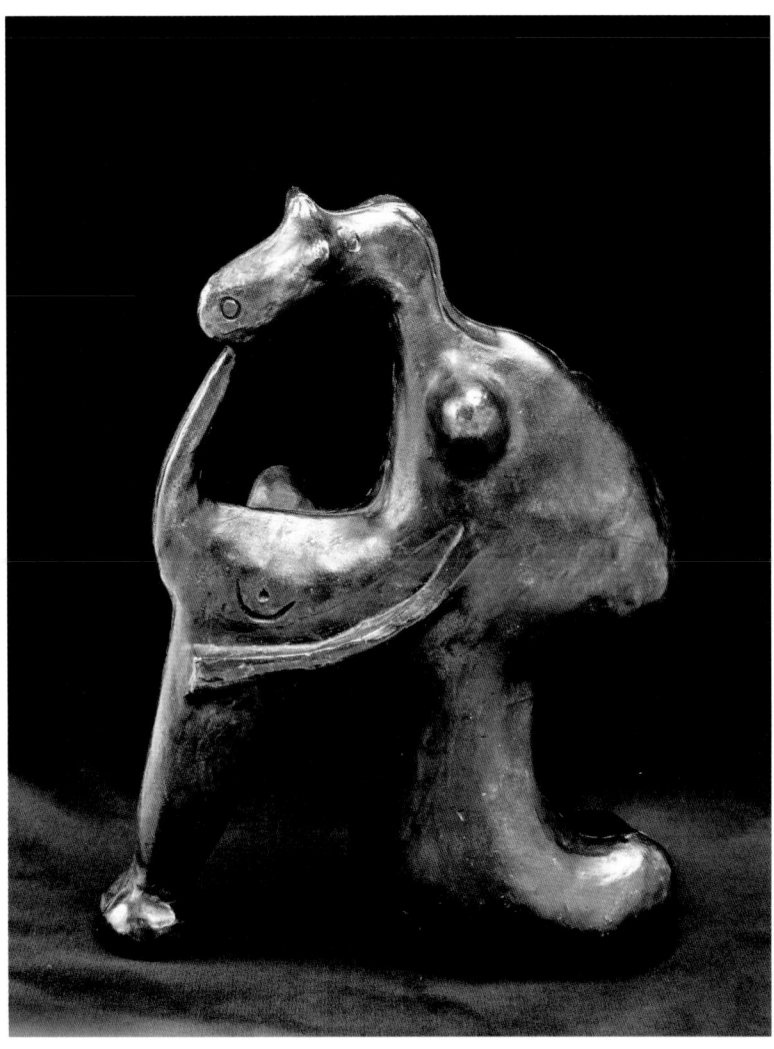

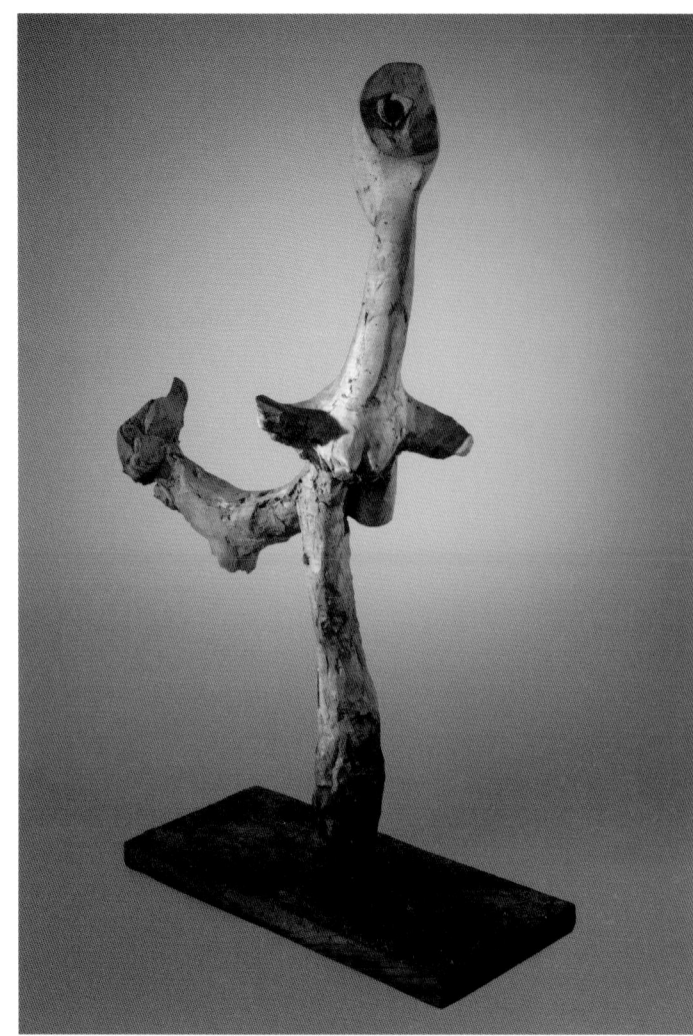

sprinting action with wild, entranced dancing.[103] Around 1924 the boundary between figures on the sand and those who dance was again very publicly blurred when Picasso's painting *Two Women Running on the Beach* was enlarged on the drop curtain for Diaghilev's new ballet, *Le Train Bleu*.[104] In a series of intriguing sketchbook drawings from 1928 Picasso continued to link these activities, some of them adding a new element in the form of a volleyball, one of Marie-Thérèse's preferred playthings.[105] Reviving the Dionysiac-Apollonian conflict that lay behind Picasso's 1925 *The Three Dancers*, these works vividly illustrated the mysterious crosscurrents of the artist's imagination and his often poetic,

sometimes agonized conflations of meaning. His bronze *Bather* summarizes this situation; imprecise by design, it is equally plausible as a lumbering beach figure or a child playing, or even as a memory of an overweight ballerina such as those in the 1919 *Two Dancers* (see 147). At least four other members of this indeterminate family were also made at Boisgeloup in the early 1930s: another work entitled *Bather* (see 174), *Running Woman* (see 170), *Bather with Raised Arms* (see 173), and *Girl with a Ball*.[106]

Varied in style and scale, all these sculptures have two features in common. In each case, the figures have one leg off the ground and where arms are discernible they reach outward or

169

Pablo Picasso

Metamorphosis I, 1928. Bronze, height: 22.8 cm. Musée national Picasso, Paris (MP 261)

170

Pablo Picasso

Running Woman, 1931–32. Plaster and wood, height: 52 cm. Private collection

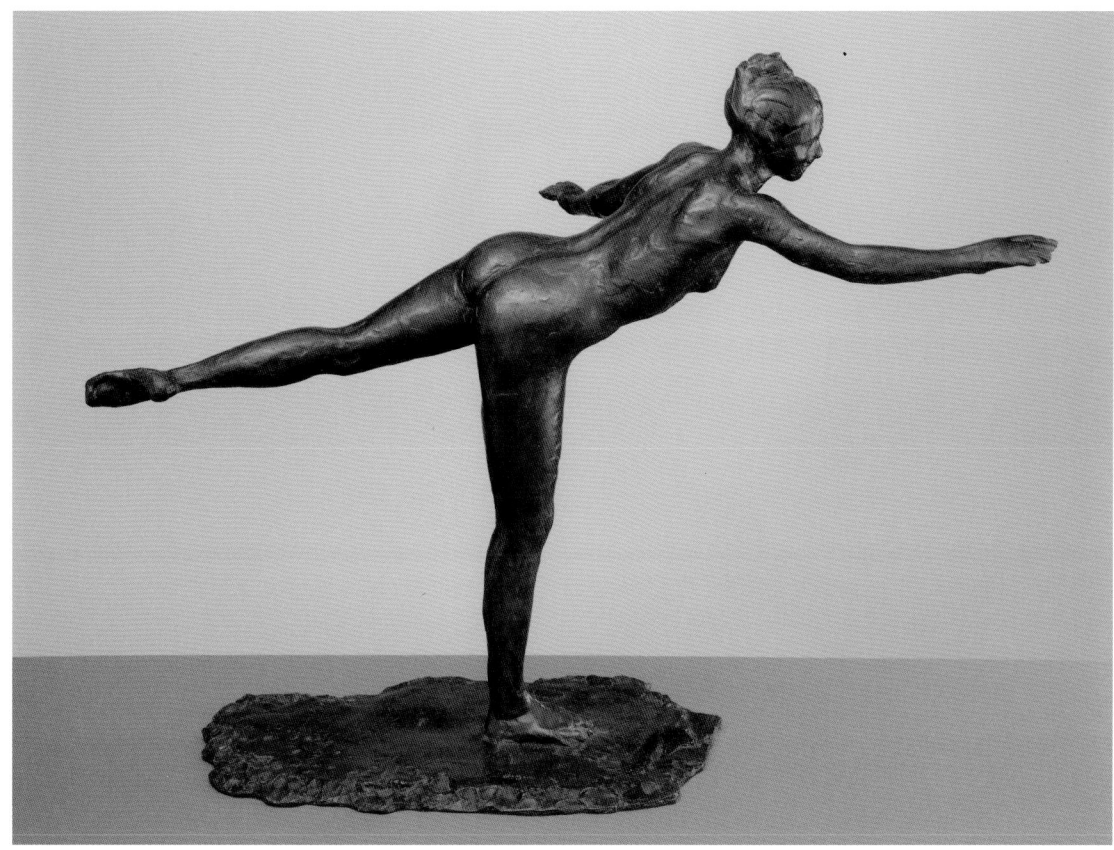

171

Edgar Degas

Grand Arabesque, Second Time, c. 1880s. Bronze, height: 48.2 cm. Sterling and Francine Clark Art Institute, Williamstown, Massachusetts (1955.47)

upward. Though greatly reduced in scale, this is the pose of the naked woman at the center of Picasso's painting *The Three Dancers*, in which the raised leg is also repeated in the adjoining "dancers," along with one or both arms lifted above their heads. In rudimentary terms, this is the language of movement as opposed to stasis, suggesting a leap into the air or a forward bound of a kind that is common to sport, exuberant display, or dance. The last and most legible of all these figures is *Running Woman* (**170**) of 1931 or 1932, where massive bulk has been replaced by extreme thinness and the lifted leg now trails behind the attenuated body. Purposefully or not, when approaching this work Picasso chose both the position and scale of one of Degas's most admired sculptures, *Grand Arabesque, Second Time* (**171**). Here, too, the body curves upward and forward in a line that begins with the foot and ends at the head, as a pillar-like leg supports

the body's weight. While the arms of Degas's ballerina are proportionate to her physique, they similarly reach out sideways to maintain balance.

In July 1931, the year in which Picasso began to make this group of figures, the first presentation of Degas's complete sculpture to be organized by the French state opened in central Paris. Picasso is known to have seen this display, which formed part of a major exhibition held at the Musée de l'Orangerie, within sight of the Louvre.[107] Entitled *Degas: Portraitiste, Sculpteur*, the exhibition ranged over almost 250 works in all media that had been loaned from public and private collections, and included the entire set of bronze casts given to the nation by the foundry of A. A. Hébrard.[108] Despite the exhibition's title and a focus on portraiture throughout the picture sections, Degas's three-dimensional work embraced all of his distinctive themes: thirty-eight figures of dancers, seventeen

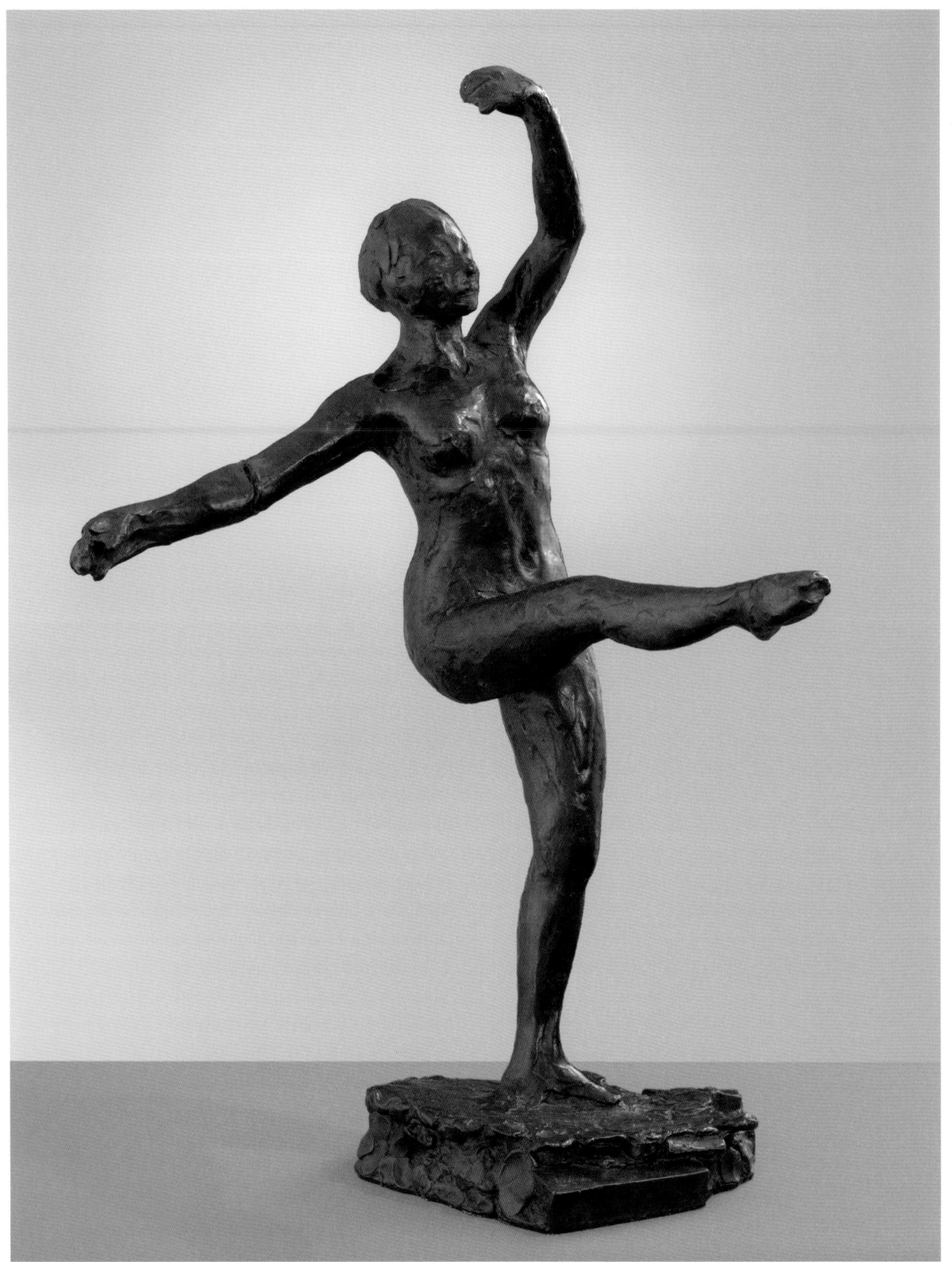

172
Edgar Degas
Fourth Position Front,
On the Left Leg, 1880s.
Bronze, height: 57.5 cm.
Sterling and Francine
Clark Art Institute,
Williamstown,
Massachusetts (1955.49)

173
Pablo Picasso
Bather with Raised Arms,
1931. Bronze, height:
32.5 cm. Musée national
Picasso, Paris (MP 304)

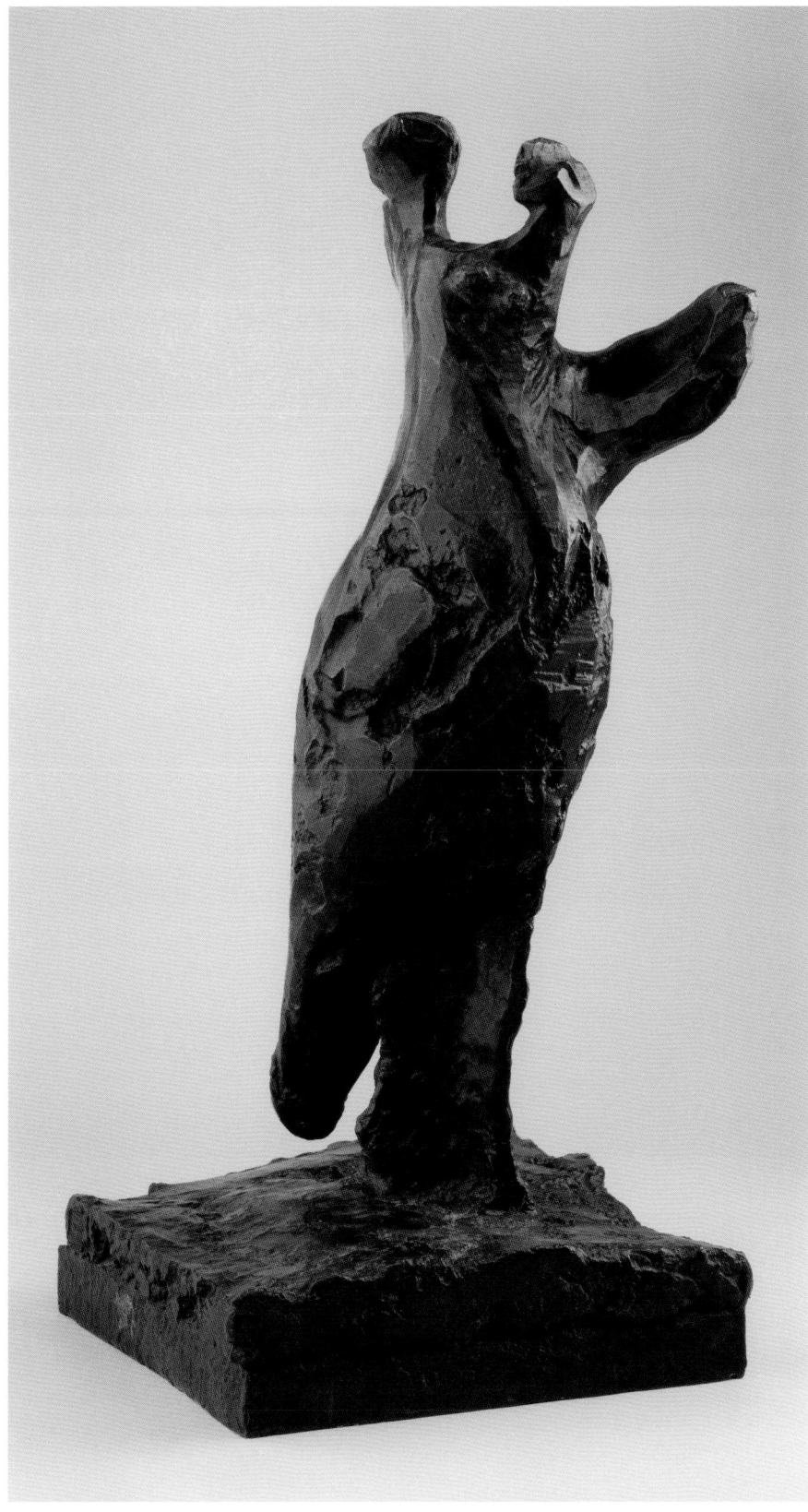

equestrian subjects, fourteen female bathers and other nudes, and some portraits and figure studies. For Picasso, the 1931 exhibition was almost certainly not his initiation into Degas's sculpture. A decade earlier, in May 1921, the full set of bronzes had been unveiled by Hébrard in their own Paris gallery, attracting widespread interest among collectors, artists, critics, and the city's population. Several illustrated essays on these works appeared immediately in the art press and comparable exhibitions were rapidly arranged in New York and London.[109] All the bronzes were again exhibited in Paris in 1924, while casts of individual sculptures were increasingly acquired by dealers and shown on their own premises.[110] Conversely, Picasso and his peers would have had no sight of the original wax and mixed-media figures that had emerged from Degas's studio at his death. While a handful had been reproduced in France before 1921, these fascinating but extremely fragile objects were retained by Hébrard as the casting process continued and later acquired for the Paul Mellon collection.[111]

Picasso's direct experience of the Degas bronzes in the summer of 1931 was extraordinarily timely. The shift from his own welded, frame-like constructions and stick-like wooden figures to what Richardson calls his "volumetric sculpture" had begun just months before, following a complex rehearsal of their subjects in drawings and some paintings of massive, ballooning figures.[112] The huge portraits and busts of Marie-Thérèse that had begun to emerge in early 1931 were larger than most of the objects in the Degas exhibition at the Orangerie, but as sculptures they shared several fundamental qualities. Both groups of works had been built up by hand in soft materials — principally wax in Degas's case and freshly-mixed plaster in Picasso's — that the artist could add to or remove from his half-finished figure as he saw fit. Different in principle from wood or stone carving, and remote from welding, the various

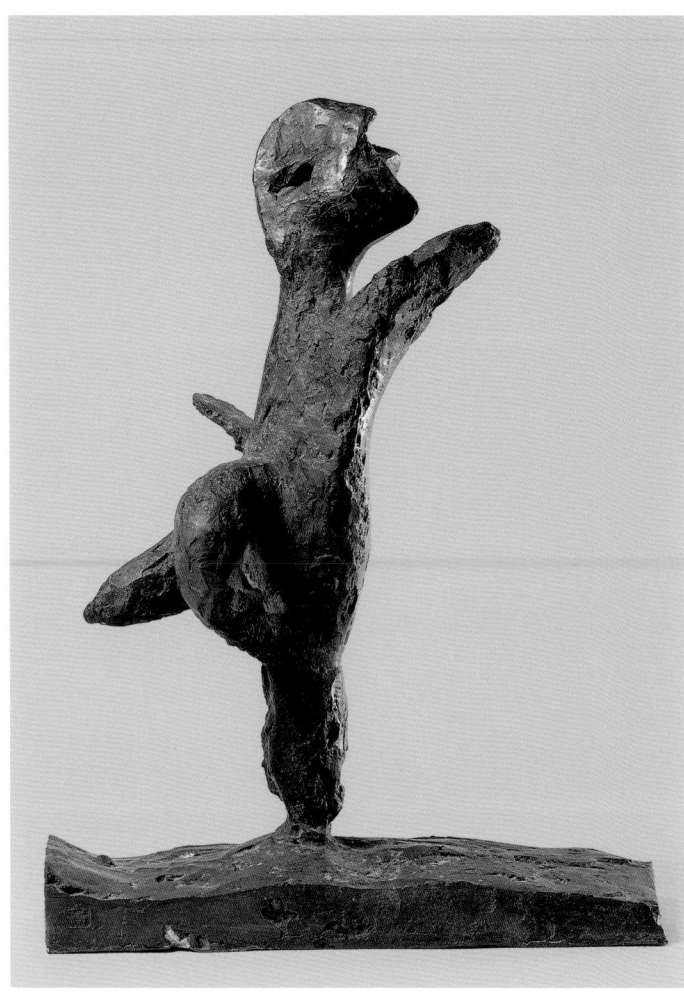

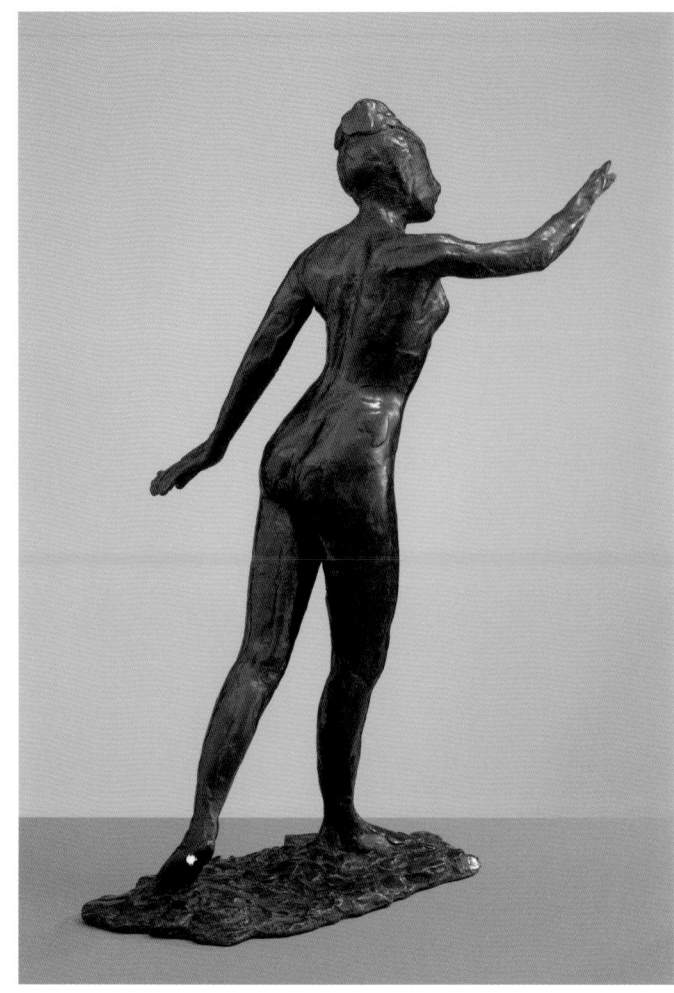

methods of modeling by hand were more directly sensuous and suited to flowing forms and surfaces, like those of the human body. Even in the bulkier works made by Degas, such as his nudes drying themselves while seated in capacious chairs, this lively sensuality of touch could animate the mass of bronze in ways that may well have intrigued Picasso.[113] The individual ballet dancers are similarly energized by their facture: in *Grand Arabesque, First Time*, the forward movement of the young woman seems to be embodied in the malleable wax and its variously smooth and taut planes, while *Fourth Position Front, on the Left Leg* (**172**) achieves a tremulousness that would be hard to equal in any other medium.

In Picasso's group of prancing female figures made from 1931 onward, he adopted an oblique approach to Degas that had become habitual, by both acknowledging and disguising his debt. Clearly invigorated by the potential of youthful athletes and performers, Picasso was also determined that his new creations should not be solemn or exquisite, and certainly not conventionally balletic. Where *Bather* (see 168) balances on one leg and raises the other — as do several of Degas's bronze dancers — Picasso's model has a body closer to a Degas bather than a member of the corps-de-ballet. In *Bather with Raised Arms* (**173**) Picasso went even further, almost caricaturing the massive bulk of this figure and reducing her head and limbs to tiny appendages, even as he insisted on her stately forward progress. *Bather* (**174**) offers another variation on this sophisticated game: now large-headed and pot-bellied, this little creature nevertheless performs a classic arabesque and even lifts her head gracefully, like the danseuse in Degas's celebrated pastel *The Star* in the Luxembourg Museum and the figure in *Grand Arabesque, First Time* (**175**).[114] Inexpertly constructed, some of Picasso's heavier figures seem to teeter rather uncertainly on their plaster or bronze bases, adding to the perceived precariousness of their actions. At the Orangerie display, Picasso would also have seen Degas's least typical ballet figure that almost falls into this same category: *Dressed Dancer, at Rest, Hands behind Her Back, Right Leg Forward* (**176**). Unique among his sculptures, this touching figure of a ballerina straining her shoulders against her back is the only case where he modeled a complete tutu in wax and similar materials. Unlike the fabric tutu on the wax and bronze variants of the *Little Dancer Aged Fourteen*, this garment can seem impossibly heavy in *Dressed Dancer, at Rest*, threatening to over-balance its wearer. Surely unintended by Degas, a comparable quality appears to have been wittily seized upon by Picasso in some of his small bather-dancers. At the opposite extreme to the Degas, on the other hand, is the superb *Running Woman*, the least bulky of all his bronze sculptures from the early 1930s and arguably one of the simplest and most effective. Almost as far removed from *Metamorphosis I* as the medium allows, *Running Woman* defies gravity and ponderousness in a single leap.

As with Picasso's 1925 drawings of dancers in the classroom, all but one of his 1931 bather-dancer sculptures were created on a small scale.[115] It is also fascinating to reflect that — at the Orangerie exhibition, if not before — Picasso had come face-to-face with the significantly larger *Little Dancer Aged Fourteen* that haunted him as a young man, to which he had never

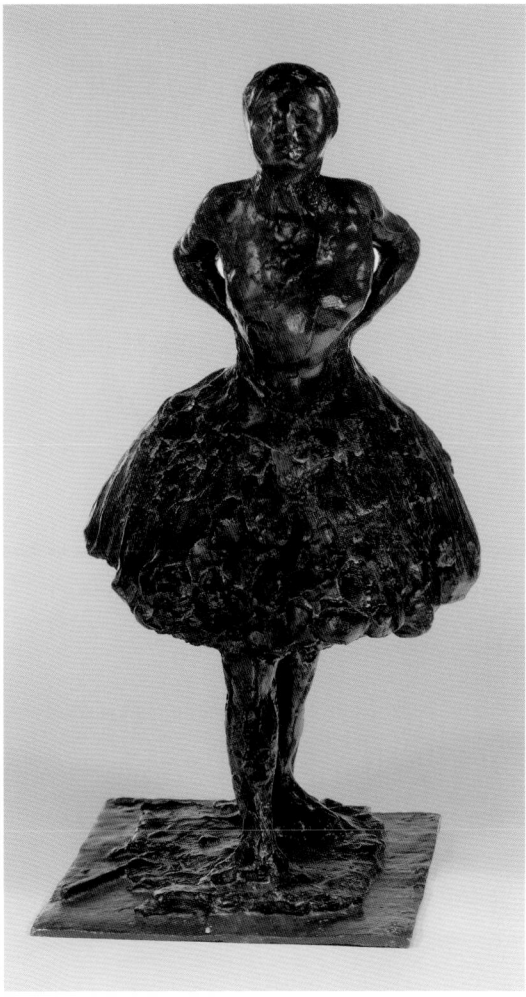

chosen to respond in a three-dimensional work of his own. Similarly, his new sculptures were never cast in an orthodox edition in the manner of Degas's bronzes and seem to have remained out of the public eye for decades. Was Picasso embarrassed by the latest evidence of his on-off fascination with "The Painter of Dancers"? What is clear is that Picasso now drifted away from the world of the ballet in his art and in his life. He and Olga finally separated in 1935, with the Boisgeloup property going to the former dancer from the Ballets Russes as part of their settlement. Already Picasso was distracted by a host of other projects, not least the two-dimensional games he was playing with Degas's bathers and women at their toilette.

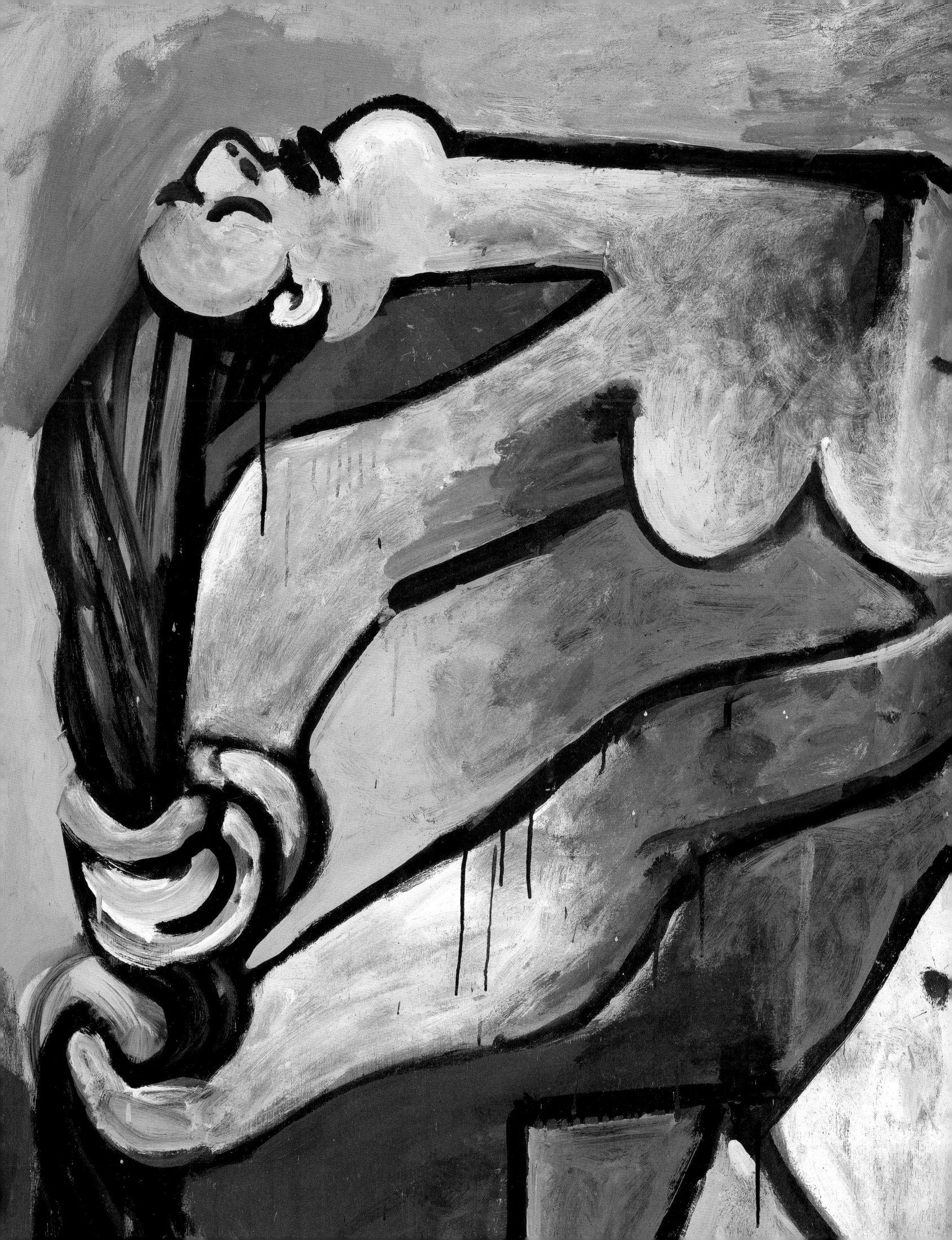

CHAPTER 4

THE REBIRTH OF VENUS: WOMEN AT THEIR TOILETTE

ELIZABETH COWLING

Hunched and concentrated on her task, a naked woman seated on a bench rubs vigorously at her right foot; her left foot plunged in a low tub full of water awaits its turn (see 224). A seated bather arches over and wrings her long mane of hair with powerful hands (see 226). Painted in 1944 and 1952, respectively, these vehemently brushed, confrontational pictures are evidence that in his sixties and seventies Picasso was still extracting high drama from two of the most commonplace motifs originating in antiquity — a woman bathing and a woman doing her hair. The female nude was of equal importance to both Degas and Picasso, but whereas Degas returned obsessively to scenarios in which nudity would occur in real life (typically the bedroom, the bathroom, and the brothel), Picasso placed his nudes in any situation with a well-worn art pedigree, showing them most frequently simply standing, seated, and reclining or, even though he rarely worked from life himself, posing for the artist in his studio. Images of women washing their bodies and combing their hair recur sporadically, rather than constantly in his work, and, when they appear, Degas was often a chosen reference point. But Degas was rarely the only reference point, for the motifs had so long and full a history that other artists, such as Ingres, often stood metaphorically shoulder-to-shoulder with him in Picasso's fertile imagination.

The Special Case of Degas

The twin themes of *la toilette* and *la coiffure* had leapt in popularity in France during the eighteenth century, not least because of her reputation as the undisputed leader in the "civilized" world in all matters relating to beauty and fashion. Although frequently given the elevating spin of a mythological or biblical pedigree — the birth of Venus, the toilette of Venus, Diana bathing with her nymphs, Susanna and Bathsheba at their baths, and so on — increasing numbers of images, especially in the domain of printmaking and illustration, depicted contemporary women in domestic settings. Inherently voyeuristic, both themes were constants of erotic art and, especially when a contemporary setting was chosen, of pornography.[1] Handled with due decorum, they could, however, be adapted to female portraiture. The nineteenth century saw the continuation and development of these traditions, academic painters tending to represent mythological and biblical heroines or to situate the bathing and hairdressing in antiquity or an Oriental seraglio, the naturalists to represent credible contemporary women in contemporary environments. Several members of the Impressionist group — Cassatt, Morisot, and Renoir among them — treated these subjects now and then, but no one came anywhere near to matching Degas's fixation.

Among Degas's first pictures to depict hair-combing were *Beach Scene* (**177**), shown in the third Impressionist exhibition in 1877, and a contemporary oil sketch of a girl in three contrasted poses attending to her long chestnut-colored hair (**178**). Simultaneously, he executed caricatural monotypes of the *pensionnaires* of brothels combing their hair and washing, occasionally in the presence of clients who had

Detail of Pablo Picasso,
Nude Wringing Her Hair
(226)

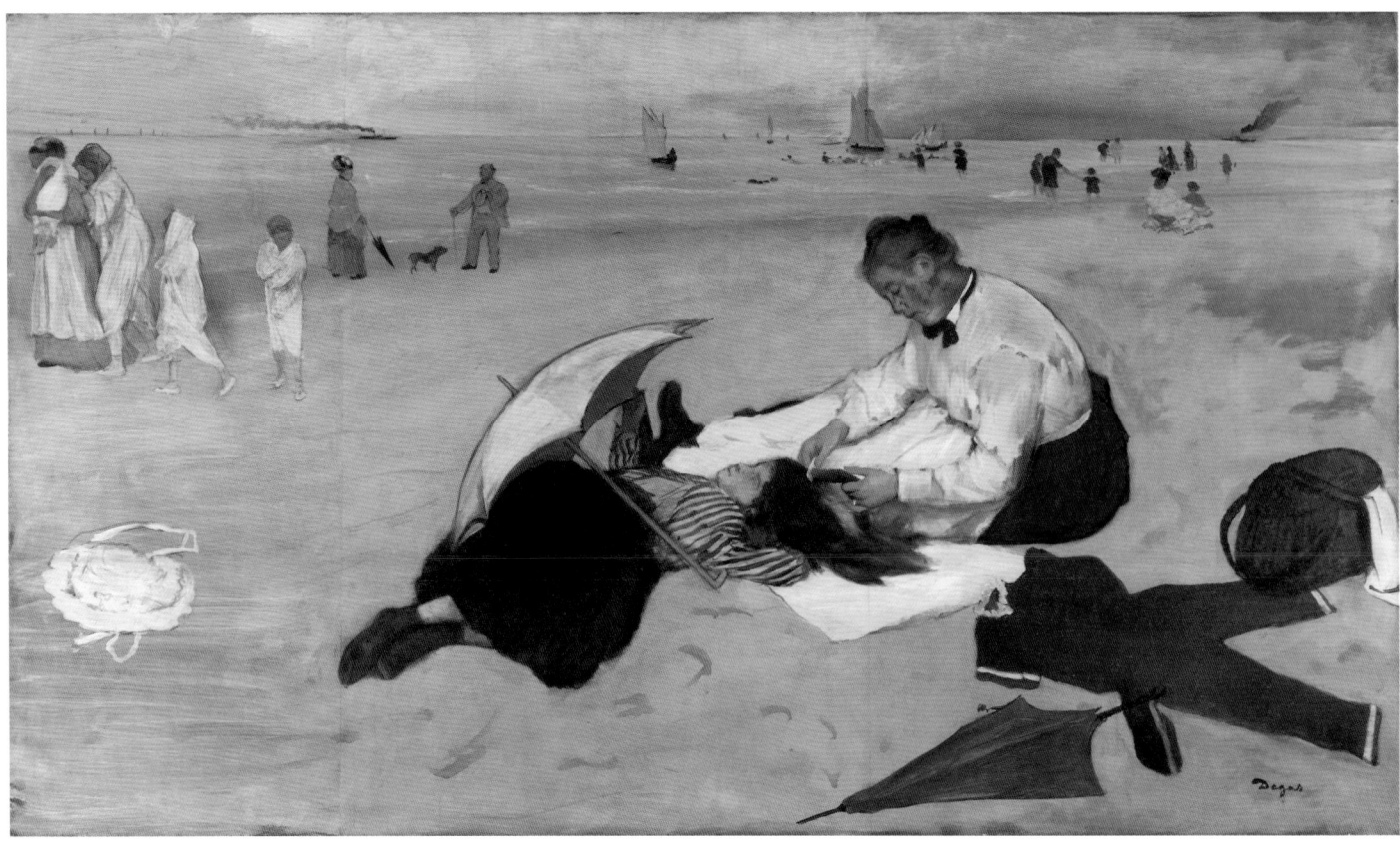

presumably paid for the privilege of watching (**179, 180**; see also 238). Plainly, during the 1870s Degas was interested in depicting women performing exactly the same daily ritual in both "innocent" (outdoors, in nature) and "vicious" (the *maison close*) circumstances. By contrast, he set the numerous, more monumental paintings and pastels that followed in the 1880s and 1890s in the morally and socially ambiguous zones of the private bedroom or *cabinet de toilette* — settings that are so ambiguous that neither contemporary critics nor recent scholars were/have been able to agree about the status ("respectable," "not respectable") of the women seen engaging in their *toilette intime*. The glowing painting in the Kreeger Museum (**181**) is a case in point: from a steeply elevated viewpoint and in near close-up, it depicts the back of a plump nude seated unceremoniously on a cushion and brushing the underside of her hair

with a gesture that is neither graceful nor flattering but perfectly observed. She might almost be the thick-set whore performing an identical action in one of the monotypes (see **180**), and her patterned cushion and carpet might well be the same as those in the brothel. It is the absence of other telltale signs — the stockings and slippers, and, above all, the client — that makes her status indeterminate and any narrative reading ultimately irrelevant. An antigoddess in that she in no way conforms to the hackneyed ideal of Classical beauty, she is nonetheless presented to us with something of the impersonality and abstraction associated with authentic Classical art — as an object of contemplation. Who she may be matters less than the refulgent spectacle conjured up by Degas's gorgeous rainbow palette and the tapestry-like weave of his brushstrokes. The painting is, furthermore, characteristic of the

177

Edgar Degas

Beach Scene, c. 1869–70. Oil (essence) on paper on canvas, 47.5 x 82.9 cm. The National Gallery, London. Sir Hugh Lane Bequest, 1917 (NG 3247)

178

Edgar Degas

*Women Combing
Their Hair*, c. 1875–76.
Oil on paper mounted
on canvas, 32.4 x 46 cm.
The Phillips Collection,
Washington, D.C.
Acquired 1940

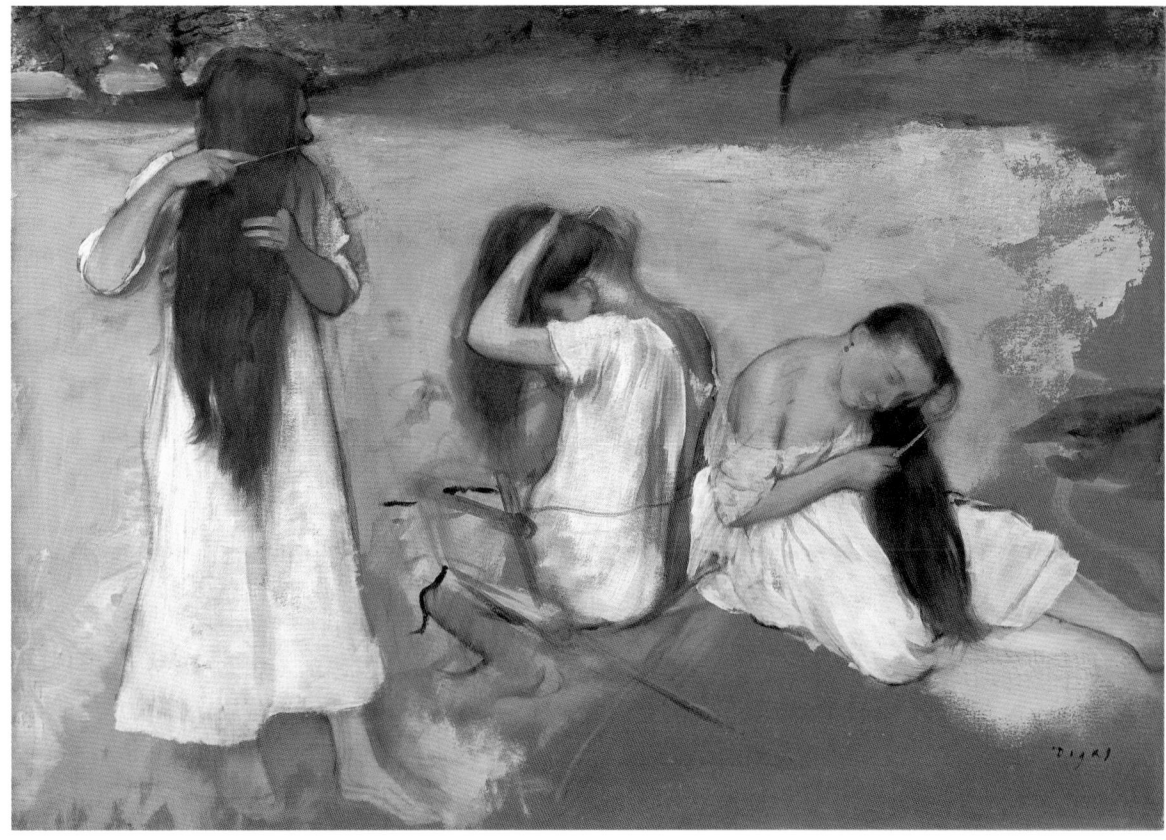

fine distinctions the class-conscious Degas liked
to draw, for, unlike Lautrec, he never dignified
the low subject of the brothel by representing it
in the reputedly high medium of oil on canvas.

At a purely personal level Degas was evidently greatly attracted to women's hair and
fascinated by its subtly changing sheen and the
natural rhythms of its sweep and flow when
being combed or brushed or coiled on top of
the head. Many of his bathers possess a cascading, rampant *chevelure* and are obliged to go
through contortions to cope with it. In a notebook used in 1868–74, he reflected upon his
powers of recall: "I can readily call to mind the
color of certain hair, for example, because I
associate it with the color of gleaming walnut
or of hemp, or indeed of horse chestnuts, real
hair, with its shimmering flow and its lightness,
or its coarseness and weight."[2] A revealing
passage, it can be set beside the soft, light,

chestnut hair celebrated in *Women Combing
Their Hair* and the Kreeger painting or the
coarse, matted hair of the prostitutes in the
monotypes. Some years later, transgressing a
social taboo, he made the daring request to be
permitted to watch Geneviève Halévy, cousin of
his friend Ludovic Halévy, brush out her hair.[3]
Contemporary manuals aimed at bourgeois
women usually insisted on the need for total
privacy, primly observing that only prostitutes
and courtesans admitted men into their presence at such unguarded, undignified moments.[4]
Degas maintained these social distinctions in his
pictures: men watch prostitutes in his *maisons
closes*, but no men are ever shown in the later,
ambiguously sited coiffure and toilette scenes.
Nevertheless, all his pictures on these themes
infringe the strict rules governing etiquette by
giving every spectator access to this normally
forbidden domain — hence the controversy

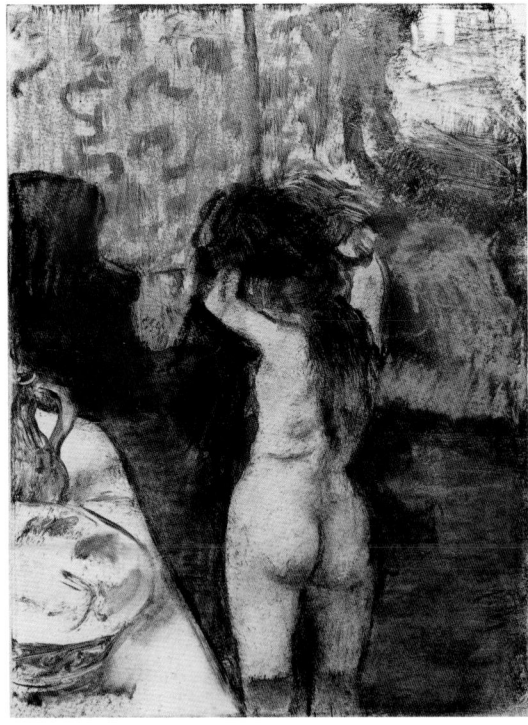

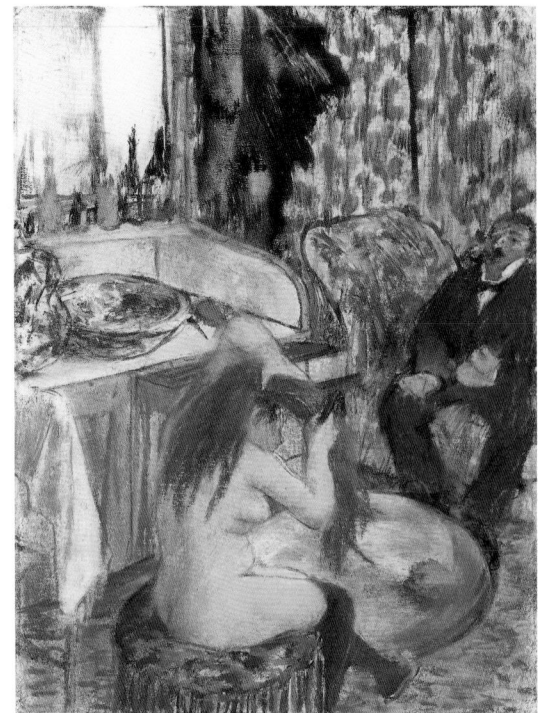

they tended to arouse whenever he exhibited them in public.[5]

Degas's predilections aside, it is significant that the steady rise in the number of his toilette and coiffure scenes from the mid-1870s onward coincided exactly with what may fairly be called a French obsession with personal hygiene. It had gradually become an obsession, in large part thanks to the fearless experimental work of Louis Pasteur and his colleagues, who in the course of the 1860s had succeeded in demonstrating that bacteria were responsible for transmitting life-threatening diseases such as cholera and typhoid. France's gravest problems — her comprehensive defeat at the hands of Prussia in 1871 and her relatively low birth rate, for instance — were commonly attributed to the supposedly poor health of the population.[6] A clamorous government campaign was mounted to combat what was described as the national malady of hydrophobia, and by 1890 hygiene and disinfection were regular topics in the health columns of ladies' magazines as well

as in innumerable self-help manuals.[7] Indeed, "microbes" became such a popular obsession that, according to Matisse, visitors to the Salon of 1897 pointed derisively to the crystal carafes depicted in his large canvas of a maid laying a dinner table and likened the spots of prismatic color to killer germs.[8]

Although all the experts agreed that regular washing with soap and water was essential, there was considerable disagreement about the frequency with which one ought to immerse oneself in water, as opposed to having a simple "sponge bath" in a basin, and about all kinds of related minutiae, such as whether the water should be cold, tepid, or hot, the duration of the bath, the best techniques for washing and drying the different parts of one's body, the value of massage, and the pros and cons of resting and taking restorative beverages after the ordeal of bathing.[9] Since private bathrooms with running water were still quite a rarity in Paris at the turn of the century — they only began to be routinely fitted into bourgeois

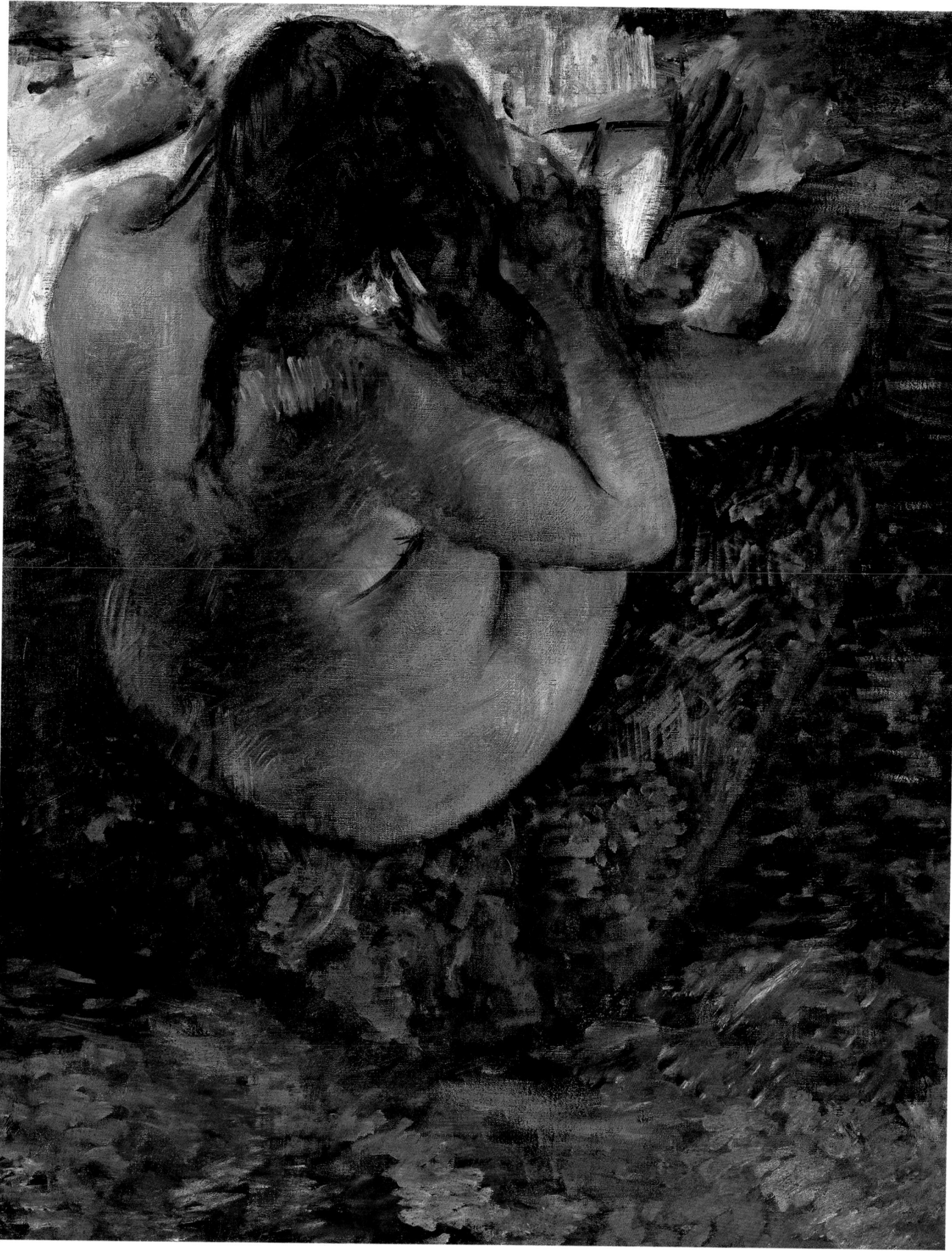

apartments during the 1880s — there was a parallel drive to construct public baths, wash houses, and swimming pools (the latter being regarded as a way of washing large numbers at the same time).[10]

Degas never concerned himself with the vulgarities of public baths and swimming pools, or for that matter with male bathing in any form, and it would be absurd to suggest that he set out like some zealous Social Realist to illustrate the hygienists' arguments. But there is a remarkable overlap between his toilette scenes and the contemporary literature on bathing. Thus, Degas depicts all the forms of equipment in use in his day from the most basic, portable zinc tub to the coveted but rare, fully plumbed-in bath with gleaming taps, not omitting that special French invention, the freestanding bidet (see 91, 180, 213, 215, 238).[11] He also depicts a wide range of the washing and drying actions minutely described in the manuals: standing, bending, and squatting in the tub; bending over the washstand basin; lying in the full bath; washing the limbs and feet; sponging the armpits and under the breasts; sponging behind the neck and reaching round to wash the back; straddling the bidet and washing the private parts; and then carefully drying everything afterward (**182–86**; see also 215, 217, 219, 225). And now and then we glimpse a padded *chaise longue* suitable for the post-ablutions rest (see 89, 198). Degas was dependent on posing models for the precision and accuracy of his bathers' gestures, and his studio was equipped with the basic props, including a portable tub and a freestanding zinc bath. To confer some degree of authenticity on the bedrooms and *cabinets de toilette* he mocked-up in his perennially untidy, dusty, gloomy studio, he would drape towels, dressing-gowns, and patterned fabrics over racks, screens, and furniture. Ironically, all these images of personal hygiene were created in a thoroughly unhygienic environment.[12]

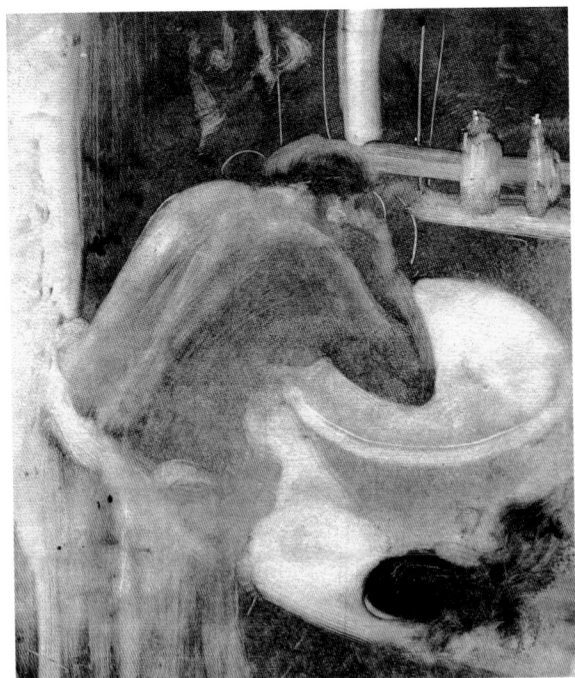

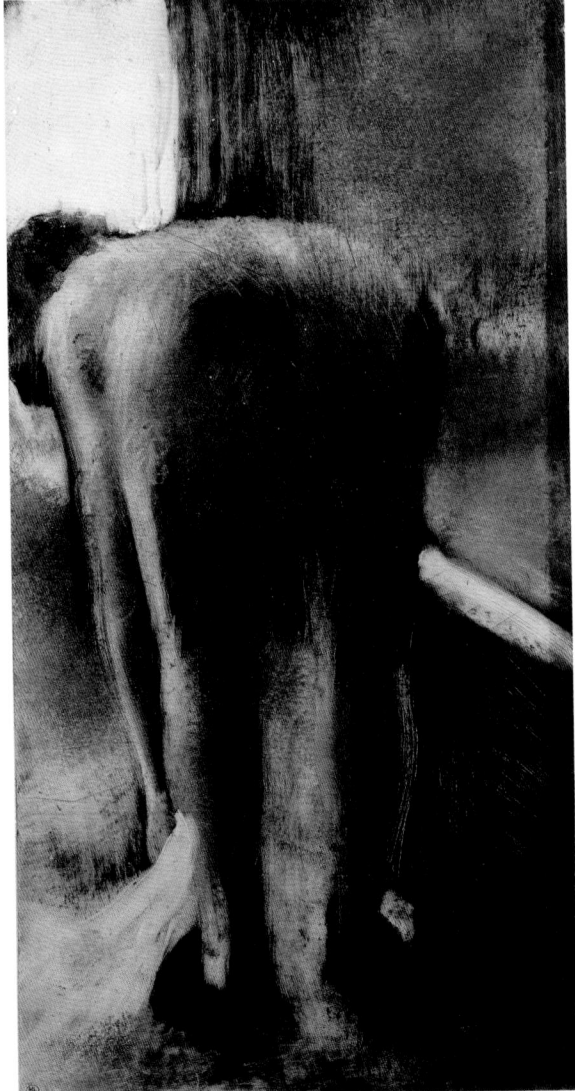

182

Edgar Degas

The Washbasin, c. 1879–83. Monotype, 31.1 x 27.3 cm. Sterling and Francine Clark Art Institute, Williamstown, Massachusetts (1962.39)

183

Edgar Degas

Woman Drying Her Feet Near Her Bathtub, c. 1879–83. Monotype, 45.1 x 23.9 cm. Musée d'Orsay, Paris, housed in the Department of Graphic Arts, Musée du Louvre. Bequest of Count Isaac de Camondo (RF 4046.B Recto)

185

Edgar Degas

After the Bath, c. 1891–92. Charcoal on yellow tracing paper, 35.2 x 25.4 cm. Sterling and Francine Clark Art Institute, Williamstown, Massachusetts (1955.1408)

186

Edgar Degas

Woman Standing in a Bathtub, 1890–92. Charcoal on yellow tracing paper, 43.7 x 30 cm. Sterling and Francine Clark Art Institute, Williamstown, Massachusetts (1955.1394)

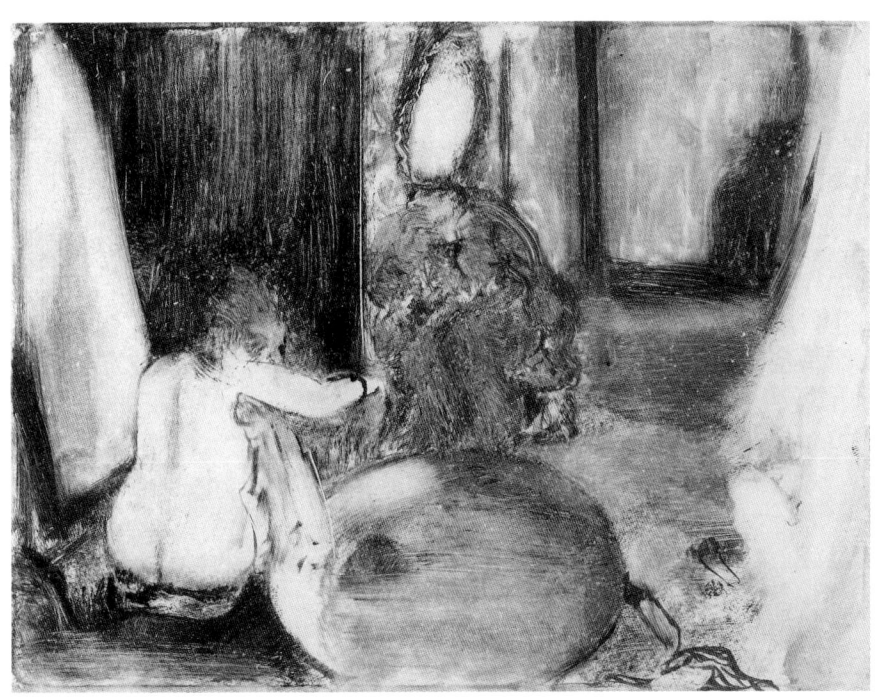

184

Edgar Degas

The Tub, c. 1878–80.

Monotype, 16 x 21.1 cm.

Private collection

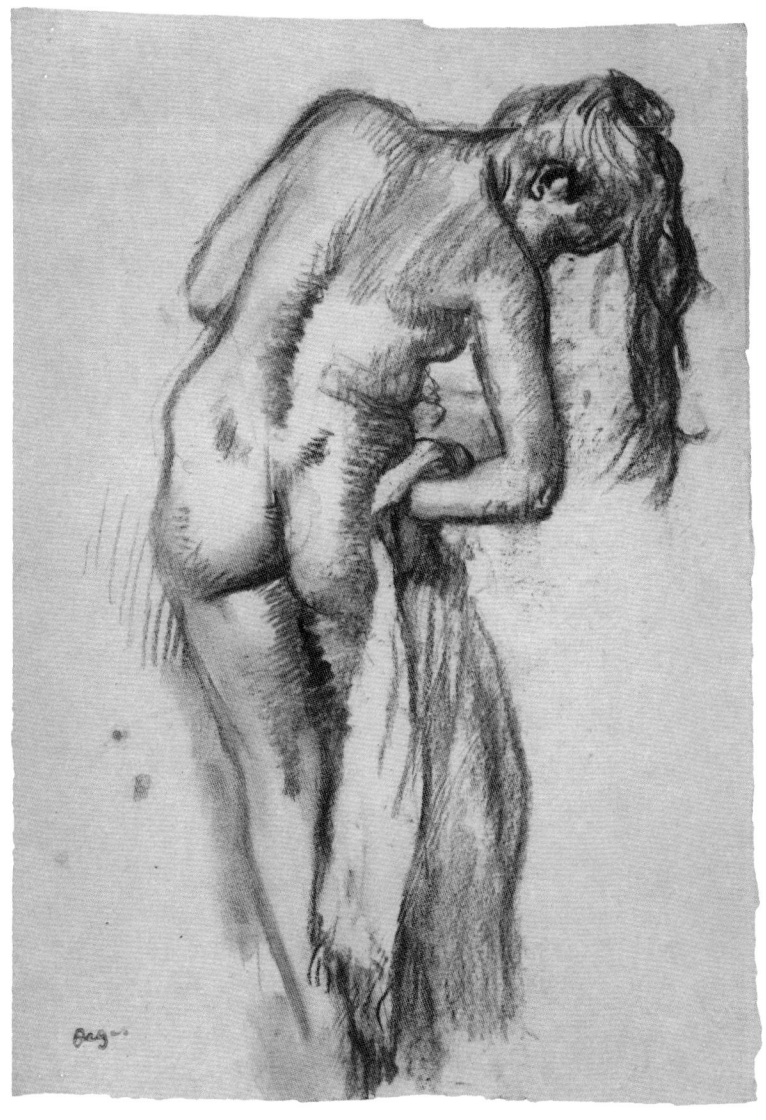

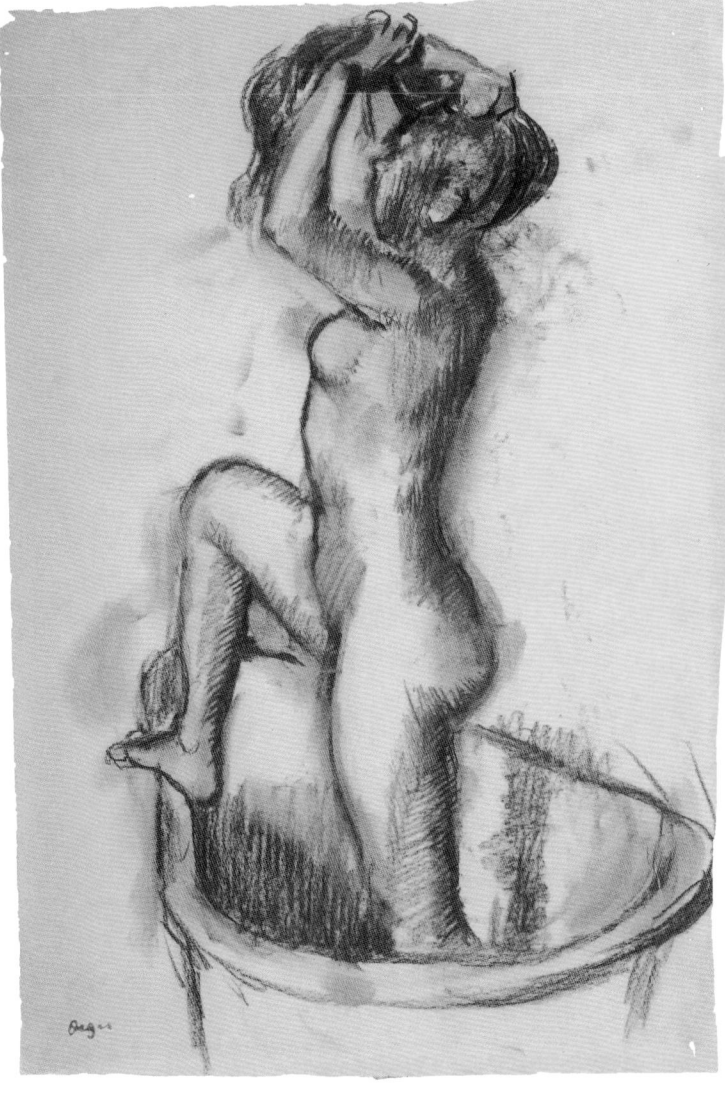

Quite often Degas depicted maidservants aiding in the complex bathing operations (see 213), bringing their mistresses sustaining beverages (see 132), or performing a massage.[13] Again, he was being strictly accurate since maids were the only people regularly admitted to the sanctum of the *cabinet de toilette*. (Célestine, the heroine of Octave Mirbeau's *Le Journal d'une femme de chambre*, is shocked and offended when a new employer insists on being left alone to bathe and care for her body.)[14] But Degas's maids appear only in scenes where a deep, full-length bath or a well-equipped washstand is depicted; in scenes with a cheap, portable tub, the woman washes unaided. He thus registered an essential economic distinction between his bathers, who in other respects are so difficult to class precisely because they are naked and observed in circumstances that are intrinsically leveling: the women with large baths, whether respectable *bourgeoises* or well-set-up courtesans, can afford to employ a maid to fetch and carry all that water; those with zinc tubs are working class and must do everything for themselves. Here, also, he was to the point, for the cleanliness of servants greatly troubled the hygienists on the grounds that dirty servants might bring disease into the most decent home.[15]

Degas's numerous scenes of hair-combing are equally topical, for human hair was deemed a prime breeding ground for the dreaded bacteria, and its proper care was therefore a matter of grave debate. Yet even as late as 1900, immersing the head in water was widely considered, in France at least, a potentially damaging and dangerous procedure, normally to be undertaken only every two or three months and never more than once a fortnight.[16] Instead, a daily regime of brushing, combing, and especially aeration was considered the best guarantee of a clean, healthy, thick head of hair.[17] As a supplement, patent lotions were recommended, to be rubbed and combed through the hair to improve its luster and texture and promote its growth while also cleaning it.[18] In line with these practices and prejudices, Degas did not depict hair-washing in the present-day sense, and his bathers often sweep up their hair to keep it out of the harmful water's way.[19] Time and again, we see them drying their necks, but never hair that is dripping wet or women with their heads swathed in towels. Instead, slow, painstaking combing, brushing, and aeration were among Degas's regular themes, and in *Beach Scene* and *Women Combing Their Hair* (see 177, 178) he depicted the much vaunted "*bain d'air*" (air bath), in which fresh air was directed to the scalp by carefully combing and spreading out the hair. In fact, both these paintings were entirely studio-based, the outdoor settings having been perfunctorily faked-up, just like the bathroom settings in the later toilette scenes.[20] And now and then the ever-alert, well-informed Degas depicted the miraculous patent lotions[21] or the hairpieces women resorted to when nature and the lotions failed them (see 84, 89).

The Role of Fernande Olivier

Toilette themes surfaced in Picasso's work at about the time of his first visit to Paris in October 1900 in a few drawings of women standing at their dressing tables (see 78) and reappeared the following year when he was preparing for his exhibition at Ambroise Vollard's gallery. Clearly Paris was the trigger, for these subjects were so typically French, and there are echoes of hard-hitting naturalist drawings by Théophile Alexandre Steinlen and the other regular illustrators of *Gil Blas Illustré*, alongside some spoofing of the pseudo-mythological nudes of Salon mainstays like William-Adolphe Bouguereau, who continued to turn out immaculate, porcelain-bodied nymphs with wondrous heads of hair almost until his death in 1905.[22] Picasso's most ambitious early essay on this subject was *The Blue Room (The Tub)* (see 88), completed after his exhibition closed on

14 July 1901. Released from the need to meet a deadline, he executed it with greater care than many of the Impressionist-style canvases included in the show, but he did not lighten or soften his heavy touch with the dense, meaty paint or sacrifice the deliberate naïveté of his drawing: the nude is oddly proportioned and seems too small in relation to the furniture; the tub wobbles disconcertingly as if, like an auto-didact, he could not control the perspective. As Richard Kendall has shown, there is good reason to believe that Picasso painted *The Blue Room* not just with Degas's celebrated pastels of women washing in portable zinc tubs in mind but also with knowledge of his lithograph of a bather drying her thigh (see 89) and of the monotype of a bather drying her back later acquired by Jacques Doucet (see 91) (or of William Thornley's reproduction of the associated pastel).[23] In its spacious setting and naturalist detail, Picasso's painting is strikingly similar to Degas's superb monotype, but he has rotated the composition by 180 degrees so that the nude is seen from the front, not the back, and her bed has moved from the foreground to the background. If, as seems likely, Degas's lithograph inspired the pose of the girl twisting and bending to sponge her thigh, then this involved an identical switch from the back to the front view of the body. Reversing the orientation of a source was a simple but effective device to assert independence, and Picasso deployed it on other occasions at this time (for instance, when switching the composition of Renoir's *Moulin de la Galette* from right to left in his remade, night-time version of the same subject [see 77]).[24] Yet although insisting on a classic frontal view of his down-market Venus, instead of the anonymous, elusive back view Degas generally preferred, Picasso followed Degas in showing her entirely absorbed in her task and chastely oblivious of the spectator. He enjoyed wrestling with the artists he admired in this way, following them in this detail, departing

from them in that, using them as a catalyst, not as a crutch.

Apart from a few drawings of an emaciated, crouching woman (perhaps a prostitute) staring disconsolately into a mirror at her sunken face and thinning hair, Picasso dropped the toilette motif until the summer or autumn of 1904.[25] By then, he had been living in the Bateau Lavoir for about six months and had decided to make his move to Paris permanent. Taking up the subject again at this watershed in his career in prefer-ence to the tragic, quasi-religious imagery of sickness, destitution, and moral dilemma typical of the Blue Period was one of several signs that he was bent on becoming a rather more French and rather less Spanish painter. A rapid brush drawing introduces a motif that reappeared in a different guise the following year: a man morosely watches a beautiful naked woman bathe and preen.[26] To judge by her body shape, this is one of the drawings to commemorate the first, casual, secretive phase of Picasso's love affair with Fernande Olivier, who at the time was living in the Bateau Lavoir with the now-forgotten sculptor Laurent Debienne.[27]

At the beginning of 1905, the real-life bed-room scene was given a romantic twist when the lovers were transformed into saltimbanques or circus performers and the drab studio con-verted into a tent. In the beguiling *The Harlequin's Family* (**187**), the stick-thin harlequin holding the couple's newborn baby watches appreciatively while his pretty wife, gazing into a mirror, arranges her hair; the bowl on the box and the towel on the ground allude to the earlier wash-ing phase of the ritual. Underlining the rejection of the robust quasi-naturalism of *The Blue Room* (see 88), the composition is centralized and symmetrical and the draftsmanship and palette exquisitely delicate. A few other works made early in 1905 pursue the same imagery of female vanity-cum-male spectatorship, but the subject did not truly take hold until the autumn of 1905, when Olivier at last heeded Picasso's

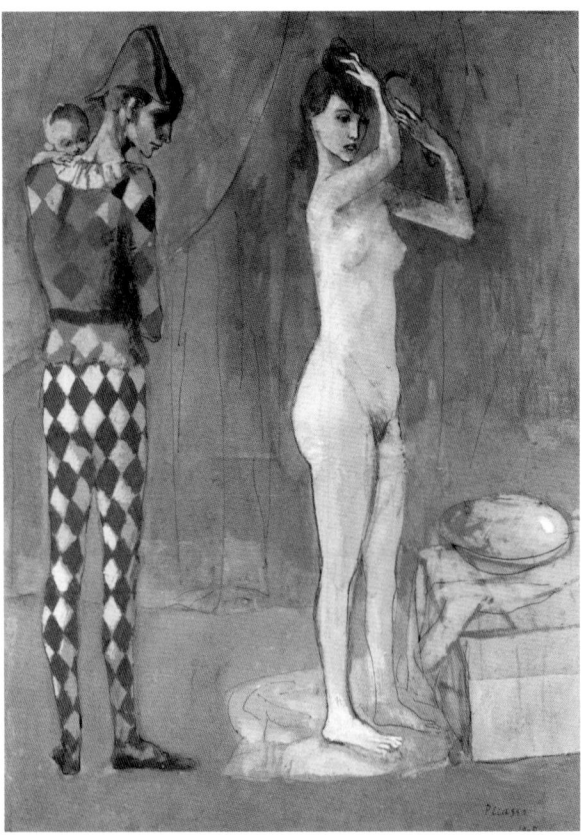

187

Pablo Picasso

The Harlequin's Family,
1905. Gouache and
India ink on paper,
58 x 43.5 cm.
Private collection

tiles," and in another, "I washed in the little lean-to that serves as a shower-room and toilet, but water has to be brought up from the kitchen."[29] Her remedy for an instantly regretted one-night stand was an ice-cold shower, and for an exhausting journey (with Picasso to Barcelona in 1906), a long, relaxing bath.[30]

Olivier first moved into the Bateau Lavoir with Debienne in the autumn of 1900. As usual, she itemized the facilities, which were dismayingly rudimentary. There was no bathroom in the "weird, squalid" building and only one tap at the bottom of the stairs for all the tenants. Worse still, there was only one toilet — memorably described in her diary as a "black recess with a door that won't shut" down a "smelly corridor."[31] Listing the miserable scraps of furniture in Picasso's studio when she first entered it some four years later, Olivier did not omit the "yellow earthenware bowl standing on a rusty little cast iron stove" that served as a wash basin and "a towel and a piece of soap on a whitewood table beside it."[32] *The Harlequin's Family* presents a generalized version of these ad hoc arrangements. Dirty water was, she says, collected in a large bucket, "which is always full to overflowing," and tipped out of the bedroom window into the gutter. A rusty frying pan served as the chamber pot.[33] Sordid, badly ventilated rabbit warrens like the Bateau Lavoir were anathema to the hygienists, and in the disgusted opinion of one regular visitor, the dealer Daniel-Henry Kahnweiler, the whole building was "the most unspeakable and unsanitary place you can imagine," a place where it was dangerous to fall ill.[34] Fortunately, there was another water supply in the form of a Wallace Fountain in the square outside, and Fernande would not have had to go far to find a public bath: by 1900, there were nine such establishments in Montmartre and twenty-five in the nearby ninth arrondissement.[35]

Writing of the period when her affair with Picasso was still only intermittent — and before

entreaties and moved in with him. Throughout the next year and more, with "*la belle Fernande*" as his constant companion and muse, the twin motifs of *la coiffure* and *la toilette* were staples of his repertoire.

When Picasso first met her, Olivier was leading the usual rackety, hand-to-mouth, promiscuous existence of a jobbing artists' model. But she had been brought up by an aunt and uncle with social pretensions and ever afterward craved bourgeois comforts and resented, and resisted, all efforts to force her to do the menial chores she considered far beneath her.[28] Her posthumously published, entertainingly gossipy *Souvenirs intimes* is punctuated by remarks about the inadequate bathing arrangements she had to cope with whenever she moved in with a new lover: in one set-up there was "no bathroom: you have to wash in the kitchen, which is so small that the tub covers all the

the artist, so fastidious in later life, had mended his ways — Olivier confided in her diary that although she was touched by his devotion, she was put off by his indifference to hygiene:

He's asking me to come and live with him, and I don't know what I should do. . . . He's kind and gentle, but he doesn't look after himself, and I find that upsetting. I don't mind untidiness, but I'm horrified by lack of personal cleanliness. I don't dare let him sense this; it's a delicate matter, but I'll get round to it.[36]

Picasso must have understood that he needed to clean up his act if he had any chance of overcoming the young woman's scruples, because on one occasion when she paid a prearranged visit she was assailed by the heady fumes of paraffin, bleach, and eau de cologne. Aided by Apollinaire, no less, Picasso had spent the day disinfecting the studio from top to bottom with this unorthodox concoction.[37] Olivier was famous for her love of perfume and the eau de cologne was evidently intended to clinch matters.

Olivier's *Souvenirs intimes* also bears witness to her preoccupation with her looks and especially her abundant hair — "the hair you loved," as she says in her opening dedication "*À Picasso.*"[38] "I have luxuriant hair," she noted proudly, "the colour of very ripe chestnuts, with big natural waves which make all the women around me jealous."[39] This was a period when the ideal *chevelure* was thick and waist-length, when no woman cut her hair unless she was ill, and when thin hair was so despised that many women resorted to the costly hairpieces that occasionally trail over washstands and chairs in Degas's candid pictures (see 84, 89). Olivier's wavy, chestnut hair — lovingly commemorated in a contemporary study by the American painter Walter MacEwan — would have made her the perfect model for Degas's coiffure scenes, and when Benedetta Canals (see 113), "a beautiful redhead" who had posed for Degas

in the past, took her to the aging artist's studio on nearby rue Victor Massé in August or September 1904, it was surely with a view to introducing her as a potential model.[40] But, Olivier noted in her diary, "I wouldn't be his type" — meaning perhaps that she was too buxom and stately to pose for the "small statuettes" that, she says, Degas was working on at the time.[41] This visit happened to coincide with the first, casual phase of her liaison with Picasso. No doubt she told him all about it, and it seems to have established a connection between her and Degas in his mind.

Unlike the legendary artist of rue Victor Massé, Picasso was enthralled by Fernande's heavy build and indolent sensuality. In his first life-size sculpted portrait of her, she has the serenity and mystique of an Archaic Greek goddess, but her features are recognizable from other portraits — long almond eyes, prominent nose, high cheekbones, lips set in a seductive, *Mona Lisa* half-smile, strong, thick neck, softly waving hair streaming down the head and over the shoulders (**188**). Thus he struck a balance between Classical idealization and reality. The sculpture was modeled in clay in the spring of 1906 in the studio of the Basque ceramist and disciple of Gauguin, Paco Durrio, who gave the inexperienced Picasso advice on modeling techniques. Perhaps it was on Durrio's suggestion that fine tulle was gently pressed into the surface of the moist clay to evoke the porous texture of skin.[42] The right side of the head looks much less finished than the other and registers the marks of the sculptor's knife and fingers; the eye is indicated with the lightest of scratched incisions — a mere beginning. The back of the head, an amorphous accumulation of hundreds of tiny patches of clay, is exploratory in a painterly fashion. By contrast, the left eye, eyebrow, and hairline are finely modeled and incised. This inconsistency was surely intentional, for it is paralleled in numerous contemporary paintings and reflects Picasso's marked preference for the dynamism of the "provisional" over the inertia of the "completed."

Rodin's notorious sketchiness may have been an inspiration, but for Rodin sketchiness has an intensely emotional, proto-Expressionist dimension alien to this sculpture by Picasso. Degas's *non finito* may be more relevant, for although it was only visitors to his studio who saw the original waxes or the handful of plaster casts, Picasso had surely heard firsthand accounts (from such mutual acquaintances as Vollard, the painter-model Suzanne Valadon, Benedetta Canals, and Olivier herself) of what the statuettes of dancers, bathers, and so on looked like, and stories of the elderly artist's chronic unwillingness to "finish" them, which apparently derived as much as anything else from the sheer pleasure of constantly reworking the material.[43] Degas's unfinished head of the ballerina Mathilde Salle (**189**), mistress of the great art collector Comte Isaac de Camondo, makes a particularly intriguing comparison with Picasso's portrait of Fernande Olivier.[44] It is equally uncompromising in its frontality and displays over its entire surface a similar exploratory roughness to the "in process" areas of Picasso's sculpture. It, too, plays off one incomplete, "blinded" eye against a hollowed-out, "sighted" eye, and the enigmatic effect of the disparity provokes similar thoughts of the contrasting public and private faces of the sitter, of the knowable and unknowable aspects of her personality, of the subtly shifting moods to which she is prone. Yet, unless it was described in some detail to Picasso, one must assume that the parallels in this case are fortuitous — a matter of affinity — since *Mademoiselle Salle* was not exhibited in Degas's lifetime or cast in bronze until after his death.

The portraits of Olivier that Picasso made after she moved in with him emphasize the beauty of her hair and record the various ways she styled it: the "cottage loaf" coiffure seen in a particularly tender print; the heavy bun at the nape of the neck seen in a half-length

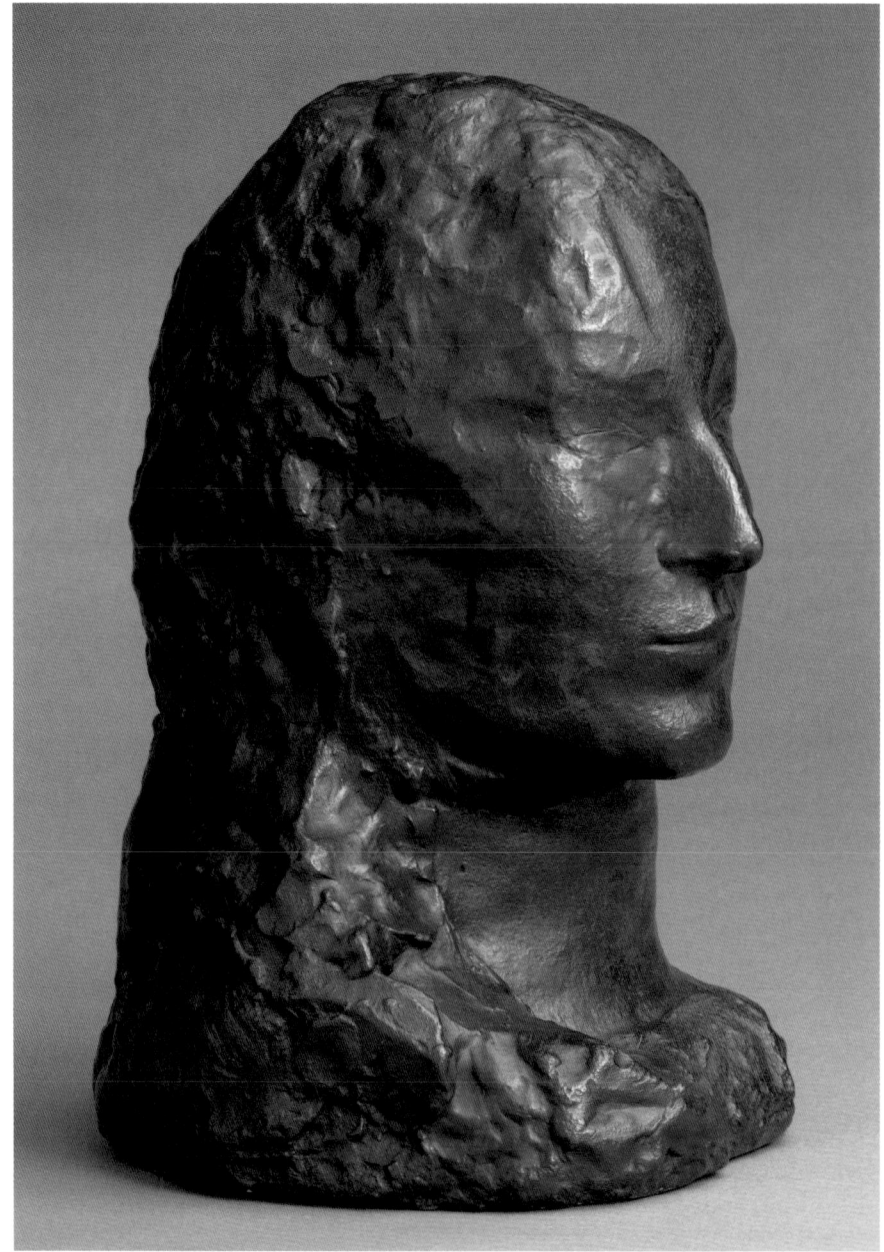

188

Pablo Picasso

Head of a Woman (Fernande Olivier), 1906. Bronze, height: 34 cm. Allen Memorial Art Museum, Oberlin College, Ohio. R. T. Miller Jr. Fund, 1955 (AMAM 1955.35)

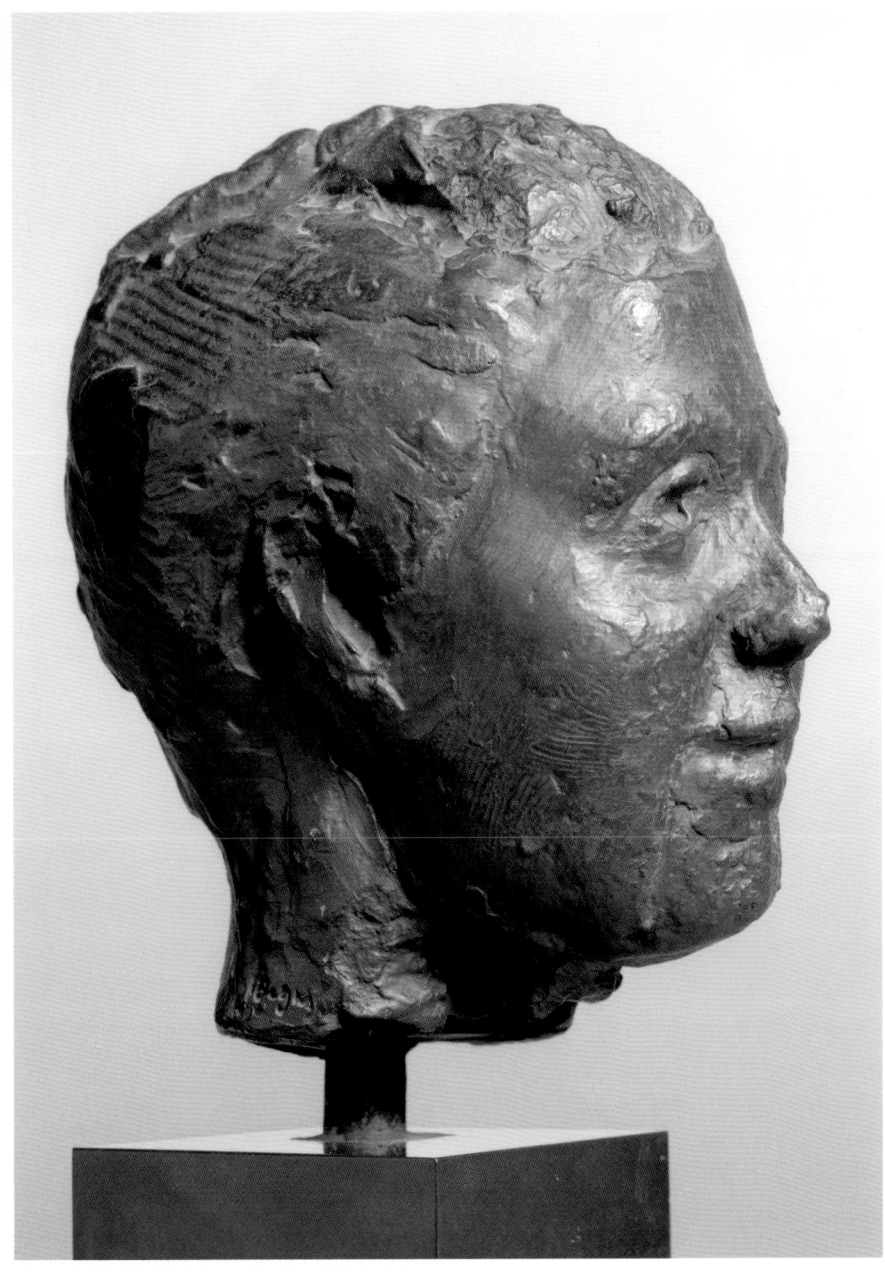

189

Edgar Degas

Head of a Woman (Mlle Salle), modeled 1892. Bronze, height: 25.5 cm. Museum of Fine Arts, Boston. Bequest of Margarett Sargent McKean (1979.509)

"unfinished" painting; with a parting and in a chignon in studies of her bent over her sewing; loose, brushed back and falling over her shoulders, as in the sculpture just discussed and in a sensual monotype depicting her noble Roman profile that Picasso printed in russet and blue gouache from glass.[45] Arguably, the monotype, which is closely related to a contemporary gouache,[46] is a sign of that association Picasso seems to have made between Olivier and Degas, for it was one of the very first of his essays in an uncommon medium that Degas had made so much his own. The very first of Picasso's monotypes, the head of a woman in a mantilla, who may be Fernande Olivier or Benedetta Canals, is more Degas-like in style and was printed with the greasy black ink Degas almost always used.[47] Other French artists in whom Picasso was much interested at this time — notably Gauguin — had also produced monotypes, so one would not be justified in concluding that these experiments are proof of firsthand knowledge of Degas's prints. But other factors described below strengthen the argument that it was indeed at about this time that Picasso's interest in them first took root.

The spectacle of Fernande arranging her hair must have fascinated Picasso, playing a significant part in his decision to paint a major genre scene on the theme of hair-combing — not, it should be noted, a likeness of her. Dating the earliest studies for the picture eventually painted in the autumn of 1906 (see 199) and attempting to reconstruct their sequence are fraught with difficulty, but some at least probably belong to the end of 1905 and the earliest oil to early 1906. A drawing representing Picasso's initial idea maps out a crowded composition depicting five women all dressed in loose-fitting gowns (**190**). Reading from left to right, a young girl seated on the ground is having her long hair attended to by a kneeling pregnant woman. In the center another young girl with her back turned to the spectator holds

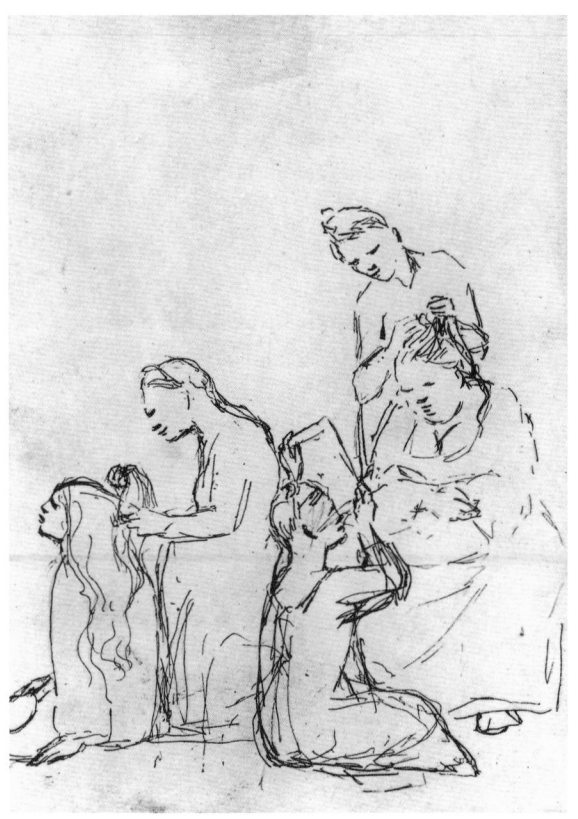

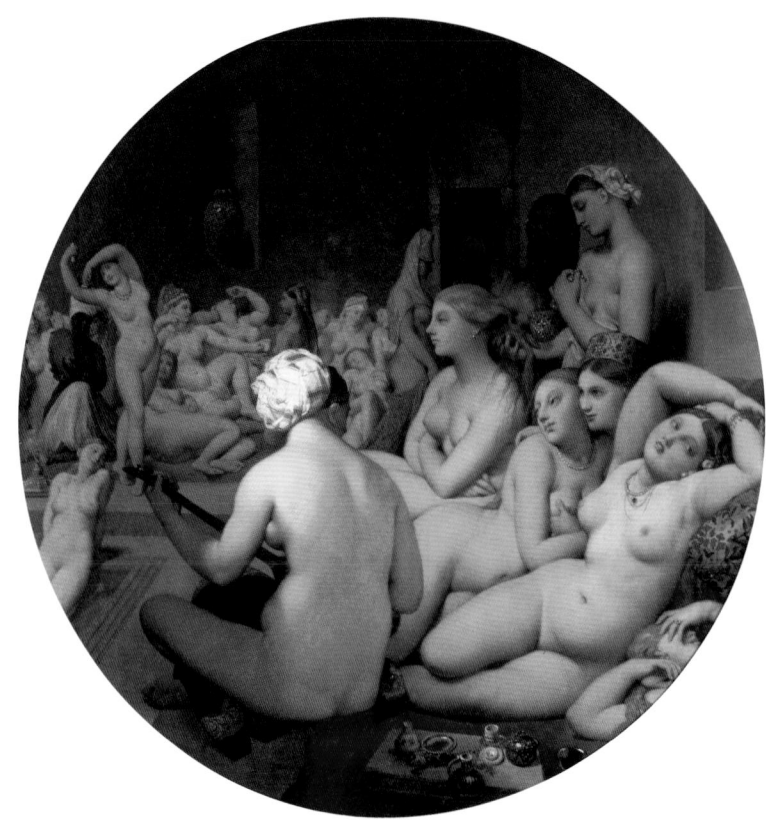

up a mirror to an obese matriarch seated on a chair, whose hair is being dressed by a standing woman.[48] There are no indications of setting in this timeless scene, but the image of cohesive group activity harks back to the *Circus Family* of early 1905.[49]

Scholars have linked the coiffure composition with Picasso's discovery of Ingres's *The Turkish Bath* (191) in the Salon d'Automne of 1905. Like many other artists at the time, Picasso was stunned by the unabashed voyeuristic sensuality, daring anatomical distortion, and extreme spatial compression of the painting, which had not been seen in public since the late 1860s and was accompanied in the exhibition by a substantial number of the preparatory studies, most of them loaned by the Musée Ingres in Montauban.[50] The crowded drawing with five figures registers Picasso's initial, cautious response and, characteristically, it involved a mixture of homage and critique. Thus, the

two women attending to their companions' hair pick up Ingres's eye-catching duo of the blond odalisque sitting patiently, arms crossed, while her friend perfumes her hair with incense, but Picasso completely altered the context and implications by clothing them and avoiding any suggestion of Sapphic eroticism. When shortly afterward he developed the motif of the matriarch having her hair dressed into an independent oil painting, he reinforced this distance from Ingres (192), modifying the pose of the blond odalisque by turning her around to face the spectator, reducing the hairdresser to a mere sign — a pair of delicate hands twisting the hair — and injecting a dose of deflationary humor, for his slouched, corpulent model is a most improbable sultan's favorite and looks indeed not unlike his new patron Gertrude Stein, who began posing for her famous, bullish portrait in the autumn of 1905.[51]

Picasso's enthusiasm for *The Turkish Bath*

190

Pablo Picasso

Women Having Their Hair Dressed, 1905. India ink on paper, 22.5 x 18 cm. Private collection

191

Jean-Auguste-Dominique Ingres

The Turkish Bath, 1862. Oil on canvas on wood panel, 108 x 110 cm. Musée du Louvre, Paris. Gift of Friends of the Louvre, with the assistance of Maurice Fenaille, 1911 (RF 1934)

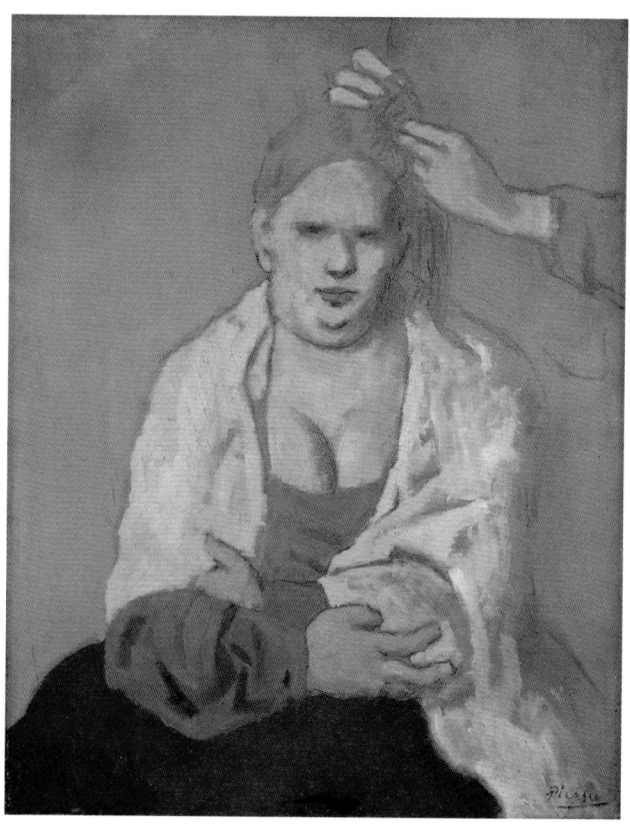

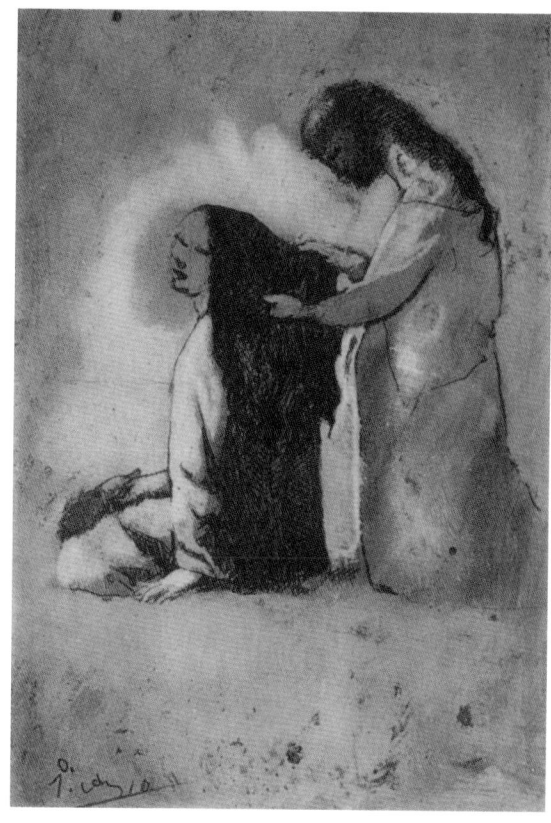

did not involve rejection of Degas's coiffure
scenes, however. On the contrary, the five-
figure compositional drawing and others that
developed the duo of the kneeling woman
attending to the young girl's hair (**193**) suggest
that Picasso was not only conversant, through
Olivier, presumably, with the doctrine of the *bain
d'air* — since that is what the young girl's hair
is receiving — but also that he had seen certain
pictures by Degas on this subject. *Beach Scene*
(see 177) was still in Henri Rouart's collection at
the time, but Picasso could have seen Thornley's
lithographic reproduction which, because it was
realized in a black-and-white drawing, is notably more draftsmanly than the painting itself.
Assuming he had leafed through the Thornley-
Degas portfolio, he would also have seen the
fine reddish monochrome reproduction of collector Roger Marx's superb pastel of a nude
woman having her hair combed by a statuesque
maid (see 198). Moreover, the generalized, sculp-

tural conception of Picasso's figures throughout
his series of coiffure drawings echoes that of
Degas's late, monumental charcoal studies in
which the women combing their hair occasionally wear similar shapeless white shifts.[52]

Anyone who visited the elderly Degas was
left in no doubt about his cult of Ingres, for
he endlessly repeated his stories of meeting
the great man and the latter's gnomic utter-
ances. (Ingres's advice to him at the start of
his career, "Always draw lines, many lines," was
engraved forever on his memory.)[53] His collection of Ingres's work was justly renowned. Yet
such devotion to the Master of Montauban had
never led to self-effacing, subservient imitation,
only to independent interpretation — a critical
attitude toward admired predecessors that was
distinctly like Picasso's own.[54] For someone with
Picasso's acute sensitivity to the creative lineage
of artists, no great strain was required to reconcile Ingres and Degas — to see, for example,

the Roger Marx pastel as a descendant of *The Turkish Bath* — and as he planned his own hair-combing picture, Picasso negotiated both exemplary predecessors. Nevertheless, it seems likely that Fernande Olivier facilitated the elision, for although she conformed remarkably to Ingres's favorite type of woman — pampered, indolent, sensual, comfortable in her replete, smooth-skinned body — her daily beauty routine and self-absorption were the stuff of so much of Degas's most personal and radical work. By a curious but productive coincidence, she had teetered on the edge of modeling for Degas at the very moment when Picasso first fell in love with her and began to make drawings of her;[55] and she took up her position at the center of his life in September 1905,[56] about a month before the opening of the Salon d'Automne, at the very time he definitively felt the impact of Ingres's work. Unconsciously, Fernande chose the perfect moment to throw in her lot with Picasso, for she incarnated his current aesthetic ideal with extraordinary completeness.

Picasso in 1906: "un primitif classique"

Picasso's circumstances changed dramatically when Ambroise Vollard descended on the Bateau Lavoir at the beginning of May 1906 and, in return for 2000 francs, walked off with twenty-seven paintings.[57] Solvent at last and buoyed up by this most promising development, the couple set off almost immediately for Barcelona, where they spent three weeks socializing with Picasso's family and his artist friends. Then, on the recommendation of the sculptor Enric Casanovas, they set off for the remote Pyrenean village of Gósol, completing the final, precipitous stage of the journey by mule. The trip to Gósol coincided with a period of intense, revisionist interest in classicism among avant-garde writers and artists in both Paris and Barcelona. Influential painter-critics such as Maurice Denis welcomed the eclipse of the sensation-based instantaneity of early

Impressionism and extolled the eternal values they believed were enshrined in the murals of Puvis de Chavannes and the late work of Cézanne, Renoir, and Gauguin, while hailing the unemotional, simplified, classicizing sculpture of Aristide Maillol as a breakthrough and model for the new generation. This vanguard classicism was to be utterly unlike the anathematized *trompe l'oeil*, often overtly titillating classicism of Salon stalwarts such as Bouguereau. The latter was much in the public eye at this moment because his death in August 1905 brought reassessment and seemed to spell the end of the era of "decadent" academic classicism. To make the distinction crystal clear, Denis emphasized the "gaucherie" of the new reforming works: Maillol was great because he was "*un primitif classique*" (a classical primitive);[58] Cézanne was great because he was "a naïve artisan, a primitive who returns to the sources of his art";[59] and Ingres was "our newest master" because of his "*bienheureuse naïveté*" (blessed naïveté).[60] The goal was to reclaim the "true" classical tradition from the "false" vulgarizing interpretation put upon it by the Salon classicists.

For an academically trained artist like Picasso, it was particularly important to eliminate any lingering corruption by direct contact with original, "primitive" sources, and to this end, Ardengo Soffici recalled, "he would pace around like a hound in search of game" in the ground-floor galleries of the Louvre where the antiquities were displayed.[61] It was in those galleries, shortly before he left for Barcelona, that Picasso discovered the archaic Iberian carvings that would have so strong an impact on his art after his return to Paris. Gósol was the chosen destination after the stopover in Barcelona because it was reputed to be completely untouched by modernity, a self-sufficient peasant community with a way of life that had hardly changed in centuries, a genuine rustic Arcadia, and Olivier's diary reveals that the village lived up to his expectations. Despite the absence of running

194

Pablo Picasso

The Watering Place, 1906.
Gouache on tan paper on
pulpboard, 38.1 x 57.8 cm.
The Metropolitan Museum
of Art, New York. Bequest
of Scofield Thayer, 1982
(1984.433.274)

195

Pablo Picasso

*Young Rider Seen from
Behind*, 1906. Charcoal on
gray paper, 46.6 x 30.4
cm. Private collection

196

Edgar Degas

*Nude Study of a Jockey
Riding a Horse, Seen
from the Back*, c. 1890.
Charcoal on laid paper,
31 x 24.9 cm. Museum
Boijmans Van
Beuningen, Rotterdam
(inv. no. F. II 129 [PK]
[Koenings Collection])

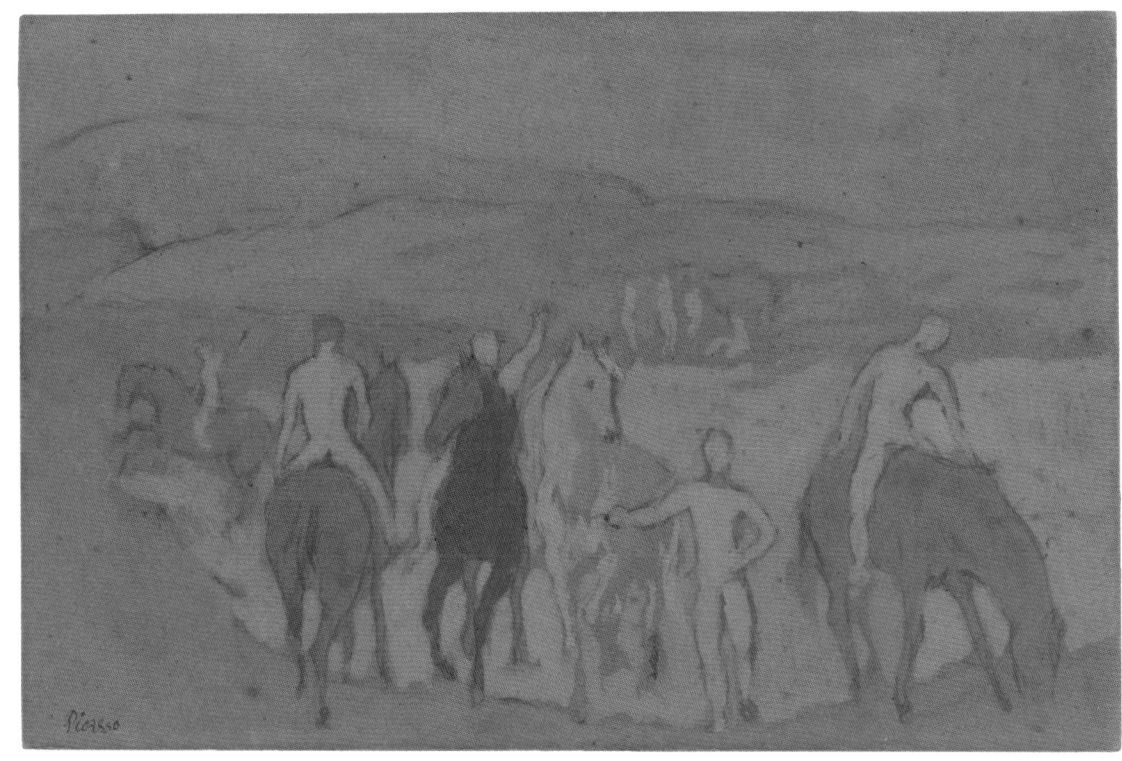

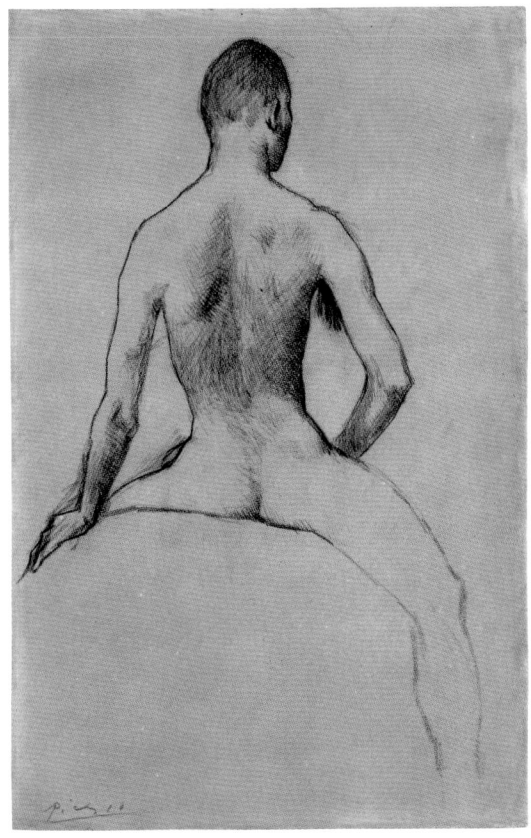

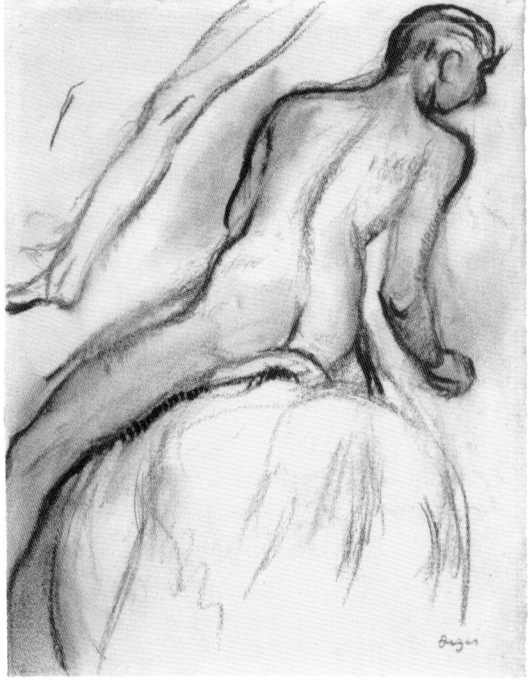

water in any of the houses, Olivier was entranced by the simple life in Gósol, reveling in the "incredibly pure" air and rugged landscape and delighted by "the clean, rustic inn" and the welcoming locals "untouched by civilization." "We have found true happiness here," she noted.[62]

Anticipating the trip to the Pyrenees, Picasso had planned a frieze-shaped Arcadian scene of naked youths watering their horses at a pond (**194**), blending reminiscences of antique sources (Archaic *kouroi* and the Parthenon frieze) with allusions to the pallid, Neoclassical murals of Puvis and the horserace scenes of Degas, with their strung-out sequences of jockeys facing both forward and backward, occasionally punctuated by a galloping steed.[63] One life drawing of a boy rider seen from the back is strikingly similar to a nude study of a jockey by Degas (**195, 196**), who, like Picasso, had not forgotten the lessons of the Parthenon frieze learned in his student years (see 3, 4): true to his classical training, even late in life Degas continued to plan modern-life genre scenes by making nude studies of the protagonists. In the end, however, Picasso decided against painting a full-scale version of *The Watering Place*, guessing perhaps that, significantly enlarged, it would have looked rather too much like a Puvis mural. Instead, he chose the more monumental option of singling out one of the striding youths with his horse and painting them life-size to create a grand but tender image of harmony between man and beast.[64] Had it been shown in one of the annual Salons, this canvas might well have drawn Denis's praise for its winning combination of the primitive and the Classical, its gaucherie and simplicity, and the absence of anecdotal detail or overt emotion. Instead, it went via Vollard into the collection of Gertrude and Leo Stein.

Picasso left for Catalonia with his head full of ideas for equally austere, archaizing paintings of nudes. It was one of the few times in his career since his student days when, under

the sway of the Louvre's collection of Egyptian, Greek, and Etruscan sculpture, the male nude rivaled the female nude as a subject for his art. He had not forgotten his plan to paint a major picture on the theme of female vanity, and in Gósol he came up with several different but interconnected compositions, each of which generated a group of preparatory studies as well as a large canvas. *The Harem* (**197**), painted under the impact of Ingres's *Turkish Bath*, was probably the first. Four identical beauties — or one beauty at four different moments — go through the daily routine of stretching or getting out of bed, washing from top to toe, combing out the tangled tresses, and gazing in rapt self-love in a mirror. A massive eunuch dozes in the foreground indifferent to their charms, having satisfied all his sensual appetites with food, wine, and tobacco. He is the only element in the composition to define the setting as a harem, and nothing could be further from the steamy luxury of Ingres's marble bathhouse than this bare, peasant room where the inmates have only an earthenware ewer and basin for their ablutions and not a single necklace to share between them. In the background, an old crone squatting beside a bucket — a cross between a shrewish procuress (known in Spain as a Celestina) and the typical cleaner employed to mop the floors in the poorest Spanish brothels — is the final anti-climactic touch, embodying both the idea of prostitution and the traditional *vanitas* moral about the transience of youth and beauty.

The satirical edge to *The Harem* and the parallel drawn with a brothel suggest that Picasso's reply to Ingres may have involved allusion to Degas's monotypes depicting *maisons closes* (see 179, 180, 238) and women whose status is more ambiguous as they are washing, dressing, or going to bed (see 91) — prints that were on the market in Paris at the time and that Picasso probably first encountered through his association with Vollard, a longstanding aficionado of Degas's erotic

197

Pablo Picasso

The Harem, 1906. Oil on canvas, 154.3 x 110 cm. The Cleveland Museum of Art. Bequest of Leonard C. Hanna Jr. (1958.45)

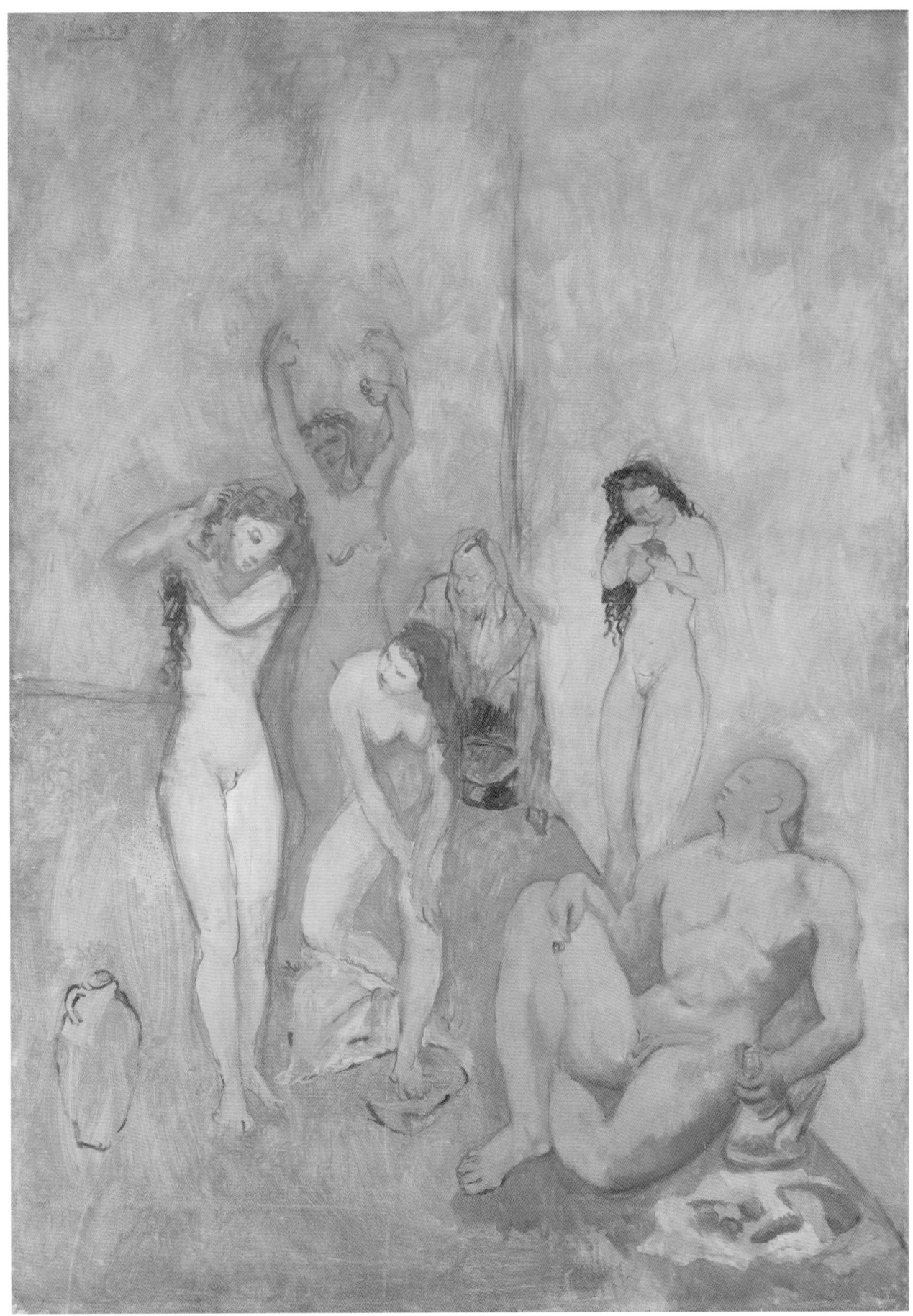

oeuvre.[65] In their own ironic fashion the brothel monotypes also toy with and puncture classical conventions by presenting a world in which women are always nude or dressed in clinging shifts — degraded nymphs whose lascivious gyrations mock the graceful, stereotyped poses of the goddesses and muses. Equally, the women in Degas's dark-field bedroom scenes often unconsciously adopt poses that are ignoble variants of canonical Classical sculptures, such as the *Spinario* and the *Callipygian Venus* (see 185). In other words, the parallel between *The Harem* and the Degas of the monotypes operates on more than one level.

Having laid in the composition, Picasso abandoned *The Harem*: after all the fuss surrounding the revelation of Ingres's masterpiece, it risked being dismissed as a clever but essentially frivolous parody. Nevertheless, just as he had removed one of the youths from *The Watering Place* and developed him in a grand, independent composition, so now he removed the elegant figure of the nude combing her hair from *The Harem* and made her the focus of two large, overtly classicizing compositions, *Girl with a Goat* and *La Toilette*. In the first, Picasso's teasing sense of humor was to the fore again, for the adolescent Venus Anadyomene, attended by an inquisitive goat, and a young boy with a vase balanced on his head look like the protagonists of a coyly titillating Bouguereau idyll.[66] And, as the side curtains and the red carpet disclose, this is pure charade, not the illustration of some authentic mythological story. Untouched by the playfulness of *Girl with a Goat* or the deflationary irony of *The Harem*, *La Toilette* achieves the dignified grandeur of *Boy Leading a Horse* through willed austerity in design, style, and technique. It, too, depends on a fusion of Classical sources — ancient Greek marbles (such as the Knidian Aphrodite and the Birth of Aphrodite relief on the famous Ludovisi Throne), red-figure vases decorated with toilette scenes, and Hellenistic Tanagra figurines — which

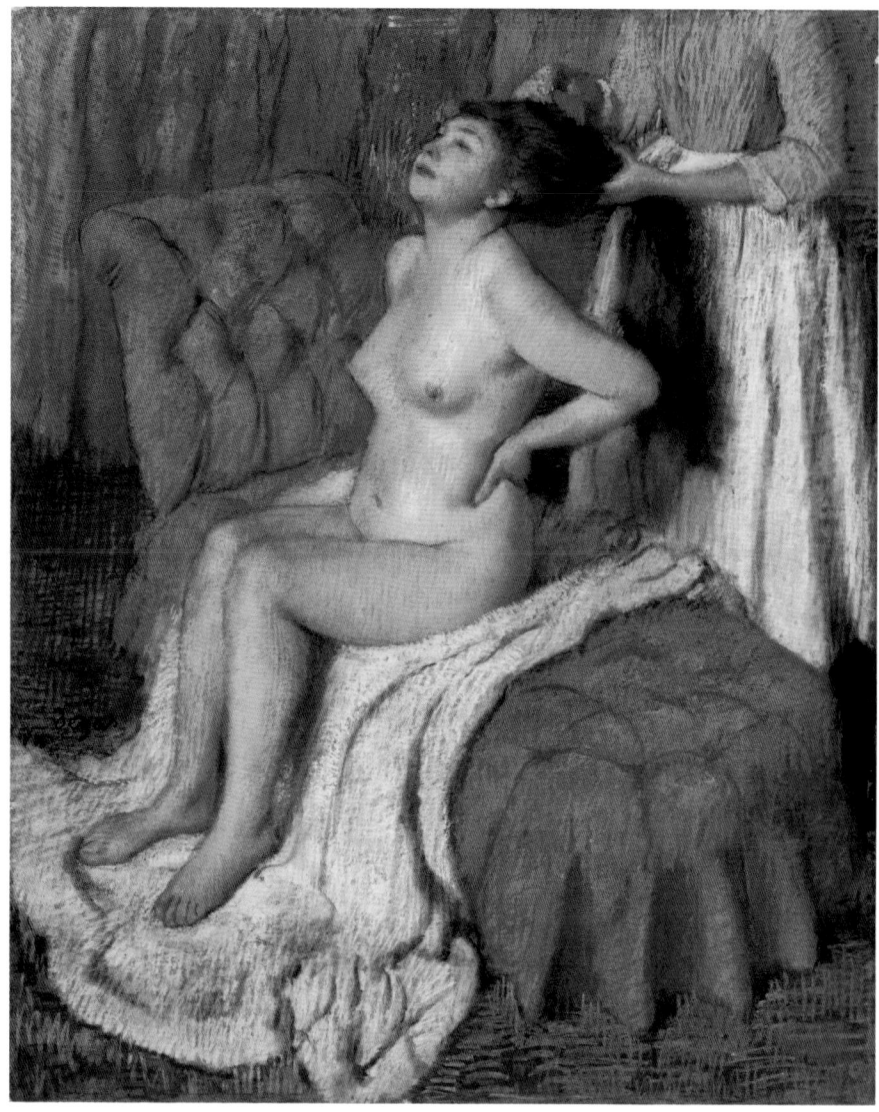

together produce something redolent of the Classical world and Classical beauty but are as far removed as can be from the archaeological "accuracy" of Jean-Léon Gérôme, another recently deceased academic painter whose star was in rapid decline. In their formal symmetry and overt Classical references, both paintings are opposed to Degas's modern-life aesthetic and oblique, fly-on-the-wall perspective, but the subject matter of *La Toilette* is fundamentally the same as the latter's representations of severely dressed maids ministering to their naked mistresses (**198**).

It used to be thought that the Metropolitan Museum's *La Coiffure* (**199**) was rolled up and brought back to Paris in an unfinished state when Picasso, alarmed by an outbreak of typhoid fever, hurriedly left Gósol in August 1906.[67] But scientific examination has revealed that it was painted in one rapid campaign after his return to Paris, on an old canvas that had already been used on several previous occasions.[68] For this new coiffure scene, Picasso turned his back on the elegant "Greek" style employed in *La Toilette*, sensing perhaps that it was too sophisticated and not as powerful as the "persistently gauche" and "incredibly awkward" painting of Cézanne that was attracting such intense interest at the time.[69] Reusing an old canvas and leaving plenty of signs that he had done so on the uneven surface were strategies to achieve uncompromising "primitive" harshness and (by contemporary standards) rank ugliness.

For the new composition Picasso returned to the pre-Gósol sketch with five figures (see 190) and systematically reworked the pyramidal group with the ungainly matriarch having her hair dressed (the heroine of that earlier essay in plain-speaking, the Baltimore *The Coiffure* [see 192]). Now he turned her around to face away from the spectator and moved the hairdresser to the left from the right. Completing the transformation, he converted the little girl seen from the back into a naked, forward-facing boy who resembles the urchin in Murillo's *The Young Beggar*, then one of the most popular paintings in the Louvre. (Being Spanish, Murillo was an appropriate source for a painting haunted by memories of Gósol.) In his quest for an authentically "primitive" note, Picasso may also have invoked the Iberian carvings discovered earlier in the year in the Louvre, for the mask-like faces of the hairdresser and the boy have something of their craggy, stony look. Although the representation of the two women as peasant types wearing the shapeless garments of the Gósol

villagers removes them as far as can be from the erotic fantasy world of Ingres's *Turkish Bath*, the motif of the hairdresser's hand cupping the long tail of hair survived and the intriguing *profil perdu* of her companion was borrowed from the seated musician in the foreground (or from her ancestor in the Louvre's *Valpinçon Bather*). But Degas once again played a mediating role between the past and the present, for the turned back and the half-hidden face recur with such obsessive frequency in his toilette scenes as to be effectively a signature motif (see 181, 184, 185, 238). Picasso heightened the innate mystery of this pose by refusing to allow us sight of the woman's reflection in the hand-mirror — a device equivalent to Degas's systematic refusal to allow the viewer to see faces that are visible, or known at least, to the secondary characters in his compositions (see 213). The mirror may be of the commonest kind, but for the women in Picasso's painting it seems to be invested with arcane significance, as if, in their innocence, they had never possessed such an object before and were hypnotized by its magical reflective properties. Their utter absorption intensifies the sense that a quasi-religious ritual is being performed — another link with Degas, whose constantly reiterated poses and gestures invest the banal routine of washing and hair-combing with the solemnity of an ancient purification rite. Without visiting Degas's studio, Picasso could not, in 1906, have seen the extraordinary *La Coiffure* now in Oslo's National Gallery (**200**), but there is a real affinity between the two pictures at the profound level of feeling and imagination, as well as in the drastic abbreviations of their drawing and uncompromising roughness of facture.[70] In ostensibly unfinished paintings like this, which emerged in the posthumous studio sales, Degas more than meets Maurice Denis's ideal of "*un primitif classique.*"

The Oslo *Coiffure* is a strikingly sculptural painting. As Richard Kendall has remarked, it

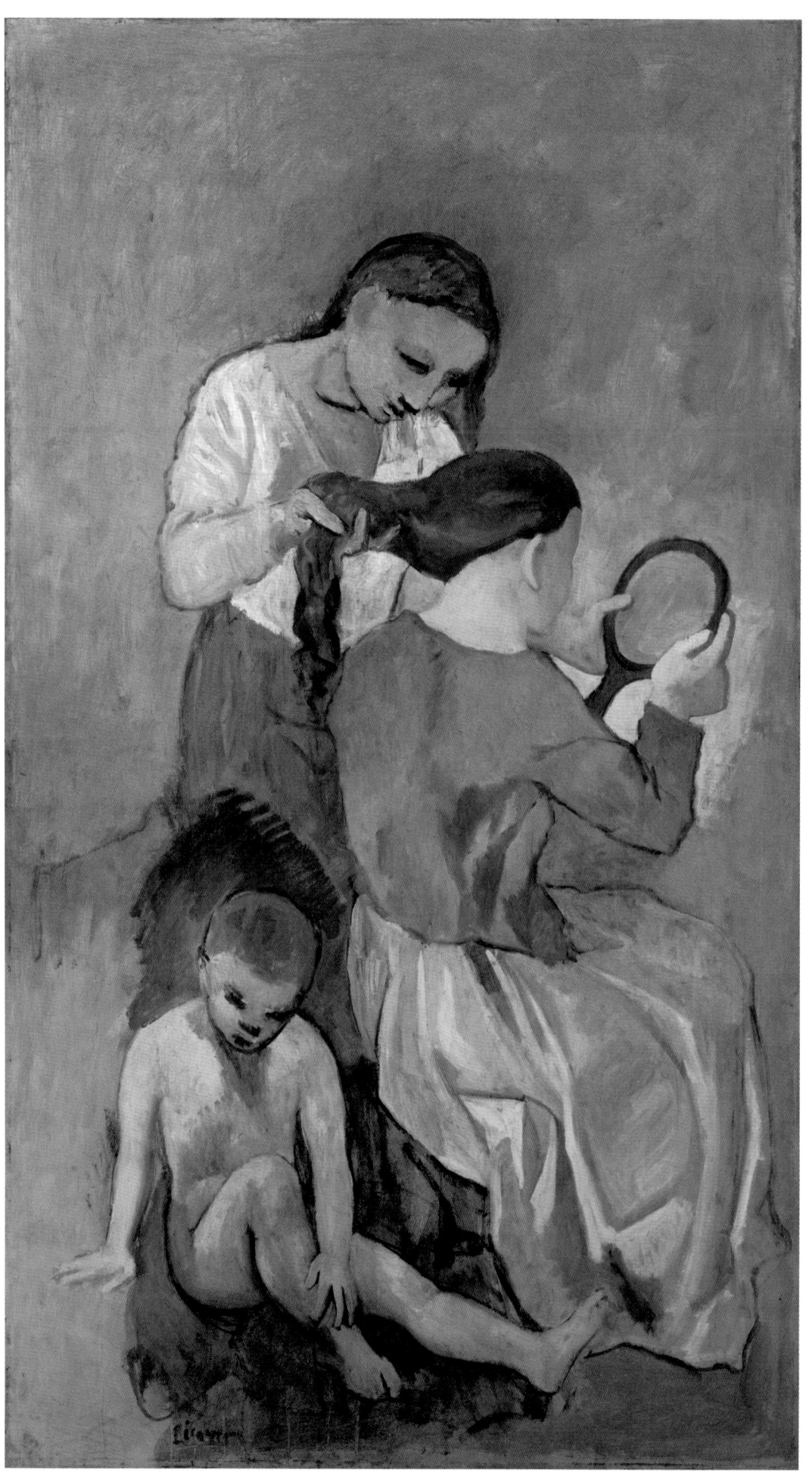

199
Pablo Picasso
La Coiffure, 1906. Oil on
canvas, 174.9 x 99.7 cm.
The Metropolitan Museum
of Art, New York.
Catharine Lorillard Wolfe
Collection, Wolfe Fund,
1951; acquired from
The Museum of Modern
Art, Anonymous Gift
(53.140.3)

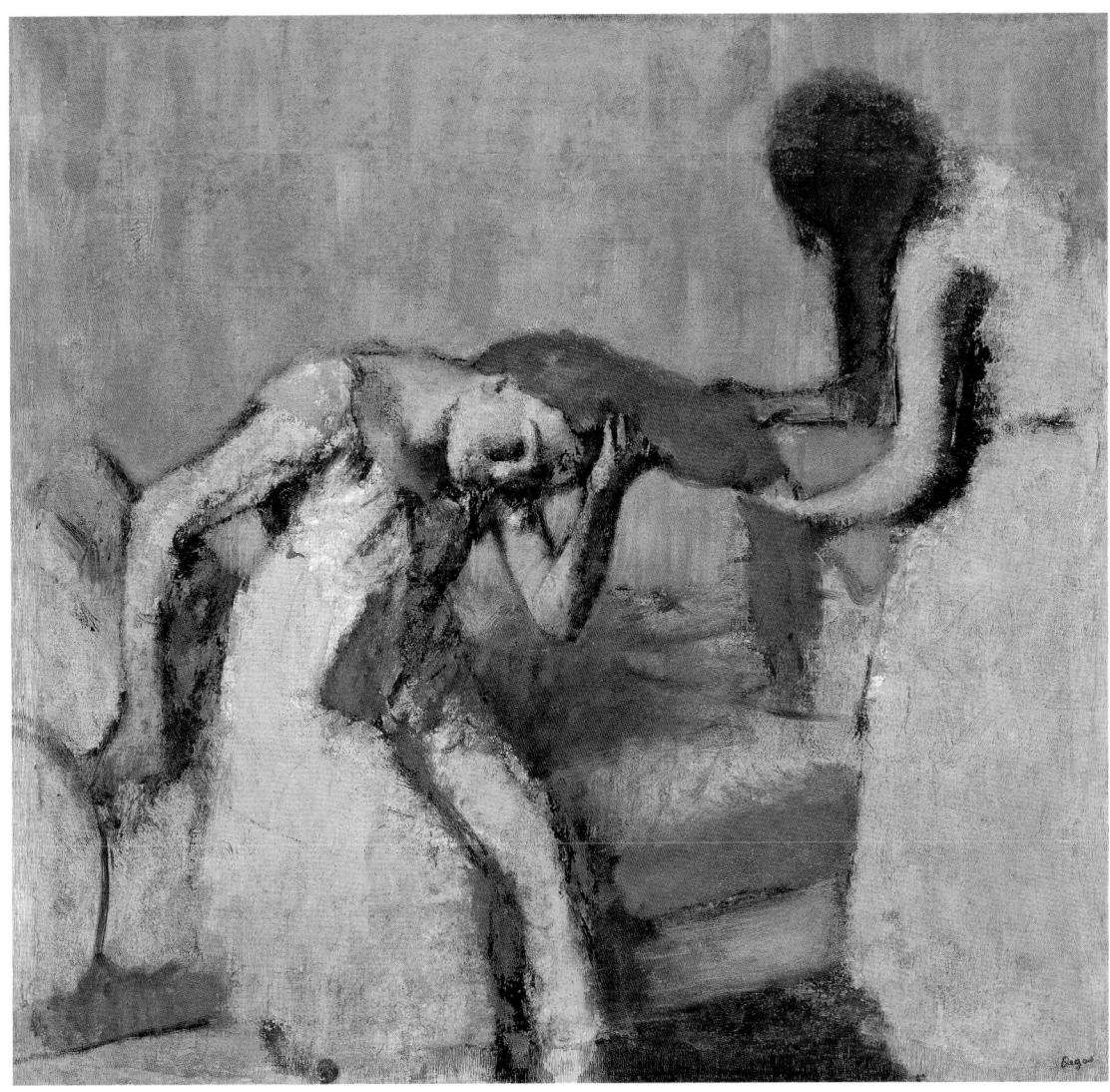

has something of the timeless and tragic quality of an ancient Greek relief, "its protagonists locked in some elemental exchange."[71] The Metropolitan Museum's *La Coiffure* is equally sculptural: the three overlapping figures are welded into a single craggy mass, but the precision of the contour uniting them and fixing them to the amorphous background creates the impression of a high relief rather than a sculpture in the round, while the tactile, patchy application of the colors and restricted palette of warm browns, creamy white, and blue call to mind the flaking paint on ancient stone or ter-

racotta. In another crucial respect Picasso was Degas's natural heir because he, too, was not content to paint in a sculptural style but felt bound to realize his ideas in three dimensions, never mind the technical difficulties. As far as we know, he had only heard of, never seen, any of Degas's wax sculptures at this point. Nevertheless, the fact that the older painter was making sculpture at all and that Renoir for one considered him "equal to the ancients," "the greatest living sculptor" — surpassing Rodin — must have been challenging, to say the least.[72] And if other incentives were needed,

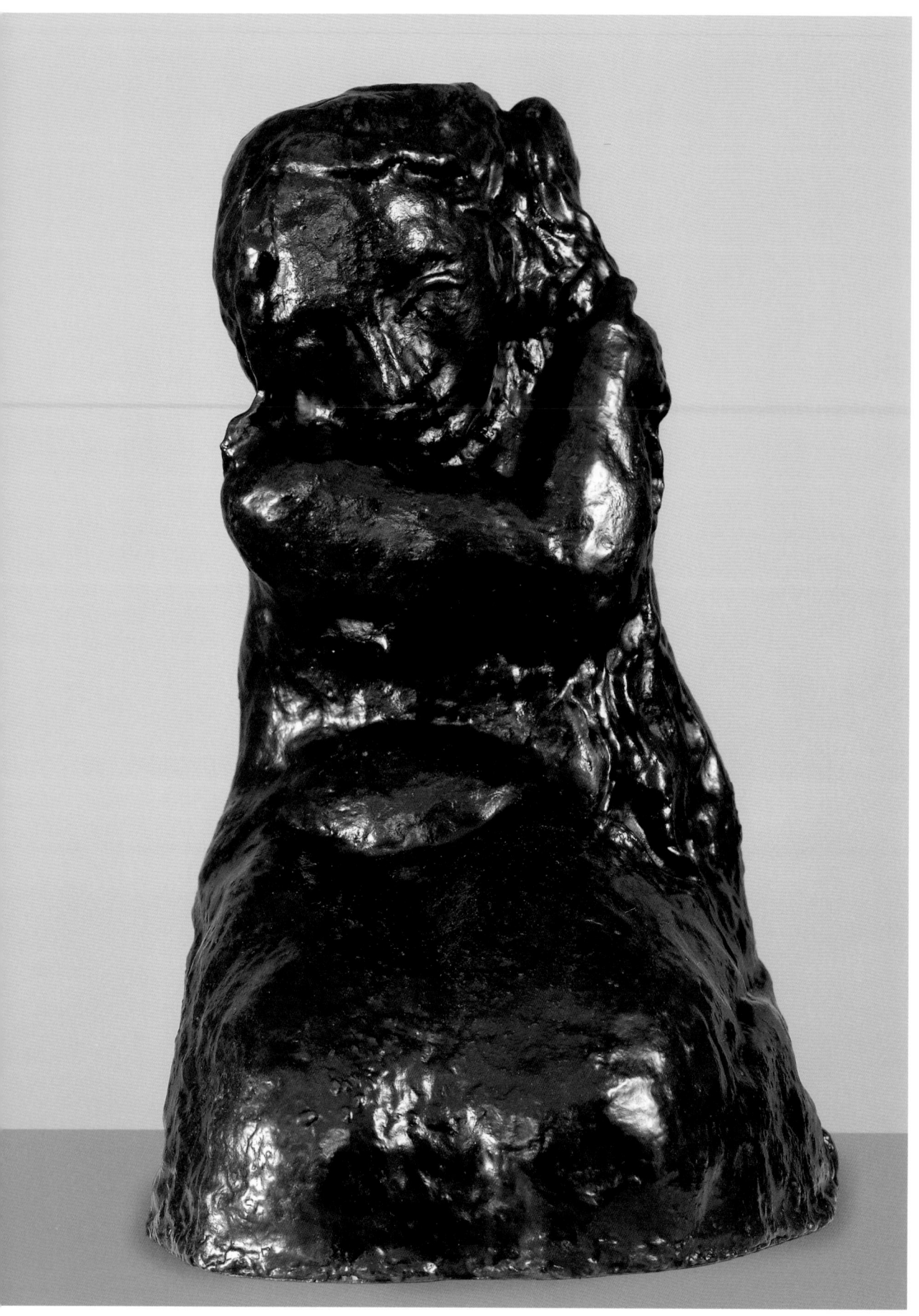

201

Pablo Picasso

Woman Plaiting Her Hair, 1906. Bronze, height: 41.6 cm. The Baltimore Museum of Art. The Cone Collection formed by Dr. Claribel and Miss Etta Cone of Baltimore, Maryland (BMA 1950.452)

202

Pablo Picasso

Woman Doing Her Hair, 1906. Pencil on paper, 31 x 22.5 cm. Hamburger Kunsthalle. Sammlung Hegewisch

203

Pablo Picasso

Woman Combing Her Hair, 1906. Pencil and charcoal on paper, 55.8 x 40.7 cm. Sainsbury Centre, Norwich, England. Robert and Lisa Sainsbury Collection (UEA 7)

204

After Doidalsas

Crouching Aphrodite with Eros, first century A.D. Roman copy from an original dating to the third century B.C. Marble, height: 122 cm. Museo Archeologico Nazionale di Napoli

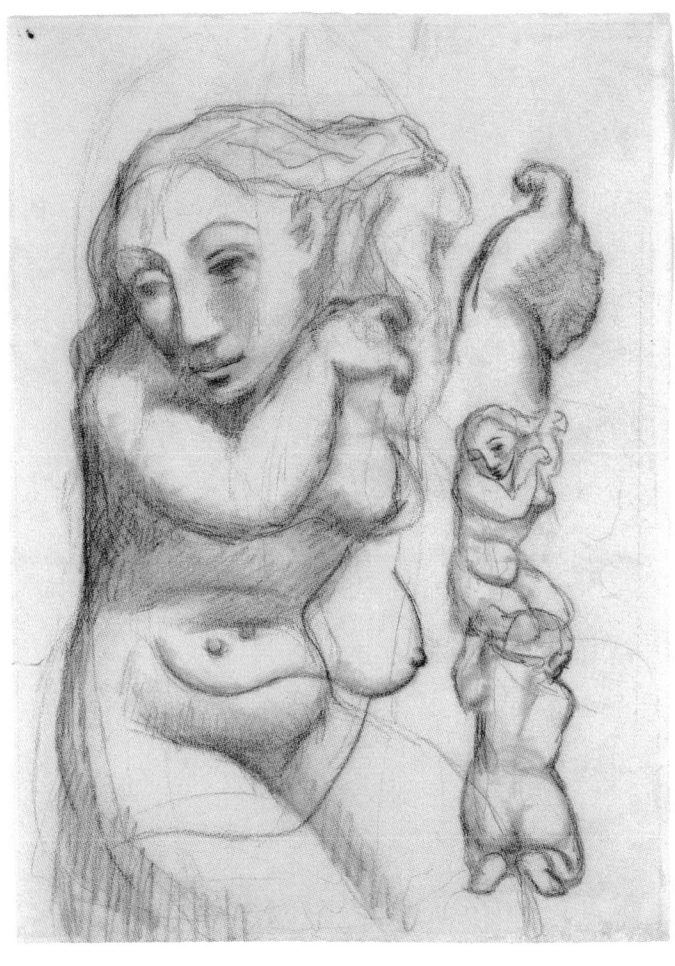

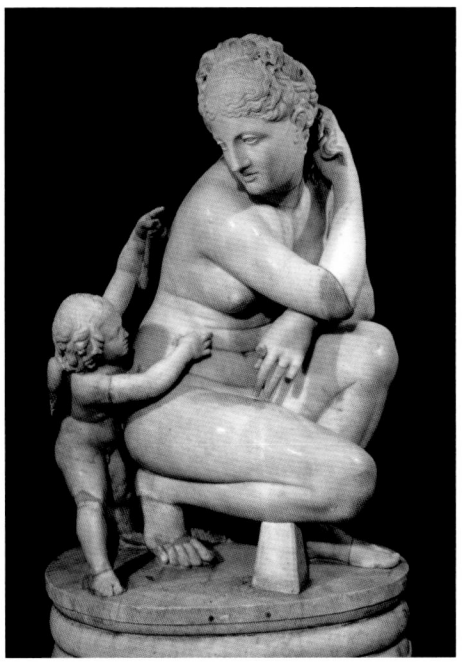

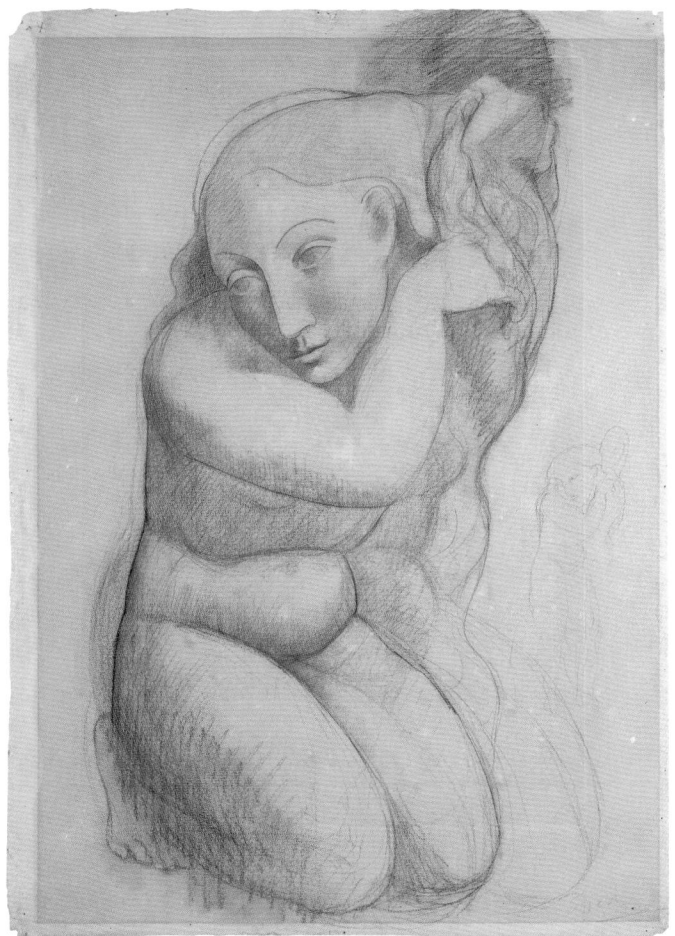

there was the example of Matisse, with whom Picasso's rivalrous friendship was developing at this time, and who stood out as another radical painter-sculptor.

Picasso's next sculpture was not derived from the Metropolitan's painting but shared its coiffure theme (**201**). Instead of being fully in the round, it took the form of a very high relief designed to be seen only from certain angles. (The back is open and in the bronze cast looks as if it has been brutally split off from its flat ground.) The proper left side of the figure — the side that illustrates the action of hairdressing — is more fully realized than the right, a disparity that recalls the earlier sculpted portrait of Fernande Olivier (see 188). One sheet of preparatory drawings does, it is true, suggest that Picasso initially thought of sculpting his crouching figure in the round because there is a view of her fully modeled back (**202**). But other preparatory drawings and paintings depict only her front and side views (including **203**). Picasso's decision to realize the sculpture in terracotta must have been made in concert with Durrio, for it was in his studio that the clay of *Woman*

Combing Her Hair was modeled and in his kiln that it was fired. Gauguin had left various works for safekeeping with Durrio when he returned to Tahiti in 1894, including several primitivist ceramic sculptures, and John Richardson is surely right to detect the influence of Gauguin's dramatic stoneware *Oviri* on the composition as well as the technique of Picasso's sculpture.[73] On the other hand, Picasso did not depict some strange, cruel, savage deity but a subject rooted in reality and, arguably, his primary point of reference was a canonical Greek sculpture familiar from numerous damaged and reconstructed Roman copies, some with, many without, an attendant Cupid: Doidalsas's *Crouching Aphrodite with Eros* (**204**).

Despite the allusion to Doidalsas, nothing could be less like finely worked marble than the soft, impressionistic surface of Picasso's sculpture. The divisions between the parts of the body are not as clearly marked as in the drawings, and the hair and legs fuse together in a molten mass, which makes it difficult to be sure whether the lower half of the figure is supposed to be draped or not. Picasso used colored glazes on the original terracotta, and the spreading form of the figure and rippling surface were no doubt created with this in mind. But it is also possible that he handled the clay in what he imagined to be the manner of the now partially sighted Degas, who — or so Vollard claimed in his engaging memoir of the artist — put it about that he was concentrating on modeling sculpture because he could feel what he was doing.[74] Although it may conceivably postdate Picasso's terracotta, Degas's *Woman Arranging Her Hair* (**205**) makes a fascinating pair with it, for more than merely the shared iconography is at stake.[75] Like Picasso's sculpture, it is closely related to (and no doubt sprang from) the artist's graphic work — among others, the lithograph (see 89) that may have been a source for the nude in Picasso's *The Blue Room* of 1901 and a contemporary charcoal

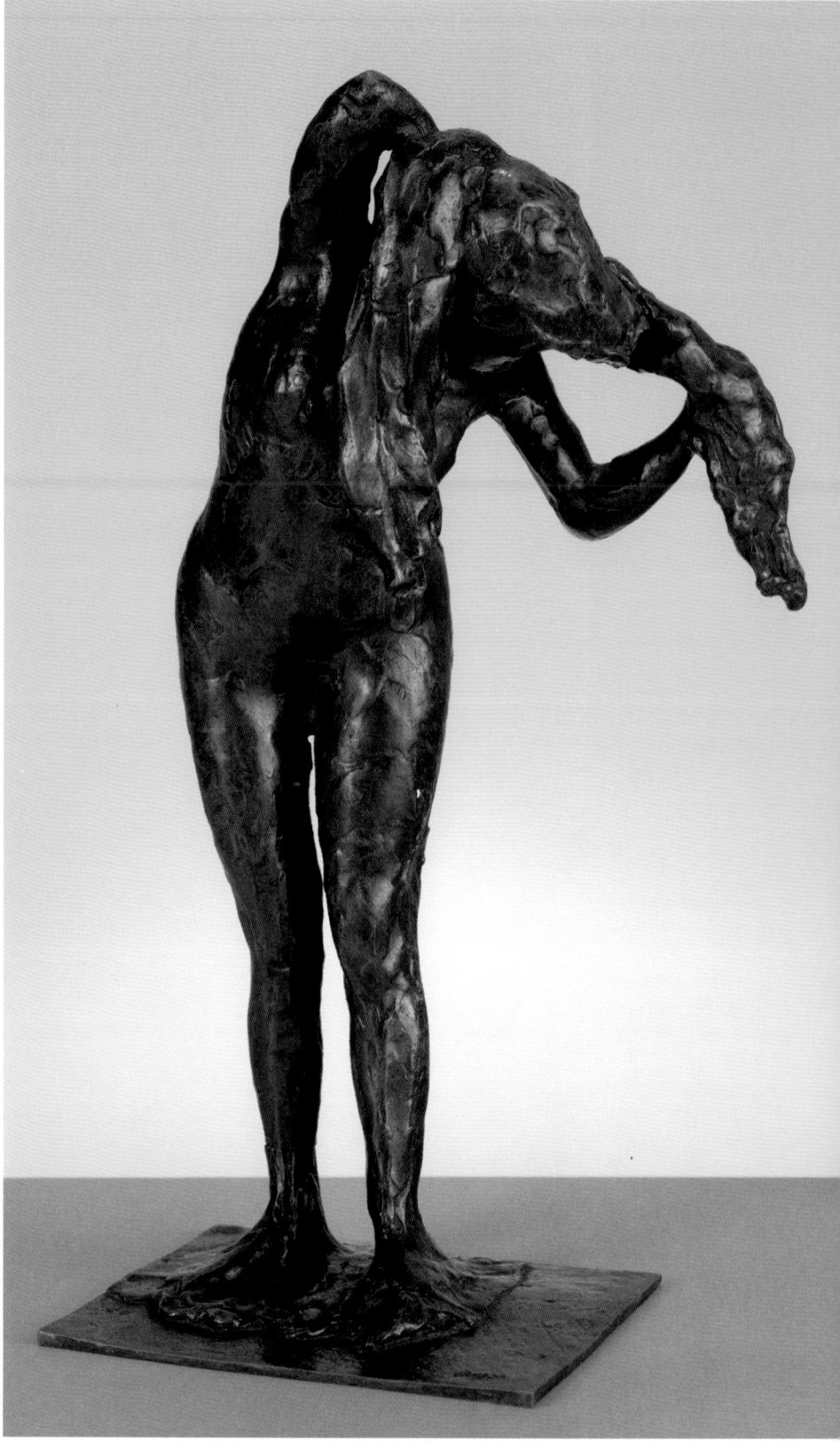

205

Edgar Degas

Woman Arranging Her Hair (La Coiffure), c. 1896–1911. Bronze, height: 46.7 cm. Hirshhorn Museum and Sculpture Garden, Smithsonian Institution, Washington, D.C. Gift of Joseph H. Hirshhorn, 1966 (HMSG 66.1305)

206

Pablo Picasso

Woman Plaiting Her Hair, 1906. Oil on canvas, 127 x 90.8 cm. The Museum of Modern Art, New York. Florene May Schoenborn Bequest, 1996 (826.1996)

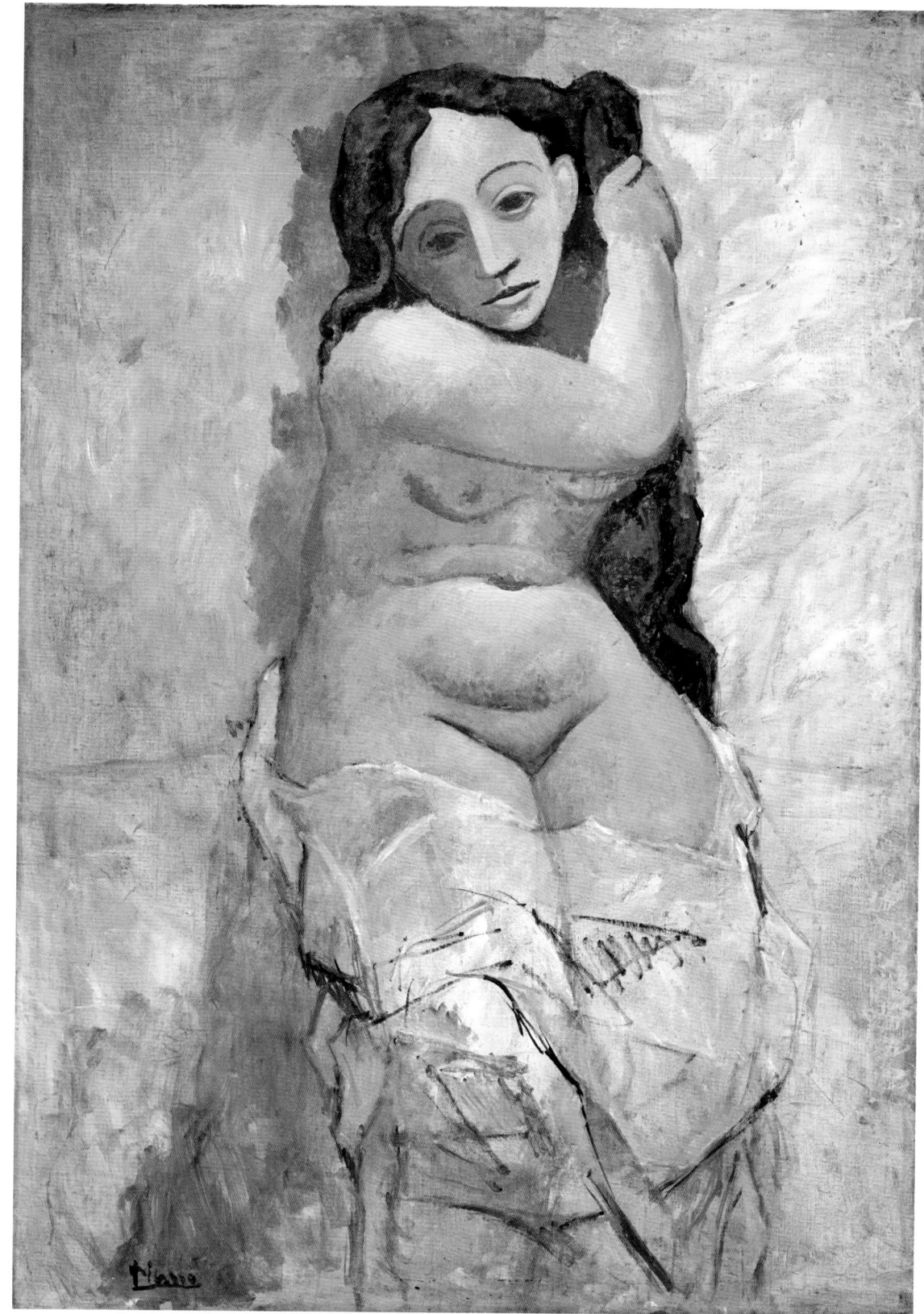

drawing (see 185). Both of these studies show the bather from the back and, although simplified and economical, pay great attention to the cleft formed by the spine and the bulging of buttocks and thighs. In Degas's sculpture, the back of the body, and these very areas, are quite naturalistically modeled, whereas the front is rougher and more abstracted (see 90), while the lumpish hair and towel look as if they were partially formed by rolling the wax between the palms of the hands. Unlike Picasso's sculpture, Degas's *Woman Arranging Her Hair* is fully in the round, but it, too, derives from a canonical antique sculpture as familiar and as often imitated as Doidalsas's *Crouching Aphrodite* — the standing figure of the goddess, hands raised to her head to wring out her streaming hair.[76] Both artists, in other words, were interpreting and updating a familiar Classical source. As this exhibition reveals, this was by no means the only occasion when their sculpture took a parallel path.

The relationship between Picasso's sculpture of a woman attending to her hair and the painting owned by the Museum of Modern Art (**206**) is debatable. Given that painting was his primary medium, it is natural to assume that (like Degas) he made the sculpture last. However, *Woman Plaiting Her Hair* obviously underwent significant modification, and it is equally possible that the two developed simultaneously, the oil in its revised form ultimately constituting in some sense a corrective to the terracotta after it was fired. Picasso was enthralled by the ancient sculptures in the Louvre, and *Woman Plaiting Her Hair* approximates much more closely their austere power and grandeur and literally, through its much greater size, their monumentality than does the retiring, gentle, rather amorphous sculpture. In reworking the painting, Picasso turned the nude to face forward and confront the viewer, framing her head like an icon within the diamond shape formed by her hair and arm, and centering her body within the

roughly brushed background, thus making her look more hieratic — more like a caryatid. By dragging the rapidly sketched white drapery down to the bottom edge of the canvas, he also lengthened her figure considerably. Rather than squatting back on her knees, she now appears, like Venus, to be slowly rising up, allowing her drapery to slip seductively down her thighs; the spectator no longer looks down upon her bent head but up at her impenetrable, mask-like face.[77] The resulting vagaries in the anatomy reflect Picasso's wish to be, not just look, spontaneous. But it is above all the impetuous physicality of the brushwork that injects drama into the ostensibly placidly serene subject: in places the surface looks not so much inconsistent and provisional as battered and abraded, like an ancient, ravaged fresco, and Picasso's contempt for conventional grace, beauty, and perfection is frankly paraded. Through Paul Durand-Ruel and Vollard, Picasso had probably come across some of Degas's coarse, urgent, at times aggressive, late charcoal drawings, many of them enhanced with fiery red, orange, and russet pastel (see 223),[78] and there are striking similarities in draftsmanship, color, and even handling of the medium between them and his painting. More significantly, there is also a shared attitude toward the female body as a vehicle for expressive drama — drama as pure energy, that is, rather than drama as narrative. This embodied drama is equally apparent in the awkward, off-balance movement, jagged silhouette, and active, tactile surfaces of Degas's statuette of the bather vigorously drying her neck.

On his return to Paris from Gósol, Picasso simultaneously explored in his new "primitive" style both time-honored variants of the coiffure motif: the woman who attends to her own hair and the woman who relies on a helper to perform the task. The next stage in his quest for fundamental simplicity was to dispense altogether with the coiffure motif. Women may raise a weighty hand to push back their hair —

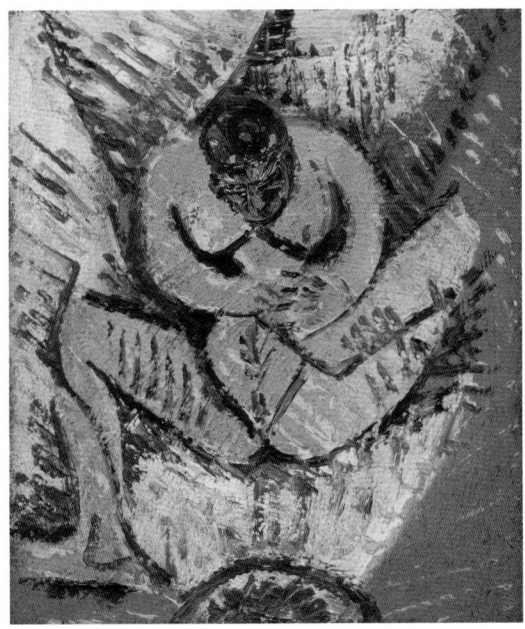

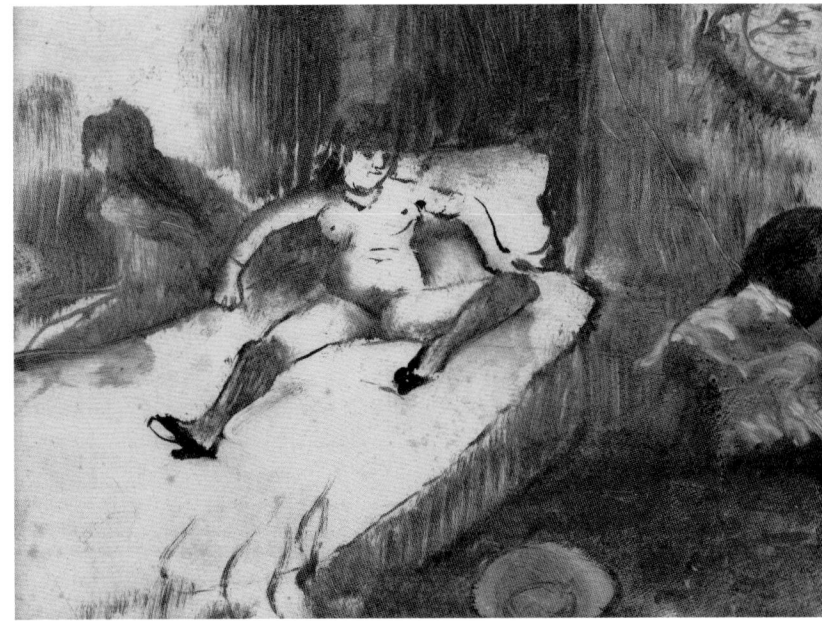

207

Pablo Picasso

Small Seated Nude, 1907.
Oil on wood, 17.6 x 15 cm.
Musée national Picasso,
Paris (MP 20)

208

Edgar Degas

Resting on the Bed,
c. 1876–77. Monotype,
12.1 x 16.4 cm. Musée
national Picasso, Paris
(RF 35783)

if that is how we should interpret the ambiguous gestures of the squat twins facing one another in *Two Nudes* of late 1906 — but there is no more combing and brushing and gazing in mirrors.[79] For, even when stripped down to its iconic essence, the coiffure motif inevitably retained some vestige of its old mythological, erotic, and allegorical connotations. By the end of 1906, it seems, Picasso desired the effect of absolute impersonality and so painted bodies devoid of transient animation and feeling, bodies that are powerful in the abstract manner of massive temple columns.

This plateau of emotional neutrality could never be a lasting ideal for the ever-restless, drama-hungry Picasso, however, and, ironically, *Two Nudes* is connected with his evolving plans to paint a major composition on the far-from-neutral theme of prostitution. Although what became *Les Demoiselles d'Avignon* (see 136) has its roots in *The Harem* (see 197), there is no sign in the hundreds of preparatory sketches that Picasso ever entertained the option of showing the whores at their toilette. Nevertheless, at about the time he completed *Les Demoiselles*, he did paint a small, vibrantly colored

panel of a seated bather intently examining her foot (**207**). An earlier drawing of Raymonde, the child Olivier and Picasso briefly "adopted" in April 1907, in exactly the same revealing pose seems to be its starting point.[80] The daughter of a prostitute, Raymonde had been "rescued" and placed in an orphanage run by nuns in Montmartre, and it was all too easy for Picasso to imagine her grown up and performing exactly the same action in a brothel.[81] Several of Degas's monotypes depict a similar scenario from a different angle (see 180, 184), and Picasso almost certainly had seen the pastelized variant of one such print that entered the Musée du Luxembourg with the Caillebotte bequest.[82] In 1958 he bought a monotype with this very subject matter, but with the *fille* facing forward (**208**), attracted to it perhaps because it anticipated his little panel (with which he had never parted). Both works turn on the same sexual pun — *bassin* in both senses of bowl and pelvis — for the basin on the floor directs attention to the whore's exposed crotch.

With this *Small Seated Nude* interior toilette scenes disappeared from Picasso's repertory, replaced by bathers outdoors.[83] The change from indoors to outdoors happened during the autumn and winter of 1907–8 under the influence of Cézanne's Bather compositions, which were well represented in exhibitions held in Paris before and after his death in October 1906. In tackling the subject Cézanne had made his own, Picasso was part of a widespread trend, for most up-and-coming painters were doing so. In his case, however, the discovery of tribal art in the Ethnographic Museum in Paris was an added incentive to abandon the urban, Degas-esque imagery of the bedroom and *cabinet de toilette* in favor of the river and the primeval forest. Bathers outdoors with their towels continued to make occasional appearances during the first half of 1909.[84] Thereafter, if Picasso gave his nudes any attribute at all, it was almost always a musical instrument, usually a mandolin or guitar. Fernande Olivier was ostensibly the subject of many of the canvases Picasso painted in the summer of 1909 in the Catalan village of Horta de Ebro (now called Horta de Sant Joan), but in stark contrast to her mood in Gósol, she was unwell, unhappy, and resentful throughout most of their stay, and her expression in his dark-toned Horta paintings is always somber or melancholy. In the one painting to include a mirror, she turns her back on it, as if grimly renouncing all concern with her looks.[85]

For the remainder of their lives together Picasso steered clear of the subjects intimately associated with Olivier at the start of their liaison. On one occasion, it is true, he painted a dressing table with its pivoting mirror and range of drawers, a glinting bottle or two, and a toothbrush in a glass of water, and now and then his nudes struck Aphrodite-like poses.[86] But the two elements were not brought together in a Cubist variant of the toilette scenes of 1906. When eventually their affair came to an end in 1912 and Eva Gouel was instated in Olivier's place, Picasso seems to have been tempted to evoke the subject by proxy in a still life on only one occasion — if, that is, one reads "*Au Bon*

Marché," the intriguing collage he constructed on the lid of a lingerie box, as a coded representation of the female body and female vanity.[87] Toilette themes resurfaced only when he began to paint and draw again in the figurative styles he had practiced before 1907, thereby reopening his dialogue with Degas and other nineteenth-century French masters.

The Aftermath of the Degas Sales

Picasso's return to what can loosely be termed naturalism did not involve renouncing Cubism, for he practiced these supposedly antithetical styles simultaneously. The phenomenon was underway by the summer of 1914 and gathered momentum during the ten weeks he spent in Italy from February to May 1917 working on the curtain, sets, and costumes for *Parade*, his first commission from Serge Diaghilev.[88] He was in Barcelona when Degas died on 27 September 1917, but in Paris for all but one of the eight sales of the artist's work and personal collection that took place in 1918–19.[89] Although earlier events — notably the auction of Henri Rouart's collection in December 1912 and the long-awaited unveiling of the Camondo bequest at the Louvre in 1914 — had brought superb paintings and pastels into the public domain, access to original works by Degas was relatively limited before the sales. Afterward, as described in chapter 3, there was an *embarras de richesse*, and when the market picked up again after the war, Picasso would quite often have seen his own pictures exhibited in proximity to Degas's in dealers' miscellanies.[90]

During the war, with Kahnweiler's gallery closed down, his entire stock sequestered by the French state, and the dealer himself in exile in Switzerland, Picasso had relied mainly on Léonce Rosenberg to buy and sell his latest work. After his marriage to Olga Khokhlova in 1918, he transferred his allegiance to Léonce's more enterprising and well-financed brother Paul Rosenberg, while maintaining friendly rela-

209
Pablo Picasso
The Bathers, 1918. Pencil on cream wove paper, 23 x 31.9 cm. Harvard Art Museum, Fogg Art Museum, Cambridge, Massachusetts. Gift of Paul J. Sachs, Class of 1900: A testimonial to my friend W. G. Russell Allen (1965.319)

210
Edgar Degas
Three Dancers, c. 1889. Charcoal and pastel on blue-gray paper, 59 x 45 cm. Museum of Fine Arts, Boston. Bequest of John T. Spaulding, 1948 (48.872)

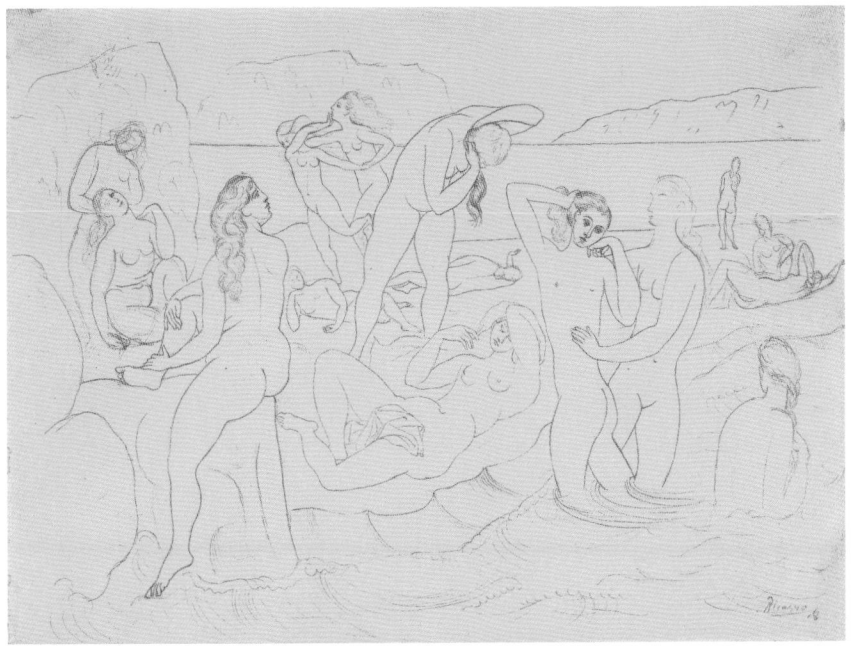

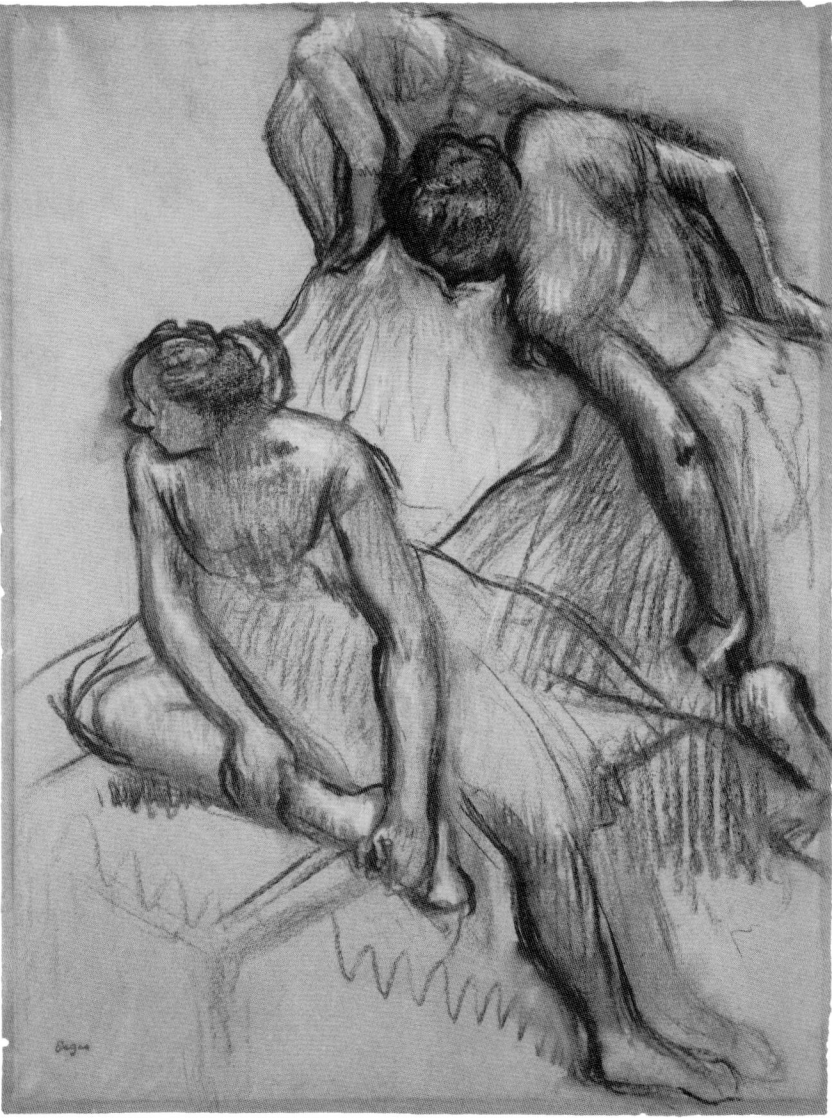

tions with Vollard, from whom he accepted commissions for *livres d'artiste* during the interwar years.[91] Vollard not only helped to organize the Degas sales, he was also one of the chief buyers, and Paul Rosenberg also bought and sold Degas's work more actively after the war. Kahnweiler, by contrast, had dealt exclusively in the work of the younger generation and in Picasso's case only in his Cubist work. It was in these radically altered circumstances that Picasso took up the toilette and coiffure themes once again.

An early instance is the masterly line drawing of fifteen bathers executed in Biarritz during his honeymoon in 1918 (**209**). The Picassos were staying with the Chilean heiress, balletomane, and art collector Eugenia Errazuriz, and in the sociable environment of her villa, with the constant spectacle of the holiday-makers on the nearby beaches, Ingres's *Turkish Bath* (see 191) insinuated itself into Picasso's mind once again. Liberating the docile and lethargic odalisques from the claustrophobic confines of the sultan's harem, he imagined them sunbathing, swimming, and frolicking outdoors under a peerless sky. But, as with most of the work he made with an eye on the art of the past, not one but a family of artists was involved in this witty transformation — antique and Neoclassical sources Ingres himself had drawn on (Greek vase painting, Etruscan mirror backs, Flaxman's illustrations to Homer), and various artists who drew on Ingres, including Renoir (the Philadelphia Museum of Art's *Bathers*, 1884–87) and Matisse (the Barnes Foundation's *Bonheur de vivre [The Joy of Life]*, 1906). In this effervescent brew there are also traces of Picasso's own earlier classicizing paintings, notably *The Harem* (see 197). With respect to Degas, although Picasso echoes some of his favorite motifs — the hairdressing couple in the background, the bather in the foreground perched on a rock grasping a raised leg, the girl in the center bending forward and wringing her hair (**210**; see also 90, 198) — it is the emphasis on split-second actions producing eccentric bodily silhouettes that is perhaps most reminiscent of his work. The range of twisting, athletic movements captured in this brilliant drawing was new in Picasso's art, which hitherto had been rather slow and stately in its rhythms — often utterly immobile — and for him, it seems, one of the great discoveries following the Degas sales was the overwhelming — one is tempted to say orgiastic — energy cumulatively expressed in the hundreds of pictures unloaded onto the market of female bodies in myriad active poses. One must not underrate the influence on Picasso's vision of the human body of the spectacle of Olga and the other dancers resting, exercising, rehearsing, and performing, but Degas was the perfect mediator between the reality of the ballet and its sublimation in the form of art.

Picasso's honeymoon in Biarritz set the pattern for his summers over the next ten years. For a couple of months a house would be rented somewhere by the sea — normally the Mediterranean, occasionally the English Channel — and there he would usually produce a series of drawings and paintings of bathers lounging by the shore, helping each other with their hair, swimming, running at high speed, and so on. Witty and amusing in their excessive anatomical distortion, they often look as if they were done casually and in spates, in a holiday frame of mind.[92] That same teasing spirit informs contemporary caricatural drawings of women in bathrooms, which strictly in iconographic terms are more closely modeled on Degas's work than anything else Picasso produced at this time. In March 1920, for example, while working in Paris on his designs for *Pulcinella*, his third ballet for Diaghilev, he produced a series of comical drawings of women in pristine bathrooms with tiled floors and up-to-date plumbing. In one, a disheveled, long-haired woman in her nightdress scrubs her teeth vigorously at the washbasin. In another, perched on the edge of a bath, a naked woman adjusts the taps. In others,

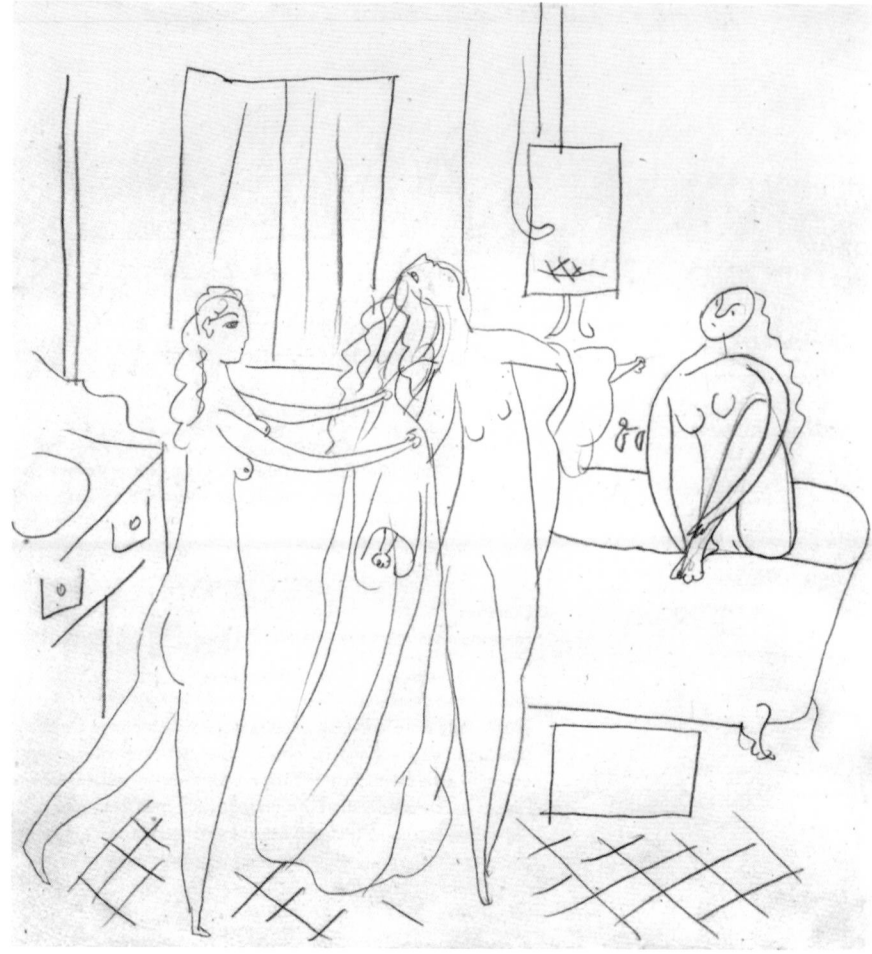

companions watch her clamber into or out of a bath and help each other take off their dressing-gowns (**211**).[93] The settings and accessories are updated, but the allusion to Degas is transparent. A few years later, in the same mocking spirit, Picasso produced a sequence of drawings of a dancer in her dressing room preparing for her next performance and then launching herself onto the stage. Intended for the 1923–24 souvenir program of the Ballets Russes de Monte-Carlo, each one is like an extremely reductive version of typical backstage and on-stage scenes by Degas.[94] Picasso surely expected his jokey *hommage* to be picked up by balletomanes who were naturally attuned to the imagery of "The Painter of Dancers."

211

Pablo Picasso

Women in a Bathroom, 15 March 1920. Pencil on paper, 25 x 23.5 cm. Private collection, Switzerland

212

Pablo Picasso

Woman in the Bath,
16 April 1921. Pencil
on paper, 16 x 12 cm.
Musée national Picasso,
Paris (MP 959)

213

Edgar Degas

Leaving the Bath,
1879–80. Drypoint and
aquatint on paper,
12.8 x 12.8 cm. Sterling
and Francine Clark Art
Institute, Williamstown,
Massachusetts
(1969.19)

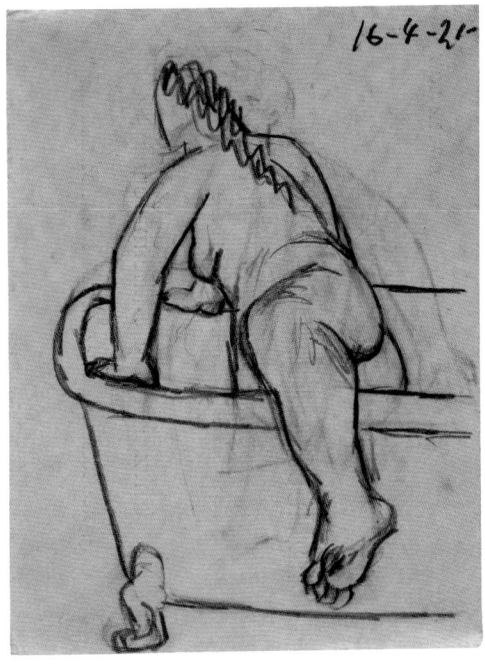

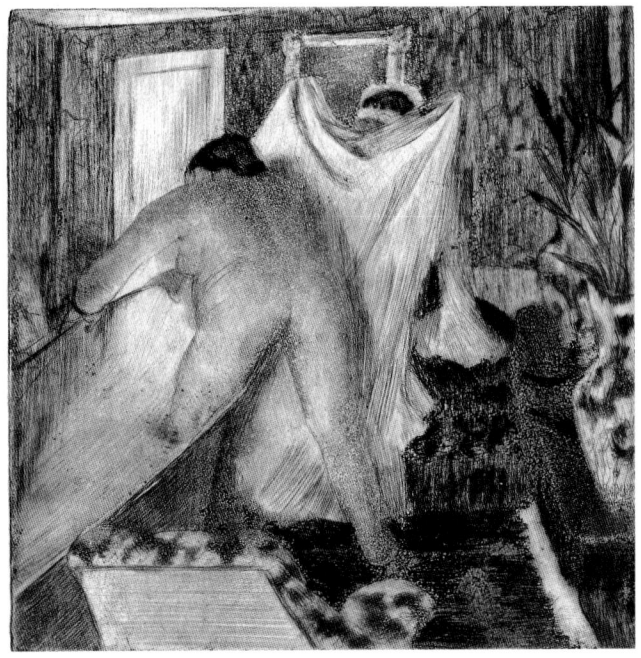

The spectacle of a woman clambering out of or into a modern bath amused Picasso. Looking like Venus was hardly possible on such occasions. In a vigorous drawing made in April 1921, a hefty woman, her hands planted firmly on the sides of the bathtub, is shown in the midst of this awkward operation, her massive left leg thrust out toward the spectator (**212**). From the faint traces of an earlier state, it looks as though originally Picasso thought of showing her not from the back but facing forward. If so, this would underline the allusion to Degas, who showed this same clambering action from both viewpoints. The wryly humorous drypoint with aquatint exhibited here (**213**) is the fourteenth of the twenty-two known states of a tiny but technically innovative print over which the artist lovingly labored in 1879–80.[95] Numerous impressions were auctioned in the sale of Degas's prints in November 1918, and it was published in Delteil's *catalogue raisonné* the following year.[96] With his passion for printmaking, Picasso may well have been intrigued by the subtle modifications the image underwent as Degas developed it — a process paralleled later in many of his

prints. He must also have seen the pastelized monotype in the Caillebotte bequest, which shows the bather facing forward and the maid on the left.[97] A further point of contact with Degas is Picasso's witty comparison between the bather's chunky foot and the claw-foot of the bathtub. It is not a joke Degas cracked in the Caillebotte monotype or in the drypoint, but something similar introduces a humorous note into many of his pictures of ballet dancers, who unconsciously imitate the splayed foot of a music stand or cheval mirror, or whose shapely legs persist in lining up and contrasting with the rigid legs of furniture.[98]

There is a crucial difference between Picasso's drawing and these works by Degas from the 1870s: where Degas pays considerable attention to the setting and structure of the room, to Picasso all that mattered is the massive bather and the cavernous, tomb-like bathtub. He used barely any shading to convey her bulk, relying simply on the weight of the emphatically redrawn contours, the breadth of limbs and torso, and the compression produced by the foreshortened perspective. In style, *Woman in the Bath* might be described as midway between the pure, fine linearism of the Biarritz *Bathers* (see 209) and the monumentality of the large charcoal drawing *Turning Nude, from the Back* (**214**), which combines strongly defined contours with zones of tonal shading to model the forms of the body. The energetic torsion of the *Turning Nude*'s body and the anonymity of the back view and *profil perdu* are signs of Degas's impact on Picasso. Either in the sales or in dealers' stock he would have seen numerous, equally tough and sculptural (although relatively more naturalistic) charcoal drawings (see 185, 186, 196), which reveal the artist's thinking process in the hesitations, revisions, additions, and smudges. Picasso was greatly interested in such drawings, and in 1937 acquired a copy of Vollard's edition of Valéry's *Degas Danse Dessin*.[99] All the drawings of dancers and nudes reproduced in the text and accompanying unbound portfolio are late, exploratory, often exceedingly free and brutal works in which color plays a secondary role; most are studies of single figures, and although dramatic in manner and mood, none has any hint of narrative content. Turning over the pages is, excitingly, like leafing through a sketchbook.

As the third largest of all Degas's paintings, *Nude Woman Drying Herself* (**215**) must have stood out at the first sale in May 1918. It had been in storage with Durand-Ruel for several years, and Picasso may have seen it for the first time at the gallery rather than at the auction.[100] Like a giant version of the monotype (see 91), which, as noted earlier, may have inspired his early painting *The Blue Room* (see 88), it must have seemed both strange and familiar. Like the monotypes, it was executed fast with extreme gestural freedom, the paint so thin that it is transparent and has dripped down the surface at various points. Degas used brushes to draw the contours and sweep on the raw and burnt umber paint, but in places he appears to have rubbed it on and into the canvas with rags —

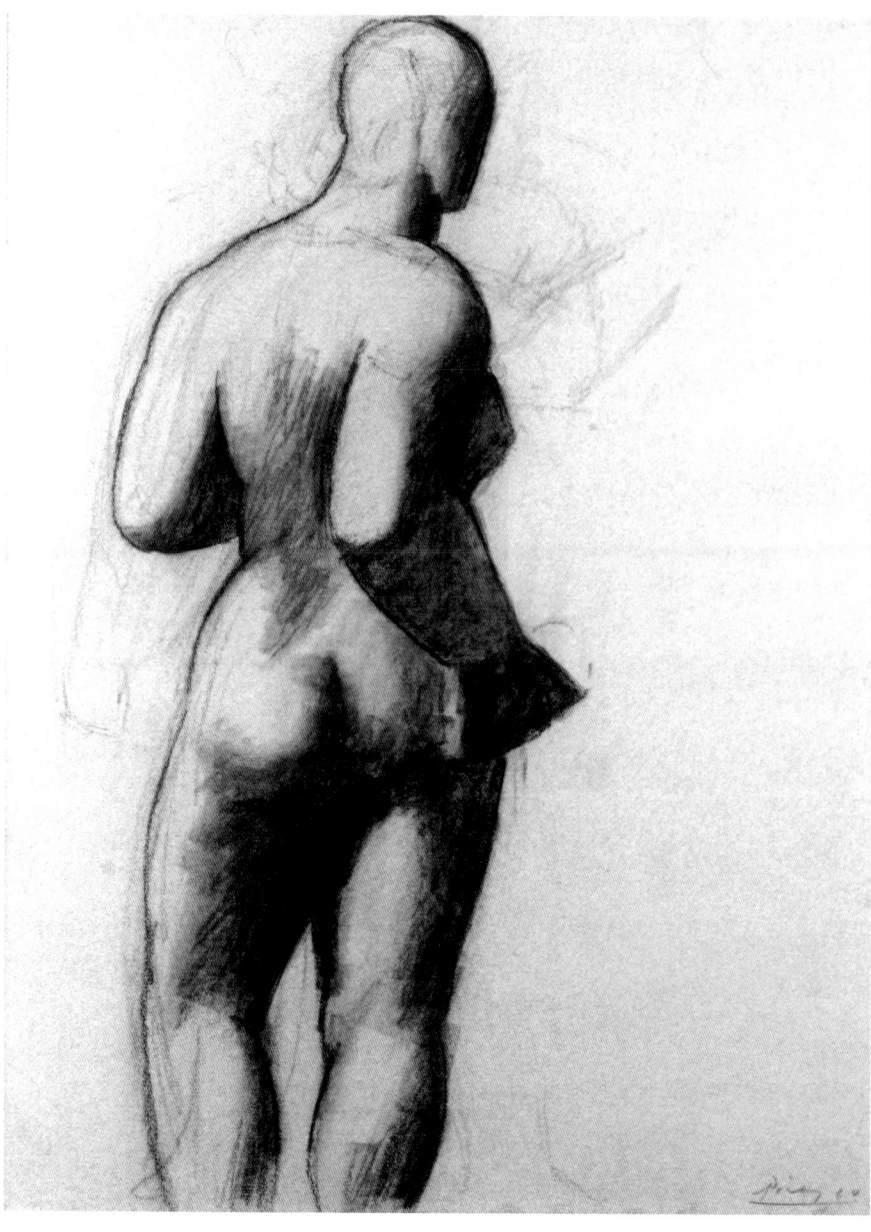

214

Pablo Picasso

Turning Nude, from the Back, 1920–21. Charcoal on paper, 63.5 x 46.5 cm. Museum Ludwig, Cologne (ML/Z 1994/31)

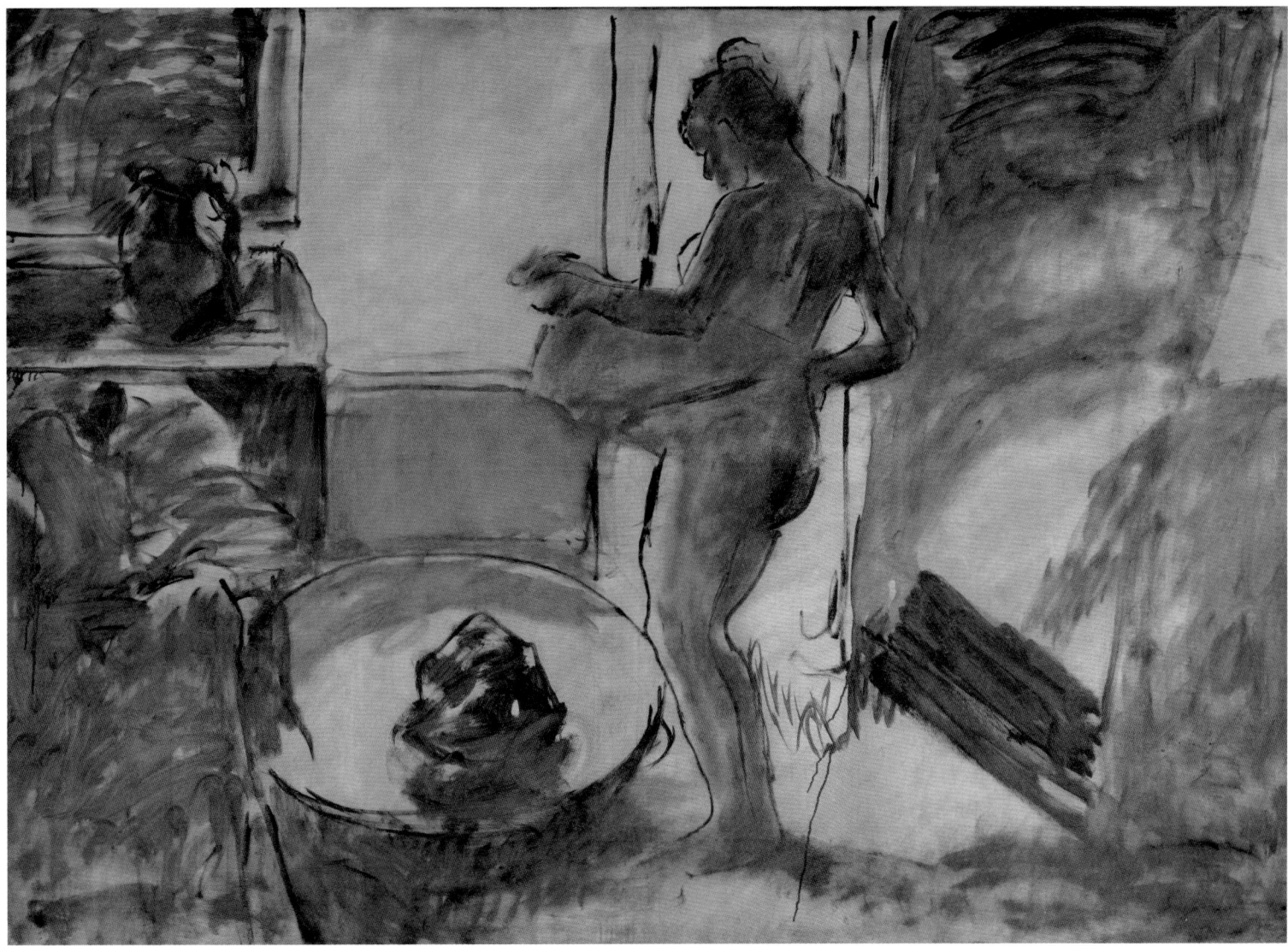

215

Edgar Degas

Nude Woman Drying Herself, c. 1884–86. Oil on canvas, 150.8 x 213.7 cm. Brooklyn Museum, New York. Carll H. de Silver Fund (31.813)

another similarity with the monotypes. Like the dark-field monotypes, *Nude Woman Drying Herself* works by suggestion rather than description, but unlike them it is unfinished, abandoned by Degas at the laying-in stage. For a fellow artist, this would have been both fascinating and moving, taking him right into the heart of Degas's studio in the way that private sketches do. And the great scale of the canvas meant that every mark Degas had made was visible: Picasso could actually gauge the pressure and speed of the hand wielding the brush or cloth, and experience almost bodily the art-

ist's impassioned élan. *Turning Nude, from the Back* may register Picasso's response to Degas's *chef d'oeuvre inconnu* because the woman's twisting movement, the angle of her arms, and the clenching of her one visible hand suggest the action of drying the back with a towel. But by omitting all explanatory accessories and treating the head as a knob, Picasso turned the body itself into the vehicle of expression and left the purpose of her movement indeterminate. Like a fragment from some ancient temple pediment or metope, this woman remains an enigma because her situation is a blank.

Picasso's use of an explicitly classical style in the postwar period is connected with his extended trips to Italy and Spain in 1917 and to London two years later. In Rome, Naples, and Pompeii, he saw famous antique sculptures and frescoes he had hitherto known in reproduction; in Barcelona, he caught up with the latest excavations; in Madrid's archaeological museum, he could revisit the impressive collections of ancient Iberian art; in London, the British Museum and the Parthenon marbles were just a brief walk away from the Savoy Hotel where he was staying. But this new classical phase was up to a point a replay of what had happened in 1905–6, when he first fell under the sway of the antiquities in the Louvre, and the rhetoric surrounding Classical art and avant-garde classicism in both Paris and Barcelona was much the same during the postwar "Call to Order" as it had been at the turn of the century. Not surprisingly, although grander, more assured and indeed more explicitly neoclassical, Picasso's postwar work is redolent of his classicizing work in 1906. *Large Nude with Drapery* (**216**), for example, is a reprise of *Woman Plaiting Her Hair* (see 206) — a bit larger, more consistent in its style and handling, a resolved "masterpiece," where the earlier painting looks as if it is still "in process." It was probably painted in Fontainebleau, where he and Olga spent the summer following the birth of their son in February 1921, and it reflects both his renewed enthusiasm for Graeco-Roman sculpture and his current interest in Mannerism — an interest apparently sparked by the collections in the nearby château and its park.[101] The comparison with *Woman Plaiting Her Hair* helps us to see that the woman in the new canvas is drying herself with a towel rather than using drapery to conceal/reveal her body. (The position of her massive left arm, swinging out from her bending torso, is consistent with the act of rubbing the right shoulder.) So, she too is a descendant of Degas's late paintings and pastels of big-boned

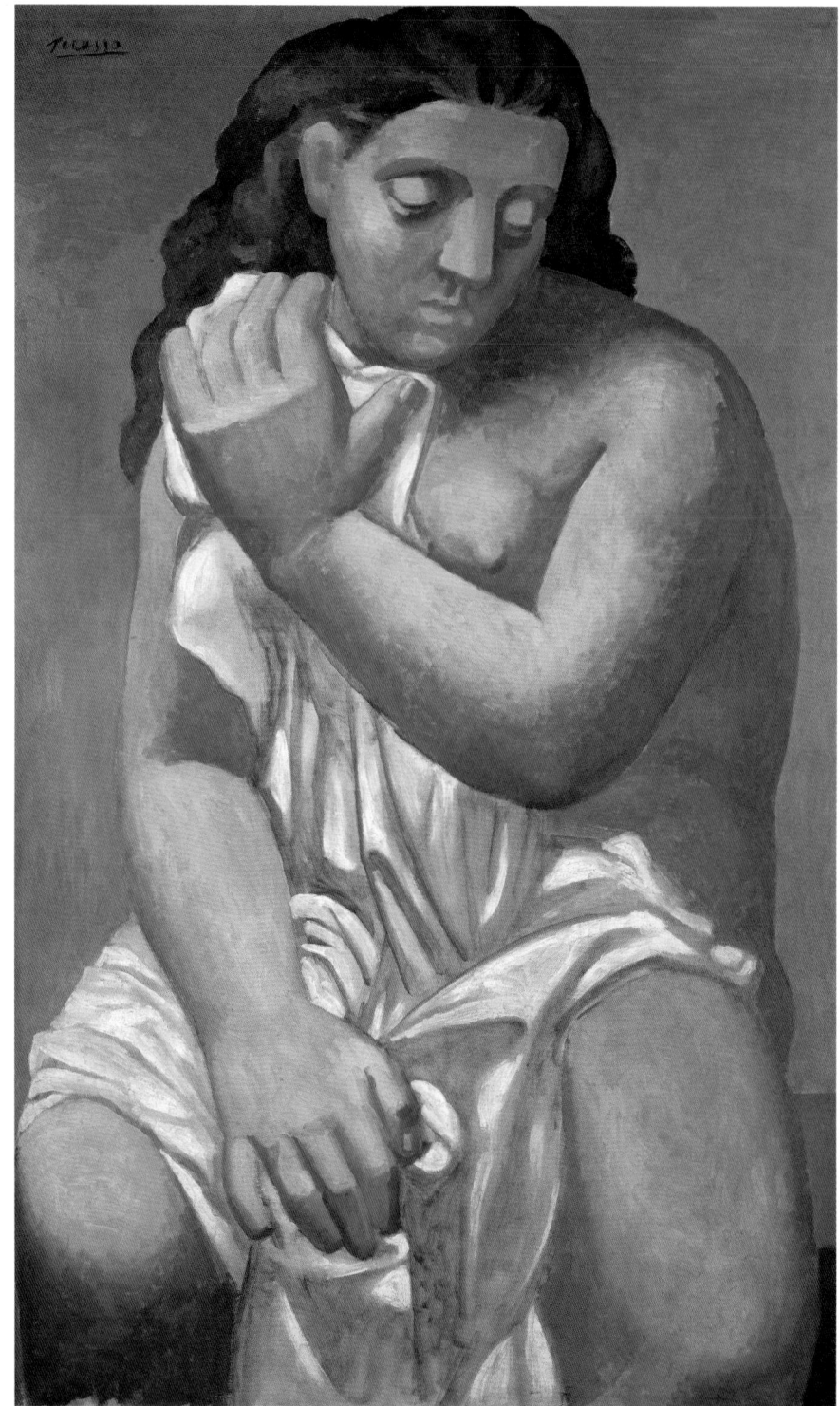

216

Pablo Picasso

Large Nude with Drapery, c. 1921. Oil on canvas, 160 x 95 cm. Musée de l'Orangerie, Paris. Walter-Guillaume Collection

217

Edgar Degas

Woman Drying Herself, c. 1893–98. Pastel and charcoal on tracing paper, 110.5 x 87.3 cm. Private collection

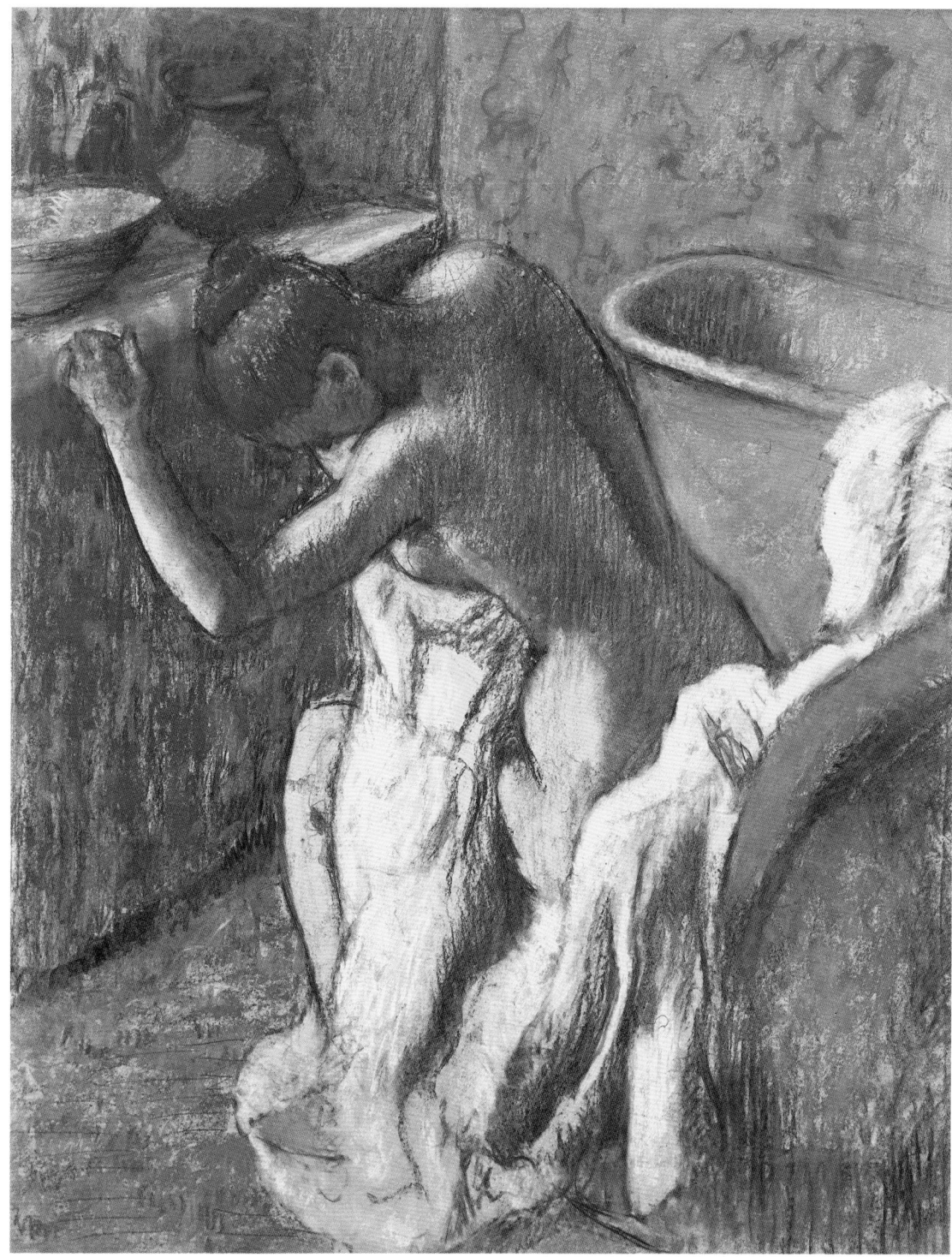

women vigorously toweling themselves, some of which are on a large scale (**217**).[102] The three-quarters angle Degas favored allows one to see the fall of the towel in front of the body and to glimpse part of a breast, thigh, and knee, so a similar tantalizing play between concealing and disclosing takes place; the difference is that Degas's bathers act within a believable, private environment, unaware of the spectator's presence, whereas Picasso's massive nude is presented to the spectator as a museum-worthy "work of art."

In Fontainebleau, Picasso made extensive use of pastel, charcoal, and sanguine as well as oils. One of his masterpieces from that summer is the two-meter-high sanguine version of *Three Women at the Fountain*, which was preceded by numerous studies of individual details (**218**).[103] In his late drawings, Degas had often used charcoal in combination with a strictly limited number of pastel colors, and in such cases, however strong the color, it is always subservient to the structural authority of the blacks and grays, the effect (even when the work is actually small) monumental rather than painterly (**219**; see also 223).[104] Picasso was attracted to pastel for the same sorts of reasons as Degas. As an artist for whom drawing was the foundation of everything he did, its draftsmanly aspect made it a natural choice, and Picasso loved the way it combined so easily with charcoal or black chalk. As a painter periodically attracted to brilliant feasts of color, he appreciated the unique, glowing intensity of hue the rich pigment was capable of generating. As a painter with a decidedly sculptural vision, he reveled in its monumental properties — the fact that he could if he wished achieve the most subtle tonal transitions and model forms to the point of *trompe l'oeil*. And there was the extreme sensuality of pastel, not just the soft, tender, velvety effects to which the crumbly medium lent itself but the fact that it invited, and at times compelled, rubbing, stroking, and blending with the fingers. Pastel never had the

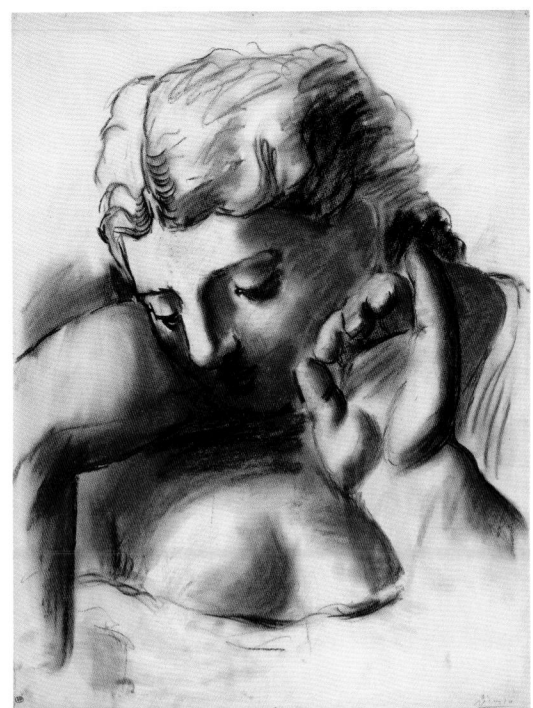

dominant role in Picasso's work that it had in Degas's, but when he did go through a phase of using it, for instance, at the turn of the century for modern-life subjects (see 68, 78, 100) and after the war, Degas, the greatest pastelist of the previous generation, was on his mind.

The special qualities of pastel are on display in another Fontainebleau work, the riveting *Seated Nude Drying Her Foot* in the Berggruen Museum (**220**). Rightly, this has often been associated with a late painting by Renoir, which Picasso had only just bought from Paul Rosenberg and that also quotes the ultra-familiar pose of the *Spinario*.[105] In the years following his death in 1919, Renoir was a recurrent reference point for Picasso,[106] but although the Berggruen pastel pays homage to the glowing, pumped-up flesh of the buxom heroine of his new acquisition, it is harder-edged and more draftsmanly, and this is where Degas's pastels of bathers come in. To judge by appearances, on this occasion Picasso drew on Degas's more meticulous works of the mid- to late 1880s: two superb

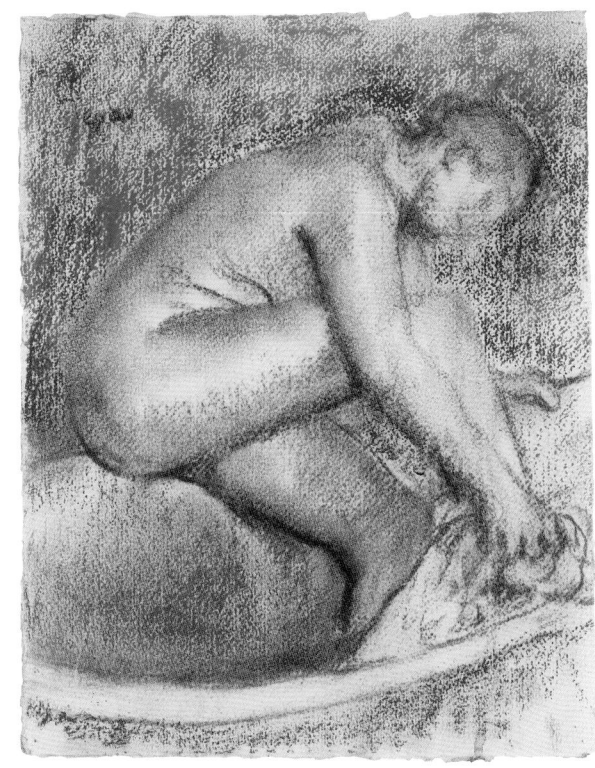

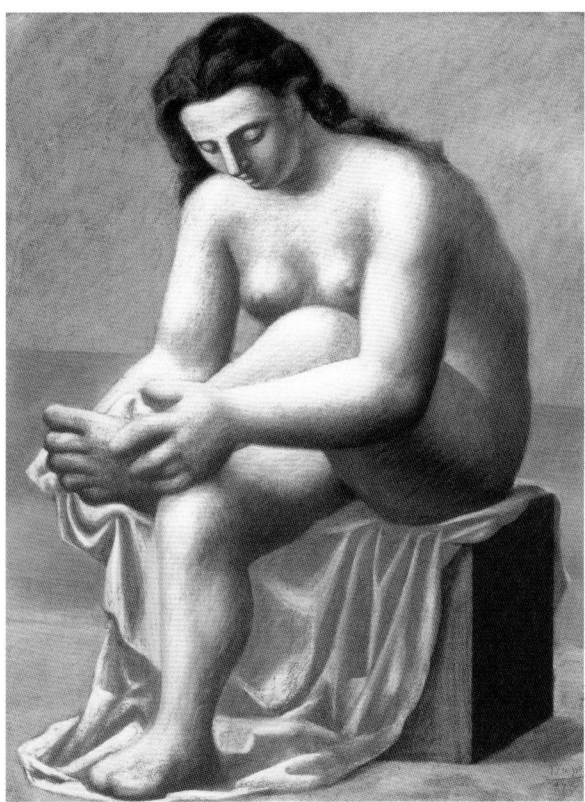

examples entered the Louvre in 1914 with the Camondo bequest (see 84).[107] What he must have appreciated about the entire series was the masterly but nevertheless personal handling of the medium, for there is nothing academic about the manner in which Degas stroked on his colors, leaving individual marks and his revisions of the contours visible, allowing the under-layers to show through and generally giving access to his method to any spectator prepared to scrutinize the surface. Picasso's pastel is more explicit in its references to sculpture — the massive bather bulges against the simplified, flattened background, the folds of her towel look crisply chiseled, her cubic seat looks as solid and heavy as a rock — but her flesh harbors a surprisingly wide and rich range of hues, and the handling of the pastel is equally nuanced.

War and the Symbolic Bather

In the Western tradition, the subject of beautiful women gazing into mirrors and attending to their looks has always been poignantly two-edged. The voluptuous motif provides an excuse to conjure up an image of alluring sensuality, but youth and beauty are transient and the reflection in the mirror may issue a ghastly warning. Picasso was well versed in the tragic potential of this iconography: in *The Harem* (see 197), the lovely girls waking to a new day may not have noticed the old hag lurking in the background, but we do. Occasionally in his "classical" phase after the First World War Picasso used the mirror to raise the old specter. In *Seated Nude* of 1922–23 a statuesque young woman at her dressing table turns to gaze back into the mirror. We can't see her face but the reflected face is sad, and there is so little paint on the canvas and that paint is so ashen that we intuit this picture is about loss or death.[108]

When the plague of war returned, there was every incentive to pursue this tragic vein. Exhibitions held in Paris in 1937, including the major retrospective at the Musée de l'Orangerie, seem

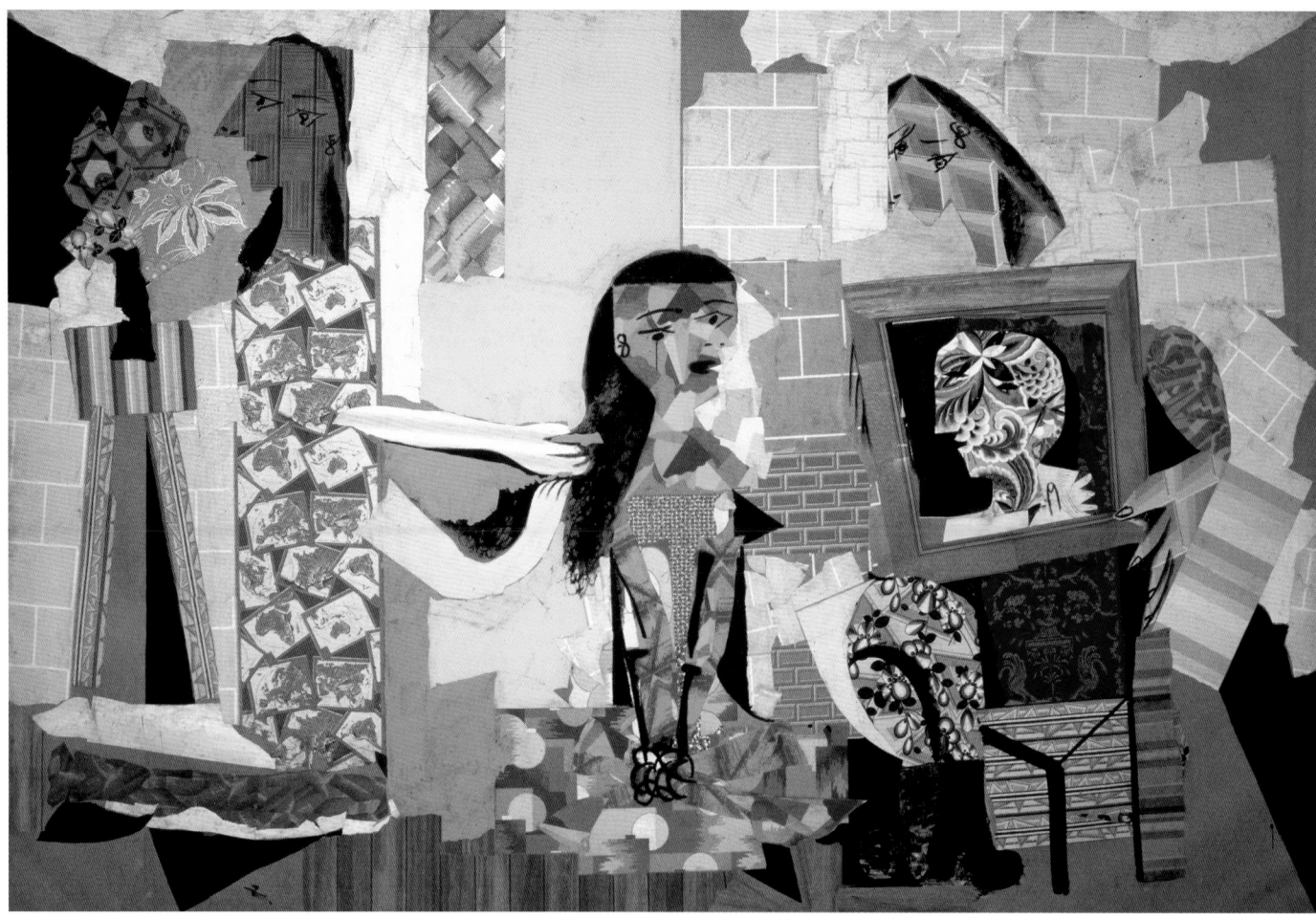

to have reignited Picasso's interest in Degas's toilette and hair-combing scenes, but since they took place against the backdrop of the Spanish Civil War and ominous political turmoil throughout Europe, he was, arguably, in the mood to see them in a much darker, more emotive light than hitherto.[109] His own work throughout 1937 was in an impassioned, angst-ridden mode: *Guernica*, the vast mural for the Spanish pavilion that absorbed him throughout May and June, was both preceded and followed by searing images of women weeping hysterically that originate in Crucifixion and Lamentation scenes. But in 1938, for his next mural-scale project, Picasso reverted to the ostensibly peaceful, private, and pleasurable subject of women at their toilette, this time, however, associating it

with distress, fear, and death. *Women at Their Toilette* (**221**), the enormous collage he made that springs entirely from cutouts of wallpaper, is the cartoon for a decorative tapestry commissioned by Marie Cuttoli, but in spite of its bright colors, garish patterns, and jazzy contrasts, it is anything but cheerfully escapist. The woman on the left combing the young girl's hair turns suddenly away, her face aghast, as if she has just become aware of a catastrophe outside. The girl herself, her skin bright red as if she has been burned and the charred bones of her arms exposed, reacts in horror to the blue specter in the mirror being held up to her by the third figure, who presumably stands for Fate. The torn and jumbled paper fragments that create the setting evoke quite literally the

221

Pablo Picasso

Women at Their Toilette, 1938. Paper, gouache, and painted paper collage, 299 x 448 cm. Musée national Picasso, Paris (MP 176)

devastation caused by bombing civilian targets, and Picasso's contemporary stream-of-consciousness poetry reveals just how panicked he was by the murderous air raids on Republican strongholds.[110]

Following the declaration of war against Germany, Picasso fled Paris with his lover Dora Maar and established himself in Royan on the Atlantic coast. They had been there less than a fortnight when he painted a gouache in cold tones of gray and blue of a woman sitting in a low tub pouring water from a jug over her feet.[111] The allusion to Degas is unmistakable, but Picasso's bather is visibly aging and decaying, and the scene takes place in so narrow and low-ceilinged a cell that, like a torture victim, she could never stand upright or stretch out. In such doom-laden circumstances, the pouring of water, traditional symbol of life and fertility, is cruelly ironic. In Royan, Picasso also created one of his most powerful wartime statements, *Woman Dressing Her Hair* (**222**). Preceded by quantities of studies and completed in May 1940 when the German army was pursuing its remorselessly efficient invasion of France, it allegorizes the terror, fury, and shame of the French people at that dreadful time in the person of a single woman wringing her hair.[112] The reference to Venus Anadyomene is pointedly sardonic in light of the monstrous ugliness of this elephantine creature and the anguish written on her bifurcated face. Like the bather in the earlier blue-gray gouache, she is entombed in an airless dungeon and, to heighten the horror of her situation, exposed to an implacable spotlight. Unlike the captive bather, however, she seems to protest and struggle, embodying resistance as well as misery. But there are no hopeful signs. How could there be when Fascism had triumphed first in Spain and now in France? Shortly after completing this masterpiece, Picasso returned to occupied Paris, remaining there for the duration of the war.

The coiffure scenes by Degas that are most relevant to *Woman Dressing Her Hair* are not those from the 1870s and 1880s, where dignity, patience, and calm seem to reign (see 198), but the later drawings and unfinished canvases in which the mood is harder to define and the hair-combing may strike the viewer as curiously brutal or painful. In a charcoal and pastel drawing once owned by Vollard (**223**), the combination of elevated viewpoint, extreme foreshortening, indecisive contours, and smudged modeling creates ambiguity that was probably not intentional but proves highly suggestive. Thus it is possible to misread the woman's pose, which is masked by her cascading hair, and conclude that her slipper-clad right leg is jerking violently upward rather than lying casually across her left leg, and that she is yanking her hair forcefully downward rather than combing it out patiently. One might, in other words, read this as an image of frustration, even anger, not of relaxed preening. Two large unfinished paintings that surfaced in the first studio sale in 1918 are equally open to differing interpretations of their mood (see 200, 227), and we can at least be virtually certain that Picasso was familiar with the one now in London's National Gallery, since it belonged to Matisse between about 1920 and 1936 and the two artists saw each other quite regularly during the 1930s.[113] For many viewers, the bedroom setting, glowing colors, sensuous handling, and stately rhythms of these two pictures will evoke the sensual pleasure of pampering and being pampered. But others may sense that the women whose hair is being combed are involuntarily flinching as they clutch at their brows and tense their straining bodies against the maids' drag on their hair. Their features are so cursorily delineated that it is impossible to read their expressions, but in one of the studies for Matisse's painting the woman's face does seem to be etched with pain or apprehension — hardly surprising given her perilously unstable, semi-reclining pose.[114] Although it is wildly exaggerated to speak of

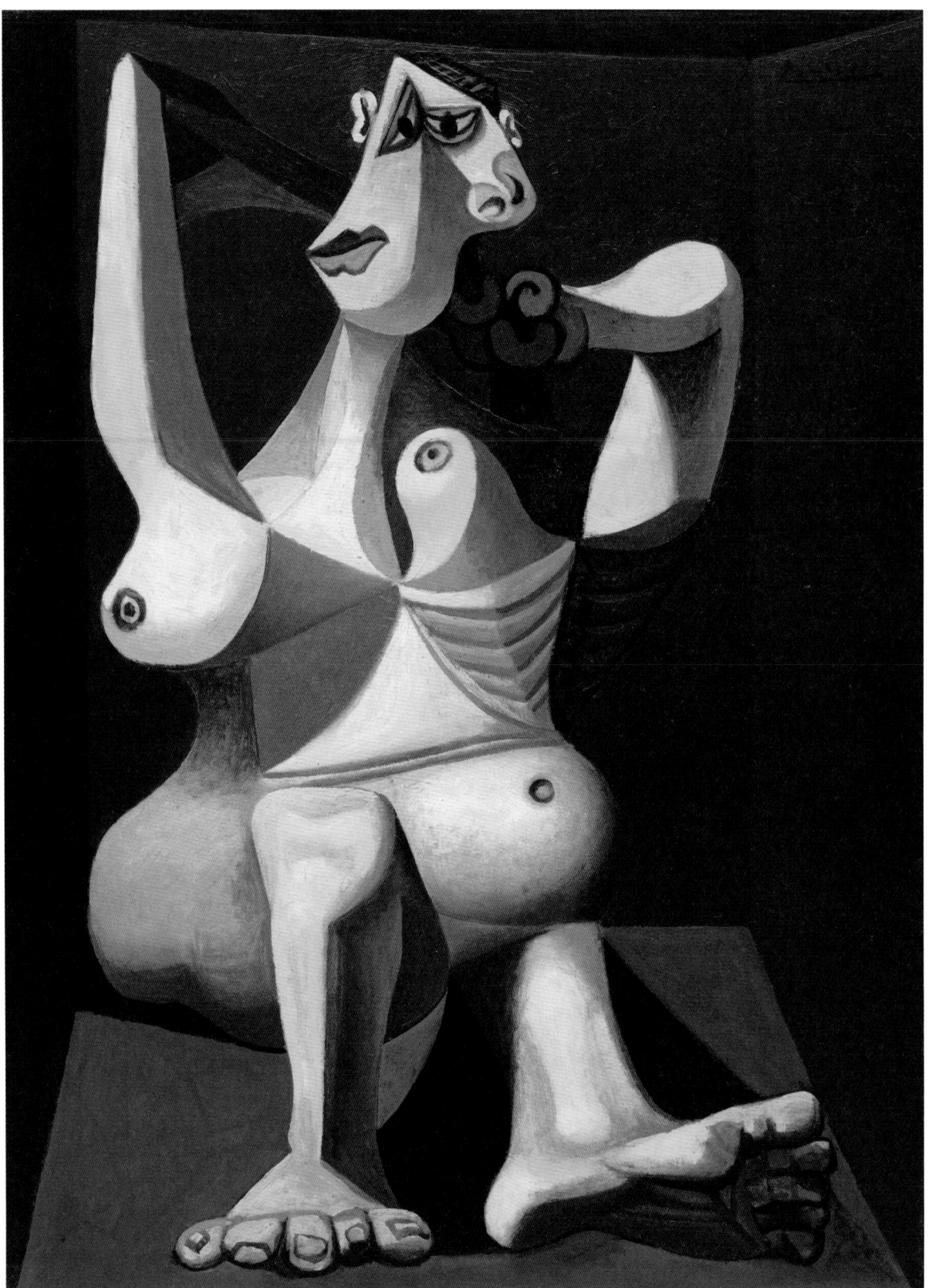

222

Pablo Picasso

Woman Dressing Her Hair, June 1940. Oil on canvas, 130.2 x 97.2 cm. The Museum of Modern Art, New York. Louise Reinhardt Smith Bequest, 1995 (inv. 788.95)

223

Edgar Degas

Woman Combing Her Hair, c. 1896–99. Charcoal and pastel on tracing paper, 109 x 76.3 cm. Private collection

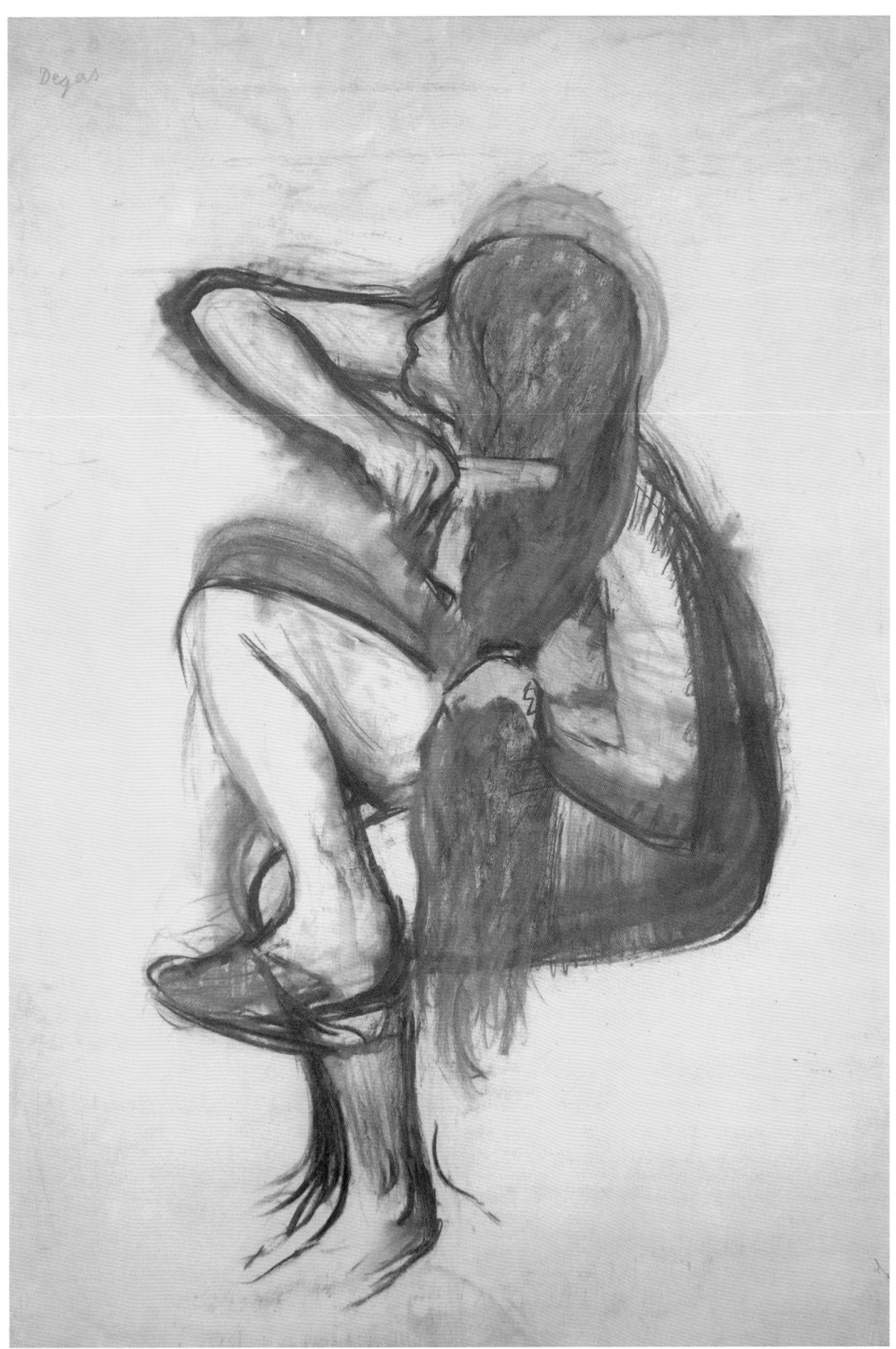
Degas

the "torture" of hair-combing, these pictures may prompt thoughts of the genuine torture of being dragged by the hair — a "negative" reading of Degas's imagery doubtless more likely at a time of war. At all events, Picasso's *Woman Dressing Her Hair* is enriched by emotional ambiguity of this kind — ambiguity that in his case was surely quite deliberate. The misshapen woman is in fact squatting on the ground with one leg bent and the other stretched out in front of her, but it looks as if she is standing on her two stumpy legs and kicking out with her left foot. The nervous knotting action of her hands is equally ambiguous: holding her hair away from her body in order to twist it into a bun (as Degas's bathers often do), or tearing violently and hysterically at it.

Between May and July 1944, in a series of brush-and-ink drawings, Picasso returned to the subject of a woman bathing in a tub (**224**). It was an extremely dangerous time to be living in Paris, with frequent Allied bombing raids during the spring, intensified Resistance activity, and reprisals by the occupying German forces. It was also a sad time, with the death that March of Max Jacob, one of Picasso's oldest friends, in the concentration camp in Drancy. Nevertheless, there was growing optimism following the Normandy landings in June, and Picasso's personal life was far from uniformly wretched, with a daily stream of friends and admirers passing through his studio and the excitement of a new love affair with the young painter Françoise Gilot. Although the brush-and-ink drawing is harsh, grim, ugly, black in mood as well as palette, there is no sign of helpless resignation, and like the heroine of the great 1940 canvas, this clumsy, bony, hunchbacked bather kicks out aggressively as if determined to break her bonds.

The viewing angle is different, but this bather's pose is almost identical to that of the woman perched on the side of a bath in Degas's abbreviated but powerful drawing in the Metro-

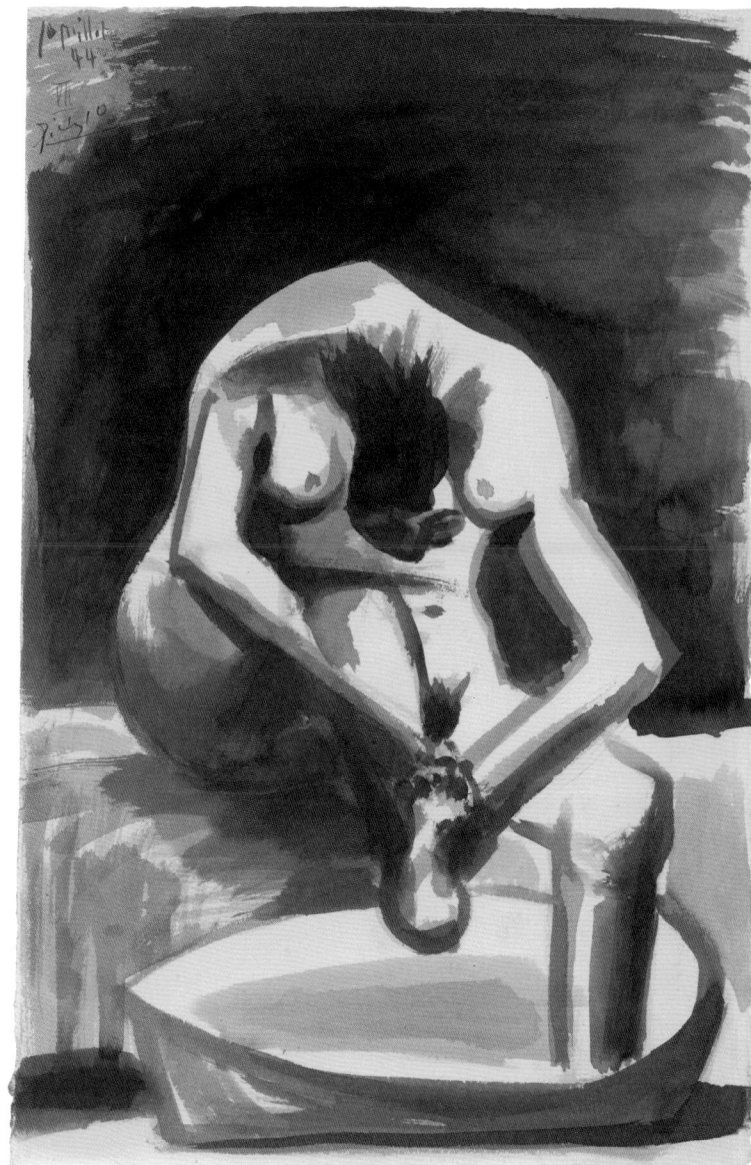

politan Museum (see 219); she, too, is completely absorbed in her task, her facial features perfunctorily indicated with a few faint marks.[115] But a more provocative parallel is with *The Tub* (**225**), Degas's most celebrated sculpture after the *Little Dancer Aged Fourteen* thanks to its unconventional mixed-media construction (discussed below): the conjunction of scrunched-up naked body, slightly misshapen tub, and crumpled towel is essentially the same as in Picasso's drawing. Like the coiffure pictures discussed

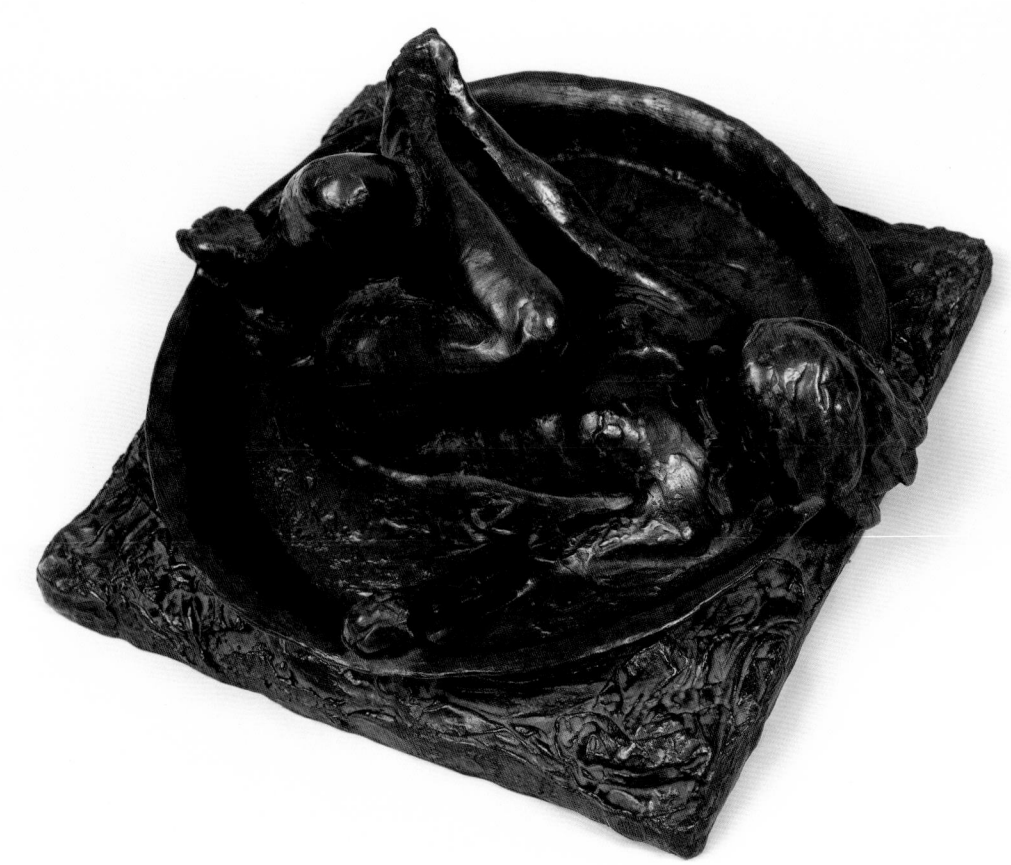

above, *The Tub* arouses different reactions and interpretations. For some it evokes the sensual delight of wallowing in a warm bath, and the svelte bather possesses a piquant, kittenish allure rare in Degas's work.[116] But others may see signs of tension, discomfort, constraint. The square plinth is only just large enough to contain the round tub and the tub is barely large enough to accommodate the bather; her head, tipped awkwardly against its top rim, is forced down onto her chest, and her right foot is squeezed up against the bottom rim. Set in everlasting bronze, the momentary pose is immutable, which — in this negative reading — heightens the sense of her vulnerability. Considerably less than life-size, pinned to her basin, she may remind one of an entomologist's specimen. In times of peace, this extraordinary sculpture might not trigger such associations, but

in times of war, thoughts of the oppression of the innocent might disturb the viewer's mind. Even if Picasso saw *The Tub* in a neutral light, this does not rule out the possibility that the brush-and-ink drawings of 1944 were conceived as a series of free variations after it and Degas's other nudes bathing in tubs, as such anticipating the many series of variations after favorite works of art from the past that he created after the war.

One of the most arresting and dramatic coiffure scenes Picasso ever painted is the large, raw oil on wood of 1952 (**226**). An essay on the time-honored theme of Venus Anadyomene, it is thus a relative of Degas's late sculpture of a bather doing her hair (see 205). But although the size of Picasso's panel and the height of the woman may lead one to infer that she is standing, in fact, like *Woman Plaiting Her Hair* of 1906

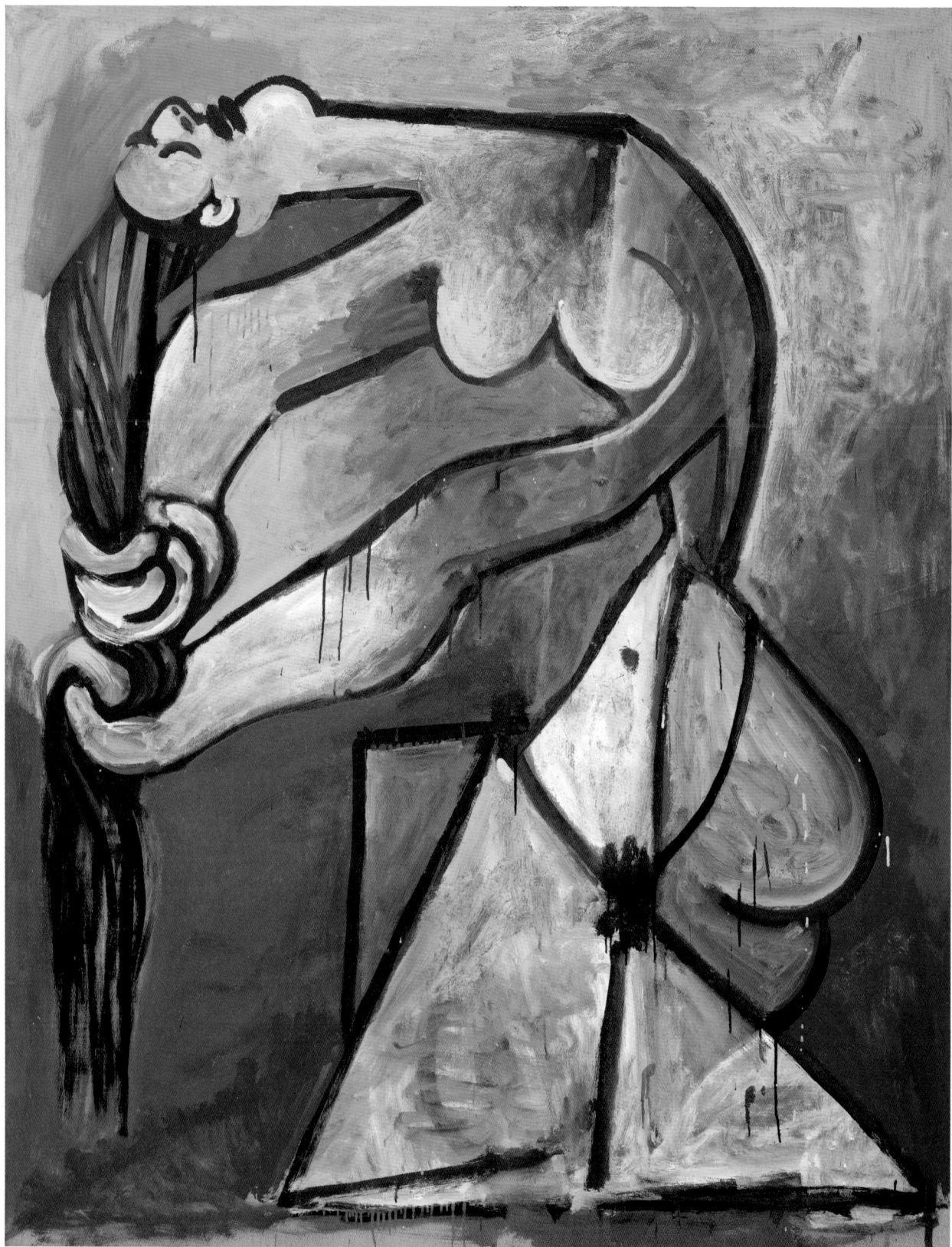

Pablo Picasso
*Nude Wringing Her
Hair*, 7 October 1952.
Oil on wood panel,
150.5 x 119.4 cm.
Private collection

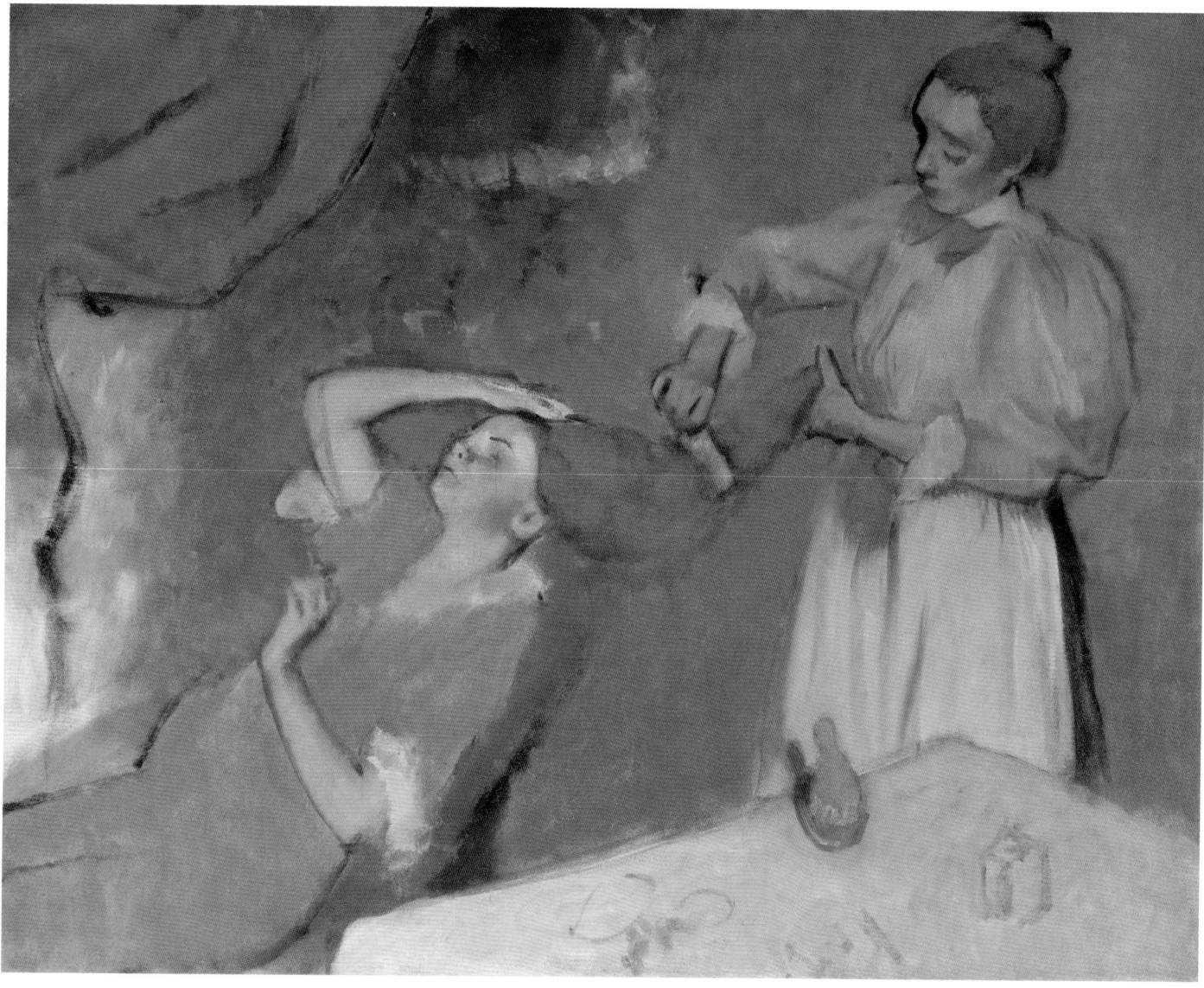

227

Edgar Degas

*Combing the Hair
(La Coiffure)*, c. 1896.
Oil on canvas,
114.3 x 146.1 cm.
The National Gallery,
London. Bought, 1937
(NGL 4865)

(see 206), she is sitting or kneeling with a shaft of drapery falling over her thighs. Although her strangely shaped arms look subhuman, like enormous pincers, and the hair-wringing seems fierce, even vengeful, the expression on her face, eyes closed, lips parted, is serene and blissful. Defining the nature of her mood — agonized, ecstatic, hysterical — is impossible, for she seems to inhabit a dreamworld where distinctions between these states of feeling have no meaning. Although Picasso executed the picture so swiftly and spontaneously that

the paint dripped and splashed, he revised the composition quite substantially, moving the arc of the woman's back away from the right edge, shrinking the mass of her torso, and reinforcing the structural geometry of the whole by, for instance, strengthening the horizontal line of her neck to echo the horizontal base of her drapery. His alterations to the head and bust greatly accentuate their phallic connotations and thus the erotic implications. He concealed these revisions to the torso by roughly brushing on gray and white paint of similar tones, and this fusion of the substance of the bather's body with the substance of the amorphous cloud-like form behind her enhances the hallucinatory quality of the work.

The action takes place not in some claustrophobic cell but outdoors against a deep blue (if stormy) Mediterranean sky, and the date inscribed on the back, 7 October 1952, confirms that Picasso painted the picture in Vallauris rather than Paris. The obvious parallel with the canvas painted in Royan in 1940 (see 222) invites the question whether it, too, may have had a political motive. Picasso was an active member of the French Communist Party at the time and sporadically produced work in support of the official Party line (although his efforts repeatedly failed to satisfy the apparatchiks).[117] It is impossible to connect it firmly to a specific incident, but in its anguished aspect it very likely embodies his adamant opposition to the Korean War and in its sublimity his passionate commitment to the peace movement. (Simultaneously, he was at work on the allegorical *War* and *Peace* murals for a deconsecrated chapel in Vallauris.)[118] As already suggested, women always allegorized the torment and vulnerability of the innocent and peace-loving in Picasso's art. But there may also be a personal motive — and the two are not mutually exclusive — for the bather in this painting has, in exaggerated and abstracted form, the long, dark hair, large breasts, narrow waist, and pliant body of Françoise Gilot. In 1952, their relationship was deteriorating, and although Françoise was not one to throw hysterical fits and tear her hair, Picasso may have found it irresistible to express the tensions within their ménage through this archetypal imagery.

The great Degas hair-combing scene formerly owned by Matisse (**227**) makes a compelling partner for this *Nude Wringing Her Hair* — the one an essay in shades of red, the other in shades of blue. The relative abstraction of Degas's canvas (the flatness of, say, the body of the woman whose hair is being combed and

the wedge of the table in the foreground), like the indecisiveness of substantial passages in the background, may be put down to the fact that it was never completed. But for another artist those very qualities are of inordinate interest. Like the giant Brooklyn sketch (see 215), it gives insight into Degas's thinking-cum-working process: the bare bones of the geometry of the composition are not concealed, nor is the spontaneous method of drawing the contours in black paint and laying in the zones of color. And the artist's second thoughts are excitingly visible in the hurried-but-incomplete painting out of the frame of what was probably a window in the background, as well as in the redrawn, step-like contour of the woman's belly. Picasso's *Nude Wringing Her Hair* is less naturalistic: whatever she signifies, his woman is clearly an archetype, not a "real" woman in a "real" situation, and the anatomical distortions are more extreme, the conceptual geometry more insistent, the sketchiness wilder and more declamatory. But the differences are of degree, not kind.

Fascinated as he was by the lives and appearance of women and with many female relatives to observe, it is not really so surprising that the supposedly aloof, caustic Degas should have depicted pregnancy in a notably sympathetic manner on several occasions.[119] His beloved aunt Laura Bellelli was pregnant when he painted the great family portrait in which she appears both regal and deeply unhappy, her swelling form discreetly indicated beneath the mourning clothes worn in memory of her father (see 10).[120] The unidentified sitter for the engagingly candid portrait of a young woman in a bright red peignoir seems to be in a quite advanced stage of pregnancy.[121] And it is possible that the model for the National Gallery's *Combing the Hair* was pregnant and that it was her changing shape that necessitated redrawing the contour of her abdomen. But nothing prepares us for Degas's startling sculpture of a completely naked woman balancing awkwardly on tired legs and gazing down at her ballooning belly, which she gently feels and cradles in a gesture typical of women close to term (228). For a number of Degas's sculptures, it is not difficult to trace a source in the art of the past, but there is no obvious precedent in this case, and so well-observed is the woman's body that one must assume a heavily pregnant model posed for him.

The circumstances surrounding Picasso's *Pregnant Woman* (229) are less mysterious. It was inspired by Françoise Gilot's two pregnancies and, according to her, his (unfulfilled) desire for a third child.[122] A fascinating sequence of photographs by Claire Batigne, taken inside and outside his studio in Vallauris, establish that the sculpture was underway in May 1950 and reveal the ad hoc methods of its construction.[123] Picasso began with a simple metal armature and gradually built up the forms in plaster around various objects purloined from the town's dumps. A large pottery vessel was used for the belly and two small pottery milk jars for the breasts; a fragment of pottery was the basis of the lower right arm and a plank of wood formed and strengthened the back. Originally the woman's hair hung down between her shoulders but, wishing for a clearer separation between the parts of the body, he decided to scoop it up into a bun at the back of the head (how Gilot normally wore her hair), modeling it roughly with scrapings of plaster that had fallen onto the wooden plinth. The conception of the figure as a rhythmic sequence of spherical and columnar forms shows that Picasso had not forgotten the lessons of African and Polynesian sculpture, although the debt is much less obvious than in the carvings made in 1907–8 in the heat of discovery when he was buying up *fétiches* for next to nothing and prowling around the crammed, dusty, underfunded galleries of the Musée d'Ethnographie du Trocadéro.

The incorporation of pottery vessels was not merely expedient. As Picasso explained to Gilot at the time, "It's not that I need that ready-made element, but I achieve reality through the use of metaphor. My sculptures are plastic metaphors." Referring to his contemporary ceramic sculptures formed with freshly turned pots, he continued:

People have said for ages that a woman's hips are shaped like a vase. It's no longer poetic; it's become a cliché. I take a vase and with it I make a woman. I take the old metaphor, make it work in the opposite direction and give it a new lease of life.[124]

He might have said much the same about the large vessel and milk jars used in *Pregnant Woman*: the symbolism is transparent but still potent. Gilot, incidentally, reacted as negatively to the sculpture as some of the first viewers of Degas's *Little Dancer Aged Fourteen* (see 141). She thought that at about half life-size it was "grotesque"; the feet were too rudimentary and the arms too long: "It always looked to me like a child-woman recently descended from the ape."[125] Perhaps what secretly offended her most was the implicit equation with the pregnant goat and pregnant baboon represented in nearly contemporary sculptures, for in both of them pottery jars were incorporated at similar strategic points.[126]

Was it pure coincidence that both Degas and Picasso tackled this highly unusual subject in sculpture? Or might the sight of Degas's sculpture have issued an irresistible challenge to Picasso, who would have had plenty of opportunities to examine it by this date? The shared, exceptional iconography aside, it is worth noting that symmetry is rare in Degas's sculpture and that the symmetry of his *Pregnant Woman* is paralleled in Picasso's. Symmetry, however, has a rather different motive in each case. In the Degas it is, one senses, dictated by the desire to find a pose that enabled him to explore not just the physical state of advanced pregnancy but also a woman's psychological state — a mixture of tender concern for the unborn child and bewilderment at the dramatic transformation of her body — whereas the symmetry of Picasso's statue reinforces its intentionally archetypal aspect: the figure is presented in a strictly hieratic manner so as to resemble a fertility goddess.

Degas did not employ *objets trouvés* in his *Pregnant Woman*. (If the original wax incorporated cork or other bits and bobs, as Degas's waxes frequently do, they served a structural rather than a representational function, and no found objects are visible in the bronze cast.) Real objects were, however, flagrantly recycled in *The Tub* (see 225) — a lead basin, cloth soaked in plaster, a wooden plank, a piece of sponge. Picasso started constructing Cubist sculptures with *objets trouvés* in 1912–13, beginning with string and cardboard boxes for his first *Guitars* and *Violins* but quickly graduating to things made of wood, metal, and fabric. *The Absinthe Glass* of 1914 incorporates a real silver-plated absinthe spoon that, rather than functioning metaphorically like the pottery vessels, stands for itself — just as Degas's lead basin, cloth, and sponge stand for themselves. The glass was modeled in wax — another obvious parallel with Degas's usual practice, despite the great difference of style.[127] In *Still Life*,[128] a contemporary relief-construction, Picasso stuck a strip of real upholstery fringe to the edge of the table top to represent the fringe on a cloth, just as Degas tied a real ribbon around the hair of his *Little Dancer Aged Fourteen*. At the time, Picasso had seen neither of Degas's sculptures, although he certainly knew by hearsay about *Little Dancer* (and maybe also about *The Tub*). In his appreciation of "la terrible réalité" (the terrible reality) of *Little Dancer*, Huysmans suggested that Degas had modernized and personalized the practice of the old Spanish masters, who clothed their statues of the Virgin and Christ in elaborate costumes, gave them wigs of real hair, and painted their faces naturalisti-

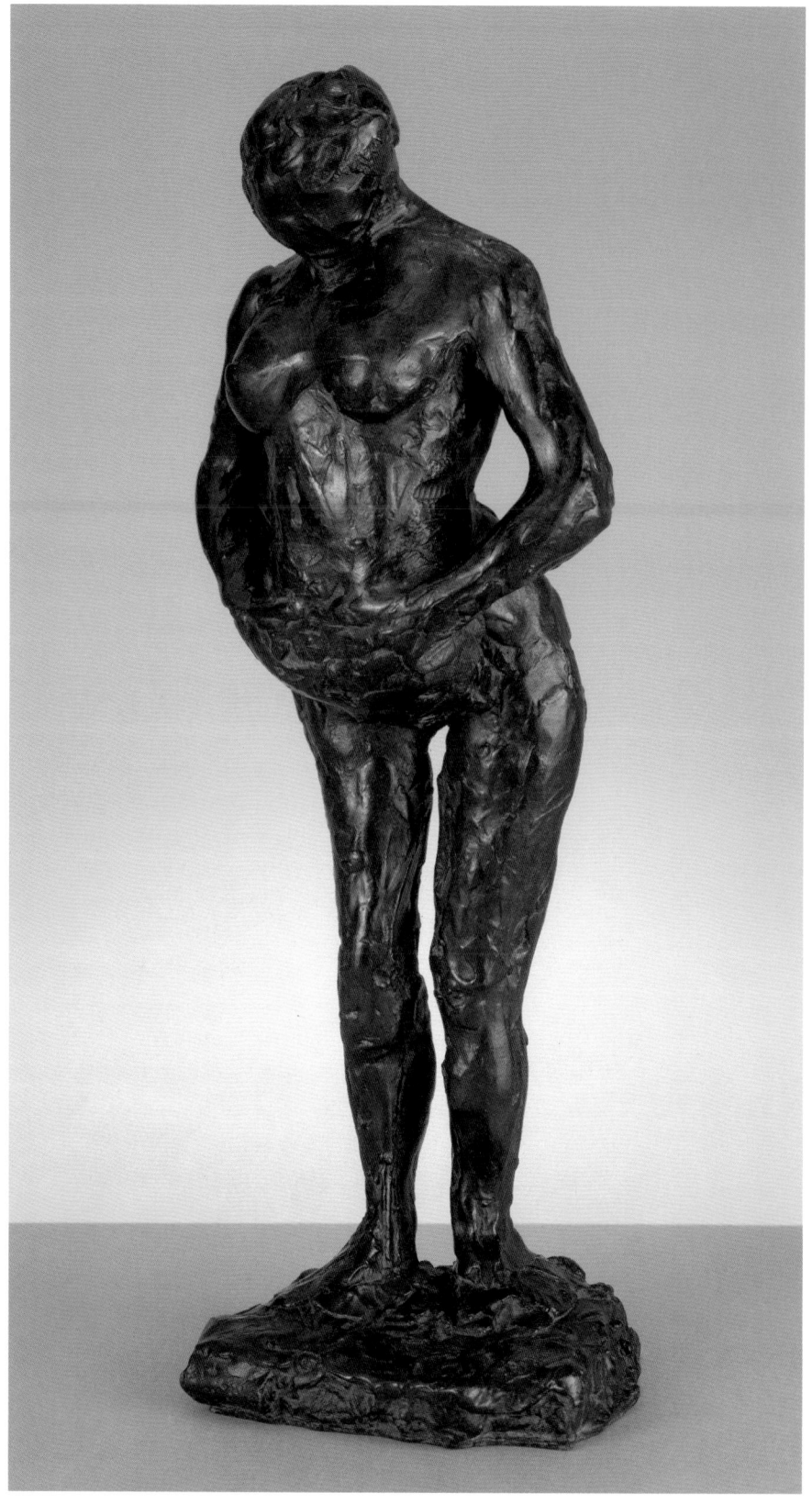

cally.[129] Picasso had been familiar with this tradition since his early childhood in Malaga — the
cathedral and churches there are full of such
sculptures — and, with or without Huysmans's
prompting, he may have made the connection
with Degas himself. But there is not necessarily
a link between Picasso's Cubist constructions
and *Little Dancer* or *The Tub*, for the incorporation of cardboard boxes and string into the first
of them was an extension of his current practice
in his two-dimensional collages and *papiers
collés*, and the use of found objects is commonplace in European craft traditions and ubiqui-
tous in African and Oceanic sculpture.

When Picasso created *Pregnant Woman* and
his other *objets-trouvés* sculptures in Vallauris,
the situation was entirely different and Degas's
precedent could not be ignored: he had joined
the canon of radical sculptors, and museums
and private collections proudly displayed the
posthumous casts alongside their Rodin bronzes;
John Rewald's complete catalogue was already
in print.[130] We know that Picasso attended the
vernissage on 11 July 1931 of the exhibition at the
Orangerie celebrating the Louvre's acquisition
of a complete set of Degas bronzes.[131] But one
would dearly like to know whether, exploiting his
contacts with Vollard and Rosenberg, he had
contrived to see any of the original waxes from
which, starting in 1919, the Hébrard foundry made
the bronze casts: he would surely have been fascinated both by Degas's manipulation of his
weird amalgams of wax, plasteline, and cork, and
also by the amateurish, sinister-looking arma-
tures sticking out of the statuettes and anchor-
ing them to their bases. In any case, Vollard may
have shown him his set of photographs of the
waxes taken soon after the artist's death, where
Degas's fondness for *bricolage* is immortalised.[132]
Improvisation was the name of the game when
Picasso returned to modeling in Boisgeloup in
1930, and he would have sympathized warmly
with Degas's uninhibited, ad hoc approach and
probably disapproved of all the tidying-up that

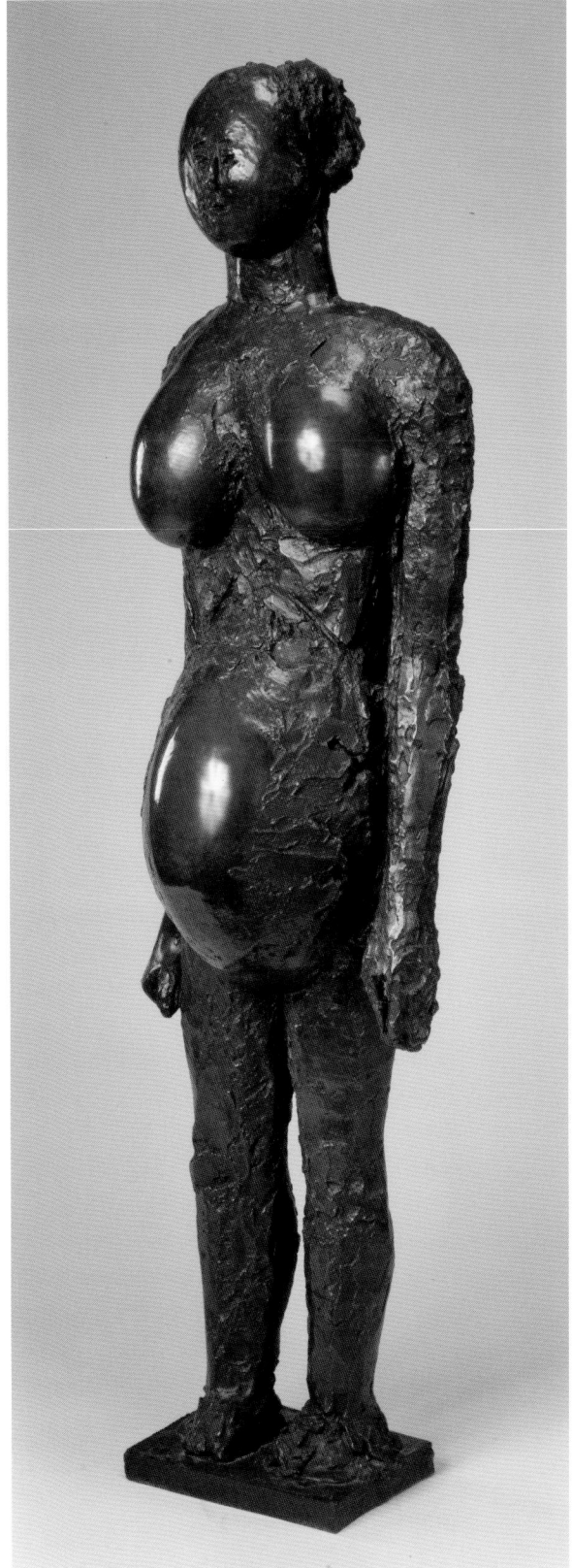

went on to make the cast sculptures more presentable (and conventional), including the elimination of the projecting supports.

Light is thrown on the role played by Degas in Picasso's late *objets trouvés* sculptures when the notorious *Little Dancer* is compared with *Little Girl Skipping* (**230**), a typical Vallauris sculpture begun in 1950 but left in a semi-finished state for several years. According to Gilot, Picasso had "always wanted to make a sculpture that didn't touch the ground" and it was the sight of a child skipping that gave him the idea of "the way to do it."[133] Picasso had been fascinated by the weightlessness and elevation of Degas's statuettes of dancers anchored only by one leg to the base, arms outstretched seeming about to take flight (see 171, 172), and the running figures he modeled in Boisgeloup in 1931–32 were made under their spell (see 168, 170, 173, 174).[134] It was perhaps at that moment that his ambition to make sculpture that defied gravity crystallized. But although ideal subjects in theory, in practice the leaping dancer and fleeing bather failed Picasso. The eureka solution was the skipping rope, which with a bit of ingenuity could provide the necessary support, and he commissioned a local blacksmith to fashion a curved iron bar that he transformed into a plausible rope by coating it in plaster and twisting pliant metal strapping around it. The little girl herself is younger than Degas's adolescent dancer, but the two shoes (not a pair) Picasso found in a dump and fixed onto her feet are surely an affectionately mocking allusion to the ballet pumps Degas fitted over the feet of the wax original. In both sculptures the imported shoes are substitutes for the modeled equivalent and lose some of their alien identity in the casting process. But the other objects incorporated in *Little Girl Skipping* involved metaphor and transformation: the cardboard lid of a chocolate box forming her face, the shallow wicker basket forming her torso and wittily evoking her knitted cardigan, the crumpled

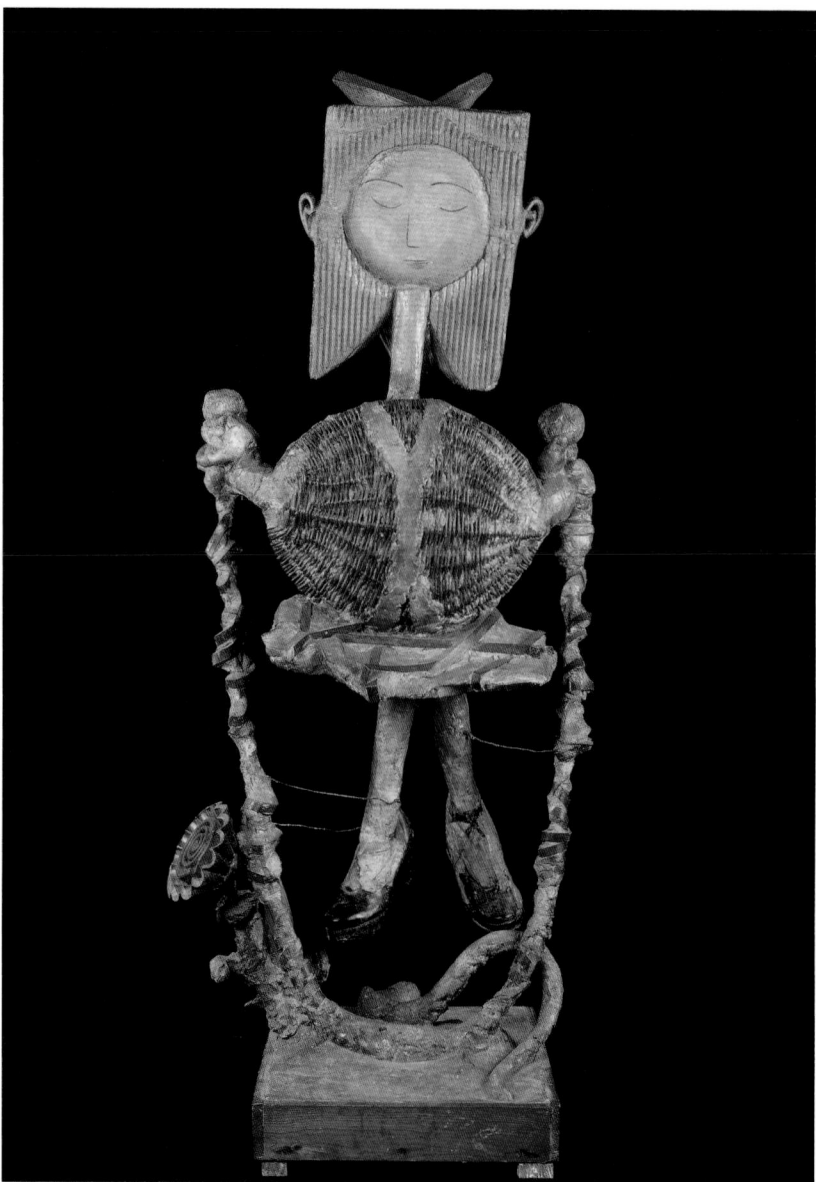

paper that was the starting-point of her flying skirt, the cake molds that stood in for the flower sprouting from the plinth, and so on. The basket/cardigan and molded paper/plaster skirt are Picasso's alternative to Degas's perfectly fitting fabric bodice and tutu and the assemblage of the child's head and body from various different materials his alternative to Degas's naturalistically modeled dancer's body. Or should one say "rejection of" rather than "alternative to," since *Little Dancer* is surely being trumped?

230

Pablo Picasso

Little Girl Skipping, 1950–52. Plaster, pottery, wicker basket, baking tins, shoes, wood, and iron, height: 152 cm. Musée national Picasso, Paris (MP 336)

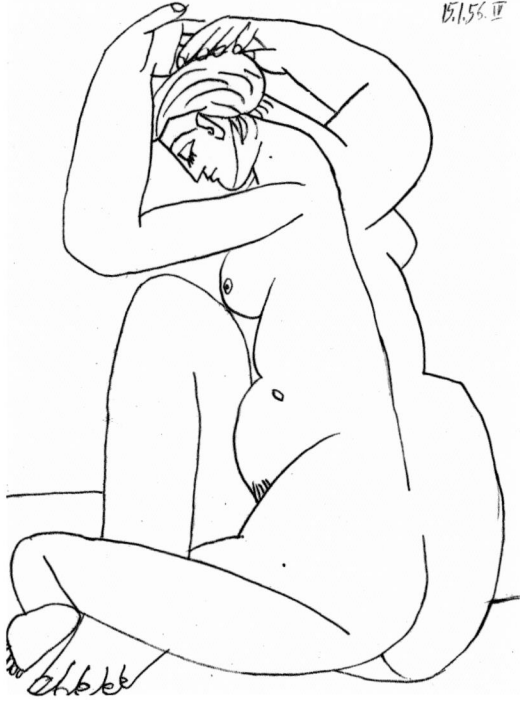

In the Vallauris sculptures, Picasso's
approach was anything but purist. The *objet
trouvé* that stood for itself rubbed shoulders
both with the *objet trouvé* that stood for something entirely different and with improvised
modeling using plaster. The effectiveness of his
"plastic metaphors" depended on visual similarities that registered quickly and engaged the
spectator's intelligence in a game of *trompe
l'esprit*, as he explained to Gilot.[135] Sometimes
clichés and traditional symbolism were involved
(like the vase/womb and milk jars/breasts in
Pregnant Woman). But frequently the spectator
is beguiled by analogies that are as imaginative
and outlandish as the conceits of Metaphysical
poetry (the wicker basket/cardigan in *Little Girl
Skipping* and the toy cars that, against all logic,
form a convincing head for the mother in
Baboon and Young). It is this "literary" aspect of
Picasso's use of *objets trouvés* that sets him
apart from Degas the sculptor. Yet Degas had a

strongly developed literary sense. Famous for
his neat turn of phrase and biting wit, like
Picasso he numbered major writers among his
friends — Mallarmé stands out among them (see
290). He himself wrote poetry, albeit carefully
crafted sonnets that are absolutely different in
form from Picasso's voluble, quasi-Surrealist
prose poems. And occasionally he used symbolic metaphors in his pictures, notably in the
surprising anthropomorphic landscapes of the
1890s.[136] In short, the two artists were united
in their desire to break down the traditional
barriers between the visual and the verbal.

Toilette and coiffure themes reappeared from
time to time in Picasso's subsequent work in
Vallauris as his relationship with Gilot crumbled.
In a painting dated 1 April 1953 a naked woman
who resembles her stands in front of a large,
deep bath, arms raised to her head.[137] The reference to Degas is unmistakable. Almost exactly
a year later, some months after she had left
him and moved to Paris with their children, he
devoted a series of drawings and paintings to
the subject of a seated nude seen from the
back piling her long hair into a bun: the back
view and *profil perdu*, relatively rare in Picasso's
work but very common in Degas's, are another
transparent *hommage*.[138] And in 1956 a carnet
was devoted to another suite of fluent drawings on this theme (**231**). But already in 1954
Picasso's life had changed radically yet again,
as Jacqueline Roque replaced Françoise Gilot
as his companion. With this change a new
phase in his dialogue with Degas opened as the
brothel monotypes assumed ever-increasing
importance. That story is the subject of the next
chapter and, like the story told here, it involves
backtracking to the beginning of the century
and the start of Picasso's long love affair with
France and French art.

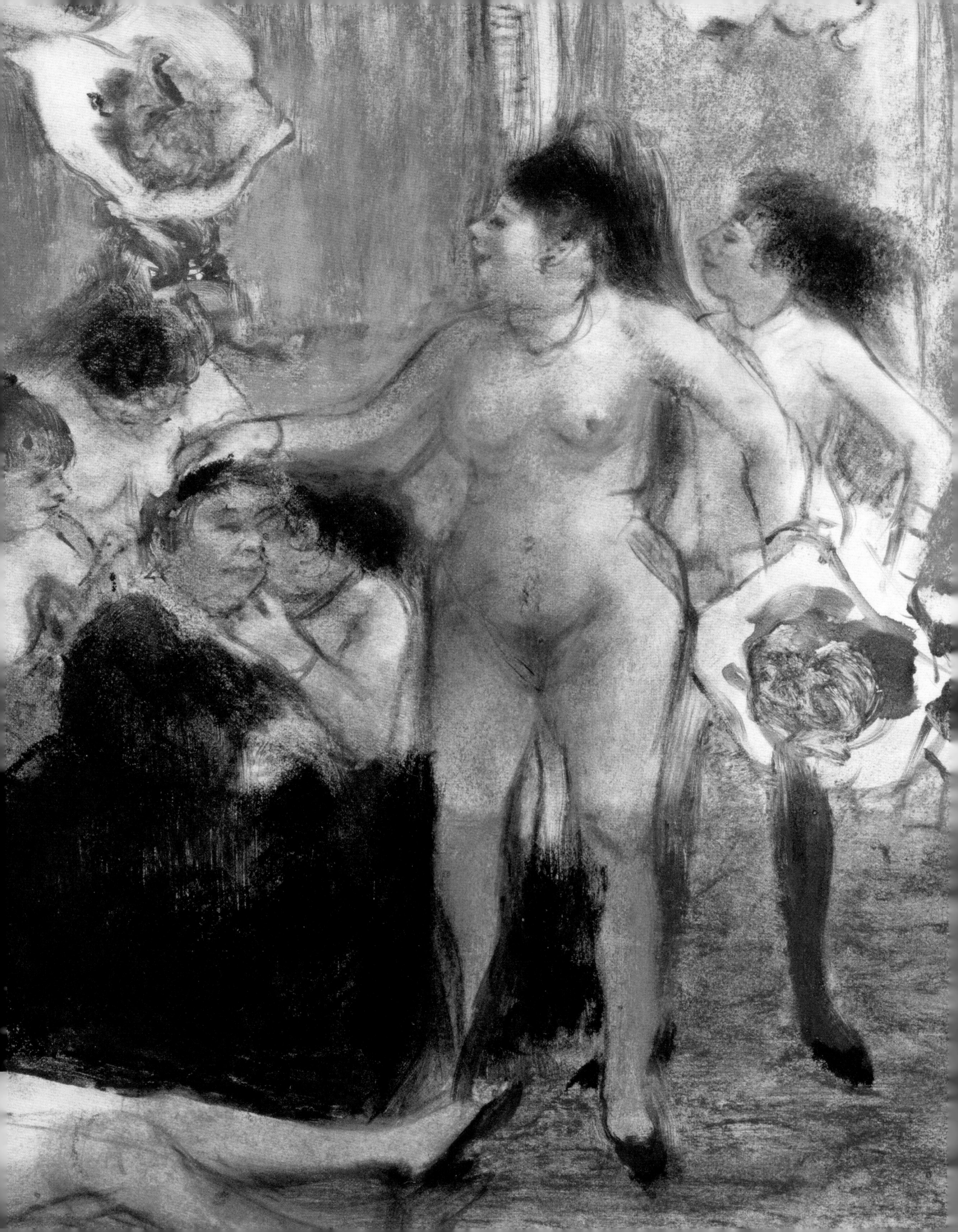

CHAPTER 5

"THE BEST THINGS HE EVER DID":

PICASSO AND DEGAS'S *MAISONS CLOSES*

ELIZABETH COWLING

When and How: Picasso's Discovery of Degas's Monotypes

The place was La Californie, Picasso's grandiose Art Nouveau villa in the hills just above Cannes, and the year 1958: "Picasso showed us some monotypes by Degas he has just bought. Magnificent. This is a Degas we didn't know. Not the Degas of the laundresses, or the drawings, or the dancers. A Degas we've never seen before."[1] The friends riveted by this private exhibition were the journalist Hélène Parmelin and her husband, the painter Édouard Pignon. The story of Picasso's acquisition of Degas's "magnificent" brothel monotypes and of their impact on his late work forms the main substance of this chapter. But unlike his two friends, Picasso had known and admired these small, piquant, reputedly marginal works for many years, and in the opening section, the knotty question of when and how he first discovered them will be addressed.

The studio sales following Degas's death generated enormous excitement and controversy not only in France but also abroad, and given Picasso's longstanding interest in the artist, he cannot have remained indifferent.[2] He was in Paris in late November 1918 at the time of the sale of Degas's prints, which was most people's introduction to the monotypes, for he was a chief mourner at Apollinaire's funeral on 13 November. If Picasso did view the sale, he would have seen most of the brothel monotypes he eventually acquired, including the most

famous of all, the richly colored *The Madame's Name Day* (see 259), which was given the accolade of a photograph in the catalogue.[3] As for Apollinaire, had he still been alive he would probably have reported the sale, for he had covered the first auction of Degas's paintings, pastels, and drawings in May 1918 at some length, describing the fierce disagreement between those who were thrilled and those horrified by the new image of Degas that emerged and deploring the fact that "the state did not make a bid for more of these infinitely precious works."[4]

Had Picasso encountered any of Degas's brothel monotypes before the sale? And had he done so by the time he started to plot a major painting on the theme of the *maison close* — a project which climaxed in the summer of 1907 in his masterpiece *Les Demoiselles d'Avignon* (see 136)? Several leading scholars have posed this intriguing question, including Robert Rosenblum, who was convinced that the visual parallels with some of Picasso's studies for *Les Demoiselles* were not fortuitous (see 242). Drawing attention to notes referring to Eugène Rouart, son of Degas's intimate friend Henri Rouart, scribbled in one of the sketchbooks Picasso used while planning the painting, Rosenblum suggested that it was Eugène who introduced him to the prints.[5] Although William Rubin was equally struck by the similarities between Degas's and Picasso's predatory whores, he thought it improbable that Rouart *fils* was the intermediary or that Picasso had

had access to any of the monotypes at this early date.[6] John Richardson also appears to rule out a connection because, despite arguing that *Les Demoiselles* was Picasso's bid to be a "painter of modern life" in the Baudelairean mold, he makes no mention of Degas as a likely visual source.[7]

The scepticism of scholars rests on the assumption that Degas's *maisons closes* were clandestine works made not for sale but for the artist's own amusement and that during his lifetime they remained unknown beyond his most intimate circle.[8] This argument does not, however, stand up to scrutiny because although the present state of knowledge is patchy, there is already a substantial body of evidence to show that Degas parted by gift or sale with a significant number of monotypes depicting prostitution and intimate toilette or bedroom scenes with brothel overtones.[9] The process started almost immediately, in fact, for the Third Impressionist Exhibition of 1877 included an unspecified number of "dessins faits à l'encre grasse et imprimés" (drawings made with greasy ink and then printed) — Degas's own definition for his monotypes. Although explicit brothel scenes were not, it seems, among those shown, there was a *cabinet de toilette* scene that, according to one critic, "scandalizes the ladies," presumably because the setting was assumed to be a brothel and the woman, although viewed from the back, to be washing her private parts.[10] Hanging nearby was one of the absolute masterpieces of Degas's entire oeuvre devoted to the lives of prostitutes, *Women on the Terrace of a Café in the Evening* (see 74). A monotype worked over with pastel, it was loaned by the painter Gustave Caillebotte and stunned critics at the time with its pinpoint accuracy of observation, becoming one of Degas's most celebrated works after it went on display in the Musée du Luxembourg in February 1897 with the rest of the Caillebotte bequest.[11] Picasso was obviously impressed: several small-scale,

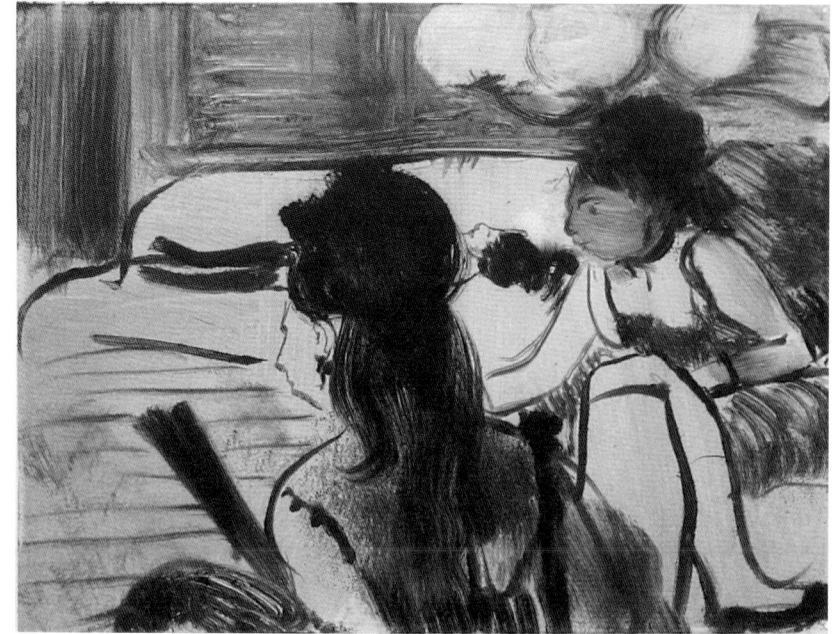

sleazy café scenes with a similar narrow horizontal format and *japoniste* composition painted during his first visits to Paris were made in emulation.[12]

Now and then during the 1880s, Degas gave monotypes to several close friends, including Vicomte Lepic, who had introduced him to the technique in the mid 1870s and supervised his first experiments, and the art critic and leading print aficionado Philippe Burty.[13] For such gifts Degas seems to have chosen sensual, voyeuristic images of nudes that were suggestive rather than explicit. Thus, the girl seated on a bed and pulling on a stocking in the print he gave Mary Cassatt may be a prostitute — she wears the telltale black ribbon round her throat and her hair dressed in the style favored by Degas's *filles* — but the setting is generalized.[14] Prints of this type were also sold to dealers and collectors: Comte Isaac de Camondo acquired in unknown circumstances one similar to but more tenebrous than Cassatt's, and a boldly simplified back view of a bather bending double to dry her feet (see 183). Alongside these ambiguous images of nudes in bed, bathing,

232

Edgar Degas

Brothel, c. 1876–77.

Monotype, 16 x 21.4 cm.

Bibliothèque de l'Insitut national d'histoire de l'art, Paris. Collections Jacques Doucet

(EM DEGAS 9)

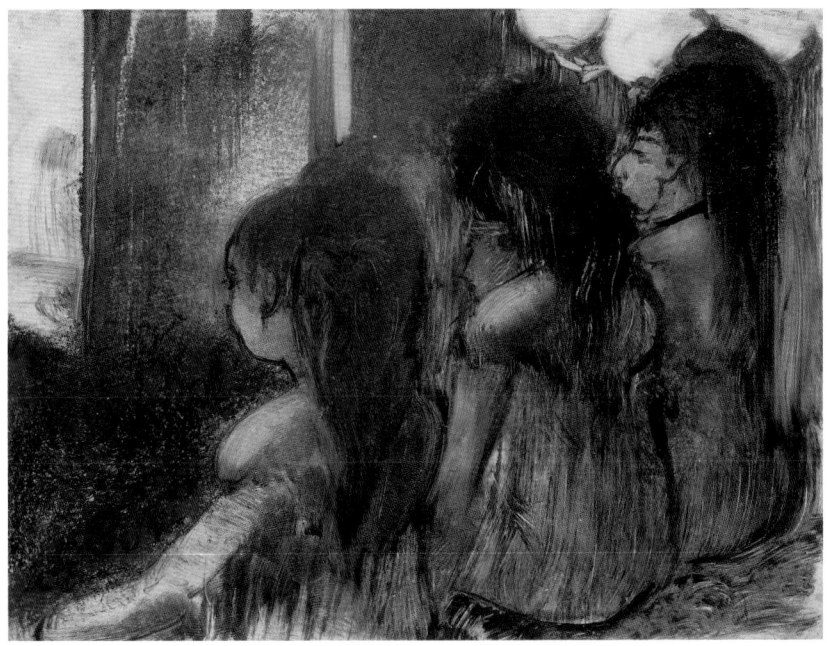

233

Edgar Degas

Three Seated Prostitutes,
Viewed from Behind,
c. 1876–77. Pastel over
monotype, 15.9 x 22.6 cm.
Musée national Picasso,
Paris (RF 35790)

and dressing, Degas also parted with a significant number of brothel scenes. An industrialist
called Dupuis, who formed an important collection of Impressionist paintings during the late
1880s, acquired two of them. Believing himself
to be ruined, he committed suicide in December
1890 and an auction was hurriedly organized
at Hôtel Drouot.[15] Thanks to the catalogue, his
Degas monotypes can be identified with virtual
certainty as the one now in Amsterdam (see
237) and the similar but notably more cheerful
Two Seated Women Facing Forward.[16] Together
they would have formed a perfect pair, the first
illustrating the weary boredom of waiting to be
picked, the other faked gaiety at the entrance
of the (unseen) client.

During the 1890s, one of Degas's principal
motives for selling his work was to finance
his burgeoning art collection, and a favorite
method was to make exchanges with accom-
modating dealers. Although his principal
agent Paul Durand-Ruel was not prepared to
handle works with flagrant sexual imagery, the
younger Ambroise Vollard, who set himself up
in a gallery on rue Laffitte in 1893, had no such

qualms.[17] On the contrary, he had a definite
penchant for prints, drawings, and literature of
this sort, and it was very likely through Vollard
that the young Picasso discovered Degas's
brothel scenes.

Vollard's first transactions with Degas date
from the autumn of 1894, and on 16 July 1895
he acquired a pastel of a nude and four brothel
monotypes in exchange for Manet's *Portrait of
Armand Brun*. Thanks to the brief descriptions
in the sale document, three of the monotypes
can be identified with virtual certainty: *Leaving
the Bath* (see 179), *Brothel* (**232**), and *Nude
Women* — a lesbian scene worked up with pastel, which was among those Picasso wanted
(but in this case failed) to buy from the Lefevre
Gallery in 1958. The fourth was probably the
sombre, autumnal *Three Seated Prostitutes,
Viewed from Behind* (**233**), which Picasso eventually acquired in 1960.[18] Although at this early
stage of his relationship with Degas Vollard did
not attempt to stockpile these "little masterpieces," as he later called the monotypes of
maisons closes,[19] he continued to buy them
whenever the opportunity arose. He may, for
instance, have handled the version of *The
Madame's Name Day* described by Renoir as
"superb" in a conversation they had "one day"
while sauntering along the *grands boulevards*
to the Place de l'Opéra.[20] Vollard's account of
their talk is typically freewheeling — it isn't clear
whether Renoir actually owned the print in
question or had merely been shown it by Degas
during a visit to his studio — but the episode
must have taken place in about 1900 at the
latest, before Renoir's rheumatism became too
disabling for rambles through the streets of
Paris. By then, print aficionados were well aware
of the existence of this "special" body of Degas's
work, for in an essay first published in 1897
the influential critic-cum-collector Roger Marx
alluded to Degas's brilliant characterization of
"the forced grin of prostitutes" and the "exaggerated truth" of "his pictures . . . of pleasure

and of vice."[21] In characterizing the prostitutes' "forced grin," Marx might have been describing the second of Dupuis's monotypes auctioned in 1891, but his devotion to Degas's work and passion for printmaking gave him privileged access to the artist's own collection and no doubt to the full range of the brothel scenes.[22]

Vollard may have been an intermediary for the brothel monotypes the couturier Jacques Doucet began buying in 1907, initially from an obscure but important prints and drawings dealer called Alfred Strölin. Strölin operated from a private address in the rue Laffitte — down the road from Vollard's gallery — and since he did not buy directly from artists and rarely at auction, he must have relied for his stock on other dealers or runners and collectors keen to sell privately.[23] At all events, one of the twelve monotypes Doucet eventually acquired (see 232) was in the original batch Vollard acquired by exchange with Degas in 1895. It is worth pointing out, furthermore, that a number of the brothel scenes Vollard published in facsimile in his *de luxe* editions of Guy de Maupassant's *La Maison Tellier* (1934) and Pierre Louÿs's *Mimes des courtisanes de Lucien* (1935) were not auctioned in the posthumous studio sale in 1918 and have no recorded history prior to their appearance in these books.[24] Clearly, Degas had parted with them before his death — maybe to Vollard, maybe to private collectors or rival print dealers and publishers such as Gustave Pellet, who was actively trading in Degas's monotypes in the early years of the century (and quite likely before 1900) and was a major buyer at the posthumous studio sale in 1918.[25]

Such was Vollard's liking for Degas's erotic prints that he chose to illustrate several of them in the album he devoted to the artist.[26] All the works reproduced were either in his current stock or had passed through his hands, and he succeeded in getting the aged Degas to "endorse" the images — and by extension the gallery — by signing all of them on the surrounding mount in a noticeably shaky hand. The album came out in 1914 and testifies to the systematic manner in which, starting in 1904 or earlier, Vollard had financed regular photographic campaigns with a view eventually to publishing complete catalogues of "his" artists' oeuvres. He was proud of this thoroughly modern enterprise, allowing visitors to consult the growing archive of photographs in his gallery and sending prints out to prospective clients.[27] In the case of Degas, an additional program of photography was undertaken at high speed in the winter of 1917–18 when the contents of his studio were being inventoried and the sale catalogues prepared.[28] But an examination of the surviving glass negatives and vintage prints reveals that the majority depict monotypes that were not in the studio sale. They must therefore have been taken before the war, although the records are too fragmentary to allow one to date them precisely.

To sum up: although Degas kept many of his erotic prints, at the turn of the century his work of this type was neither as secret nor as inaccessible as is usually claimed. The young Picasso could have seen at least a handful of the originals on visits to Vollard's gallery and more in the form of photographs — exceptionally fine photographs, what is more, for the glass negatives preserved the detail of Degas's technique with matchless fidelity. Through contacts with other dealers, collectors, and acquaintances of Degas's — since they had a surprising number of acquaintances in common — he may also have had access to other examples of these fascinating works. If, for instance, he contrived to see Camondo's collection before it was donated to the Louvre in 1908, he would have seen the intimate bedroom scenes mentioned above (see 183).[29] His pronounced interest in erotica and forays into the imagery of prostitution, which predate his first visit to Paris in 1900, surely predisposed him to

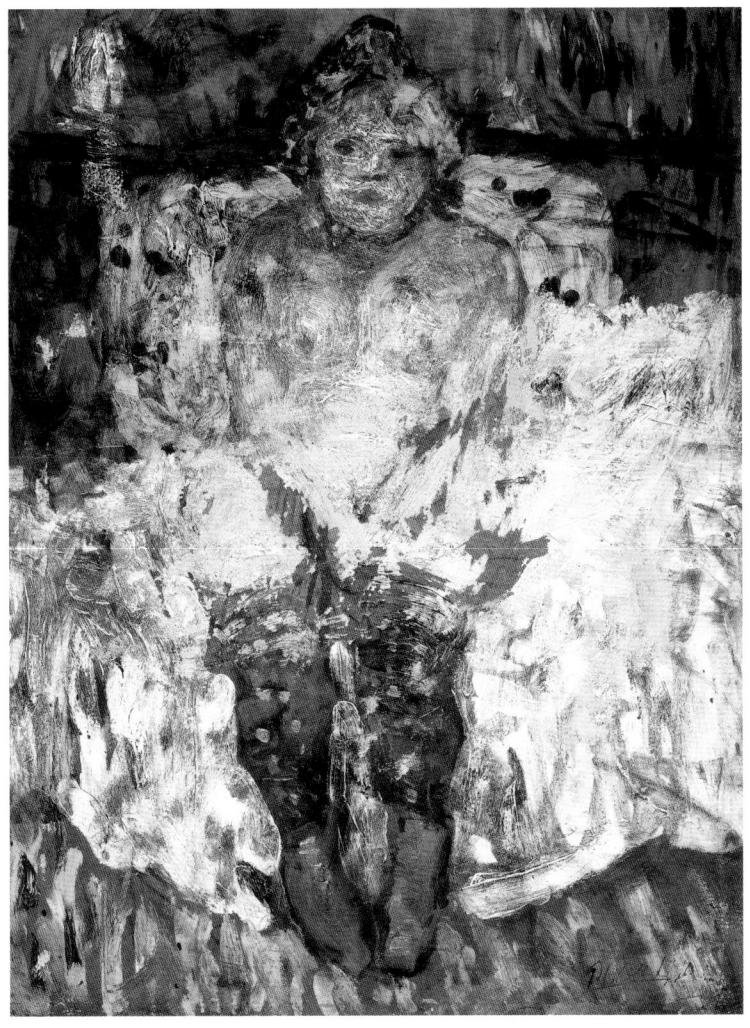

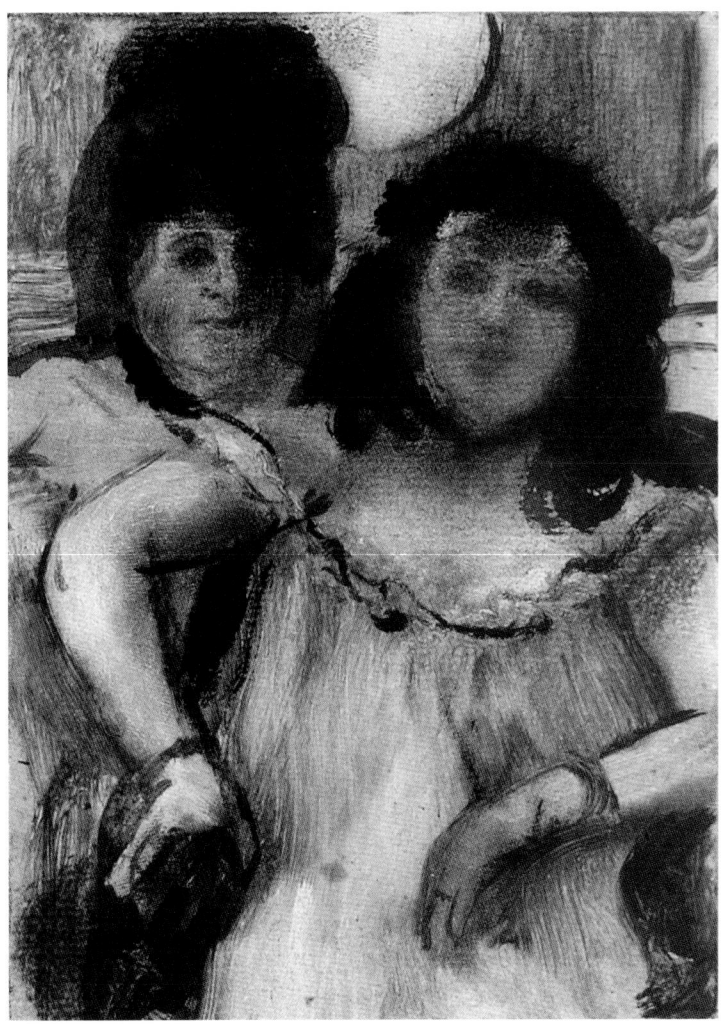

take an alert interest in anything of this sort by the French artists who most interested him, Degas among them.

Although Picasso may have dropped into Vollard's gallery on his first visit to Paris in 1900, their relationship dates from the time of his exhibition there the following summer, and to cement what he naturally hoped would be his passport to a decent living, he painted the dealer seated in his gallery surrounded by pictures hung frame-to-frame on the wall behind (see 81).[30] The exhibition was designed to make his reputation in Paris, and many of the canvases he rushed to complete before the opening on 25 June 1901 were flagrant exercises in

the style of high-profile avant-garde French artists.[31] Scenes of prostitution had a prominent place, largely no doubt because Picasso correctly identified the subject as supremely up-to-date and supremely Parisian, and estimated that his high-octane, confrontational handling would be both eye-catching and memorable. Although there are echoes of the racy subject matter and style of other artists he admired, notably Lautrec, the fat, naked whores waiting in the brothel salon and staring brazenly at the viewer just as if he were their next client (**234**) are physically like Degas's prostitutes. Even at this early stage Picasso had perhaps seen one or two of the exceptionally freely worked prints in which the whores appear in such extreme close-up that they are, as it were, within touching distance of the viewer-client (235; see also 237).[32]

Many of Picasso's early images of prostitution were not for public consumption, however, and range freely between (and also mix) descriptive realism, satire, grotesquerie, symbolism, and pornography. Sometimes the protagonists in his erotica are named and sometimes he portrayed himself.[33] Most of these images of heterosexual or lesbian lovemaking, of girls displaying their genitals or masturbating, and of prostitutes servicing their clients were executed on paper in media (like ink and watercolor) that lent themselves to fluency and speed. No doubt they were shown to cronies and then stashed away again, but now and then one would be given away or sold.[34] The graphic tradition within which Picasso was working is long, deep, and prolific, and alongside all the more or less clandestine prints and drawings he might have seen were vast numbers of pornographic photographs. Any resemblance to Degas's brothel monotypes may therefore be fortuitous, but one can imagine that Picasso would at least have been tickled by the thought that the reputedly high-minded, misanthropic, and celibate artist had been responsible for a considerable erotic oeuvre, not excluding lesbian scenes only marginally less frank than his own — that he and Degas were on the same wavelength in this dubious area as they were in others.[35]

Some of Picasso's early brothel drawings were not so risqué as to rule out reproduction in a magazine, and he may well have made them with this in mind. An early essay in this mode, *The Divan* (see 56), was probably executed even before his first trip to Paris. Although all the characters look typically Spanish, especially the rapacious Celestina, the drawing nevertheless reveals his familiarity with Steinlen's lithographs for *Gil Blas Illustré* and *Le Rire*.[36] (Such was Picasso's fascination with Steinlen at this period that he practiced imitating his

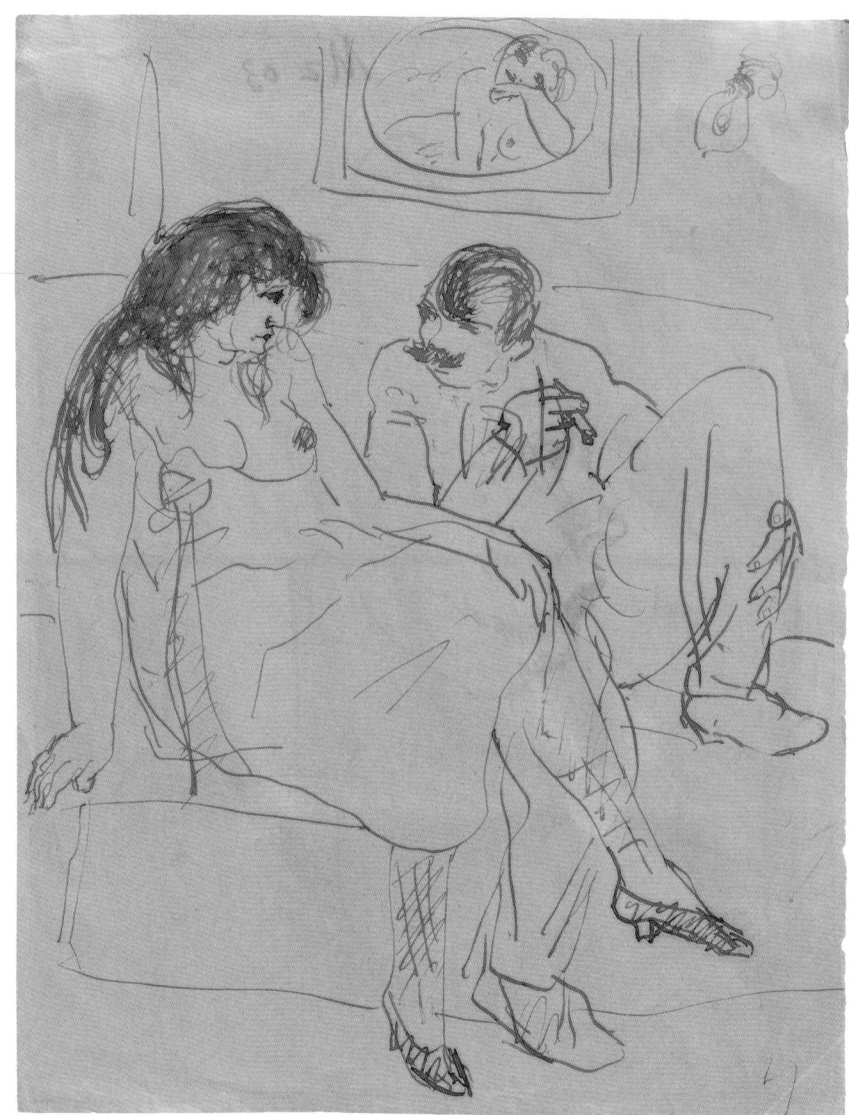

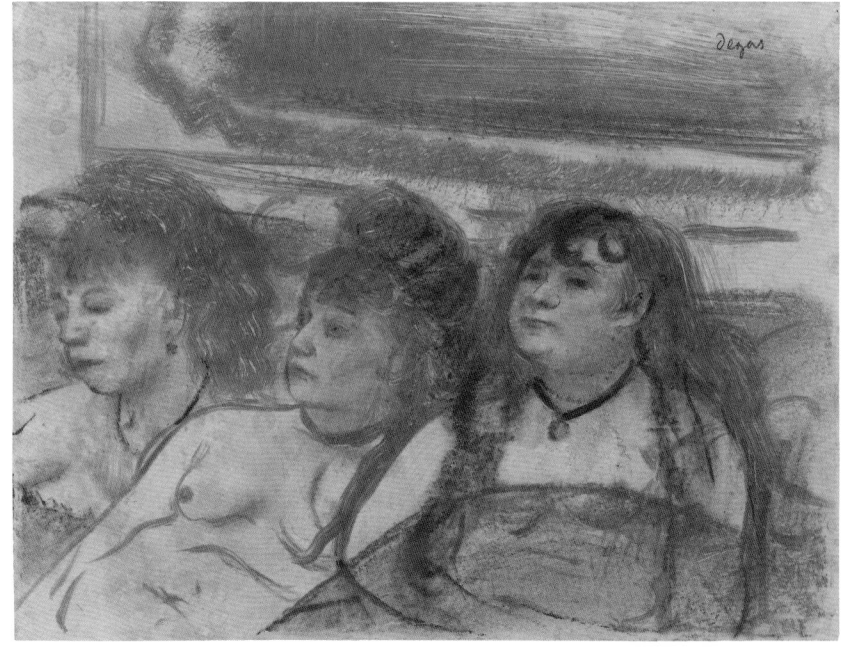

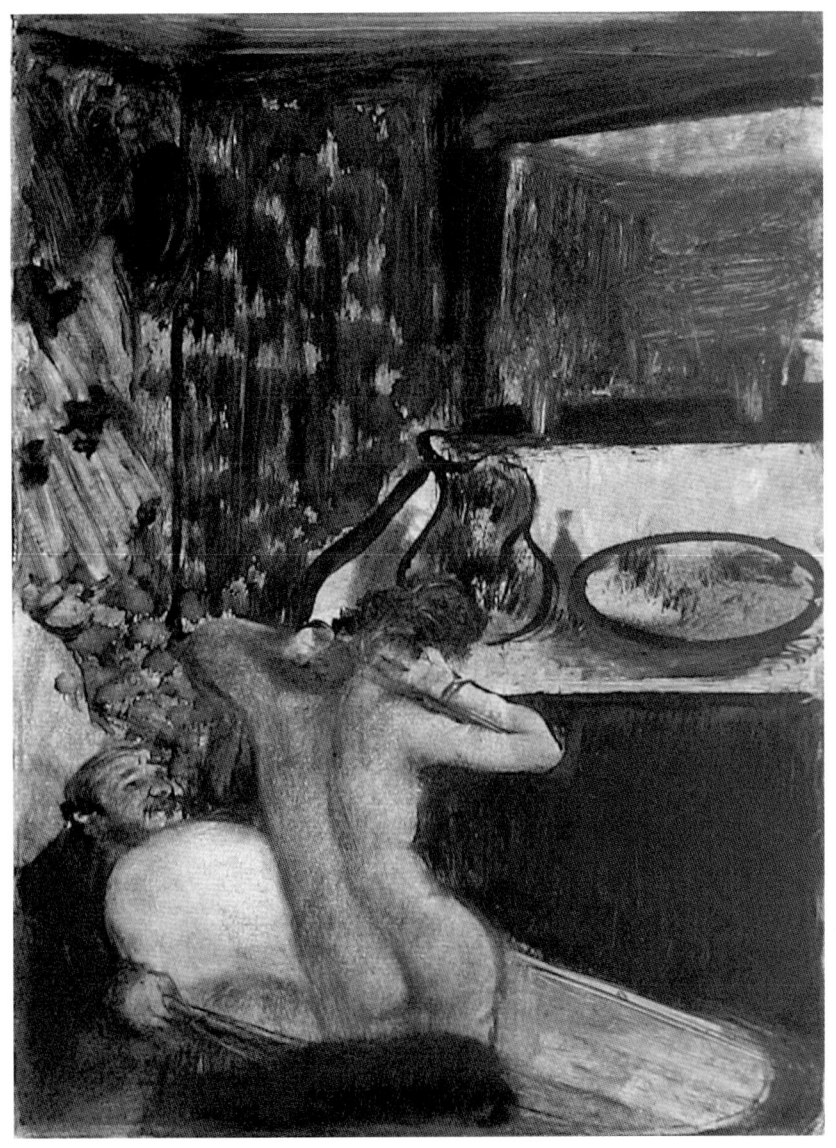

signature.)[37] A drawing with the same iconography done a few years later, after several visits to Paris, is comparatively less like Steinlen and more like Degas (**236**). Thus, at the very least, the shrewd satirical observation expressed with such economy and fluency in *The Couple* is comparable to pungently authentic brothel interiors by Degas like *Three Seated Prostitutes* (**237**), *Brothel* (see 232), and *Admiration* (**238**). Both artists' disheveled, blowsy whores and paunchy, mustachioed clients are of exactly the same conventionalized types, and both

contrive to evoke an entire, compellingly real, mini-drama through facial expression, body language, figure groupings, and the merest indications of setting. Degas may never have seriously considered publishing any of his brothel monotypes, but they do have the character of illustrations and in that sense, too, were perfect models for Picasso.[38]

Although Picasso must have visited Vollard's gallery quite regularly during his lengthy stays in Paris and after he settled in Montmartre in 1904, it was not until May 1906 that the dealer actually began to buy his work and that their relationship became closer.[39] Significantly, a mere two months before that groundbreaking first block purchase, Vollard bought back at auction a couple of the *maisons closes* prints he had originally obtained by exchange from Degas in 1895. These were *Leaving the Bath* (see 179) and *Brothel* (another of the monotypes eventually acquired by Jacques Doucet; see 232).[40] It was also around this time that Picasso made a curious series of pen-and-ink sketches of a woman lying on her back with one or both legs thrust up in the air (**239**). A more finished variant, in which the woman looks exhausted, went to his patron Gertrude Stein.[41] These were not the first drawings by Picasso to depict the body in semaphore-like movement, but in the earlier cases he usually identified the motive for the kicking, rolling, and arching as masturbation and cast the women, naked except for their stockings, as lubricious prostitutes.[42] In the 1906 sketches, Picasso may quite simply be recording a girlfriend performing stretching and limbering exercises that have nothing to do with auto-eroticism. Nevertheless, they are curiously reminiscent of monotypes in which bored prostitutes, utterly indifferent to their companions, slump, sprawl, stretch, and kick, and occasionally indulge in desultory masturbation.[43] Although most prints of this type remained in Degas's collection until his death, *Courtesans* (**240**) went to Vollard before the war. Vollard may, it is true, have acquired it after 1906, but this particular monotype must have appealed to Picasso because a photograph of it — supplied by Vollard — was discovered among his possessions after his death.[44] The grotesque, rebarbative poses of Degas's whores are another, crankier manifestation of the artist's overriding obsession with the body in motion, and if Picasso had no knowledge of *Courtesans* when he made his "gymnastic" drawings, he was certainly not ignorant of this larger dimension of Degas's work. In that more general sense, at

least, he was matching the older artist's willful exploration of the momentary, off-balance, startlingly unconventional pose.

If the "gymnastic" drawings were indeed inspired by the imagery of prostitution — what whores do in their spare time — then they may be connected with Picasso's slowly evolving plan to paint a Salon-scale picture on the theme of the brothel, for it took him some time to decide on the right subject matter as well as on the composition and poses of his protagonists. As related in the previous chapter, the sudden windfall of 2000 francs from Vollard prompted his decision to spend the summer of 1906 in Catalonia, and while staying in Gósol, he embarked on a large canvas depicting a harem-cum-brothel in which he brought together eroticized images of washing and preening that have links with Degas's many toilette scenes set in *maisons closes* (see 197). But this solution did not ultimately satisfy him, and on his return to Paris Picasso began to explore the potentially more confrontational theme of *l'attente*, the dreary waiting game played day in, day out by the *pensionnaires* of a brothel treated so often by Toulouse-Lautrec as well as Degas. His new patrons Gertrude and Leo Stein owned a major Lautrec on this very subject,[45] although the four *filles* sitting on the red plush sofa in that painting are all fully covered up by rather heavy chemises, whereas from the start Picasso followed Degas's lead in showing his prostitutes more or less completely naked.

Although it took Picasso several months and innumerable sketches to finalize the composition, he decided at an early stage that the destined masterpiece would revolve around a group of hefty naked women within a curtained interior. A small oil-on-canvas study roughly and energetically brushed in the autumn of 1906 (**241**) has qualities in common with brothel monotypes Picasso could have known and raises the question posed at the outset of this chapter about the possibility of Degas's

239

Pablo Picasso

Studies of a Reclining Female Nude in Five Positions, 1906.

Pen and black ink on paper, 23.8 x 31 cm.

Albertina, Vienna (inv. 23299)

240

Edgar Degas

Courtesans, c. 1876–77.

Monotype, 16.1 x 21.2 cm.

National Museum, Belgrade. Collection: Graphic Arts Cabinet (inv. 1632)

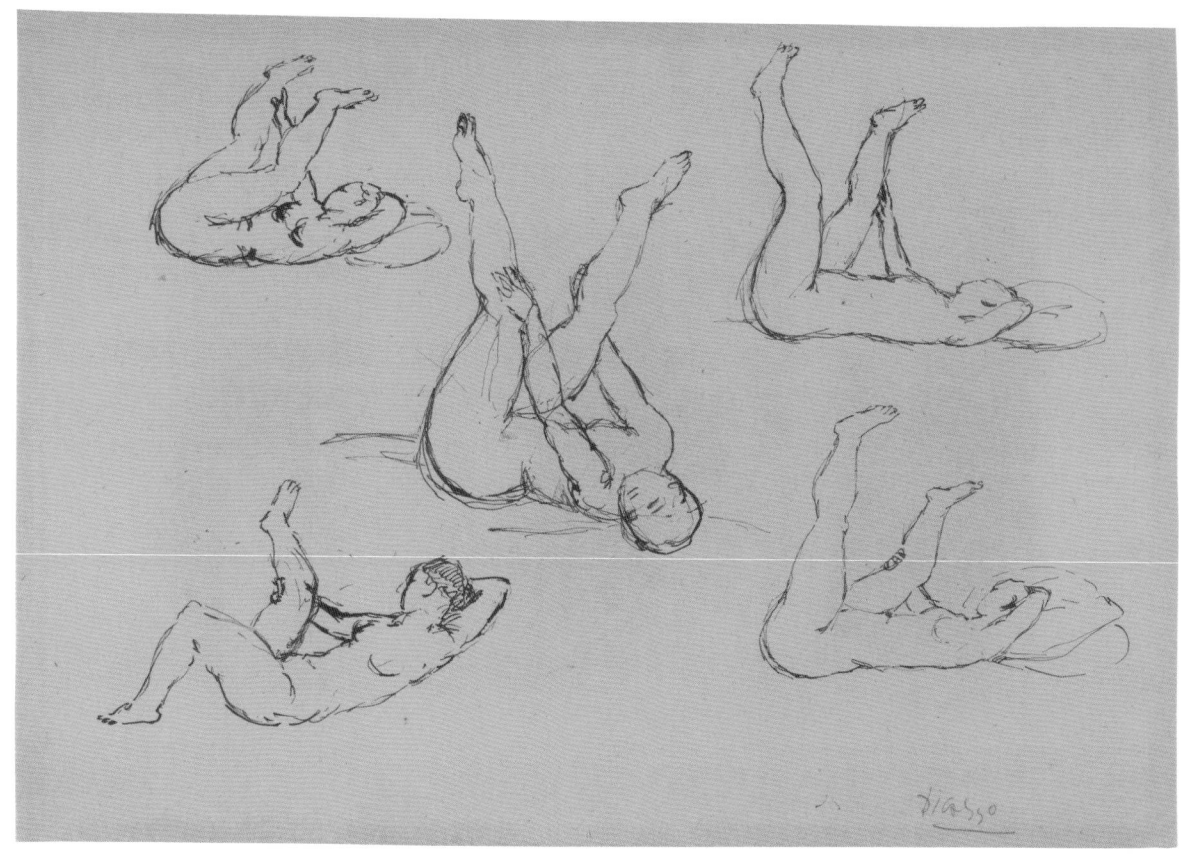

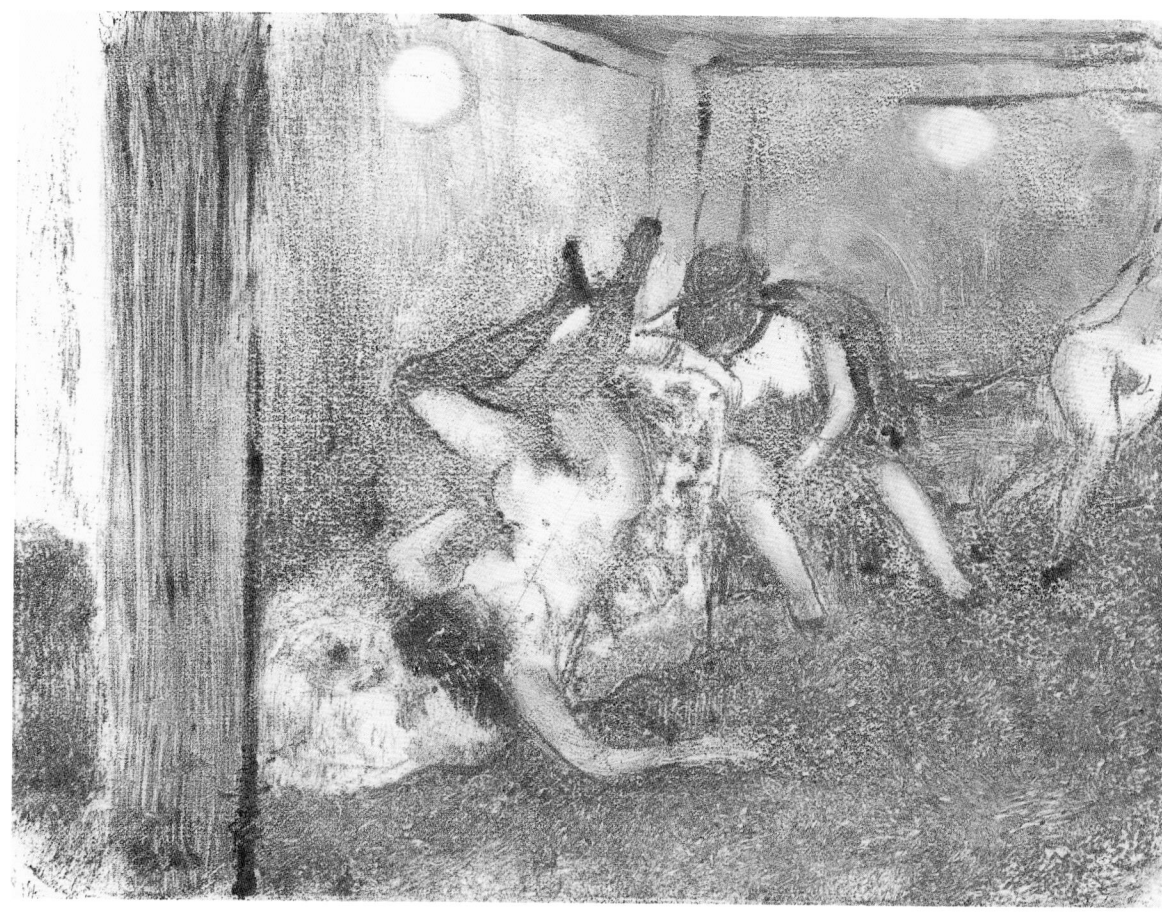

"influence" on *Les Demoiselles d'Avignon* (see 136). Thus, Picasso's three ungainly nudes have the coarse features and pudgy bodies of the three sullen whores lined up on a sofa in the searingly honest monotype now in Amsterdam that, as noted earlier, had been on the market in Paris since the Dupuis sale in 1891 (see 237). Although Picasso did not attempt to match the psychological penetration of Degas, the mood of disenchantment and the sense of time weighing heavily within the stifling world of the aptly named *maison close* are common to both. The quality of Picasso's drawing is also remarkably similar to Degas's: strongly defined contours drawn spontaneously with paint thinned so that it has the consistency of printer's ink, contrasting with, and never disappearing beneath, the dragged and smudged paint evoking the curtained setting and pitch-black shadows. The same thrilling combination of assured draftsmanship and sheer improvisation is present in *Brothel* (see 232), a more caricatural monotype on the same theme of *l'attente* that, as noted above, Vollard had bought back at auction in February 1906. What distinguishes Picasso's study from the monotypes, and indeed from similar scenes by the likes of Lautrec and Forain, is its relative abstraction: there is nothing to define the curtained interior as a brothel; the women have none of the standard attributes of whores; there is no sign that something is about to happen.

Having toyed with this narrative-free, purely suggestive image, Picasso decided to compose a scene that unambiguously declared its theme. Retaining the idea of a theatrical curtained interior, he increased the number of naked women to five, placed a sailor representing the archetypal client in their midst, and to complete his cast depicted, entering from the left, a male figure he later identified as a medical student or doctor (and who in certain studies looks quite like Picasso himself). The definitive version of this incarnation of the composition is the mag-

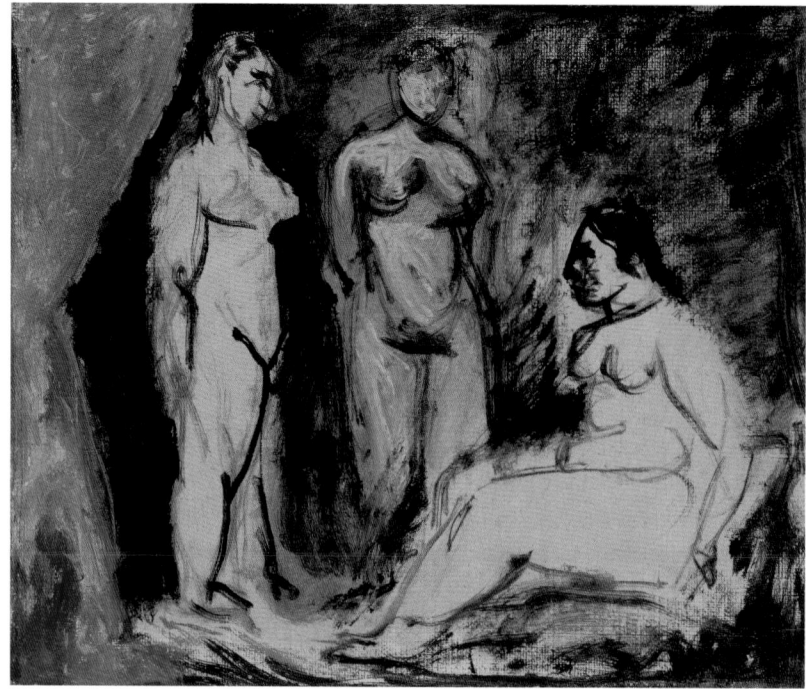

nificent drawing in Basel (**242**), which historians agree was executed in March to April 1907. In small oil studies painted at the same period, the doctor was transformed into a comic stock figure with the bald pate and dark suit of the foolish, lecherous clients in monotypes like *Admiration* (see 238).[46] The use of pastel in the Basel study to work out a bold color scheme for the painting is another obvious point of contact with Degas, who sensuously enhanced many of the brothel monotypes with passages of intense color.

In composition, the Basel drawing is closest to the more crowded and animated brothel scenes where the boredom of endless waiting is alleviated by the arrival of a client or some social occasion. Into the latter category fall the three vivacious and amusing versions of *The Madame's Name Day*. The present whereabouts of one that Picasso may conceivably have seen by 1907 is unknown, but several vintage prints and the original glass negative survive in Vollard's photographic archive (**243**).[47] In this version five prostitutes gather around and pet the

241

Pablo Picasso

Three Nudes, 1906. Oil on canvas, 25.1 x 30.2 cm. The Barnes Foundation, Merion, Pennsylvania (BF211)

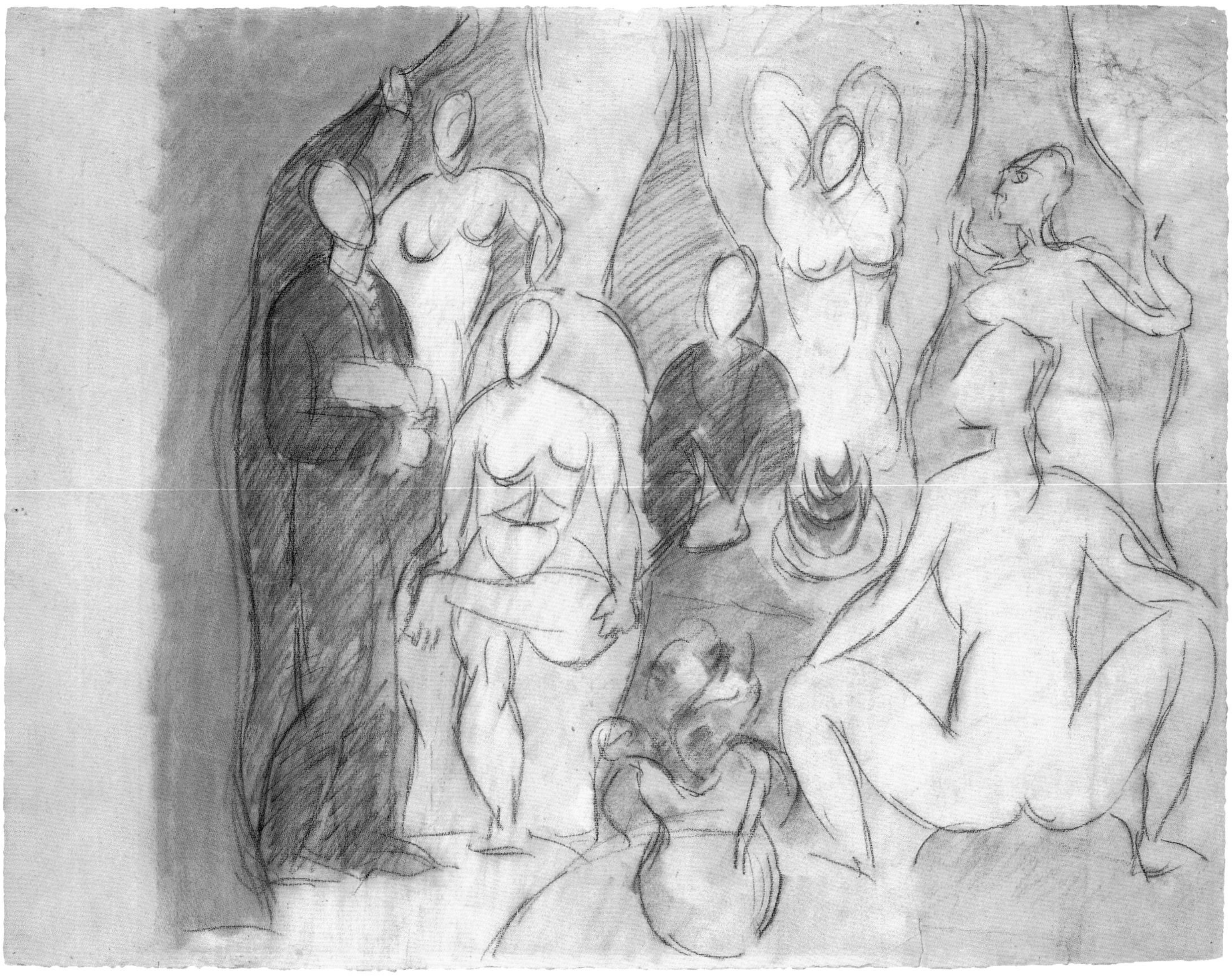

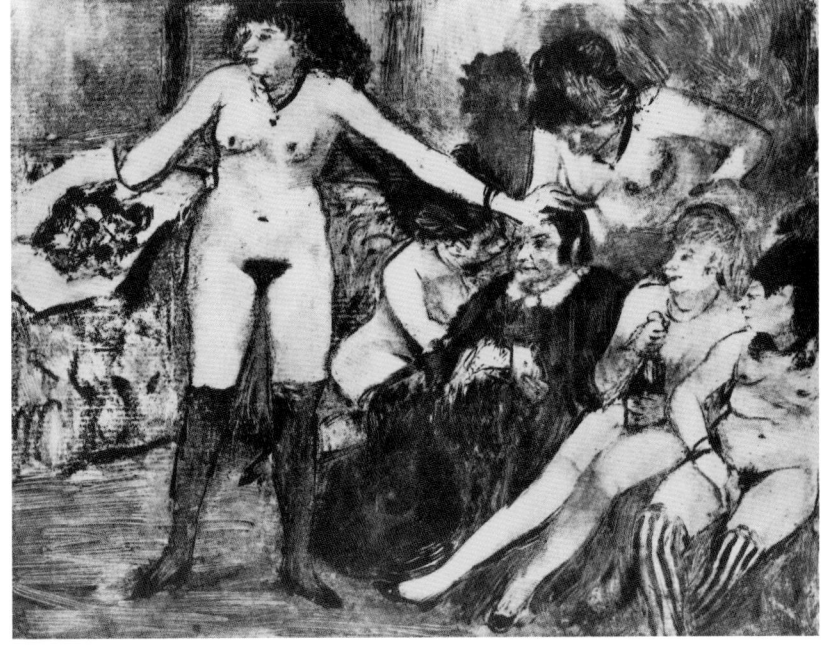

242

Pablo Picasso

Study for "Les Demoiselles d'Avignon," 1907. Charcoal and pastel, 47.7 x 63.5 cm. Kunstmuseum Basel. Kupferstichkabinett (1967.106)

243

Edgar Degas

The Madame's Name Day, c. 1876–77. Monotype, 15.5 x 20.6 cm. Location unknown

madame, who, forming a dark shape in their midst, is more or less in the same situation as Picasso's sailor. She and three of her charges look eagerly toward their right to welcome a new guest, just as the *demoiselles* and the sailor look toward Picasso's entering doctor. The dominant standing *fille* brandishes a bouquet; Picasso's equivalent is the bunch of flowers in the jug in the foreground of the Basel study. Another grasps a bottle of champagne suggestively between her legs and leers at the invisible newcomer; Picasso's equivalent is the phallic *porrón* (Spanish wine jar) on the table by the sailor. Indeed, the comparison with Degas's print brings out an aspect of the Basel study that is rarely mentioned — the fact that a party was going on when the doctor made his sudden entry.

After innumerable trials, Picasso eliminated from his composition most of the elements that have just been enumerated — the sailor, the doctor, the flowers, the *porrón* — and in the process the most obvious iconographic links with Degas's monotypes all but disappeared. But in the spring of 1907, when he had not yet reached the conclusion that illustrating a brothel scene with something like the literalness of the older naturalist generation — his father's generation — was the wrong way to proceed, Degas does seem to have been an inspiration. Moreover, the following year the instinct to "tell a story" resurfaced in small-scale compositions depicting one or two men paying homage to a reclining naked woman within an interior draped, like the brothel of *Les Demoiselles d'Avignon*, with heavy curtains (**244**). These male figures were obviously influenced by tribal carving, Picasso's latest passion, but the ceremony that turns on the offering of flowers and the crowded composition hark back to *The Madame's Name Day*.

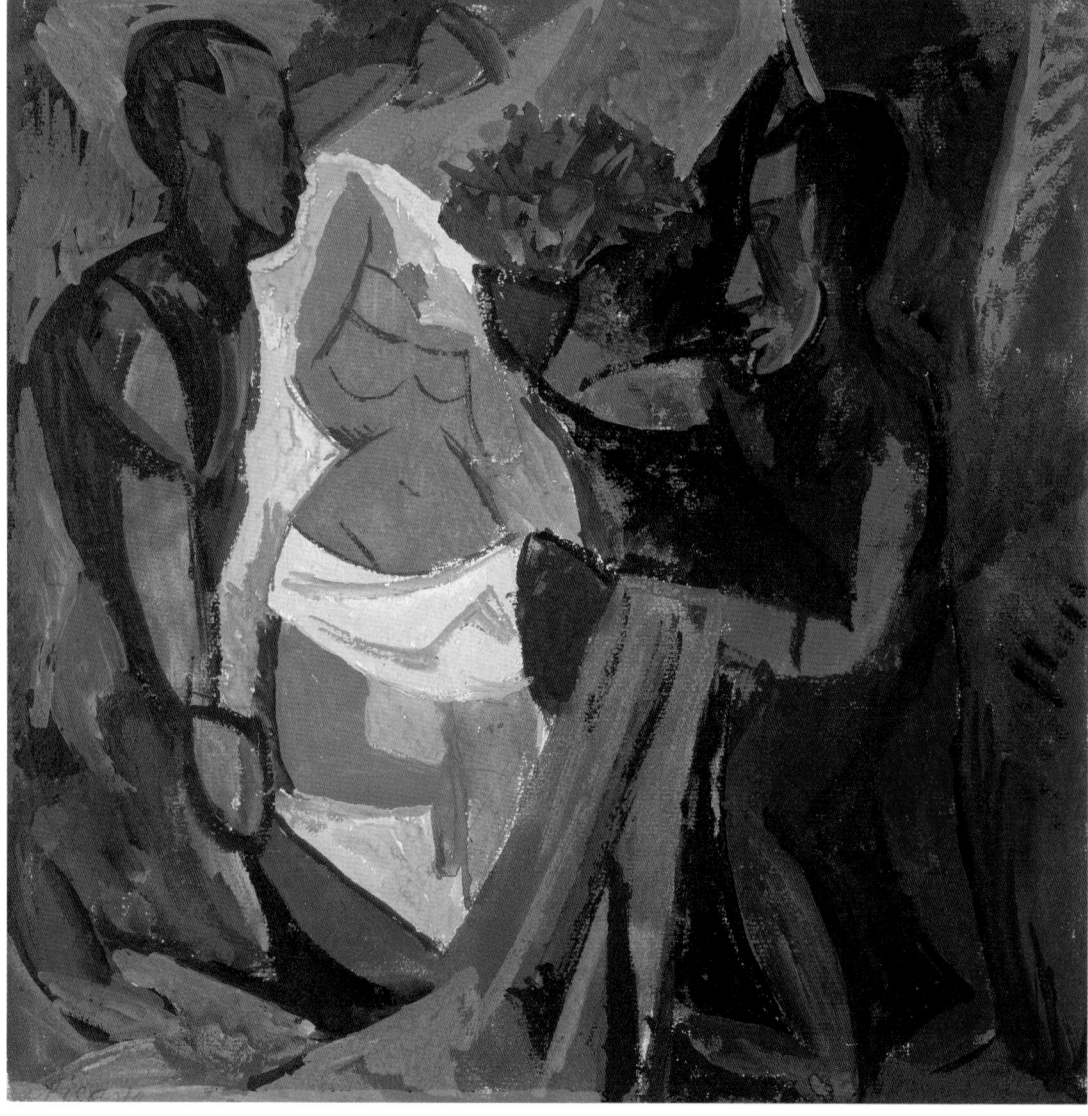

244
Pablo Picasso
The Offering, 1908.
Gouache on cardboard with white primer, 30.6 x 30.6 cm. Museu Picasso, Barcelona (MPB 112.761)

Picasso Collects Degas

In the late 1950s visitors to La Californie like Hélène Parmelin and Édouard Pignon, the couple encountered at the beginning of this chapter, might have noticed amid the bewildering chaos of the high-ceilinged ground-floor rooms a framed self-portrait photograph of Degas propped against a brass charcoal burner (**245**). It is glimpsed in a photograph André Gomès took sometime in 1958 and in several taken by David Douglas Duncan the following April (**247**).[48] How and when Picasso acquired it are unsolved questions. Nor is it known who was responsible for inking-out both Degas's redoubtable housekeeper Zoé Closier, who stands grim-faced and protective behind her employer in the original shot (see 297), and the tumbler at the left in the foreground. On the one hand, Degas is renowned for impetuously — at times ruinously — revising his own work, and it is conceivable that he was responsible. On the other hand, if Picasso did not realize the photograph was a self-portrait — he inscribed it on the back "Portrait de E. Degas," not "Auto-portrait" — maybe he was the culprit, and perhaps he eliminated Zoé and the glass in order to underline the resemblance of Degas to his own father (**246**), a resemblance that struck others and had great significance for him.[49]

Thanks to Gomès, it is certain the photograph was on display in La Californie in the very year, 1958, that Picasso acquired (in circumstances described below) his first Degas monotypes. Knowing of their arrival, perhaps somebody had just given it to him: present-giving was an important ritual at La Californie, and visitors tortured themselves trying to find something that would genuinely please. It is possible, though, that Picasso had owned it for years and unearthed it to pay homage to its maker. The photograph was not in any case the only personal item connected with Degas in Picasso's possession. His biographer Antonina Vallentin describes a visit to his former studio at rue des Grands Augustins in Paris, during which he proudly showed her a Degas frame into which he had fitted a proto-Cubist painting depicting that most typical of Degas subjects, a dancer — or what she took to be a dancer:

But it was not the picture he wanted to show me, it was the frame. "It used to belong to Degas," he said proudly. "He used to have them made specially for him. I managed to get hold of it." It was a wide, slightly convex frame and the white was lightly tinted with rose. Having dusted it and adjusted the glass, Picasso lovingly passed his hand over the gently curving wood. It was indeed the ideal frame for the rosy figures dancing in the footlights that Degas was so fond of. But Picasso's dancing girl, with her joints and movements dislocated by planes of discordant colour, struggled inside the frame as though she wanted to burst it asunder. She clashed appallingly with its elegant form and tender colouring. But Picasso gazed at her, seemingly unaware of the incongruity.[50]

As Richard Kendall has argued in this volume, this "incongruous" marriage between a gyrating *demoiselle* and Degas's ballet dancers may have been more purposeful than Vallentin assumed.

The Degas frame, along with a pile of other pictures, was stuffed behind "one of those trashy braziers that encumbered a corner of his studio at Rue des Grands Augustins," Vallentin recalled.[51] This was presumably the very brazier that ended up in La Californie providing support for the Degas photograph and other precious bits and bobs. Propping favorite pictures informally on furniture, rather than hanging them on walls, was Picasso's way of keeping them at hand and in mind, for he decried conventional methods of display as anaesthetizing. The intriguing conjunction of frame/brazier/photograph prompts the thought that he may have acquired both Degas items at the same moment and from the same source. He was a connoisseur of frames: trawling junk shops, he had started stockpiling them even before the First World War. And he had been collecting photographs of all sorts for even longer, sometimes appropriating and adapting their imagery.[52] Conceivably, he had owned both the Degas frame and the Degas photograph for decades.

Whatever the truth of the matter, in 1958–59, in the form of this altered photograph, Degas was literally present in Picasso's studio, like a silent witness or a household god. As for the Degas monotypes themselves, since one never catches sight of them in photographs taken in any of Picasso's houses, they must have been kept locked away in his "secret chamber" along with other treasures, to be brought out and discussed with the chosen few whenever he felt so inclined.[53]

Picasso was never an avid, compulsive, spendthrift art collector in the sense that Degas was during the 1890s.[54] He did not do regular rounds of the dealers' galleries with collecting in mind, or spend hours poring over auction catalogues, or haunt the salerooms, or hobnob with fellow collectors debating the pros and cons of some new purchase and bemoaning the hike, or drop, in prices. Nor, unlike Degas in the case of, say, his collection of works by Ingres, did Picasso set out to form a museum-quality collection of the painters he esteemed the most. True, he acquired pictures by favorite artists, including Renoir, Cézanne, Matisse, Miró, as well as Degas himself. But despite his enormous wealth and his numerous contacts in the art trade, he never bought anything or, as far as we know, tried to buy anything by, say, Rembrandt, Goya, Ingres, Delacroix, or Van Gogh, all of whom were among the artists he venerated most of all. Nor was he bothered about improving the standard of his collection. Some of his nineteenth-century pictures are of questionable authenticity,[55] and a good many of his tribal sculptures were produced for the tourist trade.[56] Picasso had a passion for "stuff"

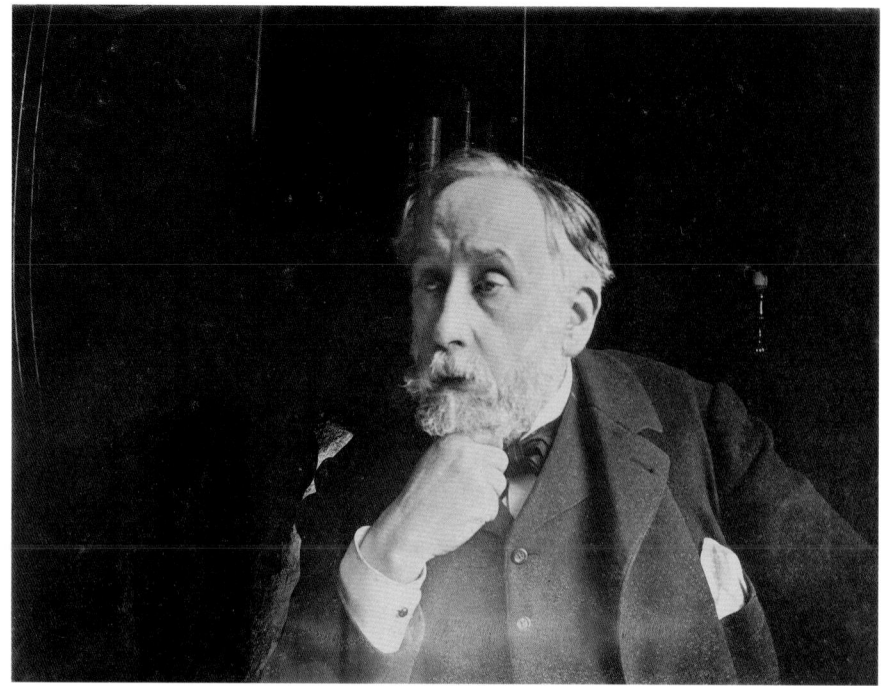

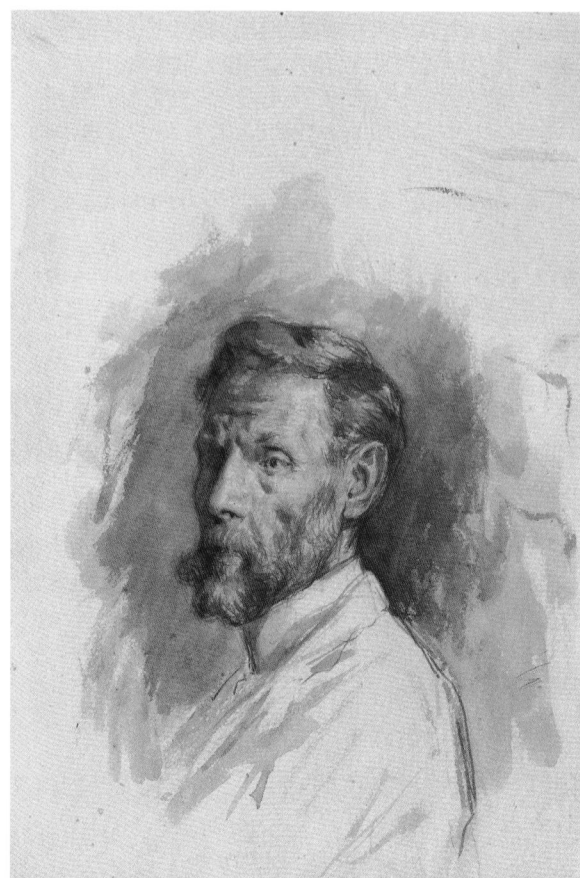

245
Edgar Degas
Self-Portrait, c. 1895.
Original photograph with modifications in ink possibly made by Pablo Picasso. Inscribed on the reverse in Picasso's hand "Portrait P. H. / de E. Degas," 20.5 x 26 cm. Private collection. Courtesy Fundación Almine y Bernard Ruiz-Picasso para el Arte

246
Pablo Picasso
Portrait of the Artist's Father, 1896. Watercolor on paper, 25.5 x 17.8 cm. Museu Picasso, Barcelona (MPB 110.331)

247

André Gomès

(French, d. 1997)

La Californie, 1958.

Photograph. Archives
Picasso, Musée national
Picasso, Paris

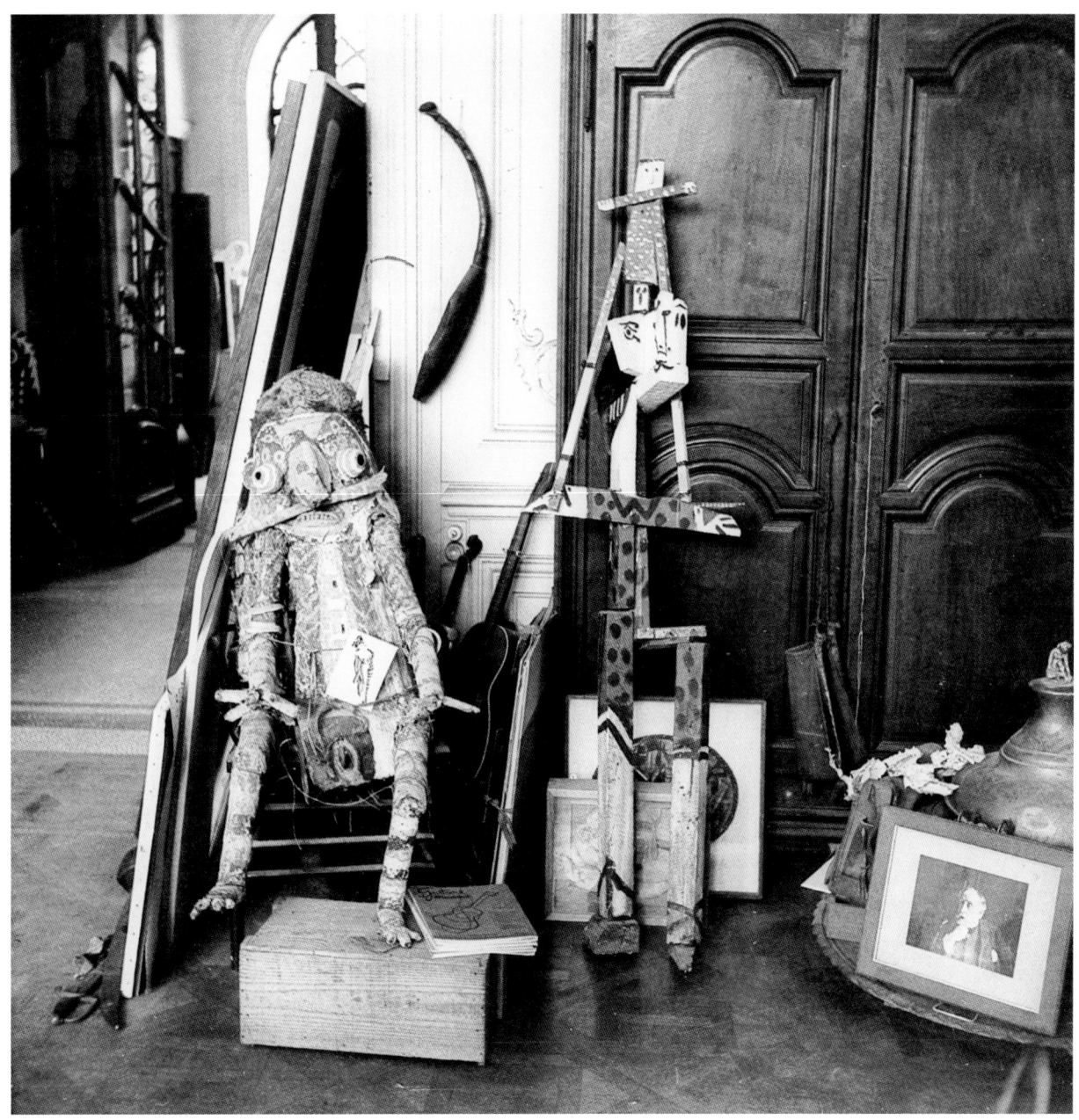

— all his homes were cluttered to a heroic, bewildering degree — but the pictures and objects in his collection were like companions and he was not ashamed of their innate shortcomings. This said, he was immensely proud of certain acquisitions, notably Matisse's *Still Life with Oranges* of 1912 and his Cézanne landscapes: friends would be invited to gaze and genuflect, Picasso enthusing, "Impossible to do anything better!" or "It's magnificent!"[57]

If Picasso's collection seems haphazard and the quality patchy — when the works donated to the French state were unveiled in 1978 there was a chorus of disappointed and disparaging comments[58] — this has much to do with the opportunistic way he went about assembling it. His preferred method was to make exchanges with dealers like Vollard, Paul Rosenberg, or Louise Leiris (who took over the running of Kahnweiler's gallery), off-setting their debts to him by taking pictures they happened to have in stock. More often than not, the dealer made the first move.[59] It was a habit that started early: Picasso's first Corot was acquired in 1910 by exchange with the German dealer Wilhelm Uhde, who got in return the splendid Cubist portrait Picasso had just painted of him.[60] In this case the dealer unquestionably came out on top because the Corot in question is a feeble work of dubious authenticity.[61] Picasso ended up with relatively high numbers of pictures by Cézanne and Renoir partly because both Vollard and Rosenberg stocked their work. If they had proposed paintings by Ingres and Delacroix, his collection might have had a rather different complexion.

When it came to Degas's brothel monotypes, Picasso seems to have taken the initiative to a greater degree than usual. He told John Richardson that he had tried to persuade Vollard to part with some but that Vollard had always refused.[62] When he first broached the matter is unknown — there is no mention of Degas in the letters from Vollard preserved in the Archives Picasso (Musée national Picasso, Paris) — but a faint echo of their wrangling survives in the form of vintage photographs of eight brothel monotypes identical to their equivalents in the Fonds Vollard.[63] Since all but one (*Courtesans*, mentioned above [see 240]) reproduce monotypes included in the posthumous sale of Degas's prints, Picasso must have obtained them at some point after November 1918. Perhaps, having refused to sell the originals, Vollard gave them to him as a sop.

There is no doubt that Picasso obtained the photographs well before June 1936, when he acquired from Vollard a copy of his edition of Guy de Maupassant's *La Maison Tellier*, with its superb reproductions of some thirty-six of the brothel monotypes.[64] Vollard lavished enormous time and effort on this and its successor, Pierre Louÿs's *Mimes des courtisanes de Lucien* (1935), and he was as proud of them as any of the *livres d'artistes* for which he commissioned original prints by Picasso, among others. In his memoirs Vollard describes the "emotions" he went through "while the reproduction of Degas's monotypes was being carried out." Few of the originals, he explains, belonged to him. Most belonged to Maurice Exsteens, who had inherited them in 1919 from his father-in-law Gustave Pellet, together with his publishing house and the entire stock of his gallery. Exsteens agreed to loan them to Vollard for as long as necessary, but Vollard lived in terror that someone would make an irresistible offer for the lot before the facsimiles were ready. In the event, it took a full six years to complete them.[65] So, between about 1928 and 1935, when *Mimes des courtisanes* came out, a substantial number of Degas's original monotypes were in Vollard's hands. These were years when Picasso's relationship with the dealer was particularly close. Not only was he at work on the etchings Vollard had commissioned for a new edition of Balzac's *Le Chef d'oeuvre inconnu* (published in 1931) but also on the one hundred prints, executed

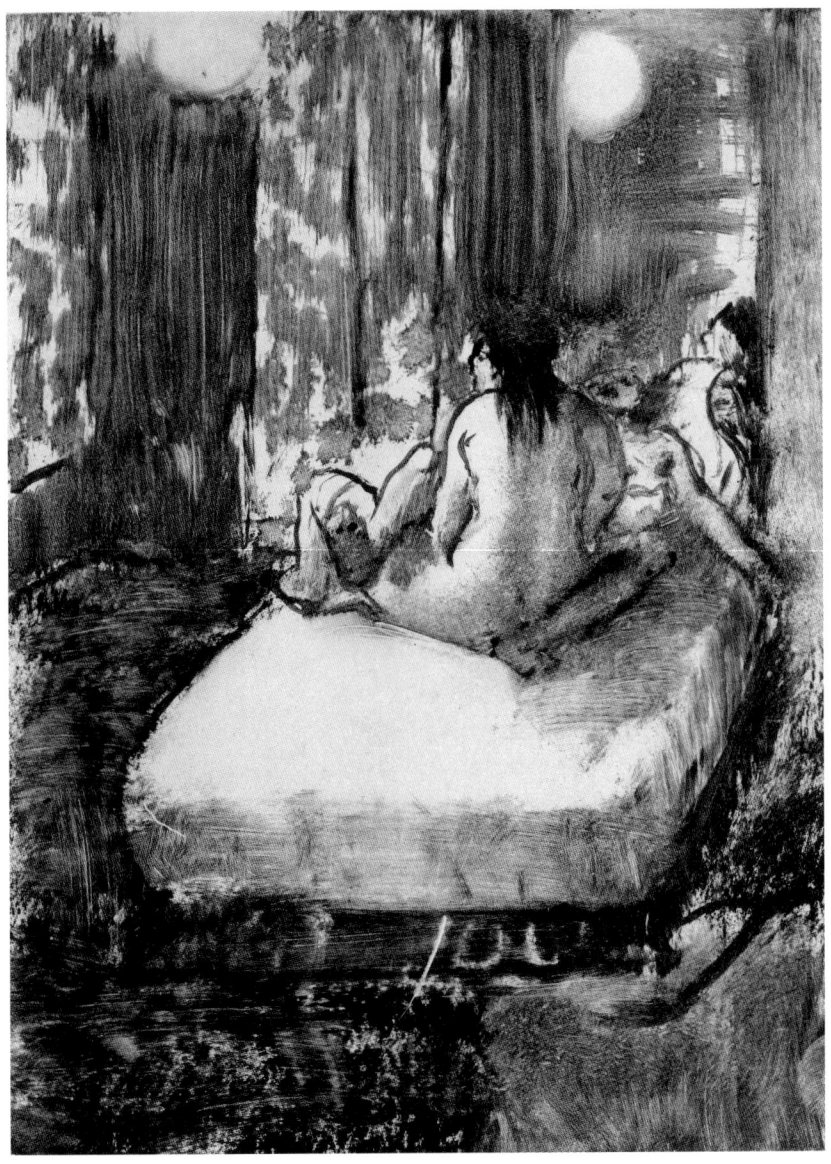

248
Edgar Degas
On the Bed, c. 1876–77.
Monotype, 16 x 11.7 cm.
Musée national Picasso,
Paris (RF 3592)

them.[66] The garrulous Vollard no doubt told all the piquant stories about Degas he tells in his various books — and more besides, for Picasso was an inveterate gossip and was fascinated by the enigma of Degas's private life.

The modest cache of vintage photographs and the copy of *La Maison Tellier* testify to the longevity and constancy of Picasso's desire to possess some of Degas's brothel monotypes — "the best things he ever did"[67] — and when the chance at last presented itself, he pounced. Richardson has described the occasion. Picasso had been invited to dinner at the Château de Castille, the flamboyant, colonnaded, Neoclassical mansion near Avignon owned by Richardson's partner Douglas Cooper, and his roving eye settled immediately on *On the Bed* (**248**), which Richardson had recently bought "for a pittance" from the Parisian dealers Paul Brame and César de Hauke.[68] One of the more sexually explicit of Degas's prints, it depicts a client flat on his back on a bed with a prostitute camped between his spread-eagled legs. One can guess what intimate service she is providing, but the act itself is screened from view by her ample back. Picasso's reaction to the print was so candidly covetous that Richardson felt he had no option but to present it to him; in return, he received a fine drawing.[69] So, a deal of the kind Picasso especially liked was struck: he had acquired his first Degas without money changing hands. What Richardson may not have known is that Picasso owned a Vollard photograph of this very monotype:[70] when he saw the original in the Château de Castille, he must have experienced the thrill of recognition. Either on this occasion or much later, "Picasso singled out the physicality of Degas's 'pig-faced whores' for admiration. 'You can smell them,' he said."[71]

The dinner probably took place in the early summer of 1958, and documents reveal the crucial role played subsequently by Douglas Cooper. On 15 January 1958 Desmond Corcoran, director of the Lefevre Gallery in London, who was in

between 1930 and 1937, that were published eventually as *Suite Vollard*. Furthermore, when in 1936 Picasso needed a refuge for his mistress Marie-Thérèse Walter and their baby daughter Maya after his separation from Olga, Vollard lent him his house in Le Tremblay-sur-Mauldre — proof if proof were needed of their intimacy, for very few of Picasso's other friends were even aware of Marie-Thérèse's existence. One can imagine Picasso's pleasure as he pored over the monotypes with Vollard, both men relishing these tasty little "*plats du jour*," as Degas called

the habit of consulting Cooper over the authenticity of works by Picasso that came his way, wrote to thank him for sorting out the latest of these questions and in closing mentioned his plan to mount a Degas exhibition.[72] Some ten days later Corcoran wrote again to describe the content of the show and to invite Cooper to "write a foreword to our catalogue, really more in the form of an essay dealing with the monotypes, and the great part they played in Degas' art." Cooper agreed and in subsequent letters advised Corcoran about possible sources of additional prints. The opening of the show was scheduled for 15 April and such was the rush in the days leading up to it that the first edition of the catalogue had a typed insert listing works added at the eleventh hour.[73] The correspondence also reveals that Corcoran had agreed in principle to take three monotypes Richardson owned and to sell them for him.[74]

The exhibition closed at the end of May. On 9 June 1958 Corcoran reported to Cooper that it had not done "too badly" from the point of view of sales and that, as regarded critical esteem, "it could not have been better." So, Cooper knew that some monotypes were still available and, witnessing Picasso's excitement in the presence of *On the Bed*, he told the artist where others could be obtained and undertook to act as intermediary: "*Only* the brothel scenes, Picasso insisted, none of the colorful landscapes, which he disdained as too 'artistic', too 'abstract.'"[75]

Picasso's instructions are worth pausing over momentarily because they tell us much about his attitude to Degas and to art in general. In his eyes, the landscape monotypes were too seductively beautiful, with their daringly simplified compositions, intense but subtle color harmonies, and "sublime" romantic mood — too much like the "Rothkos" of Degas's oeuvre. Even when still a teenager Picasso had ridiculed the fashionable cult of "art for art's sake" and he was much attracted to Degas at that time because he was not an "aesthete" but

a "painter of modern life." By 1958, Picasso's vocal hostility to abstraction had become bad-tempered: abstract art seemed to be sweeping all before it everywhere in the international avant-garde, threatening not just his reputation as the leading artist of his generation but everything he stood for.[76] In this context, the purchase of Degas's brothel monotypes has a polemical edge: they represented what art should do and be about — the open-eyed expression of smelly, brutish, ugly, carnal, "pig-faced" reality.

It was not just their fundamental realism and their hard-nosed message that sex and the sex trade are driving forces in society that appealed so much to Picasso. He also relished their picaresque aspect: the familiar cast of louche characters snapped in momentary, telling poses, pulling telling faces, making telling gestures; the sense of an on-going narrative that is left just open-ended enough for the spectator to enjoy inventing a plausible story for himself; and, last but not least, their wit and humor, occasionally benign, mostly caustic. These "novelistic" qualities have led historians to hunt fruitlessly for a specific literary source: no doubt Degas was influenced to an extent by the prevailing fashion for stories about prostitutes, but his relationship to them is oblique, not illustrative.[77] Thus there is no connection between them and Guy de Maupassant's *La Maison Tellier*, despite Vollard's determination to link the two. Much the same might be said of Picasso's relationship even to those texts, including Balzac's *Le Chef d'oeuvre inconnu*, for which he provided images on commission: he never illustrated them directly although he used the author's principal themes as his catalyst.

When Picasso was in one of his periodic phases of intensive drawing or printmaking, his (usually repressed) penchant for the narrative tradition in which he had been trained by his father tended to bubble up and he would create characters and spin amusing and picaresque story lines. The etchings collected in

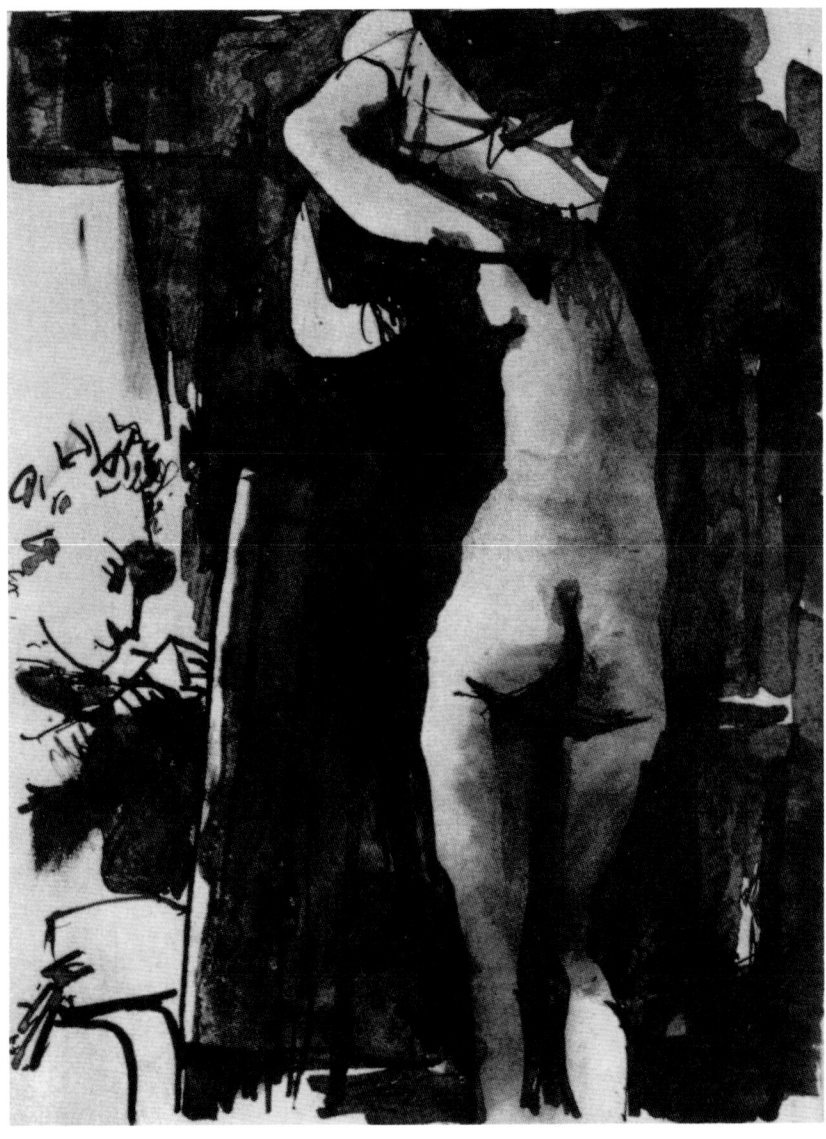

249

Pablo Picasso

Model Undressing,
28 November 1953.
Ink and wash on paper,
24 x 18 cm.
Private collection

which riff wryly on the time-honoured theme of the painter and his model and the complex relationship between desire and creativity. Many of these drawings set up humorous, stereotypical situations that invite a light, narrative reading: a beautiful young model posing before a myopic, elderly painter; a fat, droopy old model posing improbably for a classicizing allegory; a beautiful young model completely ignored while the artist listens bemused to the discourse of a pompous critic, and so on.[79] One of the first in the suite shows a model from the back pulling off her clothes within a shadowy studio (**249**) — her pose is strikingly similar to that of the nude in Degas's *Leaving the Bath* (see 179) — and the diligent painter crammed into the corner of the composition recalls Degas's ogling clients (see 238). The use of wash and the masterful speed and freedom of Picasso's brush drawing cannot but remind one of Degas's astonishingly dynamic monotype technique.

At Picasso's instigation, on 26 July 1958 Cooper opened his campaign by writing to Desmond Corcoran: "I have a friend who MIGHT be interested in some of your DEGAS monotypes. Would you let me know if any of the following are still for sale, and at what price — not too exaggerated." The whole business was to be conducted discreetly ("Please don't say anything about this to De Hauke"). There followed a list of nine prints, two of which were among those in Picasso's hoard of Vollard photographs.[80] All had been reproduced in facsimile either in *La Maison Tellier* or *Mimes des courtisanes*, so Picasso was not buying "unseen." Corcoran wrote back immediately listing the prices (ranging from £550 to £2000) of the seven that were still available and agreeing to a twenty percent discount on all but one of them.[81] The haggling continued by telephone and on 5 August the deal was concluded: the anonymous friend had rejected the monotype for which no discount was forthcoming but

the *Vollard Suite*, which were created independently of any literary text, are a case in point, and when Picasso showed them to Françoise Gilot in 1943 at the beginning of their liaison, he wove tales about the sculptor, the minotaur, and his other protagonists, commenting about their behavior and motivation just as if he were a novelist recounting a plot.[78] After the relationship with Gilot came to an end, Picasso entertained and consoled himself during the winter of 1953–54 not by painting moody landscapes but by producing 180 drawings, the majority of

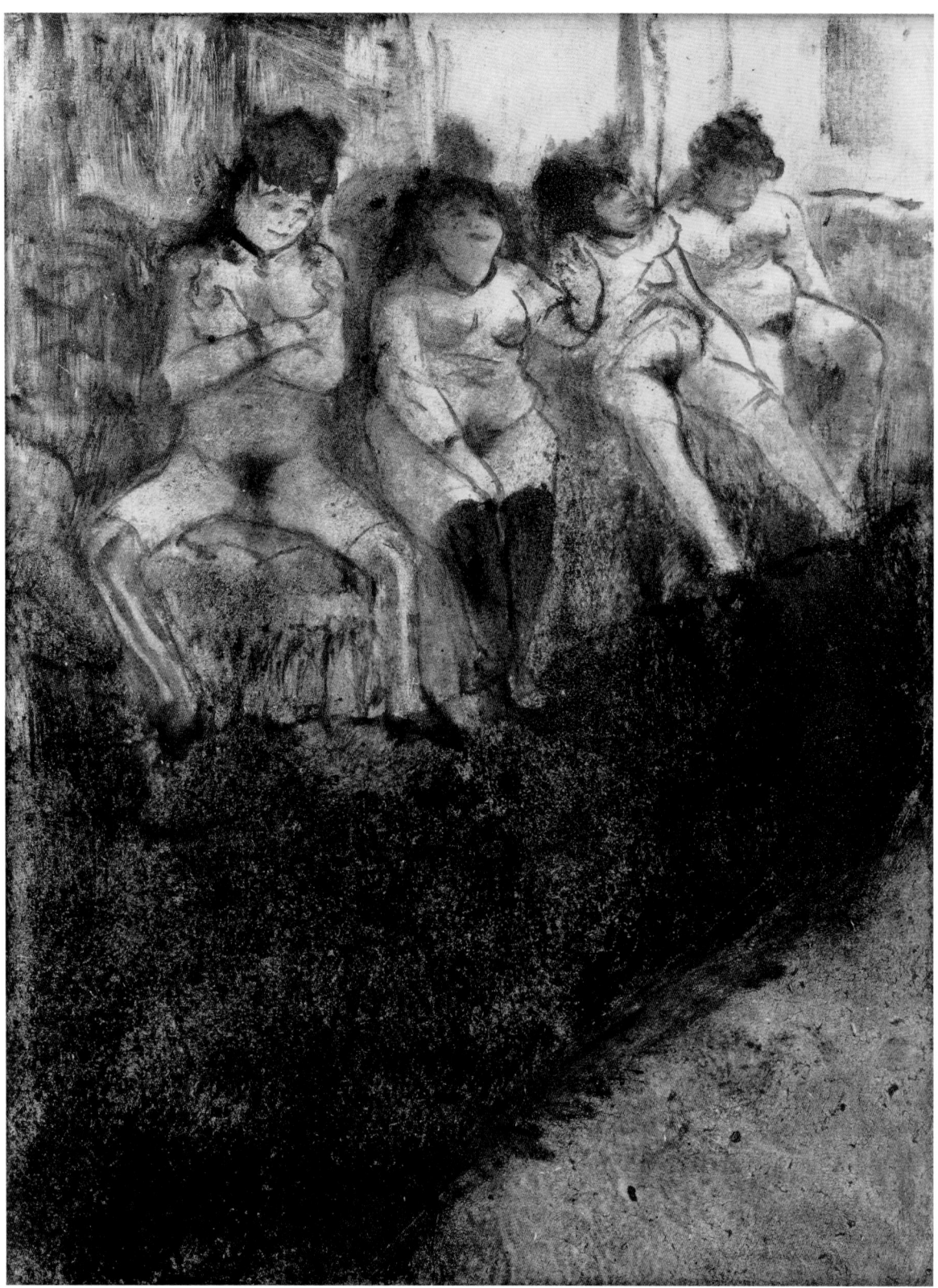

250

Edgar Degas

Waiting (Second Version),
c. 1876–77. Monotype,
21 x 15.9 cm. Musée
national Picasso, Paris
(RF 35786)

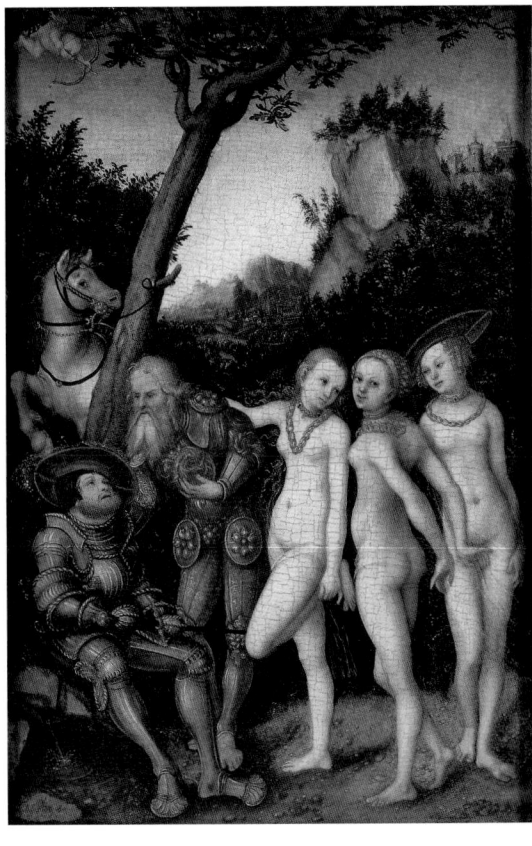

251

Lucas Cranach the Elder

(German, 1472–1553)

The Judgment of Paris,
1530. Oil on wood,
34.3 x 22.2 cm. Staatliche
Kunsthalle, Karlsruhe

would take the remaining six (**250**; see also 208, 258, 269, 272, 279). Did Picasso decide against the seventh simply because he was irked by the refusal to lower the price? Or, on second thought, did he find it the least interesting? (A plump, ungainly nude woman is seen from the back scratching between her buttocks, but there is no sign of a client and, relatively speaking, the image is less raunchy than the others he chose.) At all events, the global price for the six he took was set at £5700 — a discount of twenty-five percent and a rounded-down figure.[82] Further correspondence dealt with transport — in the car of a mutual friend, Lord Basil Amultree — and the transfer of the money.

Throughout the negotiations the identity of the buyer remained a secret. But Corcoran was not fooled: "I am glad," he wrote to Cooper, "you are pleased about everything, and if by chance it is Picasso, that he is too. There have

been rumours here about his interest in them."[83] The correspondence also reveals that Cooper made the tidy sum of 1,500,000 francs for his efforts as go-between. In a letter to Picasso confirming the deal, he mentions a global sum of "Frs. Français 8,250,000,"[84] whereas in a letter to Corcoran dated 14 August he gives the exchange rate for £5700 as "Frs. 6,750,000."[85] No doubt, both dealer and client knew that something of the sort was happening, but one can understand why Cooper wanted to keep them apart.

As a coda to the whole transaction, on 23 August Cooper sent Picasso a postcard of Cranach's jewel-like panel of *The Judgment of Paris* in Karlsruhe (**251**): "Here are some other ladies to keep the earlier ones company!"[86] He knew that Picasso was a great admirer of Cranach, but the joke was the difference between the svelte, alluring, flirtatious goddesses and Degas's jaded, unappetizing whores carelessly displaying their private parts to their petit bourgeois customers.[87] (As we shall see, there is reason to believe that Picasso did not forget Cooper's witty pairing.) By the beginning of August 1958, Picasso was, then, in possession of seven of his nine brothel monotypes. Some two years later, again through Cooper, he acquired an eighth, *Three Seated Prostitutes, Viewed from Behind* (see 233). It had been in the Lefevre Gallery exhibition but not on Picasso's original list of "wants," and Cooper's letter makes it clear that he had shown Picasso a color reproduction and was acting on behalf of the unnamed owner. The addition of pastel made it far more expensive than any of the monotypes Picasso bought in 1958: Cooper cites "9 millions d'anciens francs français," no doubt factoring in something for himself.[88] Picasso agreed. Yet, when, less than a year later, a London dealer offered to sell him the lesbian scene enhanced with pastel that had been on his list of "wants," Picasso did not take the bait.[89] Possibly he was distracted: the story of his "secret" marriage

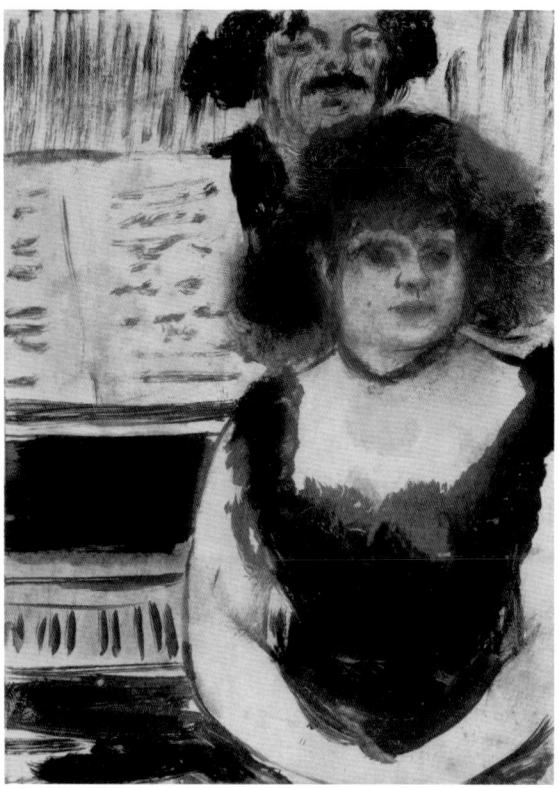

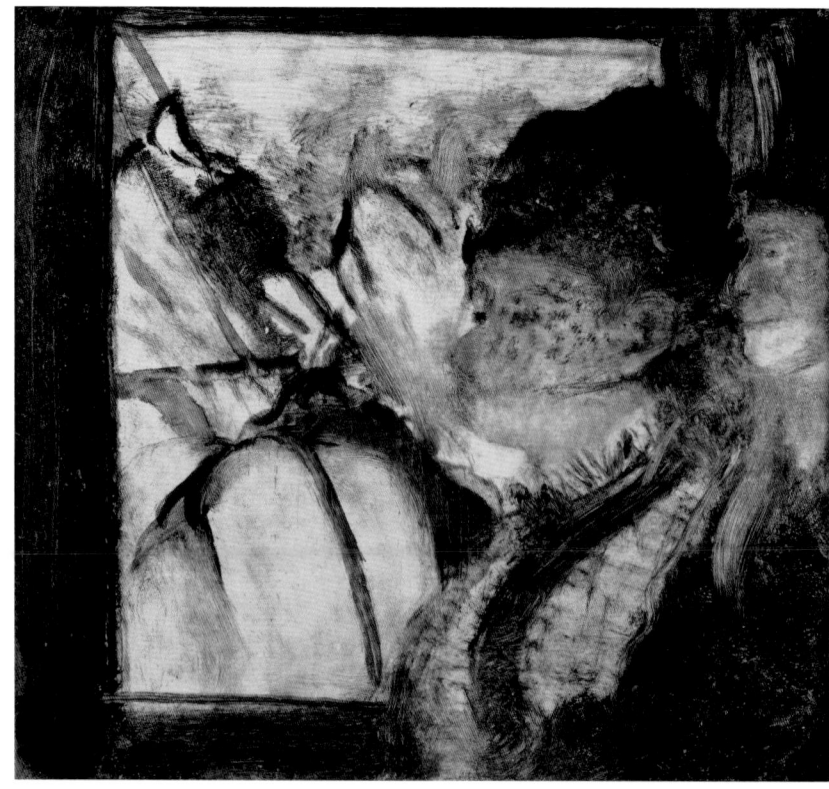

to Jacqueline Roque had just broken, and to escape the pack of intrusive journalists, the couple had fled Cannes and were keeping a very low profile.[90] But Picasso's aversion to dealers — unless the dealer happened to be a long-standing associate — is the more likely reason for his unresponsiveness. Had Douglas Cooper brokered the deal, this sale might also have gone through.

The Madame's Name Day (see 259) is the acknowledged masterpiece of the entire brothel series by Degas and, frustratingly, all efforts to discover how and when Picasso acquired it have so far proved fruitless. He owned a Vollard photograph and the facsimile in *La Maison Tellier*, but the original was not in the Lefevre Gallery show. Did he purchase it directly from César de Hauke, as Richardson surmises, and if so, was the purchase made in 1958 or later?[91] And was it on the same occasion that he bought two other monotypes said to have been in the hands of

de Hauke's business partner Paul Brame, *Pianist and Singer* (**252**) and *In the Omnibus* (**253**)? Neither belongs to the brothel series but, assuming that they were purchases rather than gifts, Picasso's interest in them is not hard to fathom. Both have the witty, observant, caricatural qualities he appreciated in the brothel monotypes, and while *Pianist and Singer* takes up the entertainment theme he himself had treated when he first came to Paris and discovered Degas's work (see 68, 75), *In the Omnibus* unmistakably pays homage to the lithographs of Daumier, an artist Picasso (like Degas) rated very highly. As for *The Maid* (see 283), the twelfth monotype in Picasso's collection, it was another present from John Richardson.[92]

If Picasso's acquisition of his Degas monotypes was largely a matter of luck, the time was unquestionably ripe, for he was then in the midst of a sustained and absorbing dialogue with favorite "Old Masters" who, as he ruefully

252

Edgar Degas

Pianist and Singer, c. 1877. Pastel and watercolor over monotype, 16 x 12 cm. Musée national Picasso, Paris (RF 35789)

253

Edgar Degas

In the Omnibus, c. 1877–78. Monotype, 27.7 x 29.8 cm. Musée national Picasso, Paris (RF 35792)

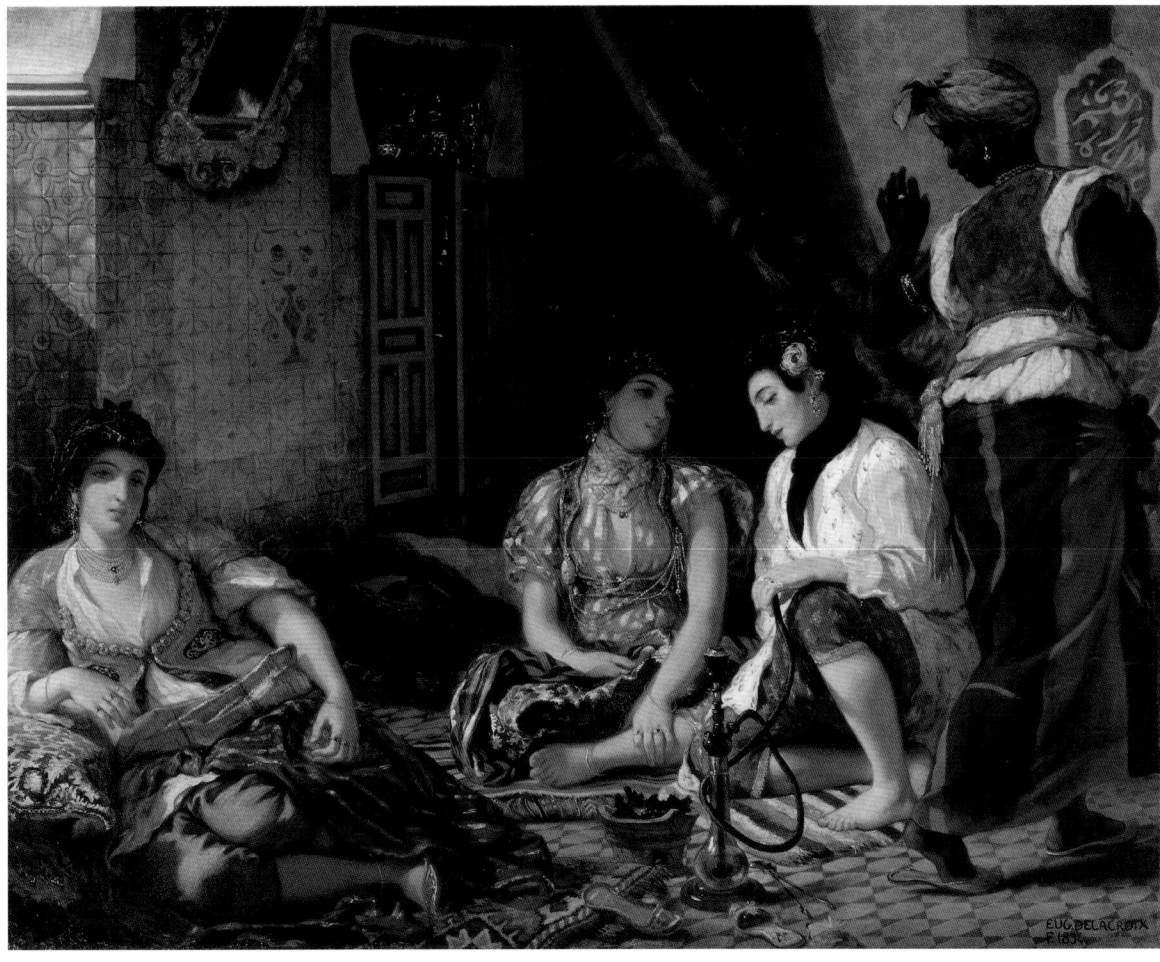

liked to say, insisted on joining him in his studio and forcing their way into his thoughts and work: "I have a feeling that Delacroix, Giotto, Tintoretto, El Greco, and the rest, as well as all the modern painters, the good and the bad, the abstract and the non-abstract, are all standing behind me watching me at work."[93]

The first of Picasso's extended series of variations was dedicated to Delacroix's great harem painting *The Women of Algiers in Their Apartment* (**254**), a subject that, as the evolution of *Les Demoiselles d'Avignon* reveals, he considered barely distinguishable from that of the brothel. Like prostitutes, odalisques live confined in a secluded, feminine environment; like prostitutes, they wait; like prostitutes, they find pleasant ways of passing the time that

will scandalize puritans. None of the Delacroix variations, not even the first, reproduces the composition of *The Women of Algiers in Their Apartment* closely, but Picasso's most dramatic invention — a naked, sleeping odalisque with a twisting torso, whose intertwined legs are flung up vertically — appeared only after a delay of about three weeks, initially in drawings and then in the third canvas in the series dated 28 November 1954 (**255**).[94] The bizarre pose of the sleeper has aroused speculation about Picasso's likely inspiration, for in all these series he dialogued with several artists simultaneously, not just with the author of his prime source. Ingres is surely involved, for the rolling, twisting motion of the odalisque and interlocking of her legs are like a Cubist interpretation of the extraordinary anatomy of his *Grande odalisque*, which Picasso had freely "copied" at about the time he completed *Les Demoiselles d'Avignon*.[95] But John Elderfield has rightly pointed to the similarity to Degas's prostitutes thrusting their legs in the air.[96] If Picasso had not seen any prints of this type in 1906 when he made the drawings described earlier (see 239, 240), he would certainly have seen several of the originals in the late 1920s and 1930s chez Vollard when the facsimiles were being prepared.[97]

Shortly after completing the Delacroix paintings and the related suite of etchings and aquatints, Picasso produced a few prints on the theme of *l'attente* (**256**). The naked women, coarse-featured and running to fat, look bored and fed up. The numbingly banal routine of life in a cheap, dozy, neighborhood brothel is evoked with devastating clarity.[98] In making this effortless transition from "high" art — the Delacroix variations — to "low" caricature, Picasso drew closer to the world of Degas's monotypes, and there is more than a whiff of imitation about them. Picasso's prostitutes are of exactly the same physical type as Degas's (see 272). Certain poses read like quotations, and the mood and atmosphere are much the same. Moreover, although Goya's use of aquatint was certainly an inspiration, Picasso's experiments with it in these prints produce lively, transitory effects comparable to those achieved by Degas through smearing, brushing, blotting, and scratching into the greasy ink. Like Degas, whose very physical approach to producing his monotypes is registered in innumerable fingerprints, "Picasso didn't mind the mess" of the aquatint process.[99]

The Delacroix variations, this mini-series of etchings, and drawings from the series created in the winter of 1953–54 (see 249) disclose that Degas was in Picasso's thoughts several years before he came into possession of any of the coveted monotypes. It was a clear case of overdetermination. That Degas should have re-entered Picasso's studio arm-in-arm, as it

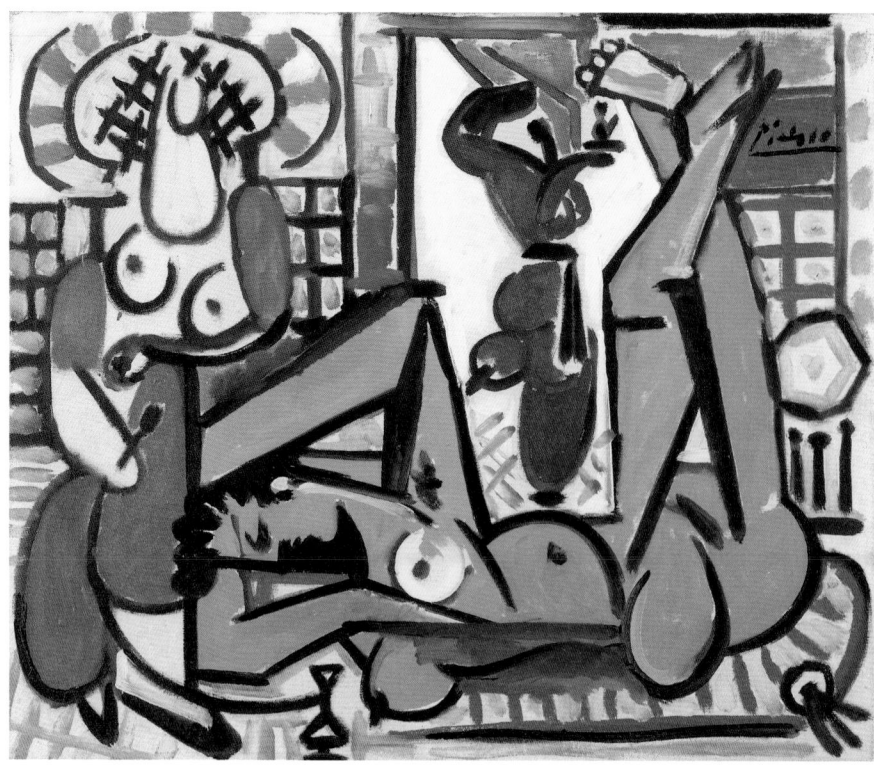

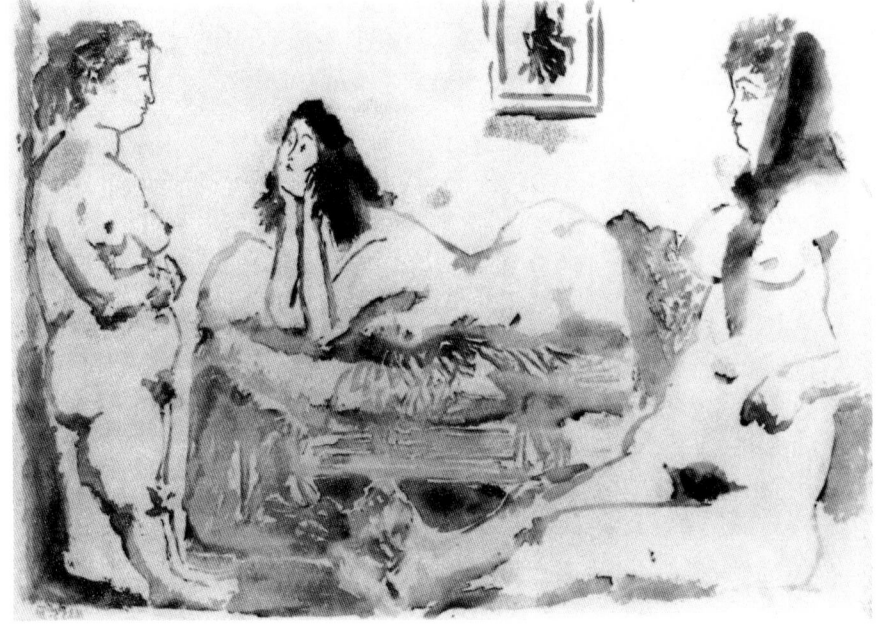

255

Pablo Picasso

The Women of Algiers,
after Delacroix, Version E,
16 January 1955. Oil on
canvas, 46 x 54.9 cm.
Museum of Modern Art,
San Francisco.
Gift of Wilbur D. May
(inv. 64.4)

256

Pablo Picasso

Brothel: Waiting I,
11 March 1955. Sugar-lift
aquatint with foul biting,
45 x 64.5 cm. Location
unknown

257

Pablo Picasso

Courtesans and
Bullfighters, 16 August
1959. Ink on paper,
50.5 x 65.6 cm.
Courtesy of Sotheby's

258

Edgar Degas

Resting, c. 1876–77.
Monotype, 16.4 x 21.6 cm.
Musée national Picasso,
Paris (RF 35787)

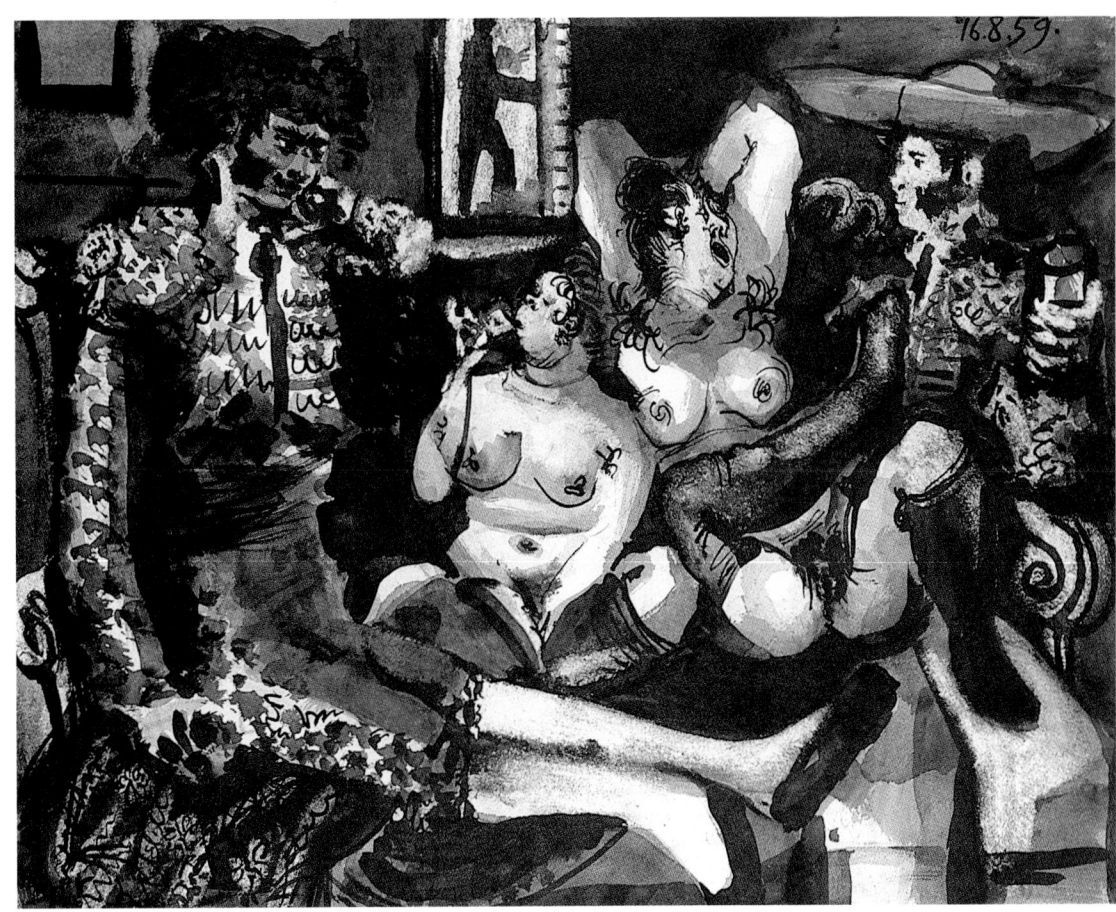

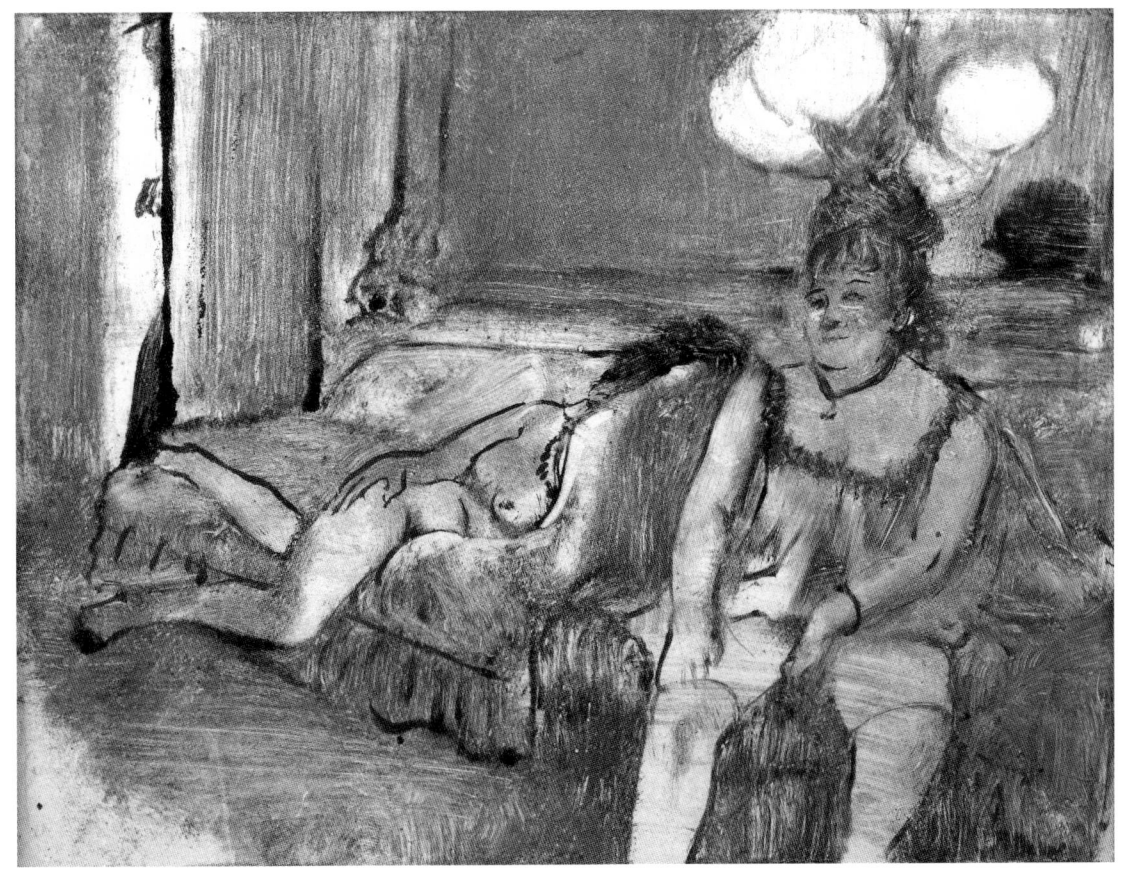

were, with Delacroix and Ingres — that this should have happened via *The Women of Algiers in Their Apartment* and Ingres's *Odalisques* — is not surprising, for Picasso was aware that Degas was passionately fond of both painters and had formed major collections of their work. Indeed, he may have concluded that Degas's *maisons closes* were conceived as a deflationary, modern-life rejoinder to their grandly romantic but passé Orientalism — conceived, that is, in the same ironic spirit as many of his abrasive, modernizing replies to Old Master paintings.

Although a decade or so passed before Picasso entered into an intensive dialogue with his Degas monotypes, a few drawings do seem to register a more or less immediate response. Thus the raucous whores carousing with a couple of bullfighters in an ink and wash drawing made in 1959 (**257**) are like their counterparts in several of the prints Picasso had recently acquired from the Lefevre Gallery (see 208, 250, 269, 272). But the comedy is broader, the effect coarser, and, avoiding obvious pastiche, Picasso transposed the scene to his native Spain. To underline this crucial change, he irreverently paraphrased the celebrated vignette of the figure silhouetted in the doorway of Velázquez's *Las Meninas*, thus identifying the top-hatted clients furtively entering Degas's brothels (**258**) with Philip IV's chamberlain.

The "actual drama of the man"

Picasso took great pleasure in displaying his brothel monotypes to friends, relishing their reaction to the subject matter and enjoying the opportunity to speculate outrageously about the artist's private motivation. Most accounts describe "exhibitions" that took place at Notre-Dame-de-Vie, the secluded old farmhouse in Mougins that became Picasso's final home in 1961 after his marriage to Jacqueline Roque. Aldo, the elder of the two Crommelynck brothers who acted as Picasso's printmakers throughout the Mougins years, recalled lengthy conversa-

tions: "He showed them to me and talked a lot about Degas as a human being as well as an artist. He appreciated how beautiful the monotypes were."[100]

Some visitors were shown the monotypes just before Picasso embarked on the suite of etchings in which Degas himself appears on stage — the first is dated 11 March 1971 (see 270) — or while he was actually in the midst of making them. The photographer Brassaï arrived at Notre-Dame-de-Vie that spring and talk turned quickly to Picasso's latest work:

*"After a period of doing only drawings," he tells me, "I've started again on a series of etchings. Wait, I want to show you something." He disappears into a cavern somewhere beyond the room in which we are gathered, and when he returns he is carrying an elaborately framed Degas monotype depicting a scene in a brothel [**259**]. The girls, clad only in long midnight blue stockings, are clustered around their madam, an old harridan dressed entirely in black, embracing her and kissing her cheeks. "It's called* La Fête de Madame,*" Picasso explains. "One of Degas's masterpieces, don't you think? It was the inspiration for the series of etchings I'm working on now."*[101]

Brassaï got the point immediately: "At the age of ninety, Picasso is returning to the theme of *Les Demoiselles d'Avignon*!" And he proceeded to comment on the exceptional intensity of Picasso's "erotic imaginings" and the sheer "lechery" expressed in these prints: "The sensuality which impregnates the drawings, etchings and paintings of these last years, the multitude of lustful attitudes, the flood of carnal embraces will probably reach its culminating point in this new series of etchings."[102]

Rightly or wrongly, William Rubin was convinced that his ribald conversations with Picasso about the monotypes were the catalyst for the Degas suite. They had three long meetings early in 1971 while Rubin negotiated the acquisition of the Cubist sheet-metal *Guitar* for the Museum of Modern Art. When the talk turned to Degas, Picasso "got very excited," went off "into a back room," and brought back the monotypes to show them to Rubin. Much of their conversation turned on Degas's mysterious sex life: "Picasso had poked me in the ribs with his elbow and said slyly: 'Hey! What do you think he was doing in those places?'" Rubin's subsequent comments give the flavor of what else must have been said: "It's well known, of course, that Degas did not have normal relations with women. He was a sort of neuter. In fact there is an essay by Paul Valéry in which there is a vague suggestion that Degas was a repressed homosexual."[103] Pierre Daix was privy to similar prurient ruminations when Picasso showed him the etching in which Degas appears formally attired and gripping a pad of paper (**260**):

"Do you think he came just to take notes? No one really knows what he did with women. . . . he would have given me a boot in the arse, old Degas, if he had seen himself like this!" Picasso then enlarged on the whole range of possibilities about Degas' sexuality: a pederast perhaps, but unaware of the fact? And of the vices he might have hoped to satisfy.[104]

The echoes of all this impertinent chatter, like the presence of Degas's photograph in the studio at La Californie, confirm that Picasso was almost as gripped by the man as by his art. Valéry's exceptionally penetrating, subtle, and vivid characterization in *Degas Danse Dessin* must have interested him deeply — may, indeed, have been a factor in his decision to acquire a copy of the book in 1937.[105] This concern with the man behind the work was typical of Picasso, in fact, tallying with his contempt for high-minded aestheticism and his identification with artists like Rembrandt who constantly drew, as he did himself, on the highs and lows of their private lives. In a conversation with Christian

Zervos in 1935 he famously remarked of two other favorite painters:

It's not what the artist does *that counts, but what he* is. *Cézanne would never have interested me a bit if he had lived and thought like Jacques Émile Blanche, even if the apple he painted had been ten times as beautiful. What forces our interest is Cézanne's anxiety — that's Cézanne's lesson; the torments of Van Gogh — that is the actual drama of the man. The rest is a sham.*[106]

According to Parmelin, Picasso venerated Van Gogh as "a sort of Christ of painting" and instead of one of his paintings, had put on display a blown-up copy of the original laconic report in an Arles newspaper of his brutal self-mutilation.[107] Degas, too, fitted Picasso's exemplary type of the anxious, driven, conflicted artist — the kind of artist who (like Cézanne) worked ceaselessly but could never "finish" anything, whose work was often "a sum of destructions" thanks to the perpetual process of revision, who was constantly experimenting yet who reverted to the same limited number of themes out of an obsession that bordered on mania. It must be the case that he settled on the brothel monotypes not just because of the qualities of subject matter and handling mentioned earlier but also because he believed that they, more nakedly than anything else Degas had created, revealed "the actual drama of the man." The landscape monotypes might be far more "beautiful," but from the human point of view, they were quite simply "a sham."

In taking so marked an interest in Degas's private life, Picasso was no different from the majority of critics. The nature of his relationships with women was a constant topic of speculation — increasingly unbuttoned speculation as the need or taste for discretion receded during the post-1945 period. That his unflattering representations of the scrawny "*rats*" of the Opéra and of mature women involved in their "*toilette*

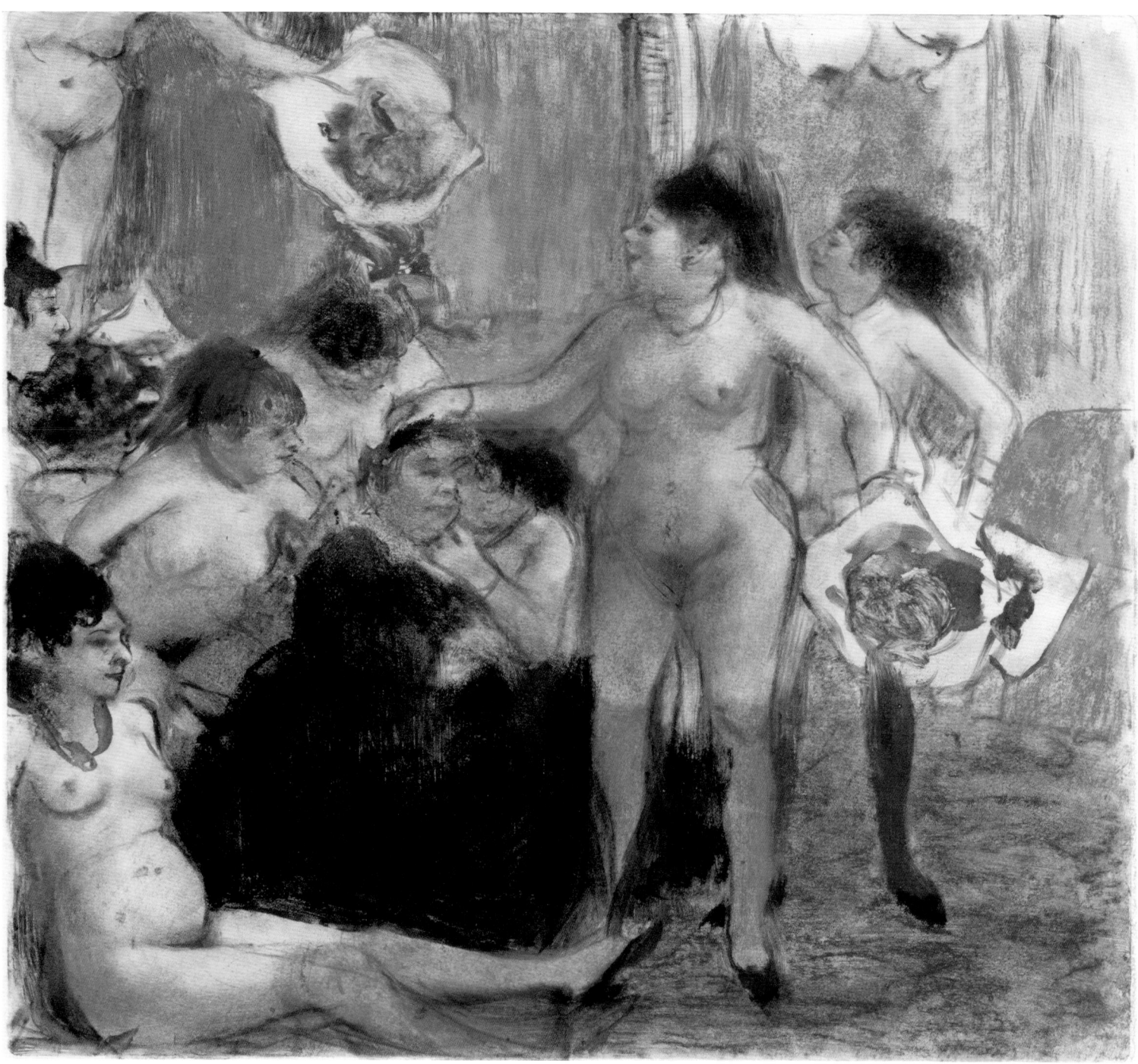

259

Edgar Degas

The Madame's Name Day

c. 1876–77. Pastel,

26.6 x 29.6 cm. Musée

national Picasso, Paris

(RF 35791)

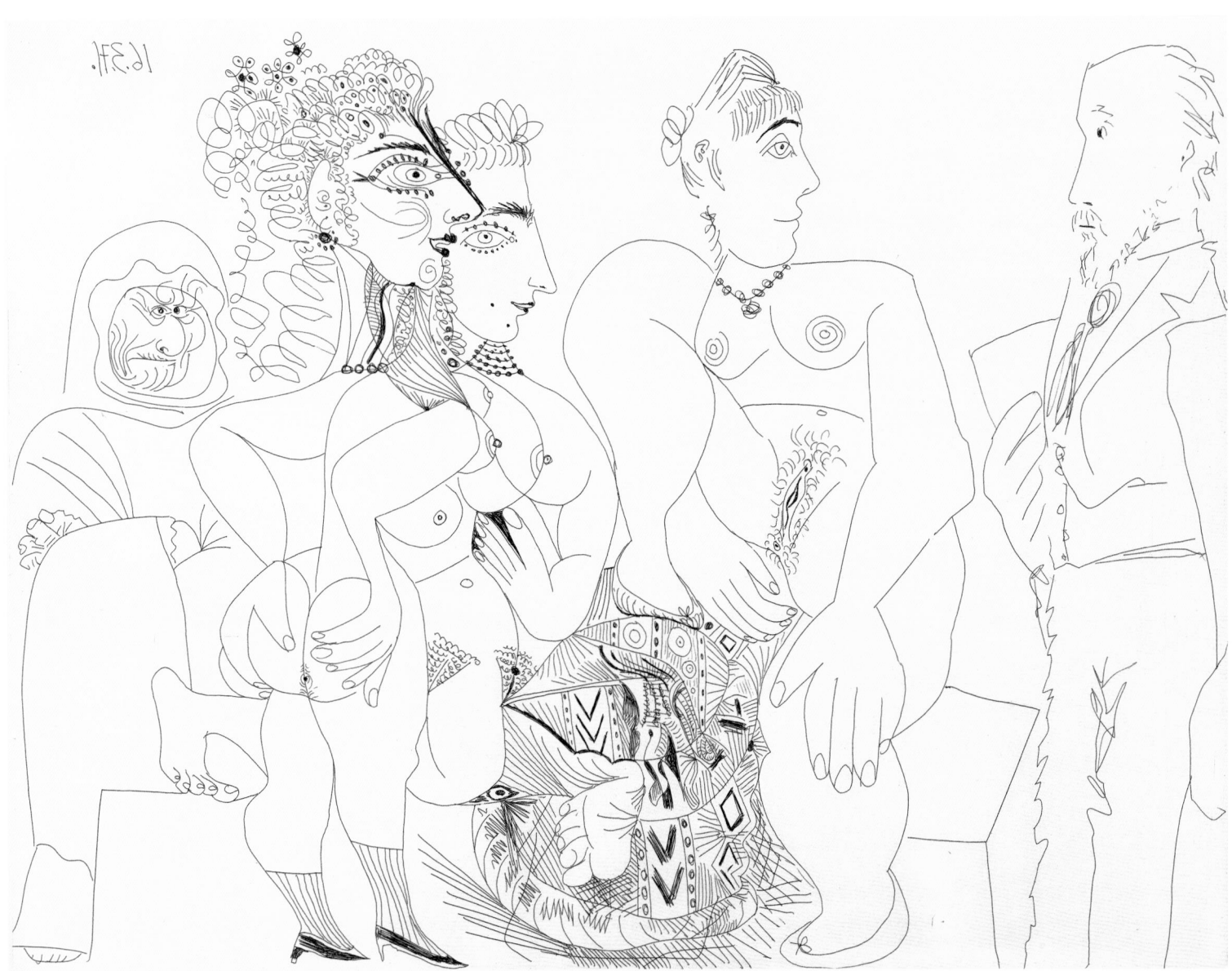

260

Pablo Picasso

*Brothel. Degas with His
Sketchbook, Celestina,
Three Prostitutes, and
a Moroccan Cushion*,
16 March 1971. Etching on
copper printed on paper
(Artist proof I/X), 36.7 x
49 cm. Museu Picasso,
Barcelona (MPB 112.232)

intime" sprang from deep-rooted "misogyny" had been a staple of Degas criticism since the 1880s, and the adjectives "pitiless," "merciless," "savage," and, above all, "cruel" were regularly trotted out by critics who admired his work profoundly.[108] The "tortured" bodies and "dislocated" poses typical of his female subjects, the critics implied, revealed a sadistic trait in the artist's nature. (Indeed, the frequency with which Degas's vision was characterized as "cruel" and his models' bodies as "tortured" deserves an essay of its own.) Recent research has modified the traditional view of Degas's sex life and proclivities quite significantly.[109] But none of that information was published during Picasso's lifetime, and he had no reason to doubt the received wisdom that Degas was literally chaste. During Degas's lifetime, studio chatter about the underlying reasons for his "chastity" was rife, and although his identity was masked when Van Gogh's celebrated letter to Émile Bernard on the subject was first published by Vollard in 1911, Picasso would have known who "X" was.[110] It is exactly the sort of tasty gossip he and Vollard enjoyed swapping.

Within a few years of Degas's death he was being defined, even by his most partisan admirers, as misanthropic and secretive, "prédestiné au célibat" (predestined to celibacy), and an artist whose vision of conjugal relationships was troublingly disenchanted.[111] Some attributed his behavior and his much-repeated, disparaging remarks about women to, in Vollard's words, "a kind of shame or modesty in which there was something like fear."[112] Not content with so abstract an account of his intimate psychology, others speculated about the likely causes of his "misogyny." Valéry, for instance, while attributing it to endemic melancholy — "His dark eye saw nothing in a rosy light" — thought that unhappy experiences with women must have played some part: "Of the sentimental side of his private life I know nothing: Our judgment of women is often the echo of our experience.

A man needs to be a kind of sage, to reproach nobody but himself when affairs of this nature leave him only with disgust, bitterness, or worse feelings still."[113]

Pierre Cabanne, who later wrote an influential biography of Picasso, could not let the subject of Degas's supposed chastity drop and came up with a mixed bag of explanations: repression following unhappy experiences, "incroyable pudeur" (incredible modesty), the "hautain" (haughty) detachment of an instinctive rationalist and moralist, and some secret physiological problem.[114] The view that Degas may have been "a repressed homosexual, who in youth perhaps . . . had closed down on his *education sentimentale* after some bitter experience, and had allowed passion to wither," was spelled out by Benedict Nicolson in an editorial published in 1963 in the august forum of the *Burlington Magazine*. Although he conceded that "there is no positive evidence whatever for this [homosexuality]," Nicolson bluntly rejected Degas's own explanation that "natural timidity" was the reason for his "failure with women": "timidity is no more than a convenient excuse for some deeper urge towards non-involvement."[115]

Cabanne's book on Degas came out in 1957 just before Picasso acquired his first brothel monotypes, and in it he posed more or less exactly the same questions about them as the artist did (albeit in rather fancier language). Did, Cabanne mused, "this prudish, chaste, 'principled' bourgeois" find "a means of liberation" in the brothels he depicted with such "implacable realism"? Was he tempted by "His Majesty Vice," by the secret world "where women, cloistered, imprisoned, delivered up to the basest instincts of men, opened up infinite horizons to the painter with keys of filth and gold?"[116] Unlike Picasso, Cabanne did not articulate what forms of "vice" Degas might have engaged in, but, like Picasso, he assumed that the brothel monotypes were not purely conventional in their imagery, that Degas was working from firsthand experience.

In Dialogue with Degas and His Monotypes: 1968

It was in 1968 that Picasso's sustained dialogue with Degas's brothel monotypes finally got underway. The immediate prelude seems to have been a recurrent anxiety dream about being robbed, which Picasso recounted to Roberto Otero on 12 March 1967. He would awake from his nightmare screaming "Stop thief!" and during periods of insomnia would fret about not having seen one of his "tiny" Degas pictures recently. Panic-stricken, he would wake Jacqueline and beg her to find it: "As soon as I see it, I can begin to think about something else. And sometimes we can't find it. That's frightful. Then I begin to suspect it was carried off by the person I last showed it to."[117] These neurotic fantasies suggest that one of Picasso's conscious or unconscious motives for cannibalizing the monotypes a few years later — especially his favorite, *The Madame's Name Day* — was the desire to keep and protect them in perpetuity by literally ingesting them.

Picasso's first move, however, was to paint what I believe to be an emblematic profile portrait of Degas — to join forces in the first instance with the man rather than his art (**261**). Dated 6 February 1968, the picture shows a bearded painter armed with his palette in the process of adding a touch to an unseen canvas. Technically, it is typical of Picasso's painting at this time: dashed off at high speed with a coarse, loaded brush and, probably, Ripolin household paint; a lot of bare white canvas; a seemingly careless, messy, childlike facture; a simple composition and stereotypical pose; highly abbreviated "signs" in lieu of naturalistic description (the Egyptian-style ideogram for the eyes, with horizontal marks to signify looking; squiggles for hair and beard; a circle and a horizontal line for the brush, and so on). The trait that identifies the painter as Degas is his extraordinary "ski-slope" nose, and when he came to depict Degas repeatedly three years later, Picasso gave him the same steeply rising

forehead, sloping nose, neat mouth, and full beard. Indeed, the Degas in the aquatint dated 11 April 1971 looks so similar to the man in the painting that the identification is confirmed beyond all reasonable doubt (**262**).[118]

Why should Degas have popped into Picasso's head on that particular day in February, momentarily ousting the musketeers and their ilk who peopled his paintings at this time? The prompt may have been a communication of some kind from the organizers of the exhibition devoted to Degas's monotypes that opened at the Fogg Art Museum (Cambridge, Massachusetts) on 25 April 1968. Although the exhibition itself was more limited in scope, its curator, Eugenia Parry Janis, had set herself to produce an illustrated checklist of the entire corpus. Picasso did not lend to the exhibition but someone must have been in touch with him, if only to get his permission to cite his name in the relevant entries.[119] He did receive a copy of the catalogue — Richardson came across it during a visit to Notre-Dame-de-Vie in 1984 — and in his late graphic work there are many echoes of monotypes he did not own himself.[120]

Within weeks of painting his portrait of Degas, Picasso began work on the great series of etchings known collectively as *Suite 347*. Between mid-March and early October 1968, all 347 were produced in a truly astounding burst of energy, and although this has been largely overlooked in the literature, the monotypes were clearly an important reference point for Picasso throughout.[121] Period and place change frequently in *Suite 347*, but naked women displaying themselves in all manner of poses and men observing the spectacle in a more or less excited state is the overarching theme. Sometimes the setting is an Ingresque harem, often a brothel with a gnarled, rapacious Celestina brokering a deal between voluptuous young prostitutes and their clients, usually costumed as musketeers. These scenes mutate easily into the primal scene of the painter with his posing

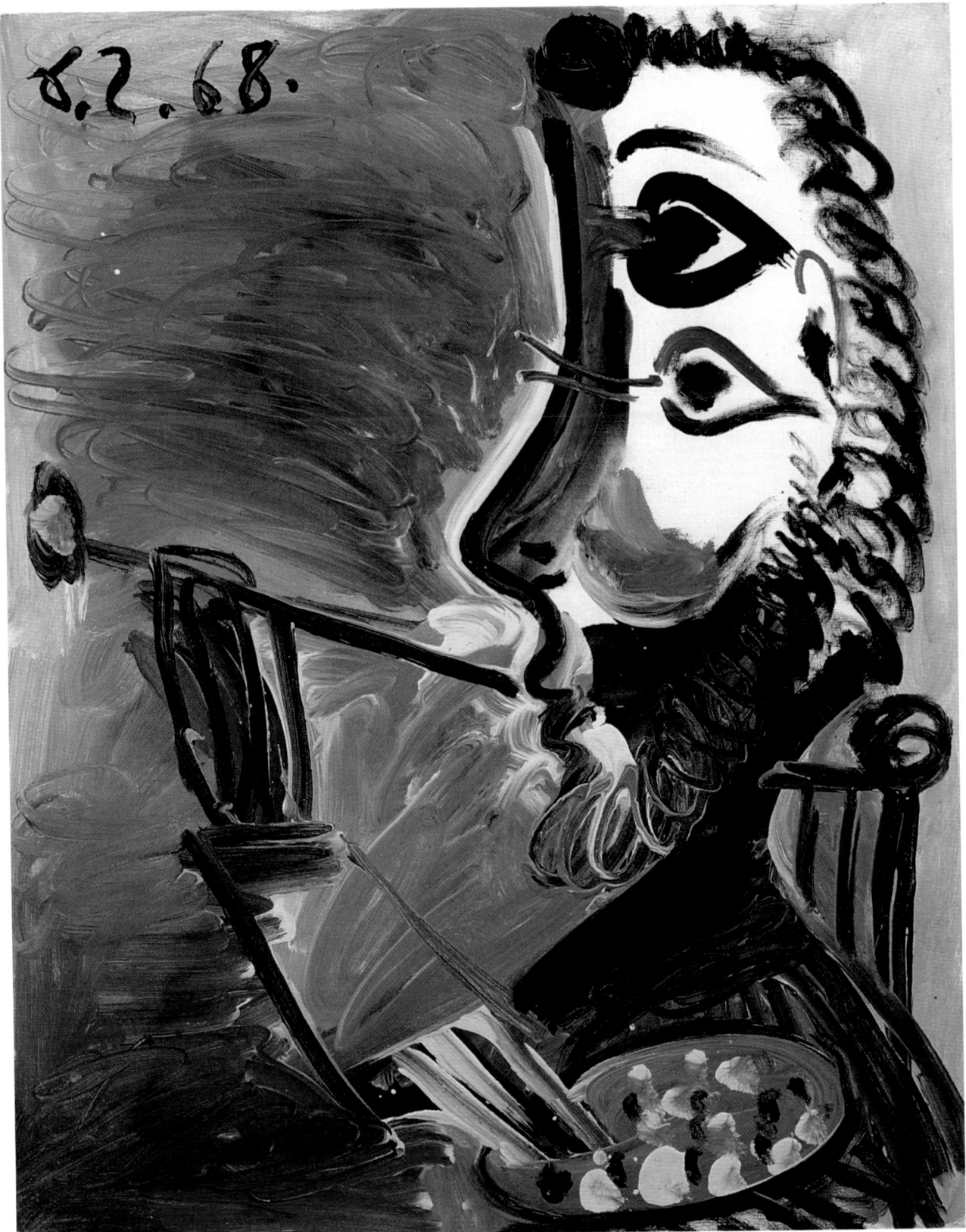

261

Pablo Picasso

An Artist (Portrait of Degas?), 6 February 1968. Oil on canvas, 81 x 65 cm. Private collection

262

Pablo Picasso

Degas Fantasizing. Faun Whispering in a Woman's Ear, 11 April 1971. Sugar-lift aquatint with foul biting on copper printed on paper (Artist proof I/XV), 36.5 x 49.2 cm. Museu Picasso, Barcelona (MPB 112.213)

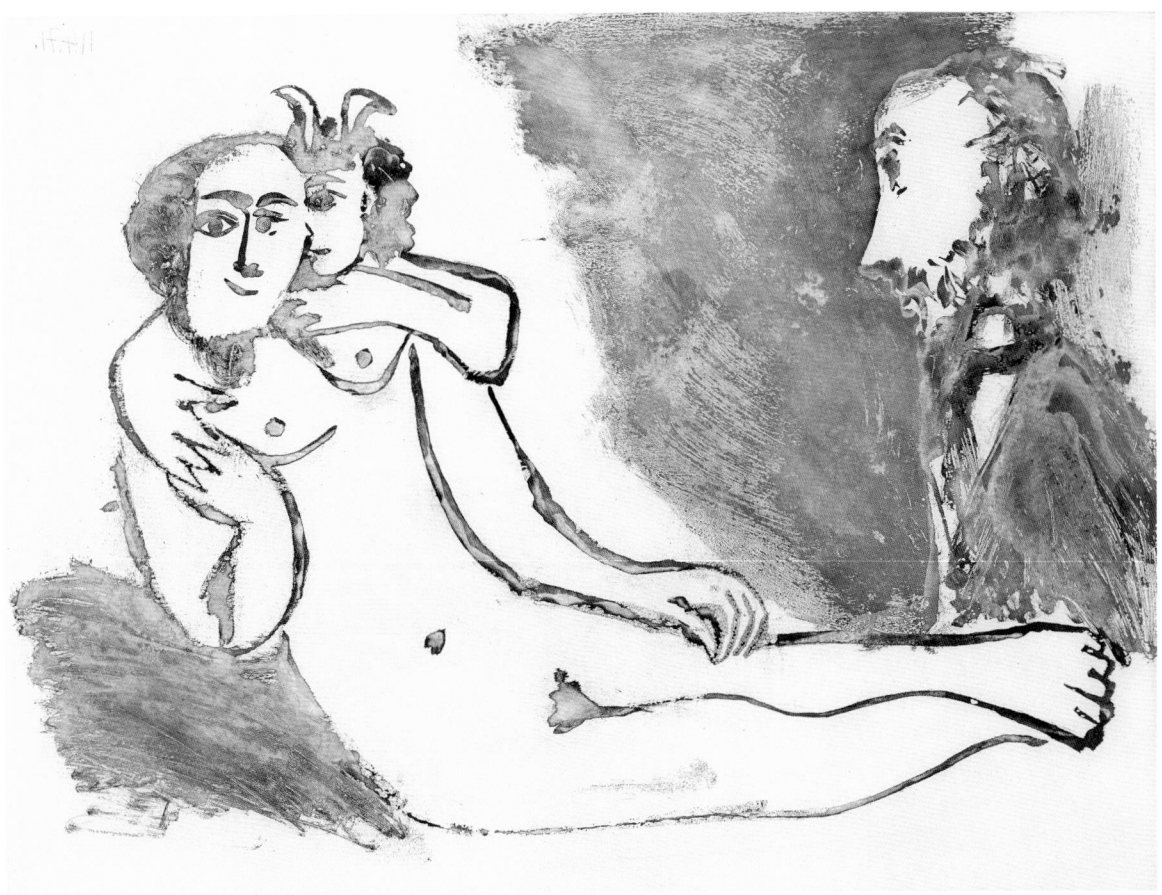

model: the voyeurism of lover and artist is hardly distinguishable as far as Picasso is concerned. In those prints where the women pass the time in loosely composed groups, standing, squatting, sprawling, scratching, maybe gossiping, maybe merely hanging around, there are echoes of *The Madame's Name Day* and Degas's many monotypes depicting the tedious routine of *l'attente* (see 250, 258, 272).[122] Like Degas, Picasso commanded a wide repertory of subtly varied gestures and movements, momentary glances and sets of the mouth with which to communicate the innate drama of the living human body in its myriad, passing moods, but he often settled on poses that fascinated Degas and recurred regularly across the brothel series. Occasionally, for example, he reverted to the quasi-gymnastic legs-aloft pose he had

explored in the Delacroix variations.[123] Sometimes he twisted a girl around and made her flaunt her behind (**263**), just as happens in Degas's *The Serious Client* (**264**).[124] And he constantly employed the pose of the recumbent girl with splayed-apart legs — a classic of pornography of the most banal variety, it is true, but nonetheless a pose that appears in no less than three of the Degas monotypes Picasso owned (see 208, 250, 269).

In all these prints Picasso was flagrant where Degas suggested. Invariably, he turned the women round so that their foreshortened bodies face the depicted voyeur or the spectator, and he rendered their genitals in florid, anatomical detail, whereas Degas shrouded them behind a black smudge of pubic hair. At one level this was simply Picasso being Picasso, flirting with the conventions of pornography and expressing his own obsessive interest in sex. But Daix asserts that Picasso believed he owed it to Degas to "restore" the "obscene" monotypes reputedly destroyed by the latter's heirs.[125] (Degas scholars have questioned the veracity of this legend of a family-led act of purification, but Picasso evidently believed it.)[126] Picasso may also have seen himself as liberating Degas from the restraints of his period by granting him the license of the permissive 1960s: "Had Degas been alive now, this is what he might have done," is the implied message. Rather than being a criticism of Degas's reticence, the unabashed projection is a measure of the completeness of the identification: through absorption, Degas has become an alter-ego.

There are salient differences at other points where the imagery of the monotypes and *Suite 347* overlaps. Thus, like Degas's, Picasso's shrewdly observed characterization of his dramatis personae is laced with ironic humor; like Degas's, Picasso's clients tend to be absurd and sexual desire has a grotesque and comic aspect. But whereas Degas conjured up the reality of the salon, bedroom, and *cabinet de toilette* of the contemporary Parisian brothel by sketching sofas, mirrors, globes, curtains, cast-off clothes, basins, and so on, Picasso invented exotic or pseudo-historical scenarios redolent of the theater, circus, cabaret, or art of the past. Degas convinces us that his is the fly-on-the-wall perspective, whereas we guess from the unstoppable flow of obsessively repetitive images and the dreamlike, irrational mishmash of allusions that Picasso is indulging in an erotic reverie fueled by intersecting memories of literature, art, movies, television, and his own experiences.[127] Both artists are masters of the "dramatic" but its quality is quite different: each of Degas's monotypes is experienced as a moment in real time — like a still from a movie, to be anachronistic; they may be miniature in scale, but the spectator feels as if he is in the room,

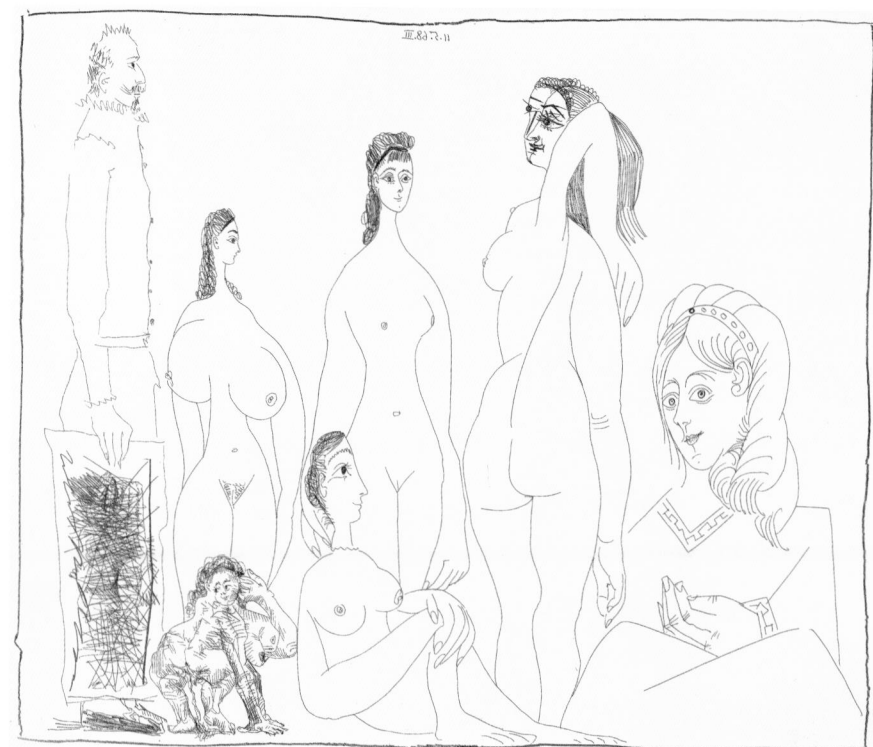

involved in the action. In Picasso's prints, by contrast, the action looks stage-managed and the set-up is theatrical; the spectator observes the surreal goings-on as if from the stalls. Ironically, his type of visual drama is more "academic" than Degas's, harking back to the old traditions of narrative painting that Degas had boldly set himself to overturn.

Picasso was equally fascinated by the technique of the monotypes, which Degas made in both the "light-field" and "dark-field" manners. In the former, the printer's ink is applied to the clean plate with various implements, as if the artist were drawing on blank paper in the usual additive manner. In the latter, the composition is made by covering the clean plate entirely with ink and then rubbing, scraping, and scratching off parts of it in order to "carve" the image from the depths of the ink and "pull" it toward the light.[128] Picasso was able to pore over the twelve he owned, registering every mark Degas had made and guessing which tools he had used

263

Pablo Picasso

Slender Painter with Women, One of Them Pissing, 11 May 1968. Etching on copper printed on paper, 41.4 x 49.7 cm. Museu Picasso, Barcelona (MPB 70.610)

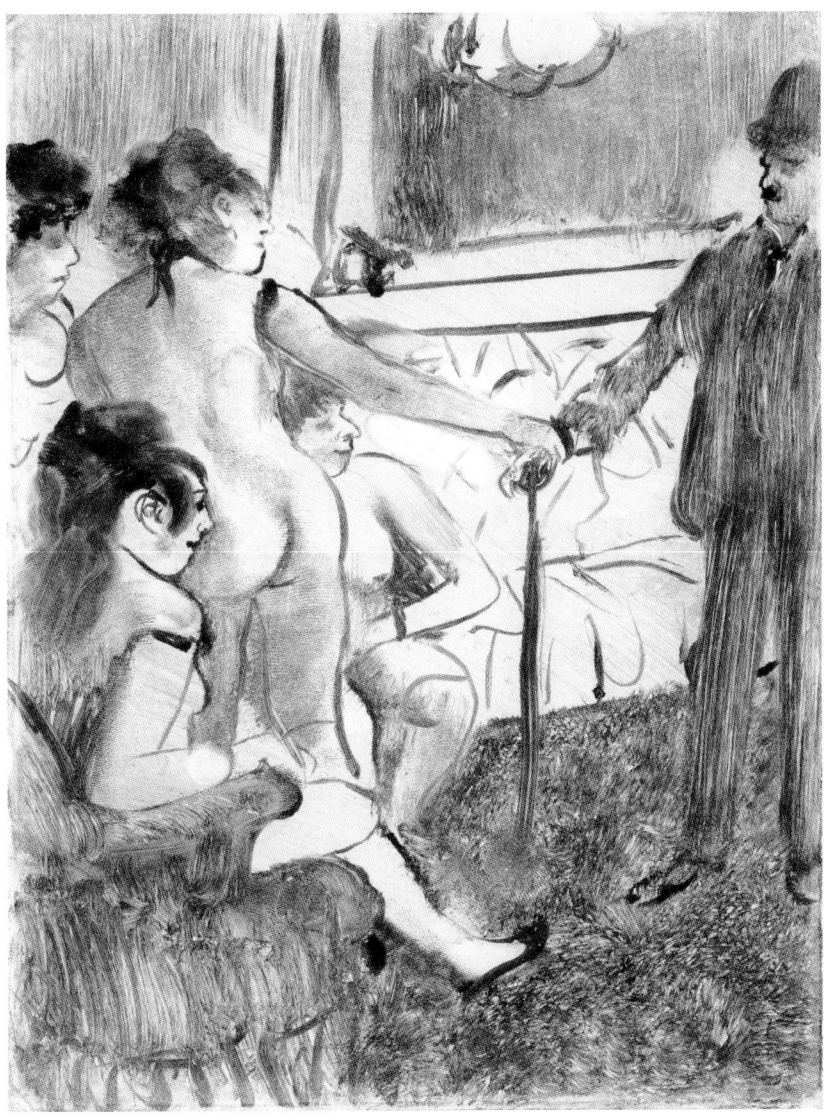

264

Edgar Degas

The Serious Client,
c. 1876–77. Monotype,
21 x 15.9 cm.
National Gallery of
Canada, Ottawa
(no. 18814)

Geiser, who began cataloguing Picasso's own prints in 1928.

Although most references to these insider conversations are of the briefest, most generalized kind, Pierre Daix has summarized one in more detail. It occurred in the spring of 1971 when Picasso was in the midst of making his Degas suite of etchings:

One day Picasso explained to me that, in his opinion, in evolving his monotype technique Degas had wanted the paper to dispute with, to interpret, his initial drawing. In an engraving, the paper reacts but it must obey. It intervenes as a developer, but a developer that is well under control. But with monotype, although the paper receives the impression of the original, it also leaves its imprint on the original. It dilutes it, subtly changing the tones.[129]

When Daix tentatively asked whether he was tempted by the monotype technique himself, Picasso replied ruefully that he was not because "he liked to dictate to his drawing and painting too much. . . . In sum, he had to have the last word." With etching, by contrast, he could make repeated revisions if he so wished. Daix concluded: "Degas was one of the very few draftsmen who really impressed Picasso and that was why the monotypes interested and excited him so much."[130] Picasso was speaking from experience: he had first experimented with the monotype technique in 1905–6 and had periodically returned to it thereafter. However, he had all but totally abandoned it in 1942.[131]

Despite being put off by the chanciness of printing from a monotype, through his virtuoso manipulation of aquatint in *Suite 347*, Picasso contrived to create effects that resemble the dark-field prints.[132] Degas tended to use the dark-field method for intimate scenes of women without men — women going to bed, getting up, resting in dark interiors lit only by the light of a fire or an oil lamp — and the predominance of

— brushes, rags, knives or palm, fingers, fingernails. As someone who had occasionally experimented with the technique himself in the past, he would have been alive to the sheer hands-on sensuality of Degas's use of the medium and must have relished the parallel between the erotic subject matter of the brothel scenes and the artist's now caressing, now aggressive manipulation of the unctuous, oozy, viscous ink and the tactility of the resulting effects. He could, moreover, analyze Degas's technique with professional printmakers like the Crommelynck brothers and specialists like Bernhard

245

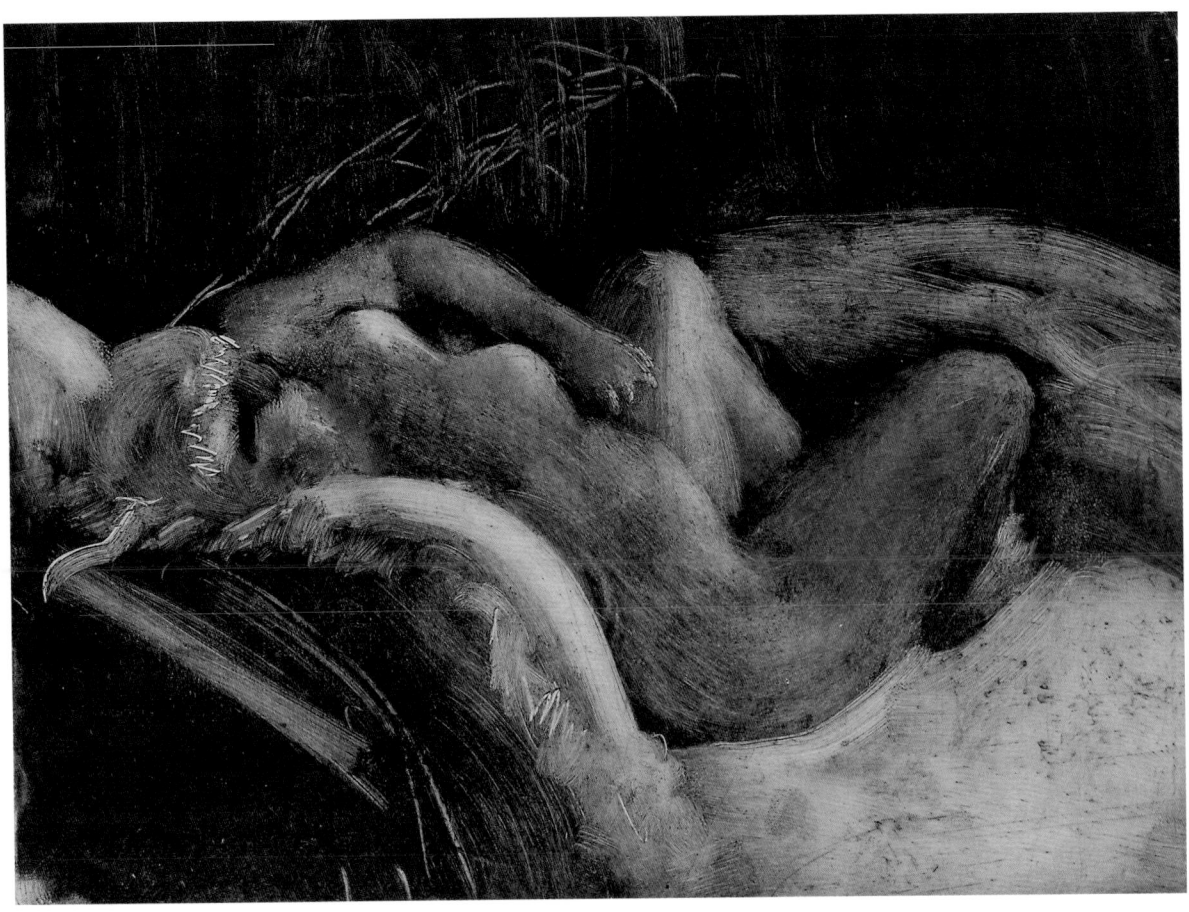

265

Edgar Degas

Sleep, c. 1879–83.
Monotype, 27.6 x 37.8 cm.
British Museum, London
(BM 1949-4-11-245)

266

Pablo Picasso

Related to "The Unknown Masterpiece": Pourbus and the Young Poussin at Frenhofer's,
30 September 1968.
Aquatint and scraper on copper printed on paper,
22.5 x 32.5 cm. Museu Picasso, Barcelona
(MPB 112.023)

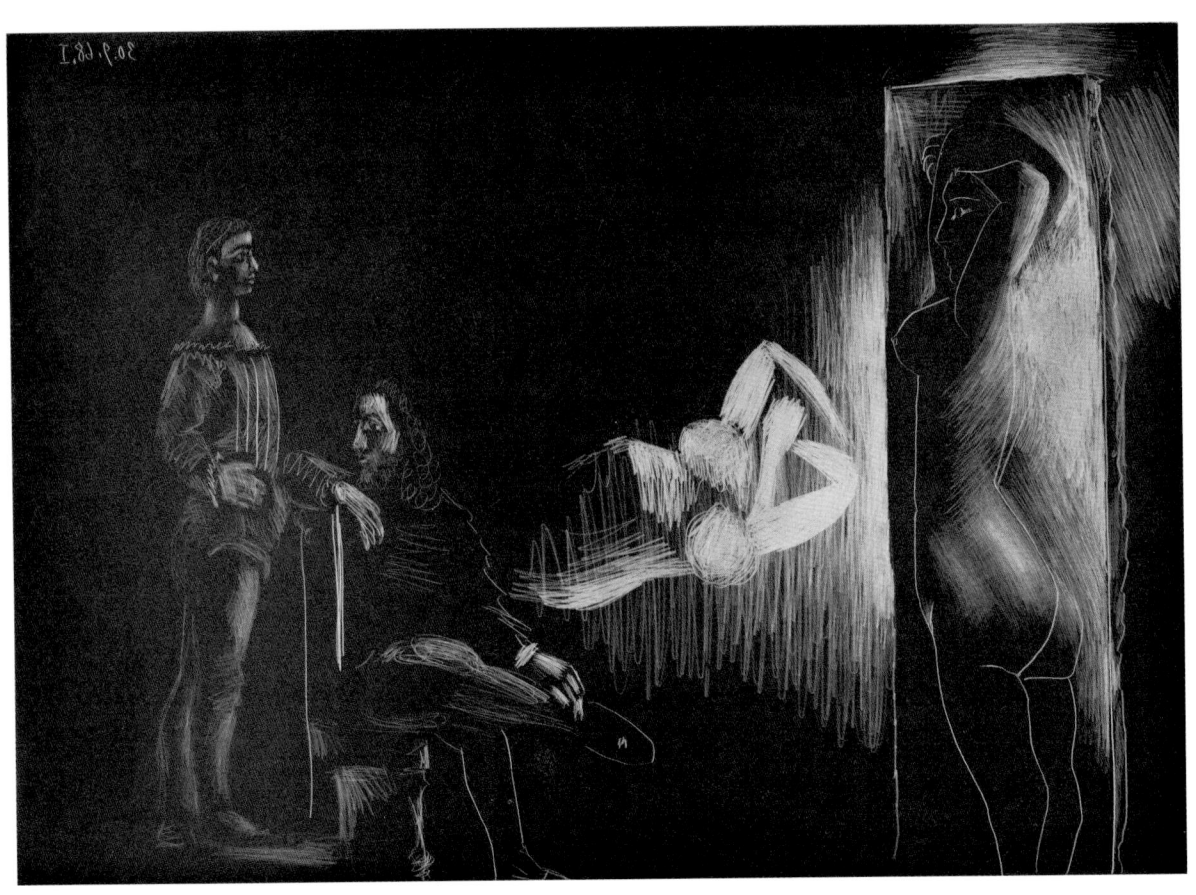

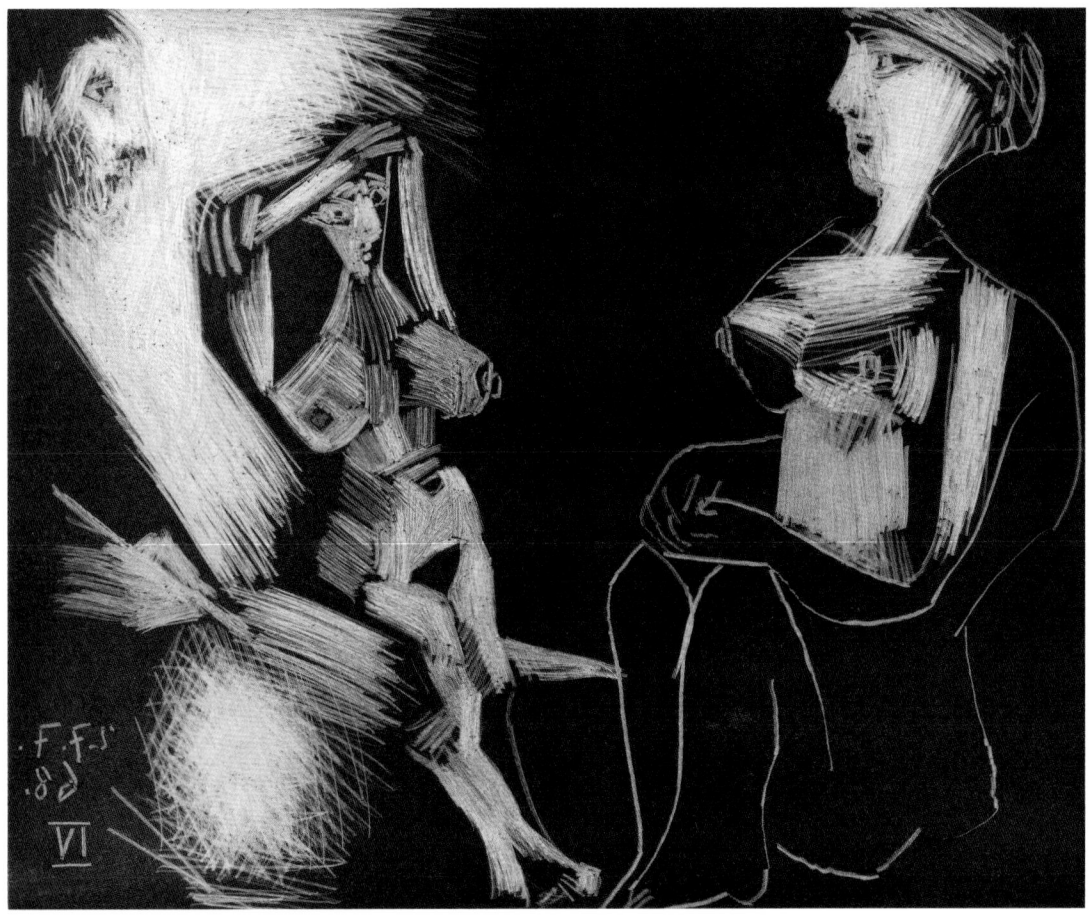

deep shadows produces a muffled atmosphere
of peculiar intensity, mystery, and privacy (see
183). Whereas in the light-field monotypes
events are described legibly, in the moody dark-
field prints things tend to be troublingly ambiguous. In *Sleep* (**265**), for instance, the cocoon of
dense shadow surrounding the tumbled bed
and the light glinting on the undulating profile
of the woman's breasts, stomach, and inner leg
create an ambience of secrecy and voluptuous-
ness. Her face is so blurred that one cannot read
its expression, and the predatory movement of
her left arm can be interpreted in different ways:
like an animal, she may simply be scratching, for
her nails are like claws; but if she is a prostitute,
then, like the *filles* in several other monotypes,
she may be masturbating, and the sinuous,
snaky undulation of her body may record ripples

of pleasure. By hiding her right arm, Degas further compromises her humanity and increases
the sense of her mutant strangeness.

Picasso owned a Vollard photograph of
Sleep.[133] The print's provocative — indeed proto-
surreal — combination of ambiguity and sensuality clearly appealed to him and is echoed in
the dramatic "black-ground" prints that punc-
tuate *Suite 347*. Rather than being in the picaresque mode of many others in the suite, the
aquatint made on 30 September 1968 is notably
dreamlike (**266**). The startling light catching
both women's bodies suggests that the source
is fire and that Picasso's theme is the irresistible power and mystery of sexual desire. In the
aquatint made on 27 July (**267**), the subject is
the artist and his model, and again the contrast
between blazing light and blackness produces

a hallucinatory effect: here desire is equated with revelation and becomes the catalyst of art — a theme that recurs constantly in Picasso's late prints. The way Picasso used his scraper in these prints to model and draw forth the figures from the deep black of the ground is also strikingly similar to Degas's use of rags, brushes, fingers, and fingernails to rub away and incise into the ink. Both artists leave a rough, active surface evocative of impatient, excited movements of the hand and the vital, uncontained process of creativity. Both leave their work looking provisional, accidental, and incomplete because to perfect and finish would be to kill off.

Degas on Picasso's Stage: The Final Act

Once Degas had lodged himself in Picasso's thoughts, he was never absent for long — when, that is, Picasso was absorbed in printmaking, for at this stage of his life it was Degas the draftsman-printmaker with whom he identified. According to Aldo Crommelynck:

> [D]rawing on the etching plate was a very casual process for [Picasso]. After the meal, lunch or dinner, but preferably late at night, he would take a small plate and work on it at the table, resting it against his knee. . . . Printmaking was quite natural for him. I believe that when he had an idea and made a drawing on the print plate, he was already thinking ahead to another possibility, which he made next. That's why there are so many plates.[134]

One is reminded of what Vollard said about the creation of Degas's little "*plats du jour,*" that "as a rule" Degas made them "after dinner, at Cadard [*sic*] the printer's."[135] Anticipating Picasso, Degas was evidently enjoying himself, able to improvise freely, messing about with the ink with untrammeled spontaneity. Again anticipating Picasso, the monotypes formed themselves into a loose, rapidly evolving, self-generating series. No wonder Picasso felt such affinity with Degas in this mode.

The 156 etchings gathered in Picasso's next suite span a longer period than those in the earlier collection, and there were gaps between the various batches: the first two date back to 1968–69; 55 were made between January and May 1970; 97 date from February to June 1971; the final two were produced in March 1972. But Picasso's predominant theme throughout is the interdependence of sexual desire and artistic creativity mediated through ardent looking, just as it had been in *Suite 347*. Essentially the same band of companion-painters from the past was at his side — El Greco, Velázquez, Rembrandt, Goya, Delacroix, Ingres, Manet — but this time Degas took pole position.

The first etching in *Suite 156* to allude explicitly to the brothel monotypes is dated 19 February 1970 (**268**). A veritable tour de force, it got more and more detailed as Picasso worked on the plate day after day.[136] The setting is an opulent late-nineteenth-century brothel decorated with arches and columns and lit by blazing, eye-like globes: Picasso was saluting Lautrec's well-known painting of the legendary brothel on the rue des Moulins.[137] Three naked whores, watched by their wizened, complacent madame, display themselves to a grotesque assortment of top-hatted *flâneurs* and a diminutive military man in Napoleonic uniform. On the other side of the stage, a lanky bohemian artist with the aquiline features of Piero Crommelynck squats beside the sofa and stares superciliously at the excitable voyeurs while drawing one of the girls. He stands in both for Picasso himself and for Degas, for there are multiple allusions to the monotypes Picasso owned: to the packed composition, the sofas and globes and the maternal madame of *The Madame's Name Day* (see 259); to the pair of on-duty but unemployed prostitutes in *Resting* (see 258); to the top-hatted smoker assessing the two tubby women in *The Client* (see 279); to the routine exhibitionism of the *pensionnaires* in *Waiting* (see 250) and *In a Brothel Salon* (**269**). Using other artists' work

268

Pablo Picasso

Painter with a Cravat Drawing His Model in the Setting of "La Maison Tellier," 19 February 1970. Etching on copper printed on paper (Artist proof I/XV), 50.5 x 63 cm. Museu Picasso, Barcelona (MPB 112.181)

269

Edgar Degas

In a Brothel Salon, c. 1876–77. Monotype, 15.9 x 21.6 cm. Musée national Picasso, Paris (MP 35785)

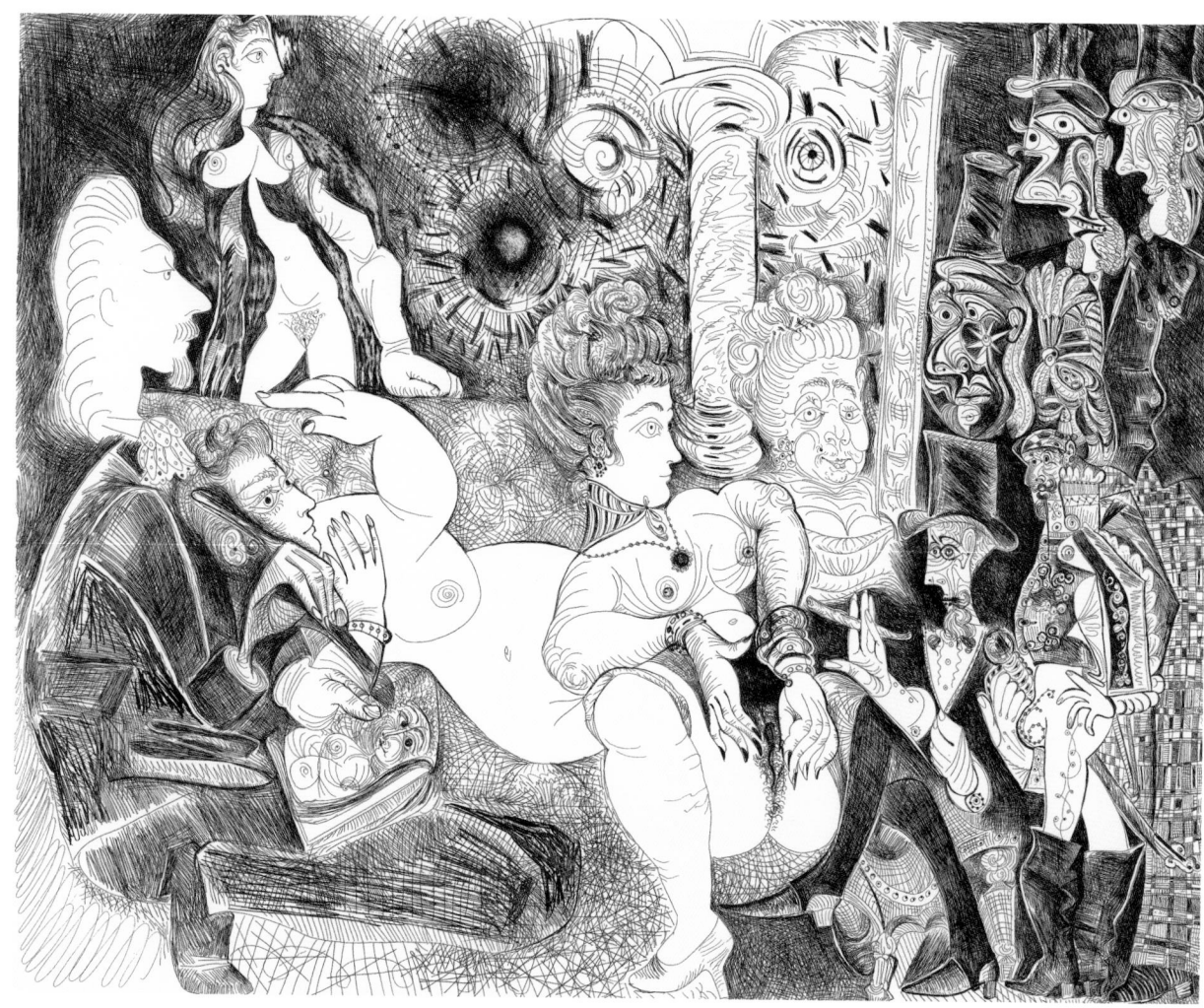

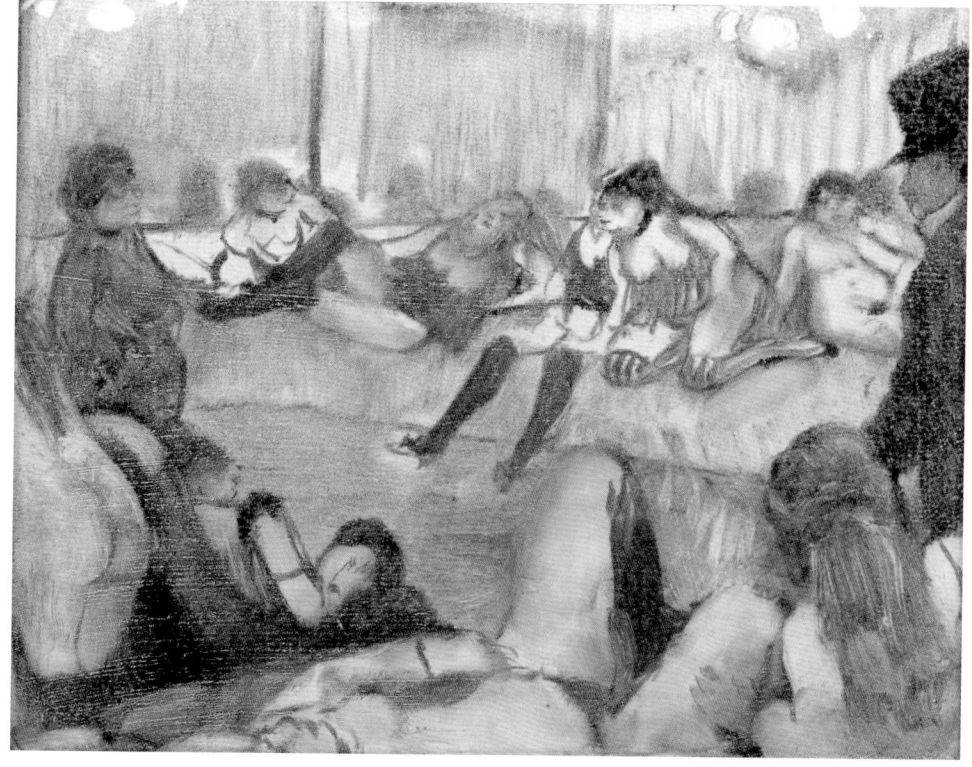

as the catalyst for his own was Picasso's standard practice after the Second World War and he was perfectly open about it. So, when less than a month after completing it, he showed this masterly print to Roland Penrose, the Swiss dealer Siegfried Rosengart and his daughter Angela, and Piero and Landa Crommelynck, he fetched the monotypes, inviting them to make the comparison for themselves and to admire the "sensual sensibility" of Degas's work.[138]

It took more than a year after the completion of this etching for Picasso to engage directly with the persona of Degas, and it was through the purely visual form of his pastiches of the brothel monotypes that he was able to express a much more subtle and sympathetic interpretation of the "actual drama of the man" than his verbal sallies might lead one to expect. Ever since Rubin's visit early in 1971, the monotypes had been on view propped against plinths in the main room in Notre-Dame-de-Vie, but Picasso continued to procrastinate — as indeed was his wont when gearing up toward the exhilarating, but mentally and emotionally draining, business of producing a suite of variations.[139] He was, Daix says, in excellent form that spring, full of energy and "serenely confident," not yet, as he would be twelve months later, painfully conscious that his time was running out. Although Daix visited the studio "almost every day" in early April 1971, when the series was in full swing, and although Picasso discussed the monotypes with him now and then, Daix had no idea what was happening in the studio.[140] Picasso was too deeply embroiled in his searching, private conversation with the ghost of Degas to allow anyone else in at this critical stage in the process of discovery.

Thanks to the meticulous dating of his work, Picasso's gradual submission to Degas's call can be charted. On 3 March and 5 March 1971 he produced a couple of his sporadic variations after Ingres's *Turkish Bath*.[141] On 8 March it was the turn of another of his favorite pictures,

Rembrandt's *"Self-Portrait" as the Prodigal Son in the Tavern* from Dresden.[142] Then, on 11 March, having already produced four other etchings, including a brothel scene with a Celestina, Picasso put Degas on stage in the character of the bourgeois client who has come to inspect the "merchandise" (**270**).[143] His features are essentially those of Picasso's earlier profile portrait (see 261) — high forehead, long sloping nose, full beard — but here the eyes are treated naturalistically and are the hooded eyes of Degas's own self-portraits. The regulation well-cut bourgeois suit approximates to Degas's garb in numerous photographs. But his stance, which is the key to his inner nature, is Picasso's invention and in modified form it recurs in many of the subsequent prints. With head erect but warily held back, eyes fixed on the naked *fille* facing him, hands locked behind his back and hidden beneath his frock-coat, Degas thrusts forward his chest and pelvis but simultaneously rocks back on his legs. His whole body expresses irresolution and conflict: the pretense of worldly masculinity and the temptation to respond to the women's blatant solicitation are fatally counteracted by the insurmountable dread of physical contact. His painful dilemma is perfectly mirrored in his clothing: hat off and coat boldly flung open, but waistcoat buttoned tightly to the neck and watch-chain secured like a padlock. The women meanwhile go through their familiar routines, displaying and offering themselves and also — Picasso makes this clear from their gestures — displaying and offering each other. The furthest one from Degas, still wearing her chemise, stands bolt upright but pivots so that he can glimpse her breasts; next to her, the most voluptuous and attractive of the four pirouettes in a parody of lascivious seduction; the third swivels around on her stool and displays her sex to him; the fourth, with the drooping breasts, slack body, and lined brow of a woman well past her prime, facetiously imitates his

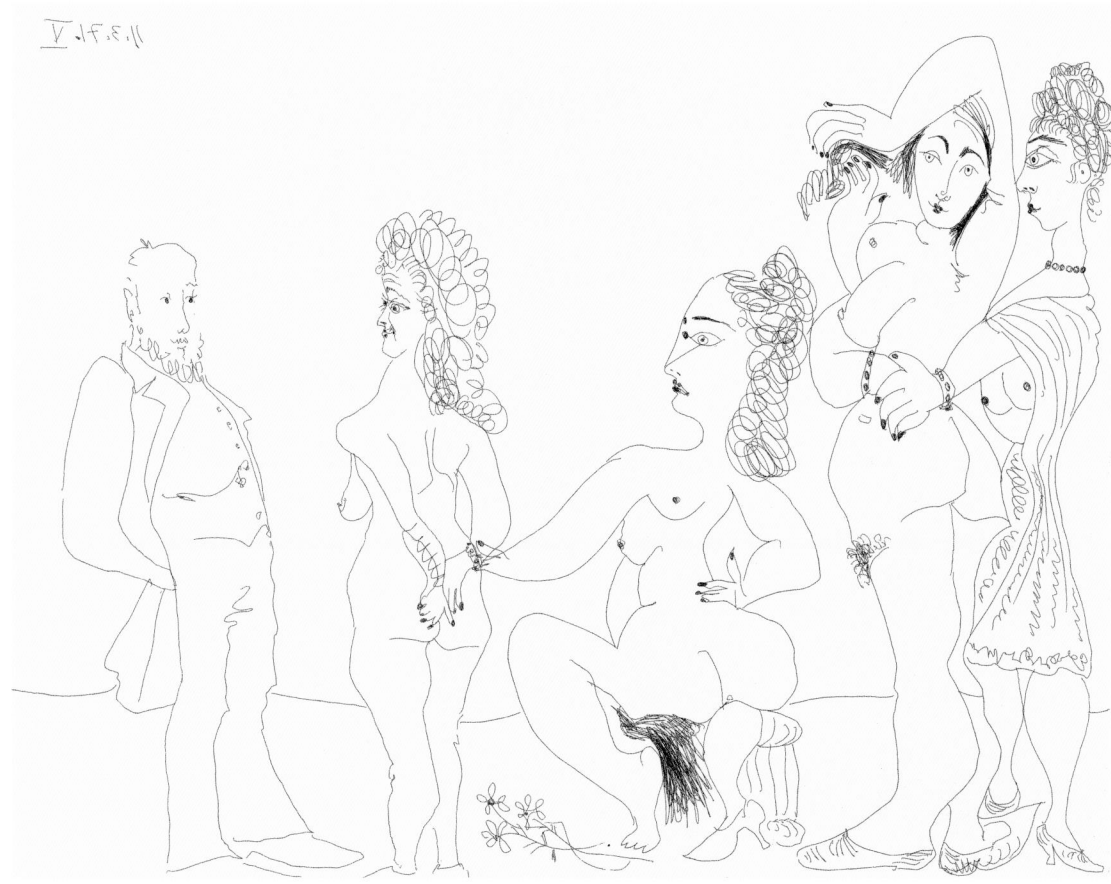

pose, standing grinning before him with her hands held behind her back. Were the flowers dumped unceremoniously on the floor Degas's placatory offering? In any case, the faces of the women express derision, indifference, or irritation: from long experience they know that this pathologically inhibited client comes only for the floor show, and going through the mock performance of a Judgment of Paris can get tiresome.

We saw how Douglas Cooper marked the completion of the successful transaction with the Lefevre Gallery by sending off a postcard of Cranach's *Judgment of Paris* (see 251). Picasso seems to have remembered this, for not only does he parody the classic subject but his lead prostitute affects a similar pose to the central goddess in Cranach's trio. This is only one of a series of knowing allusions: although the etch-ing may look lightweight and facile, its simplicity is delusive. Thus, the stance Picasso gives to Degas is not simply emblematic of his sexual peculiarities, for it also echoes the pose of one of his most famous works, the *Little Dancer Aged Fourteen* — a sculpture that, as Richard Kendall has demonstrated, had first fascinated him more than sixty years earlier (see 126).[144] By the same token, the *fille* aping Degas also apes the *Little Dancer*. The connection was not made casually because Picasso must have known of the critics' scandalized denunciations of the pre-sumed viciousness and degeneracy of Degas's adolescent model when the sculpture was first exhibited in 1881, and been familiar with back-stage scenes, such as the monotypes Degas made to illustrate Ludovic Halévy's *The Cardinal Family*, which hint at dubious liaisons between the young ballerinas and their top-hatted admirers. Already in this first print Picasso was laying his cards on the table: at the level of personal motivation and vision, he implies, the ballet scenes that made Degas's reputation were no different from the "secret" brothel monotypes that the general public barely knew.

As one would expect, in this first etching Picasso also alludes to the monotypes themselves. Degas stands in for the clients who appear at the margins of many of them, including three Picasso owned (*The Client* [see 279], *Resting* [see 258] and *In a Brothel Salon* [see 269]). Compositionally, it is closest of all to *The Serious Client* (see 264), which Picasso had wanted but failed to buy from the Lefevre Gallery. There, Degas's four prostitutes twist and turn in a similar manner and express similar amused contempt for the stiff, choosy, reluctant client, who uses his furled umbrella like a fencepost to mark a safe distance between himself and the *fille* cajoling him. And Picasso gave his prostitutes the vulgar, predatory look of Degas's: thick mats of hair, graceless bodies, cheap jewelry, pointed slippers, and high-heeled shoes.

The etching also alludes pointedly to *Les Demoiselles d'Avignon* (see 136). Degas is in the place (and outsider role) of the "doctor" entering the brothel from the left in the preparatory study (see 242). Imagine yourself in Degas's position, and the spectacle you would be presented with is essentially the spectacle presented to the viewer of *Les Demoiselles*. The *fille* standing in profile on the right is in the pose of the demoiselle on the left (they alone wear a revealing shift), and on the etched plate itself she, too, was on the left. The second and fourth *filles* resemble the two central demoiselles. Finally, the seated *fille* is heir to the notorious squatting demoiselle, and her anatomical distortions (right leg caught under a buttock; breast that is also a shoulder blade; top of the nose that starts under the eye) are not so irrational if one takes them to be the trace of her swivellng around (like the squatting demoiselle)

to display her body from every angle. *Les Demoiselles d'Avignon* has been interpreted by leading scholars as an expression of Picasso's supposedly conflicted feelings about women — desire for possession crossed with fear of annihilation. Whether or not this is valid for him, in the etching Picasso projected ambivalent emotions of this nature onto Degas.

Degas appeared in person in no less than thirty-eight of the remaining seventy-eight prints in *Suite 156*, and the majority of those that omit him manifestly sprang from the brothel monotypes, quoting figure groupings, individual poses, physical types, and so on.[145] In other words, whenever Picasso was tempted to dismiss Degas altogether or replace him with other sex-seekers (anonymous *flâneurs*, a grizzled, pop-eyed fisherman, musketeers, King Herod),[146] Degas insisted on reinserting himself: "Impossible to get rid of him," as Picasso ruefully remarked to Daix.[147] The likely reasons for this late-life obsession will be discussed shortly, but it is worth considering first some of Picasso's strategies for developing the characterization of his enigmatic predecessor.

A regular ploy was to depict Degas observing the actions represented in the monotypes and highlight his idiosyncratic reactions. For instance, in an etching dated 15 March 1971 (**271**), having seated himself on the ground to get a better view, Degas stares fixedly at the exposed behind of the bending whore — exactly the raked perspective of the artist/spectator in *Waiting* (**272**). But unlike the client in *Admiration* (see 238), who crouches in rapt adoration at the head of the bathtub while the girl, playing her part with a nice sense of style, rises like Venus from its shallows, Picasso's Degas is literally traumatized by what he sees — surely an intentional, tragicomical demonstration of Freud's theory of the "castration-complex."[148] In the etching dated 30 March (**273**), Degas, slightly more self-possessed this time, is transfixed by the girl's open legs — the perspective

271

Pablo Picasso

Women at Their Toilette with Degas Musing, 15 March 1971. Etching on copper printed on paper (Artist proof I/XV), 22.9 x 30.5 cm. Museu Picasso, Barcelona (MPB 112.273)

272

Edgar Degas

Waiting, c. 1876–77. Monotype, 12.1 x 16.4 cm. Musée national Picasso, Paris (RF 35784)

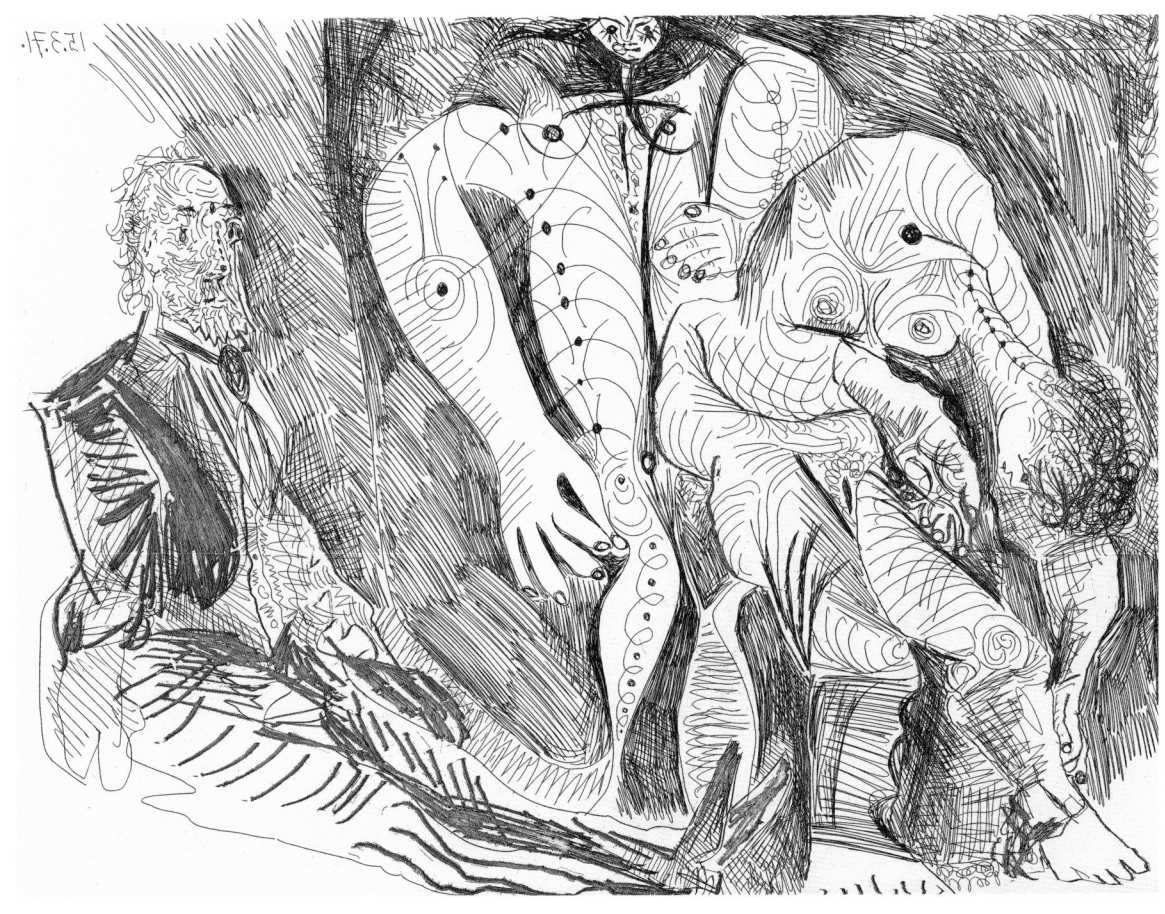

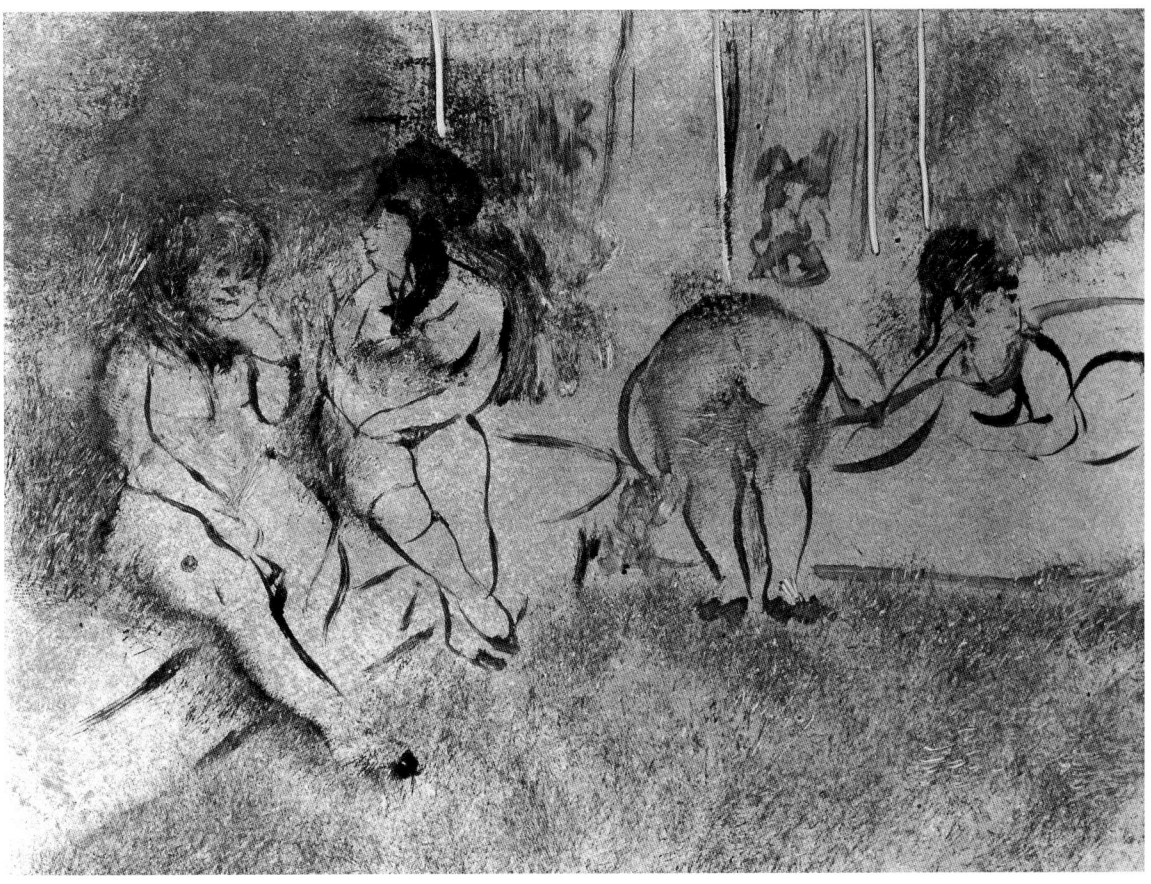

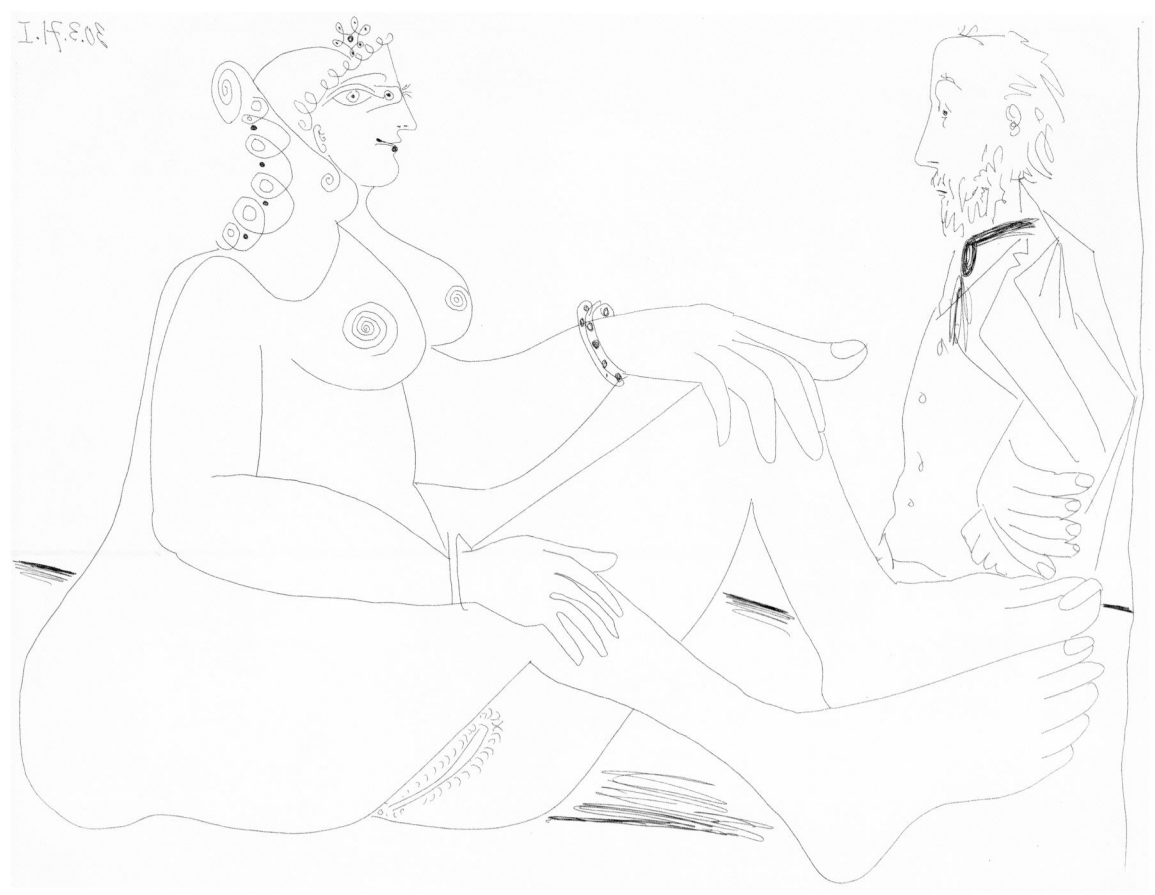

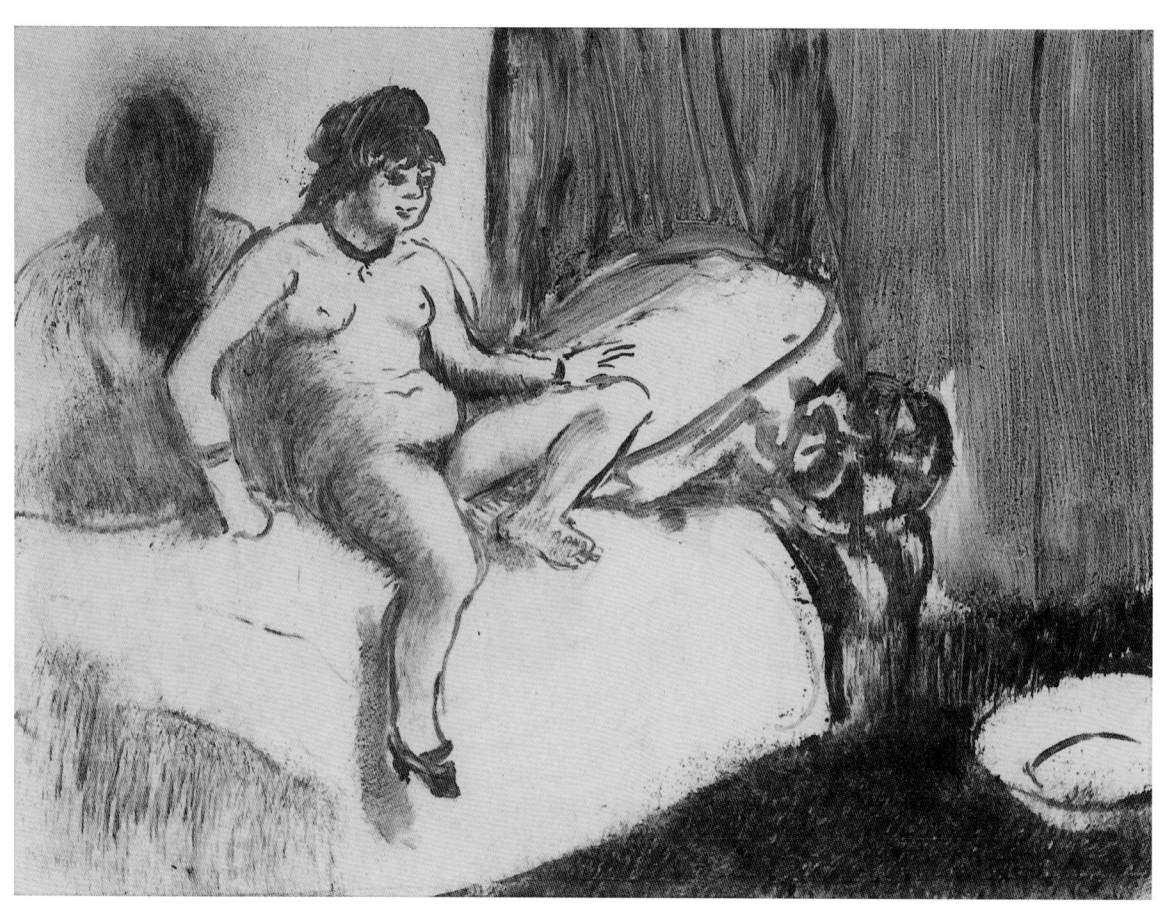

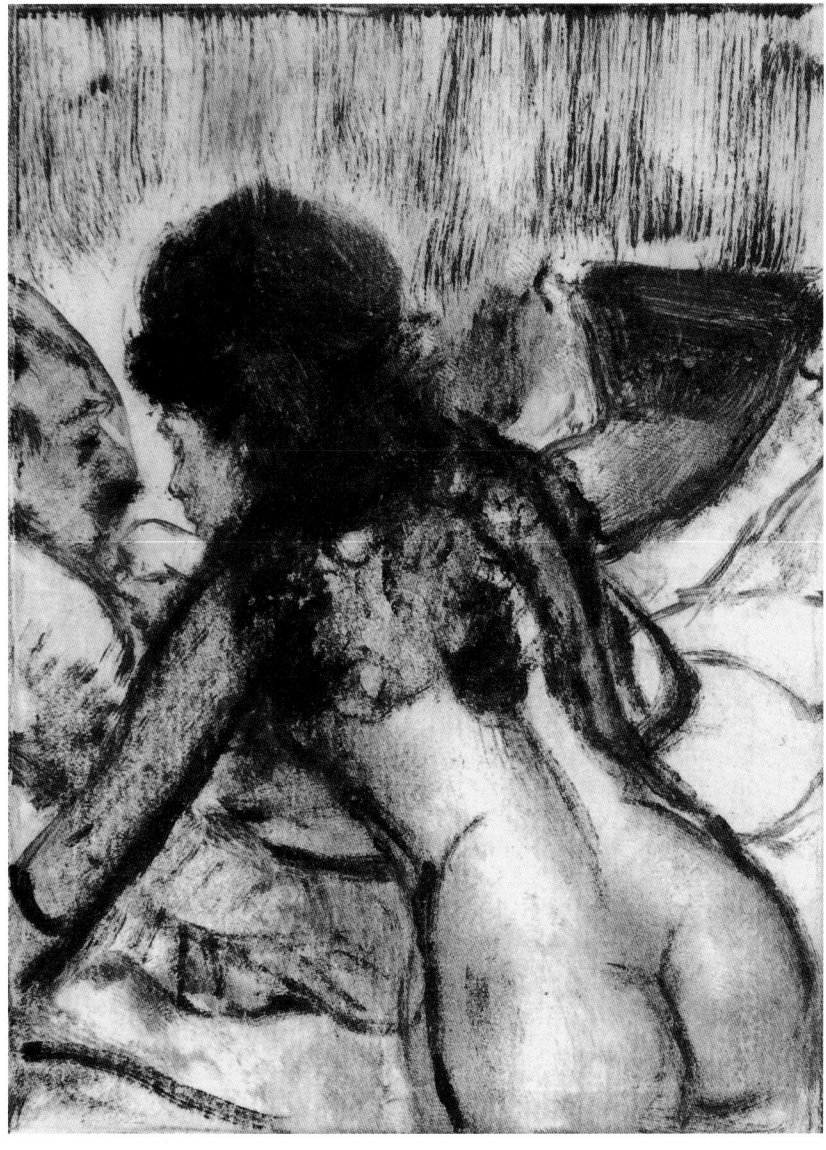

of the artist/spectator in *Resting on the Bed* (**274**; see also 208). In both these etchings Picasso considerably shortened the distance between Degas and the object of his gaze — the distance between the prostitutes and the unseen clients in the corresponding monotypes is much greater — thus highlighting his insurmountable fear of touching. In the second (see 273), Picasso has made Degas cross the threshold of the bedroom and perch beside the grinning prostitute on her bed, but his inhibitions operate literally as a straightjacket and his arms remain knotted behind his back. Not so the client in Degas's *Conversation* (**275**), who is passive and dominated, but a willing participant. The same device of imagining Degas in the midst of the scenes he depicts is used in the many prints based specifically on *The Madame's Name Day* (see 277, 280, 281). In Picasso's versions he is a habitué of the salon, observing the party from close quarters, and he looks less uncomfortable than usual, no doubt because he is there as a guest, not as an ineffectual client. These imaginative reconstructions are all based on the presumption that "old Degas" had first-hand experience of "those places."

The first etching in the series is not the only one to imply that a sexual undercurrent ripples through Degas's entire oeuvre. It has been suggested that the man in *Interior (The Rape)* was Picasso's model for the figure of Degas, who is often shown, like him, standing leaning against a wall.[149] When it became known, the imagery of *Interior (The Rape)* attracted particular interest, and although critics were divided about exactly how to interpret it, most assumed that the cowering girl was the innocent party and the man her heartless seducer.[150] In Picasso's etchings (see 260) the roles are neatly reversed: Degas, face-to-face with the prostitutes, is the "victim," they, the sexual aggressors. By quoting from *Interior (The Rape)*, he contrived to link another of Degas's most controversial but also most admired works directly to the brothel monotypes.[151] Perhaps he believed the picture was quasi-autobiographical and held the key to Degas's secret: had Degas in his youth (as Valéry and Cabanne supposed) suffered some fatal rebuff or committed some coercive act akin to rape, and become effectively impotent as a consequence? At any rate, Picasso's elision of the man in *Interior (The Rape)* with his representation of Degas implies that the former was the latter's alter-ego.

The allusion to the *Little Dancer Aged Fourteen* in the first etching was developed

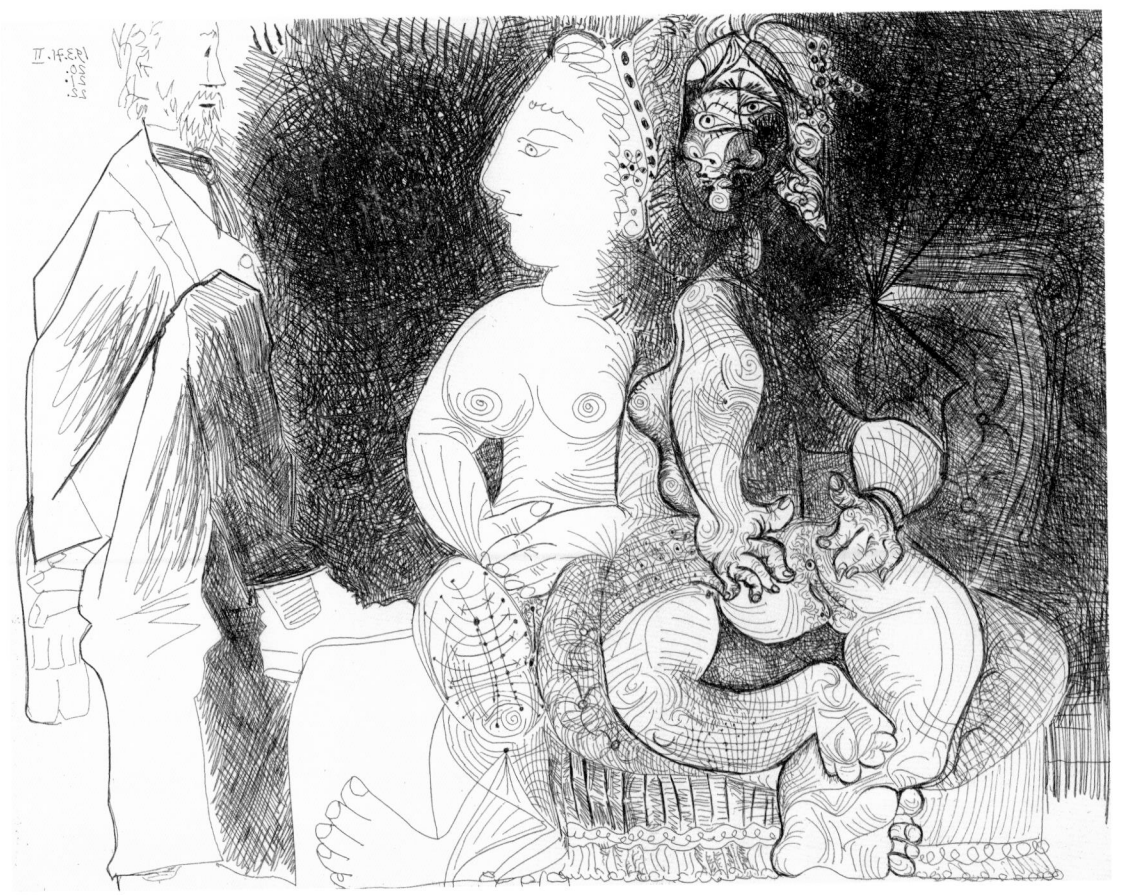

276

Pablo Picasso

Degas with Elasticized Boots and Two Prostitutes, One on an Upholstered Napoleon III Chair, 19–22 March 1971. Etching on copper printed on paper (Artist proof I/XV), 36.5 x 48.6 cm. Museu Picasso, Barcelona (MPB 112.189)

277

Pablo Picasso

The Name Day of the Madame, Flowers and Kisses, Degas Enjoying Himself, 16 May 1971. Etching on copper printed on paper (Artist proof I/XV), 36.5 x 49.2 cm. Museu Picasso, Barcelona (MPB 112.211)

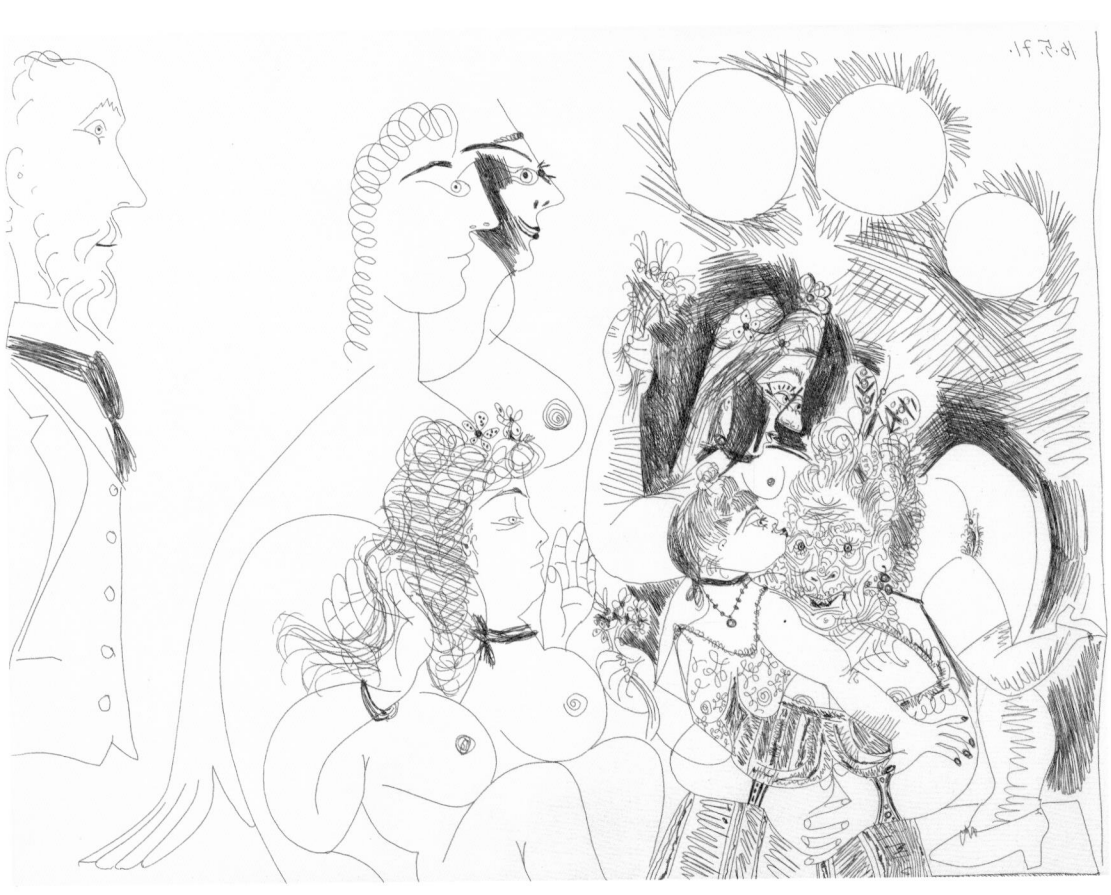

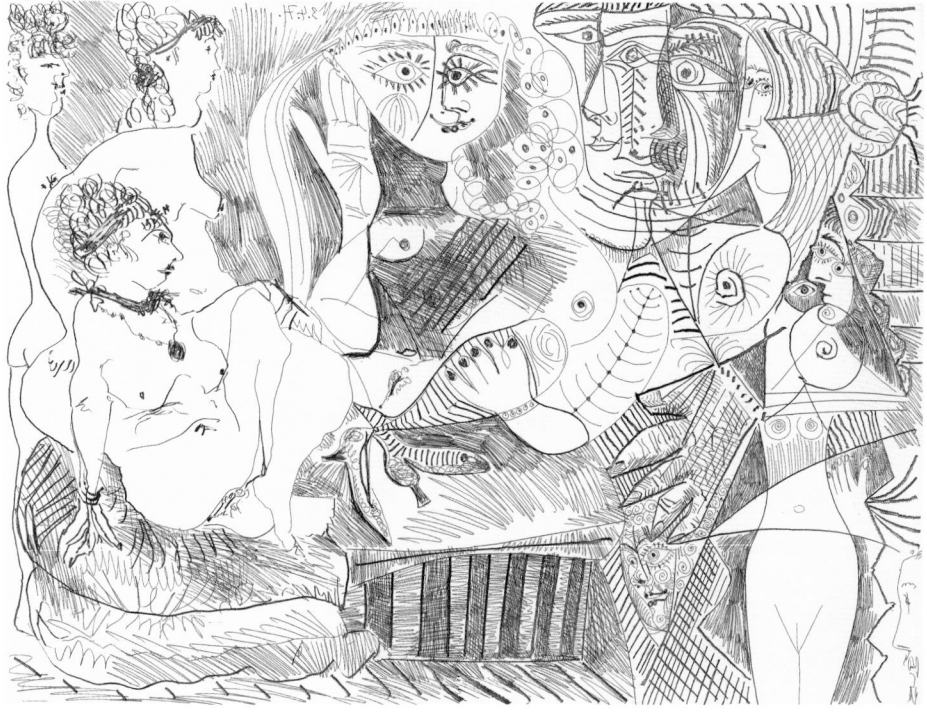

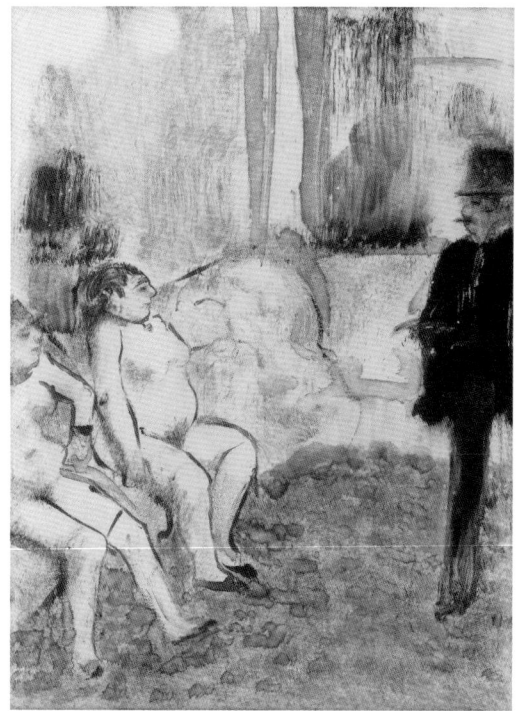

278

Pablo Picasso

Degas Having Visions.
Prostitute Listening
to the Stories of Her
Companions at Rest,
3 April 1971. Etching on
copper printed on paper
(Artist proof I/XV),
36.7 x 49.4 cm. Museu
Picasso, Barcelona
(MPB 112.207)

279

Edgar Degas

The Client, c. 1879.
Monotype, 22 x 16 cm.
Musée national Picasso,
Paris (RF 35788)

outrageously in subsequent prints where the gesture of holding the hands behind the back is obscenely transformed into a device for framing and displaying the anus and genitals. Sometimes the prostitute in these later prints prances and capers in a grotesque parody of a ballerina's pirouette (**276**) — all of which wickedly emphasizes the general point that there is nothing to choose between Degas's corps de ballet and his prostitutes. Similarly, the woman bending over to expose herself in the etching mentioned earlier (see 271) adopts an unflattering and revealing pose that crops up in many of Degas's toilette scenes, including the shadowy, pillar-shaped monotype in the Camondo bequest in which the bending bather is viewed at such close quarters that her behind seems almost to graze the surface of the print (see 183). Picasso may have believed that, privately, Degas found this taboo view of the female body peculiarly enticing, albeit troublingly so, and could not resist exploring it whenever his subject matter gave him the excuse.

In the print with the pirouetting prostitute Degas looks bemused and baffled (see 276) — an impression reinforced by giving him (for the only time in the series) the pose of Ingres's Oedipus come to solve the riddle of the deadly Sphinx. (This allusion, like that in one of the Monte Carlo drawings of 1925 discussed in chapter 3 [see 163], was probably triggered by Picasso's knowledge that Degas had owned a version of Ingres's *Oedipus and the Sphinx*, now in the National Gallery, London [see 152].) In other prints Degas behaves with aloof, patrician dignity (see 281) or appears relatively sanguine (**277**). In yet others, rather than being preternaturally unresponsive and in William Rubin's phrase "a sort of neuter," Degas seems to be experiencing a heated sexual fantasy. In the print executed on 3 April 1971 (**278**), the three prostitutes on the left are represented in the caricatural style of, say, *The Client* (**279**), whereas the women in the center and to the right are in a highly decorative, abstracted style and fused together into a jazzy patchwork.

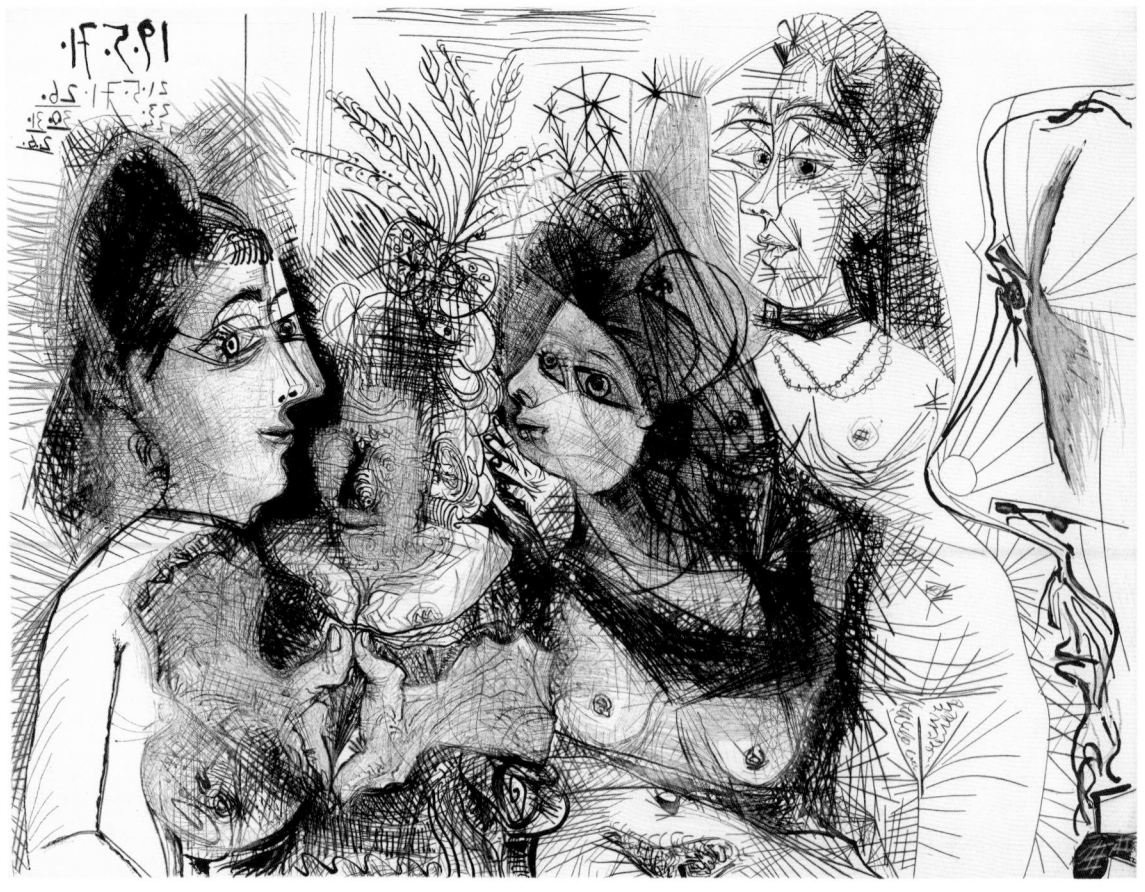

280

Pablo Picasso

Brothel. Scandal-mongering. Profile of Degas Wrinkling His Nose, seventh state, 19, 21, 23, 24, 26, 30, and 31 May and 2 June 1971. Etching, aquatint, drypoint, and scraper on copper, printed on paper (Artist proof I/XV), 36.6 x 49.2 cm. Museu Picasso, Barcelona (MPB 112.208)

281

Pablo Picasso

The Madame-Abortionist and Three Prostitutes. Degas with His Hands behind His Back, second state, 1–4 May 1971. Etching on copper printed on paper (Artist proof I/XV), 36.7 x 49 cm. Museu Picasso, Barcelona (MPB 112.234)

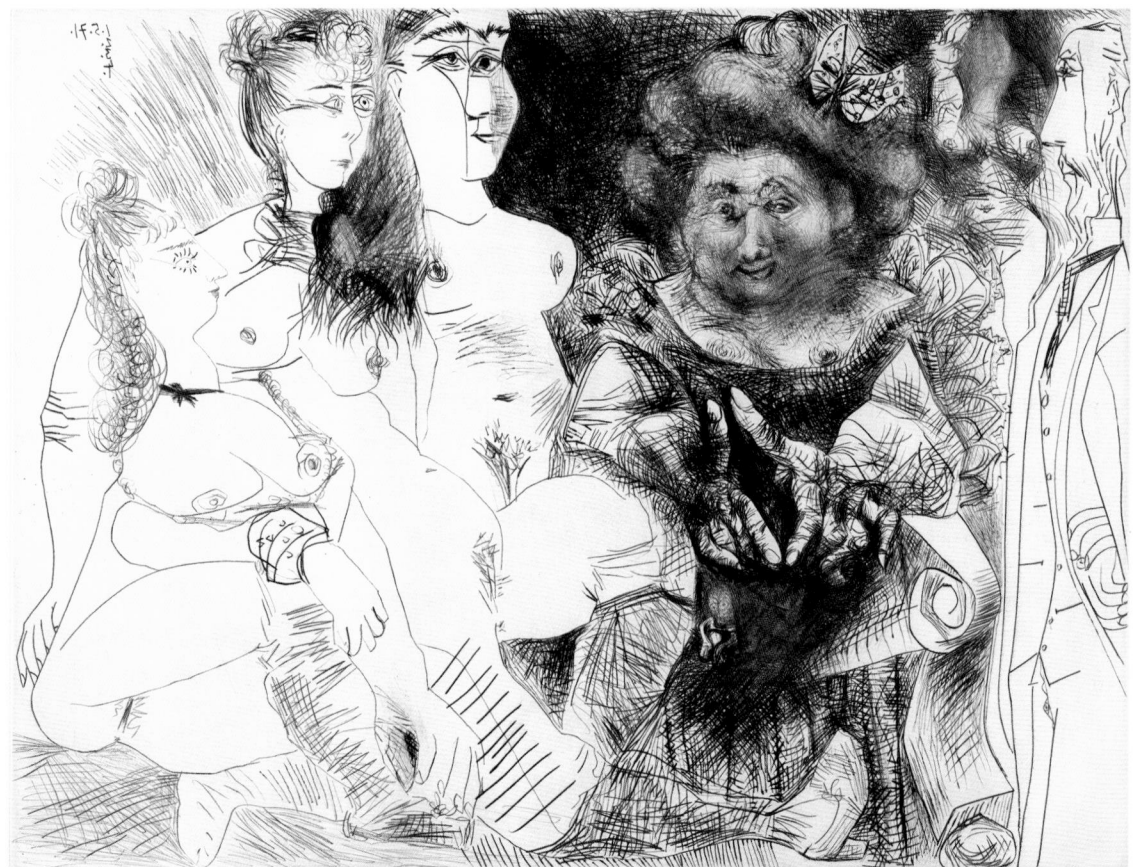

282

Pablo Picasso

"La Maison Tellier."
Prostitutes Together.
Degas Astonished, 9 April
1971. Etching on copper
printed on paper (Artist
proof I/XV), 36.5 x 49 cm.
Museu Picasso, Barcelona
(MPB 112.225)

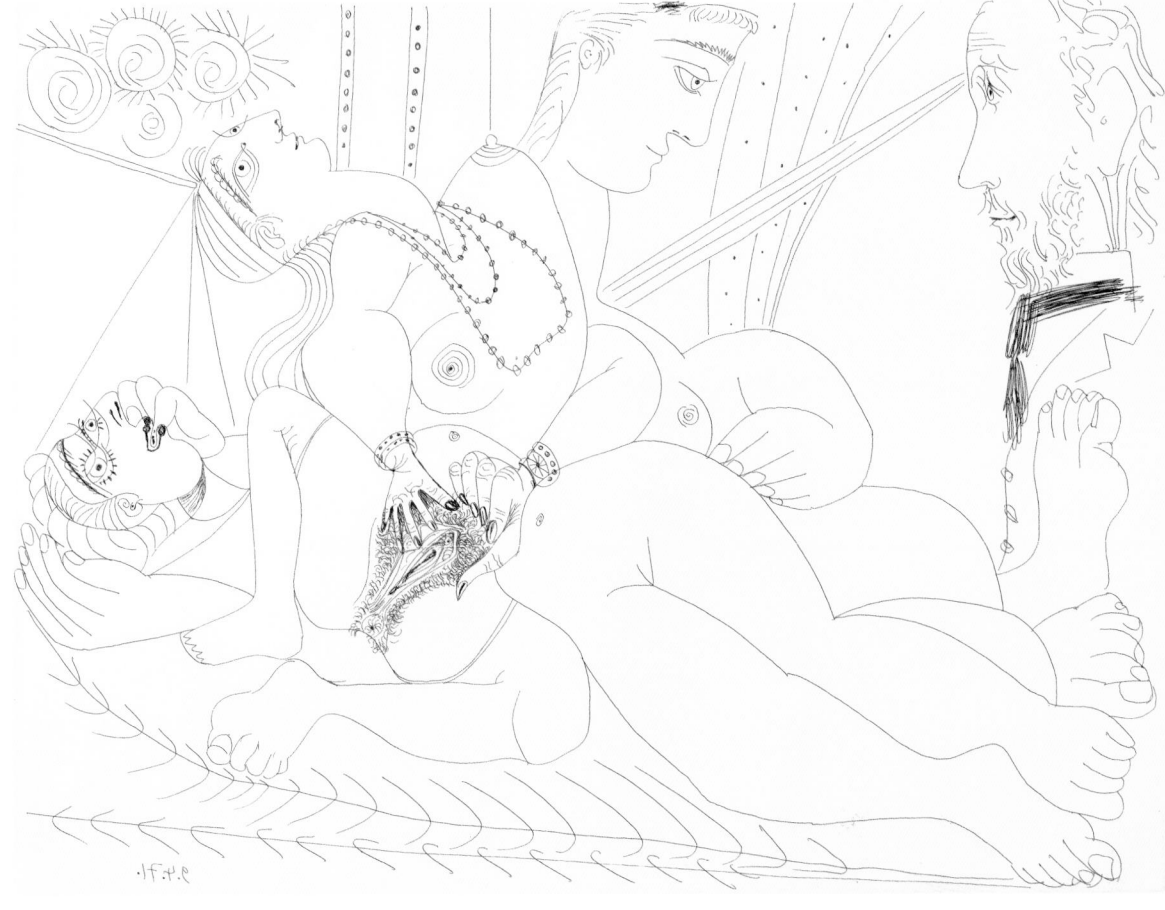

Cordoned off like a prompter in his box, Degas peeps at them from a cubbyhole at the right-hand bottom corner. A possible reading of this irrational scenario is that the sight of the "real" girls has set off a quasi-psychedelic erotic fantasy or dream. Indeed, it might be argued that in the many prints in which Degas is represented in a relatively naturalistic manner whereas the prostitutes are depicted in an excessively ornate graphic style, Picasso has "illustrated" the hallucinogenic experience of sexual fantasy allowed to run riot.[152] In a few prints where Degas's head swells to an enormous size, pressing up against the naked girls (**280**), the conventional separation of the gazer from the gazed-at collapses, as it does in those monotypes where the whores seem to push forward beyond the borders of the image and

invade the spectator's space (see 235). In the words of Gert Schiff, "In Picasso's etchings . . . the brothel becomes to Degas what it became to Bloom in Joyce's *Ulysses*: a theater of hallucinations where, in constantly shifting scenes, all the hero's secret wishes and fears take shape."[153]

The Degas of Picasso's prints has many different moods, and taken together they provided a rounded image comparable to, although different from, the complex characterization in Valéry's *Degas Danse Dessin*. If just occasionally Picasso casts Degas as the lofty, detached, moralistic puritan described by influential early biographers — arguably he is disapproving in one of the best-known prints based on *The Madame's Name Day* (**281**) — this is not his usual persona.[154] Nor is he the frosty "neuter"; nor the closet homosexual. He is painfully shy, anxious, and embarrassed, but although a martyr to chastity, his automatic response of keeping his hands perpetually locked behind his back betokens pathological repression, not indifference, and his constant attendance at the brothel and propensity to lurid sexual fantasy betray an unusually intense obsession. For Picasso, that obsession was with looking: if Degas had a "vice," the prints tell us that it was scopophilia.

In a sense, the theme of every print in the series is Degas's voyeurism: he is always the onlooker, and the women always display themselves to him as well as to us. Sometimes Picasso resorts to abstract signs to press home the point. Thus, in a print mentioned earlier (see 280), the huge looming profile of Degas is inscribed with lines radiating both from the eyebrow and up over the domed skull, and from the base of the nose up to the eye. They lend the head three-dimensionality, but their main purpose is to focus attention on Degas's eye and the direction of his gaze toward the simpering prostitutes and their ancient madame. In one of the most arresting images of the entire series (**282**), rays springing from Degas's brow beam toward the shoulder of one of the three naked girls lying in a private, curtained-off boudoir in which one assumes they have been enjoying Sapphic love. Just like the odalisques in the foreground of Ingres's *The Turkish Bath* (see 191), they are tumbled together and seem to share and exchange limbs. Knowing of Degas's inordinate admiration for Ingres, Picasso may have meant to suggest, scandalously, that the enactment of the orgiastic lesbian loves of the harem was made at Degas's demand, for in this print, against the grain, he seems to be directing and controlling events, and the dazed women react like zombies. Talking to Daix, Picasso had speculated about the "vices [Degas] might have hoped to satisfy" in visiting "those places": perhaps this is the kind of thing he had in mind. In any case, voyeurism as such is the main point, not just because of the symbolic representation of Degas's gaze but because, for the viewer of the print cast as the average consumer of popular pornographic imagery, the meticulously rendered sex and anus of one of the pseudo-odalisques are the inescapable focus of the composition. Earlier it was suggested that one of the etchings (see 271) illustrates textbook "castration anxiety." Possibly the same idea is represented more obliquely here: what we are forced to look at is what fascinates but also horrifies Degas, what draws him back again and again to the brothel but renders him sexually dysfunctional in a "normal" way.

Picasso had his own explanation for the voyeuristic character of his etchings and the Degas series in particular. When Daix remarked that in showing Degas repeatedly in the bordello, Picasso had "engraved the adventures of a voyeur as he had done with the sculptor in the *Vollard Suite*," Picasso approved of the analogy but instantly rejoined: "But the real voyeur is engraving. . . . Anyone with a copperplate *is* a voyeur. That's why I've engraved so many clinches." Referring to the ravishing aquatint in the *Vollard Suite* of a kneeling Faun reaching out toward a sleeping woman, he continued: "You say I'm the Faun. . . . But I'm also the voyeur who sees the Faun as a voyeur. . . . That's what engraving is. Whereas painting is really making love."[155] No doubt Picasso believed that when Degas took into his hands one of the small, shiny, mirror-like, metal plates he used for his monotypes, he too entered automatically into this mind-set and experienced a similar compulsion to narrate scopophilic scenes.

Just occasionally the fantasies Picasso projected onto Degas took a more serene form — a sublimated form in Freud's sense of repression of taboo sexual material. In the aquatint dated 11 April (see 262), Degas dreams of a reclining nymph fondly embraced by a charming young satyr, and for once there is nothing to upset the prudish — and nothing to upset Degas either. This print, incidentally, is an excel-

283

Edgar Degas

The Maid, c. 1876–77.

Monotype, 8.7 x 7.9 cm.

Musée national Picasso,

Paris (RF 35782)

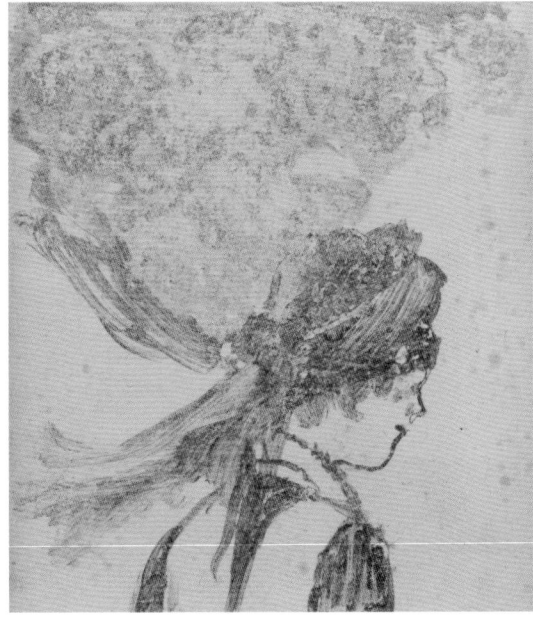

lent example of Picasso's ability, through his manipulation of aquatint, to equal the improvised, decalcomania-like effects common in the monotypes. *The Maid* (**283**) is generally overlooked in discussions of Picasso's collection because of its modest size and superficially insignificant subject matter. However, its proto-automatist technique surely fascinated him. Hovering above the maid's bowed head and seeming to emanate from it like a thought-bubble is a strange cloud-like form produced by a pool of ink that has settled into blurry, moss-like patches. Broad trailing marks describing the streamers of her cap candidly reveal the wiping action of cloth or brush. Similar pooling, spattering, and smearing make Picasso's print of Degas and the nymph look as if it were still wet and still in process.

Projection and Remembrance

Picasso was just months short of his ninetieth birthday when he made this series of etchings, and it is worth asking why Degas should have come to mean so much to him in extreme old age and why there was a long delay between the purchase of the monotypes and this com-

pulsion to identify. Picasso's personal circumstances are not irrelevant. In November 1965 he endured an emergency operation in the American Hospital in Neuilly to deal with stomach ulcers that had plagued him for a long while but flared up alarmingly in reaction to stress caused by the publication of Françoise Gilot's indiscreet memoir *Life with Picasso*, the fiasco of his failed attempt to get the French translation banned, and the prurient press coverage of the whole business, much of it hostile to him.[156] He strove to keep his operation a secret, traveled to Paris incognito, and was admitted to the hospital under the name Diego Ruiz. But news leaked out and in order to quash the rumors of cancer and dire prognostications that began to circulate, he gave upbeat reports of his state of health to journalists on his return to Mougins. In fact, however, Picasso's recovery was slow: he was eighty-four and the invasive operation felled him. He was able to resume drawing in January 1966 and printmaking that August, but there were no new paintings until early 1967. For someone with his psychological makeup — someone who equated making art with life and not making art with death — the enforced slowdown and suspension of painting were agonizing. Other indignities of old age included deafness and (so his biographers assert) impotence. He could no longer delude himself about his own invulnerability. Picasso had often complained before about not having enough time to express the images and ideas that welled up imperiously and drove him to be fanatically productive, but those complaints multiplied after his operation and he became increasingly turned in on himself, rarely leaving Notre-Dame-de-Vie and instructing Jacqueline to turn away most visitors. This is the immediate context for his late dialogue with Degas.

Like all old people, Picasso was invaded and nourished by vivid memories of the distant past. Particularly in his stream-of-consciousness-style prints and drawings, those memories surfaced in myriad glancing allusions to events, places, and people from his past and to his own earlier work.[157] Part of Degas's singular appeal in 1968–72 lay in the fact that he had been an important reference point when Picasso was young, and reminiscence was necessarily involved. The same was true of the other favorite artists who "returned" fruitfully and insistently at this juncture. But Degas was a special case for another reason. One of the people from his past who haunted Picasso in his last years was his father and first art teacher, José Ruiz Blasco. Their relationship, very close initially, had become fractious when the precocious teenager rebelled against paternal authority. Even so, there was never a total breach, and when don José died, Picasso was deeply moved. His feelings about his father remained ambivalent to the end of his life, a mixture of pride and shame according to his widow.[158] Don José was constantly in the back of his mind, so Picasso told friends: "Every time I draw a man, it's my father I'm thinking of, involuntarily. For me, a man is don José, and will be all my life. He wore a beard, and every man I draw I see more or less with his features."[159]

Don José was exactly of Degas's vintage: born in 1840, six years after Degas, he died in 1913, four years before Degas. Both dressed and behaved as men about town (see 40) and there was a striking physical resemblance, or so at least Picasso believed.[160] They even shared certain character traits: gnawing dissatisfaction with their lot that led to bouts of melancholy; disdain for those they deemed vulgar and pushy; a memorably witty but lacerating turn of phrase, which dazzled and struck fear into their acquaintances. Jaume Sabartés's description of a sardonic, middle-aged don José cannot but remind one of the often insufferable Degas: "As time passed, he learned to conceal his bitterness beneath the mocking mask of a malicious smile that, with his sophisticated bearing, underlined the sarcasm or attenuated the

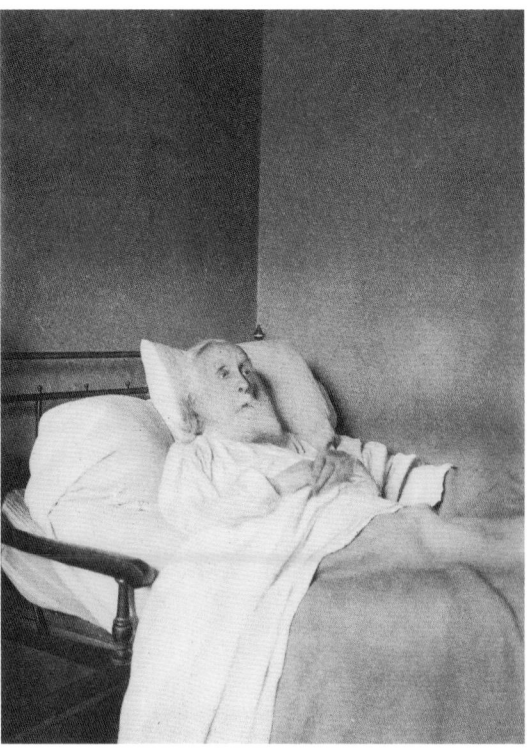

laughter which the sight of others and the idea he had of himself aroused in him."[161]

In late life both painters suffered the same tragic fate of virtual blindness, and photographs of them with their white hair and patriarchal beards staring into space are movingly alike.[162] Indeed, when Picasso rushed to his father's deathbed in May 1913, he must have been confronted with a spectacle not unlike that of the aged, bedridden, helpless Degas a few years before his death, with the difference that the ever-*distingué* don José was probably less ill-kempt (284).

For Picasso in his old age, then, Degas had a more literal father-figure role than other masters, like Rembrandt and Van Gogh, with whom he simultaneously identified.[163] He may have thought of the Degas photograph he owned (see 245) not merely as *like* his father but as in some sense *of* his father: a similar furrowed brow, distant gaze, and air of gloomy brooding are captured in sensitive and penetrating portraits the son made of the father several years before he actually discovered Degas's work (see 246).[164] There was a vast gulf between Don José and Degas at the level of artistic achievement, of course: the one a conventional painter of limited gifts and strictly local reputation, the other a groundbreaking, internationally acknowledged genius. By imaginatively eliding the two, Picasso simultaneously elevated his father's status and crushingly pointed up the absolute distinction — a distillation of that blend of pride and shame Jacqueline had noticed. But if Don José must be counted a failure as a painter, in his sex life at least he triumphed over Degas. With the reputation of a roué before his marriage to a much younger woman, he had gone on to sire not just "ordinary" children but *the* artist-genius of the twentieth century. And when Picasso placed Degas as a bystander in the brothel, he paid ironic homage to his father's bachelor escapades, for Don José had been a habitué of the Malaga whorehouses.[165]

Picasso must also have remembered his own escapades. Here the intricacies of his identification with Degas become an issue, for, to state the obvious, however much they may have had in common as artists, the history of their sex lives could hardly be more different. The most assiduous research by Degas scholars has not thrown up the name of a single mistress, whereas in Picasso's case, the list of his conquests keeps lengthening. Picasso prided himself on his potency and enjoyed drawing attention to the relationship between his art and his love affairs — how changes in his work mirrored the supplanting of one lover by another.[166] In the same spirit he wryly registered the onset of impotence. In the eighth plate of *Suite 347*, for example, he is recognizably himself but depicted as a wizened dwarf leaning on a stick.[167] In the next plate, looking like a cross between Rembrandt and Van Gogh, his alter-ego squats on the ground, arms folded to denote inactivity.[168] In both prints, the beautiful naked women perform enticingly before him, but without effect.

In a series within *Suite 347*, the notoriously bawdy prints devoted to the loves of Raphael and La Fornarina, Picasso dealt with the sexual history of another alter ego.[169] His point of departure was the group of paintings by Ingres showing La Fornarina sitting on Raphael's lap while he gazes raptly not at her but at an unfinished painting inspired by her.[170] Mischievously, Picasso crossed them with erotic Japanese prints he owned, and Ingres's decorous and sentimental image of the legendary couple is transformed into one of unbridled, athletic lust, usually observed from behind a curtain or a well-placed throne by the pope or some other dignitary, and occasionally from under the bed by an insanely jealous Michelangelo.[171] The priapic Raphael could stand in for Picasso in his heyday — with the voluptuous and compliant Marie-Thérèse Walter as his Fornarina — but not for the octogenarian Picasso. As if to acknowledge the radical change in his circumstances, Picasso lent his features to several of the aged voyeurs in these prints.[172]

The Raphael and Degas series are complementary, each coming toward the end of their respective suites, each combining the mode of cinematic, frame-by-frame narrative with obsessive repetition of the identical primal scene. The world of the Raphael suite is a world ordered and run by men, with the one woman in the story in the subsidiary, passive role. In the Degas series the situation is reversed: the brothel is a woman's world, with the madame as the matriarch and the male client as the object. Picasso's witty bracketing of the two artists has, moreover, a pleasing and deliberate art-historical symmetry: Degas the disciple of Ingres, Ingres the disciple of Raphael. One might assume that of the two great artists represented in Picasso's iconoclastic *Vite*, Raphael had by far the happier lot. But did he? After all, according to Vasari, Raphael's premature death was the consequence of his enfeeblement following a surfeit of sex: what we witness in the *Suite 347*

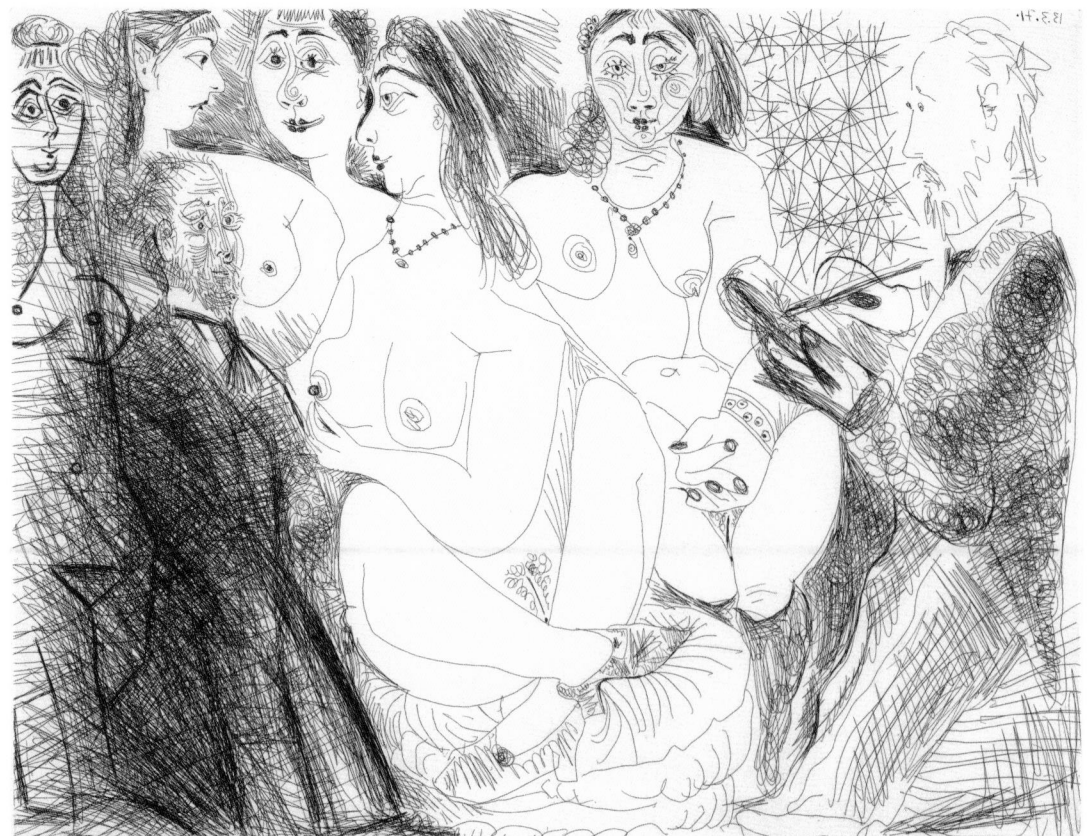

285

Pablo Picasso

Degas, in a Morning Coat,
Drawing Himself in a Suit,
among Prostitutes,
13 March 1971. Etching
on copper printed on
paper (Artist proof I/XV),
36.5 x 48.6 cm. Museu
Picasso, Barcelona
(MPB 112.228)

prints may be that final, fatally excessive bout of lovemaking.[173] By contrast, the celibate Degas was still productive in his mid-seventies.

Identifying with Degas mutated, as it was bound to, into projection, and thus the Degas series inexorably developed into a form of oblique self-portraiture. For in 1968 Picasso was in Degas's situation, condemned to look. Until that critical change overcame him, he felt no imperative need to inhabit the monotypes for weeks on end and imagine through projection what it was like to be Degas. "Condemned" is, however, the wrong word, because if the real Degas was (as far as Picasso knew) chaste owing to some obscure psychological-cum-physiological condition, this had not prevented him from producing pictures about sex that Picasso considered to be masterpieces. Viewed in this light, Degas's example was encouraging, proving that sexual dysfunction could be just

as stimulating to an artist as sexual fulfillment — provided always that the faculty of sight be not impaired. And significantly, although Degas is treated so irreverently throughout the series Picasso dedicated to him, he is invariably shown in middle age, at the height of his creative powers, never as the pathetic blind man of Degas's own version of himself, never as the Homer of painting.[174] A blind Degas would have been truly impotent as an artist, and for the notoriously superstitious Picasso, identifying with a blind painter would have been tantamount to suicide.

In Picasso's emblematic portrait of Degas (see 261), the artist is a seer. Although he is shown in iconic profile, both his eyes, hugely enlarged, are represented, one above the other, to symbolize the primacy of vision, and that area of his head is flooded by light, whereas the rest of his body is in shadow. The canvas on which he is working is not depicted, but his

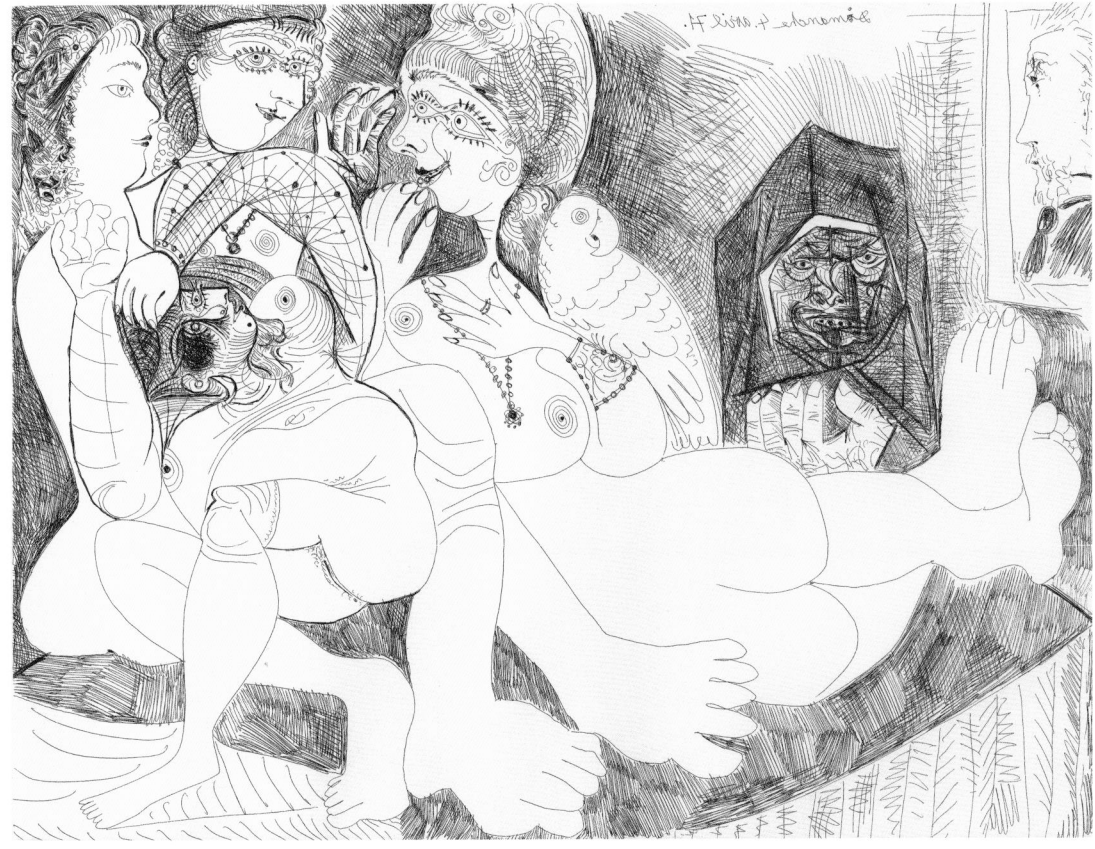

dilated gaze is directed at it. The upper eye is
stamped over the area of his brain, suggesting
that the eye controls the mind, that the artist's
power comes from his sight and the subservient
hand executes its commands. In the Degas
variations in *Suite 156*, looking is not exclusively
sexual in nature. Picasso repeatedly sets out to
"prove" that Degas's art was dependent on
looking. Hence, the device of showing Degas as
spectator at the very scenes enacted in the
monotypes: Degas was there; he saw that; he
made art — "the best things he ever did" — out
of that. On occasion, Picasso expressed this
idea more literally. In one of the first prints in
the series (**285**), Degas appears twice: first in
his traumatized state, as a rigid manikin-cum-
lay figure, in the midst of a pack of rather
friendly prostitutes, one of whom maternally
offers her nipple to him; then as himself, normal
size, leaning against a wall and calmly drawing

the scene in his sketchbook. A few days later,
Degas-the-artist was back again, looking rather
bashful with his sketchpad under his arm (see
260). The girls look at him expectantly and not
unkindly — flattered to be drawn, no doubt.
Only the old Celestina looks daggers at him:
artists don't pay! On a third occasion, in the
depths of night, by the light of an unseen lamp,
with no sign of the avaricious Celestina, Degas
works away at the portrait of a posing girl, and
for once he is in total command of the situation
and she is the modest, silent, patient model.[175]
Sublimation has occurred. In all three images
Degas is released from his usual paralysis;
instead of hiding and locking his hands away,
he uses them creatively, just as he does in
Picasso's emblematic portrait.

Degas was the ideal alter ego in this final
phase of Picasso's life, and the spate of exu-
berantly inventive prints dedicated to him may

265

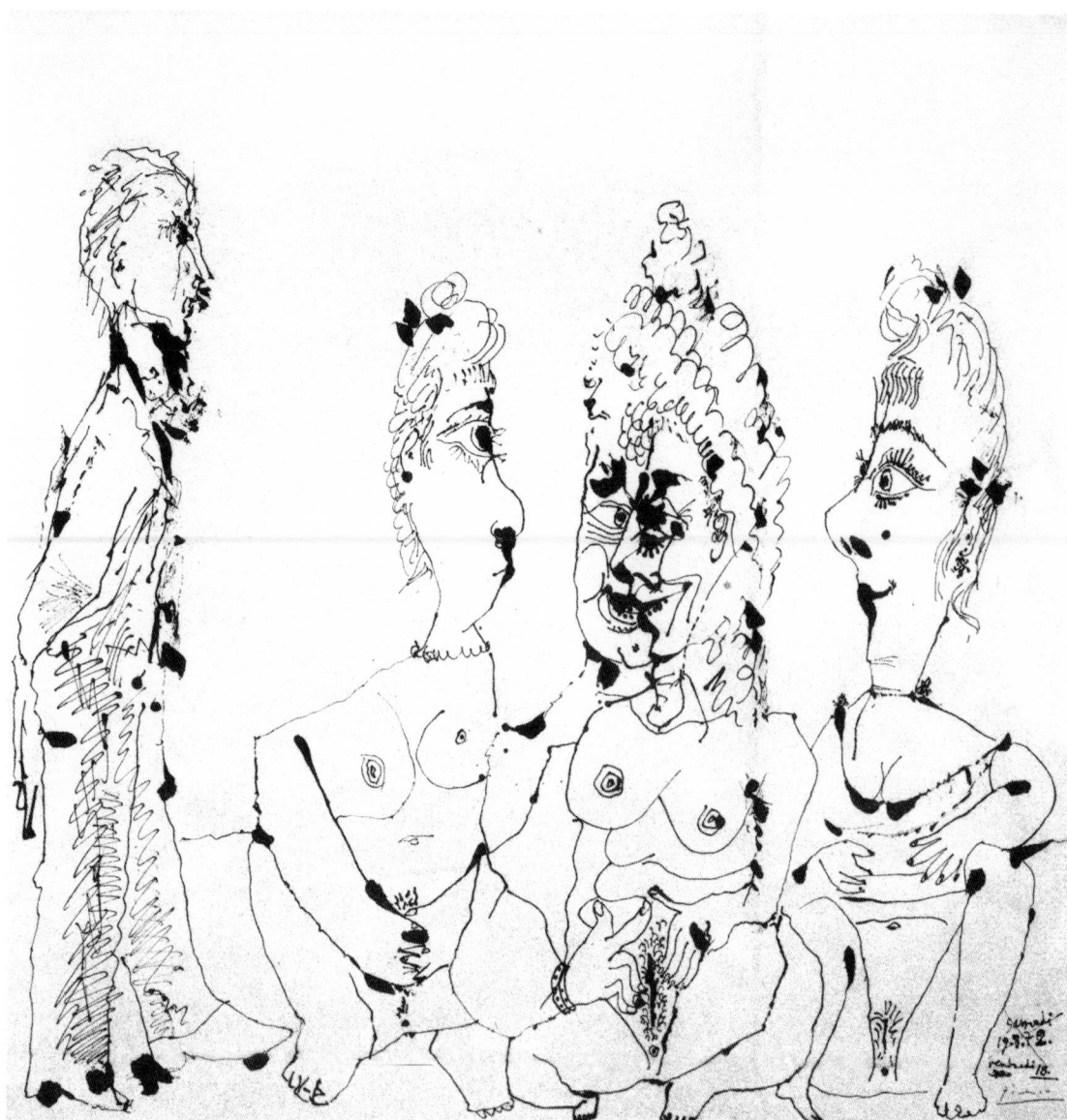

287

Pablo Picasso

Untitled, 18 August 1972.
Pen and ink on paper,
69.5 x 68.9 cm.
Location unknown

be read not as a dirge but as a celebration of vision as such and of the electrifying effect of voyeurism and fantasy fueled by voyeurism. For some spectators, the experience of looking at these prints may be daunting and shocking, for, despite their humor, they are nothing if not confrontational. Like Medusa, the prostitutes are given immense eyes with dilated pupils, the lids fringed with ray-like lashes (**286**; see 260, 278, 285); their nipples, repeatedly rendered as a spiral enclosing a pupil-like dot, stare out from their bodies (see 273); time and again the taboo zone of vulva and anus is the focus, sharply defined and brightly lit; even the complex ornamental patterns Picasso invented as he compulsively elaborated certain etchings may take an eye-like form (see 271, 278). Like the beholder of *Les Demoiselles d'Avignon*, the beholder of the prints must submit to the aggression of being stared at. But it is a reciprocal process, for the very same devices combine to lure him into looking back, and the competition among all the elaborated details means that his gaze never settles but is forever darting over the surface of the print. If the beholder does not look away in fear or embarrassment, he will be embroiled in an exercise of penetrating looking and will enter the creative, wide-awake state of both Degas and Picasso.

The final print in *Suite 156* to include Degas in person is dated 14 and 16 June 1971.[176] It did not, however, signal the end of Degas's occupation of Picasso's studio. Although the allusions are more oblique, some large late oil paintings were clearly derived from the etchings. For instance, the grisaille *Three Figures*, dated 6 September 1971,[177] omits both the madame and Degas's profile head but takes over and adapts the figures of the three prostitutes in the much reworked plate begun on 19 May 1971 and completed on 2 June (see 280). In December 1971 Picasso made several caricatural drawings of Degas in black and red crayon, all much coarser in style than the etchings and grossly comic in tone.[178] Jokey drawings of this kind — Rembrandt was a favorite butt — were a relaxation for Picasso, and he often gave them away to friends or signed books with them. In drawings made the following year when his health was beginning to fail, the dialogue with Degas continued fitfully. A pen-and-ink drawing dated 18 August 1972 shows Degas, hands locked behind his back as usual, advancing into the salon of the brothel in which three grotesquely ugly whores are squatting on the ground, all of them much larger than he, all reprising figures familiar from the prints of the previous year (**287**).[179] This time, however, the wizened madame with her towering wig is in the nude, not arrayed in the ludicrous imitation-Helena Fourment costume of the etchings — a more frightful spectacle than ever.[180] In a second drawing made that same day, she is by herself, reclining *à la* Venus, pointing obscenely with painted talons to the gash of her sex and staring in the direction of the (unseen)

door through which her next visitor — Degas presumably — is expected to enter.[181] A third drawing also dated 18 August 1972 — a mysterious carousing scene with a reclining nude and multiple profiles — includes in the top left corner the head of a wary youth, who somewhat resembles the young Degas of the 1857 self-portrait etching (see 27).[182] Perhaps Picasso was musing about what might have occurred during the artist's first visit to a brothel to determine the fatally obstructed course of his sex life ever afterward. In an even later ink drawing, the old naked man lying in the foreground looks more like Rembrandt than Degas, but there is no mistaking the reference embodied in the whore cheerfully holding her legs aloft and leering knowingly at the spectator.[183]

These very late drawings with their trembling calligraphy, drips, and blots may indicate a diminution of Picasso's hitherto exceptional manual control. But a torrent of mostly highly erotic drawings in different media was nevertheless released throughout that final summer as he fought courageously to keep creating new work as the only effective means of staving off the feebleness and inertia that would precede the end.[184] Penrose visited him twice around this time, first at the end of June 1972 and again in the middle of September, and on both occasions he was struck by Picasso's increased frailty and deafness.[185] He was not shown the extraordinary sequence of drawings depicting skull-heads produced between the end of June and the beginning of July, but Daix was and realized that, "like a good Spaniard, Picasso was looking his own death in the face."[186] For by then, there was no disguising from himself that, strive as he might, he could not cover huge canvases in the way he had the previous year and that he now found printmaking too arduous. It was in these last months of Picasso's working life that the final drawings inspired by Degas's monotypes were made. Degas was literally beside him as he contemplated his own mortality.

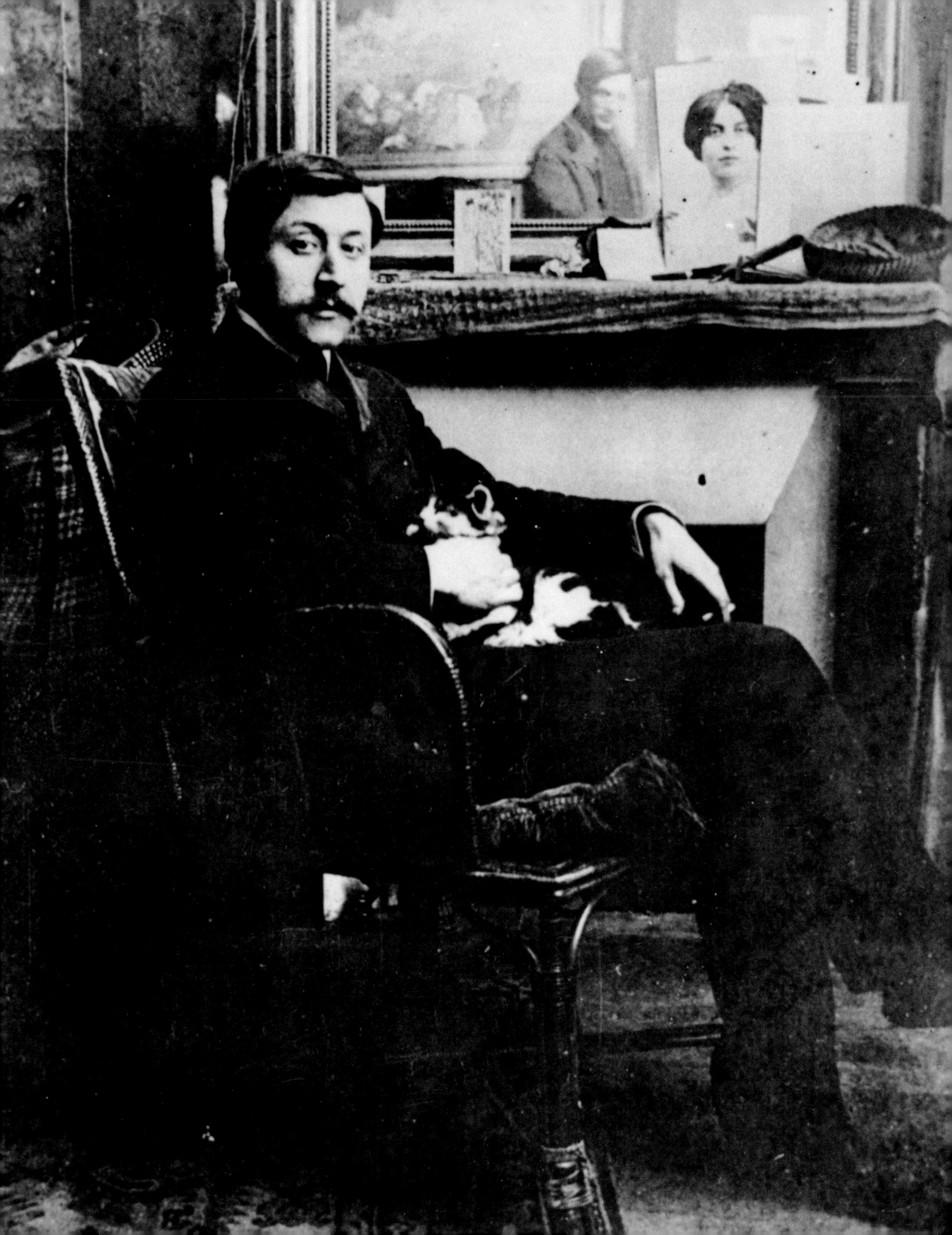

CHAPTER 6

TO PLAY WITH LIGHT AND SHADOW:

DEGAS AND PICASSO AS PHOTOGRAPHERS

SARAH LEES

The casual disarray of the corner of the room looks spontaneous, the result of a gradual accumulation of disparate objects ranging from a guitar to several canvases leaned against the walls to a brass charcoal burner. The two figures, however, one made of painted wood fragments cobbled together, the other of heterogeneous material, seem to pose openly for the camera, their painted and glued-on eyes staring fixedly outward (see 247).[1] There is another figure in this scene, and his gaze is more oblique and pensive as he rests his chin on his fist and slides a glance to the left. This is Edgar Degas, pictured in a self-portrait photograph (see 245), which is here propped up in Picasso's villa at La Californie, near Cannes, as recorded in another photograph taken by André Gomès during a visit in 1958. As Elizabeth Cowling has discussed in this volume, Gomès's visit occurred precisely at the period when Picasso purchased his first monotypes by Degas, and the presence of the literal image of the older artist confirms Picasso's fascination with him.

Degas's work as a photographer was remarkably rich, particularly given the extremely brief time span (little more than a few intensive months in 1895–96) during which he practiced it, taking up in this new medium what one observer described as "his life-work — to play with light and shadow."[2] Picasso's involvement behind the lens was somewhat more extensive, and, thanks to the mass-cultural expansion of the medium after about 1900, his role as a con-

sumer, collector, and subject of photographs was considerably more so. Both artists, that is, made use of the medium as they did almost every other artistic form, and in certain instances their approaches are remarkably similar. These instances are circumscribed by the limited number of known photographs by Degas as well as by the types of subjects he most often chose: in the catalogue raisonné published by Malcolm Daniel, only forty-four images with existing prints are listed, although several more have come to light subsequently, and textual references suggest others that have been lost.[3] Aside from a very small number of photographs that relate directly to his work in other media, Degas focused almost exclusively on a small circle of friends, and on himself. A number of Picasso's photographs take up the same sorts of subjects. Certainly portraiture was among the first and most widespread functions served by photography, so a degree of similarity between the two bodies of work is inevitable. In addition to displaying affinities in form and content, however, photographs by Degas and Picasso at times reveal related purposes both in exploring the potential of the medium and in what might be seen as attempts by their makers to record their social and artistic identities.

This brief discussion of Degas's and Picasso's photographs will consider them in parallel since, aside from the signal example of Picasso's ownership in the 1950s of Degas's self-portrait, and unlike many of the instances discussed elsewhere

Detail of Pablo Picasso,
*Ricard Canals in the
Studio* (291)

in this book, it is very difficult to document Picasso's direct contact with or knowledge of Degas's photographic output. Aside from having some of his photographs on view in January 1896 in the shop of Guillaume Tasset, an artist's supplier who sold Degas photographic material, gave him advice, and printed his negatives, Degas's photographs were not exhibited or widely circulated for many years. Since Picasso was still studying in Barcelona in 1896, he could not have seen the display at Tasset's, and when he began to make his first trips to Paris just a few years later, in 1900–1904, and to take photographs, most of Degas's prints were probably still owned by the sitters who appeared in them, many of them members of the Halévy family. Tasset's shop in Montmartre, however, was virtually around the corner from one of the studios Picasso rented during his early visits, and very close to where Degas himself lived, and discussions of the eminent artist and his work regularly took place among the younger artists in the neighborhood.[4] Moreover, Picasso gradually began to meet other owners of photographs by Degas, such as Paul Valéry and Eugène Rouart, and in 1920 René Degas, the artist's brother, donated several prints to the Bibliothèque Nationale in Paris. Picasso very likely knew at least of the existence of Degas's photographs, then, and while the connections may not be direct, the compelling visual links between certain images suggest that the two artists had a particular appreciation for the medium — and more specifically, for its capacity to capture the nuances of relations between individuals, a capacity essentially equivalent to the gaze of the artist himself.[5]

Thanks to several accounts by friends and the sometimes long-suffering sitters in his photographs, Degas's authorship of most of the images under discussion is securely documented. In the often-repeated description by Daniel Halévy of an after-dinner photography session, "Degas raised his voice, became dicta-

torial, gave orders that a lamp be brought into the little salon and that anyone who wasn't going to pose should leave. The *duty* part of the evening began."[6] In Picasso's case, the evidence of the images themselves suggests that for many of the photographs discussed here, the artist himself activated the shutter. When either Degas or Picasso appears in the frame, it is of course possible that the photograph is, strictly speaking, "by" someone else. Even in many of these cases, however, it seems most likely that the artist was still responsible for conceiving and orchestrating the image, just as Halévy's description indicates. As Anne Baldassari describes it, "Certainly, the clear intentionality that is apparent in the spatial organization, the objects, and the model himself is without any doubt enough to consider these photographs *self-portraits*, even if the artist had to have recourse to the help of a third person — a friend or companion — to accomplish the technical act of taking the picture."[7] Both artists seem deliberately to have used the ambiguity as to who authored such images, however, as a means of underscoring their role as the object of observation, as being depicted, rather than doing the depicting. I will consider most of the photographs in this essay to be by Degas or Picasso unless otherwise noted, if not necessarily in the sense of the artist as the camera operator, then at least as the author, however covertly, of the composition recorded on the plate or film.

One early photograph of Picasso was probably not taken by him but apparently by one of several Catalan friends with whom the artist spent time during his second, seven-month stay in Paris in 1901 (**288**). There are three similar photographs that show groups in the studio at 130 ter, boulevard de Clichy, where Picasso shared an apartment with Pere Mañach, who was also serving as his dealer at the time. In this photograph, Mañach appears standing at the right, while at the left Picasso slouches on a stool, staring rather balefully at the camera.

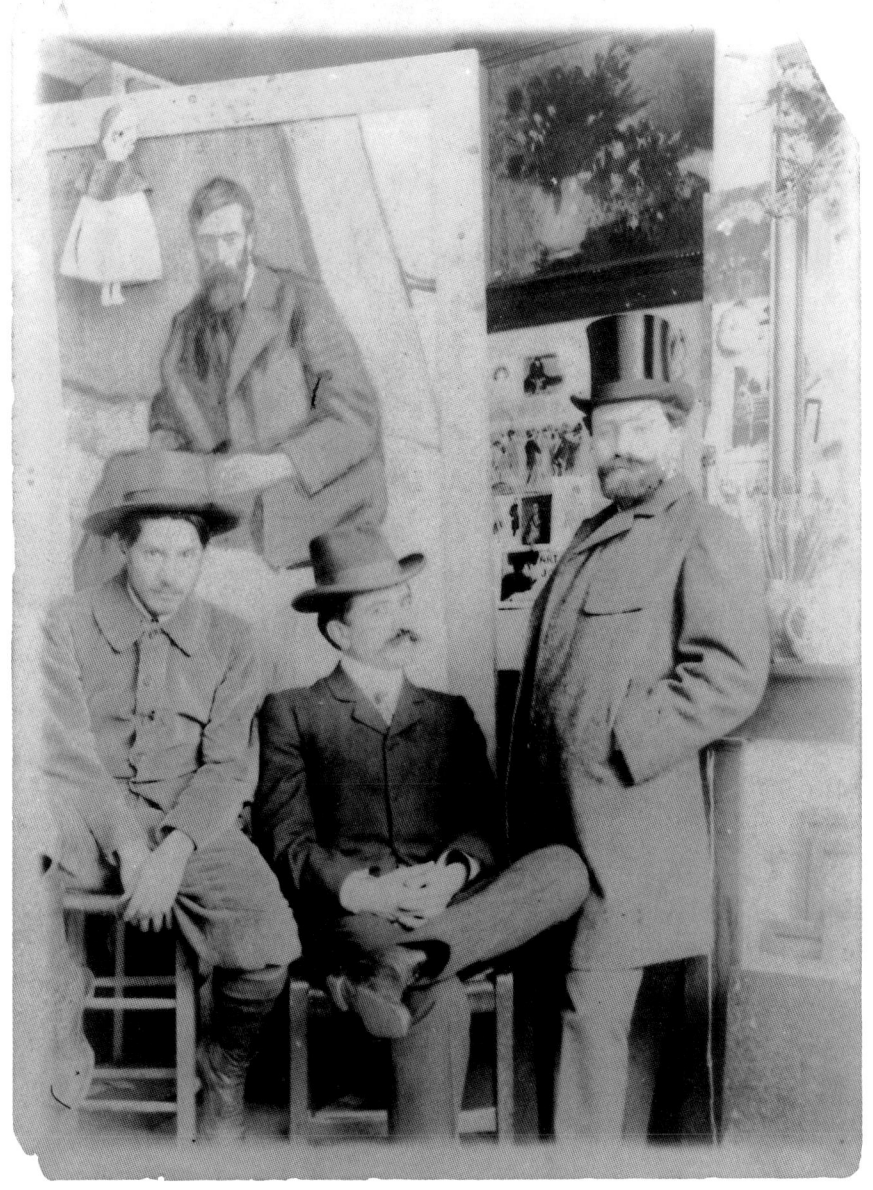

had orchestrated in 1895 after dinner at the home of his friend Ludovic Halévy, the very evening described by Ludovic's son Daniel (**289**). Here Degas appears in the foreground, his ankle on his knee much like the central figure of Picasso's friend. On the left is Jules Taschereau, a friend of Degas's (and related by marriage to Halévy), and leaning on the chair back just above Degas's head is the artist Jacques-Émile Blanche. The atmosphere is appreciably different from that in the brightly lit Montmartre studio, where the viewer is confronted by four piercing gazes (one of them painted). Here, instead, the men seemed to be wrapped not only in the dimness of the well-appointed parlor but also in the comfortable warmth of both friendship and after-dinner satisfaction, and only Taschereau may be looking outward, though it is difficult to be certain.

Yet both images convey the two artists' self-presentations at the time. Picasso looks almost like an awkward, resentful child thanks both to his posture and to his outfit, with its large rounded collar and pants that stop just below the knees. If Baldassari's dating of the image is correct, he had not yet proven himself at the Vollard exhibition, but he must have known that this display of sixty-four oil paintings, pastels, and watercolors done in a variety of styles would forcefully demonstrate his precocious virtuosity. Degas, in contrast, is clearly at home in his firmly rooted position at the center of this group, invisibly directing the somewhat more precariously posed friends who orbit around him. In the two related photographs of Picasso, in fact, he appears in a position far more similar to Degas's, confidently seated in a chair surrounded by the same friends, who are "admiring [his] paintings," as Picasso's own inscription on the reverse of one of them explains.[10] Since Pere Mañach has only a large mustache in these two images while in the previous photo he also had a beard, they were presumably taken at a different time, perhaps just before

288
Group in the Studio at 130 ter, Boulevard de Clichy, 1901. Photograph, 12 x 8.3 cm. Archives Picasso, Musée national Picasso, Paris (inv. DP 5)

The man in the center is probably the artist Antonio Torres Fuster.[8] The men pose in front of the work Picasso had hanging in his studio; Baldassari suggests that the photograph was taken shortly before several of these paintings were exhibited at Ambroise Vollard's gallery in late June 1901, in a joint exhibition of work by Picasso and Francisco Iturrino, whose large portrait hovers over Picasso's head.[9] Purely fortuitously, this grouping echoes the one that Degas

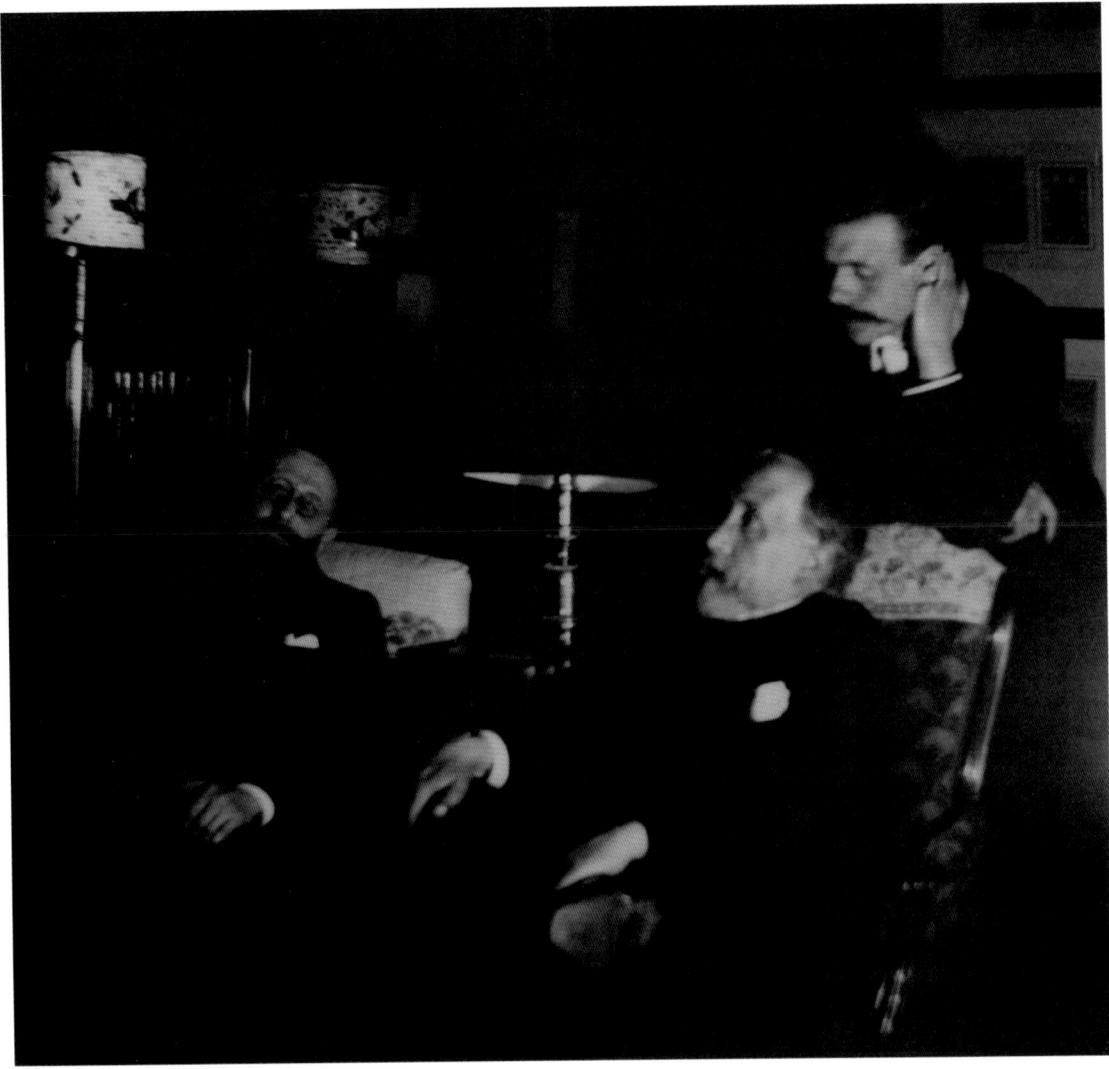

289

Edgar Degas

Jules Taschereau,
Edgar Degas, and
Jacques-Émile Blanche,
1895. Gelatin silver
print from a glass
negative, enlargement,
22.9 x 24.8 cm. Sterling
and Francine Clark Art
Institute, Williamstown,
Massachusetts
(2002.6)

Picasso returned to Barcelona, as the third print is inscribed "me in the studio. Goodbye. Picasso."[11] The presence of a second, lesser-known artist and of a supportive but non-artist friend in Degas's and Picasso's pictures suggests that both might have envisioned themselves in similar positions within a close-knit group of like-minded people of whom they were in some sense the primary focus or leader.

Both men also photographed friends without appearing in the image themselves. Picasso created a number of portraits between 1908 and 1911 in his studio at the Bateau Lavoir and then on the boulevard de Clichy of people including his old friend from Barcelona Sebastià Junyer i Vidal, the writer André Salmon, poet Guillaume Apollinaire, dealer Daniel-Henry Kahnweiler, and, perhaps most notably, Georges Braque. In virtually every one, the subject is posed in front of one or more of Picasso's paintings or drawings, suggesting the inevitable relation to his own art-making that the artist must have seen even when ostensibly devoting a photograph to a friend.[12] Degas pictured members of the extended Halévy family numerous times in their own rooms, and also recorded his brother René in his (Edgar's) studio, the collector and friend Henri Rouart in his home, and cousins Julie Manet and Paule and Jeannie Gobillard in their apartment, along with their friend Geneviève Mallarmé. These images tend to reveal Degas exploring the possibilities of the photographic medium as much as registering the bonds of family and friendship, just as he had done in the image of Taschereau and Blanche. "I'm trying to photograph almost at night," he wrote to Guillaume Tasset, and indeed many of the Halévy photographs, lit only by one or two household lamps, bear out this statement.[13] The image of Julie Manet and the Gobillards, in contrast, is nearly as brightly illuminated, at least in its upper half, as the other images are dark, thanks to the nine kerosene lamps Degas had assembled for the session, some of whose brilliance is reflected in the mirror behind the women.[14]

Two other photographs combine portraits of friends and self-portraiture in a very particular manner. Degas made his during the same session at the Manet/Gobillard residence, and it depicts the artist Pierre-Auguste Renoir and the poet Stephane Mallarmé against the backdrop of a slightly different section of the same salon as that in which the four women posed (**290**). This is perhaps the best known and most written-about of Degas's photographs, for it is filled with detail and potential meaning. At the center of the composition, Renoir gazes outward, his head tipped back perhaps to help him hold his pose but also suggestive of a level of comfort and intimacy in this company. Mallarmé leans against the wall next to him, glancing downward at his friend with what seems like solicitude. Just behind Renoir's head, reflected in a large mirror built into the wall, appear the heads of Mallarmé's wife and daughter, Marie and Geneviève, as they watch the two men being photographed. And at the left edge of the image, the camera taking this photograph appears, again in the mirror. Next to it is Degas, discernable by the dark mass of his jacket and his white collar, though his own

features are lost in the dazzling glare of one of the kerosene lamps. This image makes explicit the equivalence between the artist's gaze and that of the camera, particularly as the camera's "eye" is visible but the artist's is not, but it also complicates the subjects of that gaze. As Carol Armstrong describes it, this photograph pictures the unbridgeable divide between subject and object, between here and there; it "engenders not union between maker and mirror but a constant switching of places between the *here* and the *there*. . . . Rather than a collapse, it presents a puzzle and a paradox, a constant circle of substitutions and reversals between the act of sight and things seen in the mirror, the present and active tense of seeing and the past and passive one."[15] In this way, it records Degas investigating once again — here on an epistemological level — the possibilities of the photographic medium.

Picasso's photograph portrays Ricard Canals, another artist from Barcelona who had settled in Paris and became one of Picasso's closest friends when the latter moved definitively to the French capital in 1904 (**291**). Perhaps the photograph, taken that year, commemorates this relationship. Canals is seated comfortably in a wicker chair, holding a cat in his lap and a cigarette in his fingers. Propped up on the mantel behind Canals is a photograph of his wife, Benedetta, and just to the left appears the photographer, Picasso, reflected in the mirror above the mantel and standing in front of what looks like a large framed painting on the wall behind him. Although half of Picasso's face is lost in the glare of the light, the other half, including his signature shock of black hair, is clearly visible. He seems to be gazing as steadily at the sitter as Canals and his wife, in the image within the image, look back at him. According to an inscription on the back of this print, probably written some years later, the room is Canals's studio rather than Picasso's, the usual location of many of the other photographs Picasso took.[16] The artist is clearly exploring the nature of representation just as Degas did, if in a somewhat different way, incorporating painted, photographed, and reflected images into a single frame. The portrait of Benedetta particularly seems to complicate matters, for not only might it be placed just over the spot where Picasso's camera would appear in the mirror, but it also marks almost precisely the juncture between the space of the room and reflected space, between here and there, serving as a reminder that the two spaces are not continuous, and that each of the three figures exists in a separate sphere. This is very much like the type of paradox Armstrong finds in Degas's photograph. Picasso may be somewhat more present here than Degas is in his photograph, while the act of photographing is obscured — or rather, it is almost as if Benedetta's gaze replaces that of Picasso's camera, giving her an unexpected agency and presence even though she was literally absent — making the question of the origin of the image just as unresolvable as for the earlier photograph.

Indeed, the parallels between these two images, taken nine years apart, seem not just fortuitous but uncanny. As well as the formal similarities, both are labeled portraits of friends but also act as self-portraits, and both include the wife of the sitter, if in a separate realm. Moreover, Benedetta Canals, who would sit for her own painted portrait by Picasso the following year (see 113), had served earlier as a model for Degas and may have suggested that Fernande Olivier, with whom Picasso became involved the same year, 1904, do the same.[17] Yet, it is still almost certainly not a question of the younger artist having seen the older photograph but rather of both employing similar common conventions and compositional devices to explore in parallel ways the meaning of photographic representation and of representation in general. Certainly both artists were familiar with the mirror as a necessary tool for

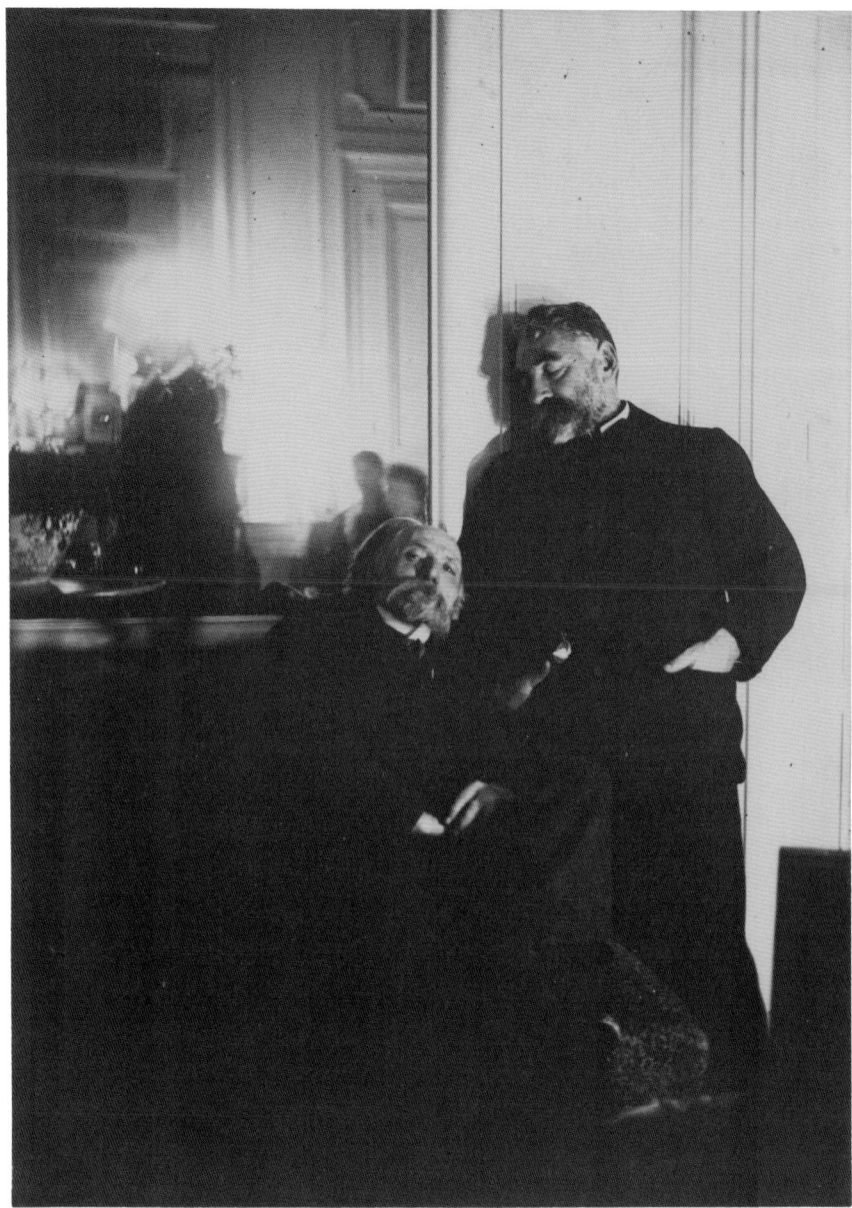

290
Edgar Degas
Pierre-Auguste Renoir and Stéphane Mallarmé, 1895. Gelatin silver print, 39.1 x 28.4 cm. The Museum of Modern Art, New York. Gift of Paul F. Walter (207.89)

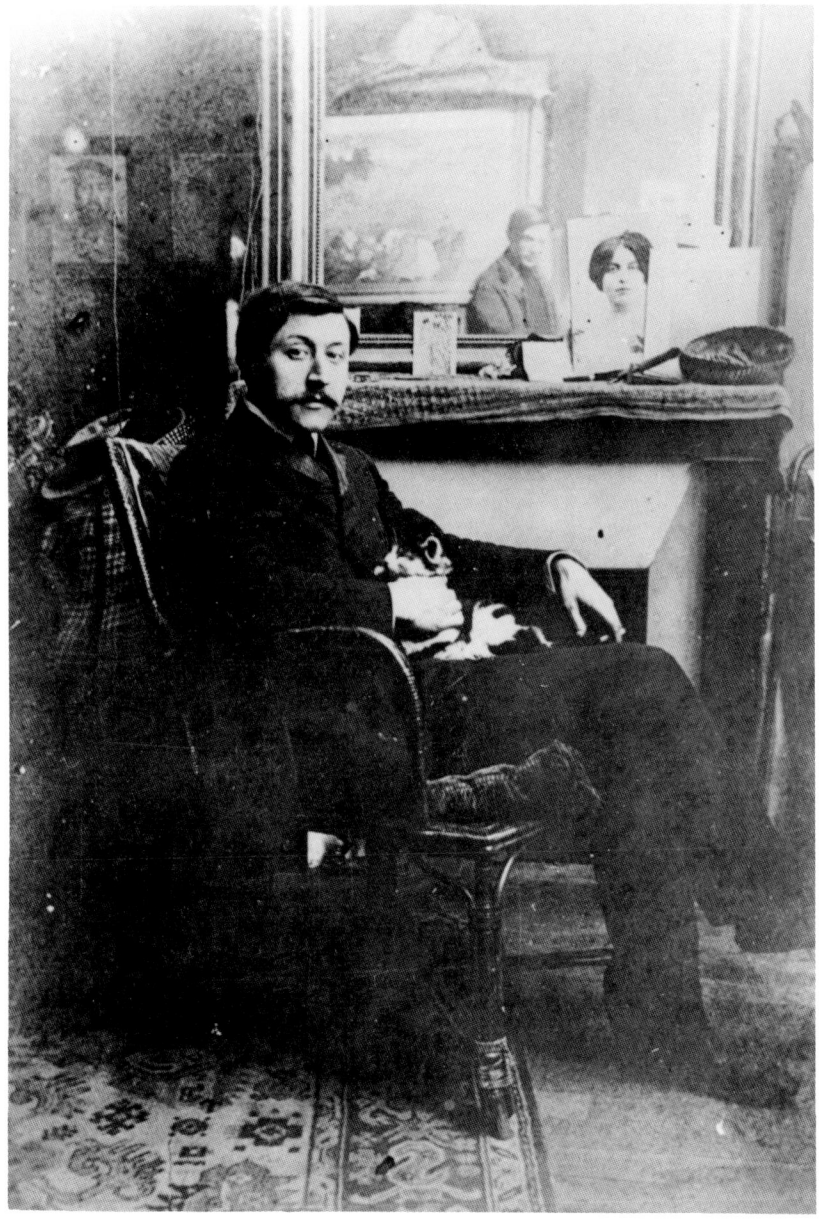

291

Pablo Picasso

*Ricard Canals in the
Studio*, 1904. Photograph
21 x 14.8 cm. Archives
Picasso, Musée national
Picasso, Paris (DP 87)

producing a self-portrait and recorded its usage here as an end in itself rather than a means for producing a painting. Degas had also counseled himself, in a now-famous remark in his notebook, to use a mirror to render unfamiliar what he looked at: "do not permit yourself to paint things except when seen in the mirror in order to habituate yourself to the hatred of trompe l'oeil."[18] In some sense, then, his photograph aligns closely with an already existing project. Picasso's compilation of different media within a single image similarly seems an early instance of an approach to image-making that would culminate in his practice of using newspaper in papier collé, or in a work like *Still Life with Chair Caning* of 1912, with its photoreproduction of the object it depicted.[19]

Another technical operation serves as a point of contact between two other photographs. In Degas's image, the scene is set once again in the Halévy apartment, where several members of the extended family pose against a wall of framed prints (**292**). But after exposing the plate once, Degas then turned it ninety degrees and exposed it again. The other image (it is impossible to determine which was made first) shows a different group in the same location. Degas then printed the double exposure. Certain passages in this double image appear sharply defined in both the vertical and horizontal orientations, while others are ghostly, the result of two coinciding areas of partial light and shadow in both scenes. This photograph and another double exposure from the same session — again mentioned by Daniel Halévy as showing "Uncle Jules [Taschereau], Mathilde [Niaudet] and Henriette [Taschereau] [seated] on the little sofa in front of the piano"[20] are often described as accidental: "Degas's preoccupation with forcing the poses he sought," Elizabeth Childs writes, "preempted his attention to technical detail."[21] But it seems equally possible that the artist was once again experimenting with the capacities of the medium,

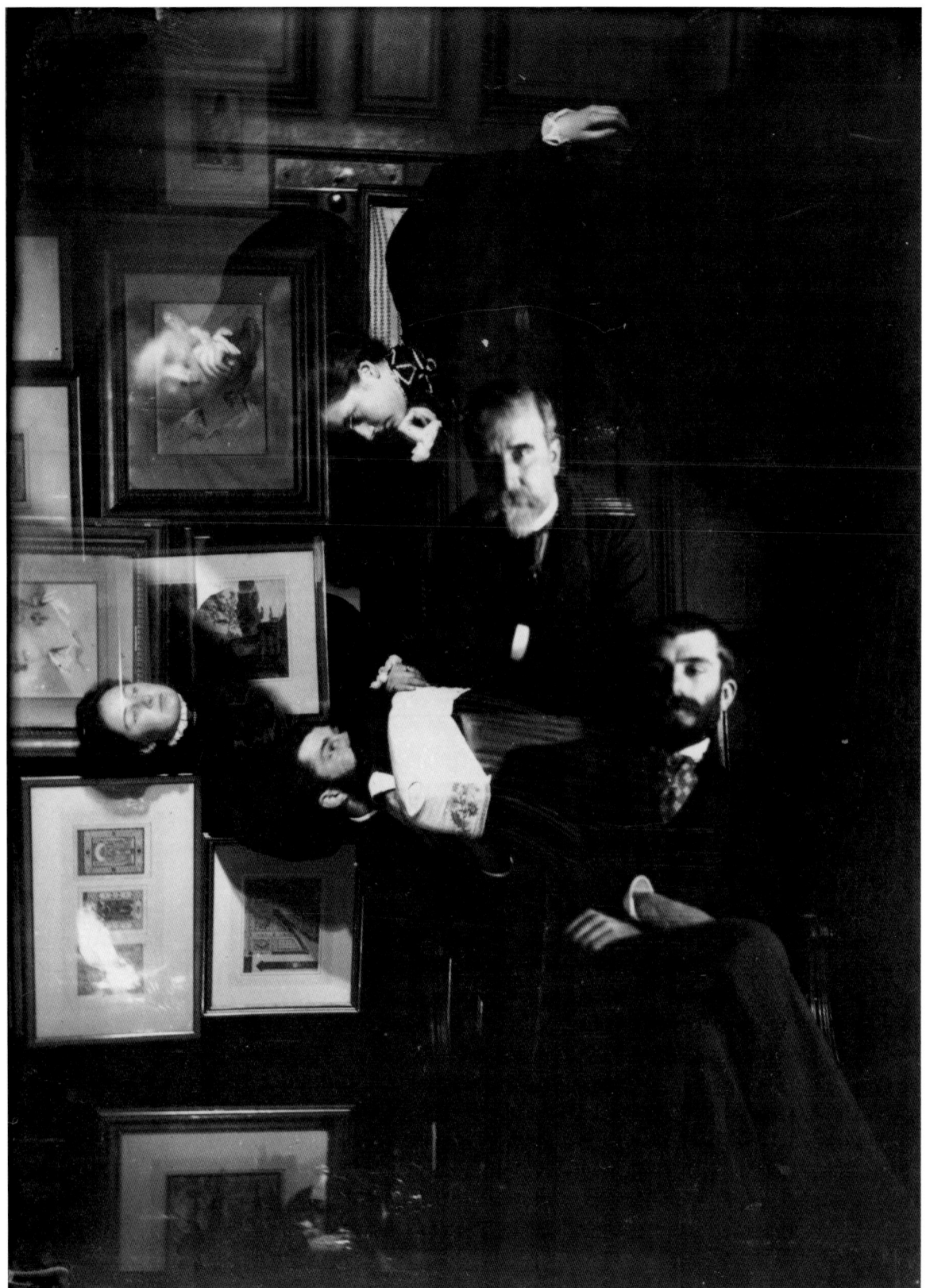

292

Edgar Degas

*Mathilde and Jeanne
Niaudet, Daniel Halévy,
Henriette Taschereau,
Ludovic and Élie Halévy*,
1895. Modern print from a
glass negative, 9 x 12 cm.
Musée d'Orsay, Paris
(PHO 1987 5)

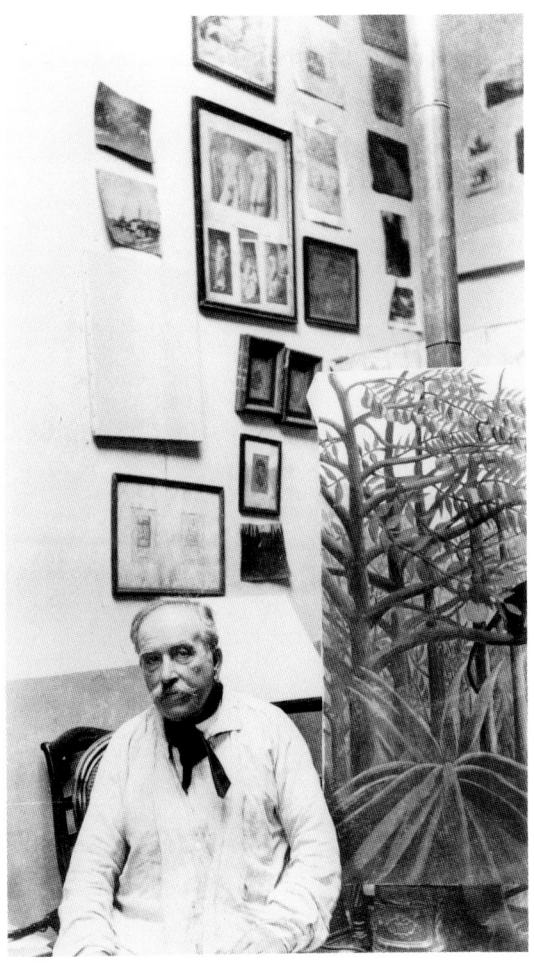

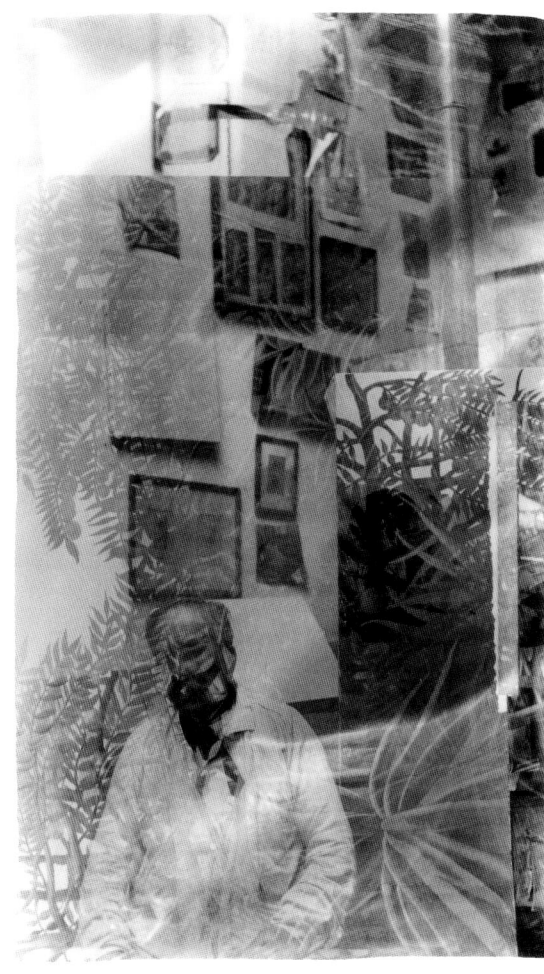

since the "accident" occurred not once but twice. Certainly once the negative was printed, Degas appreciated the strange, anti-trompe-l'oeil (or extra trompe-l'oeil) effect, since he had the negatives printed multiple times.[22]

In Picasso's case, the same operation is more clearly deliberate. Among the portraits of friends from 1908–11 is one of the douanier Henri Rousseau in his own studio, taken in 1910 (**293**). He sits dressed in a painter's smock next to his painting *Monkeys in the Virgin Forest,*[23] of which only a small slice of the left side is visible, with framed and unframed images, mostly reproductions, covering the wall behind him. The print has a somewhat unusual format, a long, narrow vertical, so that the sitter takes up only a portion of the lower left corner and

seems dwarfed by his surroundings. During this same session, Picasso also photographed the painting alone in a closer view, still not centered in the shot but this time with the lower right corner visible, along with the easel on which the canvas is resting. He then superimposed the two negatives offset by ninety degrees (**294**).[24] One of the monkeys appears directly over Rousseau's mouth, while the lush foliage seems to surround the artist, who still sits calmly within his own imaginary forest. Given the visual and conceptual aptness of the double image (Rousseau was, after all, considered a "primitive" artist), Picasso may well have intended it from the outset; further, perhaps the long horizontal format of Rousseau's painting determined the narrow vertical format of the simple portrait. Picasso must have carefully arranged the placement of the two negatives together so that the heads of the artist and monkey coincided, perhaps cutting the negative with the image of the painting, since its framing is particularly arbitrary, and it does not appear as an independent print.[25]

Once again, there is no need to suggest any direct connection between this photograph by Picasso and Degas's double images. If the latter case was possibly unintentional, the use of double exposures was well known by 1910 (and indeed by 1895), particularly for spirit photographs, which purported to record apparitions invisible to the unaided eye.[26] In fact, Picasso himself had made use of a double image a number of years earlier, to produce an unusual self-portrait (**295**). The clearest portions of this photograph show several of the artist's paintings, all dated 1901, hanging on the wall of his studio, including *Yo, Picasso* at the top, *The Absinthe Drinker* in the center, and the *Portrait of Gustave Coquiot* at the bottom.[27] Next to and partially overlapping these paintings is a shadowy figure wrapped in a dark coat and wearing a top hat, with one eye staring directly outward while the other is obscured. This image, probably created through the superimposition of two negatives, seems carefully orchestrated so that the figure appears in the empty wall space next to the paintings. If the piercing half-gaze is not sufficient to identify the artist, the parallels with several painted self-portraits of the same year, such as *Self-Portrait in a Top Hat,* reinforce the supposition,[28] and an inscription on the back of the print makes it definitive: "The strongest walls open at my approach — behold," the "my" clearly referring to the top-hatted figure in the photo, that is, to the artist himself.[29] This comment also makes clear the irresolvable nature of the double image, for if, to one observer, the ghostly artist seems to give way before the more solid wall and its vivid paintings, Picasso saw just the opposite. In some

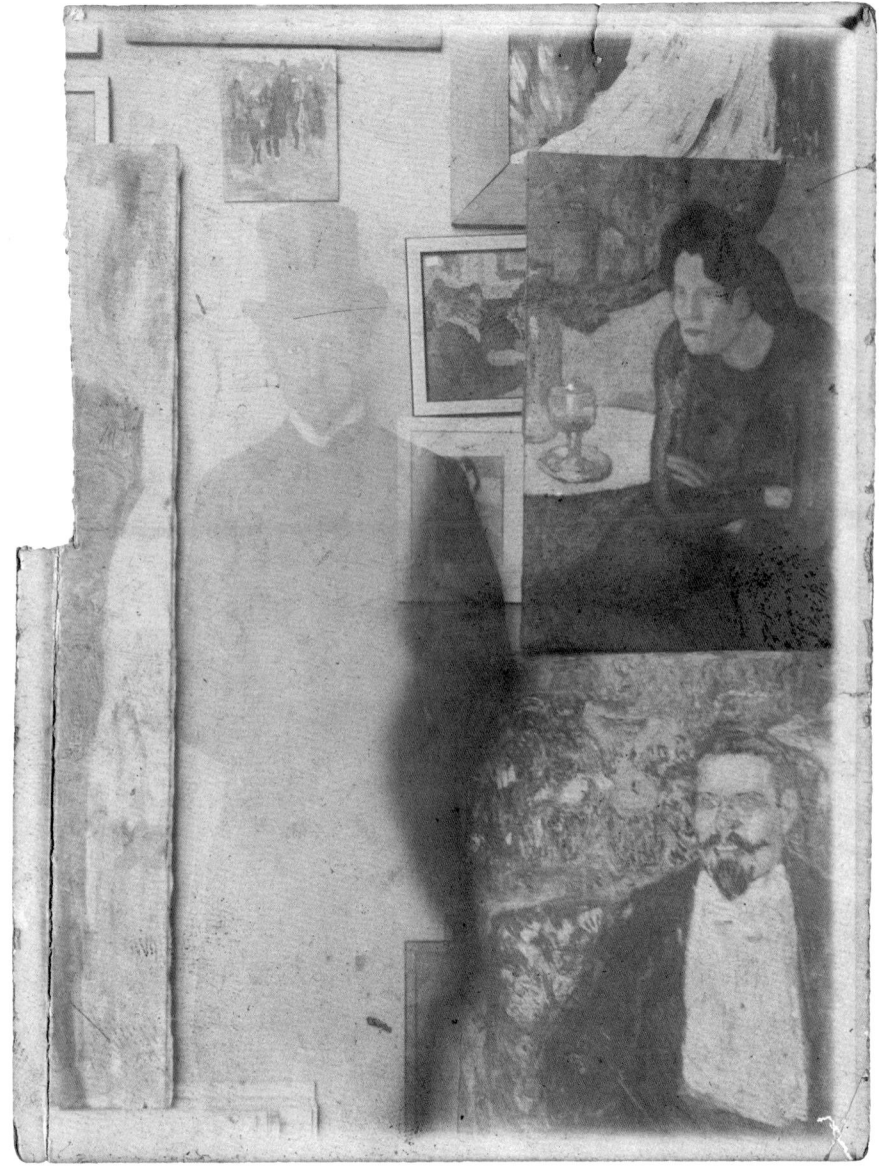

295

Pablo Picasso

Self-Portrait in the Studio,
c. 1901–2. Photograph,
12 x 9 cm. Archives
Picasso, Musée national
Picasso, Paris
(APPH 2800)

way, too, this self-portrait with paintings — which foreshadows the portraits of friends in his studio that he would make some ten years later — might serve as a multi-level exploration of his artistic identity, conflating the artist and his work in a fairly literal sense. As Baldassari comments, "[T]his interrogation uses the photograph, substituting for the mirror, as the initial site for questioning simultaneously the man, the artist, and the potential of his art."[30]

While there is no closely equivalent self-portrait among Degas's photographs, a final pair of images once again presents the artists in comparable manners. Both appear to be rather casual compositions; certainly in Picasso's photograph, which shows him with Fernande Olivier, the slightly out-of-focus quality and the presence of the large, looming bottles to the right and coffeepot directly in front of the camera suggest an impromptu photo session perhaps undertaken after a meal, much like Degas's practice (**296**). It is a standard view of a couple, she with her arms thrown around his neck, her cheek pressed to his, and both looking at the camera with a smile. Indeed, in this instance, the parallels with a photograph by Degas are fairly simple, consisting essentially of the presence of a woman with the artist, and the pyramidal shape formed by the two figures. But in Degas's *Self-Portrait with Zoé Closier* (**297**), every detail, or at least those that have caught the light, is sharply focused, and the conjunction of the seated artist placed very close to the lens and the standing figure of his servant, caught as if pausing momentarily while passing through the shot, is probably only slightly less orchestrated than the group portraits of the Halévys and their friends.[31] Furthermore, little about the relation between the two figures is standard or easily comprehensible. Their apparent estrangement from each other hints that Closier does not have the same status as the friends in all Degas's other photographs, and her expression, though she looks directly at the camera, is hard

to read — perhaps careworn, or concerned, or perhaps, given that most of her figure and parts of her face are covered in darkness, slightly haunted. Degas, for his part, gazes off to the left seemingly unaware of the person behind him, part of his face, too, nearly lost in shadow. As a reflection of the two artists' personal lives, Picasso always allied with a lover or wife, Degas always solitary, the photographs once again display more differences than similarities. Nonetheless, it is perhaps just Degas's aloofness and inscrutability, along with his proper, well-to-do appearance, that appealed to Picasso, for this is the same image, although in an altered form, that Picasso displayed in his villa at La Californie.

In the print that Picasso owned, Closier's figure has been covered over with ink (see 245). It is impossible to determine, as Cowling notes, whether Degas himself edited his photo, or whether it was Picasso who continued the process suggested by the image itself, of extending the darkness to encompass Closier entirely, rather than just partially. Picasso's singular interest in Degas is clear in either case. This interest was not only in Degas the artist, the creator of the monotypes that Picasso owned and, as the essays in this catalogue have demonstrated, the creator of a body of work from which Picasso drew a great deal of inspiration but also — as, again, Cowling has proposed — in Degas the man and the father figure both artistically and as an ideal, imagined surrogate for his own father. Degas the photographer, however, while not unknown, had yet to be fully examined in 1958. Nonetheless, complete knowledge of his photographs does not seem to have been necessary for Picasso to take up the medium early in the century and employ it in ways comparable to those his predecessor had done.

There are also considerable divergences in the two bodies of photographic work. Degas, for example, never seems to have recorded his own paintings or drawings as Picasso often did, nor did he collect photographs and postcards

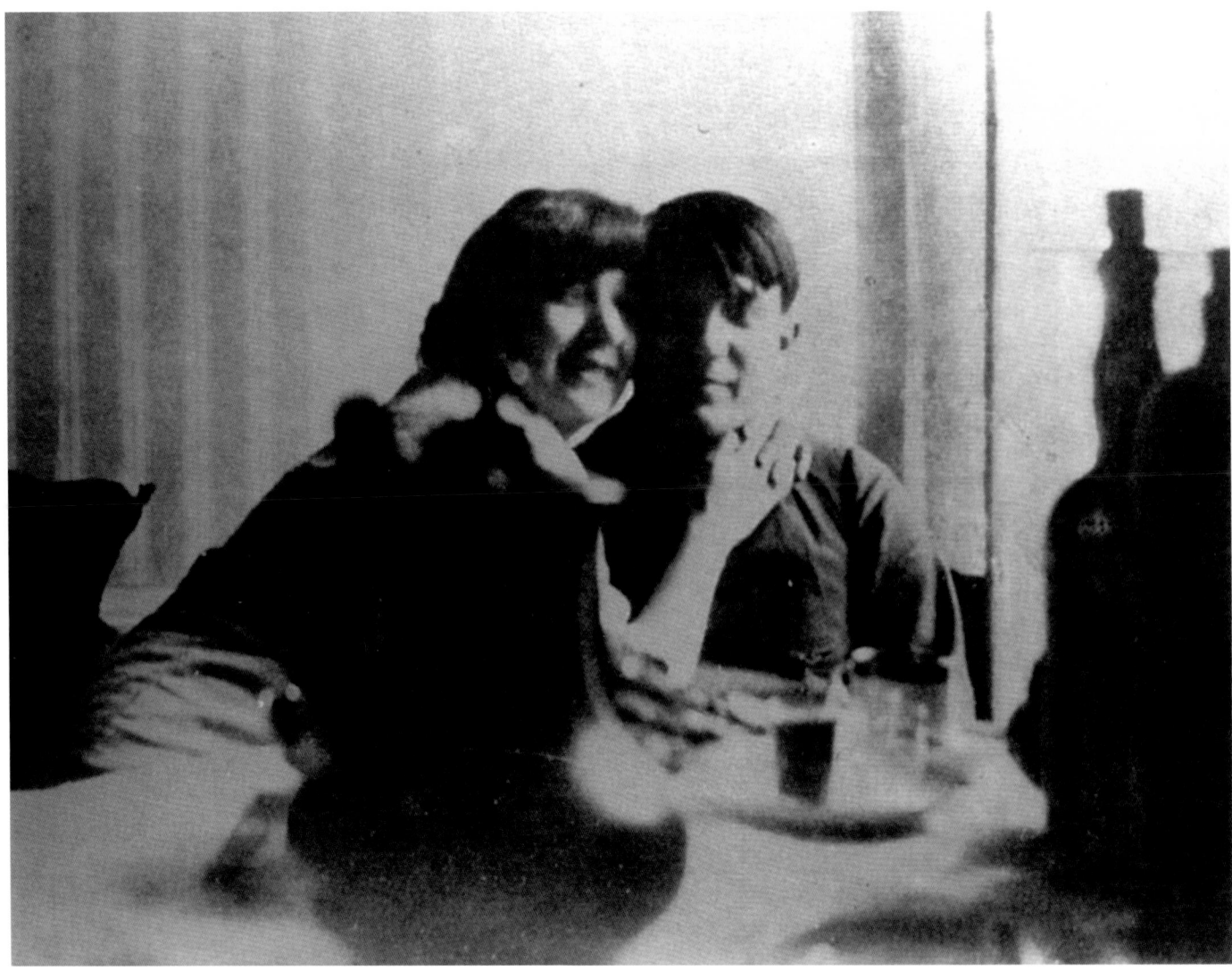

and base other works on them. In turn, Picasso did not delve into the technical possibilities and limits of the medium in creating his own photographic images as deeply as Degas did in "photographing at night," or in striving for other experimental results, such as the startling, brilliantly colored negatives of a dancer posing in the studio, which he then used as a source for works in other media.[32] In general, photography was more interwoven at different levels with Picasso's art through much of his career, as a product, source, or inspiration, than it was for Degas, whose brief, late adoption of the medium resulted in images that reveal many of the concerns he had already explored in other works. Yet, considering the areas in which their output does coincide points to an interest that both artists seem to have shared with the ways in which images generate meaning. Other artists who took photographs in this period tended to use them as tools in the working process, for their capacity to serve as documents and as tireless and infinitely adaptable models, or they investigated the more evocative and poetic possibili-

296

Pablo Picasso

Self-Portrait with Fernande Olivier, c. 1910.

Photograph,

Location unknown

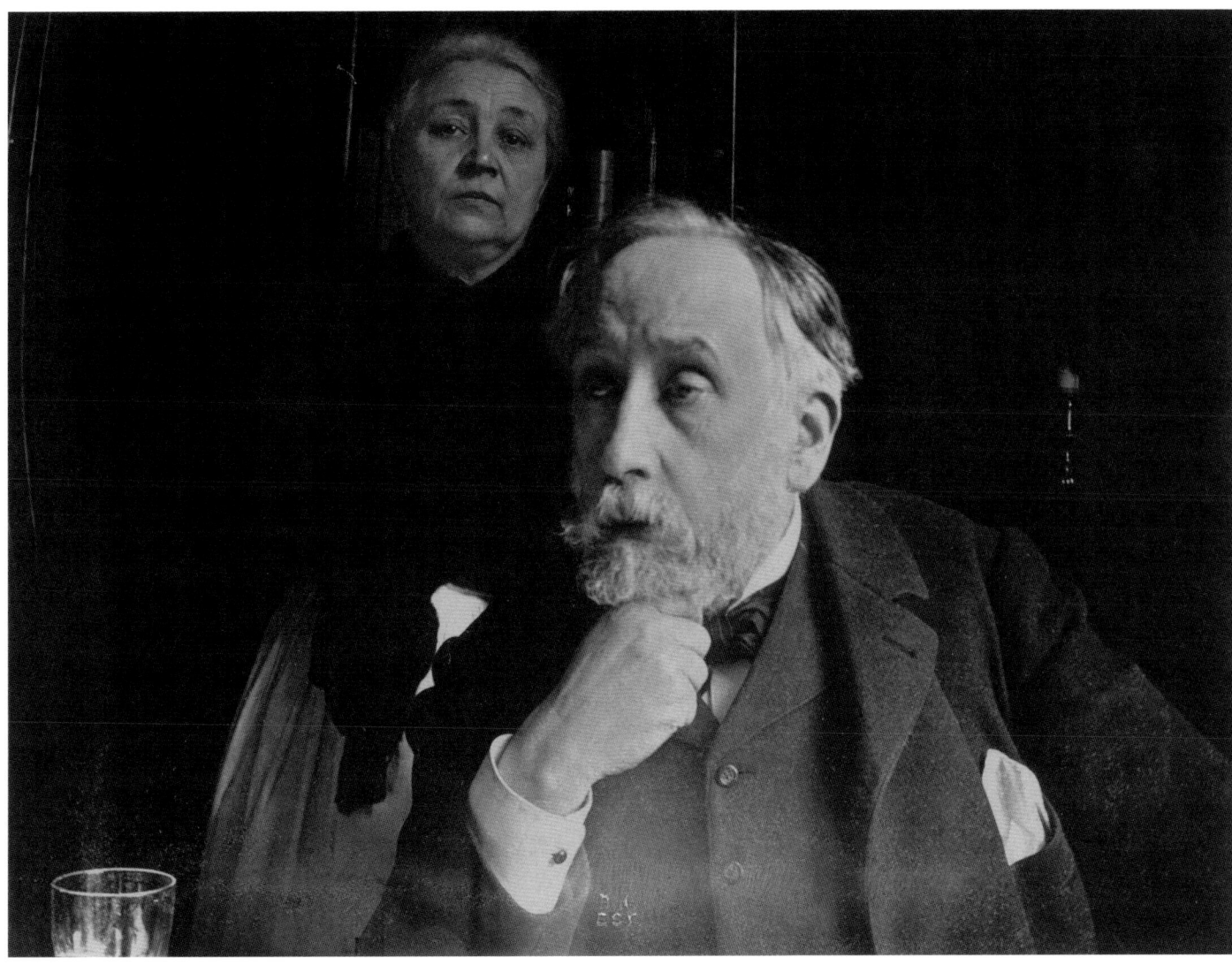

297

Edgar Degas

*Self-Portrait with Zoé
Closier*, c. 1895. Gelatin
silver print, 18.2 x 24.2 cm.
Bibliothèque Nationale
de France, Paris

ties of the medium, or simply took snapshots as part of their everyday lives. As well as exploring these aspects to a certain degree, Degas and Picasso seem to have been particularly engaged by something more fundamental about the photographed image. Antoine Terrasse identified two concepts that Degas's painted and photographic work had in common, and these ideas can also serve as a link to Picasso's output in the same media: "that is, at the point of conception, the gaze: for in one medium as in the other the observer must make a choice; and at their origin, a flat surface: a space that is no longer that of life."[33] The painted oeuvres of both Degas and Picasso have long been considered to reveal their preoccupations with the artist's gaze and with the flat surface, and it is perhaps thanks to these shared concerns that their photographic work holds such compelling parallels, harmonies, and echoes.

OLGA KHOKHLOVA, BALLERINA, AND PABLO PICASSO

CÉCILE GODEFROY

Although the place of the theater in the work of Picasso has certainly been studied,[1] the part played by the artist's first wife Olga Khokhlova (1891–1955), a dancer in the Ballets Russes, remains little known.[2] It therefore seems appropriate to recount for the first time the course of Olga's own artistic career as dancer, from her early training in Russia to her roles in Serge Diaghilev's ballets and her meeting with Picasso in 1917. The study of the young Olga's interpretations, which the artist is likely to have seen in rehearsals or in actual performances on stage, viewed together with analyses of his paintings devoted to the theme of dance, then makes it possible to reconsider the importance of "Olga the ballerina" in Picasso's work, both as subject and as muse. This examination leads us, moreover, to broaden our field of study, until now essentially pictorial, to include the influences in which the artist immersed himself beginning in 1914 and which appear more explicitly in the works dating from his first meeting with Olga and the early years of their marriage. Fostered by the Italian context, the artist's dialogue with antiquity and classicism opened a new chapter of his life involving the arts of dance and music, which Picasso discovered through his collaboration with the Ballets Russes and his love for Olga.

A Dancer with the Ballets Russes

Olga Stepanova Khokhlova was born in the city of Nezhin in the Russian Empire on 17 June 1891,[3] the daughter of Lydia Vinchenko and Stepan Vasilevich Khokhlov, a colonel in the imperial army. She grew up in Saint Petersburg with her three brothers and her younger sister.[4] Of the two elder sons, one chose a military career, while the other pursued the study of medicine. The girls turned to the arts: Nina hoped to sing and Olga chose dance.[5] In 1910, Stepan Vasilevich was transferred to the Kars region. Rather than accompany the family, Olga, who had just completed her studies at the French lycée, decided to remain in Saint Petersburg to enter the dance school of Yevgenia Sokolova.[6] Through her connections with the Konetskie sisters, she was auditioned the next year by Serge Diaghilev and engaged by the Ballets Russes.[7]

As an extension of the major exhibitions and stage productions he had organized in Russia and France,[8] Diaghilev founded the Ballets Russes, which appeared for the first time at the Théâtre du Châtelet in Paris in May 1909. With Michel Fokine, the troupe's choreographer until 1912, Diaghilev sought constantly to reinvent the form of his productions, bringing theater, music, and painting together in a dramatic unity closely akin to the Romantic principle of *Gesamtkunstwerk*. While the first season was a major success, the productions staged the following year at the Théâtre National de l'Opéra, particularly the production of *Scheherazade* with Ida Rubinstein in the title role, were a triumph, and their colorist aesthetic set off a vogue in fashion and the decorative arts. The energy of Fokine's

298

Olga Khokhlova as a wife of the sultan in *Scheherazade*, c. 1916. Reproduction from a glass negative, 11.5 x 7.5 cm. Archives Olga Ruiz-Picasso, Courtesy Fundación Almine y Bernard Ruiz-Picasso para el Arte

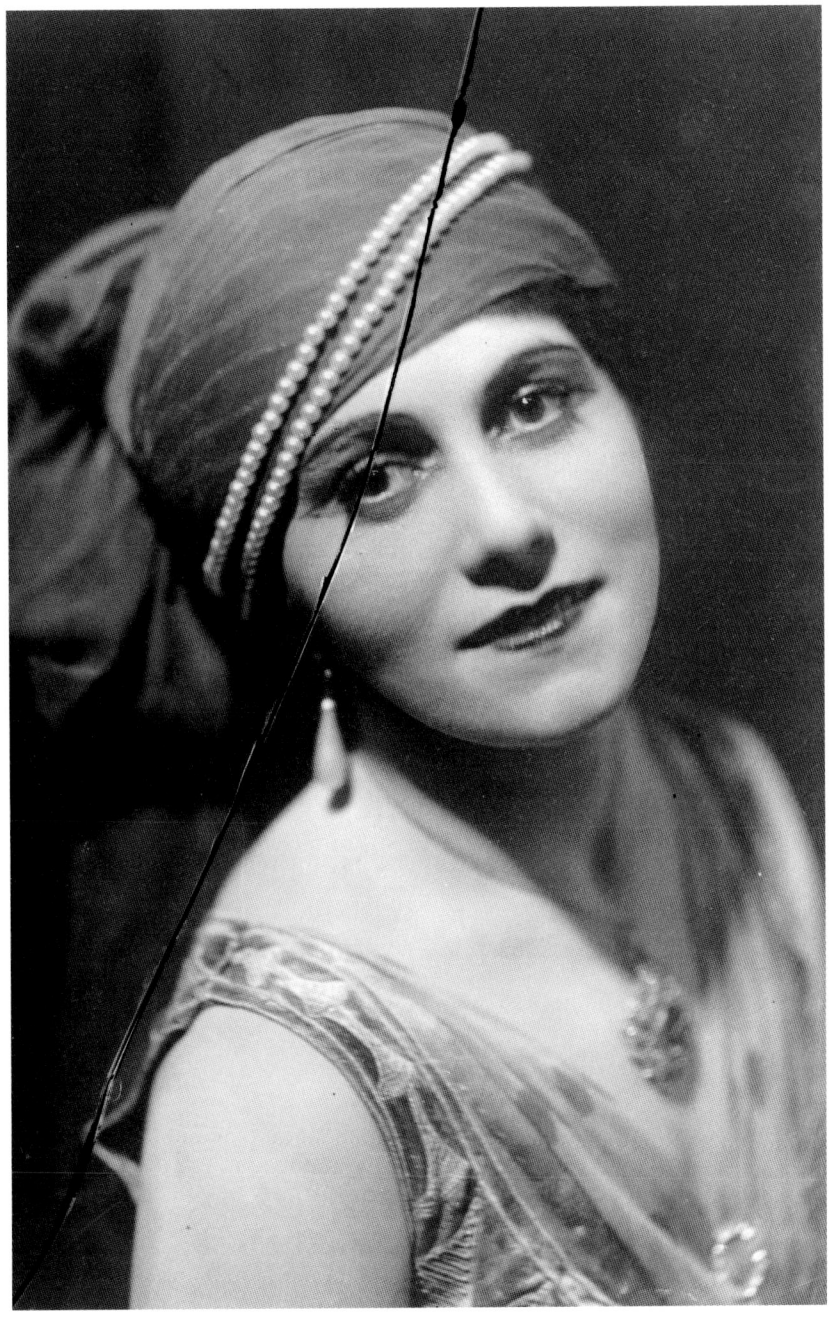

As a result, the impresario began recruiting dancers from the imperial theaters: the Mariinsky in Saint Petersburg and the Bolshoi in Moscow. He also engaged amateurs, though these dancers, too, had to attain perfect command of the arts of ballet and pantomime as taught by the great Italian ballet master Enrico Cecchetti, and meet Fokine's choreographic demands and, later on, those of Nijinsky and Léonide Massine.[9] Fokine was steeped in Russian folklore, while Nijinsky, drawn to Classical antiquity, turned the schoolroom canons of dance upside down, offering male dancers authentic dramatic roles for the first time instead of employing them merely to lift the ballerinas or in walk-on parts. Massine drew his inspiration from the study of popular dances, the circus, jazz, and the cinema. At age twenty, Olga Khokhlova, like her fellow pupil Ludmila Guliuk, a niece of Sokolova, was one of the youngest, least experienced ballerinas. Recruited with four professional dancers from the Mariinsky to join the company at Monte-Carlo in March 1911, both young women had to rapidly memorize their first choreographies.[10] Tamara Karsavina recalls that Olga "had started as a quite gifted amateur, but under the direction of the master [Cecchetti] she had revealed authentic qualities."[11]

From 1909 onward, Diaghilev ensured the troupe's success by diversifying its repertoire and by introducing a policy of presenting classic ballets and premiering works in a Russian folk style in the same program.[12] Accordingly, at the Théâtre de Monte-Carlo in April 1911, Olga Khokhlova began her career as an *artiste chorégraphique*[13] in three technically diverse ballets. In *Les Sylphides*, as one of the corps de ballet, she executed a series of steps in the pure academic tradition. She was also a slave in the *Polovtsian Dances* and a temple servant in *Cléopâtre*, a dizzying creation of Fokine's and one of the company's major successes after 1909: with sets and costumes by Bakst, the dancers executed movements inspired by

choreography, heightened to the extreme by the set designs of Alexandre Benois and Léon Bakst and the talent of the dancers — among them Anna Pavlova, Tamara Karsavina, and Vaslav Nijinsky — aroused such enthusiasm that Diaghilev decided to create a permanent ballet troupe that would perform throughout Europe.

Egyptian art and similar to the contemporary improvisations of Isadora Duncan, expanding the body language of classical ballet. Olga appeared next in Rome, Paris, and London, then at the Paris Opéra in December, where she was the slave in *Scheherazade* (**298**), another exotic and sensual Fokine choreography of the *Symphonic Suite* by Nikolai Rimsky-Korsakov.[14] After performances in Berlin, Dresden, Vienna, and Budapest, her repertoire began to expand in response to Diaghilev's wish to promote the most deserving dancers of the corps de ballet. In April and May 1912 at the Théâtre de Monte-Carlo, Olga appeared in an adaptation of *Le Lac des cygnes (Swan Lake)* by Fokine of the version by Marius Petipa and Lev Ivanov staged at the Mariinsky in 1895. She also appeared in *L'Oiseau de feu (The Firebird)* and *Petrushka*, two national masterpieces that were the fruit of a close collaboration between Fokine, Igor Stravinsky, and the troupe's three leading decorative designers, Alexander Golovin and Bakst for the first one, Benois for the latter. On 20 May, she danced the part of a serving girl in the premiere of *Thamar* at the Théâtre du Châtelet in Paris and her name finally appeared on the program of *L'Après-midi d'un faune (The Afternoon of a Faun)*, the first choreographic creation by Nijinsky for the Ballets Russes set to the *Prélude* of the same title by Claude Debussy. With the set and the Greek tunics by Bakst, Olga was one of the six young nymphs dancing barefoot, their faces turned in profile and bodies facing the stage, in a succession of slow, stylized gestures that seemed to mime the bas-relief sculptures on an ancient frieze. On 29 May, the evening of the premiere, the ballet's hieratic stylization, drawn from the pagan wellsprings of the dance, left the audience disconcerted, and Nijinsky's final gesture was deemed indecent and censured by the critics.

After touring Europe, including performances in Monte-Carlo, Diaghilev's company opened the first season of Gabriel Astruc's new Théâtre des Champs-Élysées,[15] where on 29 May 1913 it presented *Le Sacre du Printemps (The Rite of Spring)*, one of the most important works of the twentieth century. Stravinsky's composition carried experimental rhythms and mixed tonalities to paroxysmal height in a violent orchestral score conducted by Pierre Monteux, while Nijinksy's choreography broke with the academicism and the idea of grace traditionally associated with the art of ballet: instead of beginning with erect posture in "open" position, the dancers appeared onstage in a *position rentrée*, with toes turned inward and backs bent to the ground. The opening performance of this great tableau of "pictures from pagan Russia" with decor and costumes by Nicolas Roerich, in which Olga danced as one of the young maidens, created an immense scandal.

Until July 1914, the company continued its wanderings through South America and Europe, and Olga Khokhlova added to her stock of roles, appearing (in addition to the productions mentioned above) in *Le Dieu bleu*, *Carnaval*, *Daphnis et Chloé*, and in the premieres of *Khovanshchina*, *Les Papillons*, *Le Coq d'or*, *Le Rossignol*, *La Légende de Joseph*, *Midas*, *Prince Igor*, and *Nuit de mai.* In the summer of 1914, she went home to Russia but left again in November 1915 for Switzerland, where the troupe had taken refuge. This last departure from Russia was decisive both in a personal sense — she would soon become acquainted with Picasso — and in terms of her career, as Massine, now Diaghilev's leading male dancer and new artistic protégé, was preparing his first choreographic works. He was well aware of Olga's talent and within a year entrusted her with her most important roles.

In a gala benefit for the Red Cross at the Grand Théâtre de Genève on 20 December 1915, Olga appeared in *Soleil de nuit (The Midnight Sun)*, choreographed by Massine to a score by Rimsky-Korsakov. The collaboration with Mikhail Larionov, the leading exponent of the Russian Neo-primitive movement, in creating the sets and costumes gave birth to a work in which "old Russia appears through the eyes of the people, flamboyant and comic, and a Byzantine motif is peculiarly wedded to the frenzied dances of Russian workers."[16] After a performance in Paris on 29 December, the company embarked on 1 January 1916, aboard the transatlantic liner *Lafayette*, for a tour of North America, where they performed in sixteen cities in less than four months.[17] Olga, while frequently on stage during the tour, was also preparing for her first major role upon her return to Europe, in Massine's new ballet *Las Meninas (The Maids of Honor)*, the company's first production with a Spanish theme, with music by Gabriel Fauré. The premiere was presented on 21 August at the Teatro Victoria Eugenia in San Sebastian. As the maids of honor, adorned in imposing crinoline dresses designed by José-Maria Sert, Olga and Lydia Sokolova danced a pavane with Leon Woizikowski and Massine. At the official performance by the company on 28 August in Bilbao, the two ballerinas were bowed to by the king of Spain.[18] In September, the troupe split into two groups: the first left for a new tour in the United States with Nijinsky and the second, made up of some fifteen dancers, including Olga, went to Italy with Diaghilev and Massine, who entrusted to Olga the role of Felicita in his newest work, *Les Femmes de bonne humeur (The Good-Humoured Ladies)*. Based on a plot by Carlo Goldoni, the ballet evoked the atmosphere of Jean-Antoine Watteau's painting *Fêtes vénitiennes* and genre works by William Hogarth and Pietro Longhi. In the course of a comic imbroglio, the seven dancers perform solos and mimes to an orchestral setting of music by Domenico Scarlatti. Bakst, who created the decor and costumes, stressed the "touch of burlesque," the "prodigious variety," and "boisterous spirit" of the choreography.[19] The premiere at the Teatro Costanzi in Rome on 12 April 1917 was very well received by the Italian public.[20]

"Souvenir de Petrograd"

When Picasso agreed in August 1916 to design the scenery and costumes for *Parade*, with choreography by Massine based on a libretto by Jean Cocteau and an original score by Erik Satie, the artist's existing relations with Russia inclined him favorably toward the collaboration. His paintings had entered the collections of two great Russian patrons, Sergei Shchukin and Ivan Morozov, who together, up to 1914, acted as a major conduit for the dissemination of European avant-garde movements in Russia. Picasso took part in the Jack of Diamonds exhibits in Moscow in January 1912 and February 1913. In Paris, he met numerous artists from Russia, including Vladimir Tatlin (in 1914), and the Russian art critics followed the evolution of his work with interest.[21] Diaghilev's charisma, the ballet troupe's popularity and "chic" nomadic lifestyle, and his attraction to the world of the theater all provided an eminently favorable setting for his first contribution to the Ballets Russes.

Picasso arrived in Rome with Cocteau in February 1917. He first noticed Olga Khokhlova while she was rehearsing the role of Felicita in the ballet's studios on the Piazza Venezia. Charmed by her youth and beauty, the artist began an assiduous courtship, while Cocteau contrived to fall in love with a friend of hers, the dancer Maria Chabelska.[22] After Italy, the troupe returned to Paris, where its tour was marked by the scandal at the premiere of *Parade* on 18 May at the Théâtre du Châtelet. With this avant-garde work, the Ballets Russes entered a new phase of its history. That same evening, the audience warmly applauded three other works in which Olga danced: *Les Sylphides*, *Soleil de nuit*, and *Petrushka*. She also appeared in the premiere of *Contes Russes* on 11 May. The company then left for Spain, where Khokhlova's name appeared on the program for ten ballets. Despite being a rising star in the troupe, Olga decided not to go on tour in South America, in order to stay close to Picasso. By now she was

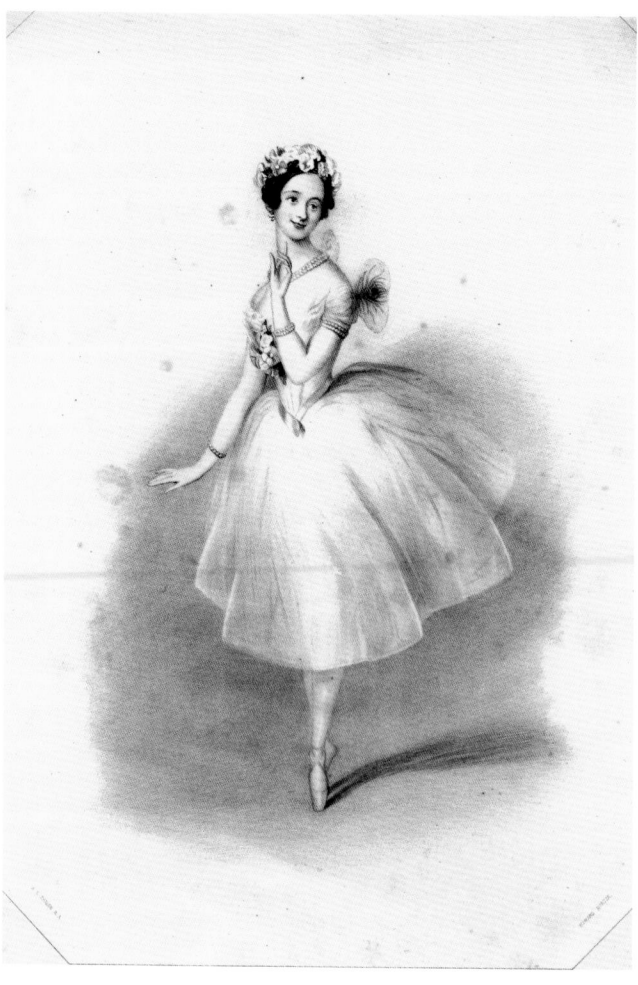

injury put her career as a dancer in jeopardy. After a long recovery,[25] the painter's wife resumed dance lessons with Cecchetti and with the master's pupil Sonia Derloff. Olga faithfully attended theater and opera productions, stayed in close touch with the dancers in the troupe, and trained regularly.[26] But, though Diaghilev, Massine, and Cecchetti all missed Olga and told her so,[27] the birth of Paulo on 4 February 1921 finally put an end to her hopes of returning to the stage. She would dance no more, save as an amateur. From 12 April 1911 to 30 June 1917, Olga Khokhlova had danced in nearly thirty Ballets Russes productions, including fifteen premieres — a career record that fully proves her range of repertoire and her talents as a performer, a dancer who participated in one of the boldest artistic ventures of the early twentieth century and left her stamp on the history of modern ballet.

"Olga the Ballerina" in the Work of Picasso
Picasso probably had the most leisure to watch his new fiancée perform from February to June 1917, when Olga danced a series of roles ranging from slave girl to "Oriental princess."[28] Considering his interest in Velázquez's great painting *Las Meninas*, her appearance in Massine's ballet of the same name at the Teatro Costanzi in Rome on 9 April must have delighted the painter, who shortly afterward painted her wearing the traditional Spanish mantilla.[29] However, Picasso's works, apart from commissions by Diaghilev, reveal that the artist was interested less in the dancer's "folkloric" or "Spanish" character than in the figure of the ballerina in the company's classical works: although marginal in Olga's own repertoire, the ballet *Les Sylphides*, which she also danced at the Teatro Costanzi on 9 April, seems more definitely to have caught and held the painter's attention.[30]

Choreographed by Fokine for the Mariinsky Theater in 1907, the ballet *Chopiniana*, renamed *Les Sylphides* by Diaghilev in 1909, was inspired

in love with the painter, who, when he introduced her to his family in Barcelona, had promised to marry her. She could not suspect that she would never dance in public again, or that political events — the First World War and the Russian Revolution in 1917 — would separate her from the land of her birth forever.[23]

After obtaining a new passport, Olga settled in Paris in November. The portraits that Picasso painted of his new muse, whether Cubist or in the "neoclassical" style of the celebrated *Olga in an Armchair*,[24] speak of the first months of a life lived partially together between the artist's house at Montrouge and the Hôtel Lutetia. A leg injury suffered by Olga in April darkened the wedding preparations, and the ceremony had to be put off until 12 July. Worse yet, the

299
Edward Morton
(British, active c. 1837–
c. 1845) after Alfred
Edward Chalon
(British, 1780–1860)
*Marie Taglioni in "La
Sylphide,"* c. 1832.
Lithograph. The Royal
Ballet School Collections,
London

300
Pablo Picasso
*Olga with a Garland of
Flowers*, 1920. Charcoal
on paper, 61 x 49 cm.
Musée des Beaux-Arts,
Lille. On loan from the
Musée national Picasso,
Paris (MP 1990-68)

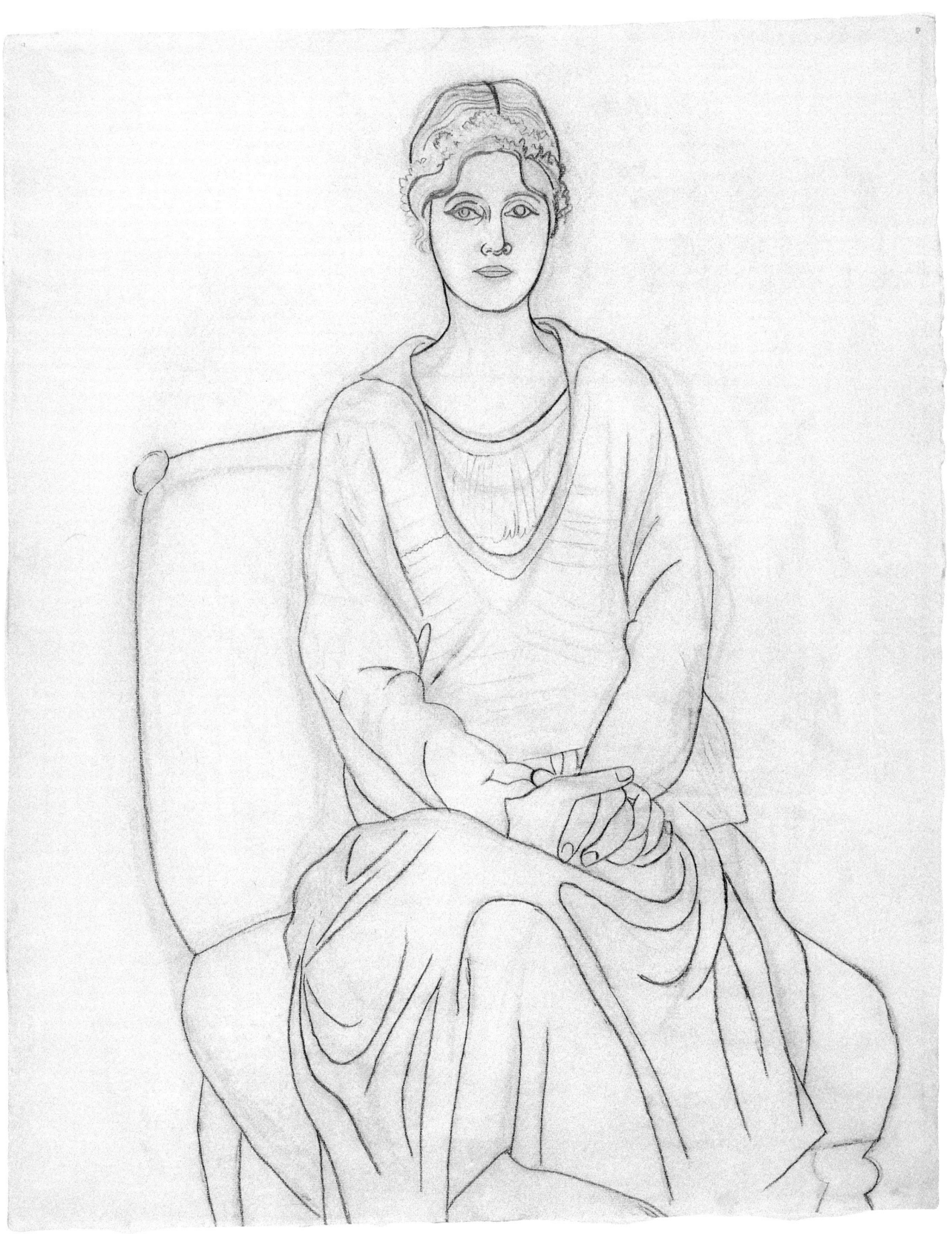

by the celebrated French ballet *La Sylphide*, created by Filippo Taglioni for his daughter Marie and presented in 1832 at the Paris Opéra. Théophile Gautier repeatedly stressed the impact and significance of this first Romantic ballet,[31] which launched the great ballerina's career and for the first time had dancers appear on stage in white tutus (designed by Eugène Lami) and satin slippers, which form the classic image of the dancer as celebrated by Degas, an identity that persists to this day. The harmonious display of the corps de ballet, the lighting effects and the elevation of the dancers seemingly up to the sky, the delicacy of the costumes, and the technical mastery of the dance on pointe by Taglioni made for the immense popularity of *La Sylphide* and raised the figure of the ballerina to the status of a fashion icon:[32] girls making their First Communion and brides soon adopted the white muslin gown and virgin's wreath of flowers.[33] Imported into Russia in 1837,[34] the ballet made a departure from the repertoire of the Paris Opéra in 1863 before its rebirth in the original adaptation by Fokine. Drawing his inspiration from *La Sylphide* — the stage settings, the "modest grace" of the dancers in "skirts of snow and feathers,"[35] and lithographic prints of the ballet's pantomime scenes (**299**) — the Russian choreographer explored the possibilities of the Romantic allusion in depth, choosing piano works by Chopin as the musical accompaniment, in orchestrations by Stravinsky, Alexander Glazunov, and others.[36] Taking the degree of abstraction a step further in his own ballet, Fokine ultimately composed a suite of dances without any definite plot line, evoking instead the poetic world of *La Sylphide* and the romantic reveries of the leading male dancer (in 1917, Alexander Gavrilov) and his female counterpart (Lydia Lopokova) surrounded by her companions (the corps de ballet, Olga among them). One of the company's greatest successes during its twenty-year history, Fokine's creation celebrated the rebirth of

Romantic ballet and restored to the spotlight one of the most idolized figures of the nineteenth century: the ballerina.

While Picasso sought to win Olga's heart in Rome, she put up a fiercely virtuous resistance. The dancer's friends who witnessed the byplay between the couple amused themselves by making specific allusions to *Les Sylphides*.[37] Most of all, the ballet's overall aesthetic — decor, costumes, music, and dance — related directly to Picasso's particular interest at the time in antiquity, Classicism, and, more generally, nineteenth-century painting. Benois's sets were inspired by a Corot landscape. The sublimation of the female bodies, from pointe shoes and diaphanous costumes to the dancers' Hellenized hairstyles, formed a tableau with a truly Classical touch. The *ballet blanc* and the classical dancer — symbol of purity and object of desire whose performance on stage draws inevitably on the presence of the male spectator in the theater and his yearning to possess this feminine ideal — are ultimately an ode to the work of Degas. As Picasso sought to master the art of stage design for the first time in his career, the phenomenon of emotional and aesthetic "crystallization" brought about by his vision of Olga in *Les Sylphides* likely stimulated the artist to reengage in the dialogue with the past that he had begun in 1914[38] and led him to associate his new muse with the Romantic image of the ballerina as ideal woman personified.

This image is observable in the portraits of Olga (**300**), whose face, with a beauty like the female figures of Ingres,[39] is tinged with a gravity that contrasts with the smile and the confidence she radiates in her photographs. The source of this Romantic melancholy, perceptible in a more general way in all of Picasso's "neoclassical" figures, may have been her appearance as the dancer of the Chopin *Nocturne* in *Les Sylphides*, in which, according to sources at that time, the music and choreography created a passage of profound sadness.[40]

301

Edgar Degas
Rehearsal of the Ballet, c. 1876. Gouache and pastel over monotype, 55.3 x 68 cm. Nelson-Atkins Museum of Art, Kansas City, Missouri. Purchase: The Kenneth A. and Helen F. Spencer Foundation Acquisition Fund (F73-30)

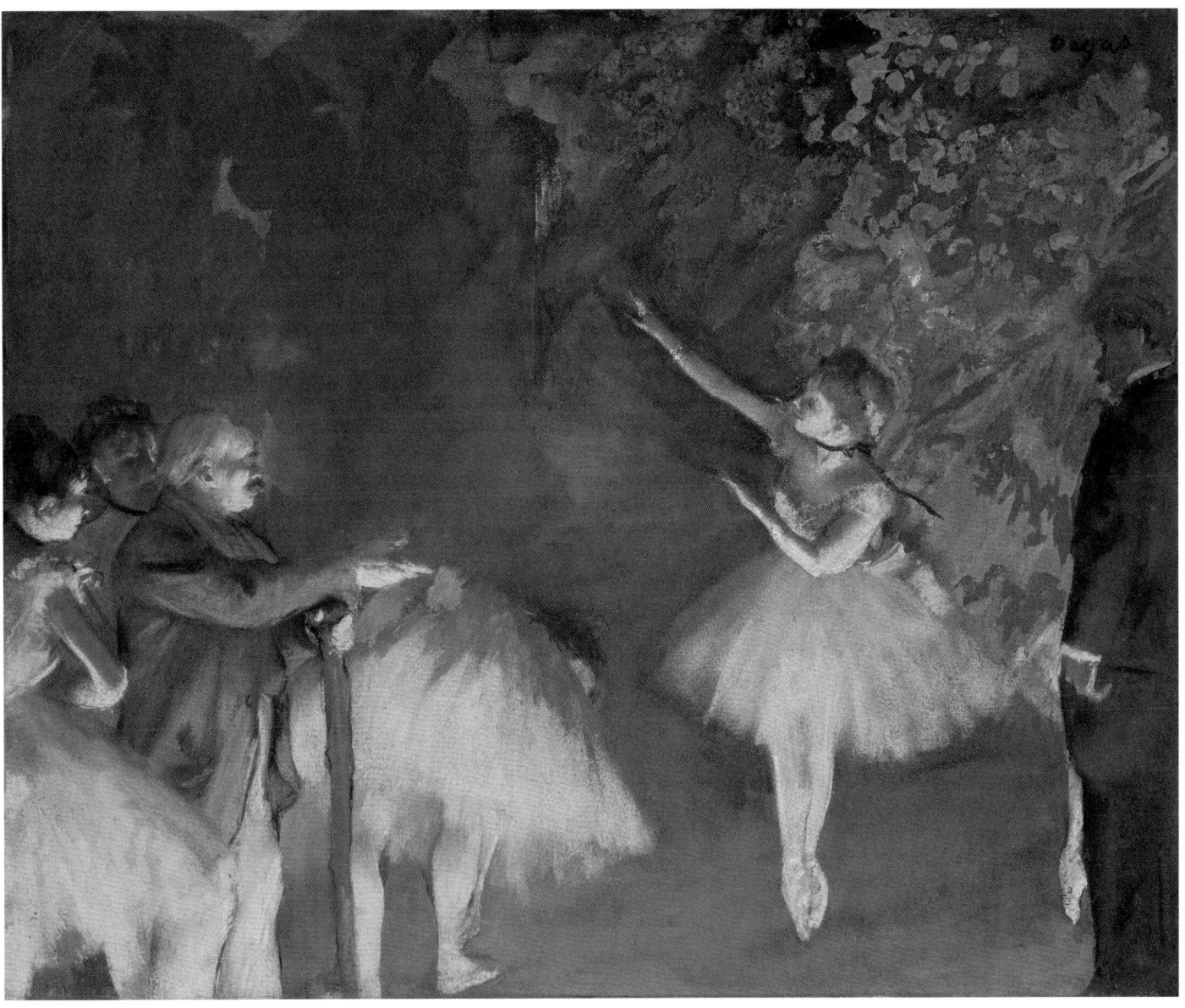

Beginning in 1917, Olga the ballerina figures in Picasso's works devoted to ballet: for example, in the curtain painting for *Parade*, where she balances, dressed in her *Sylphide* costume, on the back of Pegasus.[41] In 1919, while Olga was resuming her training, a dance session captured in photographs restores the painter's wife to her role of ballerina: Olga poses in pointes and a white tutu, and executes a variation of classic dance steps under the benevolent eye of Cecchetti (**302**). Olga in these pictures is radiant, endowing each of her poses with the artistic grace and beauty demanded by the maestro. These unpublished images immediately evoke the paintings of Degas showing the dance teacher Jules Perrot surrounded by his pupils (**301**) — paintings inspired by a daguerreotype of the former dancer.[42] Inviting comparison with Degas both in his choice of subject and in the use of photography, Picasso extracted from this sequence several drawings of the *Dancer* (**303**). That year he also did three

302

Olga Picasso and Enrico
Cecchetti, London, 1919.
Reproduction from
an original negative,
12 x 7 cm. Archives Olga
Ruiz-Picasso, Courtesy
Fundación Almine y
Bernard Ruiz-Picasso
para el Arte

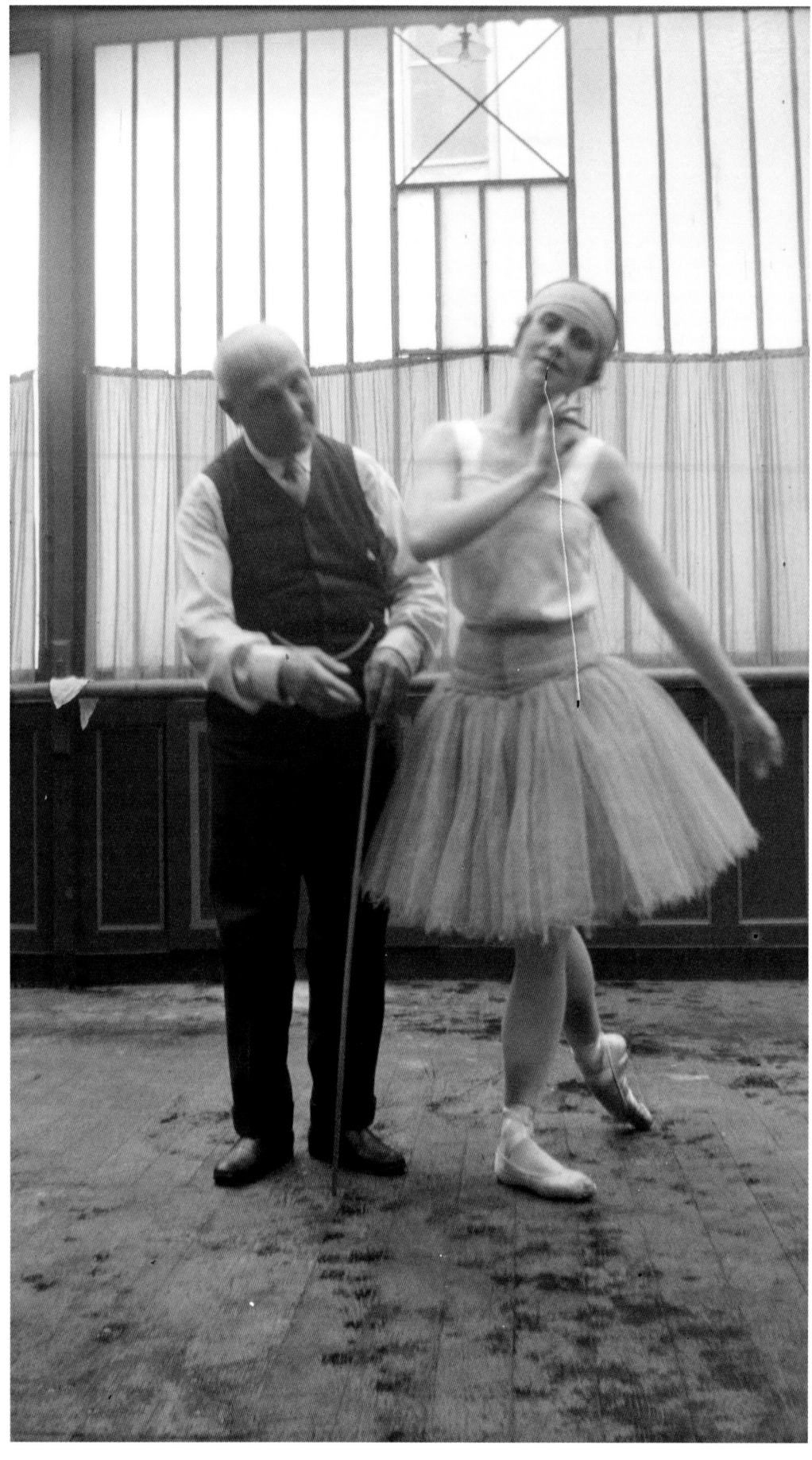

Pablo Picasso

Dancer, 1919. Pencil
and collage on paper,
40 x 22 cm. Private
collection

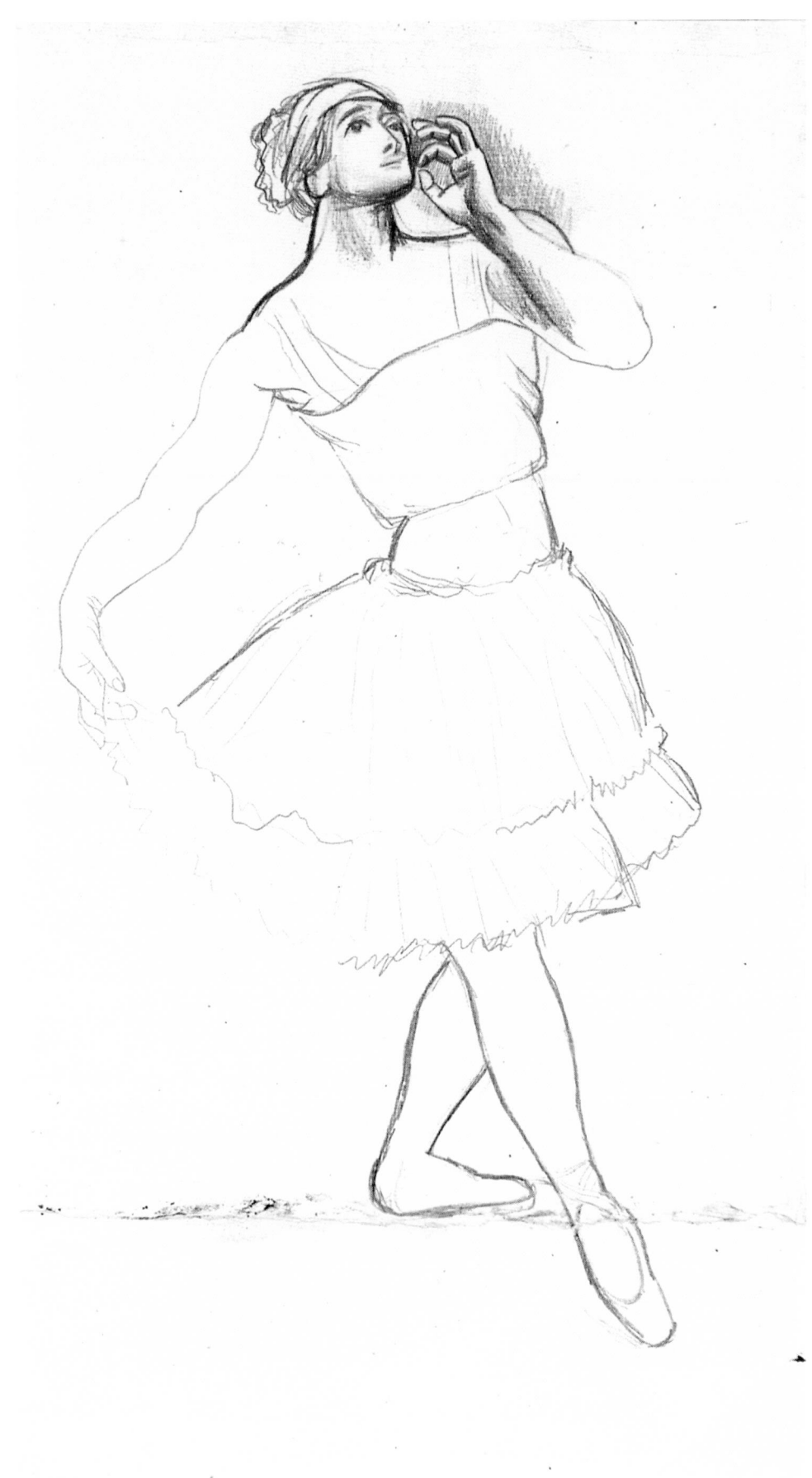

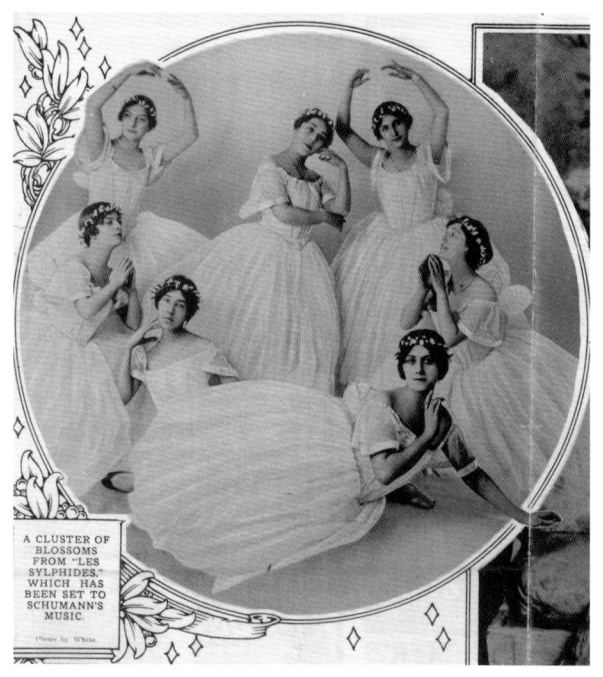

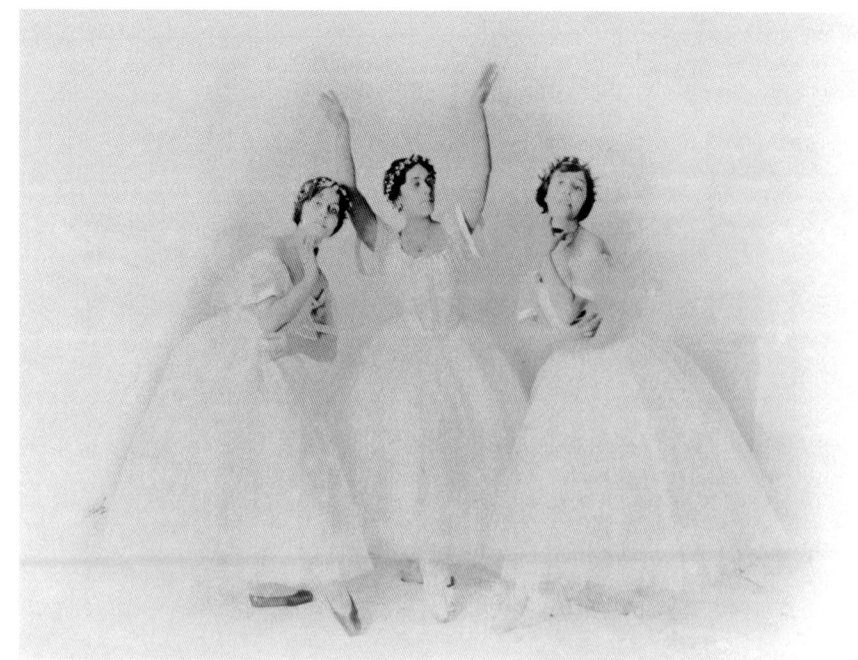

304

Ballerinas from the Ballets
Russes in *Les Sylphides*,
New York. Reproduced in
The Sun [New York],
9 April 1916. Courtesy The
New York Public Library
for the Performing Arts.
Jerome Robbins Dance
Division; Astor, Lenox and
Tilden Foundations

305

Ballerinas from the Ballets
Russes in *Les Sylphides*,
1916. Archives Picasso,
Musée national Picasso,
Paris (MP 834; DP 45)

306

Pablo Picasso

Seven Dancers, 1919.
Pencil and charcoal on
paper, 62.6 x 50 cm.
Musée national Picasso,
Paris (MP 841)

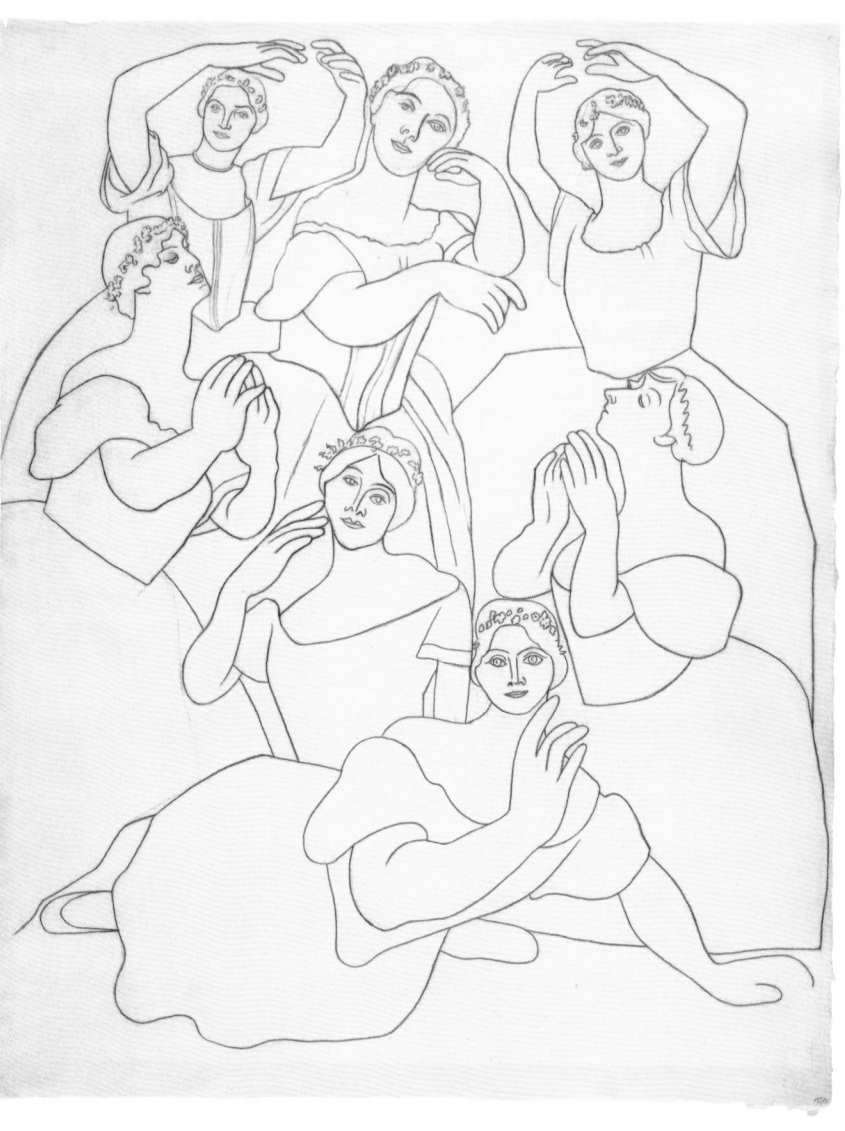

studies from a pair of printed promotional illustrations for *Les Sylphides* (**304, 305**). In the first two drawings (**306**), the seven dancers adopt poses similar to those of Marie Taglioni and her contemporaries, representing the classic gestures of a ballet finale (**307**). Olga reclines in the foreground. The third drawing shows three dancers: Olga, Lydia Lopokova, and Lubov Tchernicheva (see 149). It was reproduced in the program for the Ballets Russes' Paris season of December 1919 to February 1920. It is surely not insignificant that, in a photograph taken shortly after Paulo's birth (**308**), this same drawing hangs on the wall of the Picassos' living room near the picture of *Olga Reading*, painted when she was pregnant, especially if we recall that the figure of the dancer was originally "linked to the imitative magic of

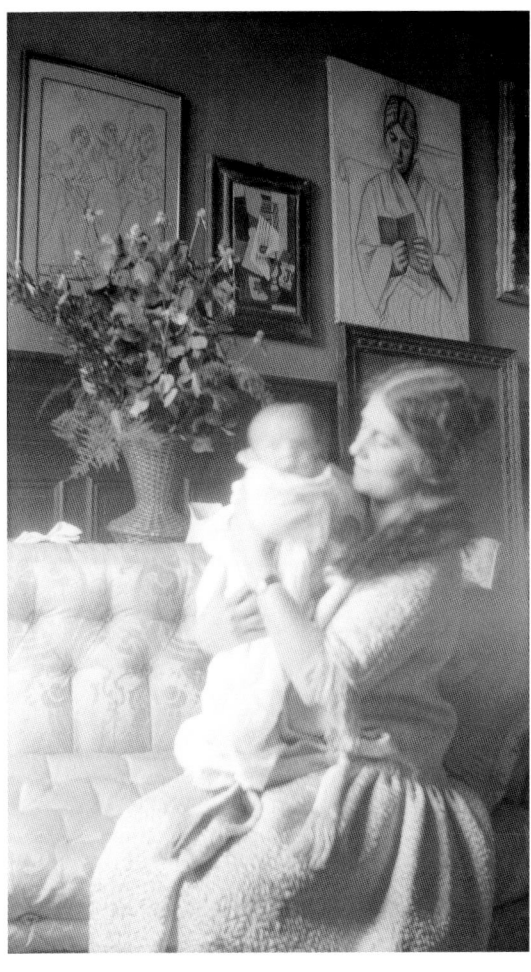

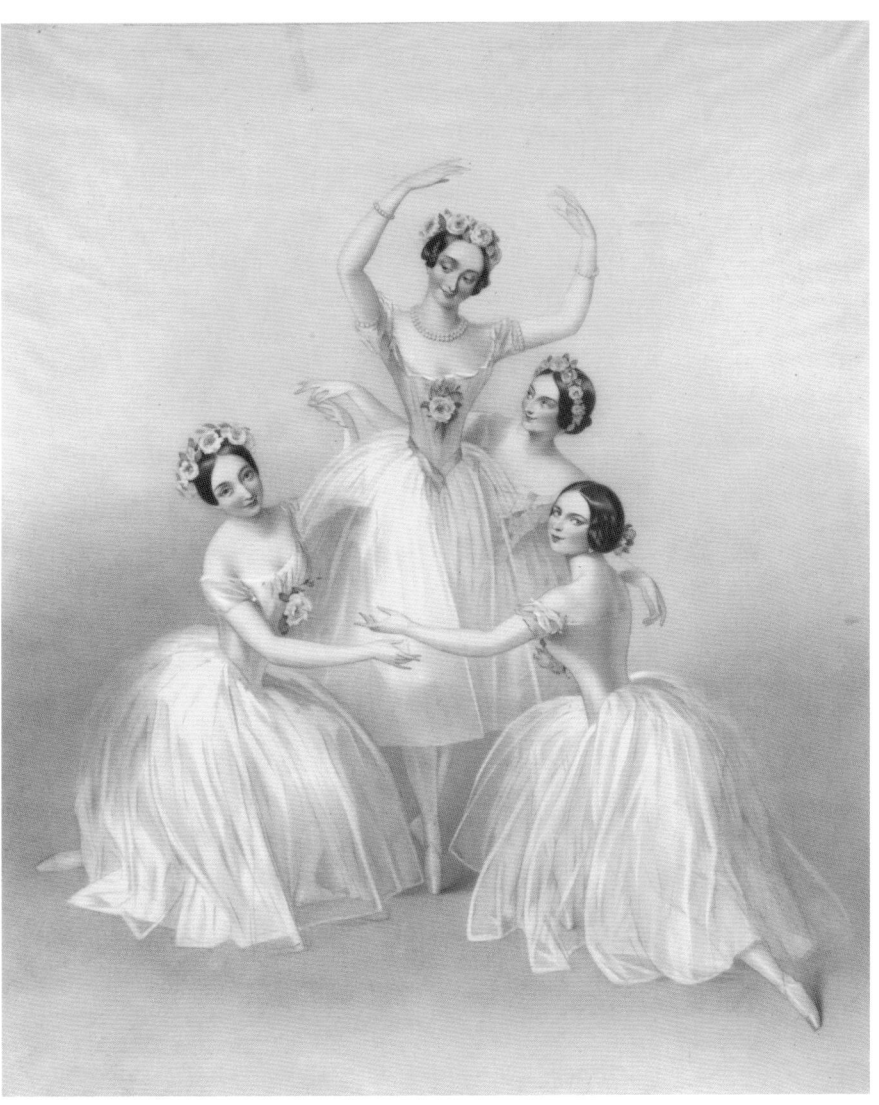

307

Thomas Herbert Maguire
(British, 1821–1895)
after Alfred Edward
Chalon, *The Celebrated
"Pas de Quatre"
Composed by Jules
Perrot, as Danced at
Her Majesty's Theatre,
July 12, 1845, by the Four
Eminent Danseuses,
Carlotta Grisi, Marie
Taglioni, Lucile Grahn &
Fanny Cerrito*, 1845.
Lithograph, 44.5 x 38 cm.
The New York Public
Library for the Performing
Arts. Jerome Robbins
Dance Division;
Astor, Lenox and Tilden
Foundations, Cia Fornaroli
Collection

308

Olga and Paulo Picasso
in the living room, rue la
Boétie, Paris, 1921 (on the
wall, from left to right:
Three Ballet Dancers
[1919], *Guitar, Playing
Card, Glass, and
Newspaper* [1914], *Olga
Reading* [1920]).
Reproduction from an
original negative,
11.7 x 6.9 cm. Archives
Olga Ruiz-Picasso,
Courtesy Fundación
Almine y Bernard
Ruiz-Picasso para el Arte

maternity or fertility";[43] this metaphor takes form naturally in the mother-and-child works (*Maternités*) done at Fontainebleau, where the painter's wife, with her hair done "à la Taglioni" and dressed in white, appears monumental and draped in antique style like a Virgin and child.[44]

During this period of Picasso's work, the preponderance of line drawings, the primary medium of pictorial representation and the "antique style" *par excellence*, also recalls the chiaroscuro effect created by the superimposition of a "white" ballet on the nocturnal scene design created by Benois. In keeping with the perceived precepts of the ancients, color, deemed superfluous and deceptive, has only a modest role in the wooded background made visible by moonlight, throwing into relief the actions of the dancers in their line of immaculate white costumes. In the same way, the absence of color in Picasso's drawings of dancers registers the purity of line, and thereby that of the forms and subject represented. Although the figure of Olga gradually disappears from Picasso's work from about 1923 onward, the ballerina remains in his program illustrations for the Ballets Russes de Monte-Carlo of 1923–24 and lives on through photography (**309**): perhaps taking directions from the artist, like one of Degas's models, Olga assumes a pose, performs curtsies and arabesques on pointe and in a tutu, and expresses in a theatrical manner the essential themes of the stage: joy, despair, abandon. Here again, the bichromatic character of black-and-white photography harks back to the polar contrasts in the scenography of *Les Sylphides*.

Historians have often taken the end of Picasso's collaboration with Diaghilev to coincide with the beginning of his estrangement from Olga, and accordingly his painting *The Three Dancers* (see 161) has long been regarded as the last great work the artist devoted to the theme of the ballet.[45] With this work, completed in May 1925 after his return from Monte-Carlo,[46]

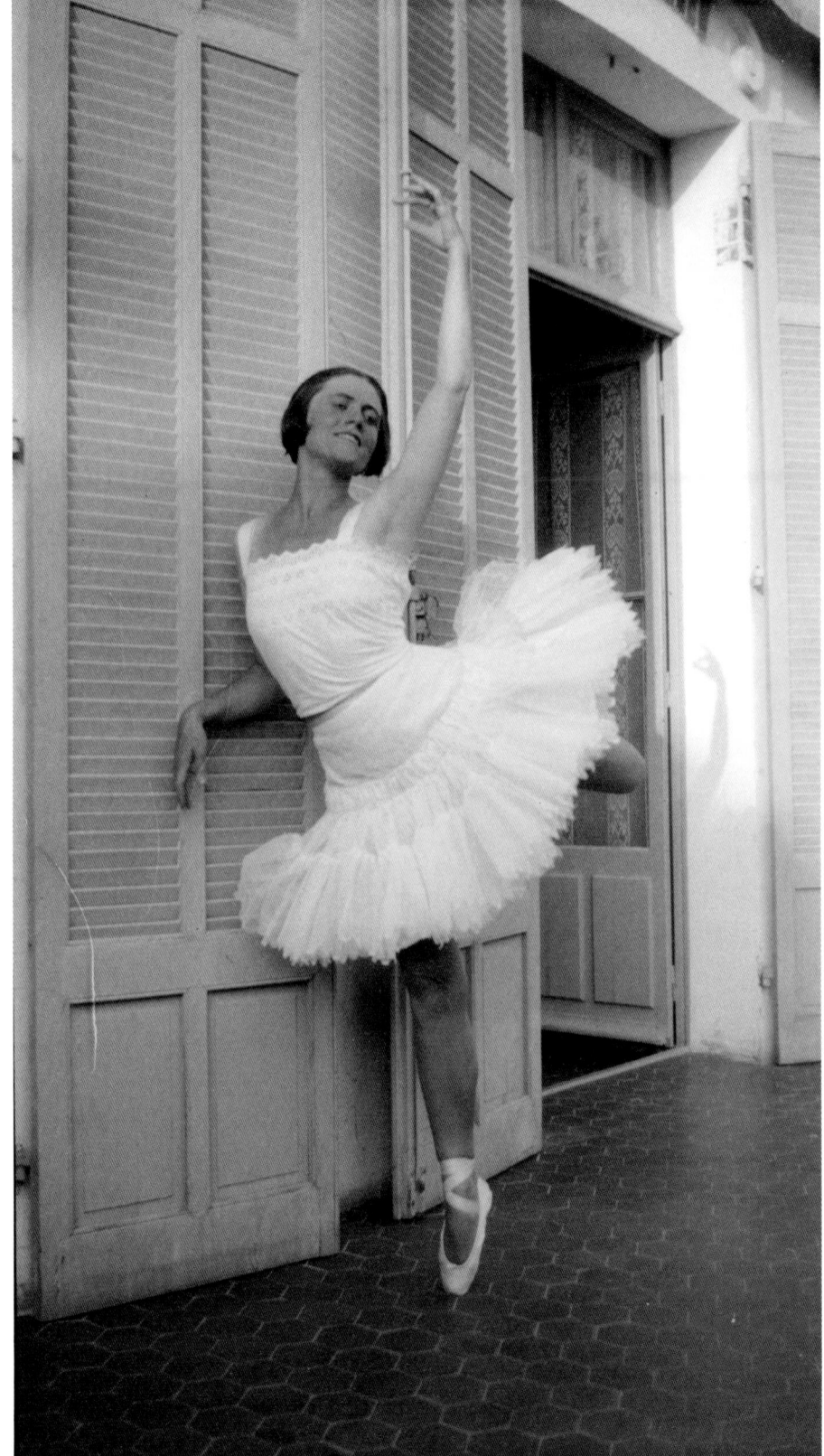

309

Olga Picasso, Villa Belle
Rose, Juan-les-Pins,
Summer 1925.
Reproduction from an
original negative,
13.3 x 6.9 cm. Archives
Olga Ruiz-Picasso,
Courtesy Fundación
Almine y Bernard
Ruiz-Picasso para el Arte

310

Pablo Picasso

*Nude Standing by the
Sea*, 7 April 1929. Oil on
canvas, 129.9 x 96.8 cm.
The Metropolitan Museum
of Art, New York. Bequest
of Florene M. Schoenborn,
1955 (1996.403.4)

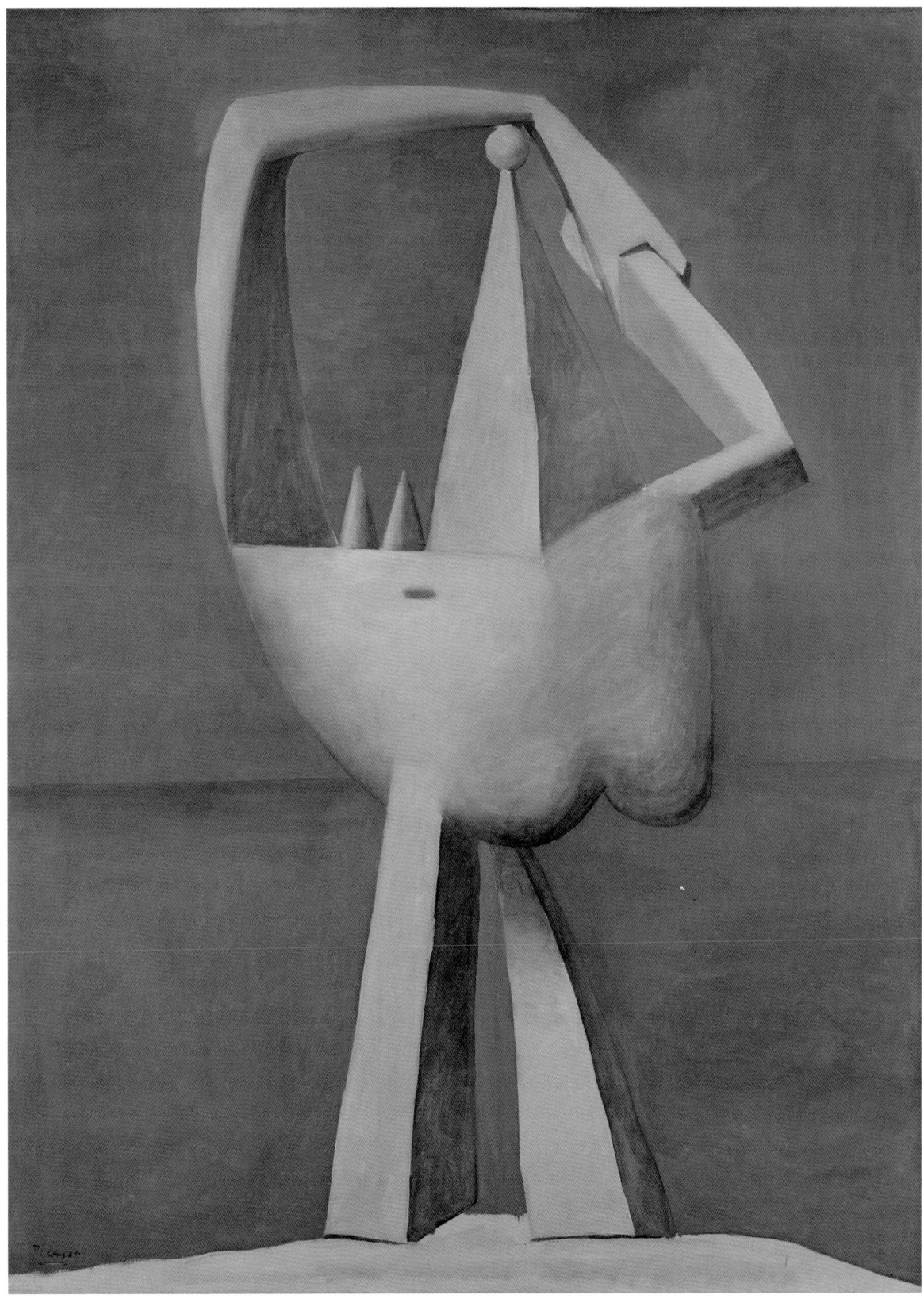

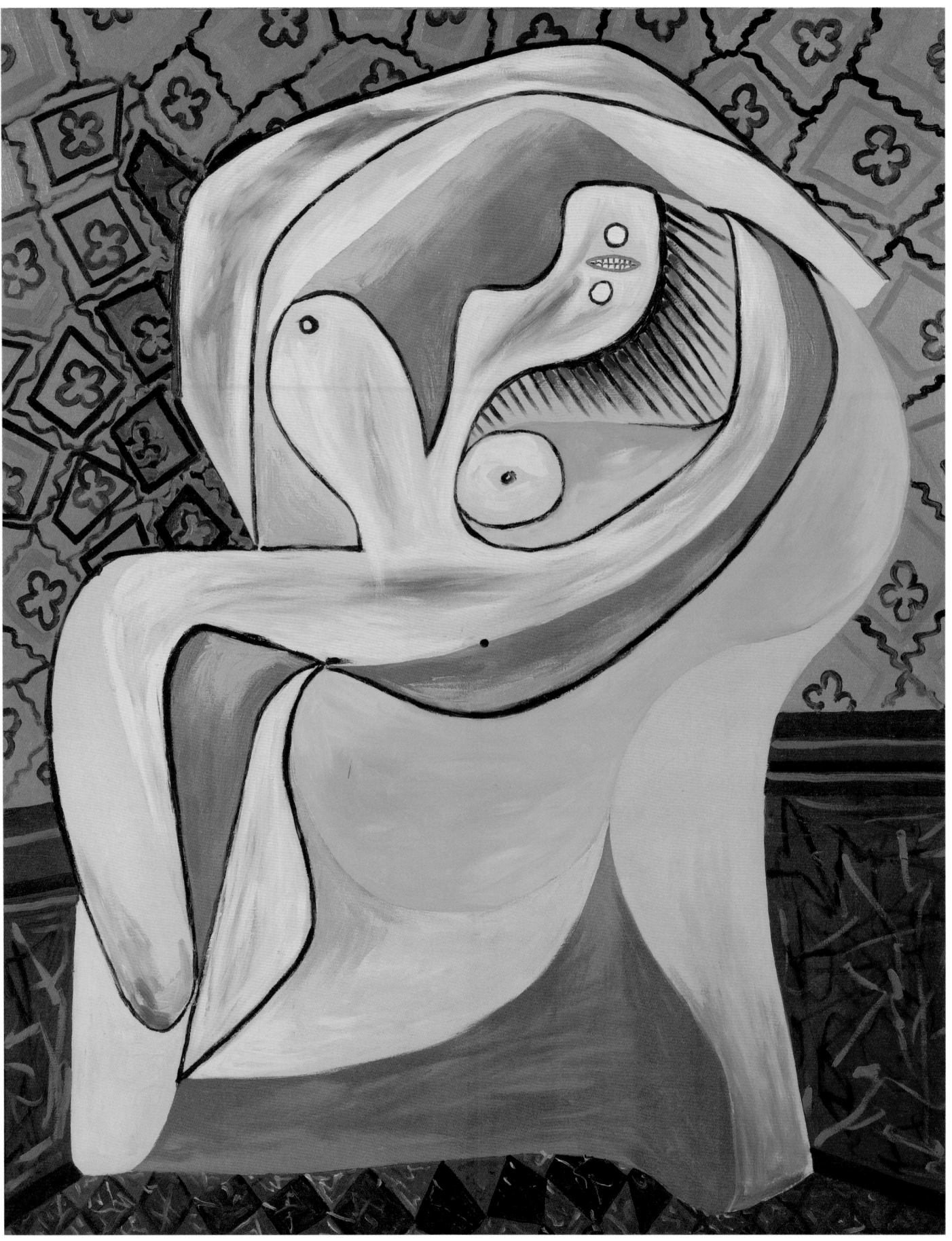

the painter inaugurated a new style that André Breton claimed for Surrealism, publishing an illustration of the picture in his review.[47] Although the biographical association of *The Three Dancers* with the death of Ramon Pichot is well attested today,[48] a parallel interpretation would tend to reconcile various theses about Olga's presence among the three figures in this round dance: sometimes perceived as the writhing maenad on the left,[49] sometimes as the flat, asexual geometric figure in the center,[50] whose Christ-like pose recalls a gesture of Lopokova's in the printed photo of 1916. Yet Olga might also be the figure on the right, whose "phantom reality"[51] evokes the ethereal character of the imaginary Sylphs, elemental spirits of the air in alchemy and Romantic mythology. The bare legs of the central figure and the figure on the right reveal the "phallic" identity of the female dancer, an object of fantasy represented from this date onward without her pointe shoes, an exclusively feminine attribute.[52] In this Dionysiac representation of the Three Graces, "Olga the ballerina" would ultimately become a mere dancer progressively stripped of her femininity and gradually obliterated in a syncopated, rotating rhythm captured in three shots like a chronophotographic image by Étienne-Jules Marey.[53]

The icon of the ballerina flirts as well with that of the bather, from the bacchanales of La Mimoseraie in Biarritz (1918)[54] and the illustrations for the May 1921 Ballets Russes program at the Gaité Lyrique, to the bathers at Dinard (1929) and certain sculptures from the artist's workshop at Boisgeloup (1931) (see 174). Long associated with Marie-Thérèse Walter, the paint-

er's mistress after 1927, certain of the Dinard bathers have recently been related more closely to the figure of the ballerina.[55] Olga's practice of her dance exercises during their summer vacations, often while wearing her bathing suit, encouraged the union of both themes and provided Picasso with a new pretext for dialogue with the painters of the nineteenth century, from Puvis de Chavannes to Cézanne. The *Nude Standing by the Sea* (**310**), for example, appears in the fifth position of classical ballet, presenting the subject to the painter's eyes with the same composure as the dancer facing the camera lens in 1916. The stiffness of the model's pose, accented by the palette of mineral colors characteristic of the Norman coast, borders on the extreme in the baleful version of the *Large Bather*:[56] the shadow that hovers about the wasted figure of the model, painted without compassion, seems an omen of the end of the dancer's reign.

On 22 January 1932 Picasso again placed Olga at the heart of his painting in a masterpiece that he entitled *Repose* (**311**): here the ballerina, the embodiment of femininity and grace, is metamorphosed into a creature both suffering and menacing, balanced on an armchair, arms arched over her head. The supernatural aspect of the *Sylphide* has definitively overridden her Romantic dimension and the aggressive colors have prevailed over the purity of the "neoclassical" line. The couple separated in the summer of 1935 and the ballerina, the painter's muse and subject of study since 1917, would be relegated to the wings, reappearing only very rarely thereafter in the master's work.[57]

REACTIONS TO THE WORK OF DEGAS
IN PICASSO'S CIRCLE (1881–1900)

MONTSE TORRAS

Félicien Fagus is considered to have been the first critic outside Spain to write about the work of Pablo Picasso. As Elizabeth Cowling and Richard Kendall have noted in their introduction to this volume, Fagus's review of Picasso's first exhibition in Paris, in which his work was shown alongside that of the Basque painter Francisco Iturrino, noted the young artist's influences:

There is no doubt that a strong family likeness marks the work of all of these [Spanish] *artists: the weight of their ancestry can be detected beneath the surface, and this is very praiseworthy. This is particularly true of the bitter, pained genius of Goya. We see it, for example, in the case of Picasso, who has just emerged as a brilliant artist. . . . [H]e is attracted by every subject, and everything can be a subject for Picasso. . . . Apart from the great precursors, it is easy to detect many likely influences: Delacroix, Manet (clearly indicated with his Spanish connection), Monet, Van Gogh, Pissarro, Toulouse-Lautrec, Degas, Forain, and Rops, perhaps.*[1]

While Picasso was clearly affected by the work of the French artists noted by Fagus, his appreciation for these artists grew from his relationship with a core group of Catalan artists of the Modernista movement at the turn of the twentieth century.

When Picasso arrived with his family in Corunna in 1891, the two main cultural centers in the city were the library of the Artisans' Circle and that of the Real Consulado (merchants' guild). Among the periodicals available in the library of the Artisans' Circle between 1891 and 1895 were *La España moderna*, *La Ilustración Artística*, *Ilustración Española y Americana*, *Ilustración Ibérica*, *La Velada*, *Galicia*, and *Revista regional de ciencias, letras, artes* or *Revista Gallega*. While it is not very likely that Picasso, then aged between ten and fourteen, would have visited the library, he did attend dancing classes for children in the same building.[2] Most of these periodicals, which his father may have read, dealt with current affairs, art, literature, and science. They were illustrated with engravings by Spanish and foreign artists, but it is highly unlikely that any of these would have been Impressionists, since the artistic trends in Spain, which essentially emanated from Madrid, were still focused on academic art.

It would appear, therefore, that if Picasso had any contact with French Impressionism while in Corunna, it must have been through the painter and sculptor Isidoro Brocos, who had lived in Paris and whom Picasso regarded as an "exceptional teacher."[3] According to Josep Palau i Fabre, it was Brocos who introduced Picasso to Impressionism.[4] It seems unlikely, however, that Picasso would have been sufficiently aware of the new trends in Europe to have considered emulating them in his own artistic development. During these early years, Picasso's father had already determined that his son's skills made him suitable for a successful career in the world of academic art, which then prevailed in the national Bellas Artes exhibitions.

Picasso left Corunna for Barcelona at the end of September 1895 and enrolled at the Escola Provincial de Belles Arts, better known as La Llotja, where his father now taught. In October, no doubt with a recommendation from his father, he requested permission to copy works of art in the museum of the Academia Provincial de Belles Arts (provincial academy of fine arts).[5] In the various classes at La Llotja, students were provided with plates from which to copy works by Velázquez, Murillo, Goya, Holbein, Lucas Cranach, Casado del Alisal, Rubens, Van Eyck, Giorgione, Proudhon, Raphael, Michelangelo, and Corot, among others. It has proved impossible to find among these engravings any that could be described, even remotely, as Impressionist.

A visit to the library of Barcelona's Reial Acadèmia de Belles Arts de Sant Jordi, which now houses the contents of La Llotja's library, gives a clear idea of the kind of art that was admired and taught in the fine art academies of the period. Of all the publications to which the Llotja subscribed, the one most concerned with contemporary French art of the period was the periodical L'Art Français. The school's archives contain only the issues dating from between May 1895 and April 1896, which include images and references to works by Puvis de Chavannes; the Impressionists Sisley, Renoir, and Morisot; and even a reproduction of Santiago Rusiñol's painting The Smile, which was shown at the Salon du Champ-de-Mars in 1895. This was the only reference to Impressionist art to be found at the library that Picasso might have been able to consult between 1895 and 1897.

In October 1897, Picasso left Barcelona to attend classes at the Academia de San Fernando in Madrid, where the teaching methods and the role models were the same as at La Llotja. In a letter to Joaquim Bas, his fellow student at La Llotja, Picasso clearly expressed

his disappointment with this style of teaching.[6] In June 1898, Picasso returned to Barcelona, having fallen ill with scarlet fever; at the end of the month he went to recuperate in Horta de Sant Joan, home of his friend Manuel Pallarès, where he painted in the open air. He returned to Barcelona in January 1899.

Palau i Fabre writes that when Picasso returned to Barcelona from Horta de Sant Joan, "He appears to have arrived with a well-established plan of campaign. . . . Undoubtedly his intention was to achieve closer contacts with the Cercle Artístic and the Quatre Gats."[7] He must be referring here to the Cercle Artístic de Sant Lluc, where Picasso again took up life drawing, as he had at La Llotja.[8] The library of the Sant Lluc arts society subscribed to most of the important art periodicals published in Catalonia and Spain, and it was also possible to consult the most influential foreign magazines of the era, such as Art et Décoration, L'Art Français, The Studio, The Art Journal, L'Image, Deutsche Kunst und Dekoration, and Die Kunst für Alle.[9] It was in these magazines that Picasso may have been able to see reproductions, in black-and-white only, of the Degas works that his new friends and colleagues would soon praise.

When Picasso returned to Barcelona, he joined the Modernista circle that included Ramon Casas, Santiago Rusiñol, and Miquel Utrillo — the very artists who would help to shape Picasso's early career and introduce him to Impressionist art and to the work of Edgar Degas. The Modernista group was centred around the café-restaurant Els Quatre Gats, established by Pere Romeu along with Casas, Rusiñol, and Utrillo in June 1897. Picasso had already heard about Modernisme before leaving for Madrid. In his 1897 letter to Joaquim Bas he wrote, "I'm going to do a drawing for you to submit to Barcelona Cómica, if they buy it, you'll have a good laugh. Modernisme it will have to be, as that is what the magazine is all about. Neither Nonell nor the Young Mystic,

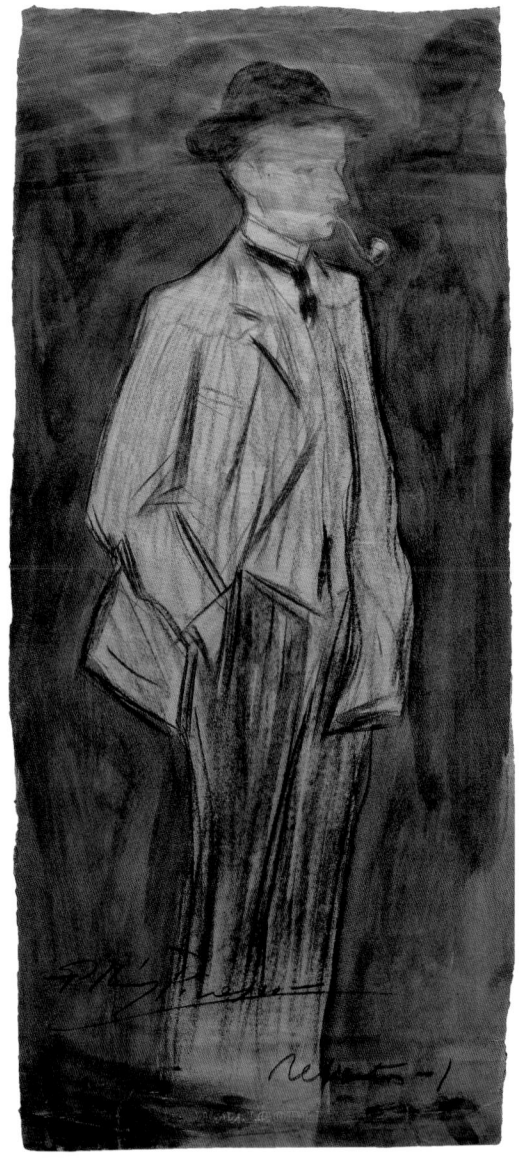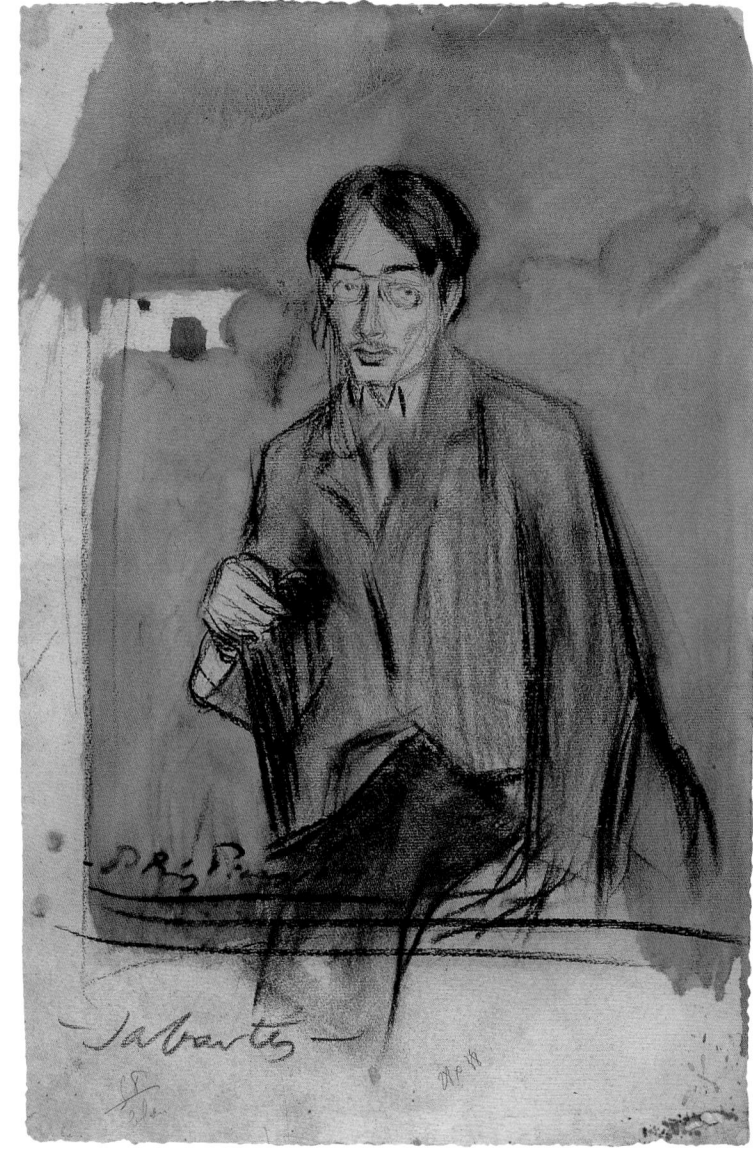

nor Pichot [Pitxot], nor anybody else has ever done anything half so shocking as my drawing is going to be. You'll see."[10] Isidre Nonell and Ramon Pitxot were younger than Casas, Rusiñol, and Utrillo but older than Picasso. Nonell had begun painting his series *Cretins of Boí* in 1896, which had proved an intolerable affront to the well-to-do society of the period. This is no doubt why Picasso cites Nonell along with Casas and Rusiñol, who were by that time already recognised and respected artists. Picasso was clearly attracted to the revolutionary nature of Nonell's

work, but his reference to these artists' works as "shocking" shows that he was still marked by the teaching he had received.

When Picasso became a member of the Quatre Gats group, he was impressed by these artists who, although they had broken with academic art, had succeeded in gaining the respect of some of the public and of the critics. They proved it was possible to make art that was different to that of the official academies and yet to be successful. At Els Quatre Gats, he was to become thoroughly acquainted with the roots

312

Pablo Picasso

*Portrait of the Writer
Ramon Reventós*, 1900.
Watercolor, charcoal, and
Conté crayon on paper,
66.5 x 30.1 cm. Museu
Picasso, Barcelona
(MPB 110.872)

313

Pablo Picasso

*Portrait of Jaume
Sabartés, Seated*, 1900.
Charcoal and watercolor
on paper, 50.5 x 33 cm.
Museu Picasso, Barcelona
(MPB 70.228)

314

Ramon Casas

Portrait of Pablo Picasso,
1900. Charcoal, Conté
crayon, and pastel,
69 x 44.5 cm. Museu
Nacional d'Art de
Catalunya, Barcelona
(MNAC/GDG 27264)

of Modernisme and come to share the movement's fascination for Paris and Parisian artists — and for Edgar Degas.

Before joining the Quatre Gats group, Picasso's awareness of Degas's work was necessarily very limited. None of Degas's work was shown in Barcelona until the Exhibition of French Art held in 1917, the year of his death, when he was represented by three pieces. References to Degas in the periodicals of the era were brief and infrequent, although those articles that did appear were universally complementary.[11] This suggests that Picasso's knowledge of Degas and the other French Impressionists came to him indirectly, via the opinions and the works of Ramon Casas, Santiago Rusiñol, and, especially, Miquel Utrillo.

Ramon Casas's most obvious influence on Picasso can be found in the portraits Picasso showed at his first exhibition: in February 1900 in the Sala Gran at Els Quatre Gats.[12] These portraits of friends (**312, 313**), like Casas's portraits of famous personalities (**314**), owe a debt to the subjective portraits favored by Degas. In a letter he sent to his friend Utrillo from Paris, dated between 1898 and 1900, Ramon Casas wrote, "I've already been to Camondo's house and it really is amazing; although I liked Monet much more than I thought (and I already knew his work), the works by Degas — apart from the drawings (and a black-and-white picture) — left me rather cold. The rest is very good, but after such a long time talking about him and wanting to see his work, frankly, the color is not what I had imagined."[13] Casas is referring here to the Camondo collection, which Utrillo reviewed in 1911, upon the death of the collector. The two are in agreement with regard to the beauty and significance of the paintings in the collection, but, unlike Utrillo, Casas is not very enthusiastic about Degas's work. It may be "very good," but Casas, who would have been accustomed to seeing black-and-white reproductions, is disappointed by Degas's colors. This is not to say,

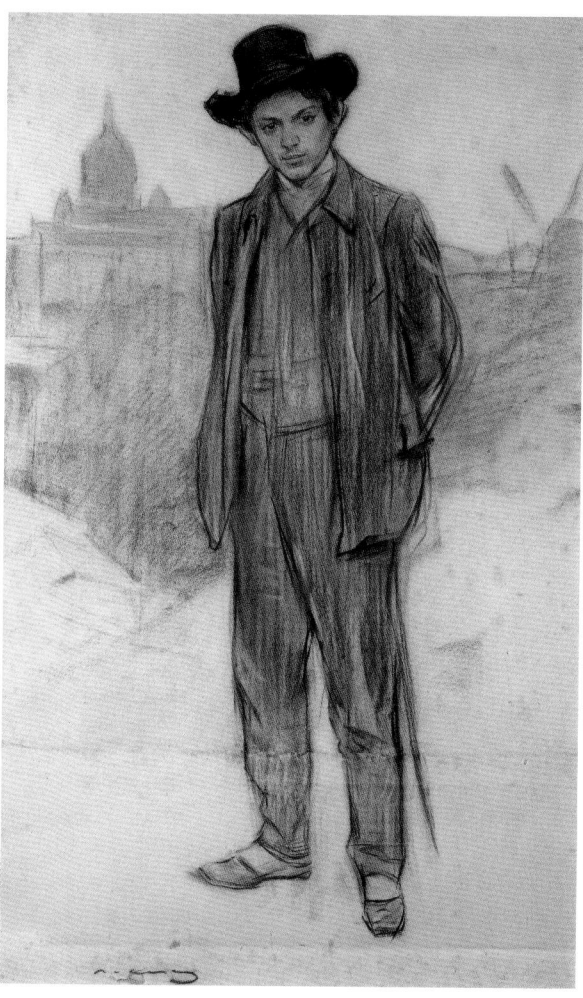

however, that Casas's work was not strongly influenced by Degas in terms of composition and subject matter, as noted by Alexandre de Riquer in 1900.[14] Degas's compositions, with their off-center framing in which elements disappear off the edge of the picture, and his subject matter of cafés and interiors served as models for Casas and Rusiñol, and, through them, for Picasso. Minor works such as the drawing *Self-Portrait in Chiaroscuro and Other Sketches* in the Museu Picasso in Barcelona give an indication of Picasso's great admiration for Casas's work.[15] In this drawing, Picasso copies Casas's signature several times and sketches, along with other figures, a woman seated at a table in a very personal Modernista style.

According to John Richardson, Picasso was more attracted to Santiago Rusiñol's personality than to his work.[16] He must have listened carefully to the older man's opinions on art, however, either at the home of Ramon Reventós or on the occasions when they met at Els Quatre Gats. Picasso made a number of sketches in which we can sense his affection for Rusiñol, such as *Portrait of Santiago Rusiñol* (see 61) and *Caricature of Ramon Pitxot*.[17] Unlike Casas, Santiago Rusiñol was not only a painter but also a writer and art critic, as well as the creator of the Cau Ferrat and the cultural festival the Festes Modernistes, which took place in the town of Sitges. Like Casas, however, Rusiñol was a fervent admirer of Degas, as his article from 1892 in *La Vanguardia* reveals:

Some by conviction and many due to powerlessness believe that art must flee reality by trying to beautify. . . . We believe, with an absolute faith, that there is nothing so beautiful as reality and that, owing to this beauty, it is impossible to succeed in anything more than a poor imitation. . . . Claude Monet in landscape and Degas in figurative painting have understood this, and out of this was born Impressionism, which seeks only to capture sensations. This school fixes on canvas those intimate subtleties that express themselves in the appearance of the line, in the essence of the color, in the nature of the form rather than in the form itself, in the soul of its much-searched-for truth, in that vague je ne sais quoi *that flows in the firmament translated into untranslatable colors.*[18]

The Catalan painter and writer Miquel Utrillo was greatly liked and respected by Picasso, and it was very probably thanks to him that Picasso had his first exhibition at Els Quatre Gats, a number of portrait drawings of Picasso's friends, executed in a style that echoes that of Casas.[19] It was also Utrillo, under the pen name of Pincell, who wrote the first major review of

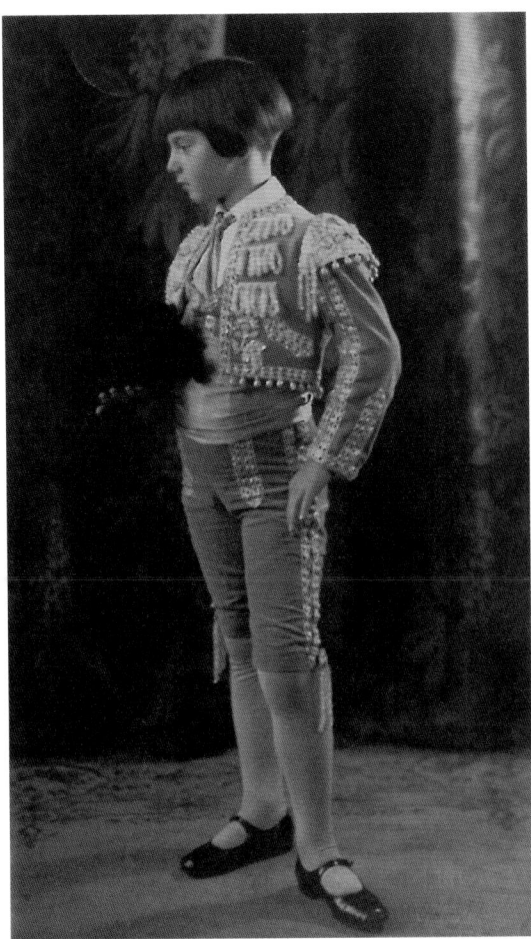

315

Paulo Picasso dressed as a bullfighter, 1929. Photograph. Inscription on back: "For Miquel Utrillo, Paulo Picasso gives you this photograph. From Paulo Picasso as a bullfighter, 31 January 1929." Museu Nacional d'Art de Catalunya (MNAC/GDG 27264)

Picasso's joint exhibition with Ramon Casas at the Sala Parès in 1901.[20] According to Pierre Daix, it was also thanks to Utrillo's efforts that this exhibition took place.[21] It would seem that Miquel Utrillo played a major role in introducing modern art to the younger generation and especially to Picasso. He was at the young painter's side while he was learning about new approaches to art in Barcelona and also during his discovery of international trends during his visit to Paris in October 1900, as we know from a drawing by Picasso in which he portrays himself alongside Utrillo, together with Ramon Casas, Carles Casagemas, and Germaine and Ramon Pitxot, coming out of the Exposition Universelle.[22]

The guidance that Utrillo seems to have

given the young Picasso may also have been thanks to Picasso's friendship with Jacint and Ramon Reventós, whose father Isidre's house provided a meeting place for personalities from cultural circles including Utrillo and Rusiñol. An indication of the relationship between Picasso and Utrillo can be found in drawings such as *Young Man with Hat and Staff* and *Various Sketches*, among others, which suggest a close friendship between the two;[23] an additional indication can be seen in a letter sent to Utrillo by Picasso when he was in Paris, in the form of a comic strip.[24] It would seem that the friendship and mutual respect between the two continued until Utrillo's death, as demonstrated by a photograph of Picasso's son Paulo, sent to Utrillo in 1929 (**315**).

Given Utrillo's role in the development of Picasso's career, it is especially telling that Utrillo was a great admirer of the work of Degas. Utrillo's admiration for the French artist is evident in articles he wrote for the periodical *Las Noticias* in 1911 about the art collection of the recently deceased Count Isaac de Camondo:

Of all the masterpieces in the Camondo collection, of most interest to the public will be the modern paintings, which were acquired long before they caused a stir and include works by Manet, Degas, Monet, Sisley, Jongkind, Delacroix, and Daumier; . . . Degas, the great complete painter of our day, will only be understood when the Camondo collection is in the Louvre. His work has never been exhibited before now, except for some works lent by a number of collectors for the glorification of French art in 1900; this collection contains sufficient works to permit us to study the artist's great personality, his noble insight into the human soul and human actions, his robust and harmonious color, and his vivid drawing; the high point of the collection is his portrait of a woman in which we can guess the terrible influence she had on the lives of a

number of men; it is a work of perfection for anyone who loves definitive painting, that which is good regardless of changing eras, without explanations, preconceptions, or points of view; it is a work that, once it is in the Louvre, will not appear to have come from nowhere, as is the case with many others. Degas's other works include studies of dancers, classrooms at the Opera, horse races, Women Ironing, L'Absinthe, *and many more.*[25]

Degas is the only artist in the Camondo collection to whom Utrillo dedicates an entire paragraph in his article.

It is not clear whether Miquel Utrillo ever met Edgar Degas personally, but there is no doubt that he had an in-depth knowledge of his work, thanks to his friendships with Suzanne Valadon, Federico Zandomeneghi, and Ignacio de Zuloaga. Utrillo had a tempestuous love affair with the model and painter Suzanne Valadon, who first met Degas in 1890, became a friend in 1894, and remained in touch until the artist's death in 1917.[26] Vinyet Panyella relates that Santiago Rusiñol often painted Utrillo and Valadon as a couple between 1890 and 1893,[27] and so Suzanne Valadon already knew Degas at the time she was involved with Utrillo and spent time with the Catalan painters of Montmartre — and at the time that Utrillo was helping to guide Picasso's burgeoning career. Degas's influence on Valadon's drawings is undeniable, as Utrillo must have been well aware.

Another of Utrillo's friends, the Italian painter Zandomeneghi, was also close to Degas. In explaining Utrillo's knowledge of Impressionist and Post-Impressionist artists, Josep C. Lapana writes:

Utrillo got his information from [Federico] Zandomeneghi, the Venetian painter whose confidence he had won as a result of accompanying him on long bicycle rides; after these excursions, the two cyclists would stop off at one of the

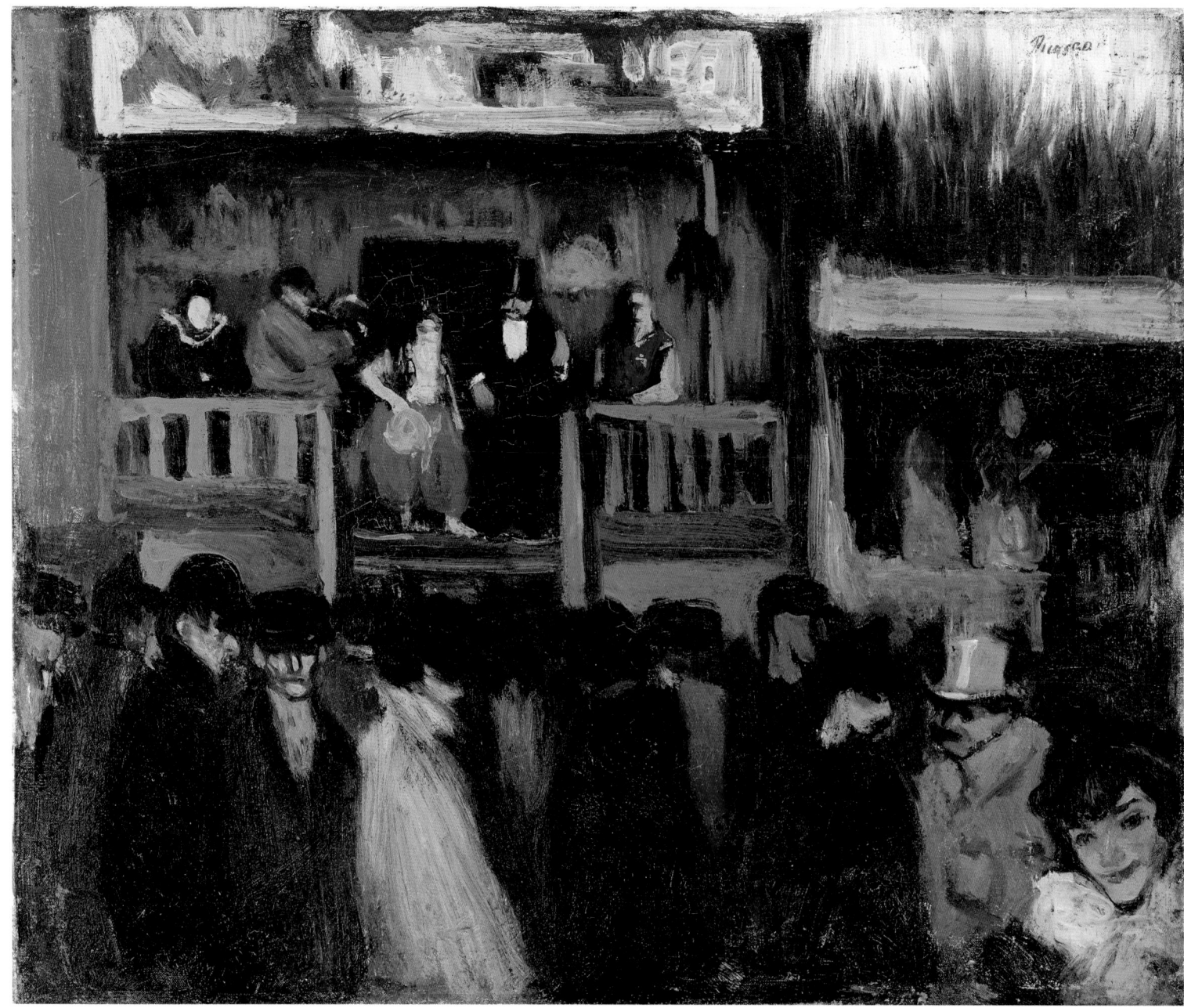

316

Pablo Picasso

Fairground Stall, Paris,
1900. Oil on canvas,
38.1 x 46.3 cm. Museu
Picasso, Barcelona
(MPB 113.113)

317

Edgar Degas

Concert at the Café des Ambassadeurs, 1876–77. Pastel over monotype, 37 x 26 cm. Musée des Beaux Arts de Lyon (inv. B 917)

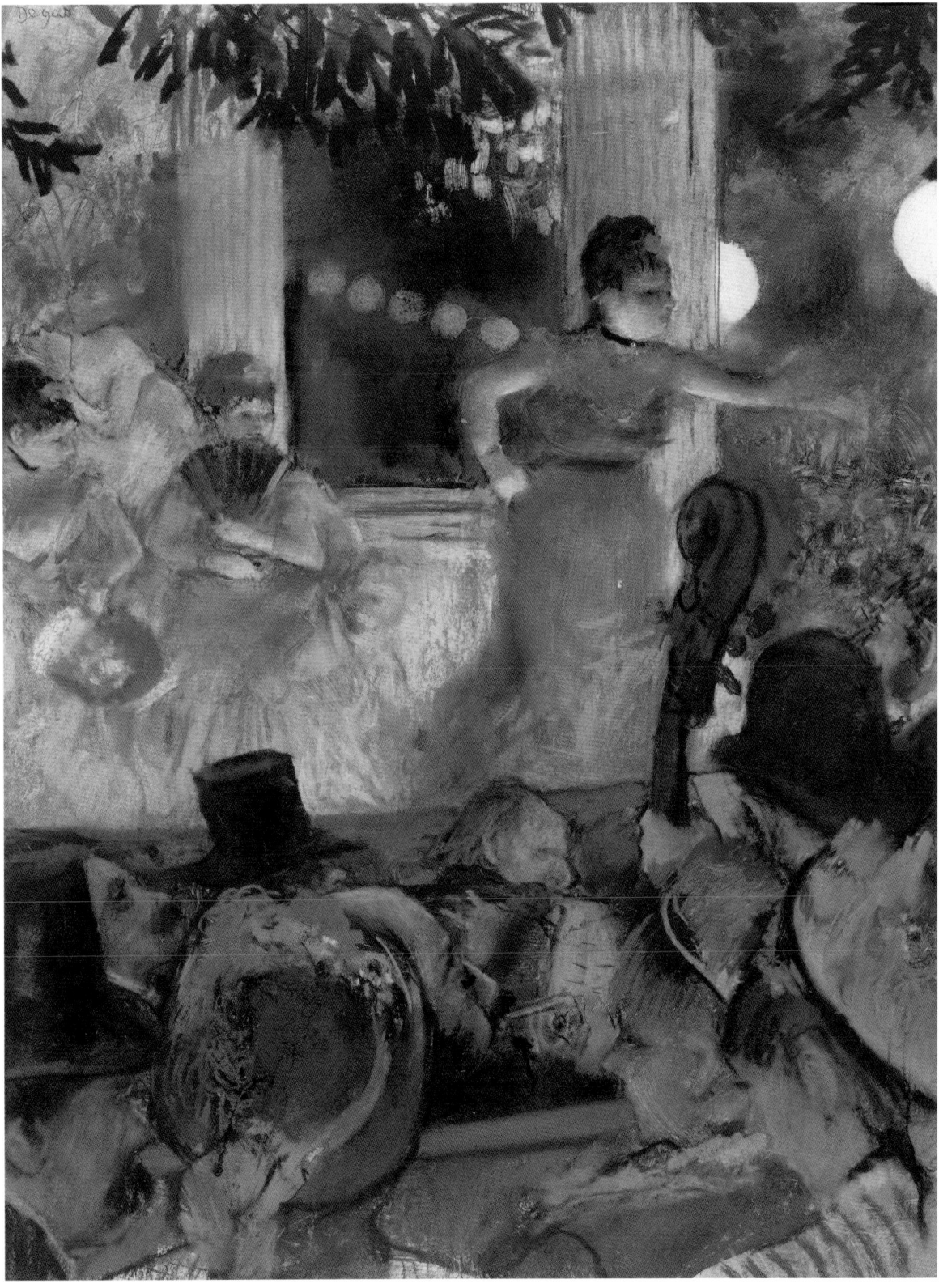

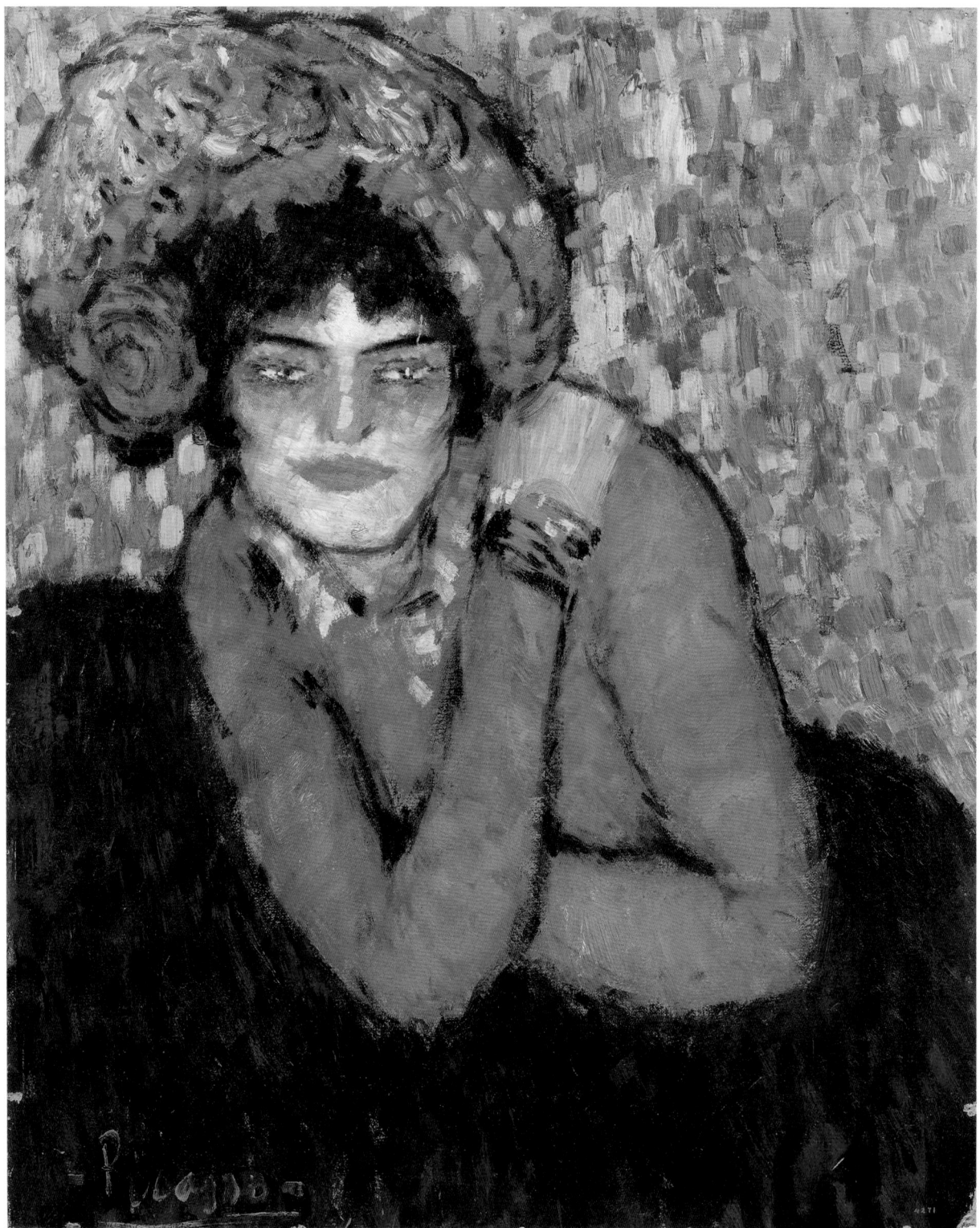

318

Pablo Picasso

Waiting (Margot),
1901. Oil on cardboard,
69.5 x 57 cm. Museu
Picasso, Barcelona
(MPB 4.271)

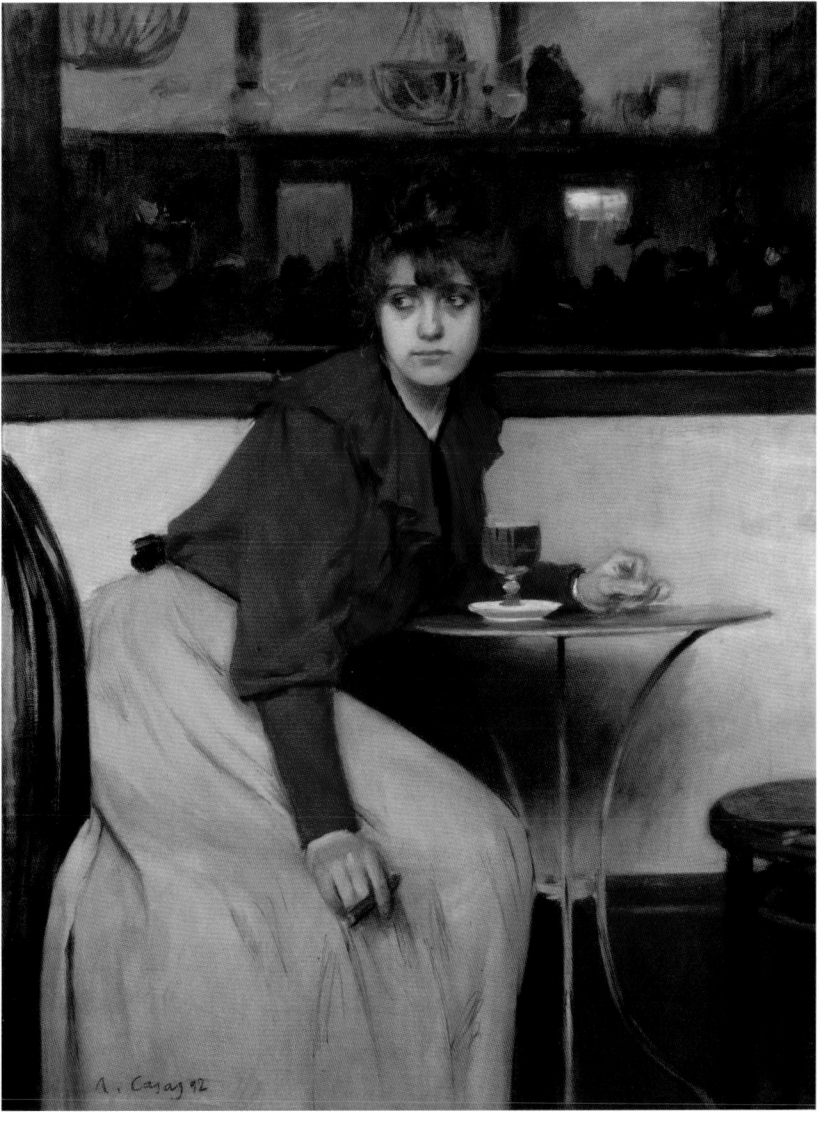

319

Ramon Casas

Madeline, 1892. Oil on
canvas, 117 x 90 cm.
Museu de Montserrat.
Gift of Joseph Maria Sala
i Ardiz (N.R 200.323)

cafés at the Porte Maillot and it was then that
Zandomeneghi would hold forth, in response to
Utrillo's skillful questioning. What he said was
this: "The entire history of French painting in the
second half of the century was set forth, narrated
by a true witness," since Zandomeneghi "knew
Manet, with whom he was close, and frequented
Pissarro, Cézanne, Desboutin, . . . Luce, Claude
Monet, Berthe Morisot, Signac, Sisley, Renoir
and many others, and in those days, he saw the
painter Degas every day."[28]

The third and final member of Utrillo's circle
to know Degas directly was Ignacio de Zuloaga,
a great connoisseur and admirer of French
painting and of the work of El Greco, and who
shared an apartment in Paris in 1892 with Santiago Rusiñol, Miquel Utrillo, and the writer and
critic Josep Maria Jordá. Degas's influence on
Zuloaga's work is also beyond question,[29] as is
the sincere friendship between the two artists;
in fact, from the time that Degas stopped working, owing to blindness, in 1912, the only visitors
he received are said by some to have been the
sculptor Bartholomé, Zuloaga, and Suzanne
Valadon.[30]

Thus, it was Utrillo who introduced modern
art to Picasso, showing him the work of the
Impressionist artists and the relationship
between art and life in those works that Utrillo
so admired. Although Picasso had frequented
museums and art schools since childhood, the
teaching Picasso received at the institutions he
attended in Malaga, Corunna, Barcelona, and
Madrid was not affected by the new international trends in art. It was not until the end of
1899, when he became a part of the famous
gatherings at Els Quatre Gats, that he began to
explore avant-garde ideas in art. Thanks to his
entry into Modernista circles through Utrillo,
Casas, and Rusiñol — the three eminent figures
of Catalan culture — Picasso began to take an
interest in the Impressionist movement and artists such as Manet, Toulouse-Lautrec, and, ultimately, Degas. And, indeed, the results were
extraordinary: it was due to his discovery of the
Modernistas and their influence that Picasso
was able to present to the Parisian public in
1901 works such as *Fairground Stall* (**316**),
whose elevated viewpoint recalls scenes like
Degas's *Café des Ambassadeurs* (**317**); portraits
such as *The Dwarf* (see 120) and *Waiting*
(Margot) (**318**), works whose psychological
insight, as well as their composition, recall not
only Casas's *Madeline* (**319**) but also Degas's
iconic *In a Café (L'Absinthe)* (see 104).

NOTES

INTRODUCTION

1. Félicien Fagus in *La Revue Blanche*, 15 July 1905, cited in Palau 1981, p. 515. The exhibition, which took place at the gallery of Ambroise Vollard, also included work by the young Spanish artist Francisco Gonzales de Iturrino.
2. Félicien Fagus, "Gazette d'art," *La Revue Blanche*, 1 September 1902, cited in Richardson 1991, p. 248.
3. Quoted in Parmelin 1965, p. 43.
4. Quoted in Vollard 1937, p. 70, and Daix 1994a, pp. 144–45: "C'est toute la différence entre un con et un peintre."

CHAPTER 1
ACADEMIES AND
"MAD REVOLUTIONARIES"

1. Charles Baudelaire, "The Painter of Modern Life," 1863, in Baudelaire 1964, pp. 1–40.
2. The drawing carries the date "November 1890"; for Picasso's later reminiscences of this event, see Parmelin 1969, p. 73.
3. Valéry 1960, p. 64.
4. Degas was admitted to the École des Beaux-Arts in Paris in April 1855; see Boggs 1988, p. 48.
5. Numerous examples of such copies are illustrated and described in Reff 1976, Notebooks 1–3.
6. Loyrette 1991, p. 29.
7. The drawing is considered to be a work

from Corunna by some authors and from Picasso's early period in Barcelona by others.
8. Valéry 1960, p. 23.
9. Degas's student work was not revealed to the public until the sales of his studio contents in 1918–19; see chapter 3.
10. Reff 1976, Notebook 11, p. 82; L.46; Reff 1976, Notebook 12, p. 63; Notebook 12, p. 74; Notebook 8, p. 41; Notebook 10, p. 31; Notebook 18, pp. 86 and 241.
11. Reff 1976, Notebook 8, p. 55; Notebook 9, p. 45; Notebook 10, pp. 17 and 45; Notebook 13, pp. 23 and 28.
12. Corunna 2002, pp. 136, 157, 159; 119, 163, respectively.
13. Corunna 2002, pp. 122–27.
14. See Reed and Shapiro 1984; Melot 1994; Kendall 2009.
15. Richardson 1991, chapter 3.
16. For Picasso's obsession with his father's paintbrushes, see Sabartés 1948, pp. 32–33, 39.
17. See Natasha Staller, "Gods of Art: Academic Education and Its Legacy," in McCully 1997, pp. 67–85; Cowling 2002b, pp. 32–43.
18. Quoted in Lemoisne 1946–49, vol. 1, p. 30: "le plus beau fleuron de ta couronne."
19. Boggs 1988, pp. 77–82.
20. Richardson 1991, pp. 52–55.
21. Ibid., p. 48.
22. Ibid., pp. 80–82.
23. Ibid., pp. 84–85.
24. Degas's mother died when he was thirteen. Doña María, Picasso's mother, was clearly important in his early emotional

life but appears to have left her son's artistic career in the hands of don José.
25. Reff 1976, Notebook 18, p. 182; Notebook 20, p. 3.
26. For several such cases, see Boggs 1988, pp. 112–14, and Thomson 1987, especially pp. 16–21, 93–99.
27. Blanc 1867, p. 13: "le culte de la beauté."
28. For paintings on view in Malaga, see Staller 2002, pp. 20–27, 107–10.
29. Staller, "Gods of Art: Academic Education and Its Legacy," in McCully 1997, pp. 68–69. Examples of Picasso's drawings from older art are in Corunna 2002, pp. 117, 151, and Museu Picasso 1985, nos. 110.140, 110.600, 110.700, 110.937, and 111.194r.
30. Richardson 1991, p. 54.
31. See Jordi Falgàs, "Greeting the Dawn: The Impact of the Renaixença in Periodicals and Architecture," and Eliseu Trenc, "Modernista Illustrated Magazines," in Robinson 2006, pp. 27–31 and 61–67.
32. *Historia y Arte*, March 1895, p. 18; December 1895, p. 196; November 1895, pp. 168–69; June 1895, p. 71.
33. *La Ilustración Artística* was launched in 1882 and published until 1895.
34. *La Ilustración Artística*, 25 June 1894, p. 408; 19 March, p. 177.
35. I am most grateful to Montse Torras for discovering this information.
36. Richardson 1991, p. 90.
37. Brown 1996; Cowling 2002b; Tinterow and Lacambre 2003.
38. Museu Picasso 1985, nos. 110.697, 111.194R, 110.860, 110.937, 111.396, 111.404.

39. Corunna 2002, pp. 144, 146; Museu Picasso 1985, nos. 110.126, 111.501r, 110.117r, 111.391.

40. Penrose 1958, p. 17. In Richardson 1991, p. 72, it is noted that Picasso in adulthood was "reticent" about his early religious studies, fearing that they "might tarnish his atheistic image."

41. *La Ilustración Artística*, 8 January 1894; 2 April; 28 May.

42. Ibid., 17 September 1894; 9 September 1895.

43. Ibid., 30 July 1894, pp. 491–93.

44. Ibid., 2 April 1894, pp. 212–15.

45. Ibid., p. 212: "Cierto que ni el número ni la importancia de las obras han podido dar una idea perfecta del admirable florecimiento actual de aquella pintura, la cual hoy ejerce su influjo soberano en todo el mundo."

46. Ibid.: "los paisajistas y marinistas, come Pissarro, Monet, Sisley."

47. Ibid., p. 214: "uno de los más acentuados impresionistas."

48. Museu Picasso 1985, nos. 111.170, 111.172r.

49. Cowling 2002b, pp. 45–46.

50. L.16–18, L.28, L.29.

51. Boggs 1988, pp. 89–92; DeVonyar and Kendall 2002, pp. 45–47.

52. The subject was suggested by a current opera by Giacomo Rossini, featuring the warlike queen who was also celebrated for her prowess as a builder of empires.

53. The battle of Covadonga was fought on the Iberian Peninsula in the eighth century, when local forces achieved a decisive victory against their Moorish conquerors.

54. Penrose 1958, pp. 33–34.

55. Robinson 2006, p. 8.

56. Marfany 1972, pp. 73–91, translated in Robinson 2006, p. 28.

57. Cowling 2002b, p. 46.

58. In Richardson 1991, p. 64, it is noted that Picasso drew "a fragment of a male nude from the western pediment of the Parthenon" for his entrance examination at La Llotja.

59. Museu Picasso 1985, nos. 110.849, 110.880.

60. For example, Museu Picasso 1985, nos. 110.048, 110.203.

61. L.35–36; Reff 1976, Notebook 10, pp. 42, 55–56, 59, 63–64, 67; Notebook 11, pp. 9, 11, 17, 21.

62. L.34; see Boggs 1988, p. 52.

63. Museu Picasso 1985, nos. 110.203, 111.203, 111.480; Z.VI.39; Z.XXI.53; Museu Picasso 1985, nos. 110.059, 111.453, 111.239, 110.101.

64. Museu Picasso 1985, nos. 110.049, 110.655, 111.391, 110.059, 110.078, 110.117, 111.453 ; see also Richardson 1991, chapter 5.

65. Richardson 1991, p. 76.

66. See, for example, Corunna 2002, pp. 136, 155, 157, 161.

67. The example of local painters working outdoors in Malaga is noted in Richardson 1991, p. 18. See also Ocaña 1994, pp. 44–49.

68. A number of broadly similar painted landscape studies, four of them dated to this same moment, are preserved in the Museu Picasso, Barcelona: nos. 110.081, 110.158, 110.167, 110.174, 110.176, 110.177, 110.186, 110.225.

69. *La Ilustración Artística*, 2 April 1894, p. 214: "la descomposition de un tono en sus colores elementales, yuxtpuestos, para que desde lejos se fundan, recomponiéndolo."

70. R. Balsa de la Vega, "Crónica de Arte," *La Ilustración Artística*, 20 May 1895, p. 354.

71. Ibid.: "El toque"; "violentos contrastes de la luz de sol."

72. A closely comparable work, *Study for "Mountain Landscape,"* measures 28.2 x 39.8 cm (Museu Picasso 1985, no. 110.081). See also Ocaña 1994, pp. 68–71.

73. Richardson 1991, p. 78.

74. Ibid.

75. Berson 1996.

76. Mendoza 2001, p. 262.

77. See Mendoza 2001; MNAC 1997; and Cristina Mendoza, "Casas and Rusiñol: The Allure of Montmartre," in Robinson 2006, pp. 42–53.

78. *La Ilustración Artística*, 1895, issues for 7, 14, and 21 January; 11 February; 18 March; 6, 20, and 27 May; 3 and 17 June; 8 July; 19 August; 30 September; 28 October.

79. Ibid., 27 May 1895, p. 374; 8 July 1895, p. 470.

80. See the detailed chronologies in MNAC 1997 and Mendoza 2001.

81. Other related scenes include Museu Picasso 1985, nos. 110.056, 110.057, 110.058, 110.059, 110.060, 110.896.

82. Sabartés 1948, p. 17; Richardson 1991, p. 65.

83. Richardson 1991, p. 67.

84. Corunna 2002, pp. 198–201; Richardson 1991, p. 41.

85. Duranty, "The New Painting: Concerning the Group of Artists Exhibiting at the Durand-Ruel Galleries," 1876, translated in Moffett 1986, p. 44.

86. [Jules-Antoine] Castagnary, *Le Siècle*, 29 April 1874, translated in Moffett 1986, p. 127; Ph[ilippe] Burty, *The Academy* [London], 15 April 1876, translated in Moffett 1986, p. 172; *La Petite République Française*, 10 April 1877, translated in Moffett 1986, p. 217.

87. Kendall 1996, chapters 1 and 2.

88. See Berson 1996, vol. 2, pp. 147–48, 180, 240–42; Kendall 1996, chapter 6 and pp. 294–95.

89. *Interior de la Moulin de la Galette* and *Au Moulin de la Galette*; see Mendoza 2001, pp. 25 and 98; *Entre Dos Luces* was shown in the Secunda Exposición General de Bellas Artes in Barcelona in 1894 (Mendoza 2001, p. 146).

90. See, for example, *Interior con Figura Femina*, 1890–91, in MNAC 1997, pp. 144–45.

91. A group of such works was shown in a joint exhibition held with Casas at the Sala Parés in Barcelona in 1891.

92. Ràfols 1948; MNAC 1997, pp. 166–67; Boggs 1988, pp. 143–46.

93. Panyella 1981, pp. 38, 60. For Degas's proximity to Puvis de Chavannes, see Kendall 1996, p. 22.

94. For example, *La Risueña*, MNAC 1997, no. 45, pp. 198–99.

95. 8 January, c. 1895, in Guérin 1947, p. 194.

96. I am most grateful to the staff of the library at the Museu National d'Art de Catalunya for providing a list of the art-related periodicals available at the Ateneo.

97. Duret 1894.

98. Roger Marx 1897, p. 323.

99. For a bibliography of Rusiñol's writings, see MNAC 1997, pp. 281–86.

100. For Chat Noir, see Kendall 1996, p. 22; Ocaña 1996, pp. 223–25; Richardson 1991, pp. 129–30.

101. Richardson 1991, p. 134.

102. Pablo Picasso to Joachim Bas, 3 November 1897, cited in Richardson 1991, p. 90.

103. Museu Picasso 1985, nos. 111.365R, 111.366, 111.368.

104. See, for example, Museu Picasso 1985, nos. 110.088, 110.097.

105. Museu Picasso 1985, nos. 110.335, 110.384, 110.752.

106. For a comparable drawing with a more fully described setting, see Richardson 1991, p. 95.

107. In this sense, Picasso's inclusion of *Gil Blas Illustré* may have been a private reference to don José's extramarital escapades, such as his frequenting of prostitutes in Malaga; see Richardson 1991, pp. 16, 20.

108. Richardson 1991, p. 154; for the importance of posters and illustrations in this milieu, see Ocaña 1996, pp. 103–11 and Robinson 2006, pp. 61–67, 69–71.

109. See Reed and Shapiro 1984; Melot 1994; Kendall 2009.

110. *Quatre Gats*, 9 March 1899, p. 3: "Aquests joves y d'altres pintors de més edat, empenyan á en Rodin á formar una nova colla, ahont entrarían en Degás, Monet y altres grans artistas desconeguts del públich."

111. For the broader role of Art Nouveau in Modernisme, see Léal 2002, pp. 108–69.

112. L.164; Boggs 1988, pp. 118–20.

113. Richardson 1991, p. 135.

114. Isidre Nonell to Raimon Casellas, 3 March 1897, cited in MNAC 2000, p. 287: "Lo d'en Millet y Corot casi ba

ferme arronsà las espatllas. . . . Quins m'han agradat de debó han sigut Puvis de Chavannes, Wisler, Sergent y Carriere. El primer sens dupte qu'es el més gran dels pintors qu'are viuen."

115. Ibid., pp. 274, 305.

116. Ibid., pp. 287–99: "Lo de C. Monet, Degas, Pissaro, Manet, Renoir, etc hasta hu trobava magre"; "Monet ja m'entusiasma y Degás també."

117. Isidre Nonell to Raimon Casellas, 26 February 1898, cited in MNAC 2000, p. 289: "Acostumat á veure la pintura mansa que sense excepció fan els pintors de Barcelona, els Degas, Monets, Pissarro y Manet van semblarme revolucionaris poca-soltas."

118. Ibid.: "D'en Degas he vist á més dels cuadros qu'exposa sovint a can Durand-Ruel, la colecció que te el Conde Camondo. La majoria son estudis de bailarinas (com vosté ja sab) admirable."

119. See chapter 2, p. 65.

120. Isidre Nonell to Raimon Casellas, 26 February 1898, cited in MNAC 2000, pp. 289–90.

121. See, for example, *Singer with a Glove*, c. 1878; L.478 bis.

122. For example, Museu Picasso 1985, nos. 110.805, 111.768, 111.792.

123. Palau 1981, nos. 334–37.

124. Moore 1918, p. 64.

125. Lecomte 1892, p. 154; Roger Marx 1897, p. 321.

126. See, for example, Museu Picasso 1985, nos. 110.056, 110.057, 110.058.

127. *Pèl y Ploma*, 6 January 1900.

128. *Pèl y Ploma*, 15 July 1899, p. 4: "un Zola, un Degas o un Mirbeau"; 5 May 1900, p. 3: "artistes com en Rodin, en Claude Monet, en Degas, en Renoir, en Besnard, en Dalou, en Sisley."

129. *Pèl y Ploma*, 1 December 1900, p. 4.

130. *Pèl y Ploma*, June 1901, p. 17: "Petit Goya," "corbates ultra impressionists."

131. See Richardson 1991, pp. 143–49; Cristina Mendoza, "Casas and Picasso," in Ocaña 1996, pp. 21–31; for Ventosa, see Richardson 1991, pp. 245–46.

132. Alley 1981, pp. 145–48.

133. Richardson 1991, pp. 152–53.

CHAPTER 2
NEIGHBORS IN MONTMARTRE

1. Sabartés 1948, pp. 19–20.

2. *Last Moments* was painted over with *La Vie*, 1903 (Z.I.179).

3. Richardson 1991, p. 172.

4. Ibid.

5. Carles Casagemas and Pablo Picasso to Ramon Reventós, 25 October 1900, cited in Richardson 1991, p. 160.

6. The café scene is Palau 1981, no. 494 (Z.VI.294).

7. Sabartés 1948, p. 22; the sketchbook is in the collection of the Museu Picasso, Barcelona.

8. For access to Durand-Ruel's collection, see Barnet 1978, p. 131; Manzi 1898.

9. Richardson 1991, pp. 152–53.

10. In Picasso 1900, pp. 26–47, the sketches are described as being executed in various combinations of pencil, crayon, pastel, and other media.

11. See also the closely related *The Comedienne* from 1901 in Museu Picasso 1985, no. 4.276 (Z.I.31).

12. The first examples appeared in the 1877 exhibition; see Berson 1996, vol. 2, pp. 72–74, where the following items in the catalogue are identified as works in pastel over print: nos. 37, 43–47, 56.

13. See Boggs 1988, no. 265.

14. *Dancer in Green*, c. 1880, is in the Museo Thyssen-Bornemisza, Madrid (L.572).

15. Richardson 1991, p. 172. Richardson incorrectly asserts that the galleries of Le Barc de Bouteville and Bernheim-Jeune were also on the rue Laffitte.

16. Their close relationship at the turn of the century is documented in numerous financial transactions (Musée d'Orsay 1989, pp. 479–509).

17. See Kendall 1993, chapters 6 and 7; Kendall 1996, p. 294.

18. Kendall 1996, p. 294.

19. Rothenstein 1931, p. 71; Vollard 1936, p. 71.

20. Vollard 1936, p. 70.

21. L.491; Monnier 1985, no. 65, pp. 72–73.

22. See Kendall 1996, chapters 3 and 4; Richardson 1991, p. 153.

23. For a technical discussion of this work, see Kendall 1996, pp. 113–14.

24. Monneret 1978–79, vol. 2, pp. 71–73.

25. For Sunyer, see Benet 1975, where his turn-of-the-century paintings of Paris streets, laundresses, cabarets, and toilette scenes are reproduced and discussed; see also Richardson 1991, p. 170.

26. Richardson 1991, pp. 167–68.

27. *Pierrot et Columbine*, 1900 (location unknown; Z.XXI.224); *French Cancan*, 1900–1901 (private collection, Z.XXI.209).

28. For example, *Dancer*, 1901 (see fig. 119); see also fig 80.

29. Palau 1981, p. 208; for Palau's discussion of Picasso's response to Impressionism and the work of Degas, see pp. 206–9.

30. *Arte Joven*, "Preliminary issue," March 1901, p. 5: "huyendo siempre de lo rutinario"; "esta caterva de impressionistas"; "barbarizando."

31. *Arte Joven* no. 3 (3 May 1901), p. 1.

32. The exhibition was shared with another Spanish painter, Francisco Iturino.

33. Vollard 1936, p. 219.

34. For a detailed summary of many of the likely exhibits, see Palau 1981, pp. 247–57.

35. For Pissarro's paintings of busy Paris boulevards from high vantage points that were shown at Durand-Ruel's gallery in 1898 or 1899, see Brettell and Pissarro 1992, nos. 44–46, 54, 58, 60, 63, 65, 68, 69, and 73.

36. Palau 1981, p. 255, no. 54.

37. Félicien Fagus in *La Revue Blanche*, 15 July 1905, cited in ibid., p. 515.

38. Berson 1996, vol. 2; the exception was the 1879 exhibition.

39. Berson 1996, vol. 2, p. 240: "Suite de nues de femmes se baignant, se lavant, se séchant, se peignant ou se faisant peigner."

40. The first, based entirely on nudes, was at the Boussod et Valadon gallery in 1888: the second was an exhibition of works by Degas at the Durand-Ruel gallery in 1896 that included a new "series of nudes" (Kendall 1996, p. 294).

41. L.872; see Boggs 1988, p. 446–68, no. 271.

42. Gustave Coquiot, *Le Journal*, 17 June 1901, cited in Palau 1981, p. 514: "savoureux"; "une fois encore la chair jeune des petites prostituées."

43. Henry Fèvre, "L'Exposition des impressionnistes," *La Revue de demain*, May–June 1886, cited in Berson 1996, vol. 2, p. 446: "Dans des boudoirs louches de maisons matriculées"; "L'Exposition des impressionnistes," *La République française*, 17 May 1886, cited in ibid., p. 472: "maritornes."

44. For example, *Crouching Nude Woman, Seen from the Back*, c. 1879 (Musée du Louvre; L.547).

45. See chapter 5.

46. Rabinow 2006, p. 152.

47. Ibid., p. 58 n. 6.

48. Ibid., p. 311.

49. Vollard 1914.

50. Vollard 1936, p. 258.

51. Ibid.; for Vollard's books, see chapter 5.

52. Gimpel 1966, p. 416.

53. Weill 1933, p. 65.

54. Duret 1894, p. 205.

55. Ibid.

56. See Kendall 1996, chapter 1.

57. The apartment at Boulevard de Clichy, 130 *ter*, overlooked the back of the building, not the boulevard itself.

58. Richardson 1991, p. 224.

59. Rewald 1944, nos. 50–51, 67–68.

60. Kendall 1996, pp. 31–38.

61. Rewald 1944.

62. Degas's decision, probably made in the late 1890s or the early twentieth century, to cast three of his waxes into plaster and display them in his apartment, is discussed in Kendall 1996, pp. 33–35.

63. Lafond 1918–19; Valéry 1960.

64. Lafond 1918–19, vol. 1, p. 114.

65. Olivier 2001a, p. 146; Vollard 1937, p. 56.

66. Valéry 1960, pp. 19, 39.

67. Lafond 1918–19, vol. 1, p. 114: "Des presses lithographiques ou à eau-fort."

68. For example, Degas seems to have given his lifelong friend and fellow artist Henri Rouart proofs of most of his major prints made during the 1870s and 1880s; see Reed and Shapiro 1984, nos. 23 onward.

69. See, for example, the sale of Roger Marx's vast print holdings: Hôtel Drouot 1914.

70. Morelon and Deconchat 2004.

71. The lithograph in question is based on Degas's pastel *Woman Drying Herself after the Bath*, c. 1876–77 (L.890) (Campbell 2009, pp. 118–23). Degas evidently supervised the making of the print as a possible inclusion in Thornley 1889 but then withheld it, along with several other such images, from the published portfolio.

72. Ganz and Kendall 2007, chapters 8 and 9.

73. Thornley 1889.

74. See Musée Goupil 1997, pp. 88–96.

75. MNAC 1997, pp. 247–48.

76. Richardson 1991, p. 290: "Yo El Greco, yo Greco."

77. Cowling 2002b, p. 88.

78. Dumas 1997, p. 67.

79. For Degas's extensive accumulation of his own works and their eventual sale, see chapter 3.

80. A study for this composition is Z.XXI.362.

81. Weill 1933, p. 61.

82. Ibid., p. 55: "Lorsqu'il passe devant mon magasin (il est mon voisin) et s'il me voit sur le seuil de ma porte, ses regards deviennent furibonds, il détourne ostensiblement la tête, salivant avec mépris."

83. Adrien Farge and Félicien Fagus, both cited in Richardson 1991, p. 248.

84. Weill 1933, p. 66: "Un de ses premiers acheteurs."

85. Richardson 1991, p. 200; in Palau 1981, p. 255, it is proposed that the "Danseuses" in the 1901 exhibition was *French Cancan* (Z.XXI.209).

86. Richardson 1991, p. 164; Weill 1933, p. 125.

87. For Haviland, see Richardson 1991, pp. 400, 479, and Richardson 1996, pp. 5–6, 183. He was related to Degas's print-collector friend Philippe Burty and to Charles Haviland, who collected Degas's pictures and owned a china factory with which Degas was con-

nected in the late 1870s (Reed and Shapiro 1984, p. 117). Paul Valéry's youthful memories of visiting Degas became part of an important memoir of the artist (Valéry 1960), and he was subsequently drawn by Picasso. Daniel Halévy, who acquired a picture by Picasso, was the son of Degas's close friend Ludovic Halévy (Loyrette 1996, p. 36).

88. Roger Marx 1897.

89. Ibid., p. 321: "Le vrai maître de Moderne"; "l'ordre intellectual et technique."

90. Weill 1933, p. 63; Richardson 1991, p. 516.

91. Richardson 1991, p. 251.

92. Z.VI.485–89.

93. Weill 1933, p. 65.

94. Private collection, 1899–1900 (Z.I.21).

95. Charles Maurice, *Mercure de France*, Paris, Dec. 1902, cited in Daix and Boudaille 1988, pp. 234–35. The reference is to Charles Baudelaire's celebrated book of poems, *Les Fleurs du mal*.

96. Richardson 1991, p. 282.

97. Adler 1986, p. 149.

98. Reff 1976, Notebook 22, pp. 19, 21, 23, 25.

99. For Degas's title, see ibid., Notebook 26, p. 74.

100. The picture was evidently not shown in the 1876 exhibition; see *Brighton Gazette*, September 1876, cited in Pickvance 1963, pp. 395–96; Boggs 1988, p. 286; Kendall 2009.

101. Duret 1894, p. 206; Hourticq 1912, p. 110.

102. Duret 1894, p. 206.

103. Sabartés 1948, p. 21.

104. Ibid., p. 20.

105. Duret 1894, p. 206.

106. X-rays made at the Los Angeles County Museum of Art suggest that the picture began as a scene of a seated man with a dog, becoming a double portrait when the figure of the woman was added at a later phase. I am much indebted to Joe Fronek for elucidating this process.

107. For studies of Degas's laundress pictures and their histories, see Boggs 1988, pp. 223–35, 424–49; Campbell 2009, pp. 94–101, 107–12.

108. The works in question were L.356, L.685, L.686, L.785; in 1900, Durand-Ruel owned all but L.356.

109. Duret 1894, p. 204; Manzi 1898, no. 8.

110. *Woman Ironing*, 1901 (Metropolitan Museum of Art, New York; Z.XXI.263).

111. The paler, more delicate lines that form the standing figure are clearly underneath the coarser marks that indicate the individual who leans forward.

112. Cowling 2002b, p. 116.

113. Boggs 1988, p. 426.

114. Z.I.248.

115. Cirlot 1972, p. 127.

116. Wineapple 1996, p. 196.

117. Ibid., p. 225.

118. Ibid., pp. 15–16.

119. See Baltimore Museum of Art 1967.

120. Olivier 2001a, p. 180. The original French text appeared in 1988; see Olivier 1988.

121. 17 August 1906, in Madeline 2005, p. 40.

122. Olivier 2001a, pp. 189–94, 227–50.

123. Olivier 2001b, p. 49.

124. Raynal 1956, p. 90; Raynal later became a writer on art.

125. Salmon 2004, p. 595.

126. Olivier 2001a, p. 199.

127. Museo de Arte Moderno de Barcelona 1976, pp. 18–20.

128. Olivier 2001a, p. 145, 147.

129. Ibid., p. 146. The reference to Suzanne Valadon is not present in Olivier 1988 (p. 170). For more on the inconsistencies between Olivier 1988 and Olivier 2001a, see Olivier 2001a, pp. 11–12.

130. Richardson 1991, p. 210.

131. Daix 1995, p. 157: "une peinture qui éclipserait toutes celles pour lesquelles elle avait déjà posé."

132. See Kendall 1996, pp. 23–25; Dumas 1997, pp. 3–73.

133. Boggs 1988, pp. 254–55.

134. Olivier 1988, p. 193: "une pointe sèche, Salomé dansant devant Hérode." This phrase is missing from the same passage in Olivier 2001a.

135. See, for example, Z.XXII.91, Z.XXII.240, Z.XXII.248, Z.XXII.256.

136. L.522.

137. Davies 1970, p. 73.

CHAPTER 3
THE BALLET

1. For a more detailed account, see Cécile Godefroy's essay "Olga Khokhlova, Ballerina, and Pablo Picasso," appendix 1 in this volume.

2. Paul Paulin to Paul Lafond, 13 September 1917, cited in Boggs 1988, p. 497.

3. See Berson 1996, vol. 2, pp. 7–8.

4. Joris-Karl Huysmans, "L'Exposition des indépendants en 1880," *L'Art moderne* (Paris: G. Charpentier, 1883), in Berson 1996, vol. 1, p. 86: "réalité absolue"; Paul Mantz, "L'Exposition des peintres impressionnistes," *Le Temps*, 22 April 1877, in ibid., p. 167: "éparse et désordonnées."

5. For studies of this subject, see Browse 1949; Lipton 1987; DeVonyar and Kendall 2002.

6. Louis Véron, cited in DeVonyar and Kendall 2002, p. 122.

7. Vollard 1924, pp. 109–10: "On m'appelle le peintre des danseuses, on ne comprend pas que la danseuse a été pour moi un prétexte à peindre de jolies étoffes et à rendre des mouvements."

8. For the suggestion that certain of these Barcelona sketches were based on other works of art, or even pictures by Degas, that Picasso had seen in reproduction, see chapter 1 in this volume.

9. Richardson 1991, pp. 182, 194.

10. L.298, L.305, L.340, L.341.

11. L.689.

12. Duret 1894, p. 206.

13. Roger Marx 1897, p. 325: "esthète"; "ironiste"; "tableaux du labeur, du plaisir et du vice."

14. L.403; Liebermann 1899, p. 13. Like the other works reproduced in Liebermann's book, this picture appeared "by permission of Durand-Ruel," who had presumably bought it from Degas.

15. Carles Casagemas and Pablo Picasso to Ramon Reventós, 25 October 1900, cited in Richardson 1991, pp. 160–61.

16. Geneviève Laporte, *Si tard le soir, le soleil brille . . . Pablo Picasso* (Paris: Plon, 1973), cited in ibid., pp. 337–38.

17. The connection was made in Penrose 1958, p. 115; the X-ray is discussed in E. A. Carmean and Anne Hoenigswald, "Study Section," in Carmean 1980, pp. 67–75.

18. Though conventional ballet dancers were often recruited at a young age, Picasso's model was almost certainly a child attached to one of the itinerant bands of jugglers, acrobats, and entertainers that could still be seen in Paris at this date: for an early photograph of such a group, see McCully 1997, p. 205.

19. For a bibliography of the principal studies of these issues, see Kendall 1998.

20. See Boggs 1988, pp. 342–53; Kendall 1998, pp. 24–43.

21. Paul Mantz, "Exposition des oeuvres des artistes indépendants," *Le Temps*, 23 April 1881, in Berson 1996, vol. 1, p. 358: "realisme à outrance"; "la vérité singulaire"; Joris-Karl Huysmans, "L'Exposition des indépendants en 1881," *L'Art moderne* (Paris: G. Charpentier, 1883), in ibid., p. 349: "la seule tentative vraiment moderne que je connaisse."

22. Mantz, "Exposition des oeuvres des artistes indépendants," *Le Temps*, 23 April 1881, in ibid., p. 358: "effrayant," "laide"; Nina de Villard, "Variétés: Exposition des artistes indépendants," *Le Courrier du soir*, 23 April 1881, in ibid., p. 371; Jules Claretie, "La Vie à Paris: Les Artistes indépendants," *Le Temps*, 5 April 1881, in ibid., p. 335: "fleurette de ruisseau"; "By Our Lady Correspondent," *Artist*, 1 May 1881, in Flint 1984, p. 43.

23. For Degas's visitors at this period, who would also have seen plaster casts of three of his sculptures displayed in his living quarters, see Kendall 1996, pp. 32–36; Vollard 1925, p. 39.

24. Havemeyer 1961, p. 255.

25. Richardson 1991, p. 372.

26. See Olivier 2001a, p. 146.

27. An extensive group of these drawings is discussed and reproduced in Kendall 1998, chapter 2; see fig. 19 and plates 30, 32–36, 38, 40–43. The work owned by Doucet, which he acquired at the Degas sales, was L.586 bis. For Roger Marx's drawing, see chapter 2 in this volume.

28. The characteristically advanced leg in certain Egyptian sculptures of standing figures was known to Picasso at this date; see Z.XXII.360, Z.XXII.362, Z.XXII.367, and sketchbook 42, F, G, in Rosenblum 1986, pp. 64–65. Some medieval and Renaissance carvings of the flagellated Christ include arms joined behind the back.

29. Rodin's work was featured at the 1900 Exposition Universelle, which Picasso saw during his first visit to Paris; for Maillol, see Richardson 1991, p. 210.

30. Cowling and Golding 1994, p. 230.

31. See also an associated drawing in Museu Picasso 1985, no. 110.509.

32. See, for example, Z.I.339, Z.I.359–60, Z.I.365, Z.VI.780, Z.VI.875, Z.XXII.409, Z.XXII.411, Z.XXII.441.

33. Other examples include Z.II.645, Z.II.647, Z.II.651, Z.VI.826, Z.XXVI.13, Z.XXVI.85.

34. Z.I.350, Z.II.3, Z.II.21, Z.II.644, Z.VI.785, Z.XXII.468, Z.XXVI.131–32.

35. See the drawings from Carnet 6 in Rubin 1994, especially p. 50.

36. See, for example, the drawings from various *carnets* in Seckel 1988, vol. 1: p. 216, Carnet 6, 24v, 25v; p. 237, Carnet 8, 26r; p. 249, Carnet 9, no. 2; p. 267, Carnet 11, 1v.

37. See *Study of a Nude Dancer* (Nasjonalgalleriet, Oslo; Vente IV, no. 287a).

38. See Pingeot 1991, p. 195.

39. Richardson 1991, pp. 385–86; see also n. 42.

40. Kahane 1998, pp. 50–62.

41. See chapter 5 in this volume.

42. Rubin 1994, p. 15.

43. Fernande Olivier to Gertrude Stein, 24 August 1907, in Olivier 2001a, p. 191.

44. Rubin 1994, p. 15; see also Richardson 2007, pp. 28–32.

45. Among the drawings for this figure are Seckel 1988, vol. 1, p. 267, Carnet 11, 1v; p. 273, Carnet 12, 3v, 4v, 5v, 6v, 7v, 8v, 9v, 13v, 14v, 14r, and 15r. Other works that relate it closely to the late stages of *Les Demoiselles d'Avignon* are Seckel 1988, vol. 1, p. 216, Carnet 7, 24v, 25v; p. 249, Carnet 9, 2; Z.II.24; Stein 1961, p. 22.

46. Rubin 1994, pp. 80–81, figs. 148–51. In his intricate reconstruction of the history of *Les Demoiselles d'Avignon*, Rubin did not consider *Standing Nude* and dealt only briefly with the "curtain-turner." This figure is considered in great detail in Seckel 1988; see n. 43.

47. See Rosenblum 1986, pp. 53–60; the inscription is reproduced on p. 68, fig. 1. In his study of this sketchbook, Rosenblum speculates that Rouart may have been responsible for introducing Picasso to Degas's brothel monotypes at this period and thus influencing the subject and composition of *Les Demoiselles d'Avignon*. Further discussion of the connection with the Rouart family is in Rubin 1994, p. 142, where the author correctly indicates that there is no evidence that Eugène Rouart or his father owned any of Degas's brothel prints, though they may well have been aware of them; see chapter 5 in this volume for a fuller account of the history of the monotypes.

48. L.293, L.373, L.1177.

49. For a summary of the family as subjects and collectors of Degas's pictures, see Lemoisne 1946–49, vol. 4, p. 42; for the Rouart dynasty, see Musée de la Vie Romantique 2004.

50. Berson 1996, vol. 2, pp. 12–13, 45, 83, 119, 156, 186–87, 251.

51. For his collection, see Manzi-Joyant 1912a and Manzi-Joyant 1912b.

52. Musée de la Vie Romantique 2004, p. 68: "entrepreneur audacieux."

53. Eugène Rouart to Pablo Picasso, 30 March 1907, in Rubin 1994, p. 150; the picture was *Acrobat and Harlequin*, 1905 (Z.I.301).

54. The same letter of 30 March 1907 (cited in the previous note) mentions a recent visit by Rouart to Picasso's studio.

55. Rothschild 1991, p. 30.

56. Penrose 1958, p. 202.

57. Richardson 2007, p. 9.

58. Rothschild 1991, p. 260; see also the essay by Cécile Godefroy in this volume (appendix 1).

59. Balanchine 1954, p. 603.

60. Richardson 2007, p. 5.

61. Rothschild 1991, p. 64, fig. 29; p. 50, fig. 11.

62. Richardson 2007, p. 14; *Harlequin and Woman with a Necklace*, 1917 (Musée National d'Art Moderne, Centre Georges Pompidou, Paris; Z.III.23)

63. Cooper 1968, p. 65.

64. Spurling 1998, pp. 304–5.

65. Penrose 1958, p. 235.

66. Cooper 1968, p. 42, figs. 148–56.

67. See Janis 1968, no. 9, see also Lafond 1918–19, vol 2, opp. p. 24.

68. Rothschild 1991, p. 31, fig. 2; p. 265, fig. 238.

69. See Madeline 2004, pp. 29–31, 60–64, 104–6, 113–14.

70. Cited in Sickert 1947, p. 151.

71. Lafond 1918–19. For the early bibliography, see Lemoisne 1946–49, vol. 1, p. 266.

72. Picasso and Olga were resident in Paris in the first half of 1918, prior to their marriage in July; the first auction took place between 6 and 8 May. After their honeymoon in Biarritz, they returned to Paris in September and remained there until May 1919; the second and third sales were held between 11 and 13 December 1918, and 7 and 9 April 1919. During the fourth sale, between 2 and 4 July, Picasso was working in London.

73. See especially Vente IV, where all but a handful of the 391 lots were works on paper.

74. See Vente I, Vente II, Vente III, Vente IV.

75. Richardson 1996, p. 99.

76. "News and Views of Literature and the Arts," 11 May 1918, in Apollinaire 1972, p. 463.

77. "The Degas Sale," 1918, in ibid., p. 469.

78. "News and Views of Literature and the Arts," 11 May 1918, in ibid., pp. 463–64.

79. "The Degas Sale," 1918, in ibid., pp. 468–70.

80. Manzi 1898, no. 15; this work was sold in Vente I, no. 161.

81. See Boggs 1988, pp. 480–607; Kendall 1996; DeVonyar and Kendall 2002, chapter 8.

82. See Kendall 1996, pp. 25–29.

83. Degas to Alexis Rouart, 11 March 1910, in Guérin 1947, p. 229.

84. For the provenance of this picture, see Lemoisne 1946–49, vol. 3, no. 944.

85. Cited in Valéry 1960, p. 17.

86. Vente I, no. 322.

87. See L.1304, L.1341.

88. See, for example, L.900, L.996, L.997.

89. The possibility that the figure at center was also posed by Marie van Goethem, the model for the *Little Dancer Aged Fourteen*, is implicit in many discussions of this work. It is further endorsed by the appearance of Marie's name and address in a notebook Degas used at this time, close to the name of the first owner of the painting, Drake de Castillo (Reff 1976, vol. 1, Notebook 34, pp. 2, 4).

90. Cowling 2002b, p. 449.

91. Gertrude Stein, *The Autobiography of Alice B. Toklas* (1931; Repr., New York: Vintage, 1961), p. 107, cited in Richardson 2007, p. 283.

92. Cowling 2002b, pp. 465, 449–50.

93. Richardson 2007, p. 277.

94. Penrose 1958, p. 258.

95. Richardson 2007, p. 277.

96. Cooper 1968, p. 65.

97. Ives 1997, p. 68, no. 616.

98. Cooper 1968, pls. 316–19, 353–84.

99. Penrose 1958, p. 251.

100. An example of the former is *Portrait of Olga in an Armchair*, 1918 (Musée national Picasso, Paris, MP 55; Z.III.83). *Still Life (Easel and Dancer's Tights)*, 1926, is Palau 1999, no. 1705.

101. An example of the former is *Guitar*, 1926 (Krugier collection; Z.VII.19); *Large Nude in a Red Armchair*, 1926 (Musée national Picasso, Paris, MP 113; Z.VII.263).

102. Reproduced in Rubin 1980, p. 266 (Z.VII.87).

103. Musée national Picasso, Paris, MP 61 (Z.III.237).

104. See Cooper 1968, pp. 347–49; *Two Women Running on the Beach*, 1922 (Musée national Picasso, MP 78; Z.IV.380).

105. See the sequence of sketchbook pages in Cowling and Golding 1994, pp. 84–87, especially sketchbook pp. 28–51.

106. *Girl with a Ball*, 1931 (S.112.II).

107. For Picasso's presence at the vernissage, see chapter 4, p. 207 in this volume.

108. Musée de l'Orangerie 1931; for the bronzes, see pp. 123–48.

109. See Gsell 1918; Lemoisne 1919; Grolier Club 1922; Leicester 1923.

110. Georges Petit 1924.

111. Some black-and-white reproductions of waxes were included in Gsell 1918 and Lemoisne 1919. The majority were bought by Mellon in 1956.

112. Richardson 2007, p. 437.

113. See Rewald 1944, nos. 69–72.

114. L.491.

115. The exception is *Bather*, 1931 (S.108.II).

CHAPTER 4
WOMEN AT THEIR TOILETTE

1. See Posner 1973.

2. Reff 1976, Notebook 22, cited in Boggs 1988, p. 255.

3. Ibid. The request was made in 1878.

4. See, for instance, Staffe 1892, pp. 11–15. According to Octave Uzanne, "Baronne Staffe's *Cabinet de Toilette* was immensely popular and influential" (Uzanne 1898, p. 167).

5. For contemporary reviews of the final Impressionist exhibition of 1886 in which Degas exhibited a series of his nudes washing, doing their hair, dressing, and so on, see Martha Ward, "The Rhetoric of Independence and Innovation," in Moffett 1986, pp. 430–34, 452–54.

6. Csergo 1988, p. 12 ff; Vigarello 1988, p. 202 ff.

7. For instance, in the December 1893 issue of *Fashions of To-Day*, the London version of the monthly, middle-market Parisian magazine *La Mode pratique*,

Dr. Guillermet devoted his regular column to the transmission of disease by microbes and the necessity for the highest standards of hygiene (p. 14). The issue for January 1894 dealt with disinfectants (p. 38).

8. Matisse 1999, p. 185. The painting referred to is *The Dinner Table*, 1897 (private collection).

9. According to Csergo, by c. 1900 most French writers agreed that one bath a week was best. Baronne Staffe was, she argues, atypical in recommending at least two baths a week (Csergo 1988, p. 73 ff).

10. See Vigarello 1988, pp. 208–9, 220–23. For the history of purpose-built bathrooms and bathroom equipment, see Wright 2000.

11. Bidets were not associated with prostitution and are discussed in Pompeillan 1898, p. 79. However, Degas confined his representation of them to his brothel monotypes (e.g., J.153, J.193).

12. Kendall 1996, pp. 25–28, 157.

13. For example, *The Masseuse*, c. 1893–98, bronze (R.73).

14. Mirbeau 1900, pp. 51–52.

15. Csergo 1988, p. 36. Célestine's mistresses invariably insist that she be "very clean" (Mirbeau 1900, pp. 308–9).

16. Csergo 1988, pp. 56–60; Vigarello 1988, p. 174; Perrot 1984, p. 125. In the December 1893 issue of *Fashions of To-Day*, the recommended period between hair washes was three weeks.

17. Staffe 1892, pp. 115–16. Mirbeau's Célestine speaks of "oxygenating" her mistresses' hair as one of her more pleasant tasks (Mirbeau 1900, p. 52).

18. Baronne Staffe provides recipes for homemade lotions (Staffe 1892, pp. 116 ff), as does the Marquise de Pompeillan (Pompeillan 1898, p. 96), and magazines carried numerous advertisements for "hair tonics" and "hair washes."

19. For example, *Woman at Her Bath*, c. 1893–98 (Art Gallery of Ontario, Toronto; L.1119).

20. Degas confirmed that *Beach Scene* was modeled in his studio (Vollard 1938, p. 112). In *Women Combing Their Hair*, the figures were modeled in the nude and the white shifts added later (Boggs 1988, no. 148).

21. In, e.g., *Woman before a Mirror*, c. 1885–86 (Hamburger Kunsthalle; L.983).

22. See also Picasso, *The Coiffure*, 1900 (Z.I.28), which, like *The Dressing-Room*, recalls Steinlen as well as *coiffure* scenes by Degas such as *La Toilette*, c. 1880 (L.749). *Seated Nude Woman*, 1901 (location unknown; Z.I.50), may have been exhibited in Picasso's show at Vollard's gallery and appears both to spoof typical Salon nudes and to refer to late drawings by Degas depicting women struggling to comb out waist-length hair.

23. See chapter 2, p. 81. *Woman Drying Herself* (see fig. 89) went through six states and some impressions were on the market. Thus, sometime between 1900 and 1910 Degas sold a significant number to the print dealer and publisher Gustave Pellet (Reed and Shapiro 1984, no. 61). *The Tub* (see fig. 91) must be one of the three monotypes entitled "Femme s'essuyant" listed in Pellet's bill of sale, dated 28 November 1911, addressed to Doucet. Pellet had purchased most if not all the seven monotypes on the list from Degas's friend Philippe Burty, who died in 1890 (More-lon and Deconchat 2004, pp. 20–21).

24. Renoir, *Le Moulin de la Galette*, 1876 (Musée d'Orsay, Paris).

25. The drawings (e.g., Z.VI.554, Z.VI.580) are connected with the tragic, huddled figures depicted in pictures in the background of Picasso's allegorical masterpiece *La Vie*, 1903 (Cleveland Museum of Art; Z.I.179).

26. *Man with Woman at Her Toilette*, 1904 (location unknown; Z.XXII.94). Anticipating the scenario of *The Harlequin's Family* (see fig. 187), a contemporary drawing depicts a thin barefoot man seated on a bed watching while his girlfriend prepares to pile her thick mane of hair into a bun (*Saltimbanques*, 1904; see Museu Picasso 1992, no. 16, p. 133).

27. Richardson 1991, pp. 309–17. Debienne's real name was Gaston de Labaume.

28. Olivier 2001a, pp. 23–32.

29. Ibid., pp. 59, 76.

30. Ibid., pp. 93, 181.

31. Ibid., p. 82.

32. Ibid., p. 139.

33. Ibid., pp. 161, 176. By contrast, the Boulevard de Clichy apartment, into which the couple moved in 1909, had every modern convenience, including running water, gas, and electricity (Crespelle 1978, pp. 213–15).

34. Kahnweiler 1971, pp. 84–85.

35. Csergo 1988, p. 322. Contemporary guidebooks listed these public facilities because only the more expensive Parisian hotels had bathrooms (Galignani 1894, p. 25; Baedeker 1904, pp. 24–25).

36. Olivier 2001a, p. 140.

37. Ibid., p. 156.

38. Ibid., p. 22.

39. Ibid., p. 109.

40. MacEwan's *Study of a Redheaded Woman (Fernande Olivier)*, c. 1903, is reproduced in ibid., p. 129. The date of Olivier's visit to Degas's studio is established by her diary (ibid., pp. 137–47).

41. Ibid., p. 146.

42. Spies 2000, p. 28.

43. See Vollard 1924, pp. 112–13, for an amusing, firsthand account of the seemingly endless cycle of construction/destruction/reconstruction that Degas's modeling typically involved. The history of the posthumous casting and public exhibition of Degas's sculpture is outlined in chapters 2 and 3 of this volume.

44. For information about Mathilde Salle, see DeVonyar and Kendall 2002, p. 220.

45. In order, the works referred to are: *Portrait of Fernande*, 1906, etching and drypoint (Baer 18bis); *Portrait of Fernande*, 1906 (private collection; Z.I.254); *Woman with Her Head Bent*, 1906 (Staatsgalerie Stuttgart; Z.I.351); *Head of Fernande, in Profile*, 1906 (Musée national Picasso, Paris; Baer 249).

46. *Portrait of Fernande Olivier*, 1906 (private collection; Z.XXII.333).

47. *Portrait of a Woman in a Mantilla*, 1905 (private collection; Baer 251). Its first owner was Vollard, the person most likely to have introduced Picasso to Degas's monotypes (see chapter 5 of this volume).

48. *Women Having Their Hair Dressed*, 1905 (private collection; Z.XXII.437).

49. *Circus Family*, 1905 (Baltimore Museum of Art; Z.XXII.159).

50. En route to Paris from Barcelona in April 1904, Picasso had made a detour to Montauban to visit the Musée Ingres and must therefore already have known some of the studies for *The Turkish Bath* (Madeline 2004, p. 5). According to Olivier, when she first started living with Picasso, he was "above all" interested in Ingres and often went to the Louvre to study his paintings (Olivier 2001b, p. 182).

51. Picasso, *Portrait of Gertrude Stein*, 1906 (Metropolitan Museum of Art, New York; Z.I.352).

52. For example, L.1164, reproduced in Vollard 1914, plate 20, and L.976, which Durand-Ruel sold to the Russian collector Ostroukoff in 1909 (Kendall 1996, p. 47). Durand-Ruel mounted a Degas exhibition in 1896 that included a new "series of nudes," and held a large stock of the artist's work (see chapter 2 in this volume). Presumably Picasso had not seen the strikingly similar *Women Combing Their Hair* (see fig. 178), as it was still in the Lerolle collection.

53. Cited in Sickert 1947, p. 151.

54. For Degas's cult of Ingres, but fundamental independence from him, see Kendall 1996, pp. 67–69, 93–94, and passim.

55. Apart from *Woman Combing Her Hair* (see note 26), these include *Meditation*, 1904 (Museum of Modern Art, New York; Z.I.235) and *The Lovers*, 1904 (Musée national Picasso, Paris; Z.XXII.104).

56. Olivier 2001a, p. 159.

57. Gary Tinterow, "Vollard and Picasso," in Rabinow 2006, pp. 105–7.

58. Denis, "Aristide Maillol," 1905, in Denis 1964, p. 149.

59. Denis, "Cézanne," 1907, in ibid., p. 164: "il est un naïf artisan, un primitif qui remonte aux sources de son art."

60. Denis, "Le Salon d'Automne de 1905," in ibid., p. 108: "Enfin, voici Ingres: c'est notre maître le plus récent." For a fuller exploration of this phenomenon and its continuation into the 1920s, see Cowling and Mundy 1990.

61. Soffici, *Ricordi di vita artistica e letteraria*, 1942, cited in McCully 1997, p. 49. The influence of Egyptian, Greek, and Iberian antiquities on Picasso's work in 1905–6 is discussed more fully in Cowling 2002b, pp. 137–52.

62. Olivier 2001a, pp. 182–83.

63. It is particularly close to *Jockeys on Horseback before Distant Hills*, 1884 (Detroit Institute of Arts; L.767), then owned by Durand-Ruel.

64. Picasso, *Boy Leading a Horse*, 1906 (Museum of Modern Art, New York; Z.I.264).

65. For Picasso's likely knowledge of these monotypes c. 1906, and Vollard's role, see chapter 5 of this volume.

66. *Girl with a Goat*, 1906 (Barnes Foundation, Merion, Pennsylvania; Z.I.249); *La Toilette*, 1906 (Albright-Knox Art Gallery, Buffalo; Z.I.325). Compare, e.g., Bouguereau's *The Return from the Fields*, 1860 (private collection); *Idyll: Family from Antiquity*, 1860 (Wadsworth Atheneum, Hartford, Connecticut); and *Young Girl Defending Herself against Eros*, 1880 (J. Paul Getty Museum, Los Angeles).

67. Richardson 1991, pp. 452–53.

68. Belloli 2005.

69. Denis writes of Cézanne's "persistante gaucherie" and "les incroyables maladresses où l'oblige sa sincérité" ("Cézanne," 1907, in Denis 1964, p. 161).

70. The Oslo *Coiffure* was auctioned in the first sale, Vente I, no. 99.

71. Kendall 1996, p. 218.

72. Renoir's comments are reported by Vollard in an account of a conversation they had, probably before the turn of the century (Vollard 1924, pp. 62–63): "capable de rivaliser avec les anciens," "le premier sculpteur." Picasso may well have heard this from the lips of Vollard, an inveterate raconteur.

73. Gauguin, *Oviri*, 1894 (Musée d'Orsay, Paris). See Richardson 1991, pp. 456–61.

74. See Vollard 1924, p. 111: "Il faut que j'apprenne un métier d'aveugle" (I must learn a blind man's trade). Degas had, of course, started sculpting years before his eyesight was seriously compromised.

75. The dates attributed to the majority of Degas's sculptures are not only approximate but also purely conjectural. Rewald dates *Woman Arranging Her Hair* to 1896–1911; in Boggs 1988, no. 284, it is dated 1900–1910.

76. The authorship and date of the "original" version of this Aphrodite sculpture are contested. See Havelock 1995, pp. 86 ff.

77. Picasso also altered the pose of the contemporary *Nude Wringing Her Hair*, 1906 (Kimbell Art Museum; Z.I.344): X-rays confirm that originally the nude was in the crouching pose of the Doidalsas *Aphrodite* (Pillsbury 1983, pp. 108–10).

78. *Woman Combing Her Hair* (see fig. 223) was illustrated in Vollard 1914, pl. 58, and glass negatives survive in the Musée d'Orsay's Fonds Vollard (ODO 1996-56-3968, 4076). The exact date Vollard acquired it is not known.

79. *Two Nudes*, 1906 (Museum of Modern Art, New York; Z.I.366).

80. Z.VI.914. When planning the figure of the squatting *demoiselle*, Picasso made drawings of this splayed frontal pose (e.g., Léal 1996, no. 9, 47r).

81. See Richardson 1996, pp. 29–32, for the adoption of Raymonde and the likely reason for her rapid resettlement in an orphanage. See also chapter 3 in this volume.

82. *La Toilette: Nude Woman Seen from the Back*, c. 1876 (Musée d'Orsay, Paris, RF 12254; L.547). See chapter 5 in this vol-

ume for the role of Degas's monotypes in the evolution of *Les Demoiselles d'Avignon*. See chapter 2 for more on the Caillebotte bequest.

83. For example, *Three Figures under a Tree*, 1907 (Musée national Picasso, Paris; Z.IIa.53); *Bathers in a Forest*, 1908 (Philadelphia Museum of Art; Z.IIa.105). These and other "Negro period" paintings are spin-offs from Picasso's protracted work on *Three Women*, 1907–8 (Hermitage Museum, St. Petersburg; Z.IIa.108).

84. Notably *Nude on the Seashore*, 1909 (Museum of Modern Art, New York; Z.IIa.111).

85. *Head and Shoulders of a Woman*, 1909 (Art Institute of Chicago; Z.IIa.167). For the melancholy tone of the Horta paintings, see Kathryn Tuma, "La Peau de Chagrin," in Weiss 2003.

86. *The Dressing Table*, 1910 (private collection; Z.IIa.220), and, e.g., *Standing Female Nude*, 1910 (Albright-Knox Art Gallery, Buffalo; Z.IIa.194).

87. *"Au Bon Marché,"* 1913 (Ludwig Museum, Cologne; Z.IIb.378). For variant readings of its imagery and hot debate about the limits of interpretation, see Zelevansky 1992, pp. 79–91.

88. See chapter 3, p. 127, and the essay by Cécile Godefroy in this volume.

89. Picasso was in London working on designs for *The Three-Cornered Hat* between late May and the beginning of August 1919, thus missing the fourth sale of Degas's work on 2–4 July. See Richardson 2007, pp. 111, 132–33.

90. For the impact of the sales, see chapters 3 and 5 in this volume. Both artists are named on the invitation cards for the following exhibitions: *Portraits*, Paris, Galerie d'Art des Editions G. Crès, 20 April–8 May 1920; *Soixante nus*, Paris, Galerie Bernheim-Jeune, 3–21 May 1921; *Les Filles*, Paris, Galerie Lucien Vogel, 1–15 December 1921 (Archives Picasso, Musée national Picasso, Paris, box 45, "Invitations expositions collectives, 1915–1945"). To my knowledge, none had catalogues.

91. For Picasso's association with Paul Rosenberg, see FitzGerald 1995. For his postwar dealings with Vollard, see Tinterow, "Vollard and Picasso," in Rabinow 2006, pp. 113–14.

92. See Conzen 2005.

93. For others in this series, see Palau 1999, nos. 696, 702, 704.

94. Cooper 1968, p. 53 and nos. 318–21.

95. See Reed and Shapiro 1984, no. 42, and Boggs 1988, nos. 192–94.

96. Vente Estampes, no. 39.

97. Degas, *Woman Climbing out of a Bath*, c. 1877 (Musée d'Orsay, Paris, RF 12255; J.175). The projecting leg and outturned foot of Picasso's bather are almost identical to those of the bather in a monotype whose first owner was Paul Lafond (Norton Simon Museum, Pasadena; J.174). Perhaps Picasso had seen it or knew it from the illustration in Meier-Graefe 1920, pl. 68.

98. For example, Degas, *The Dance Class*, 1874 (Metropolitan Museum of Art, New York; L.397); *Dance Class*, c. 1871–72 (Metropolitan Museum of Art; L.297).

99. Picasso acquired copy no. 72 of *Degas Danse Dessin* (*achevé d'imprimer* 24 February 1936) from Vollard in March 1937. I am grateful to Cécile Godefroy for this information.

100. For its provenance, see Boggs 1988, no. 255.

101. See Richardson 2007, pp. 193–94, for the influence of Jean Goujon on Picasso's Fontainebleau-period work.

102. *Woman Drying Herself* was owned by Vollard. For its provenance, see L.1342

103. *Three Women at the Fountain*, 1921 (Musée national Picasso, Paris; Palau 1999, no. 1082). The version in oil is in the Museum of Modern Art, New York (Z.IV.322).

104. For Degas's varied use of pastel in his late work, see Kendall 1996, especially chapter 4.

105. For Picasso's acquisition of Renoir's *Seated Bather in a Landscape*, c. 1895–1900, see Seckel-Klein 1998, pp. 202–11. Degas also frequently adapted the *Spinario* pose (see fig. 210, 219, 225).

106. Picasso copied Renoir's *The Engaged Couple (The Sisley Family)*, c. 1868 (Z.III.428; Z.III.429), and pastiched his late style in, e.g., *Two Women in Hats*, 1921 (Z.IV.358) and *Woman in Blue Hat with Flowers*, 1921 (Palau 1999, no. 1126). In 1919, he made a portrait of Renoir (Z.III.413) from a photograph acquired from Vollard (see Baldassari 1997b, pp. 146–47).

107. Of these, *After the Bath, Woman Drying Her Feet*, 1886 (Musée d'Orsay, Paris; L.874) is closest in iconography to the Berggruen pastel.

108. *Seated Nude*, 1922–23 (Abello Collection; Z.IV.454).

109. *Degas*, Paris, Musée de l'Orangerie, 1 March–20 May 1937. Degas was also well represented in *Chefs-d'oeuvre de l'art français*, Paris, Palais National des Arts, summer–autumn 1937.

110. Gasman 1998.

111. Picasso, *Woman Bathing in a Tub*, 19 September 1939 (private collection; Z.IX.322).

112. For the gradual evolution of *Woman Dressing Her Hair*, see Cowling 2002b, pp. 625–29.

113. Davies 1970, pp. 54–55. For Picasso's renewed friendship with Matisse during the 1930s, see Cowling 2002a, pp. 376–81. After the 1918 studio sale, Oslo's *La Coiffure* (see fig. 200) was briefly with Vollard (Boggs 1988, no. 345).

114. Degas, *La Coiffure*, 1892–95 (L.1130). Boggs, for one, believes that the woman having her hair combed in the National Gallery painting and the related studies is experiencing pain (Boggs 1988, no. 344, pp. 553–54).

115. Picasso is more likely to have known the counterproof in the Cone collection, whose first owner was Vollard (Baltimore Museum of Art; L.1407).

116. For instance, Gary Tinterow describes the bather's face as "almost captivating" and her "exaggeratedly feminine body" as "beautifully rendered" (Boggs 1988, no. 287, p. 470).

117. See Utley 2000.

118. See Musée national Picasso 1998.

119. For Degas's reputation as a celibate and misogynist, see chapter 5 in this volume.

120. See Nochlin 1992, p. 45.

121. *Girl in Red*, c. 1866 (National Gallery of Art, Washington, D.C.; L.336). Madame de Nittis also appears to be pregnant in her portrait of 1872 (Portland Art Museum; L.302).

122. Gilot 1966, p. 309.

123. Archives Picasso, Musée national Picasso, Paris.

124. Gilot 1966, p. 311.

125. Ibid., p. 310. Picasso "corrected" the feet by enlarging them in the revised version of the sculpture dated 15 March 1959 (S.350).

126. The udders of *The Goat*, 1950 (S.409.II), are formed from pottery milk jars, and the belly of the baboon in *Baboon and Young*, 1951 (S.463.II), from a large pottery jar.

127. Six bronze casts of *The Absinthe Glass* were made. Each was decorated differently and equipped with its own real absinthe spoon (S.36a–f). The original wax did not survive the casting process.

128. *Still Life*, 1914 (Tate, London; S.47).

129. "L'exposition des indépendants en 1881," *L'Art moderne* (Paris: G. Charpentier, 1883), in Berson 1996, vol. 1, p. 348.

130. Rewald 1944.

131. Paris 1931. See Richardson 2007, pp. 454–55. The bronzes were exhibited publicly for the first time at Hébrard's gallery in May–June 1921.

132. Fonds Vollard, Musée d'Orsay, Paris. Several of the photographs were published at the time by Paul Gsell (Gsell 1918, p. 373). Although it was assumed the waxes had been destroyed in the casting process, in fact the majority survived chez Hébrard, reemerging in 1955 when they were purchased by Paul Mellon (Pingeot 1991, pp. 25–28).

133. Gilot 1966, pp. 306–7.

134. See chapter 3 in this volume.

135. "I've said that a painting shouldn't be a *trompe l'oeil* but a *trompe l'esprit*. I'm out to fool the mind rather than the eye. And that goes for sculpture too" (Gilot 1966, p. 311).

136. See Kendall 1993, pp. 211–23.

137. *Woman at Her Toilette,* 1 April 1953 (Estate of the Artist; inv. 13256).

138. For example, *Seated Nude Doing Her Hair*, 7 March 1954 (Musée national Picasso, Paris; Z.XVI.251).

CHAPTER 5
PICASSO AND DEGAS'S
MAISONS CLOSES

1. Parmelin 1959, p. 143: "Picasso nous montre des monotypes de Degas, qu'il vient d'acheter. Magnifiques. C'est un Degas qu'on ne connaissait pas, ni de la repasseuse, ni des dessins, ni des danseuses. Un Degas comme on n'en a pas vu."

2. See chapters 3 and 4 in this volume. For press coverage of the sales of Degas's private collection, see Rebecca Rabinow, "The Degas Collection Sales and the Press: Selected Reviews and Articles," in Dumas 1997, pp. 302–35.

3. Vente Estampes, no. 212. For Picasso's movements in November–December 1918, see Richardson 2007, pp. 99–104.

4. "The Degas Sale," 1918, in Apollinaire 1972, pp. 463–64, 468–70. André Salmon, another intimate friend, discussed mounting excitement about the sale of Degas's private collection (Salmon 1918, pp. 388–89). See also chapter 3 in this volume.

5. Rosenblum 1986, p. 58.

6. Rubin 1994, pp. 108, 142 n. 278. For the development of Picasso's friendship with Eugène Rouart, see also Walker 2006, pp. 260–61.

7. Richardson 1996, pp. 11–14.

8. See, e.g., Françoise Cachin, "Introduction," in Adhémar and Cachin 1974, p. 75.

9. I am greatly indebted to my colleague Richard Kendall for his research into the dispersal of the monotypes during Degas's lifetime. That Degas's monotypes of toilette and bedroom scenes were commonly read as images of prostitution is borne out by Vollard's inclusion of several (including J.181, J.182, J.190, and J.192) in his illustrated editions of de Maupassant's *La Maison Tellier* (1934) and Louÿs's *Mimes des courtisanes de Lucien* (1935).

10. A. P., *Le Petit Parisien*, 7 April 1877, p. 2, cited in Gary Tinterow and Anne M. P. Norton, "Degas aux expositions 'impressionnistes,'" in Musée d'Orsay 1989, p. 312: "Pourquoi M. Degas a-t-il joint à son curieux envoi une *figure* de femme accroupie qui scandalise les dames?" Tinterow and Norton identify the work as the *Crouching Nude Woman, from the Back*, c. 1877, in the Caillebotte bequest (Musée d'Orsay, Paris; L.547).

11. The contemporary reception of *Women on the Terrace of a Café in the Evening* is briefly summarized in Boggs 1988, no. 174, p. 289.

12. For example, *In the Café de la Rotonde*, 1901 (Kreeger Museum, Washington, D.C.; Z.VI.1466). See also chapter 2 in this volume.

13. *The Reader* (National Gallery of Art, Washington, D.C.; J.141) is inscribed "Degas à Lepic." A similar dark-ground monotype (Art Institute of Chicago; J.137) is inscribed "Degas à Burty." For other recipients, see chapter 2.

14. *Girl Putting on Her Stocking* (Metropolitan Museum of Art, New York; J.169). Cassatt gave it to Mrs. H. O. Havemeyer in 1889, having presumably owned it for some time.

15. For Dupuis's collection, see Rewald 1973, p. 26 ff. At the posthumous auction of the collection on 10 June 1891, Degas's monotypes were nos. 17 and 19. Many of Dupuis's Impressionist paintings were acquired through Theo van Gogh at Boussod and Valadon, but the gallery records make no mention of the monotypes (Rewald 1973, pp. 74–76).

16. Location unknown (J.77). Glass negatives of this monotype are preserved in the Fonds Vollard at the Musée d'Orsay,

Paris (ODO 1996-56-3873, 3874), indicating that it passed through Vollard's hands at some later stage.

17. Tinterow, "Vollard and Picasso," in Rabinow 2006, p. 152. Vollard's first venture into book production, Verlaine's *Parallèlement* (1900), got him into trouble with the censors because of the "perverse" eroticism of both the poetry and Bonnard's lithographs.

18. The descriptions in the sale document are as follows: "1 zing [zinc] rehaussé femme nue vue de dos enlevant sa chemise" — *Leaving the Bath* (see fig. 179); "1 zing rehaussé trois femmes assises attendant le client" — probably *Three Seated Prostitutes, Viewed from Behind* (see fig. 233), since, as we have seen, Degas had sold *Three Seated Prostitutes* (see fig. 237) before 1891; "1 zing à fond jaune trois femmes postures différentes" — *Brothel* (see fig. 232); "1 zing entièrement repris au pastel 2 femmes sur un lit, une à la cuvette" — *Nude Women* (J.118) (quoted from Loyrette 1991, p. 791 n. 310; Loyrette does not attempt to identify the monotypes).

19. Vollard 1936, p. 258.

20. Vollard published the conversation on several occasions, notably in *Degas: An Intimate Portrait* (Vollard 1937, p. 57). There are three versions of *The Madame's Name Day*: the version sold in 1918 in the posthumous auction and much later acquired by Picasso (see fig. 259), and two smaller versions (J.88 and fig. 243), both of which passed through Vollard's hands before Degas's death.

21. Roger Marx, 1897, pp. 324–25: "le rictus forcé des filles," "vérité exacerbée," "ses tableaux . . . du plaisir et du vice."

22. Either before or after the publication of his essay, Degas presented Roger Marx with a monotype of a café-concert singer (J.42; see Jean Adhémar, "Introduction," in Adhémar and Cachin 1974, p. 17). Roger Marx owned only one other Degas monotype, described in the catalogue of the posthumous sale of his huge print collection as

"Danseuse de dos" (Hôtel Drouot 1914, no. 391. A likely candidate is J.17).

23. Strölin's archives have been destroyed. See Morelon and Deconchat 2004, p. 20. I am grateful to Simon André-Deconchat for additional information about Strölin.

24. Vollard's plan to use some of the monotypes to illustrate *La Maison Tellier* dated back to 1918 (Rabinow 2006, no. 67, p. 350).

25. After quarreling definitively with Strölin, Doucet acquired the majority of his Degas prints from Gustave Pellet. A document on Pellet's letterhead addressed to Doucet and dated 28 November 1911 lists a batch of seven Degas monotypes, but the vague descriptions of their imagery make it difficult to tie them up with those in the Doucet collection (Morelon and Deconchat 2004, pp. 20–21).

26. Notably Vollard 1914, pl. 6 (*Le Réveil*, J.164); pl. 16 (*Brothel,* see fig. 232); pl. 31 (*Leaving the Bath*, see fig. 179); pl. 44 (*Scène de toilette*, J.161). On the advertising function of the album, see Kendall 1996, p. 51.

27. Isabelle Cahn, "The Vollard Archives: Myth and Reality," in Rabinow 2006, p. 264.

28. Caroline Durand-Ruel Godfroy, "Les ventes de l'atelier Degas à travers les archives Durand-Ruel," in Musée d'Orsay 1989, pp. 266–67.

29. For the accessibility of Camondo's collection, see chapter 2 in this volume.

30. See Richardson 1991, pp. 199–200, for a confident identification of the sitter as Vollard.

31. See also chapter 2 in this volume.

32. See also *Two Seated Women Facing Forward* (J.77), mentioned above, and *Woman Seated in an Armchair* (J.78), which must have passed through Vollard's hands at some point since a glass negative survives in the Musée d'Orsay's Fonds Vollard (ODO 1996-56-4221).

33. For Picasso's sex life in early manhood, the most authoritative source is Richardson 1991.

34. For a representative selection dating from 1899–1905, see Clair 2001, nos. 2–55.

35. For the early history of the lesbian scene *Nude Women* (J.118), see above, n. 18. Similar cunnilingus scenes depicted by Picasso include *Scène érotique*, 1902 (Clair 2001, no. 24).

36. Compare, for instance, Steinlen's cover for *Gil Blas Illustré*, 9 October 1892, illustrating Guy de Maupassant's *La Maison Tellier*. See chapter 1 for further discussion of the influence of magazine illustrations on the young Picasso.

37. Richardson 1991, p. 126.

38. For parallels between Degas's brothel monotypes and nineteenth-century erotic prints and photographs, see Thomson 1988, pp. 97–117. As he points out (p. 97), several drawings in one of Degas's notebooks are loosely based on *La Fille Elisa* (1876), Edmond de Goncourt's novel about prostitution. Conceivably, Degas toyed briefly with the idea of illustrating it.

39. See Tinterow, "Vollard and Picasso," in Rabinow 2006, pp. 104–11.

40. Vollard had sold them and the pastel acquired from Degas at the same moment to Milan Obrenovic, the ex-king of Serbia, in October 1895, and bought all three back at the posthumous sale of the latter's collection (Hôtel Drouot 1906). See Anne Roquebert, "A Widening Circle: Vollard and His Clients," in Rabinow 2006, p. 223 and n. 41.

41. *Reclining Nude*, 1906 (Z.VI.881). See also the sheet of drawings on torn paper (Estate of the Artist, inv. 466; Z.XXII.201).

42. For example, *Femmes avec des bas rayés*, 1902 (Clair 2001, no. 23).

43. Degas's exploration of these bizarre poses may be indebted to the contemporary iconography of, and debates about, hysteria among women in general and prostitutes in particular (Thomson 1988, p. 102).

44. Archives Picasso, Musée national Picasso, Paris (hereafter, Archives

Picasso), APPH 12761. The broken glass negative is preserved in the Fonds Vollard (ODO 1996-56-4229).

45. Toulouse-Lautrec, *In the Salon: The Divan*, c. 1893–94, Museu de Arte, São Paolo.

46. For example, *Study for "Les Demoiselles d'Avignon,"* 1907, location unknown (Z.IIa.20).

47. Fonds Vollard, ODO 1996-56-4230 and ODO 1996-56-4469–72.

48. See Duncan 1974, pp. 84–85.

49. I am grateful to Marta-Volga Guezala for information and for sharing her thoughts about the photograph. Experts on Degas's photographs have informed her that they have not seen other prints revised in this manner by the artist himself. John Richardson remembers seeing the photograph and being struck by "a certain resemblance to Picasso's father" (John Richardson, "L'Epoque Jacqueline," in Tate 1988, p. 39).

50. Vallentin 1963, p. 82. The original text reads: "Ce n'est guère le tableau qu'il tenait à me montrer mais le cadre. 'C'est un cadre de Degas que j'ai réussi à me procurer,' expliqua-t-il avec orgueil, 'il les faisait faire spécialement pour lui.' Le cadre, d'un blanc légèrement rosé, était large, un peu bombé, et Picasso, après avoir essuyé la poussière et rajusté le verre, passait amoureusement la paume sur cette douce courbure de bois. C'était, en effet, l'encadrement idéal pour les danseuses roses à l'avant-scène que Degas affectionnait. Sa *Danseuse* à lui, violemment déhanchée, morcelée en mouvements brusques, par plans aux couleurs discordantes, s'agitait à l'intérieur de ce cadre, comme si elle voulait le faire voler en éclats; elle jurait affreusement avec sa forme gracieuse et son tendre coloris. Mais Picasso la regardait comme s'il n'apercevait guère ce que ce voisinage avait d'incongru" (Vallentin 1957, pp. 142–43). Vallentin began work on the biography in 1954 and the visit very likely took place before Picasso settled in La Californie in 1955.

Vallentin's brief description suggests that the "dancer" was a study related either to *Nude with Drapery*, 1907 (e.g., Daix and Rosselet 1979, no. 81) or *Standing Nude*, 1908 (e.g., Daix and Rosselet 1979, no. 112). For Degas's frames, see *inter alia*, Easton and Bark 2008, pp. 603–11.

51. Vallentin 1957, p. 142: "cette sorte de brasero de pacotille qui encombrait un coin de son atelier rue des Grands-Augustins."

52. No inventory of Picasso's huge collection of postcards and other forms of photography has been drawn up, but Anne Baldassari has published selected items in various catalogues (Baldassari 1994, Baldassari 1997a, and 1997b).

53. See Roberto Otero's account of one such session (quoted in Seckel-Klein 1998, p. 50).

54. For Degas's collection, see Dumas 1997. For Picasso's collection, see Seckel-Klein 1998, who reprints enlightening short memoirs by Hélène Parmelin and Jean Leymarie (pp. 21–32).

55. See Seckel-Klein 1998 on, e.g., *Tête de chamois*, attributed to Courbet "avec l'apport de mains étrangères" (no. 17), and *Paysage*, attributed to Gauguin (no. 39).

56. See Stepan 2006.

57. Hélène Parmelin, "Picasso ou le collectionneur qui n'en est pas un," in Seckel-Klein 1998, p. 22: "Qu'est-ce qu'on peut faire de mieux?" "C'est magnifique!"

58. Seckel-Klein 1998, pp. 39–42.

59. Ibid., pp. 42–45.

60. *Portrait of Wilhelm Uhde*, 1910 (The Pulitzer Foundation for the Arts, St. Louis; Z.IIa.217).

61. Seckel-Klein 1998, pp. 82–83.

62. Richardson, "L'Epoque Jacqueline," in Tate 1988, p. 39.

63. Archives Picasso, APPH 12754–12761, 12763. The one other Degas photograph in the same file is a modern ektachrome of a pastel of ballet dancers (APPH 12762; L.1281). No doubt it had been sent by a dealer angling (unsuccessfully) for a sale.

64. Picasso acquired copy no. 95 of *La Maison Tellier* (*achevé d'imprimer* 27 December 1934) on 19 June 1936. For his acquisition of the third of Vollard's books with facsimiles of Degas's drawings, Paul Valéry's *Degas Danse Dessin* (1936), see p. 190 in this volume. I am very grateful to Cécile Godefroy for this information.

65. Vollard 1936, pp. 258–60.

66. Ibid., p. 258: "dishes of the day."

67. Picasso, quoted in Richardson 1984, p. 25.

68. Richardson, "L'Epoque Jacqueline," in Tate 1988, p. 39.

69. Ibid.

70. Archives Picasso, APPH 12760.

71. Richardson, "L'Epoque Jacqueline," in Tate 1988, p. 41.

72. This letter and all the others quoted subsequently are with the Lefevre Gallery papers in the Tate Archive, abbreviated TGA (General administrative correspondence; TGA 2002/11, Box 75).

73. The copy of the Lefevre catalogue Picasso owned is in this provisional form (Archives Picasso).

74. Desmond Corcoran to Douglas Cooper, letters dated 15 April 1958, 18 April 1958, and 28 April 1958 (TGA 2002/11, Box 75).

75. Richardson 1984, p. 25.

76. For Picasso's abhorrence of "the 'artistic' attitude toward life, toward people and things," see Brassaï 1967, p. 122.

77. See Janis 1968, p. xxi.

78. Gilot 1966, pp. 41–45.

79. The drawings were first published as "Suite de 180 dessins de Picasso, 28 novembre 1953 au 3 février 1954" in *Verve*, nos. 29–30, 1954.

80. Cooper to Corcoran, 26 July 1958 (TGA 2002/11, Box 75). The list by Lefevre catalogue number was as follows: 1 (J.118); 6 (J.85); 8 (J.65); 11 (J.82); 16 (J.91); 23 (J.83); 28 (J.67); 30 (J.86); 42 (J.87). Picasso had Vollard photographs of Lefevre nos. 11 (APPH 12759; J.82) and 30 (APPH 12756; J.86).

81. Corcoran to Cooper, 28 July 1958 (TGA 2002/11, Box 75). The two that were

not available were Lefevre nos. 1 (J.118) and 30 (J.86).

82. Cooper to Corcoran, 5 August 1958 (TGA 2002/11, Box 75). The work rejected was Lefevre no. 42 (J.87).

83. Corcoran to Cooper, 8 August 1958 (TGA 2002/11, Box 75).

84. Cooper to Picasso, 5 August 1958 (Archives Picasso).

85. Cooper to Corcoran, 14 August 1958 (TGA 2002/11, Box 75).

86. Cooper to Picasso, postcard postmarked 23 August 1958 (Archives Picasso): "Ce sont des autres dames pour tenir compagnie aux précedentes!"

87. For the linocuts and lithographs Picasso made in the 1940s in response to three different paintings by Cranach, see Galassi 1996, pp. 98–113.

88. Cooper to Picasso, 21 July 1960 (Archives Picasso). *Three Seated Prostitutes, Viewed from Behind* (see fig. 233) was in the Lefevre show as no. 40, loaned by the dealers Hector and Paul Brame, the source of many of the monotypes bought for the exhibition. On 16 June 1958, Willy Peploe or Desmond Corcoran wrote to Paul Brame regretting that "we were not successful in selling your Degas monotype 'Trois filles de dos'" and thanking him for lending it "for so long" (TGA 2002/11, Box 75). Presumably, Cooper negotiated the sale to Picasso on Brame's behalf.

89. Suzanne King, of William Hallsborough Ltd., London, to Pablo Picasso, 16 March 1961 (Archives Picasso). *Nude Women* (J.118) was no. 1 in the Lefevre show.

90. Cowling 2006, p. 243.

91. Seckel-Klein cites a telephone conversation with Richardson on 11 November 1997 (Seckel-Klein 1998, p. 112 n. 15). The meager collection of cards and letters from De Hauke in the Archives Picasso contains no allusion to any transaction. Janis says that Exsteens sold *The Madame's Name Day* in 1958, but she does not say to whom and she was unaware that Picasso owned it when she compiled her checklist. There is no correspondence with Exsteens in the Archives Picasso, nor is there mention of the work in Cooper's correspondence with either Picasso or Corcoran.

92. Seckel-Klein 1998, p. 112 n. 16.

93. Quoted in Parmelin 1963, p. 77.

94. *The Women of Algiers, after Delacroix, Version C* (Z.XVI.345). For a brilliant discussion of this motif, see Steinberg 1972.

95. *Odalisque after Ingres*, 1907 (Musée national Picasso, Paris; Z.XXVI.194).

96. Elderfield, in Cowling 2002a, pp. 335 and 360 n. 16. Steinberg does not make the link with Degas.

97. For instance, both *Siesta in the Salon* (J.72) and *Resting* (J.73) were reproduced in Louÿ's *Mimes de courtisanes de Lucien* (1935).

98. Baer 923–26. Baer entitles the prints *Maison Close*: *Attente I, Attente II, La Toilette I* (all 11 March 1955), and *La Toilette II* (14 March 1955). They followed hard on the heels of brothel scenes in which a Celestina brings a pot of chocolate to a whore and her naked client (Baer 921–22).

99. Crommelynck 1995, p. 13.

100. Ibid., pp. 15–16.

101. Brassaï, "The Master at 90 . . . ," *New York Times Magazine*, 24 October 1971, cited in McCully 1981, p. 272.

102. Ibid.

103. Rubin 1973, p. 42.

104. Daix 1994b, p. 366.

105. See chapter 4 in this volume.

106. Christian Zervos, "Conversation avec Picasso," 1935, cited in Ashton 1972, p. 11.

107. Parmelin, "Picasso ou le collectionneur qui n'en est pas un," in Seckel-Klein 1998, p. 21: "une sorte de Christ de la peinture."

108. The *locus classicus* is Joris-Karl Huysmans's "Degas," first published in *Certains*, Paris, 1889 (Huysmans 1975, pp. 293–97). See also, e.g., Félix Fénéon's reviews published in 1886 and 1888 (Fénéon 1966, pp. 58–60, 103–4).

109. See, e.g., Loyrette 1991, p. 189–91, and Kendall 1996, pp. 141–57.

110. The text of the letter (datable to August 1888), as published by Vollard, runs as follows: "Mon cher copain Bernard, . . . Pourquoi dis-tu que X . . . b . . . mal? X . . . vit comme un petit notaire et n'aime pas les femmes, sachant que s'il les aimait et les b . . . beaucoup, cérébralement malade, il deviendrait inepte en peinture./La peinture de X . . . est virile et impersonnelle justement parce qu'il a accepté de n'être personnellement qu'un petit notaire ayant en horreur de faire la noce. Il regarde des aimaux humains plus forts que lui, b . . . et b . . . , et il les peint bien, justement parce qu'il n'a pas tant que ça la prétention de b . . . *Rubens*! ah! voilà! il était bel homme et bon b . . . , Courbet aussi. Leur santé leur permettait de boire, manger, b . . ." (My dear old Bernard, . . . Why do you say that Degas has trouble getting a hard-on? Degas lives like a little lawyer, and he doesn't like women, knowing that if he liked them and fucked them a lot he would become cerebrally ill and hopeless at painting. Degas's painting is virile and impersonal precisely because he has resigned himself to being personally no more than a little lawyer, with a horror of riotous living. He watches human animals stronger than himself getting a hard-on and fucking, and he paints them well, precisely because he doesn't make such great claims about getting a hard-on. *Rubens*, ah, there you have it, he was a handsome man and a good fucker, Courbet too; their health allowed them to drink, eat, fuck) (Van Gogh 1911, Lettre IX; translation from www.vangoghletters.org [letter 655]).

111. Jamot 1924, pp. 2, 4, 43 ff.

112. Vollard 1937, p. 34.

113. Valéry 1960, p. 57.

114. Cabanne 1957, pp. 6, 7, 14, 26, 36, and passim.

115. Nicolson 1963.

116. Cabanne 1957, p. 36: "Ce pudique, ce

chaste, ce bourgeois 'à principes' . . . un moyen de libération . . . réalisme implacable . . . Sa Majesté le Vice . . . où la femme recluse, prisonnière, livrée aux instincts les plus bas de l'homme, ouvre au peintre des horizons infinis aux clés de boue et d'or?"

117. Otero 1974, p. 166.

118. Degas's idiosyncratic features attracted the notice of contemporary caricaturists like Michel Manzi and Carlo Pellegrini, whose portraits of him are reproduced in, e.g., Lafond 1918–19. Picasso would also have had access to photographs of the artist in profile.

119. Picasso's correspondence from 1964 to 1973 has gone missing. No correspondence with non-lenders is preserved in the Harvard University Art Museums archive (personal communication from Jane Callahan).

120. Richardson 1984, p. 25.

121. Thus Degas is mentioned in passing only a couple of times in Holloway 2006.

122. For example, Baer 1510, 1571, 1683.

123. For example, Baer 1567, 1570, 1782.

124. See Baer 1571 and 1705. Picasso owned a Vollard photograph of *The Serious Client* (Archives Picasso, APPH 12756), as well as the facsimile in *La Maison Tellier*, and it was on his original list of wants from the Lefevre Gallery (see above, n. 81).

125. Pierre Daix, "Picasso: 44 dessins du 90me printemps," in Jan Krugier 1989, p. 25.

126. While expressing scepticism about the extent of the destruction, Gary Tinterow quotes from a diary entry for 20 March 1918 by René Gimpel in which he reports telling Mary Cassatt that Degas's "family destroyed the erotic works for fear of seeing a *Degas Erotica* published someday" ("Degas's Degases," in Dumas 1997, pp. 97 and 106 n. 37).

127. See Holloway 2006 for Picasso's allusions to literature, art, movies, and television.

128. Janis 1968, pp. xvii–xix.

129. Daix "Picasso: 44 dessins du 90me printemps," in Jan Krugier 1989, pp. 24–25: "Un jour, Picasso m'expliqua que Degas, à son avis, en développant une semblable technique avait voulu que le papier discute son premier dessin, l'interprète. Dans une gravure, le papier réagit, mais il doit obéir. Il est un révélateur, mais un révélateur solidement tenu. Tandis que dans le monotype, par l'impression, s'il prend de l'original, il en laisse aussi. Il le dilue, en change subtilement les valeurs."

130. Ibid.: "'il aimait trop commander à son dessin ou à sa peinture. . . . En somme, il devait avoir le dernier mot. . . . Degas était un des très rares dessinateurs qui en imposait à Picasso et la raison que ces monotypes l'intéressait et l'excitait."

131. Monotype was always a subsidiary medium for Picasso the printmaker. For other examples, see Baer 253–57 (1923–25), Baer 445–572 (1932–34) and Baer 712–19 (1937–42). The final catalogued monotype — apparently, a solitary case since the war — is Baer 1364 (19 August 1964), made with the copperplate of Baer 1165.

132. For a sensitive and informative summary of the technical aspects of Picasso's printmaking, see Baer 1997, pp. 55–75.

133. Archives Picasso, APPH 12754.

134. Crommelynck 1995, pp. 16–17.

135. Vollard 1936, p. 258. The correct spelling is "Cadart."

136. Brigitte Baer, "Seven Years of Printmaking," in Tate 1988, pp. 104–5.

137. Toulouse-Lautrec, *The Salon of the Rue des Moulins*, 1894 (Musée Toulouse-Lautrec, Albi). For photographs of the lavish, themed interior of the brothel, see Adriani 2005, pp. 45–47, 57.

138. See Penrose's notes of the visit dated 13 March 1970 (Cowling 2006, p. 320).

139. For instance, a notebook used between 26 and 29 June 1954 (Léal 1996, no. 50) contains, as the inscription on the cover proclaims, the "PREMIERS Dessins du Déjeuner sur l'herbe," but the

Manet series got underway only in 1959, after the Delacroix and Velázquez series were complete.

140. Daix, "Picasso: 44 dessins du 90me printemps," in Jan Krugier 1989, p. 24: "la conscience de ses réussites lui procurait alors une assurance sereine que le temps ne lui était pas encore compté"; "Il se trouve que j'ai vu Picasso presque tous les jours en ce début d'avril 1971."

141. Baer 1926, 1931.

142. Baer 1934.

143. The etching is inscribed "11.3.71.V," the Roman numeral being Picasso's standard way of indicating the sequence of works made on the same day.

144. See chapter 3 in this volume.

145. In April 1971, during a two-week break from printmaking, Picasso also made several exquisitely detailed pen-and-ink drawings depicting Degas visiting a brothel (Jan Krugier 1989, nos. 22–23 and 29).

146. The etchings referred to here are, in order: Baer 1985, 1987, 1997, 2007.

147. Daix, "Picasso: 44 dessins du 90me printemps," in Jan Krugier 1989, p. 25: "Impossible de s'en débarrasser."

148. For the link between Freud's theory and *Les Demoiselles d'Avignon*, see Bois 2001, pp. 42–44.

149. *Interior (The Rape)*, c. 1868–69 (Philadelphia Museum of Art; L.348). The parallel is drawn in Barañano 1997, p. 34. In the small print dated 12 March 1971 (Baer 1944), Picasso gave the room the patterned wallpaper of Degas's painting.

150. For example, Mauclair 1937, p. 14, where *Interior (The Rape)* is said to show Degas at his most humane and least misogynist because of the atypically sympathetic treatment of the woman.

151. *Interior (The Rape)* is often described as a "masterpiece." See Boggs 1988, no. 84, for a summary of the literature.

152. For example, Baer 1953, 1971.

153. Schiff 1983, p. 60.

154. Paul Lafond, who presents his friend Degas as a proud, refined, and

unworldly artist dedicated solely to his art and appalled by all vulgarity, describes the brothel monotypes as "réfrigérants" (icy) and insists they express not "basse curiosité" (low curiosity), but "écoeurement" (disgust) on the artist's part (Lafond 1918–19, pp. 2, 72).

155. Daix 1994b, p. 366. The aquatint concerned is dated 12 June 1936 (Baer 609).

156. For further details of this dark period in Picasso's life, see Cabanne 1975, vol. 4, pp. 151–58. For Picasso's medical condition, see Hepp 1988, pp. 16–18, 69.

157. For this aspect of *Suite 347*, see Holloway 2006. Aldo Crommelynck emphasizes the quasi-automatist, memory-based aspect of the late prints (Crommelynck 1995, p. 16).

158. Jacqueline Picasso, reported in Richardson 1996, p. 277.

159. Quoted in Brassaï 1967, p. 56.

160. Richardson 1984, p. 25.

161. Sabartés 1954, pp. 23–24: "Avec le temps, il apprit à dissimuler son amertume sous le masque moqueur d'un sourire malicieux qui, chez l'homme averti qu'il était, soulignait le sarcasme ou atténuait le rire que faisaient naître en lui la vue des autres et l'idée qu'il avait de lui-même." Valéry provides a particularly vivid and nuanced account of Degas's personality, describing him at one point as a "fidèle, étincelant, insupportable" (constant, brilliant, unbearable) guest (Valéry 1960, p. 10. See also pp. 7, 29, and passim).

162. Compare the photograph of don José with Picasso's sister Lola taken in c. 1913 (reproduced in Richardson 1991, p. 270) with photographs of Degas taken between 1908 and 1914 by Albert Bartholomé and Sacha Guitry (reproduced in Boggs 1988, pp. 496–97).

163. For the alter-ego role of Rembrandt and Van Gogh, see *inter alia* Kirk Varnedoe, "Picasso's Self-Portraits," in Rubin 1996, pp. 163–66.

164. Richardson thought ("if I remember rightly") he had seen the photograph on view in Notre-Dame-de-Vie with the monotypes early in 1971 (Richardson 1984, p. 25).

165. Richardson 1991, p. 20.

166. Ibid., p. 3.

167. Dated 25 March 1968 (Baer 1503).

168. Dated 26 March 1968 (Baer 1504).

169. Baer 1793–1817.

170. The version dated 1840 in Columbus Gallery of Fine Arts was included in the Ingres retrospective held at the Petit Palais, Paris, during the winter of 1967–68 — only months before the first etching in Picasso's Raphael series (dated 29 August 1968, I). Picasso did not see the exhibition but followed the reviews.

171. See Museu Picasso 2009, pp. 118–37.

172. For example, Baer 1812, dated 7 September 1968.

173. Giorgio Vasari, "Vita di Raffaello d'Urbino," in Vasari 1973, p. 804.

174. Degas's worsening eyesight is a constant leitmotif of his letters and the analogy with Homer was popular in accounts by early biographers (Kendall 1996, p. 52).

175. Baer 1956.

176. Baer 2017.

177. Kunstmuseum Bern (Z.XXXIII.169).

178. Including Jan Krugier 1989, nos. 40–41, both dated 11 December 1971.

179. Z.XXXIII.508. The date 19 August has been crossed out.

180. The madame's hairstyle and costume in the etchings derived from *The Madame's Name Day* parody Rubens's majestic *Portrait of Helena Fourment*, c. 1630–31 (Alte Pinakothek, Munich).

181. Private collection (Z.XXXIII.510).

182. Hakone Open Air Museum, Japan (Z.XXXIII.507).

183. Z.XXXIII.530; dated 5 November 1972, I.

184. One hundred drawings executed between 3 June and 18 August 1972 were exhibited in *Picasso: 172 dessins en noir et en couleurs, 21 novembre 1971–18 août 1972* (Paris, Galerie Louise Leiris, 1 December 1972–13 January 1973).

185. See Cowling 2006, pp. 337, 339.

186. Daix 1994b, p. 369.

CHAPTER 6
DEGAS AND PICASSO
AS PHOTOGRAPHERS

1. The painted wood sculpture is Picasso's *Woman Carrying a Child*, 1953 (private collection; S.478). The other figure is a body mask from Southern Malekula, Vanuatu (Musée national Picasso, Paris), given to Picasso by Matisse. See Stepan 2006, no. 6. My thanks to Elizabeth Cowling for these identifications.

2. Halévy 1964, p. 81.

3. See Daniel 1998, pp. 125–39. For an example of two photographs that were not listed here, see Heilbrun 2005, pp. 74–75.

4. See chapter 2 of this volume.

5. Other aspects of photography, and the idea of the photographic, in relation to both artists' work will not be addressed here, since these issues have already been discussed extensively. See, for example, Varnedoe 1980, Tucker 1982, Baldassari 1995, Baldassari 1997a and 1997b, and Kosinski 1999, among others.

6. Halévy 1964, p. 82, journal entry dated 29 December 1895.

7. Baldassari 1994, p. 39: "Certes, la forte intentionnalité qu'y manifeste la mise en scène de l'espace, des objets, du modèle lui-même, suffirait sans nul doute à tenir ces clichés pour des *autoportraits* même si l'artiste avait dû recourir à l'assistance d'un tiers — ami ou compagne — pour effectuer l'acte technique de la prise de vue."

8. Aside from Picasso and Mañach, two other men appear in these three photos: Antonio Torres Fuster and Fuentes Torres, whose first name I have not found. Since an inscription by Picasso on the back of this print notes that it depicts "Mañach, Torres, yo," standard usage of the paternal surname would indicate that it refers to Torres Fuster.

9. Baldassari 1994, p. 43. Picasso later painted over the portrait of Iturrino.

10. The two related photographs of Picasso

323

are in the Archives Picasso. See Baldassari 1994, pp. 40–41. The inscription reads, in part, "Mañach et Fuentes admirant mes oeuvres." The original inscription is in Castilian but is quoted in French in Baldassari 1994, p. 39.

11. Baldassari 1994, p. 41: "Yo en el taller. Apa Buenas. Picasso."

12. See Baldassari 1994, pp. 94–97, 113, 117, 119 for illustrations.

13. Daniel 1998, p. 23; letter from Degas to Tasset, 17 August 1895, published in French in Newhall 1963, p. 64: "J'essaie à photographier presque la nuit."

14. An inscription written by Paul Valéry on the photograph of Renoir and Mallarmé taken during this same session mentions the nine lamps: "Degas leur a infligé une pose de 15 minutes à la lumière de neuf lampes à pétrole" (Degas inflicted on them a 15-minute pose by the light of nine kerosene lamps). See 290; inscription transcribed in Terrasse 1983, p. 38 and illustrated p. 63.

15. Armstrong 1988, p. 134. Another division she finds in this photo is that of gender, reading the reflected space as feminine and the space of the room as masculine, adding yet another layer of complexity to the image.

16. For the inscription, see Baldassari 1994, p. 51.

17. See chapter 2 in this volume and Richardson 1991, pp. 137, 310.

18. Reff 1976, vol. 1, p. 134 (Notebook 30, p. 210); translated in Armstrong 1988, p. 108.

19. *Still Life with Chair Caning* (Musée national Picasso, Paris, MP 36; Z.IIa.294).

20. Halévy 1964, p. 83.

21. Elizabeth C. Childs, "Habits of the Eye: Degas, Photography, and Modes of Vision," in Kosinski 1999, p. 80. Terrasse also describes it as accidental (Terrasse 1983, p. 43).

22. See Daniel 1998, p. 33.

23. *Monkeys in the Virgin Forest*, 1910 (private collection).

24. Unlike Degas, who did not make his own prints, Picasso probably printed most of his photographs of this period himself (Baldassari 1994, pp. 25–26).

25. Baldassari has suggested that Picasso might have made the double image sometime later, perhaps in memory of Rousseau, who died that year (Baldassari 1994, p. 110).

26. According to Clément Chéroux, the photographer Édouard Isidore Buguet began producing spirit photographs in Paris in 1873 (Chéroux 2005, pp. 46–47).

27. *Yo, Picasso* (private collection, New York; Z.XXI.192); *The Absinthe Drinker* (Kunstmuseum, Basel, Inv. Im 1411; Z.I.100); *Portrait of Gustave Coquiot* (Musée national Picasso, Paris; Z.I.84)

28. *Self-Portrait in a Top Hat*, 1901 (private collection; Palau 1981, no. 1980.608); see Baldassari 1994, p. 43.

29. Ibid.: "Esta fotografía puede titularse 'Los muros mas fuertes se abren a mi paso — Mira.'" The inscription is also reproduced on the back cover of this catalogue.

30. Ibid., p. 48: "Cette interrogation trouve dans la photographie, substitut au miroir, le lieu inaugural où questionner à la fois l'homme, l'artiste, les potentialités de l'oeuvre."

31. In fact, Richard Thomson has suggested that this photograph echoes on some level Jean-Auguste-Dominique Ingres's *Cherubini and the Muse of Lyric Poetry* (1842; Musée du Louvre, Paris), a work Degas had copied as a student (Thomson 1987, p. 33).

32. The three negatives of a dancer are listed in Daniel 1998, nos. 42–44, and discussed on pp. 43–45, where he notes that their attribution to Degas has been disputed.

33. Terrasse 1983, p. 25: "La peinture et la photographie possèdent deux grands points communs. Ce sont, à leur conception, le *regard*: car il y a dans l'une comme dans l'autre nécessité d'un choix par l'observateur; à leur naissance, *la surface plane*: un espace qui n'est plus celui de la vie."

APPENDIX 1
OLGA KHOKHLOVA, BALLERINA, AND PABLO PICASSO

This is the first study based on the archives of the Fundación Almine y Bernard Ruiz-Picasso para el Arte (FABA). It was commissioned by the foundation in connection with the *Picasso Looks at Degas* exhibition and explores the preeminent theme of the dancer in the work of Degas, as well as Picasso's interest and involvement in the ballet and his images of Olga Khokhlova as a dancer. In the course of the work done for this study, FABA undertook the process of cataloguing its photographic holdings that concern Olga Khokhlova, as well as her entire personal correspondence. FABA and the author sincerely thank Evelyne Cohen, Sylvie Fresnault, and Jeanne-Yvette Sudour of the Musée national Picasso, Paris, as well as Isabelle Gaëtan of the Musée d'Orsay for their kind assistance in the preparation of this text.

1. See, for example, Cooper 1968 and Berggruen 2007.

2. The only article devoted to this subject is Baldassari 1998. Besides the Olga Picasso archives at FABA, this study relies for many details on the programs of Ballets Russes productions between 1911 and 1917. Research on these, however, remains to be completed, and the chronology may therefore be subject to revision.

3. Now Nizhyn, in Ukraine. The city lies about 150 kilometers northeast of Kiev.

4. The passport issued to Olga Khokhlova, dated Petrograd, 23 November 1915, identifies the dancer as *"La fille du colonel"* (the colonel's daughter) (FABA Archives).

5. Nikolai was stationed as an officer in Belgrade, and Vladimir studied medicine at Yaroslavl. The youngest son, Evgeny, died prematurely in October 1917. Nina enrolled in the program of the Tiflis Conservatory. A photograph taken in the apartment on the rue la

Boétie, reproduced in Baldassari 1997a, pp. 203–4, and a drawing done by Picasso at Fontainebleau (Z.IV.298) show Olga playing the piano. She seems also to have had a piano-teacher aunt named Sasha who had studied with Anton Rubinstein. Information on the Khokhlov family is based on the Russian correspondence preserved by Olga Picasso (FABA Archives), currently undergoing translation by Olga Gribenchikova.

6. Nijinska 1992, p. 333.

7. Olga would have been initiated into the dance by Matilda Konetskaya, the older sister of Olga's school friend Lubov. Originally a dancer in the Mariinsky Ballet, Matilda had joined the Ballets Russes and managed to have Olga and Lubov auditioned. See Natalya Semenova, "A Tale of Brief Love and Eternal Hatred," cited in Richardson 2007, pp. 5 and 511 n. 9. We do not know which of the two sisters appeared under the name "Konietska" in the Ballets Russes programs from 1911 to 1914.

8. Examples are the *Mir Isskustva* (World of Art) publications, the exhibition of Russian art in the Salon d'Automne of 1906, and the production of Modest Mussorgsky's opera *Boris Godunov*, presented by Diaghilev in 1908 and starring the Russian bass Feodor Chaliapin.

9. Given the chronological limits of this study, we shall not discuss the innovative choreographic work of Bronislava Nijinska or George Balanchine after 1917.

10. The professionals were Ludmila Schollar, Lubov and Nadejda Baranovitch, and Nijinska. See Nijinska 1992, pp. 332–33.

11. Karsavina 1931, p. 267: "avait débuté comme amateur assez bien doué, mais sous la direction du maître [Cecchetti], elle avait révélé de véritables qualités."

12. See Sally Banes, "Firebird and the Idea of Russianness," chapter 6 of Garafola and Baer 1999; and David Vaughan, "Classicism and Neoclassicism," chapter 8 (ibid.).

13. Olga's occupation is thus described on her identity papers reproduced in Daix and Israël 2003, pp. 52, 55.

14. For details of these tours, see Grigoriev 1953, Buckle 1979, and MacDonald 1975.

15. Located at 15 rue Montaigne in Paris, the theater was built by the firm of Perret & Frères and decorated by Antoine Bourdelle, Maurice Denis, and Édouard Vuillard.

16. Bakst 1917: "la vieille Russie apparaît à travers une vision populaire, flamboyante et comique, [et] où la note byzantine se marie étrangement aux danses frénétiques d'ouvriers russes."

17. Olga added *Le Pavillon d'Armide* and *La Princesse enchantée* to her repertoire during this tour, which included appearances in New York, Boston, Chicago, Washington, and Philadelphia.

18. Sokolova 1960, p. 84. See also Acker 1989, pp. 229–52.

19. Bakst 1917: "note burlesque," "prodigieuse variété," and " l'entrain endiablé."

20. See Massine 1968, pp. 95–98.

21. See McCully 1981, pp. 102–118 ("The War Years: 1914–1919").

22. See the *Portrait of Olga*, dedicated "Rome/1917/Pour Olga/Koklova/Picasso/Пикассо" (private collection; Palau 1999, no. 70). For an account of the meeting between Olga and Picasso, see Richardson 2007, pp. 3–30.

23. The subtitle of this section, translated as "A memory of Petrograd," is taken from an inscription in Olga's hand on the back of a photograph showing her in dance costume, attached to a letter to Picasso dated 16 March 1918 (FABA Archives).

24. 1918 (Musée national Picasso, Paris, MP 55; Z.III.83).

25. Olga was treated at the Maison de santé du Docteur Bonnet, a private hospital in Paris. Letters between Olga and Jacqueline Apollinaire make it clear that the injury was serious and the rehabilitation period was long. See Caizergues and Seckel 1992, pp. 204–11.

26. After their marriage, Picasso and Olga visited Monte Carlo to attend Ballets

Russes productions in 1919, 1923, and 1925. See ballet programs and datebooks belonging to Olga and letters from Hilda Bewicke, Lydia Sokolova, Lydia Lopokova (whose portrait Picasso drew in 1919, Z.III.298–99), Serge Grigoriev, Lubov Tchernicheva, Nicolai Sverev, Ianka and Alexander Gavrilov, Sonia Woizikowska, Bronislava Nijinska, and others (FABA Archives).

27. Massine to Picasso, 9 September 1918, Archives Picasso: "Je regrette que vous n'étiez pas avec nous et qu'Olga n'a pas fait son rôle dans *Les Femmes* mais ça viendra. . . . Comment va la santé d'Olga? Je pense qu'après la maladie elle voudra danser plus que jamais" (I'm sorry that you weren't with us and that Olga didn't play her role in *Les Femmes*, but it'll be all right. . . . How is Olga's health? I imagine after her sick leave she'll be wanting to dance more than ever). Diaghilev to Picasso, 18 October 1918, Archives Picasso: "Et Olga? A t-elle abandonné pour toujours son art de la danse ? C'est encore dommage, Massine la regrette comme chorégraphe et moi comme vieille passion" (And Olga? Has she given up her art of the dance for good? That's really too bad. Massine misses her as a choreographer, and I as an old passion). Cecchetti to Olga, 24 June 1920, FABA Archives: "Je me suis dit plusieurs fois: quel dommage! Maintenant qu['elle] commençait à faire quelques progrès voilà que de nouveau [elle cesse] de travailler !! . . . Espérons qu'en Automne, avec Mlle Sonia, vous travaillerez un peu avec elle" (I just keep saying to myself, what a shame! Here [she] was starting to make some progress, and now lo and behold, [she's stopped] working!! . . . Let's hope in the fall, with Mlle Sonia, you'll work a bit with her).

28. Olga's performances included *Les Sylphides*, *Prince Igor*, the *Polovtsian Dances*, *The Firebird*, *Les Contes russes*, *Soleil de nuit*, *Petrushka*, *Scheherazade*, *Carnaval*, *Les Papillons*,

Nuit de mai, *The Good-Humoured Ladies*, and *Las Meninas*.

29. *Olga in a Mantilla*, 1917 (private collection, Museo Picasso, Malaga; Z.III.40).

30. From Picasso's biography, it seems likely that he attended either this performance or the one at the Théâtre du Châtelet on 18 May, or else the rehearsals that, according to Prince Peter Lieven, were always held on stage (*Birth of the Ballet Russe* [London: Allen & Unwin, 1936], p. 81, cited in Gregory 1989, pp. 16–17).

31. Théophile Gautier, "1er Juillet 1844: Opéra: dernière représentation de Mademoiselle Taglioni," in Gautier 1859, vol. 3, p. 225: "Mademoiselle Taglioni a dansé *La Sylphide* — c'est tout dire. Ce ballet commença pour la chorégraphie une ère toute nouvelle, et ce fut par lui que le romantisme s'introduisit dans le domaine de Terpsichore" (Mademoiselle Taglioni danced *La Sylphide* — which says it all. This ballet opened an entirely new era for choreography and through it Romanticism made its way into the realm of Terpsichore).

32. Octave Uzanne, "Les Parisiennes de 1830," in Uzanne 1898: "Well, for my part, I'm looking forward to the pleasure of seeing Taglioni in *La Sylphide*. She is perfectly irresistible, I am told, and the house is crammed whenever she appears. — But, my dear child, do you mean to tell me that you haven't seen her yet . . .? That's perfectly absurd! You must go at once!"

33. A reversal of the influence of fashion on the theater, since the tutu derived originally from the *robes-boules* of the 1820s and pointed shoes were inspired by evening slippers.

34. Petipa created his version of *La Sylphide* in 1892.

35. Mauclair 1910: "jupes de neige et de plume."

36. The music for the original *La Sylphide* was composed by Jean-Madeleine Schneitzhoeffer.

37. See the unsigned poem in Cyrillic script on the back of a letter by Picasso to Apollinaire from Rome, in Caizergues and Seckel 1992, pp. 148–49; the French translation is by Blanche Grinbaum-Salgas: Morceau poétique./Faire des vers n'est pas difficile/En l'honneur de la beauté/Que Picasso aime à la folie./Plaisante serait l'union/De l'artiste et de la ballerine./ Que les liens conjugaux, je le souhaite,/ Vous arrachent aux sylphides./Ce morceau lyrique,/Je le dédie à l'amour nouveau,/Nous attendons que Picasso/ Avec la Khokhlova s'explique" (A bit of poetry/It's no trouble making verses/in honour of the beauty/Picasso loves so madly./It would be nice to see the artist and the ballerina together./May the bonds of marriage — I hope — /tear you away from the sylphs./These lyrics I dedicate to new love,/while we're waiting for Picasso/and Khokhlova to sort it out).

38. See, for example, *The Painter and His Mode*l, 1914 (Musée national Picasso, Paris, MP 53; Palau 1990, no. 1252).

39. See Michael C. Fitzgerald, "The Modernists' Dilemma: Neoclassicism and the Portrayal of Olga Khokhlova," in Rubin 1996, pp. 296–335; Robert Rosenblum, "Le grotesque et le beau: la deuxième rencontre avec Ingres," in Madeline 2004, pp. 59–67.

40. Olga appeared in both of the *Sylphides* sequences that bring the entire corps de ballet onto the stage: *Nocturne*, Op. 32, No. 2, the first dance, and *Valse brillante* in E-flat Major, Op. 18, No. 1, the finale. The dance critic Cyril W. Beaumont remembers the intense melancholy the ballet produced in some viewers: see Beaumont 1935, pp. 50–51. The tragic history of Olga's family after the 1917 Revolution, nearly destitute and dispersed across Russia, Georgia, and Serbia, certainly reinforced the nostalgic traits in her own personality. Although Olga during these years wrote regularly to her family, sending money and necessities, the grief, worry, and doubtless the sense of guilt at being far away and powerless to do more are visible in the studies where Picasso represents her working at her correspondence: for example, *Woman Reading*, 1917 (Musée national Picasso, Paris, MP 800; Z.III.7).

41. Overture curtain for *Parade*, 1917 (Centre Pompidou, Musée national d'Art Moderne, Paris); see Rothschild 1991.

42. DeVonyar and Kendall 2002, p. 203.

43. Souriau 1999, p. 543: "liée à la magie imitative de la maternité ou de la fertilité"; Picasso, *Olga Reading*, 1920 (Musée des Beaux-Arts, Bordeaux, on loan from the Musée national Picasso, Paris, MP 1990-7; Palau 1999, no. 933).

44. An example is *Maternité*, 1921 (private collection; Z.VI.1392). It is worth recalling here Théophile Gautier's famous distinction between *ballets blancs* and *danses nationales* and their respective types of "heroines": the "Christian" dancer Taglioni and the "pagan" Fanny Elssler (*La Presse*, 34 September 1838). See Lisa C. Arkin and Marian Smith, "National Dance in the Romantic Ballet," in Garafola 1999, pp. 45–46.

45. Cooper 1968, p. 49.

46. In the spring of 1925, while in Monte-Carlo with Olga and Paulo to attend the Ballets Russes performances, Picasso executed a series of life studies of dancers exercising at the bar or at rest (see figs. 163–67; see also Z.V.427–38; Z.V.447–50; Z.V.452–55).

47. Breton 1925, p. 17.

48. See, for example, Alley 1996.

49. Cowling 2002b, pp. 463–69.

50. Richardson 2007, pp. 282–83.

51. Levaillant 1966, p. 213: "la réalité fantomale."

52. For two discussions of gender and the symbolism of pointe shoes, see Lynn Garafola, "Reconfiguring the Sexes," in Garafola and Baer 1999, pp. 254–68; and Foster 1996, pp. 1–24.

53. According to Anne Baldassari, this "cinétisme" can also be seen in the drawing *The Three Dancers*, 1919–20 (Musée national Picasso, Paris, MP 840; Z.XXIX.432). See Baldassari 1997a, p. 173.

54. Z.III.221–230.

55. Richardson 2007, p. 334. See also the *Seated Bather*, "inspired by Olga," 1930 (Museum of Modern Art, New York; Z.VII.306).

56. Dated 26 May 1929 (Musée national Picasso, Paris, MP 115; Z.VII.262).

57. The couple remained officially married for the next twenty years. Olga died in Cannes on 11 February 1955.

APPENDIX 2
REACTIONS TO THE WORK OF DEGAS IN PICASSO'S CIRCLE (1881–1900)

1. Félicien Fagus in *La Revue Blanche*, 15 July 1905, cited in Palau 1981, p. 515.

2. Richardson 1991, p. 41.

3. Ibid., p. 45.

4. Palau 1981, p. 43.

5. According to Francesc Fontbona, "Les obres que li serviren de model no van ser cap de les pintures més il·lustres de la col·lecció acadèmica sinó un Sant Antoni de Pàdua, anònim català dels segles XVII-XVIII — que ara sabem que està basat en una composició de Carlo Maratti-, un Crist crucificat, potser d'escola valenciana del segle XVII, i alguna altra. . . . Fora del Museu de l'Acadèmia, a l'incipient Museu Municipal de Belles Arts que s'havia instal·lat al Palau, dit també de Belles Arts, que era davant el Parc de la Ciutadella, Pablo Picasso copià, i també amb llicències, un estudi d'Arcadi Mas i Fontdevila" (The works he was given to copy were by no means the most illustrious paintings in the academy's collection but included a Saint Anthony of Padua, an anonymous Catalan work of the seventeenth to eighteenth centuries — which we now know is based on a composition by Carlo Maratti — a crucified Christ, possibly of the Valencia school of the seventeenth century, and some others. . . . Outside the academy, at the municipal fine arts museum that had recently opened at the Palau de Belles Arts near the Parc de la Ciutadella, Pablo Picasso also obtained permission to copy a study by Arcadi Mas i Fontdevila) (Fontbona 2002, p. 271).

6. Picasso to Joaquim Bas, 3 November 1897, cited in Richardson 1991, pp. 90–92: "[The teachers here] haven't a grain of common sense. They just go on and on, as I suspected they would, about the same old things: Velázquez for painting, Michelangelo for sculpture, etc., etc. The other night at his life class Moreno Carbonero told me that the figure I was doing was very good in proportion and drawing, but I ought to use straight lines. . . . It's incredible that anyone should say something so stupid . . . but he is the one who is best at drawing around here, because he studied in Paris. . . . But make no mistake, here in Spain we are not as stupid as we usually appear, we are just very poorly educated."

7. Palau 1981, p. 154.

8. Palau i Fabre refers to "Cercle Artístic" without specifying if it was the Reial Cercle Artístic or the Cercle Artístic de Sant Lluc. It seems likely that he means the latter, since friends of Picasso such as Josep Cardona, with whom he shared a studio during February and March of that year, were members of that society; in addition, in 1959 Picasso gave the Cercle Artístic de Sant Lluc a drawing, now at the Museu Picasso, Barcelona (MPB 66.127), to raise funds for the society, which suggests a sentimental bond.

9. In *The Art Journal*, for example, there were reproductions of works by Degas in the issues dating from July 1894, August and December 1895, April 1896, and August 1898.

10. Picasso to Joaquim Bas, 3 November 1897, cited in Richardson 1991, pp. 90–91.

11. R. Casellas, for example, wrote in the article "El impresionismo de Velázquez" in *Hispania* 7 (Casellas 1899): "Sí. Lo hermoso y lo feo poseen idéntica belleza, cuando son transformados en arte por un pintor como Velázquez. Por esto hoy reclaman con igual derecho la herencia del gran artista, por una parte, Degas, el pintot cruel de las deformidades y miserias modernas, por otra, Whistler, el exquisito retratista de las aristocracias contemporáneas. Ambos insignes pintores representan modos de arte derivados de aquel genio, y siguen alentando con su obra esta adoración perpétua sentida por los siglos hacia la obra de Velázquez, obra duradera y serena en medio de flujs y reflujos de idealidad y de naturalismo que agitan y han agitado siempre los destinos del arte" (Yes. The beauteous and the ugly possess an identical beauty, when they are transformed into art by a painter like Velázquez. That is why the great master's inheritance is claimed by equal right on the one hand by Degas, the cruel painter of modern miseries and deformities and, on the other, by Whistler, the exquisite portraitist of contemporary aristocracy. Both of these distinguished painters represent a kind of art that is derived from that genius and they continue by their work to feed this perpetual adoration that has been felt over the centuries for Velazquez's work, abiding and serene amid the ebb and flow of idealism and naturalism that convulse, as they always have, the destiny of art).

12. See Cristina Mendoza, "Casas and Picasso," in Ocaña 1996.

13. Cited in Laplana 1993, p. 133: "Ya vaig anar a can Camondo y realment es cullunut, pro aixís com Monet em va agradar molt mes de lo que creya (y aixó que ja el coneixia) en Degas em va deixar una mica fred fora dels dibuixos (Y un cuadro blanc y negre) lo demés està molt bé pro despues de tan de temps de parlarne y desitjà coneixeu francament no es el color que em creya." Laplana provides the date for the letter.

14. Riquer 1900, p. 281: "Dintre l'obra del

nostre pintor [Casas], s'hi sent un devot d'en Degas, com s'hi endevina desseguida l'home que ha comprés maravellosament l'admirable cinisme d'en Forain" (In the work of our painter [Casas], one senses a devotee of Degas, just as one immediately perceives the man who has magnificently understood the admirable cynicism of Forain).

15. 1899–1900, MPB 110.897.

16. Richardson 1991, p. 115.

17. 1899–1900 (Museu Picasso, Barcelona, MPB 110.668).

18. Rusiñol 1892: "Unos por convicción y muchos por impotencia, creen que el arte ha de huir de la verdad tratando de hermosear. . . . Nosotros creemos con la fe más absoluta, que no hay nada tan bello cual la verdad y que por su misma hermosura no se puede llegar más que á una imitación mezquina. . . . Así lo han comprendido Claudio Monet en el paisaje y Degas en la figura, que de ahí ha nacido el impresionismo que no busca más que detener sensaciones. Su escuela es fijar sobre la tela esas íntimas sutilezas que se espresan en el aire del dibujo, en la esencia del color, en el caràcter de la forma más que en la forma misma, en el alma de sus verdad tan buscada, en ese vago no se qué que corre en el firmamento traducido en intraducibles colores."

19. See Mendoza, "Casas and Picasso," in Ocaña 1996, pp. 26–27.

20. Pincell 1901.

21. Mendoza, "Casas and Picasso," in Ocaña 1996, p. 27.

22. *Coming out of the Exposition Universelle*, 1900 (Galerie Beyeler Collection, Basel; Palau 1981, no. 481).

23. *Young Man with Hat and Staff,* 1899–1900 (Museu Picasso, Barcelona,

MPB 110.656) and *Various Sketches*, 1899–1900, (Museu Picasso, Barcelona, MPB 110.657R).

24. Richardson 1991, p. 208.

25. Utrillo 1911: "La parte que interesará más al público, entre las obras maestras de la colección Camondo, es la de la pintura moderna, compuesta por obras seleccionadas mucho antes de que metieran ruido, entre las de Manet, Degas, Monet, Sisley, Jongkind, Delacroix, Daumier; [. . .] Degas, el gran pintor completo de nuestros días, sólo se comprenderá cuando la colección Camondo esté en el Louvre. Hasta ahora, no se ha expuesto nunca exceptuando algunas obras que varios coleccionistas prestaron para la glorificación de la pintura francesa en 1900; en esta colección hay los suficientes para estudiar toda la gran personalidad del autor, su noble adivinación del alma y del movimiento humano, su color robusto y armonioso, su dibujo vital; la obra culminante es el retrato de mujer, en el que desde luego se adivina toda la influencia nefasta que ejerció en las vdas de varios hombres; obra perfecta, para todo aquél que ame la pintura definitiva, aquella que en todos los tiempos está bien, sin explicaciones, conceptos ni puntos de vista, obra que en el Louvre, no parecerá haber entrado por la ventana, como ha sucedido á muchas otras. Las demás obras de Degas, comprenden estudios completos de bailarinas, y salas de baile de la Opera, corridas de caballos, las planchadoras, el ajenjo y otras muchas."

26. See Paul Valéry in Lévêque 1978, p. 98: "[S]es camarades du temps du café Guerbois, ne l'intéressaient plus. Renoir, Claude Monet, il n'avait rien à leur dire.

Alors [Degas] reprit ses visites chez Bartholomé; — et il apparut chez ses plus jeunes amis: Suzanne Valadon et Zuloaga" (His friends from the time of the café Guerbois no longer interested him. Renoir, Claude Monet — he had nothing to say to them. So [Degas] began once again to visit Bartholomé; — and he appeared on the doorsteps of his youngest friends: Suzanne Valadon and Zuloaga). For more on Degas's friendship with Valadon, see Ronald Pickvance, "'Terrible Maria': Degas and Suzanne Valadon," and Thérèse Diamand-Rosinsky, "Suzanne Valadon's Many Identities: Marie-Clémentine, 'Biqui,' or 'Terrible Maria,'" in Marchesseau 1996.

27. Panyella 2001, p. 113.

28. Laplana 1993, p. 198: "Utrillo treia la seva informació de Zandomeneghi, el pintor venecià la confiança del qual s'havia guanyat a força de fer amb ell llargues excursions en bicicleta; de tornada, ambdós ciclistes acostumaven a fer parada en qualsevol cafè de la porta Maillol, i era aleshores quan Zandomeneghi s'explicava, responent a les hàbils preguntes d'Utrillo. Diu aquest: 'Tota història de la pintura francesa de la segona meitat del segle era descabellada, narrada per un testimoni vertader,' puix que Zandomenghi 'havia conegut Manet de qui era íntim, i es feia amb Pissarro, Cézanne, Desboutin, . . . Luce, Claude Monet, Berthe Morisot, Signac, Sisley, Renoir i molts altres, i aleshores veia el pintor Degas cada dia.'"

29. For more on Degas's influence on Zuloaga and the two artists' friendship, see Ferrari 1991 and Milhou 1991, pp. 47–51.

30. See note 26.

WORKS CITED

Acker 1989

Acker, Yolanda F. "Los Ballets Russes en España: recepción y guía de sus primeras actuaciones (1916–18)." In *Los Ballets Russes de Diaghilev y España,* ed. Yvan Nommick, pp. 229–52. Granada: Centre Culturel Manuel de Falla, 1989.

Adhémar and Cachin 1974

Adhémar, Jean, and Françoise Cachin. *Degas: The Complete Etchings, Lithographs and Monotypes.* London: Thames & Hudson, 1974.

Adler 1986

Adler, Kathleen. *Manet.* Oxford: Phaidon Press, 1986.

Adriani 2005

Adriani, Götz. *Bordell und Boudoir: Schauplätze der Moderne. Cézanne, Degas, Toulouse-Lautrec, Picasso.* Ostfildern-Ruit: Hatje Cantz, 2005.

Alley 1981

Alley, Ronald. *The Tate Gallery's Collection of Modern Art.* London: Tate Gallery, 1981.

Alley 1996

Alley, Ronald. *Picasso: The Three Dancers.* London: Tate Gallery, 1996.

Apollinaire 1972

Apollinaire, Guillaume. *Apollinaire on Art: Essays and Reviews, 1902–1918.* Ed. Leroy C. Breunig. Trans. Susan Suleiman. London: Thames & Hudson, 1972.

Armstrong 1988

Armstrong, Carol. "Reflections on the Mirror: Painting, Photography, and the Self-Portraits of Edgar Degas." *Representations* 22 (Spring 1988): pp. 108–41.

Ashton 1972

Ashton, Dore. *Picasso on Art: A Selection of Views.* London: Thames & Hudson, 1972.

Baedeker 1904

Baedeker, Karl. *Paris and Environs, with Routes from London to Paris: Handbook for Travellers.* 15th rev. ed. Leipzig: K. Baedeker, 1904.

Baer 1986–96

Baer, Brigitte, and Bernhard Geiser. *Picasso: Peintre-Graveur.* 7 vols. Bern: Kornfeld, 1986–96.

Baer 1997

Baer, Brigitte. *Picasso the Engraver: Selections from the Musée Picasso, Paris.* London: Thames & Hudson, in association with the Metropolitan Museum of Art, New York, 1997.

Bakst 1917

Bakst, Léon. "Choréographie et décors des Nouveaux Ballets Russes." Program note for *Les Ballets Russes à Paris*, Théâtre du Châtelet, May 1917.

Balanchine 1954

Balanchine, George. *Balanchine's Complete Stories of the Great Ballets.* New York: Doubleday, 1954.

Baldassari 1994

Baldassari, Anne. *Picasso photographe, 1901–1916.* Exh. cat. Paris: Réunion des musées nationaux, 1994.

Baldassari 1995

Baldassari, Anne. *Picasso et la photographie: à plus grand vitesse que les images.* Exh. cat. Paris: Musée national Picasso, 1995.

Baldassari 1997a

Baldassari, Anne. *Le Miroir noir: Picasso, sources photographiques, 1900–1928.* Exh. cat. Paris: Réunion des musées nationaux, 1997.

Baldassari 1997b

Baldassari, Anne. *Picasso and Photography: The Dark Mirror.* Exh. cat. Trans. Deke Dusinberre. Paris: Flammarion, in association with the Museum of Fine Arts, Houston, 1997.

Baldassari 1998

Baldassari, Anne. "Olga Koklova [*sic*] and Dance." In *Picasso 1917–1924: The Italian Journey*, ed. Jean Clair, pp. 96–99. Exh. cat. Milan: Bompiani, 1998.

Baltimore Museum of Art 1967

Baltimore Museum of Art. *Paintings, Sculpture and Drawings in the Cone Collection.* Baltimore: Baltimore Museum of Art, 1967.

Barañano 1997

Barañano, Kosme de. "Al voltant de la *Suite 156* de Pablo Picasso." In *Picasso: Suite 156*, pp. 11–65. Barcelona: Fundació Bancaixa, 1997.

Barnet 1978

Barnet, Vivian. *The Guggenheim Museum, Justin K. Tannhauser Collection.* New York: Guggenheim Museum, 1978.

Baudelaire 1964

Baudelaire, Charles. *The Painter of Modern Life and Other Essays.* Ed. Jonathan Maine. London: Phaidon Press, 1964.

Beaumont 1935

Beaumont, Cyril W. *Michel Fokine and His Ballets.* 1935. Repr., London: Dance Books, 1996.

Belloli 2005

Belloli, Lucy. "Lost Paintings beneath Picasso's *La Coiffure.*" *Metropolitan Museum of Art Journal* 40 (2005): pp. 151–61.

Benet 1975

Benet, Rafael. *Sunyer.* Barcelona: Ediciones Polígrafa, 1975.

Berggruen 2007

Berggruen, Olivier, ed. *Picasso and the Theatre.* Exh. cat. Frankfurt: Schirn Kunsthalle, 2007.

Berson 1996

Berson, Ruth, ed. *The New Painting: Impressionism 1874–1886; Documentation*. 2 vols. San Francisco: Fine Arts Museums of San Francisco, 1996.

Blanc 1867

Blanc, Charles. *Grammaire des arts du dessin: architecture, sculpture, peinture*. Paris: Librairie Renouard, 1867.

Boggs 1988

Boggs, Jean Sutherland, et al. *Degas*. Exh. cat. New York: Metropolitan Museum of Art, 1988.

Bois 2001

Bois, Yve-Alain. "Painting as Trauma." In *Picasso's "Les Demoiselles d'Avignon,"* ed. Christopher Green, pp. 31–54. Cambridge: Cambridge University Press, 2001.

Brame and Reff 1984

Brame, Philippe, and Theodore Reff. *Degas et son oeuvre: A Supplement*. New York: Garland Publishers, 1984.

Brassaï 1967

Brassaï. *Picasso and Co*. Trans. Francis Price. London: Thames & Hudson, 1967.

Brettell and Pissarro 1992

Brettell, Richard, and Joachim Pissarro. *The Impressionist and the City: Pissarro's Series Paintings*. Exh. cat. London: Royal Academy of Arts, 1992.

Breton 1925

Breton, André. *La Révolution surréaliste* 4 (July 1925): p. 17.

Brown 1996

Brown, Jonathan. *Picasso and the Spanish Tradition*. New Haven and London: Yale University Press, 1996.

Browse 1949

Browse, Lillian. *Degas Dancers*. London: Faber and Faber, 1949.

Buckle 1979

Buckle, Richard. *Diaghilev*. London: Weidenfeld and Nicolson, 1979.

Cabanne 1957

Cabanne, Pierre. *Edgar Degas*. Paris: Pierre Tisné, 1957.

Cabanne 1975

Cabanne, Pierre. *Le siècle de Picasso*. 4 vols. Paris: Denoël, 1975.

Caizergues and Seckel 1992

Caizergues, Pierre, and Hélène Seckel, eds. *Picasso/Apollinaire: Correspondance*. Paris: Gallimard, 1992.

Campbell 2009

Campbell, Sara, ed. *Degas in the Norton Simon Museum*. New Haven and London: Yale University Press, 2009.

Carmean 1980

Carmean, E. A. *Picasso, The Saltimbanques*. Washington, D.C.: National Gallery of Art, 1980.

Casellas 1899

Casellas, R. "El impresionismo de Velázquez." *Hispania* 7 (30 May 1899).

Chéroux 2005

Chéroux, Clément, Andreas Fischer, et al. *The Perfect Medium: Photography and the Occult*. Exh. cat. New Haven and London: Yale University Press, 2005.

Cirlot 1972

Cirlot, Juan-Eduardo. *Picasso: Birth of a Genius*. London and Barcelona: Elek, 1972.

Clair 2001

Clair, Jean, et al. *Picasso érotique*. Exh. cat. Paris: Réunion des musées nationaux, 2001.

Conzen 2005

Conzen, Ina. *Picasso: Bathers*. With contributions by Anke Spötter and Guido Messling. Exh. cat. Stuttgart: Staatsgalerie, 2005.

Cooper 1968

Cooper, Douglas. *Picasso Theatre*. London: Weidenfeld and Nicolson, 1968.

Corunna 2002

Fundación Pedro Barrié de la Maza. *Picasso Joven–Young Picasso*. Exh. cat. Corunna: Fundación Pedro Barrié de la Maza, 2002.

Cowling 2002a

Cowling, Elizabeth, et al. *Matisse Picasso*. Exh. cat. London: Tate; Paris: Galeries nationales du Grand Palais; New York: Museum of Modern Art, 2002.

Cowling 2002b

Cowling, Elizabeth. *Picasso: Style and Meaning*. London: Phaidon, 2002.

Cowling 2006

Cowling, Elizabeth. *Visiting Picasso: The Notebooks and Letters of Roland Penrose*. London: Thames & Hudson, 2006.

Cowling and Golding 1994

Cowling, Elizabeth, and John Golding, eds. *Picasso: Sculptor/Painter*. Exh. cat. London: Tate Gallery, 1994.

Cowling and Mundy 1990

Cowling, Elizabeth, and Jennifer Mundy. *On Classic Ground: Picasso, Léger, de Chirico, and the New Classicism, 1910–1930*. Exh. cat. London: Tate Gallery, 1990.

Crespelle 1978

Crespelle, Jean-Paul. *La Vie quotidienne à Montmartre au temps de Picasso, 1900–1910*. Paris: Hachette, 1978.

Crommelynck 1995

Crommelynck, Aldo. "Recollections on Printmaking with Picasso." In *Picasso: Inside the Image; Prints from the Ludwig Museum Collection*, ed. Janie Cohen, pp. 13–17. Exh. cat. University of Vermont: Robert Fleming Museum, in association with London: Thames & Hudson, 1995.

Csergo 1988

Csergo, Julia. *Liberté, égalité, propreté: la morale de l'hygiène au XIXe siècle*. Paris: Albin Michel, 1988.

Daix 1994a

Daix, Pierre. *Picasso au Bateau-Lavoir*. Paris: Flammarion, 1994.

Daix 1994b

Daix, Pierre. *Picasso: Life and Art*. Trans. Olivia Emmet. London: Thames & Hudson, 1994.

Daix 1995

Daix, Pierre. *Dictionnaire Picasso*. Paris: Éditions Robert Laffont, 1995.

Daix and Boudaille 1988

Daix, Pierre, and Georges Boudaille. *Picasso, 1900–1906: Catalogue raisonné de l'oeuvre peint*. Neuchâtel: Éditions Ides et Calendes, 1988.

Daix and Israël 2003

Daix, Pierre, and Armand Israël. *Pablo Picasso: Dossiers de la préfecture de police, 1901–1940*. Paris: Catalogues Raisonnés/Acatos, 2003.

Daix and Rosselet 1979

Daix, Pierre, and Joan Rosselet. *Picasso: The Cubist Years, 1907–1916*. Trans. Dorothy S. Blair. London: Thames & Hudson, 1979.

Daniel 1998

Daniel, Malcolm. *Edgar Degas, Photographer*. Exh. cat. New York: Metropolitan Museum of Art, 1998.

Davies 1970

Davies, Martin. *French School: Early 19th Century, Impressionists, Post-Impressionists, etc.* London: National Gallery, 1970.

Denis 1964

Denis, Maurice. *Du symbolisme au classicisme: Theories.* Ed. Olivier Revault d'Allonnes. Paris: Miroirs de l'Art, 1964.

DeVonyar and Kendall 2002

DeVonyar, Jill, and Richard Kendall. *Degas and the Dance.* Exh. cat. New York: Harry N. Abrams, 2002.

Dumas 1997

Dumas, Ann, et al. *The Private Collection of Edgar Degas.* Exh. cat. New York: Metropolitan Museum of Art, in association with Harry N. Abrams, 1997.

Duncan 1958

Duncan, David Douglas. *The Private World of Pablo Picasso.* New York: Ridge Press, 1958.

Duncan 1974

Duncan, David Douglas. *Goodbye Picasso.* London: Times Books, 1974

Duret 1894

Duret, Théodore. "Degas." *Art Journal*, 1894, pp. 204–8.

Easton and Bark 2008

Easton, Elizabeth, and Jared Bark. "'Pictures Properly Framed': Degas and Innovation in Impressionist Frames." *Burlington Magazine* 150 (September 2008): pp. 603–11.

Fénéon 1966

Fénéon, Félix. *Au-delà de l'impressionnisme.* Ed. Françoise Cachin. Paris: Hermann, 1966.

FitzGerald 1995

FitzGerald, Michael C. *Making Modernism: Picasso and the Creation of the Market for Twentieth-century Art.* New York: Farrar, Straus and Giroux, 1995.

Flint 1984

Flint, Kate. *Impressionists in England: The Critical Reception.* London; Boston: Routledge and Kegan Paul, 1984.

Fontbona 2002

Fontbona, Francesc. "El Picasso català." In *El Modernisme: Pintura i dibuix*, by Francesc Fontbona. Barcelona: L'Isard, 2002.

Foster 1996

Foster, Susan Leigh. "The Ballerina's Phallic Pointe." In *Corporealities: Dancing Knowledge, Culture and Power*, ed. Susan Leigh Foster, pp. 1–26. 1996. Repr., London: Routledge, 2005.

Galassi 1996

Galassi, Susan Grace. *Picasso's Variations on the Masters: Confrontations with the Past.* New York: Harry N. Abrams, 1996.

Galignani 1894

Galignani, A., and W. Galignani. *Galignani's Paris Guide for 1894.* Paris: Galignani Library, 1894.

Ganz and Kendall 2007

Ganz, James, and Richard Kendall. *The Unknown Monet: Pastels and Drawings.* Williamstown, Mass.: Sterling and Francine Clark Art Institute, 2007.

Garafola 1999

Garafola, Lynn, ed. *Rethinking the Sylph: New Perspectives on the Romantic Ballet.* Lebanon, N.H.: Wesleyan University Press, 1999.

Garafola and Baer 1999

Garafola, Lynn, and Nancy Van Norman Baer, eds. *The Ballets Russes and Its World.* New Haven and London: Yale University Press, 1999.

Gasman 1998

Gasman, Lydia Csató. "Death Falling from the Sky: Picasso's Wartime Texts." In *Picasso and the War Years, 1937–1945*, ed. Steven A. Nash, pp. 55–67. London: Thames & Hudson, 1998.

Gautier 1859

Gautier, Théophile. *Histoire de l'art dramatique depuis vingt-cinq ans.* 6 vols. Paris: Hetzel, 1859.

Gilot 1966

Gilot, Françoise, and Carlton Lake. *Life with Picasso.* Harmondsworth: Penguin Books, 1966.

Georges Petit 1924

Galeries Georges Petit. *Exposition Degas au profit de la Ligue Franco-Anglo-Américaine contre le Cancer.* Paris: Galeries Georges Petit, 1924.

Gimpel 1966

Gimpel, René. *Diary of an Art Dealer.* New York: Farrar, Straus and Giroux, 1966.

Gregory 1989

Gregory, John. *"Les Sylphides" — Chopiniana: Personal Reflections on Michel Fokine's Masterpiece.* Llandysul: Zena Croesor, 1989.

Grigoriev 1953

Grigoriev, Serge L. *The Diaghilev Ballet, 1909–1929.* 1953. Repr., London: Dance Books, 2009.

Grolier Club 1922

Grolier Club. *Prints, Drawings and Bronzes by Degas.* New York: Grolier Club, 1922.

Gsell 1918

Gsell, Paul. "Edgar Degas, Statuaire." *La Renaissance de l'art français et des industries de luxe,* December 1918, p. 373.

Guérin 1947

Guérin, Marcel, ed. *Degas Letters.* Oxford: Bruno Cassirer, 1947.

Halévy 1964

Halévy, Daniel. *My Friend Degas.* Trans. and ed. by Mina Curtiss. Middletown, Conn.: Wesleyan University Press, 1964.

Havelock 1995

Havelock, Christine Mitchell. *The Aphrodite of Knidos and Her Successors.* Ann Arbor: University of Michigan Press, 1995.

Havemeyer 1961

Havemeyer, Louise. *Sixteen to Sixty: Memoirs of a Collector.* New York: Ursus Press, 1961.

Heilbrun 2005

Heilbrun, Françoise. "Actualités." *Revue du Musée d'Orsay* 20 (Spring 2005): pp. 74–75.

Hepp 1988

Hepp, Jacques Gilbert. *Pablo Picasso: un mystère dévoilé.* Nanterre: Académie européenne du livre, 1988.

Holloway 2006

Holloway, Memory. *Making Time: Picasso's "Suite 347."* New York: Peter Lang, 2006.

Horticq 1912

Hourticq, Louis. "Degas." *Art et Décoration*, 1912, p. 110.

Hôtel Drouot 1906

Catalogue des tableaux modernes . . ., aquarelles, pastels, dessins . . . provenant des Successions des Rois Milan et Alexandre de Servie. Paris: Hôtel Drouot, 16–17 February 1906.

Hôtel Drouot 1914

Catalogue des estampes modernes composant la collection Roger Marx. Paris: Hôtel Drouot, 27 April–2 May 1914.

Huysmans 1975

Huysmans, Joris-Karl. L'Art moderne; Certains. Ed. Hubert Juin. Paris: Union générale d'éditions, 1975.

Jamot 1924

Jamot, Paul. Degas. Paris: Éditions de la Gazette des Beaux Arts, 1924.

Janis 1968

Janis, Eugenia Parry. Degas Monotypes: Essay, Catalogue and Checklist. Cambridge, Mass.: Fogg Art Museum, 1968.

Jan Krugier 1989

Galerie Jan Krugier. 44 Dessins de Picasso. Geneva: Galerie Jan Krugier, 1989.

Kahane 1998

Kahane, Martine, et al. "Enquête sur la Petite Danseuse de quatorze ans de Degas." Revue du Musée d'Orsay 7 (Autumn 1998).

Kahnweiler 1971

Kahnweiler, Daniel-Henry. My Galleries and Painters. With Francis Crémieux. Trans. Helen Weaver. London: Thames & Hudson, 1971.

Karsavina 1931

Karsavina, Tamara. Ballets Russes: Les Souvenirs de Tamar Karsavina. Paris: Plon, 1931.

Kendall 1993

Kendall, Richard. Degas Landscapes. New Haven and London: Yale University Press, in association with the Metropolitan Museum of Art, New York, and the Museum of Fine Arts, Houston, 1993.

Kendall 1996

Kendall, Richard. Degas: Beyond Impressionism. Exh. cat. London: National Gallery Publications; Chicago: Art Institute of Chicago, 1996.

Kendall 1998

Kendall, Richard. Degas and the Little Dancer. New Haven and London: Yale University Press, 1998.

Kendall 2009

Kendall, Richard. "'Dans un café,' 'Zigzags' and Five Recovered Impressionist Drawings." Burlington Magazine 151 (May 2009), pp. 306–11.

Kosinski 1999

Kosinski, Dorothy. The Artist and the Camera: Degas to Picasso. Exh. cat. Dallas: Dallas Museum of Art, 1999.

Lafond 1918–19

Lafond, Paul. Degas. 2 vols. Paris: H. Floury, 1918–19.

Laplana 1993

Laplana, Josep de C. Santiago Rusiñol. El pintor, l'home. Montserrat: Publicacions de l'Abadia de Montserrat, 1993.

Léal 1996

Léal, Brigitte. Musée Picasso. Carnets. Catalogue des dessins. 2 vols. Paris: Réunion des musées nationaux, 1996.

Léal 2002

Léal, Brigitte, et al. Paris Barcelona 1888–1937. Exh. cat. Barcelona: Museu Picasso, 2002.

Lecomte 1892

Lecomte, Georges. L'Art impressionniste d'après la collection privée de M. Durand-Ruel. Paris: Chamerot et Renouard, 1892.

Leicester 1923

Leicester Galleries. An Exhibition of the Works in Sculpture by Edgar Degas. London: Leicester Galleries, 1923.

Lemoisne 1919

Lemoisne, Paul-André. "Les Statuettes de Degas." Art et Décoration, September–October 1919, pp. 109–17.

Lemoisne 1946–49

Lemoisne, Paul André. Degas et son oeuvre. 4 vols. Paris: P. Brame et C. M. de Hauke, aux Arts et métiers graphiques, 1946–49.

Levaillant 1966

Levaillant, Françoise. "La Danse de Picasso et le surréalisme en 1925." L'Information de l'histoire de l'art 11, no. 5 (November–December 1966): pp. 205–14.

Lévêque 1978

Lévêque, Jean-Jacques. Edgar Degas. Paris: Éditions Siloé, 1978.

Liebermann 1899

Liebermann, Max. Degas. Berlin: Bruno and Paul Cassirer, 1899.

Lipton 1987

Lipton, Eunice. Looking into Degas: Uneasy Images of Women and Modern Life. Berkeley, Los Angeles, and London: University of California Press, 1987.

Loyrette 1991

Loyrette, Henri. Degas. Paris: Arthème Fayard, 1991.

Loyrette 1996

Loyrette, Henri, ed. Entre le théâtre et l'histoire: la famille Halévy. Paris: Fayard, 1996.

MacDonald 1975

MacDonald, Nesta. Diaghilev Observed by Critics in England and the United States, 1911–1929. New York: Dance Horizons; London: Dance Books, 1975.

Madeline 2004

Madeline, Laurence, ed. Picasso Ingres. Exh. cat. Paris: Fayard; Réunion des musées nationaux, 2004.

Madeline 2005

Madeline, Laurence, ed. Gertrude Stein, Pablo Picasso: Correspondance. Paris: Gallimard, 2005.

Manzi 1898

Manzi, Michel. Degas: Vingt Dessins, 1861–1896. Paris: Boussod et Valadon, 1898.

Manzi-Joyant 1912a

Galerie Manzi-Joyant. Collection Henri Rouart, première vente; tableaux modernes par Boudin, John Lewis Brown. . . . Paris: Galerie Manzi-Joyant, 9–11 December 1912.

Manzi-Joyant 1912b

Galerie Manzi-Joyant. Collection Henri Rouart, deuxième vente; tableaux anciens par Boilly, Breughel. . . . Paris: Galerie Manzi-Joyant, 9–11 December 1912.

Marchesseau 1996

Marchesseau, Daniel. Suzanne Valadon. Exh cat. Martigny, Switzerland: Fondation Pierre Gianadda, 1996.

Marfany 1972

Marfany, Joan Lluis. "Sobre el significant del terme 'Modernisme.'" Recerques 2 (1972): pp. 73–91.

Massine 1968

Massine, Léonide. My Life in Ballet. London: Macmillan, 1968.

Matisse 1999

Matisse, Henri, M.-A. Couturier, L.-B. Rayssiguier, and Marcel Billot. *The Vence Chapel: The Archive of a Creation*. Ed. Marcel Billot. Trans. Michael Taylor. Houston, Milan, and New York: Menil Foundation and Skira Editore, 1999.

Mauclair 1910

Mauclair, Camille. *La Revue* (Paris), 1 August 1910.

Mauclair 1937

Mauclair, Camille. *Degas*. London and Toronto: William Heinemann, 1937.

McCully 1981

McCully, Marilyn, ed. *A Picasso Anthology: Documents, Criticism, Reminiscences*. London: Arts Council of Great Britain, 1981.

McCully 1997

McCully, Marilyn, ed. *Picasso: The Early Years, 1892–1906*. Washington, D.C.: National Gallery of Art, 1997.

Meier-Graefe 1920

Meier-Graefe, Julius. *Degas*. Munich: R. Piper, 1920.

Melot 1994

Melot, Michel. *L'Estampe impressionniste*. Paris: Flammarion, 1994.

Mendoza 2001

Mendoza, Cristina. *Ramon Casas: el pintor del modernismo*. Barcelona: Museu d'Art Modern, 2001.

Milhou 1991

Milhou, Mayi. "Ignacio Zuloaga in France." In *Ignacio Zuloaga*, pp. 40–59. Exh cat. Vitoria: Gouvernement basque, Département de la culture et du tourisme, 1991.

Mirbeau 1900

Mirbeau, Octave. *Le Journal d'une femme de chambre*. Paris: Bibliothèque Charpentier, 1900.

MNAC 1997

Museu d'Art Modern, MNAC. *Santiago Rusiñol, 1861–1931*. Exh. cat. Barcelona: Museu d'Art Modern, 1997.

MNAC 2000

Museu d'Art Modern, MNAC. *Isidre Nonell, 1872–1911*. Exh. cat. Barcelona: Museu d'Art Modern, 2000.

Moffett 1986

Moffett, Charles S., et al. *The New Painting: Impressionism, 1874–1886*. Exh. cat. San Francisco: Fine Arts Museums of San Francisco; Washington, D.C.: National Gallery of Art, 1986.

Monneret 1978–79

Monneret, Sophie. *L'Impressionnisme et son époque*. 4 vols. Paris: Robert Laffont, 1978–79.

Monnier 1985

Monnier, Geneviève. *Musée du Louvre, Cabinet des Dessins, Musée d'Orsay: Pastels du XIXe siècle*. Paris: Ministère de la Culture, Réunion des musées nationaux, 1985.

Moore 1918

Moore, George. "Memories of Degas." *Burlington Magazine* 32 (February 1918): pp. 63–65.

Morelon and Deconchat 2004

Morelon, Dominique, and Simon André-Deconchat. "Edgar Degas et Jacques Doucet: ombres et lumières entre un artiste et un collectionneur." In *Degas: blanc et noir*, pp. 7–24. Exh. cat. Avignon: Musée Angladon, 2004.

Musée de la Vie Romantique 2004

Thierry, Solange et al. *Au coeur de l'impressionnisme: la famille Rouart*. Exh. cat. Paris: Musée de la Vie Romantique and Paris-Musées, 2004.

Musée de l'Orangerie 1931

Musée de l'Orangerie. *Degas: portraitiste, sculpteur*. Exh. cat. Paris: Musée de l'Orangerie, 1931.

Musée d'Orsay 1989

Musée d'Orsay. *Degas inédit: Actes du Colloque Degas, Musée d'Orsay, 18–21 avril 1988*. Paris: La Documentation française, 1989.

Musée Goupil 1997

Musée Goupil. *Degas, Boldini, Toulouse-Lautrec. . . . Portraits inédits par Michel Manzi*. Paris: Somogy éditions d'art, 1997.

Musée national Picasso 1998

Musée national Picasso. *La Guerre et la paix*. Exh. cat. Paris: Réunion des musées nationaux, 1998.

Museo de Arte Moderno de Barcelona 1976

Museo de Arte Moderno de Barcelona. *Canals*. Barcelona: Junta des Museos de Barcelona, 1976.

Museu Picasso 1985

Museu Picasso. *Catalogo de pintura y dibujo*. Barcelona: Museu Picasso, 1985.

Museu Picasso 1992

Museu Picasso, Barcelona. *Picasso 1905–1906: From the Rose Period to the Ochres of Gósol*. Exh. cat. Barcelona: Electa, 1992.

Museu Picasso 2009

Museu Picasso, Barcelona. *Imágenes secretas: Picasso y la estampa erótica japonesa*. Exh. cat. Barcelona: Museu Picasso, 2009.

Newhall 1963

Newhall, Beaumont. "Degas, photographe amateur." *Gazette des Beaux-Arts* 61 (January 1963): pp. 61–64.

Nicolson 1963

Nicolson, Benedict. "Editorial: Degas as a Human Being." *Burlington Magazine* 105, no. 723 (June 1963): pp. 239–40.

Nijinska 1992

Nijinska, Bronislava. *Early Memoirs*. Trans. and ed. by Irina Nijinska and Jean Rawlinson, with an introduction and special consultation by Anna Kisselgoff. Durham, N.C., and London: Duke University Press, 1992.

Nochlin 1992

Nochlin, Linda. "A House is Not a Home: Degas and the Subversion of the Family." In *Dealing with Degas: Representations of Women and the Politics of Vision*, ed. Richard Kendall and Griselda Pollock, pp. 43–65. London: Pandora, 1992.

Ocaña 1994

Ocaña, Maria-Teresa. *Picasso Landscapes, 1890–1912: From the Academy to the Avant-Garde*. Boston: Little, Brown, 1994.

Ocaña 1996

Ocaña, Maria-Teresa, ed. *Picasso and Els Quatre Gats: The Early Years in Turn-of-the-Century Barcelona*. Exh. cat. Barcelona: Museu Picasso, 1996.

Olivier 1988

Olivier, Fernande. *Souvenirs intimes*. Paris: Calmann-Lévy, 1988.

Olivier 2001a

Olivier, Fernande. *Loving Picasso: The Private Journal of Fernande Olivier.* Trans. Christine Baker and Michael Raeburn. Originally published 1988 as *Souvenirs intimes.* New York: Harry N. Abrams, 2001.

Olivier 2001b

Olivier, Fernande. *Picasso et ses amis.* Ed. Hélène Klein. Paris: Pygmalion/Gérard Watelet, 2001.

Otero 1974

Otero, Roberto. *Forever Picasso: An Intimate Look at His Last Years.* Trans. Elaine Kerrigan. New York: Harry N. Abrams, 1974.

Palau 1981

Palau i Fabre, Josep. *Picasso. Life and Work of the Early Years, 1881–1907.* Trans. Kenneth Lyons. London: Phaidon, 1981.

Palau 1990

Palau i Fabre, Josep. *Picasso Cubism, 1907–1917.* Trans. Susan Branyas, Richard Lewis-Rees, and Patrick Zabalbeascoa. Barcelona: Ediciones Polígrafa, 1990.

Palau 1999

Palau i Fabre, Josep. *Picasso: des ballets au drame (1917–1926).* Trans. Robert Marrast. Cologne: Könemann, 1999.

Panyella 1981

Panyella, Vinyet. *Epistolari del Cau Ferrat: 1889–1930.* Sitges: Grup d'Estudis Sitgetans, 1981.

Panyella 2001

Panyella, Vinyet. *Paisatges i escenaris de Santiago Rusiñol: Paris, Sitges, Granada.* Montserrat: Publicacions de l'Abadia de Montserrat, 2001.

Parmelin 1959

Parmelin, Hélène. *Picasso sur la place.* Paris: Julliard, 1959.

Parmelin 1963

Parmelin, Hélène. *Picasso Plain: An Intimate Portrait.* Trans. Humphrey Hare. London: Secker & Warburg, 1963.

Parmelin 1965

Parmelin, Hélène. *Picasso: The Artist and His Model and Other Recent Works.* New York: Harry N. Abrams, 1965.

Parmelin 1969

Parmelin, Hélène. *Picasso Says . . . .* London: Allen & Unwin, 1969.

Penrose 1958

Penrose, Roland. *Picasso: His Life and Work.* London: Victor Gollancz, 1958.

Perrot 1984

Perrot, Philippe. *Le Travail des apparences, ou les transformations du corps féminin, XVIII–XIXè siècle.* Paris: Seuil, 1984.

Picasso 1900

Picasso, Pablo. *Carnet de Paris (facsimile).* Graz: Academische Druck- u. Verlagsanstalt, 2006.

Pickvance 1963

Pickvance, Ronald. "'L'Absinthe' in England." *Apollo* 77 (May 1963): pp. 395–98.

Pillsbury 1983

Pillsbury, Edmund. "The Rebirth of Venus." *Art News* 82, no. 4 (April 1983): pp. 108–10.

Pincell 1901

Pincell [Miquel Utrillo]. "Pablo R. Picasso." *Pèl & Ploma* 77 (1 June 1901): pp. 15–17.

Pingeot 1991

Pingeot, Anne. *Degas: sculptures.* Photographs by Frank Horvat. Paris: Réunion des musées nationaux, 1991.

Pompeillan 1898

Pompeillan, Marquise de. *Le Guide de la femme du monde, précédé du Guide de la jeune fille, suivi du Guide de l'homme du monde.* Paris: Pontet-Brault, 1898.

Posner 1973

Posner, Donald. *Watteau: A Lady at Her Toilette.* London: Allen Lane, 1973.

Rabinow 2006

Rabinow, Rebecca A. *Cézanne to Picasso: Ambroise Vollard, Patron of the Avant-Garde.* Exh. cat. New York: Metropolitan Museum of Art; New Haven: Yale University Press, 2006.

Ràfols 1948

Ràfols, J. F. "Degas y Rusiñol." *Anales y Boletín de los Museos de Barcelona,* July–December 1948, pp. 503–4.

Raynal 1956

Raynal, Maurice. *Modern Painting.* Lausanne: Skira, 1956.

Reed and Shapiro 1984

Reed, Sue Welsh, and Barbara Stern Shapiro. *Edgar Degas: The Painter as Printmaker.* Exh. cat. Boston: Museum of Fine Arts, 1984.

Reff 1976

Reff, Theodore. *The Notebooks of Edgar Degas.* 2 vols. Oxford: Clarendon Press, 1976.

Rewald 1944

Rewald, John. *Degas, Works in Sculpture: A Complete Catalogue.* New York: Pantheon Books, 1944.

Rewald 1973

Rewald, John. "Theo van Gogh, Goupil, and the Impressionists." *Gazette des Beaux Arts* 31 (1973): pp. 1–108.

Richardson 1984

Richardson, John. "The Catch in the Late Picasso." *New York Review of Books,* 19 July 1984, pp. 21–28.

Richardson 1991

Richardson, John. *A Life of Picasso. Vol. 1, 1881–1906.* With the collaboration of Marilyn McCully. New York: Random House, 1991.

Richardson 1996

Richardson, John. *A Life of Picasso. Vol. 2, 1907–1917: The Painter of Modern Life.* With the collaboration of Marilyn McCully. London: Jonathan Cape, 1996.

Richardson 2007

Richardson, John. *A Life of Picasso. Vol. 3, The Triumphant Years, 1917–1932.* With the collaboration of Marilyn McCully. London: Jonathan Cape, 2007.

Riquer 1900

Riquer, Alexandre de. "Exposició Casas." *Joventut* 18 (14 June 1900).

Robinson 2006

Robinson, William H., Jordi Falgàs, and Carmen Belen Lord. *Barcelona and Modernity: Picasso, Gaudí, Miró, Dalí.* Exh. cat. Cleveland: Cleveland Museum of Art, in association with Yale University Press, 2006.

Roger Marx 1897

Roger Marx. "Cartons d'artistes: Degas." *L'Image,* October 1897, pp. 320–25.

Roger Marx 1914

Roger Marx. *Maîtres d'hier et d'aujourd'hui.* Paris: Calmann-Lévy, 1914.

Rosenblum 1986

Rosenblum, Robert. "The *Demoiselles* Sketchbook No. 42, 1907." In *Je suis le cahier: The Sketchbooks of Picasso,* ed. Arnold Glimcher and Marc Glimcher, pp. 53–60. Exh. cat. London: Royal Academy of Arts, 1986.

Rothenstein 1931

Rothenstein, William. *Men and Memories, 1872–1900.* London: Faber and Faber, 1931.

Rothschild 1991

Rothschild, Deborah M. *Picasso's Parade: From Street to Stage.* New York: Sotheby's Publications, 1991.

Rubin 1973

Rubin, William. "Visits with Picasso at Mougins." *Art News* 72, no. 6 (Summer 1973): pp. 42–46.

Rubin 1980

Rubin, William. *Pablo Picasso: A Retrospective.* Exh. cat. New York: Museum of Modern Art, 1980.

Rubin 1994

Rubin, William. "The Genesis of *Les Demoiselles d'Avignon.*" In *Les Demoiselles d'Avignon,* by William Rubin, Hélène Seckel, and Judith Cousins, pp. 12–144. Studies in Modern Art, special issue. New York: Museum of Modern Art, 1994.

Rubin 1996

Rubin, William, ed. *Picasso and Portraiture: Representation and Transformation.* Exh. cat. New York: Museum of Modern Art, 1996.

Rusiñol 1892

Rusiñol, Santiago. "Filosofías que como tales no han de servir de gran cosa." *La Vanguardia,* Barcelona, 21 August 1892.

Sabartés 1948

Sabartés, Jaume. *Picasso: An Intimate Portrait.* New York: Prentice-Hall, 1948.

Sabartés 1954

Sabartés, Jaume. *Picasso: Documents iconographiques.* Geneva: Pierre Cailler, 1954.

Salmon 1918

Salmon, André. "La collection Degas et le mouvement contemporain." *L'Europe nouvelle* 2 (March 1918): pp. 388–89.

Salmon 2004

Salmon, André. *Souvenirs sans fin, 1903–1940.* Paris: Gallimard, 2004.

Schiff 1983

Schiff, Gert. *Picasso: The Last Years, 1963–1973.* Exh. cat. New York: George Braziller, in association with Grey Art Gallery and Study Center, New York University, 1983.

Seckel 1988

Seckel, Hélène, ed. *Les Demoiselles d'Avignon.* 2 vols. Paris: Réunion des musées nationaux, 1988.

Seckel-Klein 1998

Seckel-Klein, Hélène. *Picasso Collectionneur.* Paris: Réunion des musées nationaux, 1998.

Sickert 1947

Sickert, Walter. *A Free House.* London: Macmillan, 1947.

Sokolova 1960

Sokolova, Lydia. *Dancing for Diaghilev.* London: Murray, 1960.

Souriau 1999

Souriau, Étienne. *Vocabulaire d'esthétique.* Paris: Quadrige/PUF, 1999.

Spies 2000

Spies, Werner. *Picasso: The Sculptures.* With the collaboration of Christine Piot. Ostfildern/Stuttgart: Hatje Cantz, 2000.

Spurling 1998

Spurling, Hilary. *The Unknown Matisse.* London: Hamish Hamilton, 1998.

Staffe 1892

Staffe, Baronne. *The Lady's Dressing-Room.* Trans. Lady Colin Campbell. London: Cassell & Co., 1892.

Staller 2002

Staller, Natasha. *A Sum of Destructions: Picasso's Cultures and the Creation of Cubism.* New Haven and London: Yale University Press, 2002.

Stein 1961

Stein, Gertrude. *The Autobiography of Alice B. Toklas.* New York: Vintage, 1961.

Steinberg 1972

Steinberg, Leo. "The Algerian Women and Picasso at Large." In *Other Criteria: Confrontations with Twentieth-Century Art*, pp. 124–234. Oxford: Oxford University Press, 1972.

Stepan 2006

Stepan, Peter. *Picasso's Collection of African & Oceanic Art: Masters of Metamorphosis.* Munich and New York: Prestel, 2006.

Tate 1988

Tate Gallery. *Late Picasso: Paintings, Sculpture, Drawings, Prints, 1953–1972.* Exh. cat. London: Tate Gallery, 1988.

Terrasse 1983

Terrasse, Antoine. *Degas et la photographie.* Paris: Éditions Denoël, 1983.

Thomson 1987

Thomson, Richard. *The Private Degas.* London: Thames & Hudson, 1987.

Thomson 1988

Thomson, Richard. *Degas: The Nudes.* London: Thames & Hudson, 1988.

Thornley 1889

Thornley, George William. *Quinze lithographies d'après Degas.* Paris: Boussod et Valadon, 1889.

Tinterow and Lacambre 2003

Tinterow, Gary, and Geneviève Lacambre. *Manet/Velázquez: The French Taste for Spanish Painting.* Exh. cat. New York: Metropolitan Museum of Art, 2003.

Tucker 1982

Tucker, Paul Hayes. "Picasso, Photography, and the Development of Cubism." *Art Bulletin* 64 (June 1982): pp. 288–99.

Utley 2000

Utley, Gertje R. *Picasso: The Communist Years.* New Haven and London: Yale University Press, 2000.

Utrillo 1911

Utrillo, Miquel. "Crónica de Arte." *Las Noticias,* April 1911.

Uzanne 1898

Uzanne, Octave. *Fashion in Paris: The Various Phases of Feminine Taste and Aesthetics from 1797–1897.* Trans. Lady Mary Loyd. London: Heinemann, 1898.

Valéry 1960

Valéry, Paul. "Degas, Dance, Drawing." In *Degas, Manet, Morisot,* pp. 1–102. Trans. David Paul. Vol. 12, *The Collected Works of Paul Valéry.* London: Routledge & Kegan Paul, 1960.

Vallentin 1957

Vallentin, Antonina. *Picasso.* Paris: Albin Michel, 1957.

Vallentin 1963

Vallentin, Antonina. *Picasso.* Trans. London: Cassell & Co., 1963.

Van Gogh 1911

Van Gogh, Vincent. *Lettres de Vincent van Gogh à Émile Bernard.* Paris: A. Vollard, 1911.

Varnedoe 1980

Varnedoe, Kirk. "The Ideology of Time: Degas and Photography." *Art in America* 68 (Summer 1980): pp. 96–110.

Vasari 1973

Vasari, Giorgio. *Le vite dei più eccellenti pittori, scultori e architetti.* Ed. Licia Ragghianti and Carlo L. Ragghianti. Vol 2. Milan: Rizzoli, 1973.

Vente I

Catalogue des tableaux, pastels et dessins par Edgar Degas. . . . Paris: Galeries Georges Petit, 6–8 May 1918.

Vente II

Catalogue des tableaux, pastels et dessins par Edgar Degas. . . . Paris: Galeries Georges Petit, 11–13 December 1918.

Vente III

Catalogue des tableaux, pastels et dessins par Edgar Degas. . . . Paris: Galeries Georges Petit, 7–9 April 1919.

Vente IV

Catalogue des tableaux, pastels et dessins par Edgar Degas. . . . Paris: Galeries Georges Petit, 2–4 July 1919.

Vente Estampes

Catalogue des eaux-fortes, vernis-mous, aquatintes, lithographies et monotypes par Edgar Degas, et provenant de son atelier. Paris: Galerie Manzi-Joyant, 22–23 November 1918.

Vigarello 1988

Vigarello, Georges. *Concepts of Cleanliness: Changing Attitudes in France since the Middle Ages.* Trans. Jean Birrell. Cambridge: Cambridge University Press, 1988.

Vollard 1914

Vollard, Ambroise. *Degas: quatre-vingt-dix-huit reproductions signées par Degas.* Paris: Galerie A. Vollard, 1914.

Vollard 1924

Vollard, Ambroise. *Degas (1834–1917).* Paris: G. Crès et Cie., 1924.

Vollard 1925

Vollard, Ambroise. *Renoir: An Intimate Record.* New York: A. A. Knopf, 1925.

Vollard 1936

Vollard, Ambroise. *Recollections of a Picture Dealer.* Trans. V. M. Macdonald. London: Constable, 1936.

Vollard 1937

Vollard, Ambroise. *Degas: An Intimate Portrait.* Trans. Randolph T. Weaver. New York: Crown Publishers, 1937.

Vollard 1938

Vollard, Ambroise. *En écoutant Cézanne, Degas, Renoir.* Paris: Grasset, 1938.

Walker 2006

Walker, David H., ed. *Correspondance: André Gide, Eugène Rouart.* Vol. 2. Lyon: Presses Universitaires de Lyon, 2006.

Weill 1933

Weill, Berthe. *Pan! . . . dans l'oeil . . . ou trente ans dans les coulisses de la peinture contemporaine, 1900–1930.* Paris: Librairie Lipshutz, 1933.

Weiss 2003

Weiss, Jeffrey. *Picasso: The Cubist Portraits of Fernande Olivier.* Exh. cat. Washington, D.C.: National Gallery of Art; Princeton: Princeton University Press, 2003.

Wineapple 1996

Wineapple, Brenda. *Sister Brother: Gertrude and Leo Stein.* New York: G. P. Putnam and Sons, 1996.

Wright 2000

Wright, Laurence. *Clean and Decent: The Fascinating History of the Bathroom and the Water-closet.* London: Penguin, 2000.

Zervos 1932–78

Zervos, Christian. *Pablo Picasso.* 33 vols. Paris: Cahiers d'Art, 1932–78.

Zelevansky 1992

Zelevansky, Lynn, ed. *Picasso and Braque: A Symposium.* New York: Museum of Modern Art, 1992.

CHECKLIST OF THE EXHIBITION

WORKS BY EDGAR DEGAS

Study after a Rider from the Parthenon Frieze, 1855. Pencil on gray paper, 23 x 30.2 cm. Kunsthalle Bremen — Kupferstichkabinett — Der Kunstverein, Germany (1956/536)
Fig. 3 / Barcelona only

Study for "Dante and Virgil," c. 1856–57. Pencil and chalk on paper, 30.8 x 22.5 cm. Sterling and Francine Clark Art Institute, Williamstown, Massachusetts (1955.1403) [Vente IV.109f]
Fig. 29

Two Portrait Studies of a Man, c. 1856–57. Pencil and stumping with slight touches of white heightening on burnt-rose paper, 44.8 x 22.6 cm. Sterling and Francine Clark Art Institute, Williamstown, Massachusetts (1955.1393) [Vente IV.67]
Fig. 94

Roman Beggar Woman, 1857. Oil on canvas, 100.3 x 75.2 cm. Birmingham Museums and Art Gallery, England (1960P44) [L.28]
Fig. 21

Self-Portrait, c. 1857. Etching and drypoint, 23 x 14.4 cm. Sterling and Francine Clark Art Institute, Williamstown, Massachusetts (1955.1402) [R.S.8]
Fig. 27 / Barcelona only

Self-Portrait, c. 1857–58. Oil on paper, mounted on canvas, 26 x 19 cm. Sterling and Francine Clark Art Institute, Williamstown, Massachusetts (1955.544) [L.37]
Fig. 26

Giulia Bellelli, Study for "The Bellelli Family," c. 1858–59. Essence and pencil on buff wove paper, 36.2 x 24.8 cm. Dumbarton Oaks House Collection, Washington, D.C. (HC.P.1937.12.[E]) [L.69]
Fig. 9 / Williamstown only

Two Women Restraining Horses, c. 1860–62. Pencil on tracing paper, 30.6 x 31 cm. Musée d'Orsay, Paris, housed in the Department of Graphic Arts, Musée du Louvre (RF 15 528)
Fig. 23 / Barcelona only

Standing Nude, c. 1860–65. Pencil on paper, 29.2 x 21.7 cm. Sterling and Francine Clark Art Institute, Williamstown, Massachusetts (1955.1847) [Vente IV.109d]
Fig. 48

Portrait of Thérèse Degas-Morbilli (Study for "Portrait of M and Mme Morbilli"), c. 1865. Pencil and charcoal on paper, 35.2 x 23.3 cm. Musée d'Orsay, Paris, housed in the Department of Graphic Arts, Musée du Louvre. Gift of Mme Arlette Devade, neé Nepveu-Degas, 1990 (RF 42 663)
Fig. 51 / Barcelona only

Portrait of a Woman in Gray, c. 1865. Oil on canvas, 91.4 x 72.4 cm. The Metropolitan Museum of Art, New York. Gift of Mr. and Mrs. Edwin C. Vogel, 1957 (57.171) [L.128]
Fig. 114 / Barcelona only

At the Café Châteaudun, c. 1869–71. Pencil and oil (essence) on paper, mounted on canvas, 23.7 x 19 cm. The National Gallery, London. Presented by Mr. and Mrs. Charles Wilmers, 1991 (NGL 6536) [L.215]
Fig. 101

The Dance Class, 1873–75. Pastel and gouache on paper, 29.8 x 21 cm. Private collection. Courtesy of the Halcyon Gallery, London [L.375]
Fig. 122 / Barcelona only

In a Café (L'Absinthe), 1875–76. Oil on canvas, 92 x 68.5 cm. Musée d'Orsay, Paris. Bequest of Count Isaac de Camondo, 1911 (RF 1984) [L.393]
Fig. 104

Woman with an Umbrella (Berthe Jeantaud), c. 1876. Oil on canvas, 61 x 50.2 cm. National Gallery of Canada, Ottawa. Purchased 1969 (inv no. 15838) [L.463]
Fig. 115 / Williamstown only

Carlo Pellegrini, c. 1876–77. Oil on paper mounted on board, 63.2 x 34 cm. Tate, London. Presented by the Art Fund, 1916 (N03157) [L.407]
Fig. 63

Song of the Dog, c. 1876–77. Crayon lithograph, 37 x 26.6 cm. Lent by Nicholas Stogdon [R.S.25]
Fig. 71

Admiration, c. 1876–77. Monotype, 21.5 x 16.1 cm. Bibliothèque de l'Institut national d'histoire de l'art, Paris. Collections Jacques Doucet (EM DEGAS 3) [J.184]
Fig. 238 / Williamstown only

Conversation, c. 1876–77. Monotype, 16 x 12.1 cm. Private collection, Switzerland [J.106]
Fig. 275

Courtesans, c. 1876–77. Monotype, 16.1 x 21.2 cm. The National Museum in Belgrade. Collection: Graphic Arts Cabinet (inv. 1632) [J.74]
Fig. 240 / Barcelona only

Resting on the Bed, c. 1876–77. Monotype, 12.1 x 15.9 cm. Private collection, Switzerland [J.92]
Fig. 274

The Tub, c. 1876–77. Monotype, 42 x 54.1 cm. Bibliothèque de l'Institut national d'histoire de l'art, Paris. Collections Jacques Doucet (EM DEGAS 4) [J.151]
Fig. 91 / Williamstown only

Two Women, c. 1876–77. Monotype, 16.3 x 11.9 cm. Bibliothèque de l'Institut national d'histoire de l'art, Paris. Collections Jacques Doucet (EM DEGAS 10) [J.76]
Fig. 235 / Williamstown only

Woman Ironing, 1876–87. Oil on canvas, 81.3 x 66 cm. National Gallery of Art, Washington, D.C. Collection of Mr. and Mrs. Paul Mellon (1972.74.1) [L.685]
Fig. 110

Singers on the Stage, 1877/79. Pastel over monotype on ivory wove paper, laid down on board, 16 x 21 cm. The Art Institute of Chicago. Bequest of Mrs. Clive Runnells (1977.773) [L.455/J.30]
Fig. 76 / Williamstown only

Mlle Bécat at the Café des Ambassadeurs, c. 1877–78. Lithograph in black on grayish white wove paper, 20.5 x 19.3 cm. The Art Institute of Chicago. William McCallin McKee Memorial Collection (1932.1296) [R.S.31]
Fig. 70 / Barcelona only

Nude Study for "Little Dancer Aged Fourteen," c. 1878. Bronze, height: 72.4 cm. The National Gallery of Scotland, Edinburgh (NG 1624) [R.XIX]
Fig. 128

Studies for the "Little Dancer Aged Fourteen" (Nude), c. 1878–80. Charcoal heightened with white chalk on gray paper; stamped with red signature lower right, 48 x 63 cm. Private collection, London [Vente III.386]
Fig. 127

Café-Concert Singer, c. 1878–80. Monotype in black on cream laid paper, 8 x 7.2 cm. The Art Institute of Chicago. Potter Palmer Collection Fund (1963.822) [J.50]
Fig. 69 / Barcelona only

Three Ballet Dancers, c. 1878–80. Monotype, 20 x 41.7 cm. Sterling and Francine Clark Art Institute, Williamstown, Massachusetts (1955.1386) [J.9]
Fig. 148

The Tub, c. 1878–80. Monotype, 16 x 21.1 cm. Private collection [J.189]
Fig. 184 / Williamstown only

Leaving the Bath, 1879–80. Drypoint and aquatint, 12.8 x 12.8 cm. Sterling and Francine Clark Art Institute, Williamstown, Massachusetts (1969.19) [R.S.42]
Fig. 213

Little Dancer Aged Fourteen, 1879–81. Bronze, with gauze tutu and silk ribbon, on wooden base, height: 99 cm. Sterling and Francine Clark Art Institute, Williamstown, Massachusetts (1955.45) [R.XX]
Fig. 141

Sleep, c. 1879–83. Monotype, 27.6 x 37.8 cm. British Museum, London (BM 1949-4-11-2425) [J.135]
Fig. 265

The Washbasin, c. 1879–83. Monotype in black on laid paper, 31.3 x 27.3 cm. Sterling and Francine Clark Art Institute, Williamstown, Massachusetts (1962.39) [J.36]
Fig. 182 / Barcelona only

Dancers in the Classroom, c. 1880. Oil on canvas, 39.4 x 88.4 cm. Sterling and Francine Clark Art Institute, Williamstown, Massachusetts (1955.562) [L.820]
Fig. 158

Fourth Position Front, On the Left Leg, c. 1880s. Bronze, height: 57.5 cm. Sterling and Francine Clark Art Institute, Williamstown, Massachusetts (1955.49) [R.XLIII]
Fig. 172

Grand Arabesque, First Time, c. 1880s. Bronze, height: 48.2 cm. Sterling and Francine Clark Art Institute, Williamstown, Massachusetts (1955.46) [R.XXXV]
Fig. 175

Grand Arabesque, Second Time, c. 1880s. Bronze, height: 48.2 cm. Sterling and Francine Clark Art Institute, Williamstown, Massachusetts (1955.47) [R.XXXVI]
Fig. 171

Entrance of the Masked Dancers, c. 1884. Pastel on gray-brown paper, 49 x 64.7 cm. Sterling and Francine Clark Art Institute, Williamstown, Massachusetts (1955.559) [L.527]
Fig. 157 / Williamstown only

Nude Woman Drying Herself, c. 1884–86. Oil on canvas, 150.8 x 213.7 cm. Brooklyn Museum, New York. Carll H. de Silver Fund (31.813) [L.951]
Fig. 215

Woman Brushing Her Hair, c. 1885–90. Oil on canvas, 74 x 61 cm. The Kreeger Museum, Washington, D.C. (1964.4) [L.642]
Fig. 181 / Williamstown only

Two Dancers in the Wings, c. 1888. Pastel on paper mounted on cardboard on a wooden stretcher, 59 x 46.4 cm. Private collection [L.944]
Fig. 154

The Tub, c. 1889. Bronze, height: 22.2 cm. The National Gallery of Scotland, Edinburgh (NG 2286) [R.XXVII]
Fig. 225

Nude Study of a Jockey Riding a Horse, Seen from the Back, c. 1890. Charcoal on laid paper, 31 x 24.9 cm. Museum Boijmans Van Beuningen, Rotterdam (inv. no. F II 129 [PK] Koenings Collection) [Vente III.131 (2)]
Fig. 196 / Barcelona only

Woman Standing in a Bathtub, 1890–92. Charcoal on yellow tracing paper, 43.7 x 30 cm. Sterling and Francine Clark Art Institute, Williamstown, Massachusetts (1955.1394) [Vente III.327 (2)]
Fig. 186

After the Bath, c. 1891–92. Charcoal on yellow tracing paper, 35.2 x 25.4 cm. Sterling and Francine Clark Art Institute, Williamstown, Massachusetts (1955.1408) [Vente III.327 (1)]
Fig. 185

Woman Drying Herself, c. 1891–92. Lithograph, 33.1 x 24.8 cm. Sterling and Francine Clark Art Institute, Williamstown, Massachusetts (1962.38) [R.S.61]
Fig. 89

Head of a Woman (Mlle Salle), modeled 1892. Bronze, height: 25.5 cm. Museum of Fine Arts, Boston. Bequest of Margarett Sargent McKean (1979.509) [R.XXX]
Fig. 189

Jules Taschereau, Edgar Degas, and Jacques-Émile Blanche, 1895. Gelatin silver print from glass negative, enlargement, 22.9 x 24.8 cm. Sterling and Francine Clark Art Institute, Williamstown, Massachusetts (2002.6) [D.6b]
Fig. 289

Dressed Dancer at Rest, Hands behind Her Back, Right Leg Forward, c. 1895. Bronze, height: 42.9 cm. The Metropolitan Museum of Art, New York. H. O. Havemeyer Collection, Bequest of Mrs. H. O. Havemeyer, 1929 (29.100.392) [R.LII]
Fig. 176

Self-Portrait, c. 1895. Original print with modifications, possibly made by Picasso. Inscribed on the reverse in Picasso's hand "Portrait P.H. / de E. Degas," 18.2 x 24.2 cm. Private collection. Courtesy Fundación Almine y Bernard Ruiz-Picasso para el Arte [D.20]
Fig. 245

Combing the Hair (La Coiffure), c. 1896. Oil on canvas, 114.3 x 146.7 cm. The National Gallery, London. Bought, 1937 (NGL 4865) [L.1128]
Fig. 227

Woman Combing Her Hair, c. 1896–99. Charcoal and pastel on tracing paper, 109 x 76.3 cm. Private collection [L.933]
Fig. 223 / Williamstown only

Pregnant Woman, c. 1896–1911. Bronze, height: 43.2 cm. Hirshhorn Museum and Sculpture Garden, Smithsonian Institution, Washington, D.C. The Joseph H. Hirshhorn Bequest, 1981 (HMSG 86.1415) [R.LXII]
Fig. 228

Woman Arranging Her Hair (La Coiffure), c. 1896–1911. Bronze, height: 46.7 cm. Hirshhorn Museum and Sculpture Garden, Smithsonian Institution, Washington, D.C. Gift of Joseph H. Hirshhorn, 1966 (HMSG 66.1305) [R.L]
Fig. 205

Group of Dancers, c. 1900. Charcoal and pastel on paper on board, 57.2 x 69.5 cm. Private collection. Courtesy of the Halcyon Gallery, London [Vente I.228]
Fig. 155 / Barcelona only

PRINTS AFTER DEGAS

La Maison Tellier by Guy de Maupassant. Photogravures by Maurice Potin (French, b. 1874) after monotypes by Degas, some with additions in pochoir. Wood engravings by Georges Aubert (French, 1886–1961) after drawings by Degas. Paris: Ambroise Vollard, 1934. Sterling and Francine Clark Art Institute, Williamstown, Massachusetts

Les Mimes des courtisanes de Lucien, by Lucian of Samosata. Trans. by Pierre Louÿs. Photogravures by Maurice Potin after monotypes by Degas, some with additions in pochoir. Paris: Ambroise Vollard, 1935. Sterling and Francine Clark Art Institute, Williamstown, Massachusetts

WORKS BY PABLO PICASSO

Academic Study: Greek Horseman (Copy of a Plaster Cast; Parthenon, West Frieze [VI], Figure 11), 1895. Pencil and Conté crayon on paper, 28.3 x 29.9 cm. Museu Picasso, Barcelona (MPB 110.694V)
Fig. 4 / Barcelona only

The Old Fisherman, 1895. Oil on canvas, 83 x 62.5 cm. Museu de Montserrat. Gift of X. Busquets (N.R. 200.502) [Z.I.1]
Fig. 19 / Barcelona only

Academic Study from Life: Male Nude, from the Side, with a Pole; Sketch of Head and Bust of Male Figures, 1895–97. Pencil, Conté crayon, and ink on paper, 48.3 x 31.5 cm. Museu Picasso, Barcelona (MPB 110.849)
Fig. 28

Battle of Covadonga, 1895–96. Pen and sepia ink on paper, 17.9 x 22.4 cm. Museu Picasso, Barcelona (MPB 110.639)
Fig. 24 / Barcelona only

Portrait of the Artist's Father, 1896. Watercolor on paper, 25.5 x 17.8 cm. Museu Picasso, Barcelona (MPB 110.331) [Z.XXI.28]
Fig. 246

Self-Portrait, 1896. Oil on canvas, 32.9 x 24 cm. Museu Picasso, Barcelona (MPB 110.076) [PF1.154]
Fig. 25

The Artist's Father, with a Copy of the Magazine "Gil Blas" in His Pocket, 1899. Crayon on paper, 30.5 x 24.7 cm. Museu Picasso, Barcelona (MPB 110.032)
Fig. 40

Lola, the Artist's Sister, 1899. Charcoal and colored pencil on paper, 45 x 29.5 cm. Museu Picasso, Barcelona (MPB 4.265) [Z.I.29]
Fig. 50

The Divan, c. 1899. Charcoal, pastel, and colored pencil on varnished paper, 26.2 x 29.7 cm. Museu Picasso, Barcelona (MPB 4.267) [Z.I.23]
Fig. 56

Female Nude, c. 1899. Charcoal on paper, 48.5 x 33 cm. Museu Picasso, Barcelona (MPB 110.595) [PF1.292]
Fig. 49

Joan Vidal i Ventosa, 1899–1900. Charcoal, black pencil, and wash on paper, 47.5 x 28 cm. Museu Picasso, Barcelona (MPB 70.802) [Z.VI.252]
Fig. 60 / Williamstown only

Self-Portrait, 1899–1900. Charcoal and crayon on paper, 22.5 x 16.2 cm. Museu Picasso, Barcelona (MPB 110.632) [PF1.357]
Fig. 53

Stuffed Shirts, 1900. Oil on panel, 13.6 x 22.5 cm. Museum of Fine Arts, Boston. Gift of Mrs. Charles Sumner Bird (Julia Appleton Bird) (1970.475) [Z.I.35]
Fig. 75

Portrait of Santiago Rusiñol, c. 1900. Charcoal and watercolor on paper, 33 x 23 cm. El Conventet Collection
Fig. 61 / Barcelona only

The Blue Room (The Tub), 1901. Oil on canvas, 50.5 x 61.6 cm. The Phillips Collection, Washington, D.C. Acquired 1927 (1554) [Z.I.103]
Fig. 88

The Dwarf, 1901. Oil on cardboard, 105 x 60 cm. Museu Picasso, Barcelona (MPB 4.274) [Z.I.66]
Fig. 120

The End of the Performance, 1901. Pastel on canvas, 73 x 47 cm. Museu Picasso, Barcelona (MPB 4.270) [Z.I.30]
Fig. 68

Boy's Head, December 1902. Conté crayon and charcoal on paper, 31.2 x 23.5 cm. Museu Picasso, Barcelona (MPB 110.529) [PF1.809]
Fig. 95

Study of a Head Gazing Upward, December 1902. Conté crayon on paper, 31.2 x 24.3 cm. Museu Picasso, Barcelona (MPB 110.530) [PF1.812]
Fig. 96

The Couple, 1903. Pen and sepia ink on gold, yellowish paper, 23 x 18 cm. Museu Picasso, Barcelona (MPB 110.499) [PF1.939]
Fig. 236

Portrait of Sebastià Junyer i Vidal, 1903. Oil on canvas, 126.4 x 94 cm. Los Angeles County Museum of Art. David E. Bright Bequest (M.67.25.18) [Z.I.174]
Fig. 105

Three Studies of a Nude Woman, c. 1903. Pen and ink on paper, 17.9 x 23 cm. Museu Picasso, Barcelona (MPB 110.496)
Fig. 131

The Frugal Repast, 1904. Etching and scraper on zinc printed on laid Arches paper, 46.1 x 37.8 cm. Sterling and Francine Clark Art Institute, Williamstown, Massachusetts (1962.89) [Baer 2]
Fig. 116 / Williamstown only

The Frugal Repast, 1904. Etching and scraper on zinc printed on laid Arches paper, 46.3 x 37.7 cm. Museu Picasso, Barcelona (MPB 110.011) [Baer 2]
Barcelona only

Woman Ironing, 1904. Oil on canvas, 116.2 x 73 cm. Solomon R. Guggenheim Museum, New York. Thannhauser Collection, Gift, Justin K. Thannhauser, 1978 (78.2514.41) [Z.I.247]
Fig. 109 / Williamstown only

Portrait of Benedetta Canals, 1905. Oil and charcoal on canvas, 90 x 69.5 cm. Museu Picasso, Barcelona (MPB 4.266) [Z.I.263]
Fig. 113

Studies of a Reclining Female Nude in Five Positions, 1906. Pen and black ink on ocher paper, 23.8 x 31 cm. Albertina, Vienna (inv. 23299)
Fig. 239 / Barcelona only

Woman Doing Her Hair, 1906. Pencil on paper, 31 x 22.5 cm. Hamburger Kunsthalle. Sammlung Hegewisch [Z.VI.751]
Fig. 202 / Barcelona only

Woman Combing Her Hair, 1906. Pencil and charcoal on paper, 55.8 x 40.7 cm. Sainsbury Centre, Norwich, England. Robert and Lisa Sainsbury Collection (UEA 7) [Z.I.341]
Fig. 203 / Williamstown only

Woman Plaiting Her Hair, 1906. Bronze, height: 41.6 cm. The Baltimore Museum of Art. The Cone Collection formed by Dr. Claribel and Miss Etta Cone of Baltimore, Maryland (BMA 1950.452) [S.7.II]
Fig. 201

Woman Plaiting Her Hair, 1906. Oil on canvas, 127 x 90.8 cm. The Museum of Modern Art, New York. Florene May Schoenborn Bequest, 1996 (826.1996) [Z.I.336]
Fig. 206

Head of a Woman (Fernande Olivier), c. 1906. Bronze, height: 34 cm. Allen Memorial Art Museum, Oberlin College, Ohio. R. T. Miller Jr. Fund, 1955 (AMAM 1955.35) [S.6.II]
Fig. 188 / Williamstown only

Head of a Woman (Fernande Olivier), c. 1906. Bronze, height: 35.7 cm. Museu Picasso, Barcelona. (MPB 113.035)
Barcelona only

Standing Nude, 1907. Oil on canvas, 93 x 43 cm. Museo del Novecento, Milan (8750) [Z.IIa.40]
Fig. 140 / Williamstown only

Yellow Nude, 1907. Watercolor, gouache, and India ink on paper, 59.8 x 39.5 cm. Gretchen and John Berggruen, San Francisco [Z.XXVI.281]
Fig. 139 / Barcelona only

Study for "Les Demoiselles d'Avignon," 1907. Charcoal and pastel, 47.7 x 63.5 cm. Kunstmuseum Basel, Kupferstichkabinett (1967.106) [Z.IIa.19]
Fig. 242 / Williamstown only

The Offering, 1908. Gouache on cardboard with white primer, 30.6 x 30.6 cm. Museu Picasso, Barcelona (MPB 112.761)
Fig. 244 / Barcelona only

Two Dancers, 1919 (Summer). Pencil on paper, 31 x 23.9 cm. The Museum of Modern Art, New York. The John S. Newberry Collection, 1963 (178.1963) [Z.XXIX.430]
Fig. 147

Seven Dancers, 1919–20. Ink and watercolor on paper, 26.3 x 39.5 cm. Private collection [Z.III.355]
Fig. 150

Three Dancers, 1919–20. Pencil on paper, 39.5 x 26.3 cm. Private collection. Courtesy Fundación Almine y Bernard Ruiz-Picasso para el Arte (2304) [Z.XXIX.415]
Fig. 160 / Barcelona only

Seated Woman (Olga Picasso), 1920. Crayon and gouache on paper, 63 x 48 cm. Collection of Marina Picasso [Z.IV.97]
Fig. 144 / Barcelona only

Turning Nude, from the Back, 1920–21. Charcoal on paper, 63.5 x 46.5 cm. Museum Ludwig, Cologne (ML/Z 1994/31) [Z.III.435] Fig. 214

Woman in the Bath, 16 April 1921. Pencil on paper, 16 x 12 cm. Musée national Picasso, Paris (MP 959) [Z.XXX.222] Fig. 212

In the Wings, 1925. Pencil on paper, 50.9 x 40.5 cm. Collection of the Vanech Family Fig. 167

Three Dancers Resting, 1925. Ink on paper, 35 x 25 cm. Private collection [Z.V.429] Fig. 163 / Barcelona only

Two Dancers, 12–13 April 1925. Pencil on paper, 51 x 41 cm. National Gallery of Ireland, Dublin (NGI.3271) [Z.V.453] Fig. 166 / Barcelona only

Two Seated Dancers, 1925. Pencil on paper, 50 x 40 cm. Private collection Fig. 165 / Williamstown only

Bather, 1931. Bronze, height: 40 cm. Private collection. Courtesy Fundación Almine y Bernard Ruiz-Picasso para el Arte (55297) [S.113.II] Fig. 174

Bather with Raised Arms, 1931. Bronze, height: 32.5 cm. Musée national Picasso, Paris (MP 304) [S.114.II] Fig. 173

Running Woman, 1931–32. Plaster and wood, height: 52 cm. Private collection [S.137.I] Fig. 170

Woman Washing Her Feet, 10 July 1944. Ink on paper, 50.8 x 33.6 cm. The Museum of Modern Art, New York. Purchase, 1953 (186.1953) Fig. 224

Pregnant Woman, 1950. Bronze, first state, height: 104.7 cm. Hirshhorn Museum and Sculpture Garden, Smithsonian Institution, Washington, D.C. Gift of Joseph H. Hirshhorn, 1972 (HMSG 72.232) [S.349.II] Fig. 229

Nude Wringing Her Hair, 7 October 1952. Oil on wood panel, 150.5 x 119.4 cm. Private collection Fig. 226 / Williamstown only

An Artist (Portrait of Degas?), 6 February 1968. Oil on canvas, 81 x 65 cm. Private collection [Z.XXVII.222] Fig. 261

Man with Two Nude Women, 27 July 1968. Mezzotint printed on paper with a watermark, 31.5 x 39.5 cm. Museu Picasso, Barcelona (MPB 70.566) [Baer 1718] Fig. 267

Related to "The Unknown Masterpiece": Pourbus and the Young Poussin at Frenhofer's, 30 September 1968. Aquatint and scraper on copper printed on paper, 22.5 x 32.5 cm. Museu Picasso, Barcelona (MPB 112.023) [Baer 1841] Fig. 266

Painter with a Cravat Drawing His Model in the Setting of "La Maison Tellier," 19 February 1970. Etching on copper printed on paper (Artist proof I/XV), 50.5 x 63 cm. Museu Picasso, Barcelona (MPB 112.181) [Baer 1876] Fig. 268 / Barcelona only

Degas among the Prostitutes. First Appearance of Degas, 11 March 1971. Etching on copper printed on paper (Artist proof I/XV), 36.5 x 49 cm. Museu Picasso, Barcelona (MPB 112.231) [Baer 1942] Fig. 270

Degas, in a Morning Coat, Drawing Himself in a Suit, among Prostitutes, 13 March 1971. Etching on copper printed on paper (Artist proof I/XV), 36.5 x 48.6 cm. Museu Picasso, Barcelona (MPB 112.228) [Baer 1945] Fig. 285

Women at Their Toilette with Degas Musing, 15 March 1971. Etching on copper printed on paper (Artist proof I/XV), 36.5 x 49 cm. Museu Picasso, Barcelona (MPB 112.273) [Baer 1948] Fig. 271

Brothel. Degas with His Sketchbook, Celestina, Three Prostitutes, and a Moroccan Cushion, 16 March 1971. Etching on copper printed on paper (Artist proof I/XV), 36.7 x 49 cm. Museu Picasso, Barcelona (MPB 112.232) [Baer 1951] Fig. 260 / Barcelona only

Degas with Elasticized Boots and Two Prostitutes, One on an Upholstered Napoleon III Chair, 19–22 March 1971. Etching on copper printed on paper (Artist proof I/XV), 36.5 x 48.6 cm. Museu Picasso, Barcelona (MPB 112.189) [Baer 1955] Fig. 276

Prostitute with a Bracelet and Degas with His Hands behind His Back, 30 March 1971. Etching on copper printed on paper (Artist proof I/XV), 36.7 x 49.1 cm. Museu Picasso, Barcelona (MPB 112.233) [Baer 1966] Fig. 273

Degas Having Visions. Prostitute Listening to the Stories of Her Companions at Rest, 3 April 1971. Etching on copper printed on paper (Artist proof I/XV), 36.1 x 49.5 cm. Museu Picasso, Barcelona (MPB 112.207) [Baer 1972] Fig. 278

Brothel. Gossip, with a Parrot, Celestina, and the Portrait of Degas, 4 April 1971. Etching on copper printed on paper (Artist proof I/XV), 36.5 x 49 cm. Museu Picasso, Barcelona (MPB 112.184) [Baer 1973] Fig. 286

"La Maison Tellier." Prostitutes Together. Degas Astonished, 9 April 1971. Etching on copper printed on paper (Artist proof I/XV), 36.5 x 49 cm. Museu Picasso, Barcelona (MPB 112.225) [Baer 1975] Fig. 282 / Barcelona only

Degas Fantasizing. Faun Whispering in a Woman's Ear, 11 April 1971. Sugar-lift aquatint with foul biting on copper printed on paper (Artist proof I/XV), 36.5 x 49.1 cm. Museu Picasso, Barcelona (MPB 112.213) [Baer 1978] Fig. 262

The Madame-Abortionist and Three Prostitutes. Degas with His Hands behind His Back, second state, 1–4 May 1971. Etching on copper printed on paper (Artist proof I/XV), 36.7 x 49 cm. Museu Picasso, Barcelona (MPB 112.234) [Baer 1981] Fig. 281

The Name Day of the Madame, Flowers and Kisses, Degas Enjoying Himself, 16 May 1971. Etching on copper printed on paper (Artist proof I/XV), 36.5 x 49.2 cm. Museu Picasso, Barcelona (MPB 112.211) [Baer 1993] Fig. 277

Brothel. Scandalmongering. Profile of Degas Wrinkling His Nose, seventh state, 19, 21, 23, 24, 26, 30, and 31 May and 2 June 1971. Etching, aquatint, drypoint, and scraper on copper, printed on paper (Artist proof I/XV), 36.6 x 49.2 cm. Museu Picasso, Barcelona (MPB 112.208) [Baer 1995] Fig. 280

ARCHIVAL MATERIALS

Nymphs. L'Après-midi d'un Faune. Ballets Russes. Serge Diaghilev's Ballet Russe, 1916. Postcard photograph by Jean de Strelecki, 8.7 x 13.7 cm. Archives Olga Ruiz-Picasso, Courtesy Fundación Almine y Bernard Ruiz-Picasso para el Arte

Olga Khokhlova as a Nymph in "L'Après-midi d'un Faune," c. 1916. Photograph (modern print from a glass negative), probably by Jean de Strelecki (French, active in New York, c. 1915), 11.9 x 7.4 cm. Archives Olga Ruiz-Picasso, Courtesy Fundación Almine y Bernard Ruiz-Picasso para el Arte Fig. 118

Olga Khokhlova as a Wife of the Sultan in Scheherazade, c. 1916. Photograph (modern print from a glass negative), 11.5 x 7.5 cm. Archives Olga Ruiz-Picasso, Courtesy Fundación Almine y Bernard Ruiz-Picasso para el Arte Fig. 298

Olga Khokhlova, Pablo Picasso, Maria Chabelska, and Jean Cocteau, Paris, 1917. Photograph, 10.9 x 7.1 cm. Archives Olga Ruiz-Picasso, courtesy Fundación Almine y Bernard Ruiz-Picasso para el Arte

Letter from Jean Cocteau to Pablo Picasso, Paris, 12 May 1918. Pen and ink on paper, 26.5 x 19.8 cm. Archives Olga Ruiz-Picasso, courtesy Fundación Almine y Bernard Ruiz-Picasso para el Arte

Olga and Pablo Picasso, Villa La Mimoseraie, Summer 1918. Photograph (modern print from an original negative), 14.8 x 9.1 cm. Archives Olga Ruiz-Picasso, courtesy Fundación Almine y Bernard Ruiz-Picasso para el Arte

Olga Picasso and Enrico Cecchetti, London, 1919. Photograph, 11.4 x 6.8 cm. Archives Olga Ruiz-Picasso, Courtesy Fundación Almine y Bernard Ruiz-Picasso para el Arte Fig. 302

Olga Picasso, Enrico Cecchetti, and an Unknown Dancer, probably Sonia Derloff, London, 1919. Photograph, 6.8 x 11.4 cm. Archives Olga Ruiz-Picasso, Courtesy Fundación Almine y Bernard Ruiz-Picasso para el Arte

Pablo Picasso, Serge Diaghilev, and Olga Picasso behind the Casino at Monte-Carlo, c. 1920. Photograph, 11 x 7 cm. Archives Olga Ruiz-Picasso, courtesy Fundación Almine y Bernard Ruiz-Picasso para el Arte

Paulo and Olga Picasso, c. 1921. Photograph, 14 x 9 cm. Archives Olga Ruiz-Picasso, courtesy Fundación Almine y Bernard Ruiz-Picasso para el Arte

Olga and Pablo Picasso, La Garoupe, Cap d'Antibes, Summer 1923. Photograph, possibly by Gerald Murphy (American, 1888–1964), 12.8 x 17.5 cm. Archives Olga Ruiz-Picasso, Courtesy Fundación Almine y Bernard Ruiz-Picasso para el Arte

Doña María Picasso y López, the Artist's Mother, and Olga Picasso, c. 1923. Photograph (modern print from an original negative), 11.3 x 6.9 cm. Archives Olga Ruiz-Picasso, courtesy Fundación Almine y Bernard Ruiz-Picasso para el Arte

Olga Picasso, c. 1924. Photograph, 12.1 x 7.4 cm. Archives Olga Ruiz-Picasso, courtesy Fundación Almine y Bernard Ruiz-Picasso para el Arte

Boris Kochno, Serge Diaghilev, Paulo Picasso, and an Unidentified Man, Monte-Carlo, 1925. Photograph, 6.6 x 11 cm. Archives Olga Ruiz-Picasso, courtesy Fundación Almine y Bernard Ruiz-Picasso para el Arte

Olga Picasso, Villa Belle Rose, Juan-les-Pins, Summer 1925. Photograph, 11.9 x 7.5 cm. Archives Olga Ruiz-Picasso, Courtesy Fundación Almine y Bernard Ruiz-Picasso para el Arte

Enrico Cecchetti, c. 1926. Postcard photograph inscribed "À Mlle Kohlova [sic] / Souvenir de son / prof : E Cecchetti 1926," 13.5 x 8.8 cm. Archives Olga Ruiz-Picasso, Courtesy Fundación Almine y Bernard Ruiz-Picasso para el Arte

INDEX